This day in Baptist History III

David L. Cummins

Libary of Congress Cataloging-in-Publication Data
Cummins, David L., 1929-
This day in Baptist history III : 366 daily devotions / David L. Cummins
p. cm.
Includes bibliographical references (p.) and index.
ISBN 0-9774362-0-9
1. Devotional calendars-Baptists. 2. Baptists-Prayer books and devotions-English. 3. Baptists-History. I. Title: This day in Baptist history 2. II. Title.

This Day in Baptist History III
Edited by David L. Cummins

Cover design by Kip Pelton
Cover picture *Resurrection Morn* by Hong Min Zou* is copyrighted by www.HongminZou.com

*On November, 1963, General Lee's Army moved into winter quarters on the south side of the Rapidan River. The Union army moved up to the north side.

The pickets on each side of the river were within speaking distance of each other. My command camped on the north side of Clark's Mountain and was composed of the following regiments of infantry: 58th, 42nd, 49th, 32nd and 13th Virginia, General A. P. Hill's old regiment. This was the 4th Virginia Brigade, commanded by General Pegram, who was killed at Hatcher's Run.

"While in camp our chaplain, Reverend Willie Ragland, preached very faithfully the gospel of Christ to our command, the 13th Virginia, that loved and honored him as a servant of God. One of the converts, Goodwin, of Company A, of Orange Courthouse, living in the lower part of the county, wished to be baptized in the Rapidan River; but the enemy was just on the other side, and our officers feared that we might bring on trouble. But finally they gave their consent. We marched very scatteringly, about fifty strong; and the enemy, seeing that we had no arms, did not fire on us, but seemed grearly puzzled and watched us closely. As soon as we reached the water's edge we began to sing that grand old hymn, "*There is a Fountain filled with Blood*," and at once the enemy began to leave their works and hasten to the riverside, and many voices in the Northern army joined in the song. Both armies were at peace as they witnessed the death of the old man into the resurrection of the new man through Jesus Christ our Lord."

Printed in the United States of America

ISBN 0-9774362-0-9

Contents

Preface

Solomon has well said, "*. . . of making many books there is no end. . . .*" Surely that statement could be said of Baptist history alone. The subject is so vast and is such a rich field of study that one could easily become enamored with the past and dwell upon it to the exclusion of present day challenges and opportunities. The authors of volume three of *This Day in Baptist History* are well aware of that danger. It is not our purpose to glory in the past to the exclusion of seeing the vision of the present and/or the future. Our desire has been merely to look into the past, honor those who have gone before us, and gain enthusiasm from their exploits for the challenges of the day in which we live.

The Scriptures often call upon God's children not to forget the ancient landmarks. For instance, in Joshua 4:15-22 the Lord instructed the children of Israel to make a memorial that future generations might pause to reflect upon God's faithfulness in His dealing with their forefathers. The Psalmist reminds us in Psalm 78:4-7 that we are to instruct our children as to the past, and they in turn are to instruct their children. The Lord would have us instruct our children as to His blessings historically upon His people, and then He desires that our children should instruct our grandchildren. In other words, from generation to generation we are to rehearse the blessings of God. That is what the authors of volume three have attempted to do.

Fearfully, in this "throw away" society, the past is often neglected and totally forgotten. This trend has resulted in present day congregations completely dropping the name "Baptist" from their ministries. We do not believe that Baptist people who are properly aware of the sacrifices made by our forefathers could possibly participate in such a practice. We rejoice in the price that those who have gone before us have paid for our religious freedom. It is the desire of the present authors to reinforce our gratitude for those who have gone before.

David L. Cummins
Deputation Director
Baptist World Mission

Acknowledgments

Volume III of *This Day in Baptist History* has been totally unplanned. A continual barrage of notes such as the following made the project a necessity. "When will Dr. Cummins' 3rd volume of *This Day in Baptist History* be ready? We have used volumes I and II in our daily devotions twice over and are anxious for volume III to be available." With continual calls such as the above, we seemed to have no alternative but to research and write this third (and last) volume of the set.

When my former partner, Dr. E. Wayne Thompson, was unavailable to participate, the overwhelming task seemed almost oppressive. However, I am greatly indebted to others who have assisted in this project. The author of each entry is designated by his initials. I must express gratitude to: Dr. David C. Baughn (DCB - South Carolina); Rev. Robert P. Bixby (RPB - Illinois); Dr. Ron A. Brooks (RAB - South Carolina); Dr. Edward G. Caughill (EGC - Virginia) ; Dr. Fred J. Moritz (FJM - Alabama); Dr. Larry R. Oats (LRO - Wisconsin); and Dr. David R. Potter (DRP - Hungary). Of course, my contributions are denoted by my initials: DLC.

My secretary at the time of the commencement of this project was Miss Sheri Decker. She was a great assist in those early days, but left our employment to marry. Her able replacement, Miss Jodi Scorpil, has been a continual blessing in the tedious labors required. Other personnel of our Baptist World Mission staff have graciously proofread entries, and I am indebted to: Mrs. Anita Knighten, Mrs. Judy Moritz, Mrs. Judy Owens, and Miss Beth Prahl.

I am greatly indebted to Dr. Mary Kraus, college professor, for her helpful suggestions and final proofing of the manuscript.

Once again, I must confess that I am greatly indebted to my dear wife, Mary, for her understanding as many hours of research were taken from "family time." She not only participated without complaint, but she encouraged me onward when I was ready to despair.

Without these helpers, this project could never have been completed. I thank the Lord for each one.

About the Authors

Dr. David C. Baughn (DCB). David Baughn has pastored two historical Baptist churches in South Carolina and West Virginia. He has been used of God in the field of evangelism and has served as professor of Baptist History in four Bible colleges. He is often invited to serve as an evangelist, and he conducts Baptist Heritage conferences.

Rev. Robert P. Bixby (RPB). Robert Bixby serves as pastor of Morning Star Baptist Church in Rockford, Illinois. Previously, Brother Bixby served as a missionary in France.

Dr. Ron A. Brooks (RAB). Ronald Brooks has served for twenty years as a missionary and field administrator with Baptist World Mission. Prior to his present position, he ministered as an assistant pastor, school administrator, and college professor. He served two tours of duty in Vietnam, retiring from the Army with the rank of Major.

Dr. Edward G. Caughill (EGC), is associate pastor of Tabernacle Baptist Church, Virginia Beach, Virginia. Dr. Caughill has served as professors at Pillsbury Baptist Bible College in Owatonna, Minnesota, and Maranatha Baptist Bible College in Watertown, Wisconsin, and as Dean of the Tabernacle Baptist Bible College in Virginia Beach, Virginia.

Dr. David L. Cummins (DLC). David Cummins has served the past eight years as deputation director of Baptist World Mission. His ministry has consisted of service as pastor, evangelist, and church planter. He has co-authored volumes one and two of *This Day in Baptist History* with Dr. E. Wayne Thompson and has also written *A Brief History of Baptist Missions*.

Dr. Fred J. Moritz (FJM). Fred Moritz is executive director of Baptist World Mission, Decatur, Alabama. He has previously served in pastorates in Minnesota, Illinois, and Indiana, as well as laboring as an evangelist. Dr. Moritz has authored two volumes and is a continual contributor to Christian periodicals.

Dr. Larry R. Oats (LRO), is a professor at Maranatha Baptist Bible College, Watertown, Wisconsin. His expertise in Baptist History is well known in fundamental Baptist circles.

Dr. David R. Potter (DRP), is a missionary serving in Pecs, Hungary, with Baptist World Mission. He previously served as a professor at San Francisco Baptist Seminary in California.

January 1

The Boy Preacher

Scripture: Titus 3:1-15

January 1 symbolizes new beginnings. We start a new year with a new calendar and often a new hope. So it was with David Marks, the "Boy Preacher."

Marks, of Junius, New York, was saved in 1816 when he was ten years old. He desired to be baptized, but for some reason his Calvinistic Baptist church rejected his request two or three times. Although not yet a teenager, Marks believed that God was calling him to the ministry. He and his parents believed that a good education would be a very important part of his preparation. Believing that he could obtain an education at no charge because of the poverty of his family, he left home in 1819, when but thirteen years of age, and went to Brown University. How disappointed he must have been when the president informed him that only the tuition would be free. He had no alternative but to return home with a heavy heart.

Shortly after his return, two Freewill Baptists, Zebulon Dean and Samuel Wire, heard of his situation and traveled thirty miles to see him. This meeting began his connection with the Freewill Baptists. He requested baptism from them, and on July 11 he followed the Lord in believer's baptism.[1]

He traveled to New Hampshire on a preaching tour when he was 15. As a result, he was offered six months' support at school and all his tuition free, if he would dedicate himself to study. Believing, instead, that he should devote his time and effort to preaching, he declined the offer. How frequently today does this same attitude keep many a promising young preacher from further education.

On January 1, 1821, he left home again at the request of Rev. Zebulon Dean and spent a few weeks with him in protracted meetings, usually giving an exhortation after the sermon. Being only fifteen years of age, he was called "the boy preacher" and was sometimes treated with coldness and at other times with abuse. While on a later western preaching tour, he learned that his father's house with all its contents had been consumed by fire, but he continued his meetings. Then he received by letter the painful news of his mother's death. This brought him back to Junius, where he mingled his tears and prayers with surviving friends over their loss.

In June 1822, Marks left for Sandusky City, Ohio, by boat. The captain refused to land him at Sandusky but set him and four others ashore on a peninsula six miles across the bay. The keeper of the lighthouse was the only person on the peninsula, and his supply of provisions was nearly exhausted. It was sunset, and Marks had eaten but one meal in the last forty hours and was now without money or provisions. He said of that event, "I lay down on the floor, and closed my eyes to sleep, hoping to forget my hunger. But recollections of kind brethren in New York, contrasted with my present situation, drove slumber from my eyes. When the men who landed with me had fallen asleep, the keeper, remembering the poor boy that had come far from a father's house to preach the Gospel, brought me a cracker and half a pint of milk. This was a delicious morsel, and I received it with thanksgiving."[2]

Wisely, Marks later changed his view toward the necessity of an education.[3] He felt constrained to preach, but could he not study, too? He took a job on the Erie Canal for the purpose of buying books. His fellow-laborers recognized "the boy preacher," and, learning of his desire to purchase books for study, they took up a collection; in return, he preached to them in the evening. After that, while on the road from one appointment to another or in his room after a meeting, he applied himself to personal study.[4]

Perhaps you know some young man who desires to preach but is struggling with the cost of a Bible college education. What an encouragement you could be to him!

LRO

---

[1] I. D. Stewart, *The History of the Freewill Baptists* (Dover: Freewill Baptist Printing Establishment, 1861), 324.

[2] Ibid., 423.

[3] Ibid., 367.

[4] Ibid., 402.

January 2

Do You Love Your Pastor?

Scripture: Hebrews 13:7, 16-18

There is an interesting anecdote concerning one of the early black Baptist churches in America. But let us first consider the black Baptist beginnings in our land. Prior to the Civil War, Baptist slaves who trusted Christ as Savior united with the white Baptist churches as members. Usually they were seated in "slave balconies," but they were part of the congregation. Often the black slaves outnumbered the white members of those churches. But God mightily gifted some former slaves to preach the Gospel, and gradually a desire developed among the slaves that they might have their own churches.

The first black Baptist church in America was formed in Savannah, Georgia, on January 20, 1788. Abraham Marshall (Vol. 1:127-128), who was the white pastor of the Kiokee Baptist Church in Appling, Georgia, and Jesse Peter (black) instituted the work. The first black pastor was George Lisle (Vol. 1:26-27; 206-207), who ultimately traveled to Jamaica and built an outstanding black Baptist church there. He was succeeded by Andrew Bryan (Vol. 1:27, 162). The First African Baptist Church of Savannah, Georgia, continued to grow.

On December 26, the Second Baptist Church was organized with two hundred members, and on January 2, 1803, another church was formed. It was called the Ogeechee Colored Baptist Church, and it began with 250 members. In 1805, the Joy Baptist Church was established in Boston, Massachusetts, and that was followed in 1808 by the Abyssinian Baptist Church of New York City.

However, the birth of the sixth black Baptist church is the focal point of our interest today. In June of 1809, the First African Baptist Church of Philadelphia was organized. The first pastor of this church was Rev. Henry Cunningham. Not much is known of Cunningham's early days, but in 1802, his name appeared in church records as a deacon of the First African Baptist Church of Savannah.

Later, he requested a letter from that church to join the white Savannah Baptist Church.[1] From there he became the pastor of the Second Baptist Church in Savannah. The membership consisted of "intelligent domestic servants and some mechanics."[2] In time Rev. Cunningham was invited by Rev. Henry Holcombe, pastor of the First Baptist Church of Philadelphia, to accept the pastorate of the First African Baptist Church in that city.

There was really only one problem. Reverend Henry Cunningham was still a slave! Some preacher/slaves had been given their freedom by their masters. This had been true of George Lisle and John Jaspers. But such was not the case with Reverend Cunningham. The members at the Second Baptist Church in Savannah asked his master to allow him to go North and raise the money to purchase his freedom. The request was refused unless Reverend Cunningham could furnish security.

What could be done? There was no way he could provide security! But thank God for faithful members. Two members of his congregation, men who were free-born, bound themselves into servitude in his stead that their pastor might go to the North and raise the necessary finances.

Upon successfully raising the money, Reverend Cunningham informed his bondsmen and expressed a willingness to return. This offer was refused, the money was sent, and the two bondsmen were freed. They joined their pastor in Philadelphia to assist in forming the nucleus of the First African Baptist Church of Philadelphia.[3]

What love those members showed their pastor. I wonder how many church members who read this volume would be willing to make such a commitment for the man of God who serves them as God's undershepherd. May the Lord grant such a love among the children of God in this twenty-first century.

DLC

---

[1] Leroy Fitts, *A History of Black Baptists* (Nashville, TN: Broadman Press, 1985), 48.

[2] Ibid., 48.

[3] N. H. Pius, *An Outline of Baptist History* (Nashville, TN: National Baptist Publishing Board, 1911), 60.

January 3

Confirming His Death, Burial, and Resurrection

Scripture: Matthew 3:13-17

I am amused and quite amazed when I read certain professed religious historians who claim that immersion was unknown among Baptists until 1641. The members of the Westminster Assembly who presented the famed Presbyterian Westminster Confession of Faith, came within one vote of demanding immersion as the Presbyterian form of baptism.[1] When the Presbyterians gained ascendency in Great Britain, they reversed the law of 1534 that had enforced immersion. Reverend J. F. Bliss in his *Letters on Christian Baptism*, summarized the acts of Parliament as follows: "The original law of 1534 enforced immersion, and those who were not baptized were to be treated as outlaws. The law was passed when the Roman Catholic Church was abandoned and the present Established Church inaugurated in its stead. However, this law was repealed by an act of Parliament in 1644, at least so much of the old law as enforced immersion, and they passed an act enforcing sprinkling in its stead, and left the original penalty annexed to outlaws, being deprived of the inheritance of the state, the right of burial, and in short, of all of the rights to other sprinkled citizens of the realm . . . After 1648 immersion was prohibited and for many years made penal."[2]

The purpose of passing the above mentioned law was to choke the Baptist cause that was prospering in the land. The actual wording of the law that was passed on January 3, 1644 or 1645 follows: "Then the minister is to demand the name of the child, which being told him, he is to say (calling the child by name) I baptize thee in the name of the Father, of the Son, and of the Holy Ghost.

"As he pronounceth the words, he is to baptize the child with water; which for the manner of doing it is not only lawful but sufficient and most expedient to be, by pouring or sprinkling of the water on the face of the child, without adding any other ceremony."[3]

Previously to that time in Great Britain all denominations in Christendom had practiced baptism by immersion. The introduction of pouring and sprinkling was a novelty in Great Britain. Previously, the Roman Catholic Church had practiced sprinkling, but that practice had been unknown in Great Britain among the Protestants until it was introduced by the Presbyterian practice.

Dr. W. H. King of London made a complete search of the subject of baptism in the pamphlets found in the British Museum. He reported as follows: "I have carefully examined the titles of the pamphlets in the first three volumes of this catalogue, more than 7,000 in number, and have read every pamphlet which has seemed by its title to refer to the subject of baptism, or the opinions and practices of the Baptists, with this result: that I can affirm, with the most unhestitating confidence, that in these volumes there is not a sentence or a hint from which it can be inferred that the Baptists generally, or any section of them, or even any individual Baptist, held any other opinion than that immersion is the only true and Scriptural method of baptism, either before the year 1641 or after it."[4]

Surely baptism has nothing to do with one's salvation. The Lord Jesus Christ was not baptized to make Him the Son of God. He was baptized to manifest the fact that He was the Son of God. For that reason we who are trusting Jesus Christ alone as our Savior are to be baptized. Our Savior left us an example that we should follow in His steps. Surely we ought to follow as perfectly as possible, and that calls for the immersion of the believer as he or she is buried in the likeness of the Savior and raised to walk in newness of life. We thank God for this beautiful ordinance as it pictures our lovely Savior.

DLC

---

[1] Thomas Armitage, *A History of the Baptists* (New York: Bryan, Taylor & Co., 1890), 438.

[2] John T. Christian, *A History of the Baptists* (Texarkana: American Baptist Association, 1922), 1:296.

[3] Ibid., 1:196-297.

[4] Ibid., 1:298.

January 4

Paul or John the Baptist?

Scripture: 1 Corinthians 14:8-12

It is amazing and assuring to realize how our God uses such varied personalities and diversely gifted men to preach the Gospel. After all, it is not the messenger but the message that is important. Doubtless one of the finest orators to grace a Baptist pulpit in America was William Staughton. He was born in Coventry, England, on January 4, 1770, and his brilliance was revealed early when at the age of twelve he published poems in Goldsmith's *Animated Nature*. He was saved early in life, and baptized by Reverend Samuel Pearce of Birmingham. In 1792 he graduated from Bristol Baptist College, but, while a student, he attended the organizational meeting of the first modern-day missionary agency in the world. Though still a youth, he sat in company with William Carey and Andrew Fuller. Following his academic training, he served briefly as pastor in Northampton, and then sailed to America in 1793.

Richard Furman requested him to serve as pastor of the Baptist church in Georgetown, South Carolina, and he remained their briefly. Ordained on June 17, 1797, he served two churches in New Jersey. He assisted in establishing a seminary, and, though he was only twenty-eight years old, his work was so impressive that he was awarded an honorary doctorate from Princeton in 1798. From 1805 to 1823, he served as pastor of First Baptist and Sansom Street Baptist churches in Philadelphia. During that period he also served as principal of a Baptist theological institution, taught botany in area schools, and founded the Philadelphia Bible Society. During that time he also served as corresponding secretary of the American Baptist Board of Foreign Missions. In 1823 he was appointed the first president of Columbian College in Washington, D. C. In 1829 he accepted the offer to become president of Georgetown College. He sent his library ahead in preparation of the move, but was never able to fulfill that commitment. He became ill, and passed into the presence of his Lord on December 12, 1829.

The erudite William Staughton surely was not surpassed by any Baptist preacher in America in mental ability, and it is questionable that any were more adroit in speech. But in addition to all his learning, William Staughton spoke with spiritual authority, and the blessings of God were attendant upon his multi-faceted ministry.

With that in mind, it is thrilling to realize that the man of God was not an elitist. He realized that the Lord of the Harvest prepared his laborers for various fields of ministry. While pastoring the prestigious Sansom Street Baptist Church, Reverend Staughton invited an old-fashioned minister from what was considered the "boonies," the wooded area of western Pennsylvania, to preach in his pulpit.

"The old gentleman dressed in his sheep's gray, and buttons to match, went through the preliminary exercises very acceptably; but when he came to the preaching, feeling that he must be particularly fine, he was in danger of making an entire failure. The intelligent audience could hardly restrain their laughter. Doctor Staughton was sitting on nettles, and inwardly asking what should be done? Knowing that the old gentleman was "a good deal of a man when he was himself," the Doctor nervously pulled the speaker by the coat, and hurriedly whispered, "Brother! Brother!! Give it to them bush fashion." The old gentleman swung off into the same style in which he preached in the woods of western Pennsylvania, and was then perfectly irresistible. The audience which had commenced with laughing ended with praying; and 'Give it to them bush fashion," grew into a proverb which is doing its work of profitable admonition even to this day."[1]

Baptists have more variety in preaching styles than any other religious group in America. I have been blessed while enjoying sound exegetical treatment of God's Word, but I have also been thrilled with simple, home-spun, soul-stirring, gospel preaching. In these days when we hear much about "cloning," it is well that each God-called preacher develop his ability to its greatest extent without being forced into a mold that promises success. May God, in our day, raise up Dr. Staughtons along with back-woods preachers who are all true to His Word.

DLC

[1] Joseph Belcher, *The Religious Denominations in the United States* (Philadelphia: John E. Potter, 1856), 188.

January 5

Who Were the Anabaptists?

Scripture: Matthew 5:10-11; Luke 6:26

I weary of reading current-day historians who faithfully read Anabaptist antagonists of the past but who never give attention to the more recent historical findings. I feel like saying, "Shame on you! You ought to do your homework. Your personal bias is showing!" On this date in 1527 two outstanding Anabaptists paid the price for their faith. Felix Manz, known as the Apollo of the Anabaptists, was drowned in Lake Zurich for his testimony. George Blaurock, considered the Hercules of the movement, was stripped to the waist and severely beaten. Many church historians speak of the Anabaptists as mere heretics. But is this a true evaluation? Have current Baptists any "spiritual" relationship to them? Early in this volume I want to honor the sacred memory of the spiritual Anabaptists with whom fundamental Baptists today have much in common. This will prepare the reader for the history of a number of these stalwarts of the faith whose memory is honored in this volume.

A reputable historian has said: "Information on the groups [of Anabaptists] has been notoriously scarce and has rested in the main upon hostile polemics."[1] It is apparent that the Anabaptists in the days of the Reformers realized their principles had long endured. They maintained the "...principle that the True Church could not have been destroyed since the founding . . . ."[2]

Dr. Roland H. Bainton connects Anabaptists with the ancient Donatists when he acknowledges that "The parallels between the Anabaptists and Donatists were however, more than superficial."[3] I am not implying that Bainton claimed an actual relationship between the Donatists and the Anabaptists of the Reformation period. But he wrote of their similar persecutions: "To call these people Anabaptists, that is rebaptizers, was to malign them, because they denied that baptism was repeated, inasmuch as infant baptism is no baptism at all. They called themselves simply Baptists, not re-Baptists. The offensive name was fastened on them in order to bring them under the penalty of the Justinian Code against the Donatists." It is interesting that those known as "Anabaptists" were willing to assume the simple name of "Baptists."

Leonard Verduin, historian of the Christian Reformed Denomination stated: "We know that at the time of the birth of the Hybrid [the Anabaptists of the days of the Reformation] there were already people who were called 'Anabaptists.'"[4]

Interestingly, C. A. Cornelius (1819-1903), a Roman Catholic scholar, was among the first historians to call for modern research of the Anabaptist movement. Prior to that time, professed historians followed the deliberations of hostile polemics.

"Scholars of preceding generations have leaned heavily upon the highly partisan and quite unreliable accounts of sixteenth-century Anabaptism in the writings of Ulrich Zwingli, Justus Menius, Heinrich Bullinger, and Christoph Fischer, to say nothing of the milder but just as erroneous accounts of Martin Luther and Philip Melanchthon."[5]

Unfortunately, some professors of Church History in fundamental schools are guilty of continuing the quotations of the enemies of these stalwart heroes of the faith who gave their lives for truth. In his scholarly work of 1882, Henry Burrage wrote: "No one among us would be satisfied with a history of the Reformation in Germany, prepared by Dr. Eck, or any other of Luther's opponents; but works concerning the Anabaptists, written by their bitterest enemies, are received by writers of almost every name as trustworthy history."[6]

We are not calling for a direct link with the Anabaptists, but we praise the Lord for our spiritual affinity with the faithful in their ranks.

DLC

---

[1] Franklin Hamlin Littell, *The Origins of Sectarian Protestantism* (New York: The Macmillan Company, 1964), Introduction XIIV.

[2] Ibid., 81.

[3] Roland H. Bainton, *The Reformation of the Sixteenth Century* (Boston: Beacon Press, 1985), 98-99.

4 Leonard Verduin, *The Anatomy of a Hybrid* (Grand Rapids, MI: William B. Eerdmans Publishing Company, 1976), 149.

5 William R. Estep, *The Anabaptist Story* (Nashville, TN: Broadman Press, 1963), 1.

6 Henry S. Burrage, *A History of the Anabaptists in Switzerland* (Philadelphia: American Baptist Publication Society, 1882), 1.

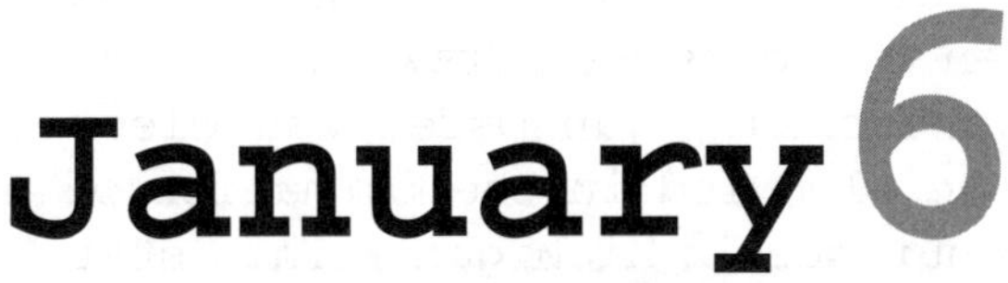

A Faithful Soldier

Scripture: Philippians 2:25-30

The last ministry of Pastor Oliver Willis Van Osdel is worthy of a separate study. (Mar. 7)

In 1909, at age sixty-two, Van Osdel was called to return to Grand Rapids, Michigan, to again pastor the Wealthy Street Baptist Church.[1] That a church he had formerly served would think enough of him to call him again is a wonderful compliment to this man. His ministry in Grand Rapids is noteworthy, but his leadership in Baptist circles in the North is most significant.

The years in the Grand Rapids pastorate were characterized by the same building, evangelism, and growth that distinguished the first thirty-five years of Dr. Van Osdel's work for Christ. In 1895 the church had been unwilling to build. By 1909 they had experienced sufficient growth to know they must build. Through much sacrifice and hardship, the new edifice was constructed in phases. The completed building, seating 1300 for worship and providing classrooms for 1000, was built from 1912-1917.[2] It served the congregation until 1982.[3] Van Osdel also devoted himself to leading the church in evangelism and missions outreach. At the end of his ministry, eighteen people from the church were serving the Lord as missionaries, thirteen of them in foreign countries.[4] "He seems, for instance, to have played some part in the organization of . . . Baptist Mid-Missions."[5]

We must also understand Van Osdel's influence among fundamentalist Baptists of his day. The modernist-fundamentalist war raged from the early 1900s, and Van Osdel was a staunch fundamentalist. There seem to have been strong differences with his son, because Edgar was more tolerant of modernism than his father.[6]

Van Osdel provided strong leadership for Baptists in the fight with modernists within the Baptist groups in the North. Because of the modernism in the Grand Rapids Baptist Association, fourteen churches withdrew and formed a new area association of churches. Van Osdel was elected as the first moderator. He also led in the formation of a new state association of churches in Michigan. This statewide association was a protest of and separation from modernism in Baptist circles.

The battle also raged on the national scene. In 1920 fundamentalists within the Northern Baptist Convention met in a Conference on Baptist Fundamentals in Buffalo, New York. That organization survives as the Fundamental Baptist Fellowship. Van Osdel was not against this movement, but he was skeptical of its prospects for success, viewing it as a "smiling protest."[7] Compromises by leaders within the movement, most notably by Jasper C. Massee, doomed any hope the Fundamentalist Fellowship within had for success. Massey "betrayed" the fundamentalists who had named him to lead them.[8]

In 1922 another group called the Baptist Bible Union was formed. This movement spread its influence farther than the Northern Baptist Convention. T. T. Shields from Canada, William Bell Riley from Minnesota, and J. Frank Norris from Texas were the dominant leaders in that movement. The story of the Baptist Bible Union and its tragic demise is too long to tell here. Van Osdel was the only Baptist leader who was part of the Union from its birth in 1922 until its end in 1930.

Another movement was to grow out of the ruins of the Baptist Bible Union, and the aging Van Osdel was the driving force behind it. On May 15, 1932, the General Association of Regular Baptist Churches was formed in Chicago. It maintained a consistent separatist, fundamentalist, Baptist testimony for many years.

Van Osdel resigned from the Wealthy Street Church on August 20, 1934. He died January 1, 1935. There is no written account of the memorial service for him. On Sunday, January 6, 1935, David Otis Fuller preached a memorial sermon, "Home - to Be With Jesus."[9] Van Osdel fought modernism, encouraged fundamentalists, and helped to establish a fellowship of Baptist churches. At a memorial service for him, J. Frank Norris said: "I didn't grieve for him. When he went home I said, 'Hail, victorious soldier!'"[10]

FJM

---

[1] Kevin Thomas Bauder, "Biography of O. W. Van Osdel" (unpublished Th.M. Thesis, Denver Baptist Theological Seminary, 1983), 17. I am indebted to Dr. Bauder for the use of this thesis, from which all the information in this entry is taken.

[2] Ibid., 23.

[3] Ibid., 24.

[4] Ibid., 26.

[5] Ibid., 26.

[6] Ibid., 18-19.

[7] Ibid., 49.

[8] Ibid., 56.

[9] Ibid., 99.

[10] Cited in Bauder, 99.

January 7

From Deism to Theism; From Medicine to Ministry

Scripture: Philippians 1:21

Ezekiel Skinner, the only child of Ezekiel and Mary Skinner, was born in Glastenbury, Connecticut on June 27, 1777.[1] By the age of ten both of his parents had passed away, and young Ezekiel was left orphaned. His uncle apprenticed the lad to a blacksmith, but Ezekiel's mental ability caused his disinterest in the trade. Through his efforts as a young man, Ezekiel was enabled to purchase his last year of apprenticeship, thus allowing him to complete his educational background. As time passed he entered the study of medicine, attending medical schools at both Hebron, Connecticut, and Philadelphia.

At this period of his life, Ezekiel became a Deist, and he became bold in asserting that position. On one occasion he declared that he wished to have his infidel sentiments engraved on his tombstone.

In 1801 Mr. Skinner was licensed to practice medicine, and on November 22, 1801, he married Sarah Mott of Chatliam, Connecticut. His medical practice took him to Granville, Massachusetts, and it was there the young doctor came to a personal saving knowledge of the Savior. At the time he united with the Congregational church, and he remained a Congregational member for the next few years of his life. After carefully examining the matter of immersion, Dr. Skinner became convinced that he ought to obey the Lord in the waters of immersion, and in 1807 he united with the Baptists in Lebanon, Massachusetts.

During the War of 1812, Dr. Skinner enlisted as a foot soldier and joined the troops on the Canadian border. However, when it was discovered that he was a physician, his services were demanded in military medicine. Following the War, the Skinner family moved to Stafford, Connecticut, and while residing there, Dr. Skinner began to preach. His ministry was such that he was licensed to preach in 1819. With continued confidence that the Lord had indeed called him, his ministry became more and more acceptable. In time the congregation of the Baptist Church in Ashford, Connecticut, called the gifted Doctor to become their pastor, and he was ordained in 1822. For the next nine years he pastored the Ashford church, and a second ministry was carried on concurrently in the Baptist Church in Westford. The Westford ministry continued for another eight years.

The Skinner home surely was spiritually oriented for God and blessed with at least two sons. A son named Benjamin Skinner was born on January 7, 1803. That son grew up with a heart burdened for missions, and after being trained for Christian service in Hamilton, New York, he was ordained and was accepted as a missionary to Liberia on October 12, 1830. Before a year had passed, Benjamin, his wife and child, succumbed to a tropical disease and died. Doubtless the severe weather had entered into the problem, but undaunted, Dr. Ezekiel Skinner determined that the Lord would be pleased to have him replace his son in Liberia. Though the good Doctor was almost sixty years of age at the time, in 1834 he sailed for Liberia. He served in that difficult place for three years before returning to the States. He had determined to remain until a suitable replacement could be found, and he persisted in that task. Upon his return to the States, he assumed once again the role of physician and minister, and labored as such until a couple of months before his home-going. In April 1855, having resigned the pastoral charge at Westford, he took up his residence with a surviving son, Dr. E. D. Skinner, who was a physician in Greenville, Long Island. Dr. Skinner's health continued to decline, but even then he preached as occasions came up until two weeks of his home-going on Christmas, 1855.

Dr. Skinner surely lived an exciting life, but best of all, once he was saved, he determined that he would live his life to the full for the glory of our Savior. In reading a summary of Dr. Skinner's life, we ought to ask ourselves if what we are living for is worth dying for. At best, life is short, and only what we do for Christ will endure. May we today dedicate ourselves anew to God's will for our lives. As our Scripture verse indicates, may He be our source, our sustenance, our substance, and our satisfaction.

DLC

---

[1] William B. Sprague, *Annals of the American Pulpit* (New York: Robert Carter & Brothers, 1865), VI 695.

January 8

Never Too Late

Scripture: 2 Timothy 2:15

It would be difficult to imagine one in more extreme financial straits than those faced by our subject of this entry. He was born into poverty on January 8, 1852, in Monticello, Arkansas.[1] His parents, Benajah and Mary Carroll had married in North Carolina, and had moved first to Mississippi and then to Arkansas. From there, when our subject was six years old, the family moved on westward to Burleson County, Texas. There were twelve children in the Carroll family. In Burleson County James Milton Carroll obtained the little education available in small country and village schools. Due to the turbulent times in which he grew to manhood, his education was sadly wanting. However, he had an excellent mind. Mr. and Mrs. Carroll's estate was primarily wrapped up in the slaves that they owned, and with the Civil War and freeing of the slaves, the family was impoverished. Benajah Carroll died during the Civil War when James was only ten years old, and, in 1868, when the lad was sixteen, his mother, Mary, died. Thus James Carroll was cast upon his own ingenuity as a teenager.

Before his nineteenth birthday, James married sixteen-year-old Sudie Wamble. The teenage couple settled down to farming on rented property. Early in their marriage, James responded to the call of God to preach, and was licensed to do so by the Liberty Baptist Church in Burleson County. Soon he realized the limitations of his education, and determined to do something about it. He had not finished the seventh grade, but he determined to attend Baylor University, entering in January of 1873. His wife also decided she would further her education, and enrolled in Baylor College. It is difficult to understand how, but by taking double courses every semester, in five years James graduated with a Master of Arts degree. During college days he had taken Latin, Greek, and Hebrew. Furthermore, he had a multitude of honors in many varied subjects.

His gifts soon became apparent. He became pastor of the Baptist Church in Anderson, Texas, and served there for two years. During that period he served as Corresponding Secretary of the Sunday School Convention of Texas. He was then sent as a missionary to establish a ministry in Corpus Christi, Texas. Upon the completion of that task, he went to Lampasas, Texas to pastor. The young preacher was greatly concerned for prohibition, and he resigned his pastorate to work diligently on that project. Following successful work there, he accepted a call to reestablish the Baptist church in Taylor, Texas. During the next period of his life he served as agent of Foreign Mission work for Texas; agent for Baylor Female College; and then he became the Corresponding Secretary of the Texas Education Commission. When he was able to talk his brother, B. H. Carroll, into assuming that role, James was elected pastor of the First Baptist Church of Waco. He resigned that assignment when solicited by the board of trustees of Baylor University to begin work for the endowment of the school. It is difficult to picture James Carroll as a teenager with only seven grades of education, when one considers what he accomplished in life. Prayer, hard work, determination, and grit paid off.

Overshadowed by his more famous brother, Benajah Harvey Carroll, J. M. Carroll's contributions to the Baptist denomination have all but been eclipsed.[2] His most outstanding literary achievements were *A History of Texas Baptists*; and the biography of his older brother, *B. H. Carroll, the Colossus of Baptist History*. However, posthumously, he authored a small paperback that has been treasured by many throughout our land. I allude to the booklet, *The Trail of Blood*.

Perhaps someone is reading this account whom God has burdened for the ministry or for missions. You realize that your education has been limited. May I suggest it is not too late. If you have the faith, determination, and grit, you can still obtain an education and excel. God is no respecter of persons. He will see you through too, IF you are willing to expend the energy and remain faithful to the task. Let J. M. Carroll be a stimulus in your life.

DLC

---

[1] B. J. W. Graham, *Baptist Biography* (Atlanta, GA: Index Printing Company, 1923), 2:47.

[2] W. R. Estep, Jr., *Encyclopedia of Southern Baptists* (Nashville, TN: Broadman Press, 1958), 1:233.

January 9

Victory Over our Last Enemy

Scripture: Matthew 10:17-21

Hunters of our Anabaptist forefathers usually captured the so-called heretics singly, but on January 9, 1558[1], the police broke into a small congregation of twelve in Aachen on the Rhine and seized all who were present, even an infant still in a cradle.

As was often the custom, individual members of the congregation were tortured on the rack, and some were suspended from the ground by their arms with heavy iron weights attached to their feet. Of the group, one man recanted, but five remained steadfast. Six women were flogged and exiled and five men were strangled and burned in October 1558. The leader of the group was Hans Schmidt, a missionary who had traveled down the Rhine River to Aachen and the Netherlands. Elsewhere we have mentioned the missionary efforts of the Anabaptists, and Hans Schmidt had been given to that ministry. Of course, as leader of the captured group, he would be the first one to be executed.

As they awaited martyrdom, Anabaptist prisoners were detained in separate cells. Their days were filled with torture as their captors attempted to gain information concerning others of the Anabaptist assemblies. To encourage one another, the prisoners would sing hymns as loudly as possible.

Prior to his execution, and while suffering the various procedures of torture, Hans Schmidt composed hymns and was able also to smuggle several dozen letters out of the prison. These hymns and letters provided many details concerning torture, interrogation, and life as it was experienced while incarcerated.

It is well to remember that martyrdom became an Anabaptist hallmark. People from every walk of life gave their lives rather than recant. Many unknown heroes and heroines became unforgettable witnesses of God's grace in the hour of death. The Anabaptists referred to a glorious death as a "good witness." Men would prepare the message they were determined to give at the time of their execution, and for this reason,

Michael Sattler's tongue was cut out that he might not speak. The Anabaptists seized upon the time of execution for evangelizing. Hans Schmidt was no exception. As he went to death, Hans Schmidt's voice rang with a hymn of joy he had composed.

In you, O Father
Is my joy,
Though I must suffer here!
Let me be scorned
By everyone
If your grace still is here!

It has well been mentioned that "The Anabaptists saw themselves living again the painful persecution of the apostolic church, hounded by cruel political and religious lords who had no mercy . . . . The true follower of Jesus will not hesitate to drink the cup He drank (John 18:11); indeed he will expect it. 'For whosoever will not suffer with Christ also will not rule with Him, and whosoever does not have this Holy Spirit is no Christian. . . . Thus the Anabaptists developed a theology of suffering, transforming the persecuted remnant into a triumphant church, rich in historical significance . . . . The idea of suffering became their moving power and hope . . . .'"[2]

Most Christians today are unaware that sufferings and martyrdoms are still present in the world. Accurate reports are squelched by our liberal media, but martyrdoms still take place. The persecution of Christians was renewed in the 20th century and witnessed more than 100 million Christians persecuted and martyred in Africa, Asia, and even Europe. In Sudan, followers of Christ among the tribes of the central and southern areas of the nation have engaged in a life-and-death struggle against radical Moslem invaders from the north. There have been reports not only of martyrdoms, but of believers in the Nuba mountains in southern Sudan who have been sold into slavery.

From the former Soviet Union and Eastern Europe to Africa, Asia, and Latin America, thousands of believers have disappeared into Gulags, been gunned down by dictators, and decapitated by Moslem fanatics from the north.

What if martyrdom became common in America? How would modern-day believers respond? This question must be considered. Surely our Lord gives us grace for living, but He is able to provide us with grace for dying as well.

DLC

---

[1] John S. Oyer and Robert S. Kreider, *Mirror of the Martyrs* (Intercourse, PA, Good Books, 1990), 32.

[2] Frankling Hamlin Littell, *The Origins of Sectarian Protestantism* (New York: The Macmillan Company, 1964), 131-132.

January 10

Faithfulness to the Word

Scripture: Nehemiah 8:1-18

From the earliest days of the British and Foreign Bible Society (founded in 1804) and the American Bible Society (founded in 1816), Baptists supported and encouraged the translation of the Bible into numerous languages. However a conflict eventually developed, which caused the Baptists to withdraw from fellowship with these interdenominational Bible societies. In the 1830's the British and Foreign Bible Society refused to support Carey's Bengali translation and the American Bible Society refused to support Judson's Burmese translation because they both had translated the Greek *baptizo* as "immerse." As a result, on both continents, the Baptists moved their support to new Bible societies that would be true to the original meaning of Scripture.

During the half century after these two divisions, the Baptists had occasionally sought to restore fellowship between the various Bible societies. While at times some headway was made, the refusal to recognize the actual meaning of *baptizo* continued to create a barrier to reunion.

In 1886 the Anglican Bishop of Rangoon, Burma, and the British and Foreign Bible Society sent a request to the American Baptists for permission to reprint Judson's Burmese translation, but with one change - replacing "immerse" with the transliteration "baptize." Judson's reply to an earlier similar request had been: "I would rather lose my right hand than tamper with the Word of God."[1]

The reply from the American Baptists, written on January 10, 1887, deserves quotation as an epitome of the sentiment of the Baptists of that day:

> We understand that you ask our consent to change Dr. Judson's translation of the word "baptize" and its cognates, either "by transliterating the Greek word," after the manner of the English version, or by adopting "a neutral term which all denominations might use." . . . You make this request not on the ground that the present rendering is an incorrect or inadequate translation of the Greek word, but because it is not acceptable to other denominations of Christians. You seem to regard it as more important to please these other denominations than to make the Burman version mean the same thing to the Burman that the Greek Testament means to the Greek. . . . We are compelled to decline:
>
> 1. Because we cannot consent to obscure or neutralize the plain meaning of our Lord's command. The leading authorities, both in classical and New Testament Greek, define the word "baptize" by words signifying to "immerse" or to "dip." In such a question we must be guided simply by a sense of loyalty to Him who gave the word, and not by a desire under other conditions to meet their wishes. We cannot, we dare not, deliberately obscure or neutralize any word of Christ.
>
> 2. Because Judson's translation describes the act of baptism as it was accepted and practised by the apostles and their immediate successors, the New Testament and all credible church historians being witnesses.
>
> 3. Because Judson's translation follows the precedents established by versions of the best repute, both ancient and modern, made by men who acted without bias before any question had arisen about baptism, and with a single purpose to express the real meaning of the Greek text. . . .
>
> 4. Because the rule which you have adopted is invidious to the extent of positive injustice, in that it discriminates, not against a novel and unauthorized rendering of the word "baptize" and

its cognates, but against a numerous and influential body of Christians who conform to the New Testament law of baptism and the practice of the primitive ages of the church....

Of course you do not mean to say that the British and Foreign Bible Society will not join in circulating a version which translates "baptize" by a word meaning immerse. . . . What you really mean is, that you will not circulate such a version if it be made by Baptists, for a people whose practice it would be likely to shape or determine. You will circulate it if made or used by a people who say, "I immerse thee," when they simply apply their wet fingers to the forehead of the candidate....

J. N. Murdock, *Cor Secretary*.[2]

May we be as faithful as these Baptists in upholding the truth of God's Word!

LRO

---

[1] C. C. Bitting, *Bible Societies and the Baptists* (Philadelphia: American Baptist Publication Society, 1897), 77.

[2] Ibid., 77-79.

January 11

A Gifted Orator

Scripture: 1 Corinthians 1:11-18

One of the early Baptist "evangelists" in America was Thomas Jefferson Fisher. He was born on April 9, 1812, in Mount Sterling, Kentucky. His father was of German extraction and had moved to Kentucky from Pennsylvania. Young Mr. Fisher made a profession of faith when he was sixteen and united with the Presbyterian church at Paris, Kentucky. A year later, however, he was baptized with believer's immersion by Jeremiah Vardeman. He then united with the Baptist church in Davids Fork, Fayette County. Being from a large family of thirteen children, educational opportunities were very limited. Having an insatiable desire to learn, young Mr. Fisher became a tailor and paid for his own schooling.

He traveled to Middletown, Pennsylvania, and entered a private academy remaining there until 1831. At that time he removed to Pittsburgh to study under another private tutor, a Baptist preacher. During his second year in Pittsburgh, Thomas Fisher was licensed to preach by the church of which his tutor was pastor. In 1834, the young twenty-two-year-old man was ordained at Lawrenceburg and the following February he accepted a call to pastor the Mill Creek Baptist Church near Bardstown. But it soon became apparent that Thomas Fisher was really not gifted with a pastor's heart, and he resigned that pastorate. From that time onward his ministry was primarily that of an evangelist.

He has been described as "a strangely gifted orator."[1] Though he made his home in Kentucky, most of his "protracted meetings" were held in the South. Vast crowds gathered to hear him preach, and it is estimated that 12,000 professed conversion under his ministry. On one occasion as he was returning from the Southland where he had ministered during the winter, he stopped on a Saturday night in Bowling Green, Kentucky. The Methodists were holding a protracted meeting, and they invited him to preach. In as much as he was so weary, he declined the invitation, but he agreed to preach on Monday morning.

"'I went to the meeting early,' said Mr. Wilkins, 'and took a seat by the side of the pulpit where I could observe the audience. The house was crowded. Mr. Fisher arose, read his text and started off happily. The audience was at once enchained, and, within forty minutes, the orator had lifted them to their feet. Every individual in the house, as far as I could see, was standing up and leaning forward, with open mouth, towards the speaker, apparently oblivious of all his surroundings, and so stood until the discourse was finished.'"[2]

Another described his ministry thus: "He was holding one of those characteristic revivals of his at Hardingsburg, Kentucky. . . . Fisher was in the height of all his peculiar glory, scattering 'star-dust' in the eyes of the astonished hearers, or pouring streams of sulfurous flames into their ears. The wild beauties, the extravagant imagery, the resounding pomp of words and scraps of sublime poetry . . . [held the audience]."[3]

For thirty-four years, Mr. Fisher traveled throughout the southern States in evangelism, but he devoted most of his time to meetings in Kentucky. He had extraordinary success in his labors, but his untimely death terminated his ministry on January 11, 1866. The great evangelist was shot in the head by an unknown assailant in Louisville, Kentucky, where he died three days later.

Few men are gifted as orators, but we are reminded that God used men of various gifts in the early days of the church. Paul and Peter had contrasting styles, and then we read of Apollos who was "eloquent." Some of the early saints began to exalt the messenger, and the saints in Corinth became divided by that practice. But more important than the style was that Paul, Peter, and Apollos were all men of God whom He had sent to honor the Book. Let us thank God for men whom He has gifted differently, but let us honor the message first, and lift high the Savior.

DLC

---

[1] William Cathcart, *The Baptist Encyclopaedia* (Philadelphia: Louis H. Everts, 1881), 1:396.

[2] J. H. Spencer, *A History of Kentucky Baptists* (Printed by the Author, 1886), 71-72.

[3] S. H. Ford, *Christian Repository*, (August 1871), 104.

January 12

Persevering For Truth

Scripture: 2 Corinthians 4:16-18

There is no doubt that the Commonwealth of Virginia provided the greatest challenge for Baptist advancement of any colony in early America. No denomination suffered at the hands of the gentry and clergy in Virginia as did the Separatist Baptists. A complete roster of persecutions among our forefathers in Virginia during the last half of the eighteenth century is impossible. Lewis Peyton Little's book, *Imprisoned Preachers and Religious Liberty in Virginia,* is the most integral study to date, but even that volume fails to chronicle every account of abuse.

Samuel Harris championed the cause of Separate Baptists in Virginia. January 12, 1724, marks the date of his birth, but he was not saved until 1758. He was a man of prestige, holding several positions of prominence. He served as sheriff, colonel of the militia, and captain of Mayo fort. But under the preaching of the Murphy boys, Harris found that "the arrow of the Almighty stuck fast,"[1] and he was gloriously saved. Daniel Marshall baptized him, and early it was apparent that the Lord's hand was upon him. He began preaching before his ordination, which took place in 1769. Though a leader, Harris' pathway was not easy. In 1765 he first preached in Culpepper County, but he was driven out of town by a mob. In Orange County he was pulled from the platform by a roughneck and abused until rescued by friends. On another occasion he was knocked down while preaching. However, it has been said that "Colonel Harris did not suffer as many persecutions as some other Baptist preachers. Perhaps his bold, noble, yet humble manner dismayed the ferocious spirits of the opposers of religion."[2]

Consider John Waller. He was on a grand jury at the trial of the Separatist Baptist, Lewis Craig. Mr. Craig told the jury: "I take joyfully the despoiling of my goods for Christ's sake. While I lived in sin the jury took no notice of me." That sweet testimony led to John Waller's salvation. In time he became an honored Separatist Baptist preacher. On one occasion as Waller was preaching, he was assaulted by a parson and a sheriff. The parson actually stuffed his whip handle down Waller's throat, but the man of God arose and returned to preaching the Gospel. John Taylor, John Koontz, William Webber, David Barrow, Lewis Lunsford, John Pickett, James Ireland, and Elijah Baker all suffered at the hands of mobs as they attempted to preach the Gospel.

On several occasions snakes were thrown into the midst of their audiences, and yet those dear preachers persisted in the task before them. Many attacks were made upon preachers and candidates when the ordinance of baptism was observed at a river. To further ridicule the ordinance of believer's immersion, at times Separatist Baptist preachers were plunged into mud with a threat of drowning them in the mire.

It must be reiterated that forty-four Baptist preachers were incarcerated. While imprisoned, an attempt was made to blow James Ireland up. Yet all of the attacks against them did not hinder the work of the Baptists. These stalwarts endured such trials with thanksgiving.

John Leland served in Virginia for fourteen years, and in that time he preached about three thousand sermons and baptized over seven hundred people. Prior to his salvation, John Waller was known as "swearing Jack Waller," but God wondrously transformed his life. During his ministry, Waller baptized in excess of two thousand people. At times he served five congregations simultaneously, and, he assisted in establishing eighteen churches. Waller's daughter, Ann, became the wife of Abraham Marshall, son of Daniel Marshall. Abraham followed his father as pastor of the Kiokee Baptist Church in Georgia and strengthened the cause of the Separatist Baptists there.

Surely the faithfulness of these men should stimulate us to faithfulness in these days when our enemy is not persecution from the world as much as apathy among the saints.

DLC

---

[1] Garnett Ryland, *The Baptists of Virginia 1699-1926* (Richmond, VA: The Virginia Baptist Board of Missions & Education, 1955), 38.

[2] Robert B. Semple, *History of the Rise and Progress of the Baptists in Virginia* (Layette, TN: Church History Research & Archives 1976), 383

January 13

Freedom in Russia?

Scripture: Genesis 10

When the iron curtain came down in 1991, many believers in America experienced euphoria thinking that total religious freedom would be experienced in Russia. They reasoned that Communism had failed and people would automatically turn to God and His Word. Indeed a semblance of freedom was allowed, but religious freedom was a totally new concept in the world's largest country. Russia was and is primarily Russian Orthodox, and the hierarchy of the Russian Orthodox church treasure a religious monopoly. With the crumbling of the USSR, Russia adopted a constitution officially allowing freedom of religion. However, that freedom has not been consistently respected across the country. Unlike most of the former Soviet republics, Russia has not established a central agency to deal with religious affairs. The result has produced a wide variation of perceived freedom, with regional authorities often harassing Baptists and other non-traditional groups.

In 1997, a national religion law was passed. It required churches to have existed in the country for fifteen years before being permitted to register. Without registration, churches had great restrictions placed upon them. This was particularly an issue for Baptist groups who refused state registration on principle. Remembering the abuses of official registration under the former Soviet Union, even if Baptist congregations met the fifteen year ruling (which was impossible), they still wanted nothing to do with registration. In September 2003, *The Moscow Times* reported that one non-registered, independent Baptist church was refused permission to rent any public buildings. The result was they had to meet outdoors in a city park. This requirement for registration was amended to allow for a re-registration for groups who were registered prior to the implementation of the 1997 law, but this, of course, gave no relief to independent Baptist congregations. Christian leaders have noticed an increasing intolerance toward non-Orthodox believers. New visas and visa renewals have been regularly denied for foreign religious workers.

In Tula, Russia, a Baptist church building of an independent Baptist congregation was blown up on January 13, 2004. Local authorities made the claim that the explosion was caused by faulty equipment within the building, but in a January report by the Union of Councils for Soviet Jews, witnesses testified to having seen a group of men around the building and the sound of breaking glass just before the explosion. The Baptists also established that the gas pipes were not damaged. The pastor had also recently received anonymous threats. City building experts have ruled that the building is beyond repair.

This Day in Baptist History III

Well-taught believers in America thrilled at the open door for evangelism when the iron curtain came down. There was a rush to strengthen the fundamental, unregistered Baptist churches. A spirit of urgency swept many Christians in an effort to get the printed Word of God into the hands of the Russians. Thank God for the progress that has been made in training young Russian Baptist pastors to reach and teach their own people. But most well-informed believers realized that the door was not being permanently opened. Communism is not dead, and the prophecies of the Scripture concerning the power of the North will be fulfilled. The nouns in Ezekiel 38 and 39 have for years been understood for to be Russia: Rosh or Gog for Russia; Meschech for Moscow; and Tubal for Tobolsk, the largest state. Genesis 10 is of help in establishing the identity of these names. Magog was the second son of Japheth who settled north of the Black Sea. Tubal and Meschech were the fifth and sixth sons of Japheth, whose descendants settled south of the Black Sea. These people intermarried and became known as Magog, the dominant tribe. When the nation was almost totally bankrupt, the hierarchy of the USSR realized that they must allow a bit of freedom temporarily and some capitalism. However, though communism surely failed, the socialistic dream that calls for a mighty amalgamated force from the North, lives on. We need to pray that our sovereign God shall protect and encourage His own in these days. And while the Lord keeps the door partially opened, we need to do all possible to support and send missionaries to evangelize and equip the saints with God's Word for the terrible days that await that land.

DLC

January 14

Not Only Faith, but Also Practice

Scripture: Revelation 2:1-7

The basic premise of Baptists has always been that the *"Bible is our only rule of faith and practice."* Historically the Bible has been foundational to everything Baptists believe. However, the Bible is not only the basis of our belief; it is also to be the fabric of our behavior. Whenever Baptists cease to uphold that principle in practice, trouble is bound to occur. Following the Civil War, great devastation was experienced throughout the South. As southern civilians fled before advancing Union armies, they left everything behind - including scores of abandoned Baptist buildings. In many parts of the country, law and order were non-existent. Anarchy ruled supremely in sections of the South, and widespread confusion ruled the day. In 1864 the American Baptist Home Mission Society noted: "In almost every city, town and village taken by our army, there has been found a deserted Baptist meeting-house. In many places these houses have been stripped of all that was movable, or converted into hospitals, stables, storehouses."

What was to be done to preserve those buildings? The Bible principle is, of course, the precious distinctive we know as the autonomy of each local church. The members of each of those church buildings were therefore responsible to care for God's property. They would surely return to their own houses and renovate their church building. But sincere men doubtless thought they had a plan that was a temporary fix during an emergency. When men ignore God's Word, or think they have a better idea than that expressed in the Bible, man is always proven wrong.

Perhaps with honorable intentions, the Home Mission Society asked the War Department in Washington for authority to take over abandoned Baptist buildings in the South. On January 14, 1864, the War Department notified its military personnel: "You are hereby directed to place at the disposal of the American Baptist Home Mission Society all houses of worship belonging to Baptist Churches South, in which a loyal minister does not now officiate."[1] The Home Mission Board appointed J. W. Parker of Boston to oversee the work. Soon he reported that about half of the Baptist meeting-houses in the South had been abandoned, but in essence the War Department gave authority for the Society to seize almost any Baptist building. All buildings were to be surrendered except where "a loyal minister" was to be found. But according to Washington's standards, surely very few existed in the South. In actuality, the very request of the Home Society at that point seemed to be logical, but it was not biblical, and it could only lead to added confusion!

Again, it is not my purpose to impugn motives. The intention of the well-meaning members of the Home Mission Society might have been totally unselfish. However, as one would expect, there were many abuses to the plan. Furthermore, that action stirred much indignation among the Baptists of the South, and served further to divide Baptists throughout America.

How many times Baptist history reveals failure among Baptist people when the Bible has not been accepted as the "only rule of . . . practice!" Associations and conventions have ended up preempting local congregations and confiscating the very buildings the people of God have sacrificially erected.

Space does not permit an inventory, but many illustrations of this truth could be presented. For instance, a local professed Bible-believing Baptist church may find itself in financial difficulty. Rather than urging God's children in the practice of voluntary tithes and offerings, some have reverted to the wisdom of the world in having bake sales, chili suppers, and other of the world's favorite fundraisers. When this happens, the needed money might ultimately be realized, but the testimony of the local church has been seriously injured.

May we learn well the lesson that we must not only TRUST (our only rule) but OBEY (our only practice) God's Word if we are to realize God's blessing.

DLC

---

[1] H. Leon McBeth, *The Baptist Heritage* (Nashville, TN: Broadman Press, 1987), 403.

January 15

Confessions of Faith

Scripture: Romans 11:33-36

The primary distinctive of Baptists is the bold assertion that the Bible is their only rule of faith and practice. However, mankind's attempt to completely systematize theology leads to the realization that a finite mind can never fully comprehend the infinite God. By faith we accept what we cannot reconcile, and we take comfort in the statement of God through Moses in Deuteronomy 29:29. *"The secret things belong unto the LORD our God: but those things which are revealed belong unto us and to our children for ever. . . ."* However, it is often true that the limited mind of man seems never willing to stop short of dogmatism. Extremism becomes the norm, and from time to time it becomes necessary to modify growing emphatic excesses.

Illustrations are apparent in Baptist history. In the late seventeenth century, Thomas Collier, the English "Apostle of the West," issued a "a Short Confession." This was "what one historian called 'the remarkable current away from Calvinism' by Collier and his western churches."[1] In the late eighteenth century, Andrew Fuller led in the modification of an extreme theological system [hyper-Calvinism] and prepared the way for the rebirth of missions. Baptists had gone to "seed" over Calvinism. Fuller said: "had matters gone on but a few years the Baptists would have become a perfect dunghill in society."[2]

Baptists have long prided themselves on not being a "creedal people," but Baptist confessions of faith have been with us since Hubmaier's Eighteen Dissertations of 1524, and Michael Sattler's Schleitheim Confession in 1527. A confession of faith affirms what Baptists of a local church or area believe, whereas a creed prescribes what members must believe. The confession is inclusive while a creed is exclusive.

Historians have distinguished the theological beliefs of our Baptist family using the terms "particular" or "general." Particular Baptists are so designated for their faith in a "particular redemption" including only the "elect." Whereas others are delineated as "General Baptists," believing in a "general redemption," meaning that Christ died for all mankind. Other differences are apparent, but the names of the two groups were fashioned by this distinctive.

As intimated with reference to Thomas Collier and Andrew Fuller, from time to time it seemed that a "correction" was needful. Both Collier and Fuller were "Particular Baptists," but they sensed that the emphasis was becoming too pronounced. A similar situation existed among American Baptists in the nineteenth century. This resulted in the New Hampshire Confession of Faith which was drawn up to modify what was perceived as a growing extreme emphasis of Calvinism. In June of 1830, "the Baptist Convention of New Hampshire appointed a committee to prepare and present at the next annual sessions 'such a Declaration of Faith and Practice, together with a Covenant, as may be thought agreeable and consistent with the views of all our churches in this state."[3] The purpose of tempering is apparent for the "...Calvinistic Baptists in the New Hampshire area had been considerably modified after 1870 ...."[4]

Various men worked on the drafting of the Confession, and on January 15, 1833, the copy was presented to the Board and approved with slight modifications. On the *Freeness of Salvation*, the Confession states: "We believe that the blessings of salvation are made free to all by the Gospel; that it is the immediate duty of all to accept them by a cordial, penitent, and obedient faith; and that nothing prevents the salvation of the greatest sinner on earth except his own inherent depravity and voluntary refusal to submit to the Lord Jesus Christ, which refusal will subject him to an aggravated condemnation."[5]

Adding a premillennial clause, fundamental Baptist groups throughout America soon adopted the Confession. In 1925 the Southern Baptist Convention adopted this Confession with slight modifications. This confession is perhaps reflective today of the theological position of a majority of Bible-believing Baptists in America. As Scripture admonishes, may we endeavor to keep the unity of the Spirit . . . till we all come in the unity of the faith.

DLC

---

[1] H. Leon McBeth, *The Baptist Heritage* (Nashville, TN: Broadman Press, 1987), 67.

[2] Thomas Armitage, *A History of the Baptists* (Watertown, WI: Baptist Heritage Press, 1988), 584.

[3] William L. Lumpkin, *Baptist Confessions of Faith* (Philadelphia: The Judson Press, 1959), 360.

[4] Ibid.

[5] Ibid., 363.

January 16

Serving the Lord in Extraordinary Days

Scripture: Psalm 37:18

In December of 1754, twelve years before the signing of the Declaration of Independence, Stephen Nixon was born in Sumter District, South Carolina. We should note as well that this was eleven years prior to the founding of the Congaree Baptist Church, the congregation that Stephen Nixon would one day pastor. The old church records of the Congaree Baptist Church reveal the fact that Stephen Nixon was saved sometime after 1774 through the ministry of Richard Furman, pastor of High Hills of Santee Baptist Church. In quick order Stephen was baptized, licensed, and ordained by the High Hills church.

At the outbreak of the Revolutionary War, young Mr. Nixon felt constrained to serve the newly forming nation, and he enlisted in the military. Initially he served as a horseman under General Thomas Sumter, and after 1780 his commanding officer was General Nathanael Greene. As he continued in the military, he was appointed Sargeant under Colonel Harry in 1781, and he fought in the Battle of Eutaw Springs.

When he was a little over twenty-five years old, on April 10, 1780, Stephen Nixon married Martha A. Nettles in Sumter District, South Carolina. Until Stephen's death thirty-six years later, Martha stood faithfully at his side. Ten children graced the home of the Nixons.

In all Stephen Nixon was greatly used of the Lord in a ministry that spanned thirty-seven years. In 1779, for the first time, he served as a messenger from the High Hills of Santee Baptist Church to the Charleston Baptist Association, and between 1785 and 1796 he served in that role seven times. In 1792 Stephen was licensed to preach by the High Hills church. It is apparent that he had become fully accepted with his preaching ability, for in 1797 he was listed in the Association minutes as the minister of the High Hills church. For the next five years, between 1797 and 1802, he preached at various places in the Midlands of South

Carolina. In 1802 he was called as pastor of the Congaree Baptist Church in Richland County. The Congaree Baptist Church was quite famous, for it had been established in 1765 as the result of the itinerant ministry of Philip Mulkey and Daniel Marshall, great Separatist Baptist preachers. Early in its history, the Congaree Church had been served by another outstanding pastor, Joseph Reese. Upon being called as pastor to that historic church, Stephen Nixon served well until his death on February 4, 1816. While serving there, Pastor Nixon actively engaged in his vision of church planting by assisting in the establishment of several churches. He was a prime mover in the establishment of the First Baptist Church of Columbia, South Carolina, which was started in 1809, and then later the Amelia Township Baptist Church.

The only physical violence that Baptists in South Carolina had experienced had taken place in Cheraw Hill. It must have been a highlight when the Charleston Association held their annual meeting at the Cheraw Hill Church in Marlborough District, South Carolina, in 1816. Pastor Stephen Nixon had doubtless looked forward to that meeting, but the Lord had other plans. His servant was transported to his heavenly home on February 4, 1816, in the sixty-first year of his life. In the minutes of the Association for that year it is stated on page 2, section 18, that "the humility and piety of Rev. Stephen Nixon, were of an extraordinary character." In his will, which was probated on April 27, 1816, is a note concerning his small library of books. He wished them to be distributed to his children after his death. The author takes notice of the fact that though most of these farmer-preachers were not afforded the opportunity of a formal education, many were excellent students of the Bible and readers of good books.

Pastor Stephen Nixon was called of God to serve the Lord in an exciting period of our American history. Following the Revolutionary War, he witnessed the unfolding of the great missionary program with which he was an encouraging leader. He was enabled to labor with other great men such as Richard Furman. May the Lord remind us that each of us is one called "for such a time as this." May He encourage us to faithfulness in the time and place that He has assigned us until He calls us to Himself.

DCB

January 17

The Music of Martyrs

Scripture: Hebrews 12:2

Genuine Christianity has truly been known for its Christ-exalting music. In the time of deepest sorrow, our Lord can provide His saints with a song. Church history is replete with examples of the saints, such as Paul and Silas, who, though in stocks in prison, "...sang praises unto God...." The writer's love of the Anabaptists may, in part, be attributable to this very truth. We first hear of George Blaurock in connection with the discussion of the Anabaptists concerning infant baptism, January 17, 1525. We might point out that the basic principle of soul liberty is at the very heart of infant baptism. This was clearly seen by the Anabaptists before and during the days of the Reformation. Pilgram Marpeck put the issue of voluntaryism and coercionism thus: "By infant baptism men coerce people to enter the Kingdom of God; and yet there should be no coercion there. All they have eternal punishment awaiting them who seek to sustain the Kingdom of God with recourse to the civil power . . . the magistry has no assignment touching the Kingdom of God." Hans Denck, another of the Anabaptists wrote: "Let everyone know that in matters of faith things ought to be on a voluntary basis, without coercion." Seeing this principle clearly, George Blaurock gave expression to this truth as he set forth the heart desire of the Anabaptists "to gather by ourselves as Paul has it."[1]

The repudiation of infant baptism in January of 1525, led to the banishment of Ludwig Hetzer, William Reublin, and others, and ultimately to the imprisonment of Grebel, Blaurock and Manz. Of course, after incarceration, martyrdom would follow.

Blaurock had been a monk, but he had renounced the religion of ritual for one of reality. He became closely related in the ministry of Conrad Grebel and Felix Manz, and following their deaths he became a leader among the Swiss

Anabaptists, until he was burned at the stake in Claussen. His martyrdom was called for because "...he had forsaken his office as priest, which he had formerly exercised in popery; that he disregarded infant baptism, and taught people a new baptism; that he rejected the Mass; that he likewise rejected the confession of the priests as founded by them, and that the mother of Christ is not to be invoked or worshiped....On the place of execution he earnestly spoke to the people, and pointed them to the Scriptures."[2]

In his death, Blaurock exemplified the truth set forth in one of his hymns. He had written: "Blessed are those in all tribulation who cling to Christ to the end." Because of his zeal he became known by the brethren as the second Paul, and historians have referred to him often as "the Hercules of the Anabaptists."

I do not believe the assumption of some that the Anabaptists relished martyrdom! Surely they would have delighted in the privilege of living a full life of soul liberty and religious freedom. However, martyrdom was to be chosen before a life of sensual pleasure that ended in eternal flames of hell fire.

At any rate, Blaurock's great hymn is thrilling indeed, for he wrote:

As he himself our sufferings bore
When hanging on the accursed tree
So there is suffering still in store
O pious heart, for you and me.[3]

May we learn with our Savior to "...Who for the joy that was set before Him endured the cross, despising the shame...." And may we "...consider Him that endured such contradiction of sinners against Himself, lest [we] be wearied and faint...."

DLC

---

[1] Leonard Verduin, *The Reformers and Their Stepchildren* (Grand Rapids, MI: William B. Eerdmans Publishing Company, 1964), 74-75.

[2] Thieleman J. van Braght, *Martyrs Mirror* (Scottdale, PA: Herald Press, 1950), 430.

[3] Henry Burrage, *Baptist Hymn Writers and Their Hymns* (Portland: Brown Thurston & Company, 1888), 18.

January 18

Another Look at the First Amendment

Scripture: John 8:32

Baptist historians have unitedly expressed great interest in the First Amendment to our national Constitution. A meeting is reported to have taken place between Reverend John Leland, a Separate Baptist preacher and James Madison, primary author of our Constitution. In an interesting article published on this date by Sightler Publications in Greenville, South Carlina, additional confirmation of that meeting has been further established.

It is known that the Baptists of Virginia, along with Patrick Henry, initially stood in opposition to the ratification of the constitution. Our forefathers feared a constitution that did not have a means of specifically limiting the powers of a centralized government. Without definite assurance otherwise, a centralized government could impose a "state church" upon the entire nation! Such was unconscionable. Being the leading voice among the Baptists of Orange County, his cohorts wanted Reverend Leland to run as a candidate for the state convention. This body was slated to debate and vote on the matter of ratification of the legal instrument. Two delegates were to be chosen from each county to form the state convention, and surely with Leland's mind, as he represented Orange County, and Patrick Henry's oratory, as he represented his country, the chance of defeating ratification was almost assured.

James Madison is recognized as the primary author of the Constitution. His residence was in Orange County, and when he was informed by Joseph Spencer that the Baptists opposed the ratification, and that Reverend John Leland was leading the efforts to defeat ratification, he made his way to the Leland home. Mrs. Leland informed Mr. Madison that her husband was studying in the woods across the road from his house. Mr. Madison entered the wooded area and met the Baptist preacher. They spent considerable time together, and Mr. Leland explained the Baptist's hesitancy in accepting the Constitution. Mr. Madison promised that a Bill of Rights would be appended to the Constitution, and the First Amendment would prevent the establishment of an official state church for the nation.

Mr. Leland withdrew his name as a candidate and encouraged the election of James Madison from Orange County to the state convention. He urged the Baptists to support Mr. Madison for that post, and this action assisted in the ratification of the Constitution by a vote of 187 to 168. This was only a margin of nineteen votes out of 355.

"There are two witnesses who confirm that such a meeting took place. One was George Nixon Briggs, a Baptist and governor of Massachusetts, who spoke with Leland in 1837 about the matter after Leland had retired to Massachusetts, and the other was John Strode Barbour, a native of Orange County. These witnesses are named in an article by Samuel Chiles Mitchell, Professor at the University of Richmond, which appeared in the *Religious Herald* of October 18, 1934. . . . The article is entitled "JAMES MADISON AND HIS CO-WORKER, JOHN LELAND." Mr. Mitchell's article was a transcript of an address he gave at the Bicentennial of Orange County on September 26, 1934, in the Grove at Gum Spring on the site of John Leland's home. The meeting of Briggs and Leland is also recounted in the biography of Leland in the *Annals of the American Pulpit*. A stone monument with a bronze bust of Leland was placed at the Gum Spring by the Sons of the American Revolution of Berkshire County, Massachusetts, the home of John Leland. The Gum Spring monument is on Virginia State Highway 20, a few miles Northeast of Charlottesville, not far from Jefferson's home at Monticello and even closer to Madison's home, Montpelier."[1]

Our current Supreme Court, using a convoluted system of legal hermeneutics, has distorted the First Amendment. They have totally denied the original intent of that important addition to our national constitution. In fact, they have seemingly determined to completely reverse the meaning of the First Amendment.

Let us pray that the Lord of Heaven will once again give us judges who are strict constructionists. The Constitution was never meant to be a "living document," but rather it was meant to be a "lasting document" providing safeguards of total religious freedom.

DLC

[1]Research paper by James H. Sightler, M.D., Sightler Publications, January 18, 2004, Greenville, South Carolina.

January 19

The Three-Year-Old Orphan

Scripture: Psalm 68:5

Due to the length of this testimony, this story is found in two entries of this volume. Dr. E. Robert Jordan was saved on January 19, 1948. January 22, 1949, marks the date of the wedding of Dr. and Mrs. E. Robert Jordan, and we shall conclude this exciting material on that date.

When he was only two years old, our subject's mother had an adulterous affair, ending an abusive marriage. The lad's father remarried, but the step-mother was cruel. When only three years old, the boy and his five-year-old sister ran away, taking turns carrying their one-year-old sister. They somehow managed to carry their sister across Dayton, Ohio, and found their way to their grandparent's home. The children were taken to court, and all three were sent to an orphanage.

There the three-year-old boy learned the "pecking order" of the system. He suffered many beatings administered by older boys, but he learned to fight back. As he matured, his goal was to be the "big boy" of the orphanage. Gradually he fought his way to that goal, beating the "big boys" in nine other cottages. The youth hated school and was a constant irritant to his teachers. At fifteen he was in the sixth grade, and the future seemed futile. But then came the world-changing news of Pearl Harbor, December 7, 1941. Everything altered. E. Robert Jordan was now sixteen, but his "cottage father" signed for him, and in 1942 the lad found himself aboard a train headed for the Great Lakes Naval Station.

He was now rudely awakened to the "pecking order" in the military. Early he determined he would climb up the ranks.

Drinking became a way of life for him. After getting into a fight, he was ordered by his commanding officer to represent the Navy against the Marines in boxing competition. He set a goal to become the middle weight boxing champion of the Navy, and in time he accomplished his desire.

Jordan was assigned to the Pacific theater of the war. He soon observed first-hand Japanese suicide attacks. Leading a squadron, he witnessed a suicide bomber destroy his gun turret, killing all his men. His drinking habit worsened, but even more than his hatred of the Japanese was his deep-seated animosity toward his stepmother. During a furlough he decided to kill her, but time and again his plan was thwarted.

Jordan re-enlisted for six years and was assigned to a cruiser in Philadelphia. He was disgusted, however, to discover that he had the duty of training 72 new recruits. With a vitriolic spirit, he soon selected a smiling recruit to be the recipient of his anger. He heaped abuse upon the young sailor, but rather than driving the young man to anger, the recruit merely smiled in return. In time, Tim, the young recruit, became the Chief's companion. He accompanied the Chief to saloons, drank only milk, and then helped his drunken leader back to the ship. Tim insisted on giving the Chief the business card of his preacher brother, asking him whenever he needed a friend to visit his brother.

While docked in Bermuda, the Chief drank excessively and got into a fight. This landed him in jail overnight. He realized he had destroyed his hope for promotion, and despaired for his future. When back in his home port, the Chief went to Atlantic City, and spent a weekend drinking. Out on the boardwalk he discovered he was temporarily paralyzed. A hippie taunted him with a statement God would use to change Chief's life. The hippie said: "You are who you are when you are totally alone!" The Chief had pretended to be macho, but when alone, he knew insecurity and fear. He could not shake that statement!

Upon deciding to return to his ship, he reached in his pocket for trolley fare, but found the business card of Tim's brother. Why not get a free meal? He had nothing to lose. Thus he boarded a street car and arrived at Tim's brother's door close to midnight! (To be continued on the January 22 entry.)

DLC

January 20

The Gospel Among Black Slaves

Scripture: Ephesians 4:1-16

A complete history of the working of God among slaves in America has never been possible due to the failure of adequate record keeping. We know that "the earliest church organization among them [black Baptists] was the First African Baptist Church of Savannah, Georgia, instituted January 20, 1788, at Brampton's barn, three miles west of Savannah, by Abraham Marshall [white] and Jesse Peter [black]. Its first pastor was George Lisle, who was liberated by Mr. Henry Sharp of Burke County, Georgia, and afterward became pastor at Kingston, Jamaica."[1]

In other entries we have rejoiced in being reminded of the ministries of George Lisle, John Jaspers, Lott Cary, and Colin Teague, but in this entry I invite you to visit a scene in North Carolina. It is well to realize that "the foreign slave trade was closed in 1808 by Congress. By 1860, however, slaves numbered 331,059 or about one-third of the total population."[2]

One of the freed slaves who gained a position of influence in his day was Ralph Freeman, or Rolf, as it often appears. Ralph had been enslaved in Anson County, North Carolina. Soon after he had made a profession of faith and was baptized, he expressed a desire to preach. In time he was licensed by the church of which he was a member, and it was apparent that, indeed, the Lord had gifted him. Ralph became a good reader, and he was very much at home in the Scriptures. His owner decided to sell him, but the brethren gathered the funds necessary and purchased Ralph's freedom. With his new-found freedom, Ralph began to travel and preach. Soon the local congregation recognized his call as from God, and he was ordained to the gospel ministry. Often Ralph was called upon to preach at funerals, and, on one occasion, he was asked to bring the key-note Sunday message at the association meeting of the churches. Ralph was of average size, but his smiling countenance won the hearts and respect of his hearers. His humility literally shone through while he preached.

Elder Joseph Magee, a white preacher, befriended Ralph, and they traveled and preached together. Their friendship grew, and in time they agreed that the one surviving would preach the funeral of the first to die. Elder Magee moved to the west of the state and continued his ministry, and in time the Lord called His servant home.

"Upon his deathbed, he bequeathed to Ralph his riding horse, overcoat, Bible, and fifty dollars in cash, and requested his family to send for Ralph to come and preach at his funeral. In company with a white brother, Ralph went to the West and preached the funeral sermon from a text that the deceased had selected. The brother who went with Ralph stated that he never before saw so large a congregation. At the conclusion of the sermon, Elder Magee's brother stated to the congregation what provision his deceased brother had made for Ralph, and added, 'If any of you would like to give him any amount, it would be thankfully received.' The congregation soon made up fifty dollars, which was given to him."[3]

Following that occasion, the Legislature of North Carolina passed a law forbidding black men from holding public services. Ralph was mortified, and his ministry was curtailed.

At his death, Reverend Ralph Freeman was buried in the churchyard of the Bethlehem Baptist Church. In 1907, the Honorable Eugene Little erected at his grave a granite headstone, and on it were these words: "He was a Primitive Baptist preacher of much force and usefulness."[4]

DLC

---

[1] N. H. Pius, *An Outline of Baptist History* (Nashville, TN: National Baptist Publishing Board, 1911), 58.

[2] M. A. Huggins, *A History of North Carolina Baptists* (Raleigh: The General Board Baptist State Convention of North Carolina, 1967), 263.

[3] George W. Purefoy, *A History of the Sandy Creek Baptist Association* (New York: Sheldon & Co., 1859), 329.

[4] Mullins, 172.

January 21

Prayer Makes History

Scripture: Philippians 4:6-7

What makes an event historically significant? Perhaps one of the surprises of heaven will be the discovery of Divine perspective on history that readjusts our ideas of historical significance. Major battles, revolutions, and even national revivals might yield their dominance and significance in the minds of men to humble prayer meetings.

Perhaps the world has yet to understand the significance of such events as that which took place on January 21, 1788. Four Baptist ministers met together for a day of prayer and fasting. The thrilling thing about this humble prayer meeting was that none of the four men who gathered that day in the study of College Lane Baptist Church in Northamptonshire, England, dreamed that in the future each would be memorialized in biographies! Such would become their significance in history! But on this day, they met as four friends who shared a longing for greater personal godliness, holiness in their churches, and the evangelism of the world. They met as humble men with no other ambition but the glory of God. They met as men who knew that even as Aaron and Hur held up Moses' petitioning arms, they would hold each other up for the sake of Christ. They met as brothers. And the brotherly love that drew them to the study that winter morning in 1788 would endure until the close of their lives. Who were these men? They were none other than John Ryland, Jr., John Sutcliff, Andrew Fuller, and William Carey. They were the founders of the modern missionary movement!

John Ryland recorded this holy event in his private journal. "Brethren Fuller, Sutcliff, Carey, and I, kept this day as a private fast, in my study: read the Epistles to Timothy and Titus; [Abraham] Booth's charge to [Thomas] Hopkins; [Richard] Blackerby's Life, in [John] Gillies; and [John] Rogers of Dedham's Sixty Memorials for a Godly Life: and each prayed twice - Carey with singular enlargement and pungency. Our chief design was to implore a revival of godliness in our souls, in our churches, and in the church at large."[1]

A thoughtful analysis of Ryland's entry is helpful here. Notice, first, the teachability of these men. They had no audio recordings in that day, so they did the next best thing: they read the message of one of their very own contemporaries (Abraham Booth). How often Christians get together to talk about their contemporary preachers instead of humbly gleaning from them! God gives grace to the humble. Secondly, notice the orderliness of this prayer gathering. They read material that was suited to their intentions. The Scripture reading was the Pastoral Epistles. (They wanted revival in their churches and they were pastors). The other reading was from what is considered the first work on revival, and the Sixty Memorials were on godly living. Very likely, their seasons of prayer (they each prayed twice) were interspersed among the reading as if they were responding to God's work in them. Thirdly, notice the two words that John Ryland used to describe William Carey's praying, and remember that this was before anyone had an inkling of Carey's future fame. He said that Carey prayed with "singular enlargement and pungency."

We don't use these words very often in our day, especially in the description of prayer. The wording is a bit old fashioned. Sadly, another reason we might not use them in this context is because that kind of prayer is also old fashioned. The idea of "enlargement" in Ryland's day meant freedom. The idea of "pungency" meant pointed and aggressive. We do not know what Carey said - oh! to have heard that prayer! - but we do know that one godly man sensed that the humble cobbler was unleashing his soul in uninhibited expressions, calling out to his Lord with clear, pungent prayer, boldly making his requests. We do not know what was said, but we know what they wanted! And God surpassed their expectations when he used them to start a missionary movement that continues to this very day. What is more, if your heart is stirred to pray by this simple recalling of their winter meeting, then their godliness is still bearing fruit over two hundred years later. Certainly, the prayer meeting in Ryland's study was an historical event!

RPB

[1] Michael A. G. Haykin, *One Heart and One Soul, John Sutcliff of Olney, his friends and his times* (Durham, England: Evangelical Press, 1994), 168.

January 22

A Trophy of God's Grace

Scripture: Romans 3:21-26

This entry is continued from that of January 19 and deals with the salvation experience of Dr. E. Robert Jordan.

E. Robert Jordan, the Naval Chief, rang the doorbell around midnight, and introduced himself. "Your brother, Tim, said that you would like a visit from me. Well, here I am." Immediately Tim's brother, Frank, asked, "Bob-where are you going when you die?" The question took the Chief by surprise and he responded with a bit of profanity, but claimed he was going to heaven because he was not bad enough to go to hell!

Frank rankled the Chief by insisting that he was going to hell because he had not received Jesus Christ as his Savior. All of this transpired at the door. As the conversation continued, Frank invited his guest in for something to eat. The Chief agreed, and after enjoying the meal, he pushed back from the table and said, "Now you can go ahead and talk about religion." Frank insisted he was not interested in talking religion, but wanted to explain the reality of a personal relationship with God. The Chief did not know the difference, but Frank explained that religion is man's futile attempt to reach God by his own effort. Whereas Bible Christianity is God reaching out to man with the free gift of salvation.

The two talked until eight in the morning, and Frank invited the Chief to return. And return he did! Night after night, the two men talked. While the conversations were taking place, the Chief found himself drawn to the environment. For the first time in his life, he was witnessing love.

In time, Frank invited Bob to attend evangelistic services at his church, but that was too much. In fact, Bob walked with Frank and his wife to the church doors, but as they entered, he left to return to his ship. However, his desire for real peace overwhelmed him, and Bob returned to the church and slipped in. The hymns were attractive, but as the sermon developed, Bob almost exploded in anger. The service being over, Bob tried to slip out, but Frank caught him. Frank expressed thankfulness that Bob had returned, but Bob, in a fit of rage, said: "I will never come back . . . .You two betrayed me. . . ."

When Frank asked how that could be, Bob explained that they told the preacher all about his drinking, gambling, and wickedness. Frank assured Bob that nothing had been said to the preacher, but the Holy Spirit was bringing conviction. Still Bob determined never to return, but he did. Evening after evening, he attended. He had no mother, no father, no family, and he wanted to believe that life could be better.

As the preacher declared truth, Bob, for the first time, acknowledged his sinfulness and realized his inability to do anything about it. Returning to his ship, he was unable to sleep. Bob determined to return to the church and respond to the invitation the next night. But as the invitation was given, he froze. As the preacher talked with him at the door Bob explained that he had come that night to be saved but was too proud to respond. The preacher suggested they go to the study to talk, and he invited Tim to join them.

Amazingly, as the pastor dealt with Bob, Tim also realized he had never really been saved. That night a down-and-outer and an up-and-outer both received the divine forgiveness of sin! Bob returned to his ship. He awakened his men at 4:30 in the morning to tell them how he was gloriously saved!

The next Sunday Bob was appointed by the pastor to preach in a rescue mission. Sixteen people were saved, and some of them went on to Bible colleges. That night Bob also met his wife, Margie. God gave Bob and Margie five children. The first son, Tim, was named after the sailor who pointed Bob to Christ. Bob completed college; pastored Calvary Baptist Church in Lansdale, Pennsylvania for nearly fifty years; helped in establishing 100 churches; and founded the Calvary Baptist Seminary.

Friend, God's mercy and grace are sufficient for your need today as well.

DLC

January 23

Vermont Yankee in the Southland

Scripture: 2 Timothy 4:5-7

Charles Dutton Mallary was born in West Paultney, Rutland County, Vermont, on January 23, 1801. In his early years he had come under deep religious impressions. He credits these impressions to the pious influence of his parents, especially his mother. When he was sixteen years of age, during a revival, he experienced the saving grace of Jesus Christ in his life. After a period of searching, reflection, and visiting various churches, in June of 1822, he was immersed and entered the fellowship of the Baptist church in West Paultney, pastored by Clark Kendrick.

After finishing the usual studies as a youngster, he entered Middlebury College in August 1817. After graduation from school, Mr. Mallary spent a year as a teacher of young people in Vermont. During that period he became exercised about preaching the Gospel. In October, 1822, he relocated in Charleston, South Carolina. In time he moved from there and settled briefly at Cambridge, Abbeville District, South Carolina. There he began preaching, was licensed by the local church, and in 1824, received a call to pastor the First Baptist Church of Columbia. At that time, the church was only about fifteen years old, having been founded in 1809. Mallary was ordained in April of that year and began his ministry in Columbia.

There on July 11, 1825, Reverend Mallary married Miss Susan Mary Evans, granddaughter, on the maternal side, of the eminent man of God, Edmund Botsford. Two sons, Charles and Rollin, were born to this couple. Unfortunately, they did not have many years together, for Susan died in 1834. In December of 1840, C.D. Mallary married his second wife, Mrs. Mary E. Welch, of Twiggs County, Georgia. They were together for a little over twenty years. She died suddenly on August 28, 1862, almost two years before his death, which took place July 31, 1864.

This Day in Baptist History III

After ministering for two years in Columbia, the Lord directed Pastor Mallary to go about 20 miles southeast of Columbia to an area known as the "Fork" named for the joining of the Wateree and Congaree Rivers. He then became pastor of two churches, Beulah and Congaree Baptist Churches. In 1830 he accepted a call to the First Baptist Church in Augusta, Georgia. In 1834 he removed from Augusta and went to Milledgeville to pastor, but because of poor health, was able to stay less than two years. His attention was turned to working with Mercer University where he served as an agent from 1837 to 1839. With a passion to preach, in 1840 he accepted the position as Missionary for the Central Association. This has been acknowledged as the most effective time in his ministry. He engaged in extensive preaching tours and protracted meetings that resulted in great revivals in the central part of Georgia.

From 1840 until his death in 1864, he spent the remaining days of his ministry in Twiggs and Sumter Counties, Georgia. He resided in Jeffersonville for several years, ministering in a number of churches until 1848. In that year, he was called to preach at the LaGrange church, which he did until 1852. But again, failing health caused him to retire from the pastorate for good. He moved to the neighborhood of Albany in 1852. Even though he was unable to pastor again, he preached till the end of his life.

Besides his ministry as an outstanding preacher, C. D. Mallary was a gifted writer. Two of his works have come down to us as outstanding volumes. They are *The Life of Edmond Botsford* and *The Memoir of Mercer*. A number of other writings of various kinds have survived to this day.

He finished his useful sixty-three years at Magnolia Springs in Sumter County, Georgia, on Sunday noon, the 31 of July. It is said that the last day of his life was like the close of a beautiful day. He talked about the Lord, spoke much of his old friends, living and dead, alluding particularly to Mercer, Sanders, Dawson, and others who had gone before. His last words were, "SWEET (clapping his hands,) HOME!"

What a wonderful way to close one's life! We should pray that God will allow us to finish our course in such a fashion.

DCB

January 24

Rightly Dividing the Word

Scripture: 2 Peter 1:19-21

Clarence Larkin, who became well known for his ministry of writing, was born on October 28, 1850 in Chester, Pennsylvania. We know little concerning his early life, but when he was nineteen, he was converted and became a member of an Episcopal church. Knowing that his sins were forgiven, he immediately desired to preach, but the opportunity to attend college was not available. He secured employment in a bank, and in a few years he was able to leave the bank and enter college. He possessed a methodical mind, and graduated as a mechanical engineer. He served as a professional draftsman, before becoming a teacher of the blind.

The Lord was surely preparing Clarence Larkin for a unique ministry. First his mechanical drafting mind gave him ability to organize matters well. As a teacher for the deaf he cultivated his descriptive ability. In that capacity it was necessary to visualize what he wanted to communicate. But when Clarence's health began to fail, it was necessary for him to give up his teaching position. When his health improved, he became a manufacturer, but this did not bring satisfaction of heart. Clarence desired to preach.

In 1882, when he was thirty-two, he embraced Baptist convictions, was immersed and united with a Baptist church. Two years later he was ordained. He went from the business world to the labor of ministry as he accepted a call to pastor the Baptist church in Kennett Square, Pennsylvania. His second pastorate was at Fox Chase, Pennsylvania, where he pastored for twenty years. At the time of his ordination, Clarence Larkin was not a premillennialist, but as he studied the Bible and interpreted the Scriptures literally, he was forced to reconsider his position concerning prophecy. For years postmillennialists had taught that the world was getting better and better, and that the church would convert the world and Christ would then return. However, one could not read the Bible in one hand and the newspaper in the other and come to that conclusion. In fact, Dr. A. T. Robertson told Dr. H. A. Ironside that "I have never definitely declared myself as a premillennialist, but I think if I had my life to live over again, I would be much more positive concerning this, for I have never in all my ministry known a premillennialist who was a Modernist." Dr. Ironside had said: "There is about the premillenial position that necessitates a belief in the full inspiration of this Book. Everything is based upon that."[1]

After adopting the Premillenial understanding of the Scriptures, Reverend Larkin, with draftsmen skills, began making large wall charts, which he entitled, "Prophetic Truth." He used these charts in teaching from the pulpit. This means of presenting prophetic truths became very popular. Area believers soon heard of this unique way of presenting God's Word. In time Reverend Larkin was invited to teach in two Bible institutes. Soon the man of God began publishing his charts. They were circulated widely even before World War I. Prior to that war, the battle between Fundamentalism and Liberalism was just heating up. Prophetic preaching was gaining great interest, and Reverend Larkin was invited to bring addresses on the war in light of prophecy. It was at that time that he began the work of preparing his book on *Dispensational Truth* (*or God's Plan and Purpose in the Ages*) which contained a number of charts depicting a graphic portrait of Biblical truths. The volume was first published in 1918 and went through several editions. This was the crowning work of Reverend Larkin's literary efforts, though he also wrote *The Book of Daniel*, *Spirit World*, and the *Second Coming of Christ*.

Often it has been suggested that one is dispensationally correct while being dispositionally mean spirited. Those who knew him best reported that Reverend Larkin always exhibited a gracious spirit. The demands of his books made it necessary for the man of God to devote full time to that ministry, and thus for the last five years of his life, he did not pastor. His Lord saw fit to take his servant home on January 24, 1924.

Those who do not understand dispensation truth tragically roam through the Bible in a maze of confusion. Thank God for this Spirit-taught truth.

DLC

[1] H. A. Ironside, *The Lamp of Prophecy* (Grand Rapids, MI: Zondervan Publishing House, 1962), 129.

January 25

She Would not Budge

Scripture: Esther 4:16b

As the sixteenth-century Anabaptists expanded, martyrdom was almost expected. One of the early martyrs of the movement was the daughter of Hans Hut, outstanding evangelist leader. Han's daughter is unnamed in history, but she died on January 25, 1527,[1] being drowned for her faith. Her martyrdom took place in Bamberg, about thirty miles north of Nuremberg.

The Hut household is of interest, for before his conversion, Hans Hut possessed an exuberant personality and was known for his enthusiasm. After being led to Christ Jesus through the ministry of Hans Denck, his continued effervescence was directed toward his personal witness of the Savior. On May 26, 1526, Hans Hut witnessed his faith in believer's baptism. He immediately began sharing the truth of the Gospel with his own family, and then his usefulness was greatly extended as he preached the glorious Gospel at every open door.

His unnamed daughter was greatly impressed by the fact that her father, whose restless spirit had been so evident, now possessed a tranquility of spirit. Soon his daughter saw her personal need of the Savior, and she too was saved.

We do well to realize that the Anabaptists' attitude toward women was far superior to others. They referred to the ladies in their assemblies as "sisters," and the women were encouraged to witness for Christ personally. To be sure, the men were in positions of leadership, but the godly ladies also had a ministry to perform. Misunderstanding or devilish desire caused their enemies to suggest that the Anabaptists practiced a version of so-called "free-love." Historic enemies of our heroes and heroines perpetrated that lie. That lie had no basis in reality. In fact, the high standard of morality of the Anabaptists was mentioned often by sincere historians of that era.

As we check the dates of Han's baptism and of his daughter's martrydom, we observe that she had but a few months to live following her conversion. It is apparent that Hans was accompanied by his family when he traveled to Bamberg to do some evangelist work. He met with considerable success as during his stay he led several outstanding leaders to Christ, but leaving his family at Bamberg, Hans left for an evangelist stint to Augsburg. It was while he was away that his daughter was arrested. She had participated in many Anabaptist meetings and indeed had a fine grasp of the New Testament.

Upon her arrest she was severely confronted by church leaders, and as she was accosted, she gave lucid answers about her faith in Christ Jesus as Savior. She refused to disavow her Lord. The result was that she was found guilty and sentenced to death by drowning. This followed the pattern usually practiced by the Sacral churches. The custom was to burn male Anabaptists at the stake and to drown females who would not abjure their faith in Christ alone. On January 25, 1527, Hans Hut's daughter was led to the river where she was placed in a bag. After heavy weights were attached, she was thrown to her death in the waters of the river.

As we have observed, Hans Hut was not present at the time, and we can only imagine the heartache he must have endured when informed of the facts. However, he had little time to mourn, for the next months found him laboring in the Gospel in Bavaria and Austria. He attended the so-called Martyr's Synod in Augsburg, August 20, 1527, and in a short time he, too, was arrested and imprisoned in Augsburg.

Hans was terribly abused by his inquisitors and suffered horrendously on the rack. However, Hans would not repudiate his faith. On December 6, 1527 while imprisoned, a fire began in his cell, and Hans was almost asphyxiated. He died as a result. It had been less than a year since the martyrdom of his daughter, but on that date, Hans and his daughter were reunited for eternity to joy around the throne of the Lamb.

May God grant courage that we who know Christ might be faithful in the reality that we do know Him Who holds our future, and our all-glorious eternity in His Hands.

DLC

---

[1] Myron S. Augsburger, *Faithful Unto Death* (Waco, TX: Word Books, 1978), 74.

January 26

He Gradually Became a Baptist

Scripture: Acts 18:24-28

Joseph Grafton was born on June 9, 1757, in Newport, Rhode Island. His father was a mariner. Joseph's mother was a serious lady, intent on spiritually catechizing her children. Educational advantages were limited, but Joseph remained in school until he was fourteen. Unfortunately, he came into contact with his father's naval peers, and he soon picked up their vices.

When Joseph reached his eighteenth birthday, an extensive religious revival prevailed in Providence. The Lord was moving in the Congregational church and in the Baptist congregation. Joseph Grafton came under conviction, and in time was saved. He had full assurance of salvation. Immediately he considered church membership and decided upon the Congregational church. However, in studying the Scriptures, he became convinced that immersion was the biblical form of baptism, so he was baptized by immersion and united with the Congregational church.

The young man wanted to serve the Lord, and began to wonder what the Lord would have him do. He battled the idea as to whether he should enter the ministry, but he could not decide. He made up his mind, however, that he ought to marry, and on December 12, 1779, he was wed to the daughter of an army officer. Soon the deacons of the Congregational church became convinced that he ought to preach. Joseph was reluctant to yield, but a succession of trials caused him to reconsider. In May of 1783, his oldest child died. A few weeks later, his second child died. Soon thereafter his wife passed away. He was still unconvinced. In July of 1874 he was seized with a severe attack of bleeding from the lungs. There seemed little hope of recovery, but he gradually improved, and yielded to the claims of Christ. The Congregational church granted him a license to preach, and in time he was invited to preach at Plainfield, Connecticut, to a congregation of Separatists, and he continued with them for fifteen months. During that time he considered the ordinance of communion, and soon found that he actually agreed with the Baptists. Thus he asked the Congregational church to dismiss him, and united with the First Baptist Church in Providence.

He began now to preach in Baptist circles, and was called by the Baptist church in Newton, Massachusetts, to serve them. He accepted the call on June 18, 1788, and Reverend Grafton served the Lord there for nearly fifty years. Soon after his call he married Mrs. Sally Robinson, a widow with seven children. She served with her husband until her home-going in June of 1804. In time the pastor married for the third time. This time he married Hannah Parker, and she served with him until her death on January 26, 1835.

The Baptist Church in Newton experienced numerous revival seasons during the pastorate of Reverend Grafton. His gracious and humorous approach to the ministry was well received by the people. As age began to take a toll, he asked that the congregation accept his resignation and call a younger pastor who could better care for the needs of the church family. This was done, but Pastor Grafton's occasional services were always thankfully received.

I have mentioned the pastor's humor, and a couple of anecdotes may illustrate this truth. On one occasion he was addressing a mission conference. He spoke on the Great Commission, and then, at the close of the meeting, he received an offering for missions. He said: "And now let every gentleman reach in his pocket, and every lady in her purse, and see if there be not there a piece of money, as there was in the mouth of Peter's fish." It is reported that at that rally one of the largest offerings ever was received.

Within Pastor's membership was a man distinguished by his greedy spirit. He was doing well financially, but he had resolved not to give any more than necessary for charitable or religious purposes. The gentleman's store was broken into, and a considerable amount of merchandise and cash was taken. The next day, the pastor called to console the man, and in his witty way he remarked, "What the Lord didn't get, the devil did."

Reverend Grafton passed into the presence of the Lord on December 16, 1836. He was a man whose convictions grew stronger as he studied. His life counted for the Lord. May that be true of our lives as well.

DLC

January 27

A Baptist by Conviction

Scripture: Ephesians 2:8-9

Old fashioned revival meetings were a standard part of summertime in fundamental churches in the 19th and 20th centuries regardless of the denomination. John A. Winstead was converted as a 22-year-old -man in such a meeting held in the Bunn Methodist Church in the summer of 1949. He was born near Bunn, North Carolina, in Franklin County on March 16, 1927. On the very night he accepted the Lord as his Savior, he accepted the call to preach the Gospel.

John grew in the Lord as he studied the Scriptures and decided there was no Scriptural reason for denominations to have the power to govern local churches. He came to the conclusion that churches should be autonomous and govern themselves. As a result he left the Methodists in 1952. He was encouraged to return but remained steadfast in his decision and others began to leave as well. This group started an independent church, the Union Gospel Tabernacle, in an old chicken house on Mr. Willie Jeffrey's farm. When people laughed at John for starting a church, he told them that people laughed at Noah too, and he kept right on building. Young people came by often and John led many to the Lord at the site of the old chicken house. A permanent building was erected and in 1970 the church was renamed Calvary Baptist Tabernacle.

John began Bible training at Bob Jones University in 1954 and became a diligent student of the Scriptures and a man of convictions. While a student he was busy outside of his studies. One of the highlights of his academic career was being elected chaplain of the senior class in 1958. His job as campus maintenance worker helped him financially to get through college. His wife, Lucille Jeffreys Winstead, worked for Oliver B. Greene's "Gospel Hour." During this time John pastored the El Bethel Baptist Church in Swainsboro, Georgia, for two years.

Mr. and Mrs. Winstead were childhood sweethearts and were reared in the same fundamental Methodist church. They were baptized Biblically at the same time in an old pond by a

Baptist preacher, and were married on January 27, 1947. Even though they had no children of their own, they have many spiritual children born into the kingdom of God as a result of their 25 years in evangelism. They traveled for twelve years living out of suitcases and staying wherever the churches housed them. After purchasing a trailer, they traveled another thirteen years before leaving the field of evangelism.

Winstead's first revival meeting was held in Clinton, Pennsylvania, in a Presbyterian church February 8-22, 1959. The two-week meeting resulted in the salvation of many souls and the founding of an independent Bible-believing church. Some of the people left the Presbyterian Church and identified themselves with the new church because they could no longer support the apparent liberalism of their former church. Several new churches started from Winstead's evangelistic meetings. John came to the conclusion that Baptists were Biblicists and became a Baptist by conviction.[1]

Tabernacle Baptist Church in Bunn, North Carolina, began in an old store building after a two-week revival meeting in 1963. John's brother, Bill, played the piano for him. Property was purchased near Perry's pond in Franklin County, North Carolina, a building built, and the church is still going today.

On May 19, 1983, John organized the Maranatha Baptist Church in Bunn, North Carolina, his home. Land was purchased in November 1985, and on April 21, 1991, the church dedicated its present building of worship. John pastored there until his death on February 8, 1992.

Fifty-three pastors, evangelists, and missionaries were among the several hundred who attended John's memorial service at the Maranatha Baptist Tabernacle. At the Winstead's request, an offering for missions was taken at his funeral. John was buried in the Bunn Cemetery on February 11, 1992,[2] but his spirit is rejoicing, and he is surely singing his favorite song, "Amazing Grace."

Let us pray that God will raise up more evangelists like Brother Winstead who will stand firm on the great doctrines of the Bible, have a heart for church planting, and never lose their zeal to see souls saved.

DCB

---

[1] Telephone interview with Lucille Winstead Newell by Bettye Baughan on August 10, 2004

[2] *The Franklin Times*, February 29, 1992

January 28

Suffering According to the Will of God

Scripture: 1 Peter 3:14-17; 2 Corinthians 4:17

As one reads the accounts of imprisonments of Russian Baptist saints under the wicked hand of communism, one theme emerges. Whether it was preacher or layman, man or woman, young or old, all seemed to echo the same message: These heroes and heroines of the faith looked upon their suffering as being the will of God! They fully accepted the sovereignty of God in the matter, and knew that if He willed, their terms could be shortened or completely terminated in a moment of time. But, if they were called upon to fulfill the entire term, or if while imprisoned they were retried again and an additional term was given, with complete confidence in God's providential leading, these saints suffered willingly.

For we who have experienced the total religious liberty of America, this may be incongruous to our thinking! Perhaps our freedom has lulled us into the false philosophy that causes us to believe that we deserve special privileges. If a city so much as attempts to restrict parking that affects members of a congregation, a cry may well go up suggesting that we are being persecuted. We live in a society that is used to demanding its "rights," whatever that means!

Such is not the attitude among believers in most of the world, and surely it was not the case in Russia during its most recent sordid history. Valentina Saveleva, a secret courier of Christian literature, was arrested in January of 1982. A twenty-seven-year-old college graduate, her future appeared bright, but from the outset of her detainment, she knew she would receive a five-year sentence in the Russian penal system. This assurance did not cause Valentina to succumb to the communist court system in a fatalistic manner, but she knew full well that her future was in the hands of the Lord and not her captors.

The brilliant defense Valentina presented meant nothing to the puppet judge. The KGB had already determined the sentence, and Valentina made that clear to her court-appointed, atheistic attorney. At one point, the attorney became indignant with the entire proceedings and told Valentina that she was helpless to assist her. Valentina responded: "Don't worry. I understand. They're going to give me five years, no matter what."

Her interrogator became interested in Valentina's Bible, and especially wanted to read of the trial of Christ. Directing him to the portion, Valentina said, "As you can see, history repeats itself." When asked what she meant, she responded: "Just as there were no grounds to condemn Christ to death, and his enemies had to find false witnesses, so you look for false witnesses against me. They said that he was acting against Caesar, and you say that my activities are against the government. Pilate washed his hands, saying that he found no guilt in Christ, but he handed him over for crucifixion anyway. You tell me, 'We're sorry this is happening to you,' but at the same time you promise me a five-year sentence." How cleverly she superimposed the Scriptures upon her current scene. But it was all in vain.

After the verdict of five years had been given, on January 28, 1983, her long trip began that would deliver her to a distant prison camp near Irkutsk in Siberia. The miserable journey took over a month with stops in prisons in Pyatigorsk, Aktyubinsk, Orenburg, Chelyabinsk, and Irkutsk. She finally arrived at the prison camp in Bozoi on March 3, 1983.[1] The geographic area was known as "The Valley of Death," and living conditions were desperate, but accepting the will of God allowed Valentina to endure victoriously. Continual efforts by the KGB to break Valentina's spirit and will were in vain. She had a resolute assurance that she was exactly where God wanted her, and though she suffered greatly, the Lord provided grace and grit for every trial. Valentina persevered, and the Lord made her "more than a conqueror."

I must ask myself, could I endure what she did? What about you?

DLC

---

[1] Georgi Vins, Compiler, *Let The Waters Roar* (Grand Rapids, MI: Baker Book House, 1989), 35.

January 29

A Full-Sized Crown

Scripture: Daniel 12:3

Back in 1949 when Bill Hopper, missionary in the Philippines, determined to carry the Gospel to the Negritos, he was informed that it was a useless venture. After all, he was told, the Negritos did not possess a soul. But believing that Jesus Christ had tasted death for every man, Bill Hopper went forth to those whom one of the encyclopedia describes as "...physical weaklings, of low, almost dwarf, stature, with very dark skin, closely curling hair, flat noses, thick lips and large clumsy feet." As he made his initial contact with the Negritos, the missionary climbed from the valley below. However, before reaching the tribe, he was confronted by a menacing chief standing straight and tall in his pathway in all five feet of his stature. Even in his tattered shorts and "tattletale gray" t-shirt, there was a regal air about the chief. There was no doubt as to why he had been chosen chief. He knew no fear.

In time, the missionary broke down prejudices and gained the confidence of the people. He was able to gather a group of the Negritos and begin sharing with them the love of God expressed in the Son's death. As the Gospel was faithfully preached, Chief Severo was the first to respond to the invitation. He cautiously raised his hand indicating his desire to experience peace with God. Severo became a student in the Bible school, and he bore personal testimony of a transformed life to his people. The Lord burdened his heart to preach the Gospel, and before long he was traveling throughout the islands of Panay and Guimaris to the scattered Negritos.

Missionary Hopper realized that missions are not merely evangelism. It is discipleship that leads to the establishment of local churches that can multiply over and over again. Thus in 1950 the Nagpana Fundamental Baptist Church was formed, and Chief Severo became pastor of the little congregation that met in a bamboo/palm leaf structure. The establishing of a church was one of the factors that caused the people to change from a nomadic tradition and begin to establish barrios. Loin cloths and bare breasts gave way to modest apparel, and cruelty was converted to civility and peace.

With the passing of years, Bill and Naomi Hopper retired, but their heart was ever with the Negritos. As often as possible they returned from the States to encourage and fellowship with their spiritual children. Thus in January of 2004 as the elderly couple planned to return to the Philippines, they were alerted to the fact that the Nagpana Baptist Church would be celebrating its Golden Anniversary on January 29-30. However, upon contacting their friends assuring them of their plans to attend the anniversary, they were informed that on Thursday, January 15, Chief Severo had graduated to glory. Furthermore, they learned that the Chief's funeral would be conducted along with the Golden Anniversary. Making their way along the tedious route, they arrived at Nagpana, now a barrio of between 700 and 800 people.

Of course, Bill Hopper participated in the lengthy funeral service. Many gave testimony of their admiration of Chief, Pastor Severo – a little man of stature but a spiritual giant before his God. Many told of his encouragement during their days in the Bible school as he had faithfully guided them into the service of the Lord. The municipal council had prepared a resolution of condolence for the family. This was read by the vice mayor and presented to the Chief's daughter. Along with the challenge of Missionary Hopper, the pastor of the Nagpana Baptist Church presented the various meanings of the word "departure" from the Greek Testament as he challenged his people to faithfulness to the Lord.

From raw heathenism to faithful service, Mr. Hopper had witnessed the grace of God in the lives of many Negritos. Now at the graduation of a great man of God, he wondered, in his own words, "How many stars does Severo have in his crown?" Friend, if you are saved, you would do well to ask yourself, "Will I have any stars in my crown?"

DLC

January 30

Foundation of Truth

Scripture: Psalm 12

Basil Manly, Jr. was born in the county of Edgefield, South Carolina, on December 19, 1825. His boyhood years were spent in Charleston, South Carolina, where his father was pastor of the First Baptist Church. When Manly was fourteen, his father was chosen to serve as president of the University of Alabama, and the family moved to Tuscaloosa, Alabama. He matriculated in the University of Alabama immediately, and graduated when he was only eighteen. Young Manly was licensed to preach on May 13, 1844, by the Baptist church in Tuscaloosa, and he began studies at the Newton Theological Institution in Newton Center, Massachusetts. When the Southern Baptist Convention came into being in May of 1845 he left Newton and entered Princeton Theological Seminary to complete his studies there.

His ordination took place on January 30, 1848, at Tuscaloosa, Alabama, and he immediately undertook the pastoral care of three churches in Alabama and Mississippi. Shortly thereafter his health failed, and for two years his ministry was somewhat curtailed. When his health was restored, Reverend Manly accepted a call to pastor the First Baptist Church of Richmond, Virginia. Richmond's First Baptist Church was perhaps the most prestigious congregation in the Southern Baptists at that time. He served there until October 1, 1854, when he became president of the Richmond Female Institute. Even while serving in that capacity, he ministered in a county church as well.

In 1859, when the Southern Baptist Theological Seminary was founded, Reverend Manly was chosen to write the "Abstract of Principles" (articles of faith) for the newly established school. He was selected as one of the four founding faculty members of the new seminary which was located initially in Greenville, South Carolina. Reverend Manly briefly provided instruction in Old Testament studies and the Hebrew language at the seminary until the Civil War made it necessary to temporarily close the seminary. Following that dreadful war, in 1871 Mr. Manly accepted the position of presidency of Georgetown College, Georgetown, Kentucky. But in 1879, when the Southern Baptist Theological Seminary relocated in Louisville, Kentucky, he returned to the faculty of the seminary. He devoted much of the remainder of his life to ministerial education.

The man of God also had a serious interest in Gospel music, and he wrote nearly forty hymns. A number of these compositions appeared in *The Baptist Psalmody*. He edited this volume with his father.

However, the most important writing of Basil Manly, Jr. is *The Bible Doctrine of Inspiration*. Basic to all theology is what one believes about God's Word. In his presentation, Mr.

Manly clearly understood this fact, and he emphasized this truth as he explained the difference between an inspired and uninspired Bible. This is foundational truth! It is the determining factor as to whether we are following God or men, and whether our religion is of divine or human origin. Manly argued that without an inspired Bible we would have no infallible standard of truth, no authoritative rule for obedience, and no ground for confident and everlasting hope.

The close of the twentieth century and the opening of the twenty first century have brought Baptists full circle again in this battle for truth. Either the Bible is truly God's inspired, infallible, inerrant, integral Word, revealing our loving Heavenly Father to mankind, or the Bible is an empty volume of meaningless platitudes that lead us to despair. How wonderful it is to be able to take the Bible in hand with the full realization that it is indeed God's Word. Surely as He promised in our Scripture reference for the day, "The words of the Lord are pure words, as silver tried in a furnace of earth, purified seven times." We can declare with the Psalmist that God has "preserved them from [his] generation forever."

Tragically many Baptist colleges and seminaries have drifted from this foundational truth. Pray today that God the Holy Spirit might bring refreshing revivals to such campuses. This would result in a large group of young Baptist preachers going forth declaring anew with confidence the edict of "Thus saith the Lord." This is America's need in this day!

DLC

January 31

Local Church Autonomy

Scripture: 1 Samuel 5:1-9

On May 16, 1926, Reverend Ford Porter became pastor of the First Baptist Church of Princeton, Indiana. This church held membership in the Northern Baptist Convention and its affiliated organizations, the Indiana Baptist Convention, and the Evansville Baptist Association. The great battle between modernism and fundamentalism had recently begun. Pastor Porter soon became aware of serious modernistic inroads into the Northern Baptist Convention. Believing in the verbal, plenary inspiration of the Bible, he determined that he would position the congregation solidly upon the inerrant, infallible Word of God. Therefore, early in his ministry he thoroughly grounded the saints in solid Bible teaching. His ministry was Gospel-centered, and the Lord blessed the church with growth. In 1932 during the heart of the national financial depression, more than 200 professed conversion or united with the church.

With growing conviction, the leadership of the congregation came to the realization that something must be done concerning their alignments. Thus the deacons called for a special meeting of the congregation that the issue might be discussed and a decision made as to what to do. On January 31, 1938, in a specially-called meeting, the congregation voted 92 to 18 to concur with the pastor and deacons and withdraw from the Convention and its affiliated organizations.

On February 1, Pastor Porter wrote the congregation urging them to: ". . . join hands and be united in heart, praying earnestly, and go after lost souls that many who are on the road to Hell may be saved."[1]

However, the minority did not admit defeat. Convention leaders had guided them into writing letters to various churches of the association stating, "We now constitute, and since the 31st of January, 1938, have constituted the true First Baptist Church of Princeton, Indiana, and we have not withdrawn fellowship from the Northern Baptist Convention, the Indiana Baptist Convention and the Evansville Baptist Association."[2]

Twice this group of dissidents met with Pastor Porter. The first time accompanied by their attorney, they asked for the resignation of the pastor. On their second visit, Pastor Ford invited them into his study where they might pray about the matter. They refused the invitation. The minority group then called for an ex parte council to be composed of the pastor and two messengers from the associated churches.

Such a "packed" council convened and voted 17 to 3 to override the majority of the First Baptist Church membership. The council was repudiated by the church membership, but still the convention-inspired minority persisted. Two court cases ensued, but the Baptist distinctive of the local church autonomy was upheld, and First Baptist Church of Princeton continued as an independent, fundamental Baptist church.

On the last day of the second trial, March 11, 1940, an interesting event transpired. Dr. R. T. Ketcham, then director of the General Association of Regular Baptists, had been summoned as a witness in the case. He had spent the night with the Porter family, and as the family was enjoying devotions that morning, the passage to be read was from 1 Samuel 5. Each member of the family led in reading a verse aloud. Dr. Ketcham was assigned verse five. But as Pastor Ford's 13-year-old son read verse four, Dr. Ketcham broke into laughter and could not immediately gain his composure. What was so funny? Verse four reads: "And when they arose early on the morrow morning, behold, Dagon was fallen upon his face to the ground before the ark of the LORD; and the head of Dagon and both the palms of his hands were cut off upon the threshold; only the stump of Dagon was left to him." Dr. Ketcham said: "Ford, that's what's going to happen today! The convention is going to fall on its face . . . and break its neck."[3]

Praise the Lord. The victory was won that very day, and the Baptist distinctive of local church autonomy had once again been vindicated. May we today stand upon the age-old Baptist distinctives as we impact the world with the Word.

DLC

---

[1]Ford Porter, *We Still Have An Autonomous Church* (Monrovia, IN: Lifegate, Inc., 2003), 13.

[2]Ibid., 14.

[3]Ibid., 78.

February 1

The Reformers' Dilemma

Scripture: Acts 5:29

The apostles faced a dilemma in the early days of Christianity: whether to obey divinely appointed authority or to hearken to the voice of God Himself. When put to the test in Acts 5, they passed, because they adhered to the principle implied in Peter's challenge to the rulers in Acts 4:19, "Whether it be right in the sight of God to hearken unto you more than unto God, judge ye." Even though the apostles had lived under the God-ordained Old Testament theocracy, the choice for them was obvious: obey the clear command of God.

Now, imagine that you live in the Reformation era. Instead of the Council of Elders in Jerusalem, centuries of tradition and a corrupt state church oppose the preaching of the pure Gospel of grace. John Hus had been burned at the stake because the Emperor Sigismund was not able to give Hus the safe conduct he had promised in 1411. Wycliffe had survived in England because of the protection afforded by his friend John of Gaunt, the king's uncle. State protection seemed to be the key to survival for any reform movement. Luther, for instance, enjoyed the protection of the Electors of Saxony and others of the German nobility.

Now consider Ulrich Zwingli, the Swiss Reformer. By his own testimony, Zwingli, in 1523, held that it would be better to baptize children when they had come to years of understanding . . . because [t]here is no clear utterance in the New Testament that commands the baptism of children. Yet just two years later, Zwingli said that this view was an error.[1]

The Biblical Anabaptists opposed infant baptism and resented the name Anabaptist which their opponents had imposed on them. Anabaptism means re-baptism. One cannot be baptized a second time if one has never been scripturally baptized the first time. The Anabaptists of Zurich agreed to debate Zwingli on the subject in January of 1525, provided that the only authority to which the debaters could appeal was the Bible. Reneging on his promise, Zwingli defeated his Anabaptist opponents by shouting them down. The Zurich City Council declared him the victor and decreed that the Anabaptists should have all their children baptized within a week or suffer banishment.

The Anabaptists refused to comply, so on February 1, 1525, the Council ordered them arrested and that each of their children should be baptized as soon as it was born. After they were fined 1,000 gulden plus costs, all were released except Felix Mantz and George Blaurock. In the next few years, the Council imposed confiscation of property, imprisonment, torture, and death upon the Anabaptists of Zurich. The severity of punishments meted out to people who were no threat to public order shows the weakness of the arguments used against them. The Reformation in Zurich had turned into a Protestant inquisition.

What caused Zwingli to change from the opinion he held in 1523 to the one he embraced in 1525? Here was his dilemma. On the one hand, he believed and taught that salvation is by faith alone apart from baptism. On the other hand, infant baptism was at the heart of the union of church and state. Believer's baptism means that no one is united to the church until he voluntarily chooses to follow Christ. Union of church and state is unworkable under such a system, because in a state-church union, every citizen must be a church member whether he is born again or not. Zwingli and the Council recognized this fact. The choice before them was whether to follow the traditions of men or to follow the teaching of Scripture, wherever it leads. Following the Scripture meant abandoning the security of state protection. Ironically, Zwingli's embrace of the state church concept led to his own death in a religious war with a neighboring Roman Catholic Swiss canton.

As we thank God for our religious freedom, let us also remember that this heritage of freedom does not come to us from the Reformers, but from men of conviction like Mantz and Blaurock, who, at the cost of their lives, decided to obey God rather than man.

DRP

---

[1]Thomas Armitage, *A History of the Baptists* (Watertown, WI: Maranatha Baptist Press, 1973), 330.

February 2

Another Victorious Prisoner

Scripture: Proverbs 21:1; Zechariah 4:6

Pastors of independent Baptist churches in Russia during the days of the zenith of communism lived in the constant realization that they could well be incarcerated at any time. Such was the experience of Veniamin Markevich, the pastor of the Baptist church in Ordzhonikidze. Pastor Markevich had been released from prison in the summer of 1982. But now in October, as he walked along the street, two shouting men dashed across the street and a police car pulled alongside simultaneously. Pastor Markevich was unceremoniously thrown into the car and taken to prison. He was unaware at the time that two other Baptist pastors were concurrently taken into custody, and all three were put on trial together. Pastors Markevich, Veniamin Chistyakov, and Vasily Mikhin were given four days to prepare for trial late in December of 1982.

The actual trial lasted from January 24 to February 2, 1983. The testimony of the state witnesses makes clear why KGB agents were so determined to incarcerate the three Baptist preachers. One teacher declared, Our school has a great atheistic program, but because of the activities of the defendants, practically nothing comes of it![1] Of course the defendants knew full well that, as in all such cases, the KGB had already determined guilt and the duration of the sentence. The elderly judge seated before the defendants would merely recite their verdict.

Politically, an important change had just taken place in Russia. Leonid Brezhnev, leader of the Soviet for eighteen years, died on November 10, 1982. Two days later, the Soviet Communist Party's Central Committee appointed Yuri Andropov as General Secretary. Andropov had been head of the KGB and was in charge of both foreign espionage operations and internal security. In his speeches, Andropov lashed out at the Western powers. He said: We know well that the imperialists will never meet one's pleas of peace. It can only be defended by relying on the invincible might of the

Soviet armed forces.[2] Thus the flexing of muscles and show of force among the people seemed to be essential to the new administration. As pre-determined, the three men were found guilty, and Vasily Mikhin received a three-year term; Veniamin Chistyakov, four years, and Pastor Markevich five years.

The vast nation of Russia includes eleven time zones, and it took one hundred days to transport Pastor Markevich from the Caucasus to Yakutia in Siberia. How does one cope with such imprisonment? The Russian believers recognized the sovereignty of their God, and thus it is thrilling to read that even during the times of darkest distress, prayers of thanksgiving ascended to the Heavenly Father.

While he was in transit, somehow Pastor Markevich's wife was able to discover his location. She traveled six hundred miles to visit her husband, and she was granted thirty minutes with her beloved. At that time she informed him that one of his daughters planned to marry Pastor Chistyakov's son. When first he had been imprisoned, Pastor Markevich's daughter was only thirteen years old, but now she was mature and planning marriage, and that, without him. Rather than concentrating on the awful persecution that Russian believers experienced in prison, meditate for a moment on one's separation from family during vital days of familial blessing. How that must stir our hearts.

Pastor Markevich was moved from time to time to different prisons, but in the will of God, he was ultimately released eight months early in February 1987. Andropov lived but a short time and was followed to the Soviet leadership by Konstantin Chernenko. But he too had died and Mikhail Gorbachev followed him as General Secretary. Immediately Gorbachev submitted calls for reform, and to paint a picture of improving public relations, several prisoners were released.

Surely it is wonderful to know that our God is omnipotent and the king's heart is in the hand of the LORD . . . He turneth it whithersoever He will (Prov.21:1). May we live our lives in that quiet confidence.

DLC

---

[1]Georgi Vins, compiler, *Let the Waters Roar* (Grand Rapids, MI: Baker Book House, 1989), 95.

[2]Clifton Daniel, Editor-in-Chief, *20th Century Day by Day* (London: Dorling Kindersley, 2000), 1212.

February 3

The Eternal Optimist

Scripture: Ephesians 4:11

It was into a Catholic family of both German and Irish descent that Glen H. Schunk was born in Scales Mound, Illinois, on February 3, 1918. His mother's Irish maiden name of Flannigan spoke volumes of her descent. Glen's father, had been a professional ballplayer, but he became a mechanic to support four children.

Glen met Irma Hartwig, an honor student from his local school in Freeport, Illinois, on a blind date, and thus they became high-school sweethearts. After two years of courtship, they married August 29, 1938, in Dubuque, Iowa, before she finished nursing school. Glen found employment in a sandwich shop. Irma had been converted at the age of thirteen, but she had never grown significantly in the things of God. Glen was enthusiastic in his new-found faith, and through his personal witness he led some family members to the Lord.

America's involvement in World War II was brought about by the attack on Pearl Harbor on December 7, 1941, and soon after that Glen was drafted into the army. He was sent to Camp Walters, Texas, for basic training. Following his training, his military experience took him to many parts of the world. Being on the front lines, he was often in foxholes, and on such occasions, as the bullets flew overhead, he would take out his New Testament for consolation. Other soldiers thought Glen lived a charmed life, and as a result, many wanted to share his foxhole. During those experiences, Glen won many fellow soldiers to Christ. Needless to say, with a heavy heart he also witnessed the death of some.

On one occasion Glen was wounded in action and sent to a military hospital in Naples, Italy. There he was placed in a ward with 1,000 men. While hospitalized, Glen attended services at the chapel regularly. It was at that time that he saw the tremendous spiritual needs of men, and he prayed concerning the possibility of the Lord leading him into full-time Christian service. The Lord was moving in Glen's heart, and when he concluded that God wanted him to preach, he took his stand for the Lord and won many to Christ. He began a Bible study for the new converts, and before he was discharged from the hospital, over 400 men were in attendance at the classes. Some of those converts ended up in the ministry.

Glen was uncertain as to how Irma would accept the idea of his becoming a preacher. There was apprehension in his heart as he wrote her to explain what he sensed was God's will in the matter. How thrilled he was when Irma wrote back stating, "If the Lord has called you, He has called me!"

That was the beginning of a life of service in the field of evangelism for Glen and Irma Shunk. They traveled together for twenty-two years. In nearly 900 revival meetings, it is estimated that they witnessed the salvation of over 60,000 people. Irma was a faithful prayer warrior as her husband stood in pulpits across the land. Evangelist Schunk preached the love of God and surely declared concisely the gospel of grace, but he also preached tenderly on a regular basis emphasizing an eternal Hell. But Evangelist Schunk's most unique trademark was his ability to give the invitation. When he drew the net, one sensed the working of the Holy Spirit with great convicting power.

The man of God was scheduled to bring the commencement address at Pillsbury Baptist Bible College early in June of 1978. But the Lord had other plans, and on June 6 of that year the Lord called His servant home. An amazing number of preachers attended his funeral in South Bend, Indiana, and the auditorium was filled with those who wished to pay respects to a man who had faithfully proclaimed the Gospel. Glen's contagious optimism had encouraged many pastors through troubled waters. In 1991 his body was moved from Osceola, Indiana, to Greenville, South Carolina. Irma died on August 12, 1999, and is buried beside him waiting the resurrection of the saints.[1]

Let us pray that the Lord of the Harvest will raise up many evangelists who will labor in local churches, stirring the members in a soul-winning effort as they continue the ministry of perfecting the saints.

DCB

[1]*The Unforgettable Glen Schunk* (Frontline Magazine, January-February, 1991) 28-33.

February 4

A Name of Honor

Scripture: Proverbs 22:1

John Dillahunty, who is our subject of interest, descended from a noble French family. His grandfather, David de la Hunte, was a Huguenot and was expelled from France because of his religious beliefs. He fled to Holland and then later made his way to Ireland. John's father, Daniel Dillahunty, came to America in 1715 and settled in Kent County, Maryland. It was there that John was born on December 5, 1728. When grown, John Dillahunty married Hannah Neal, a Quakeress. This marriage was not pleasing to John's parents, and when the couple sought reconciliation with them in vain, John and Hannah left their Maryland home and moved southward settling near New Bern, North Carolina.[1]

It is probable that John and Hannah heard the celebrated George Whitefield preach in February of 1755 when that great preacher ministered in New Bern. At that time John was serving as the sheriff. Following his ministry in New Bern, George Whitefield confessed that the hearers were totally indifferent, and he poured out his heart in intercessory prayer for the area. He requested the Lord to send someone to move the hardened hearts of the citizens there. That prayer was answered as the Lord of the Harvest sent the Separate Baptists. The Separate Baptists had moved to Sandy Creek, North Carolina, in 1755, and from their home base, Shubal Stearns, Daniel Marshall, and others went in every direction preaching the Gospel. Under the preaching of these men, John and Hannah were soundly converted and adopted Baptist principles. In due time, they were baptized by another Separate Baptist preacher, Reverend Philip Mulkey. When a Baptist church was organized, John had matured spiritually to a sufficient degree to be made a deacon. As he continued to grow in grace, and as he evinced much ability, the church congregation granted him a license to preach.

Before the opening of the Revolutionary War, Dillahunty preached frequently but like most Baptist preachers of the time, he was engaged actively in the war. When the pastor of the Chinquapin Chapel Church of the Church of England (Reverend James Reed) fled to England where his sympathies dwelt, a strange thing happened. John Dillahunty was asked to preach there, and the congregation grew very fond of Baptist doctrine. Following the close of the conflict, the vestry met, and, having determined that the right to the property was with them, they unanimously gave the whole of the property to John Dillahunty and the Baptists. In fact, the congregation affiliated with the Baptists, and Mr. Dillahunty became the stated pastor. In time the Methodists disputed their right to the property on the ground that, as part and parcel of the Episcopal Church, they were themselves its legal representatives and successors; but their claims were summarily and successfully opposed by the old Vestry, and Reverend Dillahunty and the congregation were allowed to proceed unmolested in their labors.[2] He continued to serve in that capacity until 1794 when he led a group of about six families to relocate in the rich hill country of Middle Tennessee west of Nashville. The work of God continued at the Chinqauapin Chapel as Pastor John Koonce became the pastor.

Upon their arrival in Tennessee, Pastor Dillahunty established the Richland Creek Baptist Church. One can only surmise the names of those who accompanied Pastor Dillahunty by the names that appear in the county records of Tennessee and once were prominent in the records of Jones County, North Carolina: Martin Stanley, Jesse Blackshear, Abraham Little, Charles Huggins, and others. These were descendants of large landowners in North Carolina who had begun to scout for new land which their children could establish. Thank God, as they went westward they carried the transforming message of the gospel. Reverend John Dillahunty continued to serve the pastorate of the Richland Creek Baptist Church until his death in Nashville on February 4, 1816.

DLC

---

[1]George Washington Paschal, *History of North Carolina Baptists* (Raleigh: The General Board North Carolina State Convention, 1930), 1:305.

[2]Ibid., 1:315-316.

February 5

A Diligent Soul Winner

Scripture: Romans 12:1-2; Proverbs 11:30

Patience is not a virtue many possess, perhaps not even the subject of our entry today. However, those who traveled with Bernard H. Frey had quickly to learn that lesson because of his intense love of witnessing. Bernard would often keep companions waiting while he witnessed to waitresses, attendants, or clerks about their eternal destiny. From the day he came to know Christ as Savior, Bernie, as he was affectionately called, felt compelled to share the Gospel.

Born into the family of John and Bena Marie Frey on September 22, 1914, in Rushmore, Minnesota, Bernard was the eighth of nine children. Bernie's father passed away when the lad was only nine, and his dear mother reared all nine children alone.[1] Growing up on a farm, Bernie learned the value of hard work, and that held him in good stead while in the Lord's work. On May 18, 1936, Bernie married Miss Emma Anfinson, and she became his faithful partner. Following his conversion, Bernie and two other men organized the Calvary Baptist Church in his hometown. He taught the men's Sunday school class, ministered as Sunday school superintendent, served as a deacon, and led the way as a soul-winner. More than twenty men went into the ministry from that church, primarily from Bernie's influence.

Bernie was not a young man when God called him to preach, but he entered Northwestern College in Minneapolis, Minnesota, simultaneously with his oldest daughter. Both father and daughter transferred to Pillsbury Baptist Bible College in Owatonna, Minnesota, upon its opening in 1957. Bernie was among Pillsbury's first students, and he became the first grandfather to graduate from the institution. He was greatly influenced by Dr. Monroe Parker who became President of Pillsbury on February 5, 1958. While still in college, Bernie pastored a Baptist church in Canon City, Minnesota. Following their Dad's example, his younger children also attended Bible college. His ministerial history included four churches in Minnesota and South Dakota.

The area of his ministry was difficult soil for Baptists because of both the Lutheran and Catholic culture. As Dr. R.V. Clearwaters used to say, You have to carve them [new converts] out of a rock. Bernie's wife and family played a vital role in these ministries—teaching Sunday school, visiting, playing musical instruments, and singing.

In the spring of 1972, Bernie was chosen coordinator of the New Testament Association of Independent Baptist Churches. The tribute given by Pastor Gerhard Raske at the time of Bernie's home-going, sets forth his accomplishments in that ministry.

The Association "suffered an immense loss at the home going of its coordinator, Rev. Bernard Frey. In many respects, our coordinator was the NTA. At a time when the association seemed to approach a standstill, our dear brother, Bernard Frey, was led of God to accept the position of coordinator, being elected by the constituency in the spring of 1972 . . . . It was not an easy task, yet in these two years this man of God encouraged and inspired every church and individual that he met. Under his leadership . . . he gave the constituency more unity and direction and provided counseling and special meetings for many. . . . He preached with the love of God and the power of the Holy Spirit, and winning souls was his number one concern. . . . He loved his work . . . and gave himself to it, much of the time laboring beyond the call of duty. Let's all praise the Lord for the privilege that we had being under the influence of this great man of God, and let us continue to be faithful to the Lord and His work . . . even as our dear brother was."[2]

April 17, 1974, is a date indelibly stamped on the minds of his children—Barbara, Duane, Marcia, and Debra—as the day they said goodbye to their father. As of this writing, three of Bernie's children are serving the Lord in full-time service as a direct result of their father's example of godliness. His children testify that he was a loving father, a great preacher, and that he possessed a pastor's heart. He loved to spend time with God's people inspiring them to share the good news to men and women in need of the Savior. May we today determine to tell someone of our Savior.

DCB

[1] Telephone interview with Marcia Frey Schearer by Bettye Baughan, July 20, 2004.

[2] *New Testament Association of Independent Baptist Churches*, Spring 1974.

February 6

God's Call is to Faithfulness - Not Fame

Scripture: Matthew 25:21

While we rightly celebrate the memory of those servants of God whose ministries made a large impact on the world, we must not forget the work of thousands of Baptist pastors who labored all their lives in obscurity. Christ rewards faithfulness, not fame. Daniel Erastus Burt is one example of these unsung heroes.

Daniel Burt was born in Cambridge Springs, Pennsylvania, on November 4, 1835, in one of the buildings of his father's tannery plant. He received his theological training in Lewisburg, Pennsylvania, at what is now Bucknell University. During 35 years of pastoral ministry, he served small rural churches in western New York and northwestern Pennsylvania. Because several of these churches were unable to afford a full-time pastor, he often doubled as the local schoolmaster as well. When times were tough his farmer parishioners would supply him with food in lieu of a salary.

After his retirement, a newspaper asked him to write a series of articles summarizing his years in the ministry. The yellowed clippings of these reminiscences, still treasured by his descendants, contain many interesting anecdotes. I will let him tell one of them in his own words. It begins with evangelistic meetings held at his church.

"One Monday evening two sisters, professed infidels, were going past the meeting house during the services, and the younger one said, 'Let us go in and see them make fools of themselves.' The next evening, they were actors and in earnest. Both of them continued going forward every evening during the week. The older one professed to have found the Savior. Saturday afternoon was the covenant meeting. At the close, after all had gone home, except the younger sister and two lady members of the church, the evangelist and myself, she said 'I cannot leave this house until this burden is removed.' As in the days of Jesus at the home of Jairus when he took with him Peter, James and John and the parents into that death chamber and spoke the word that gave life again to the girl of twelve summers, so here as we few were there upon our knees He who is the resurrection and the life said to the burdened one 'Thy sins be forgiven thee.' The next day the evangelist baptized the two sisters and others. This younger sister was a maiden of twenty-six summers. Two or three months after her baptism she asked me why it was that she heard the same thing in every sermon? I was surprised and told her that I tried to have more diversity about me than that. She said that was not it. It did not matter who was preaching. It was the same in every prayer, in the songs we sung, in the reading of the Bible. I said, 'My sister, that could not be unless it was some duty. Why,' I continued, 'that was the way God called me into the ministry. Every sermon, every prayer, and every hymn said duty. The more I pleaded inefficacy, the more impressive came the same thing in every sermon. I imagined that other people could see what the pastor was hinting at the same as I did.' The younger sister replied, 'That is it exactly.' It was a call to some foreign land as a missionary.

"A correspondence was started with Mrs. Hovey, who advised that her pastor should take the lectures that he received while in college and give her a course in theology. So it was arranged. She was to come to the parsonage every week day morning at nine o'clock. For five days we took theology, on Saturday we took up the Sunday school lesson. This continued for over eight months. The last month we added Greek. Then came her commission from the Woman's Mission Society, to go to Yokohama, Japan."

That faithful pastor, Daniel Burt entered into the joy of his Lord on July 29, 1908. His faithful wife,

Orpha, followed her husband into the eternal land of joy on February 6, 1922.

Faithful service always produces spiritual results. May our Lord find us faithful to His call in our lives.

DRP

February 7

Were the Reformers Spiritual Men?

Scripture: Isaiah 54:2-3

Some time ago while ministering to a group of pastors, I inadvertently mentioned the fact that the reformers (I.E. Luther, Calvin and Zwingli) could hardly be considered spiritual men. The statement was unrelated to the message, but surprisingly, following the session several pastors approached to question me concerning that statement. I reminded the men that the reformers actually led in the persecution of the Anabaptists. I believe that most Christians today equate the Reformers as being comparable to our Lord's apostles. However we do well to realize that while the Reformers, in the rediscovery of ancient spiritual truths, had some similarities to our Baptist forefathers, in no way can they be considered as "spiritual men."

Consider the following statements and actions.

In 1807 Dr. Samuel Jones, pastor of the Baptist Church in Lower Dublin, Pennsylvania, preached a Century Sermon commemorating the Centennial of the Philadelphia Baptist Association. Dr. Jones was one of the most influential Baptist ministers in the Middle Colonies, and he served as pastor of the Lower Dublin church for over fifty years until his death in 1814. In his famed message he presented a properly focused appreciation for the Reformation. He recognized the eventual blessings that came out of the Reformation, but he did not set the Reformers up as paragons of spiritual enlightenment men whom we replicate. He said, "The reformation, which has been so much gloried in was but a poor piece of business, although it has been attended with valuable consequences. The reformers shook off the Papal yoke, but in the main retained its principles and spirit. They did not establish the right of free inquiry, liberty of conscience, and the word of God as the only rule of faith and practice: but, on the other hand, opposed ... a thorough reformation. They were influenced by worldly motives, connected religion with world establishments, were the abettors of tyranny and oppression, and even of persecution by fire and the sword."[1]

Freedom of religion in America came not through the theology of the reformation, but rather through the influence of our godly Baptist forebears. The historian, Leonard Woolsey Bacon put it this way: "Other sects, notably the Presbyterians, had been energetic and efficient in demanding their own liberties; the Friends and the Baptists agreed in demanding liberty of conscience and worship, and equality before the law, for all alike. But the active labor in this cause was mainly done by the Baptists. It is to their consistency and constancy in the warfare against the privileges of the powerful Standing Order of New England, and of the moribund establishments of the South, that we are chiefly indebted for the final triumph. . . ."[2]

Religious freedom was not the product of the reformation. In this day when our freedoms are being eroded by governmental edicts, limitations and controls, it is time again for Baptists to express their determination to maintain this basic tenet which is clearly enunciated in the Scriptures. May the Lord find each of us faithful.

DLC

---

[1]A. D. Gilllette, Editor, *Minutes of the Philadelphia Baptist Association 1707 to 1807* (Springfield, MO: Particular Baptist Press, 2002), 466-467.

[2]Leonard Woolsey Bacon, *A History of American Christianity* (New York: The Christian Literature Co., 1897), 221-222.

February 8

Missionary to the Outcasts

Scripture: John 4:1-42

We are familiar with many of our great forefathers. Frequently, however, we are unaware of some of those who assisted and worked alongside those better-known men. George Dana Boardman is such a person. He was born in Livermore, Maine, on February 8, 1801, the son of a Baptist pastor. He was ordained at North Yarmouth, Maine, on February 16, 1825. With his wife, he sailed on July 16 of that same year for Calcutta, India. There they remained until March 20, 1827, when they embarked for Amherst, Burma, to assist the well-known Adoniram Judson.[1] They arrived in Burma only days after the burial of Mrs. Ann Judson.

It was decided that the Boardmans should move to the province of Tavoy and establish a mission at its principal town, which was also called Tavoy. In April 1828, they began their missionary work in that place. Tavoy was a place of upwards of 9000 inhabitants. It was one of the principal strongholds of Buddhism, filled with temples and shrines dedicated to that religion. Within the limits of the town there were nearly a thousand pagodas. As soon as his zayat was built, Mr. Boardman began his work with great zeal and with a firm trust in God that this work would not be in vain. The Karens seemed ripe for the gospel, while among the proud Burmese only a few became believers. The Karens had long been oppressed by the Burmese and lived in the hills and forests. The Karens of the vicinity held a tradition that at some time messengers from the West would bring to them a revelation from God. Hence, they were prepared to receive our missionaries with open arms and to accept their message.[2] Two converts were soon won, and a wide-spread interest in the new religion began very soon to show itself in Tavoy.

One of those converts was Ko Thah-byu, who served as an evangelist to his own people. Although Boardman's health was poor, he agreed to travel to a Karen village and minister to the new converts there the rite of Christian baptism. Lying on a cot carried on the shoulders of the Karens and accompanied by Mrs. Boardman, he set out on his journey. For three days they traveled until they reached the zayat, which the faithful disciples had built for them. More than a hundred were already assembled, nearly half of whom were candidates for baptism. At the close of the day, just as the sun was sinking behind the mountains, his cot was placed at the riverside, in the midst of the assembly that had gathered to witness the first baptism ever held in that region. As Boardman watched in silent gratitude upon the scene, he felt that his work among these people was finished, and he was ready to depart in peace. The next day the missionaries left to return to Tavoy, hoping to reach the home of Mr. Boardman while he was still alive. But before the end of the second day's journey, February 11, 1831, the end had come, and the spirit was released from its weary body. Boardman's body was taken to Tavoy and laid in a tomb, in what was at one time a Buddhist grave, beside a forsaken pagoda.[3] Mr. Judson's feelings on hearing of his death are expressed in his journal of February 28th: One of the brightest luminaries of Burmah is extinguished. Dear brother Boardman has gone to his eternal rest. He fell gloriously at the head of his troops, in the arms of victory. . . . Disabled by mortal wounds, he was obliged, through the whole of his last expedition, to be carried on a litter; but his presence was a host, and the Holy Spirit accompanied his dying whispers with almighty influence. Such a death, next to that of martyrdom, must be glorious in the eyes of Heaven.[4]

LRO

---

[1] William Cathcart, *The Baptist Encyclopedia* (Philadelphia: Louis H. Everts, 1881), 109.

[2] Thomas Armitage, *A History of the Baptists* (New York: Bryan, Taylor, and Co., 1890), 819.

[3] Cathcart, 109.

[4] J. Clement, *Fifth Thousand Memoir of Adoniram Judson: Being a Sketch of His Life and Missionary Labors* (Auburn: Derby and Miller, 1853), 191-192.

February 9

Mr. Missions - A Statesman

Scripture: 2 Timothy 4:6-8

It would be well to read the entries of November 16 and December 8 with this material as it all pertains to Fred Donnelson, Mr. Missions.

In our entry of December 8, we left the Donnelsons in a Japanese internment camp just outside of Shanghai. The group of internees was comprised of some professional and skilled workers along with several missionaries. Through American diplomatic intervention, the internees were allowed to exercise some self-government. There were, however, many trials of cold, insects, and lengthy political haranguing. The food was not good, but for twenty-two months as prisoners of war, they endured the adverse circumstances. Fred had lost forty-five pounds.

The Donnelsons were repatriated and returned to America on the Swedish liner *Gripsholm,* boarding the ship on October 19[1]. This was the second furlough for the Donnelsons, But what of the future? After a lavish welcome home to America, and after regaining strength, the Donnelsons were able to go back again to Shanghai. They returned to the Shanghai Baptist Tabernacle, and it was even possible for their son Paul and his wife to join them. They began a radio ministry, and the church grew rapidly.

But the Communists began driving into south China. Seeing the impending problems, Fred sent his son and daughter-in-law back to the States, but he and Effie determined to remain. The members of the Tabernacle pled with the Donnelsons to leave, and finally they relented. At the last minute, in 1949, they evacuated. Fred was now in his fifties, and it would be the last time he and Effie would see their adopted land! But God was not done with His servant.

Upon returning again to America, Brother Donnelson settled briefly in Ottumwa, Iowa, with their only plan being to visit the churches that had graciously supported them. But in 1950 a split developed in the World Fundamental

Baptist Missionary Fellowship, and the Baptist Bible Fellowship was formed. Within a matter of weeks the missionaries who had served under the World Fundamental Baptist Missionary Fellowship declared their intention to become part of the Baptist Bible Fellowship. Soon Fred Donnelson was asked to assume the role of mission director for the Baptist Bible Fellowship. His work would be that of organizing, promoting, and directing the missionary efforts.

Donnelson desired to join his son and daughter-in-law and go to serve in Formosa (now Taiwan), but leaders of the new fellowship assured him that he could do more by staying in the States and promoting missions. His was a decision somewhat like that of Luther Rice in another era. For eighteen years Donnelson oversaw the mission program of the Baptist Bible Fellowship. During those years the missionary family grew from fewer than twenty serving in four fields to over three hundred serving in twenty-six fields. His impact was surely blessed of God, and the Lord used him to challenge countless young people to lift up their heads and look upon the fields of the world.

In time Fred Donnelson became known as Mr. Missions in the Baptist Bible Fellowship. But the years have a way of catching up with all earthlings, and in 1968 Fred Donnelson stepped down from the role in which God so used him. His influence surely did not cease, for he continued to speak in Christian colleges and churches urging young people to consider preaching the Gospel where Christ is not known. On February 9, 1974, the Lord saw fit to call His servant home. We have no doubt that his was a grand entry into glory. Doubtless his home-going was something like being repatriated. Surely in the host lined up to meet him were many Chinese whom he had led to the Lord. And sprinkled midst the throng there were some missionaries whom he had challenged to serve.

Every child of God is hastening toward Heaven. Perhaps it will be in the rapture, or perhaps it will be with a visit of the death angel. But what kind of reception will be ours when we are repatriated to glory? May we be found faithful.

DLC

---

[1]Fred Donnelson, *Finding Freedom In A Japanese Prison Camp* (Chicago: World Fundamental Baptist Missionary Fellowship, n.d.), 92.

February 10

Faithful to the End!

Scripture: Galatians 5:7, 15

As one reads early American history, it is interesting to note the varied spellings given the same individual in various journals. Of concern in our entry today is John Meglamare, one of the early Baptist preachers in Virginia. James B. Taylor, noted biographer of Baptist preachers in the Commonwealth, spelled the name as it appears above. However, the historian of the Baptists of Virginia, Robert Baylor Semple, spells it McGlamre. The later historian, Garnett Ryland, uses the spelling adopted by Semple. There is no question, however, that these men are speaking of the same individual.

John Meglamare was born on June 7, 1730[1], and even the state of his birth is unknown. Though we cannot ascertain the spiritual condition of either of his parents, we do know that they were Presbyterians. During his youth, John gave serious thought to spiritual matters. Prior to his conversion, John Meglamare moved to Halifax County, North Carolina, and there he became acquainted with God's method of salvation. When he was 34, he experienced the regenerating work of God, was baptized, and united with the Kehukee Baptist Church. The church was well established, having been founded on December 11, 1755. John Meglamare was blessed of God to mature spiritually in such a setting, for the Kehukee church became mother to several churches, and John was blessed in witnessing such growth.

Soon after his conversion, John began preaching, and the congregation soon observed God's hand upon him. Thus on Saturday, February 10, 1767, he was ordained. When his pastor, Elder Thomas Pope, died, the congregation looked to the newly ordained man of God to assume the pastorate. He did so, and served the church faithfully until 1772. His removal to Virginia came about through his evangelistic efforts while still serving as pastor.

During preaching excursions to Sussex county, Virginia, the blessings of Heaven were known in the salvation of many.

For several months the pastor made continued incursions into Virginia, and many desired baptism. Among them was James Bell, an influential citizen of the area. These young converts urged the man of God to move to Virginia and establish a church for them. Believing this invitation was of the Lord, he accepted. Soon a church of eighty-seven was formed, and the Lord added to the church daily such as should be saved.

John Meglamare had experienced God's blessing in evangelism, and thus he traveled extensively through adjacent counties. Soon four other churches came into existence at Mill Swamp, Black Creek, Sea Cock, and High Hills. With tireless energy he continued to pastor and serve in an itinerant role of evangelism until his age made it impossible to continue such a strenuous pace. His last pastorate at Blue Run could well have been his most fruitful. I wish that we might conclude on such a note of victory, but such is not the case.

In 1786, John Meglamare moved to Kentucky. From that time, he seemed somehow to become a bitter old preacher! He apparently developed a censorious temper. He wrote a pamphlet in which he condemned preachers for receiving regular salaries. Seemingly he could not allow the subject to drop, and he became known for his caviling spirit until his death in 1808.

The author of these lines has passed the desired three score years and ten. Well over fifty years of my life have been invested in the work of God. My horizon is bright, but not with additional prospects of pastoring, though I could wish for that; but, I am closer to the reality of Heaven than ever before! Whether it be in the rapture or in death, I cannot lose! But until that time, it is my desire to be an encourager of young, fundamental, Baptist pastors. Perhaps these lines are being read by a retired preacher who no longer is able to pursue an active ministry of preaching. Let me challenge you to be an encourager of young preachers by prayer and word. Your encouragement could make the difference between victory and failure!

DLC

---

[1]James B. Taylor, *Lives of Virginia Baptist Ministers* (Richmond: Yale & Wyatt, 1838), 1:60.

February 11

The Battleground of Baptism

Scripture: Romans 6:1-10

How interesting to note how those of other denominations profess to seek continually for assured results of scholarship. In one important tenet, the Bible's clear teaching is rejected for the endless research of so-called scholars. Every major doctrinal section of theology has been carefully scrutinized; however, scholarship concerning the doctrine of baptism is completely overlooked.

For years, Dr. Alexander McLaren, outstanding Bible expositor from Manchester, England, wrote for *The Sunday School Times*. Dr. McLaren was a Baptist. McLaren's life spanned a period when Great Britain produced fine Bible teachers. He was born on February 11, 1826, and lived until May 5, 1910. In one of his articles for the Sunday school publication, he commented on the immersion in the Jordan. Immediately, the editor of *The Sunday School Times* was bombarded by pedobaptists for allowing such a statement to go unrebuked. The editor, himself a Presbyterian, replied that though he was not a Baptist, he concurred that Dr. McLaren was correct in his interpretation.

When Dr. McLaren used the phrase, "the immersion in the Jordan" for a second time, the editor of *The Sunday School Times* was attacked by another Presbyterian editor for allowing the expression to be printed. In the charge, the writer wrote, "We deny that there was an immersion in the baptism of Jesus, and we do not care to have the young people of Presbyterian churches taught that there was. This is not undenominational teaching, but sectarian of the strictest sort. Our Sunday School literature is the safest and best for our churches and schools."

To this rebuff, the editor of *The Sunday School Times*, himself a Presbyterian, made the following reply: "There is food for thought in that Presbyterian editor's conclusions. One morsel difficult of digestion is as to how he would comment on some of the statements of Dr. John D. Davis,

Professor of Oriental and Old Testament Literature in the Theological Seminary at Princeton, NJ, as given in his *Dictionary of the Bible*, published by Westminster Press, and copyrighted by the Trustees of the Presbyterian Board of Publication and Sabbath School Work. Professor Davis says: "The mode of John's baptism is not described; but, as Jesus entered into the Jordan, it was probably by affusion (pouring) or immersion . . . . The word is derived from the verb, *baptizo* which means, etymologically, to immerse. This Bible Dictionary stands at the head of a list of Books for Sunday School Workers, recognized by the Presbyterian Committee of Publication, at Richmond, V.A. It would seem, therefore, to meet with the approval of those who have at heart the training of the the young people at Presbyterian churches in both the South and the North. As the editor of *The Sunday School Times* is a Presbyterian, he is glad to be able to assure readers of his own denomination there is some Presbyterian literature which is safe for their church and schools. Professor Davis is in agreement with many Christian scholars of various denominations in finding that the primary meaning of *baptizo* is to immerse, and very many who are not Baptists agree with Dr. Davis and Dr. McLaren in believing that John's form of baptism was, or may have been, immersion."[1]

Those words were originally written in the nineteenth century. We are now in the twenty-first century, and it well to realize that the Greek word *baptizo* is still understood as immersion.

All the lexicons of worth translate the word simply, "to dip, to immerse, to submerge." Let me quote three of the outstanding lexicons. *Thayer's Lexicon*: "To dip, to immerse, to submerge." *Liddell and Scott*: "To dip under, overhead and ears, to overwhelm." *Bagster's Greek New Testament Lexicon* renders the word as follows: "to dip, to immerse." The order of the Book of Acts is very clear. Those who **believed** unto salvation were **baptized** as witnesses, and then they **belonged** to the local church as a place of service. Friend, have you been obedient to the Lord in the matter of believer's immersion? If not, I urge you not only to **trust**, but to **obey**!

DLC

[1]J. B. McInturff, Editor, *The Old Paths* (Woodstock, VA: Power Print, 1905), 164-165.

February 12

Songs in the Night

Scripture: Acts 16:25

In just six days, February 18th, Luba Skvortsova would celebrate her twenty-fourth birthday[1], but it would not be in freedom. Luba was visiting in the home of a Christian friend when police raided the premises. Miss Skvortsova was arrested, and her confinement began. She was jailed locally until her trial finally began. Luba was driven to the court building. As the vehicle approached the building, Luba could see her parents and a multitude of church friends. The prison van stopped, for something was not quite right. Rather than taking the prisoner into the court, the guards informed Luba that the trial had been postponed. They then returned to the prison. Following lunch, Luba was returned to the court. But this time, the street was full of police, and her friends were not allowed near. Guards finally allowed her parents into the courtroom for the two-day trial, but other believers were forced to remain outside. Finally when the verdict was delivered, the believers were allowed to enter. As the judge read the sentence of three years imprisonment, church friends began throwing flowers at Luba. They shouted, Take courage! Be faithful unto death. The barrage of flowers continued until Luba returned to the van.

The thought of confinement in prison for three long years was sobering, but Luba prayed the Lord would provide Christian fellowship. Arriving at the prison camp, Luba was escorted to her cell on the top floor of the prison. Entering the cell, she discovered six women prisoners, and one asked what such a young child was doing there. Luba told them she was a Christian, but inasmuch as she had not slept for twenty-four hours, she asked them to let her sleep and assured them she would provide all the details in the morning.

Soon she discovered that she was in the same prison in Voroshilovgrad that housed a number of the independent Baptist pastors; Pavel Rytikov, Stepan Germaniuk, Pavel Sazhnev,

Ivan Tyagun, and Anatoly Balatsky. When these men learned that Miss Skvortsova was there, they determined to get a message to the young lady. As she walked one day in the exercise yard, she saw some graffiti on the wall. It read: Be faithful unto death! In the courtroom her friends had uttered those words, and now again she was reminded of her commitment. Is it any wonder she testified that while in prison her favorite Bible verse was Revelation 2:10?

Upon sharing her testimony with cell mates, Luba was thrilled to hear that there was another believer in the prison. She was introduced to Maria Didnyak, who became like a mother to Luba. Luba and Maria encouraged each other by sharing portions of Scripture and even singing quietly together. In time, the warden ordered the ladies not to meet, but they were inseparable.

On one occasion, the guards discovered their small Gospel and a notebook of poems. The material was confiscated, and the ladies prayed they might be given strength to endure the expected punishment. Promptly, they were summoned by the camp director, but in an effort to frighten the ladies, she told them they were to return the next day and meet all the camp administrators. The next day the administrators were called in and were told that the search of the two ladies had produced a Gospel. Amazingly, everyone seemed interested. They asked to see the Gospel. The administrators passed it among themselves. Though highly educated in atheism, this was the first time that they had seen a Gospel! They asked many questions, and the ladies shared their testimonies. Luba and Maria were shocked that their only punishment was the denial of having extra money to spend in the camp store.

After Maria's release, God gave grace to Miss Skvortsova, and she was able to help many. Mrs. Ulyana Germaniuk, pastor Germaniuk's wife, was incarcerated, and had to be placed in the infirmary. Luba tended to her physical needs, nursing her back to health.

Luba lived out her favorite Bible verse throughout her three-year imprisonment. What would we be willing to endure for our Savior?

DLC

---

[1]Georgi Vins, Compiler, *Let The Waters Roar* (Grand Rapids, MI: Baker Book House, 1989), 83.

February 13

A Warm-Hearted Pastor

Scripture: 1 Samuel 18:1-4

We possess little knowledge of Benjamin Miller's early life. Knowing his age at the time of his death, we calculate that our subject was born in 1715. In a volume concerning the Baptists of New Jersey, the author tells us, "Rev. Mr. Miller . . . when a young man was said to be 'wild and forward,' which means that he was a forceful man, and had in him the making of a man, and all of his life he proved him to be a man among men."[1]

Another historian reports that Mr. Miller, " . . . met with a sudden and surprising change under a sermon of Rev. Gilbert Tennent: [Presbyterian preacher of the Great Awakening] Mr. Tennent [it is said] christened him; and encouraged him to study the languages, to qualify him for the ministry. However that be, Mr. Miller did spend some time at learning under the tuition of Rev. Mr. Biram. It was there he embraced the sentiment of the Baptists, owing to a discourse of Mr. Biram at the christening of a child, and a conversation that followed between him and his pupil."[2]

In the course of time, Mr. Miller offered himself for membership in the Baptist church at Piscataway and was immersed in 1740. On September 8, 1747, some of the members of Piscataway, who had requested dismissal in order to form themselves into a church at Scotch Plains, spent the day in solemn prayer to accomplish that purpose. One of the number was Benjamin Miller. When he was twenty-five-years old, the Scotch Plains church called him to be pastor, and he was ordained on February 13, 1748. Mr. Miller served that congregation as pastor until his homegoing on November 14, 1781.

Elsewhere in this, and our earlier two volumes, we related how Daniel and Martha Marshall left their ministry among the Mohawk Indians (because of warfare), and made their way into what is today West Virginia. They became associated with the Mill Creek Baptist Church, pastored by Samuel Heaton.

There they were immersed, and "Marshall's ability was recognized . . . and he was soon licensed by the church to the unrestrained exercise of his gifts. Preaching as opportunity came, Marshall found a warm response in the community. In fact, Robert Semple, the Virginia historian, says his preaching stirred such excitement that some of the more cold-hearted church members were shocked. Some even complained to the Philadelphia Association of what appeared to be disorder.

"The Association sent Benjamin Miller to investigate the report. To the evident disappointment of the cold hearted, Miller could find nothing disorderly. Instead, he was delighted with what he saw and joined heartily in the revival services. In his report to the Association he stated that such warm-hearted Christians as he found in the Mill Creek church were worth more than gold."[3]

Thus we learn of the warmth of heart in the ministry of Benjamin Miller. Though he was not part of the Separate Baptist movement, it is apparent that he was an evangelistic pastor, and his congregation experienced continual growth.

Mr. Miller was a close friend of two other warm-hearted Baptist preachers of that day: John Gano, chaplain in the Revolutionary War, heard of Mr. Miller's death after the surrender of Cornwallis at Yorktown. He said: "Never did I esteem a ministering brother so much as I did Mr. Miller, nor feel so sensibly a like bereavement." His second close companion was Reverend Benjamin Stelle. Mr. Miller pastored Scotch Plains for thirty-four years, while Reverend Stelle pastored the Piscataway church for twenty-nine years. The men were inseparable.

Morgan Edwards summarized it well when he wrote: "Lovely and pleasant were they in their lives and in their death, they were not much divided, the one having survived the other but thirty-five days."[4] May the Lord raise up warm-hearted gospel pastors in these days of trial.

DLC

[1]Thomas S. Griffiths, *A History of Baptists in New Jersey* (Hightown, NJ: Barr Press Publishing Company, 1904), 263.

[2]Morgan Edwards, *Materials Towards A History of the Baptists* (Danielsville, GA: Heritage Papers, 1984) 1:106.

[3]William L. Lumpkin, *Baptist Foundations in the South* (Nashville, TN: Broadman Press, 1961), 27-28.

[4]Edwards, 106.

February 14

Publishing Glad Tidings

Scripture: 2 Corinthians 9:6

On this date in 1824, Reverend Noah Davis sent a tremendously important message to a former classmate, the Reverend James D. Knowles of Washington, D. C., urging that consideration be given for the establishing of a publishing house for Bible literature among the rapidly growing ministry of the Baptists in America. As the nation expanded westward, Mr. Davis recognized the importance of under-girding young converts in biblical truth. This is what he wrote: "I have been thinking for some time, how a Tract Society can be gotten up in Washington, which shall hold the same place among Baptists that the American Tract Society does among the Congregationalists. I now feel very much, the necessity of having tracts to scatter in the waste places. It is a plan of doing good scarcely thought of among Baptists."[1]

I am certain that Reverend Davis bathed his appeal in prayer, for on February 25, 1824, a company of twenty-five Baptists met at the house of Mr. George Wood in Washington D. C. to consider the appropriateness of the formation of a Baptist General Tract Society. The call that brought them together was the result of the letter sent by the Reverend Noah Davis of Maryland.

Because Philadelphia offered greater advantages for publishing and distributing its tracts throughout the county, in 1826 the society was transferred there. Mr. Davis was asked to assume the management of the society. Growth was slow, but it was steady. Mr. Knowles gave this tribute to Reverend Davis: "His heart was in the work; a qualification, without which, no man ever accomplished much. He possessed unusual talents for business. He was active, affable, and prompt. He spoke with fluency, and when excited, with much power and eloquence. His full, loud, and sonorous voice, his manly person, his simple, direct, and forcible diction, gave him great advantages in preaching, and especially in occasional addresses."[2]

Later the society began to print bound volumes (primarily to promote and support Sunday schools) and to prepare books and other publications that would be used primarily in the pioneer ministries of the West. In 1840 traveling salesmen were employed to circulate their publications and educational materials. With the establishment of the Southern Baptist Convention in 1845, the name of the society was changed to The American Baptist Publication Society. Its objective, according to its constitution, was: To promote evangelical religion by means of the Bible, the printing press, colportage, and the Sunday school.[3]

Pastor Davis sought to rouse the Baptists to regard their obligations. He said, "There is great responsibility resting on the Baptists of the United States, for to whomsoever much is given, of him shall be much required. At least two million of the population of this country are so connected with us, that the work of preaching the gospel to them must be done mainly through our efforts. Many millions in other portions of the earth are accessible to the ministers of Christ, to whom men should be sent from us with the word of life. Are we exerting ourselves to fulfill our duty to these dying millions? The Baptists of this land, because of their numbers and resources, are capable of doing great things. We profess purity of faith. Our holy lives, and zealous endeavors to convert souls ought to show it. Is it then our duty, or is it not, to pray and labor, and give of our substance, that the way of God may be known upon earth, and his saving health among all nations. The field is the world, and it is already white unto the harvest. The Master requires us to publish, or aid in publishing the gospel to every creature, and until some other method of imparting it, than the one pursued, is shown to be according to the dictates of scripture and common sense, we must believe that this work is to be done by men full of faith, and of the Holy Ghost, going forth with the Bible and tracts into every corner of the world, and proclaiming salvation to the lost."[4]

Although spoken by Pastor Davis many years ago, is it not still our obligation? Surely the least we can do is share the Gospel by means of gospel tracts everywhere we go.

EGC

---

[1]James B. Taylor, *Virginia Baptist Ministers*, (Richmond: Yale and Watt, 1837), 372.

[2]Ibid., 373.

[3]W. Cathcart, *The Baptist Encyclopedia*, (Philadelphia: The Baptist Standard Bearer, 1881), 948.

[4]Taylor, 375.

February 15

A House For A Church

Scripture: 1 Corinthians 16:1-12

From nearly the beginning of the Massachusetts Colony until 1769, the Baptists had been persecuted in various ways in the city of Boston and, indeed, throughout the entire colony. The first record in the books of the First Baptist Church in Boston reads thus: "The 28th of the third month, 1665, in Charlestown, Massachusetts, the Church of Christ, commonly, though falsely, called Anabaptists, were gathered together, and entered into fellowship and communion with each other; [they] engaged to walk together in all the appointments of our Lord and Master, the Lord Jesus Christ, as far as he should be pleased to make known his mind and will unto them by his word and Spirit, and then were baptized, Thomas Gould, Thomas Osborne, Edward Drinker,

John George, and joined with Richard Goodall, William Turner, Robert Lambert, Mary Goodall, and Mary Newell, who had walked in that order in Old England, and to whom God hath since joined Isaac Hull, John Farnham, Jacob Barney, John Russell, Jr., John Johnson, George Farley, Benjamin Sweetzer, Mrs. Sweetzer, and Ellis Callender, all before 1669."[1]

This was not a large group, but considering the danger of being part of something besides the Congregational Church of Massachusetts, it is significant.

This infant church was first organized in Charlestown near Cambridge. Thomas Gould became its pastor. He and his members paid dearly. They lost the right to vote, were fined and imprisoned, and were threatened with banishment. Gould was brought before both the secular courts and the church courts and charged with Anabaptism. This Baptist church came into existence under the influence of Henry Dunster, the first president of Harvard College, who had adopted baptistic principles.[2] The church moved from Charlestown to Noddle's Island and then dared to enter Boston sometime after Gould's death in 1675. John Russell became the new pastor. Philip Squire and Ellis Callender built a small meetinghouse. This building was so plain that it did not attract the attention of the Boston authorities until it was completed and the church began to use it for worship on February 15, 1679. In May the General Court passed a law forbidding the use of a house for public worship without the consent of the court or a town meeting on forfeiture of the house and land. Because of this, the Baptists stopped using their own church edifice until King Charles II required the authorities to allow liberty of conscience to all Protestants. With this approval, the Baptists went back to using their building again. In spite of the king's permission, the Court charged them with a crime and on March 8, 1680, ordered the marshal to nail the doors closed, which he did, posting the following notice on the door: "All persons are to take notice that, by order of the Court, the doors of this house are shut up, and that they are inhibited to hold any meetings therein, or to open the doors thereof, without license from authority, till the Court take further order, as they will answer the contrary to their peril. Edward Rawson, Secretary."[3]

The Baptists quietly petitioned the Court in May asking simply for the right to meet in their own building, but the Court continued to prohibit them as a society by themselves, or joined with others, to meet in that public place they have built, or any public place except such as are allowed by lawful authority.[4] The next Sunday the members of the church held public services in the yard. That week they prepared a shed for use on the next Sunday, but when they came to their property, they found the doors open! Never stopping to ask whether the marshal had opened them or the angel, which threw open the iron gate for Peter, they went in boldly and held their services in their own building. For nearly 70 years this was the only Baptist church in Boston.[5] Since that day, there has always been a great door and effectual opened to Boston Baptists.

LRO

---

[1] Thomas Armitage, *A History of the Baptists* (New York: Bryan, Taylor, and Co., 1890), 699.

[2] Ibid.

[3] Ibid., 703.

[4] Ibid.

[5] David Benedict, *A General History of the Baptist Denomination in America* (Boston: Lincoln and Edmands, 1813), 398.

February 16

Is Church Membership Important?

Scripture: Acts 2:41-47

The Baptist Church of Charleston, South Carolina, was established when William Screven led his congregation to flee the persecution in Kittery, Maine, and they relocated in Charleston in 1683. Through the following years, that congregation had outstanding pastoral leadership such as Oliver Hart who began his ministry there on February 16, 1750, and Richard Furman, who pastored there beginning in 1787.

This Day in Baptist History III

Church membership was important in those days. The following were the rules for membership:

> First: When a person desires to join the church, the desire shall be made known to the Pastor a sufficient length of time before the communion season, to allow of conversation and acquaintance; and for further satisfaction, the Pastor may appoint the deacons, or any other of the brethren he may think proper, to visit the Candidate, for the purpose of obtaining all needful information concerning his or her experience and faith, character and life.
>
> Second: The Pastor, and those he may have sent to visit and converse with the Candidate, shall meet together, at such a place as he may appoint, to consider the qualification of the Candidate, and after which conference, the Pastor shall give such advice to each as may appear suitable. In the meantime, any of the members may visit the Candidate or Candidates, for the purpose of forming acquaintance, and obtaining fellowship, before the period of their reception into the church.
>
> Third: If the Candidate or Candidates be thought to possess those qualifications which may entitle them to a participation of the privileges of God's House, they shall appear before the church; which (as it is a garden enclosed) shall be privately convened for said purpose, and none but the members be present, and each Candidate will then relate the reason for his or her hope, and give such answers to questions respecting their Christian knowledge, repentance and faith, as may afford consistent evidence of a gracious state; after which, satisfaction being obtained, they shall be baptized, and admitted to all the privileges of the church.
>
> Fourth: After each Candidate has been examined before the church, he or she shall be requested to retire to the vestry, while the church considers the case; which done, the Can-

> didate shall be called in and the Pastor shall make known the decision of the church, which if favorable, they shall be kindly received; but if there should appear to be any deficiency in the knowledge and experience of the Candidate, and it may be thought advisable to wait sometime longer, or in order to get better information, the Pastor will, in a kind, affectionate and encouraging manner, present this advice.
>
> Fifth: In case of Candidates coming from the country, or under any peculiar providential circumstances, where the above course cannot be pursued, the Pastor, and those he may consult, must act as may seem most for the glory of God, and the welfare of the church. (Rules for the Admission of Members into the Baptist Church of Charleston, 1828).[1]

God has Divinely ordained three bodies to which man may serve Him. He created the home, civil government, and the local church. The local church is the pillar and ground of truth. During the close of the twentieth and now at the opening of the twenty-first centuries, I fear that local assemblies have become number-conscious. Church membership has become cheapened, and it means little today to be a church member. Many join the church one Sunday and become active participants in the invisible church almost immediately.

I realize the local church is not an exhibit of perfected saints, but is rather a workshop for strengthening believers. But perhaps it is time for Bible believing Baptists to rethink the process of membership that once again such a status might be meaningful. Personally, I belong to the three units that God established. I thank God for family, I praise the Lord I am an American, and I am pleased to acknowledge that I am a member of a local Baptist church. Thus, I am accountable to a loving pastor and people. What kind of a church member are you?

DLC

---

[1]John T. Christian, *A History of the Baptists* (Nashville, TN: Broadman Press, 1926), 2:155-156.

February 17

A Rich Jungle Experience

Scripture: Romans 12:1-2

Being called upon by one's country to serve in the armed forces in time of war is part of the responsibility of good citizenship. For a Christian, the responsibility is a double challenge. The first focus of God's child must be to serve the Lord well and be His witness. Then the child of God needs to serve his country well and do his assigned job to the best of his ability.

In early 1968, as a pilot, flying missions in Cambodia, I was sent to the Philippines to go through Jungle Survival School. The school was used to prepare one in the event one was shot down in enemy jungle territory. Tactics were taught to assist in evading the enemy and get out safely.

The concept was excellent, and the schooling provided practical experience. To say the least, the reality training made for some exciting experiences. Romans 12:1-2 talks about our bodies being living sacrifices. While in the survival training, I met a young Negrito man in the jungle who taught me what being a living sacrifice really means.

As we were dropped off in the jungle, we were warned that our troops would be searching for us as the enemy would in actual combat. We were warned too that cannibals still inhabited the jungle. Along with these challenges, the ever-present snakes and wildlife added to the living danger. Needless to say, a young army pilot feels a bit apprehensive alone in the dark, dank jungle. For several days I had averted danger, but hunger became a very real enemy. As I hunkered down after several days of safely evading the enemy, I prepared for my first meal. I carefully lit a small fire which was necessary to cook the morsels I had secured in the jungle. All of a sudden a sound foreign to my ears alerted me to the fact that someone or something had encroached upon my space. Fear gripped my mind as I observed the small native who entered the circle of light made by my little fire. Who was he? I was soon to find out.

His first words to me were, "Is that a Bible you are reading"? After I answered "Yes," he continued with, "Are you a Christian"? What a wonderful relief and blessing to discover that he was a fellow believer. It amazed me the more to find Christian fellowship in the middle of the jungle during jungle survival training. I asked him how he came to know Christ as Savior. Following is the thrilling answer he related to me.

His tribe worshiped the sun god, and his father was the spiritual leader of the tribe. They practiced a rite of passage to manhood that required young men to leave their mountain home and go to the jungle valleys below to steal certain items without being detected or caught. While watching a village in the jungle, he noticed a small white building in the middle of the clearing. Every evening people entered the building, and he heard strange noises. The noise, he later discovered, was the singing of gospel hymns. The building was a mission church. Curiosity caused him to go to the door of the building to listen and to see what was going on. There was a man in the front who spoke from a Book about a God who created the sun, moon, and stars. He said this God loved the world and sent His Son to pay the price for sin. The man who was speaking saw this young man, and after the meeting invited him to his home. There he presented Christ fully to the Negrito, and he received Jesus Christ as his Savior.

Immediately the young Negrito realized he had a mission. He was challenged by the Lord to return to his village with the good news of salvation. He immediately set out for home. He first approached his brother, and told him of Jesus. But his father, having seen them leave the village, followed them into the jungle. The old chief told his son that he could never speak of this God again in this village, and if he did, he would be cast out of the village. To be cast out meant to be thrown over a 300 foot cliff to one's death. The young Negrito's heart burned with the message of Christ, and he had to tell his brother. Again, his father followed, and just as he said, the young man was cast out of the village and over the cliff to die.

By the grace of God, the young Negrito was able to catch hold of several tree limbs and rocks, thus breaking his fall. He awakened some time later, badly battered and with a broken leg and arm, but he was alive.

I could but praise God as I learned first hand what it meant to be a living sacrifice for Jesus Christ, but there was yet more to the lesson, and we will reveal that in the devotional material tomorrow.

RAB

February 18

Other Vital Lessons From the Jungle

Scripture: Mark 16:15

In yesterday's devotion, we left our young Negrito friend alive, but badly battered having been thrown over a 300 foot cliff to his apparent death.

The young national Negrito related that he remembered grabbing for a tree limb, a rock, or anything he could grasp, but he continued the plummet. Apparently his alertness slowed the rate of his fall, and he awakened later, badly battered, and with a broken leg and arm. Miraculously, he was alive. Somehow the young man crawled down the remainder of the mountain to the village where the missionary held forth the Word of God. He was gradually nursed back to health. As his body healed, he learned more and more about the glorious Gospel, and he delighted to rejoice in the Lord. As he grew in grace he was more determined than ever to share the Gospel with his people.

When he was healed, he told the missionary that he must return to his village to tell his people about Jesus. The missionary was greatly concerned thinking that they would kill him for sure this time. The young man responded however by saying, You do not understand. No one has ever lived when cast out of the village. They will think I have come back from the dead.

That is exactly what happened. They must have at first thought he was an apparition, but in a period of several weeks the entire village came to know Christ as Savior. The young man's father grew in grace and in time became the pastor of the church in that former heathen village. Ah, yes, I learned more from that young man about being a living sacrifice than I had ever known before.

Out of fairness, I must also relate the fact that because of his assistance I escaped other jungle dangers. When I reported back, I was thoroughly debriefed, for, you see, I was the only pilot who had been undetected during the test phase. The young Negrito knew the jungle as one might know his hometown. He took me to the hulk of an old army tank that remained from World War II and showed me places where freedom fighters had set up ambushes for the Japanese during the war. He assisted me in learning how to acquire the food needed to live in the jungle and helped me avoid ambush sites set up to capture me. I was thankful for the lessons the young Negrito taught me concerning how to survive in the jungle and how to avert the many dangers there.

But there is one other lesson he taught me that I must share. He taught me first hand the importance of the gospel preaching, church-planting missions. I later learned that when the first Bible-believing missionary determined to take the Gospel to the Negritos, he was repudiated and told that the Negritos did not possess a soul! Now there is a church in a Negrito village with a former witch doctor as the Pastor. I could not help but think of many professed Christians in the twenty-first century who seemingly believe that as long as people are happy with their religion, they need not take the glorious Gospel to them. If only those Americans could visit heathen mission fields of the world, they would understand our Lord's Great Commission that the Gospel be taken into all the world. Whether it be heathen crawling the so-called Holy staircase on their knees, or heathen washing in the filthy waters of a polluted river, or Tibetan nationals praying on their prayer beads, the need is the same. The heathen rituals in the heart of Africa, or the formalistic ceremonies of the proud European can never bring peace. The empty call to prayer heard repeatedly in many parts of the world, or the incantations of the priests in Cambodia or Thailand are useless. The despair written upon human hearts exhibits itself in the faces of nationals around the world. But introduce the true Gospel of the Son of God, and transformation takes place.

Would to God you could talk with my Negrito friend. Though I possessed the polished education that many would treasure, he, a simple-minded national, became my tutor, and I thank God for the lessons he taught me.

Be sure to pray today for faithful missionaries who continue to labor in third world countries of the world. And, could it be that the Lord would call you to go?

RAB

February 19

America's First Missionary Sacrifice

Scripture: Philippians 2:14-30

Six young people were sitting in a small cabin on board the ship *Caravan*. Two were the well-known Ann and Adoniram Judson. Two were young men on board only to say goodbye to the others. The last two were Harriett and Samuel Newell. The former Harriett Atwood was the youngest of the group. Her love for Samuel and for her Lord led her to pursue the difficult life of a missionary. The six spoke of their high hopes for a great work to be achieved in Christ's name in the needy countries of the Far East. They sang hymns from an old songbook long since forgotten, and they prayed in quietness and confidence, which was their daily strength. A little after sunrise on February 19, 1812, the ship spread her sails to the wind. Harriet and Samuel Newell, along with the Judsons, set sail for the mission field.

Their arrival in India was not welcomed. However, William Carey and his fellow missionaries opened their homes and hearts to the new missionaries, but the East India Company was far less accommodating. The new arrivals were soon told they could not remain in India and that they must prepare to return to America. There seemed to be but one way of escape: to seek some other heathen country outside the jurisdiction of the East India Company. So, with sudden, desperate purpose they asked permission to embark for the Isle of France, five thousand miles southwest, near Madagascar. Their request was granted, and on August 4 Samuel and his frail wife sailed away from all their friends in a small ship bound for Port Louis on the Isle of France. The vessel could accommodate only two passengers, and the Newells were chosen because Harriet's health made a home an urgent necessity.

The ship was battered mercilessly by winds and waves, so that the voyage of a few weeks lengthened into three anxious months. Far out on the Indian Ocean a baby girl was born in the little cabin on the ship's deck and given her mother's name, Harriet Atwood Newell. For a few days joy and hope abounded in the hearts of the parents, but cold and rain fell upon the ill-fated ship, and the baby, unable to endure the exposure, died in her mother's arms. After the child's death Harriet showed the first signs of the fatal disease which rapidly consumed her life.

When the dreadful voyage was finally over and the ship came to port, a British surgeon and a Danish physician ministered to the sick wife, but to no avail. Gradually her strength waned until the last flicker of hope for her recovery vanished. Night and day Samuel Newell sat by the bedside of his beloved wife, trying to catch every precious word she spoke. Her thoughts seemed to dwell with perfect peace upon Christ and heaven, although at times Harriet spoke of her mother across the seas in the Atwood homestead in Haverhill. "Tell my dear mother," she said, "how much Harriet loved her. Tell her to look to God and keep near to Him and He will support and comfort her in all her trials. Tell my brothers and sisters, from the lips of their dying sister, that there is nothing but religion worth living for. Tell them, and also my dear mother, that I have never regretted leaving my native land for the cause of Christ."[1]

On a November afternoon, death sealed Harriet's brown eyes, and there, in a little mud-walled cottage, she quietly breathed her last. In a land of strangers, without one friend to weep with him, her husband followed the body of his wife to the graveyard of Port Louis, where, in the heathery ground, under an evergreen tree, that suggested her New England home, the young woman who was the first American to give her life for the cause of Christ in the non-Christian world was buried.

LRO

[1] Ethel Daniel Hubbard, *Ann of Ava* (Philadelphia: Missionary Education Movement of the United States and Canada, 1913), 63-64.

February 20

Prospering Amid Persecution

Scripture: Acts 5:40-41

King Charles I of England believed in the divine right of kings, and the divine right of bishops, and he exercised authority accordingly. With his ascension to the throne in 1625, the real power of the Church of England began. Bishop William Laud became the Bishop of London in 1628, and in 1633 he was appointed the Archbishop of Canterbury and began work as head of the established Church. He established his position with great zeal and determination. Immediately he attempted to force ritualism on the Scottish Presbyterian Church. This led to rioting in the churches, and a flare of rebellion swept the entire land of Scotland. When the king endeavored to squelch the rebellion, trouble broke out at home, and the Civil War of 1642 to 1649 followed. Laud's severe program against the Puritans incurred their hostility, and his dealings with the Queen, who was Roman Catholic, stirred her hatred. In 1640 he was impeached for treason, and imprisoned in the Tower of London. He was tried in 1643, and was hanged on the scaffold in the Tower. However, during his rule his enmity against the Baptists raged.

By 1626 twenty-one General Baptist churches are known to have existed, and by 1633, when Laud was appointed Archbishop of Canterbury, another nine Baptist churches had come into being.[1] By persecution and imprisonment, the Archbishop was determined to bring the land into subjection.

"Early in his reign Laud gave the Baptists a taste of his cruelty. Three of their most popular ministers in Kent, Thomas Brewer, Turner and Fenner were arrested and placed in prison, where Brewer remained no less than fourteen years. Two years later, 1627, Laud mentions to the King these persons in prison and says: I must give your Majesty to understand, that at about Ashford, in Kent, the Separatists continue to hold their conventicles, notwithstanding the examination of so many of them as have been discovered. They are all of the poorer sort, and very simple, so that I am utterly to seek what to do with them."[2]

It is amazing to realize that the hatred and persecution of the Baptists by the King and his Archbishop did not retard or stop their growth! Historical proof exists to reveal that Baptists were present and growing in number in London and throughout the land. The *Calendar of State Papers* of February 20, 1635, reveals the fact that: Baptists "refuse on Sundays and other festival days to come to their parish churches, but meet together in great numbers on such days, and at other times, and in private houses, and places, and there keep conventicles and exercises of religion, by the laws of this realm prohibited. For remedy whereof, taking with him a constable and such other assistance as he shall think meet, he is to enter into any house where such private conventicles are held, and search for such sectaries, as also for unlawful and unlicensed books and papers; and such persons, papers and books so found, to bring forthwith before the writers to be dealt with as shall be thought fit."[3]

Another phenomenon comes to light in one's study of history. The Edict of Toleration in 1689 granted Baptists some semblance of freedom. They could meet without recrimination, and yet in the days immediately following the Edict of Toleration they did not grow rapidly. It would appear that opposition stirred commitment.

That observation is interesting in light of America today. We have guaranteed religious freedom, and yet to many Americans freedom of religion seems to mean freedom from religion. Without fear of police surveillance we can gather in buildings dedicated to our worship of God. I am not advocating that we pray for persecution in our day, but let us surely pray for revival that we might be found faithful unto the coming of our blessed Lord Jesus Christ.

DLC

---

[1]John T. Christian, *A History of the Baptists* (Texarkana: American Baptist Association, 1922), 284-285.

[2]Ibid., 285.

[3]Ibid., 286.

February 21

England's Great Baptist Orator

Scripture: Acts 18:24-28

Robert Hall, Jr., was born at Arnsby, near Leicester, England, on May 2, 1764. He was the youngest of 14 children, and at the age of two he could neither speak nor walk. Nevertheless he learned to read through the efforts of an intelligent nurse who took him for frequent walks to a small cemetery near his father's residence. From its gravestones she taught him the alphabet, spelling, and reading, and he quickly made up for lost time. When he was eleven his teacher, Mr. Simmons, dismissed him from his school because he was further advanced in education than his instructor.[1]

At the age of 15, he entered Bristol College to study for the ministry. According to the custom of the college, he was required to give an address in the vestry of Broadmead Church before his instructors and fellow-students. He began brilliantly, but he soon became too nervous to continue, and covering his face in an agony of shame, he exclaimed, Oh! I have lost all my ideas.[2] He was instructed to deliver the same address the next week, and the second time was a failure worse than the first. Hall was extremely sensitive, and these discouragements, while intensely mortifying, only made him more determined to succeed.

In the mid 1770s John Ryland was influenced by Jonathan Edwards' *Inquiry into the Freedom of the Will*. He recommended this combination of theological Calvinism and evangelical enthusiasm to his colleagues, including Robert Hall, Sr. Hall held what was called by the Calvinists of his day an Arminian view of the atonement. He believed that Christ died for the entire world. Hall Sr. spoke scornfully of the works of John Gill, the strong Calvinistic Baptist theologian. He also believed that unbaptized persons might come to the Lord's table. In 1799 he preached a sermon from Isaiah 57:14 in which he portrayed hyper-Calvinism as a barrier which prevented sinners from coming to their Savior. This was printed and when William Carey read it, he stated, "I do not remember to have read any book with such raptures."[3] It was this book which persuaded the great William Carey to become a Baptist. This was the theological climate in which Robert Hall, Jr., grew up.

In 1781 Hall, Jr. went to Aberdeen where he served as pastor for four years. In 1785 he became the assistant to Dr. Caleb Evans, pastor of Broadmead Church, Bristol. Hall's preaching soon attracted large congregations and an unusual amount of interest. Many of the leading men of Bristol, and a large number of Episcopal clergymen, came to hear this great preacher. In 1791, the year in which his father died, he accepted a call to succeed the learned, but erratic, Robert Robinson as pastor of the church in Cambridge. Robinson had been leading his church into Unitarianism, and the congregation believed that Hall would continue in that direction. However, they were soon disappointed. Their spiritual coldness had the effect of curing Hall's free thinking. Notwithstanding the difficulties which orthodoxy presented to his intellect, the truth of Scripture was so powerful that Hall could not distance himself from it.[4] In the city of Cambridge, famous for its Episcopal university, Hall soon acquired the reputation of being the most finished scholar and eloquent preacher in the British Isles.

From this time on Hall was spoken of as the prince of preachers, and his opinions and sayings were collected and quoted by Baptists and non-Baptists alike. He spent 15 years at Cambridge and nearly 20 at Leicester. In 1825 he returned to Bristol. His life came to a close on February 21, 1831.

Robert Hall, Jr. zealously promoted all the great philanthropic and religious institutions of his day. He provided influence and assistance for the Bible and missionary societies in their infancy. He studied for his sermons with the greatest care, but he, unlike many of the preachers of his day, never read his sermons and seldom wrote them in their entirety. He was viewed as the greatest preacher that had ever spoken the English tongue.

LRO

---

[1] William Cathcart, *The Baptist Encyclopedia* (Philadelphia: Louis H. Everts, 1881), 488.

[2] Ibid.

[3] H. Leon McBeth, *The Baptist Heritage* (Nashville: Broadman, 1987), 180.

[4] William Landels, *Baptist Worthies* (London: Baptist Tract and Book Society, 1883), 202.

February 22

A Mother's Prayer

Scripture: 1 Samuel 1:28

Thomas W. Roberts was born February 22, 1817, into a godly home in Nelson County, Virginia. When he was a small child, his mother often took him up on her lap and prayed that God would make him a Christian minister. This made a tremendous impression upon her son, and years later, after his mother's prayers were answered, he would relate to others his mother's concern and parental practice in prayer on his behalf.

At the age of fifteen, he was baptized into the fellowship of Mount Shiloh Baptist Church. Not long after this, he felt called to preach and made plans for college and ministerial preparation. However, his education was interrupted by failing health, and for a period he became a teacher. Finally, in 1841 his health improved and he was ordained to the Gospel ministry.

From the very beginning of his ministry, he was involved in pioneer work. For many years he was a missionary for the State Mission Board. He was the first minister to immerse a candidate in the town of Waynesboro. He described the service this way: A large crowd assembled on either side of the river to witness the novel sight, but there was no disturbance; the crowd behaved with perfect decorum, but there was no singing. In his annual report for the year of 1852, he stated that he aided in the founding of two new churches, new Sunday schools, preached 126 sermons, 48 addresses, and baptized 47 people.

Dr. Cornelius Tyree said of him and his work: "No minister of the Albermarle Association for the last thirty years has done more to spread Christianity than this good man. He was not only a good evangelist and protracted-meeting preacher, but was one of the best pastors that God has ever given to the churches of that region."[1]

In the course of time, physical problems returned, and Pastor Roberts developed a severe bronchial problem, making actual preaching impossible. His physical problems did not interfere with wedding plans, however, and he was married to Miss Annie M. Thomas of Fluvanna County, Virginia, on January 25, 1866. Soon thereafter he founded a school for girls, and it proved to be a very successful endeavor. He sought to keep the costs reasonable enough so that many young ladies who could not attend larger and more expensive schools could get a good, solid education.

Surely we would observe that his godly mother's prayers were answered. She certainly shared the love and dedication to the Lord as expressed in Hannah's song in 1 Samuel 1:28. "There is none holy as the LORD: for there is none besides thee: neither is there any rock like our God." As Hannah was willing to give Samuel into the Lord's service, so she offered her son to the Lord.

Those of us who have been privileged to have such godly mothers surely ought to praise the Lord for such a godly heritage. Mrs. Roberts considered it a great privilege to be the mother of one of God's servants.

Tragically, in these days of materialism, many parents are desirous that their children follow a course that will provide financial security. Some such parents, though professing to love the Lord, will even attempt to dissuade their offspring from Christian service, particularly foreign missions. Perhaps some parents, who have been negligent in praying that the Lord would take their children for His service, are reading these lines just now. May I remind you that even as Pharoah's daughter assured Moses' mother that if she would take Moses and raise him for her, wages would be assured. In essence the Lord asks us to take the children He gives us and to raise them for His use. You can be sure He will reward all such service.

As Pastor Roberts' health worsened, he spoke words of cheer to those around him. He gave directions for his funeral and testified of his hope beyond the grave. As death approached, he declared with assurance that his preparation for eternity was sure through the finished work of Christ at Calvary. The man of God was buried on September 17, 1876, and the text used for his funeral was Romans 8:18: "For I reckon that the sufferings of this present time are not worthy to be compared with the glory which shall be revealed in us."[2]

EGC

[1]George Braxton Taylor, *Virginia Baptist Ministers*, (Lynchburg, VA: J. P. Bell, Company, 1912), 250.

[2]Ibid., 251

February 23

The Baptist Nurseries

Scripture: Philippians 1:27; 4:1

An interesting phenomenon that resulted from the Great Awakening was the growth of the so-called New Light or Separate churches. The preaching of George Whitefield was primarily among the Congregationalists during those thrilling days of the moving of the Spirit of God in early America. The Congregational denomination had fallen into apostasy as infant baptism had abolished any hope of a regenerate church membership. However, during the Great Awakening many Congregationalists came to know the reality of salvation by faith in the shed blood of Jesus Christ. The impact of the Great Awakening produced new converts, and it has been estimated that perhaps as many as fifty thousand were converted. In a period of twenty years, more than one hundred and fifty new regular Congregational churches were established.[1] However, young converts were often repudiated upon returning to their Congregational churches, and in time, many of these left their churches to form an entirely new denomination. These churches were soon known as Separates. In all, about one hundred such churches came into being.

Following is a partial list of Separate preachers who came out of the regular Congregational churches in New England from 1745 to 1751: "John Hovey, of Mansfield, October 1745; Solomon Paine was ordained at Canterbury, September 10, 1745; Thomas Stevens at Plainfield, September 11, 1745; Thomas Dennison at Norwich Farms, October 29, 1745; Jedidiah Hide at Norwich Town, October 30, 1745; **Matthew Smith at Stonington**, December 10, 1745; John Fuller at Lyme, December 25, 1745; Joseph Snow at Providence, February 12, 1747; Samuel Wadsworth at Killingly, June 3, 1747; Paul Park at Preston, July 15, 1747; **Elihu Marsh, at Windham**, October 7, 1747; Ebenezer Frothingham at Weathersfield, October 28, 1747; Nathanael Shephard at Attleborough, January 20, 1748; **Isaac Backus at Bridgewater**, April 13, 1748; John Paine at Rehoboth, August 3, 1748; **William Carpenter at Norton**, September 7, 1748; **John Blunt at Sturbridge**, September 28, 1748; **Ebenezer Mack at Lyme**, January 12, 1749; Joshua Nickerson at Harwich, February 23, 1749; Samuel Hide at Bridgewater, May 11, 1749; John Palmer at Windham, May 17, 1749; **Samuel Hovey at Mendon**, May 31, 1749; **Samuel Drown at Coventry**, October 11, 1749; **Stephen Babcock at Westerly**, April 4, 1750; **Joseph Hastings at Suffield**, April 17, 1750; Nathanael E. Ewere at Barnstable, May 10, 1750; **Joshua Morse at New-London**, May 17, 1750; Jonathan Hide at Brookline, January 17, 1751; Ezekiel Cole at Sutton, January 31, 1751; Ebenezer Wadsworth at Grafton, March 20, 1751; **Shubael Stearns at Tolland**, March 20, 1751; **Nathanael Draper at Cambridge**, April 24, 1751; **Peter Werden at Warwick**, May 17, 1751."[2]

It is interesting to note of the 33 preachers listed above who became part of the Separate denomination, we are assured that at least fourteen of these left that denomination to become Separate Baptist pastors. These are designated in bold print above. Two of these men of God became prime movers in revival throughout New England and in the Southland. Of course, these two men were Isaac Backus and Shubael Stearns.

Goen presents two primary reasons that caused this phenomenon of Separates becoming Baptists. First, the

Separates had come to a position of Biblicism. The Bible became the only rule of faith and practice, and infant baptism could not be defended Scripturally. Baptists were also congregational in church order, and the change then seemed easily accomplished. Secondly, there was the economic consideration. Baptists at the time were permitted to claim the Act of Toleration and be excused from paying taxes to support the State church. The Separates were not allowed such a privilege, and some, doubtless, would easily be persuaded to become Baptists for this reason. However, it must be pointed out that Quakers too were excused from state church taxation, and the Separates could just as easily have joined with them if that was the reason for their defection.

Only eternity will reveal the reasoning of all involved, but Separate Baptists became the stimulus of providing the ongoing of the Great Awakening as it moved into the Southland. Backus and Stearns are names that every Baptist in America ought to know.

DLC

---

[1]C. C. Goen, *Revivalism and Separatism in New England, 1740-1800* (Middletown: Wesleyan University Press, 1987), 8-9.

[2]James Beller, *America in Crimson Red* (Arnold: Prairie Fire Press, 2004), 127-128.

February 24

Shine as the Stars

Scripture: Psalm 126:5-6

How unlikely that a pastor who lived his entire life from birth to death in a rural area would ever have such godly influence as to baptize almost 5,000 people. But such is the man we consider in our devotional today. In the country churchyard of Bethel Baptist Church in Charlotte County, Virginia, a modest grave marker designates the resting place of the body of the beloved pastor, Elijah White Roach. How fitting that the words of Daniel

12:3 have been incised on the marker: "They that turn many to righteousness shall shine as the stars forever and ever."[1]

Elijah's parents owned a farm, and they sought to provide as complete an education as possible for their children. However, E. W.'s quest for learning made him willing to relinquish all claims to the estate to be enabled to obtain more training. He remained on the farm until he was seventeen. At that juncture in his life, a teacher came to the area who was proficient in the classics but lacked a thorough knowledge of mathematics. Seventeen-year-old E. W., being very capable in mathematics, proposed to exchange his knowledge of algebra and geometry for the privilege of studying the classics with the new tutor. Young Mr. Roach proved to be an excellent student, and was ever seen with a book in his hands. This led in time to his obtaining a position as a teacher. However, as he continually studied at night without sufficient lighting, his eyesight became seriously impaired. In the course of time he was forced to abandon all hopes of extending his education.

In coming to maturity, E. W. made a profession of faith and became a member of the local Baptist church. On June 13, 1819, E. W. married Miss Anne R. Harvey, daughter of Colonel Isham Harvey. The Lord blessed that union with twelve children, all of whom were trained to love and serve the Lord. E. W. was a faithful father, and he was loyal, as well, to the house of God. As he matured spiritually and developed leadership, he was invited occasionally to preach. At that time, a seasoned pastor, Abram Poindexter, took E. W. under his wing and began to train him for Christian service. In 1832, the local church licensed E. W. to preach, but even then the man of God requested that the congregation seriously consider the matter for three additional months.

From that time on, E. W.'s ability in the pulpit grew, and the following year a church building was constructed in Midway and thirteen members constituted the new church. E. W. was ordained, and became the pastor of that congregation. The church grew immediately. In that era, most ministers supplemented their salaries. E. W. farmed and taught school to eke out a living. Yet during that period of time, he preached two hundred times a year and kept up with pastoral visitation. Other congregations were formed, and in time E. W. was pastoring four such churches. Along with that pattern of service, E. W. entered the field of evangelism, and his service took him westward as far as Kentucky.

I have mentioned the faithful role of a loving father that E. W. fulfilled. Not only was he a faithful father, but, following a business meeting in the Salem Baptist Church, he felt constrained to report that his youngest daughter was in need of church discipline. The week previously she had gone out dancing. The church dealt with the matter, and his daughter said: "I was dumbfounded, for I did not even know that my dancing was known to him. I promised never to do so again and kept my word."

E. W. Roach preached into his eighty-seventh year. In fact on the Lord's Day before his home-going, he preached at the Midway Baptist Church. Then arriving home on Monday, he fell asleep in Jesus. Great crowds gathered for his funeral, and the text used was the goal of his life. "They that turn many to righteousness shall shine as the stars forever and ever."

May the Lord burden our hearts to be faithful witnesses and soul-winners wherever He may place us.

DLC

[1]George Braxton Taylor, *Virginia Baptist Ministers* (Lynchburg, VA: J. P. Bell Company, 1912), 3:359.

February 25

Circuit Riding Preacher

Scripture: 1 Corinthians 1:21, 26-29

How would you like to be a circuit riding preacher with the responsibility of five churches that you would have to serve on horseback? That is the responsibility that faced Thomas Scrivner from his home in Glasgow, Kentucky, every Saturday. To reach these churches from his home, he had to ride to Dover, four miles; to Peters Creek, ten miles; to Mt. Gilead, twenty-two miles; to Fountain Run, twenty miles, and to Indian Creek, twenty miles.[1] The weather did not detour the man of God as he faithfully kept his appointments. And the size of the churches? In all, Elder Scrivner had the oversight of over nine hundred members! The records reveal that the Dover church listed 232 members, the Peters Creek church had 125 members, the Mt. Gilead church recorded 147 members, the Fountain Run church consisted of 208 members, and the Indian Creek church family comprised 194 members.

With the care of five churches upon him, Elder Scrivner scheduled preaching two days per month to each congregation, and between every Sunday and the following Saturday, he would visit destitute neighbors, and preach in school-houses or in the open fields. When there were not five Sundays in a month, Elder Scrivner would preach two weekdays at the Indian Creek church. During the course of this ministry, the man of God baptized 2000 people. When Elder Scrivner was not ministering to the spiritual needs of the saved or witnessing to the lost, he was studying and preparing sermons. Of course, his studying often had to be done in the saddle. It might shock one to learn that Elder Scrivner was 54 years old when he accepted the charge we have described!

Let me share a bit concerning God's dealing in the life of this circuit-riding preacher. Thomas Scrivner was born in Rowan County, North Carolina, on February 25, 1775. He had only sufficient education to learn how to read and write. When he was nineteen years of age, he moved to Madison County, Kentucky, and there he professed salvation. He was baptized and united with the Tates Creek Baptist Church. A couple of years later he returned to North Carolina to marry Miss Esther Hamilton. To this couple were born three sons. In 1799 the family returned to Kentucky, and Mr. Scrivner was elected a deacon of the Viney Fork Baptist Church near Richmond. In 1816 they lost their property due to a prior claim, and thus they moved to Tennessee. When the family seemed to experience sickness due to the climate, Mr. Scrivner decided to move his family to Missouri. Upon arriving in Barren County, Kentucky, his wife and one son became deathly ill. While waiting for physical recovery, the couple fell in love with the area. Thus it was that he purchased property, and they settled near Glasgow and united with the Mt. Pleasant Baptist Church.

In the course of time, Mr. Scrivner established prayer meetings for neighbors, and the deacon began reading portions of God's Word to those who gathered to pray. Then he began commenting on the Scripture portion. He began thinking of poor perishing sinners, and yet he felt incompetent to preach the Gospel to them.

However in 1827 the church licensed him to preach, and he entered into the ministry with zeal. Revival fell, and among the converts were his three sons. In June 1829, he was ordained to the full work of the ministry. On July 4, 1829, with twelve converts he established the Fountain Run Baptist Church and pastored until 1858, when the feebleness of old age induced him to resign. On July 16, 1864, the Lord called His servant home. But what an investment he had made as he labored faithfully with the gifts he had. His greatest ability was his dependability.

The question is, can the Lord depend upon us to be faithful with the gifts He has given us?

DLC

[1]J. H. Spencer, *A History of Kentucky Baptists* (Gallatin, TN: Church History Research & Archives, 1984), 444.

February 26

Another Crown of Life

Scripture: James 1:12; Revelation 2:10

In an impoverished home in Cape Town, Mississippi, a godly mother prayed that God would grant the desire of her heart. And what was the request? She prayed that one of her children would become a missionary with the good news of the Gospel. The ravishes of the Civil War were still being experienced when on February 26, 1883, the Lord answered that petition, and a baby daughter was born into the Maxville home. The baby's name was Selma Martha Maxville, but the prospects of her getting to the mission field seemed remote indeed.

At the age when potential missionaries would be in college, Mrs. Maxville became a shut-in, and Selma was consigned to caring for her mother. The hopes of her ever performing missionary service certainly must have vanished, as the years ticked by. In fact, Mrs. Maxville lived until Selma was thirty years old when education would have seemed impossible to most, and Selma was needed at home. But with the passing of her mother, Selma enrolled in a medical school. Then, she attended a Bible college in Kentucky. Finally, in 1916, at the age of thirty-three, Selma left her homeland and headed for the field of Burma. Her assignment took her to labor among the Mons people in Moulmein, a city that had been pioneered by Adoniram and Ann Judson. There she served in the Ellen Mitchell Memorial Hospital, then known as the American Hospital. Faithfulness was the hallmark of Miss Maxville, and she served there for thirty-three years.

Retirement beckoned, but Miss Maxville opted to remain, and in 1940 she opened a hospital in the township of Mudon. When the Second World War began in 1941, Miss Maxville fled to India as a refugee. After the war, in 1947, she returned to Teingone, Kamarweit, and re-opened the hospital. Her last letter to the mission was dated January 9, 1950. She wrote: "I would like to humbly request you to allow me to serve as a nurse if there is no other nurse to take my place. . . . I would continue my service without pay."

Thus at the age of sixty-seven, Miss Maxville continued with the work to which the Lord had called her. On February 18, 1950, she took a thirteen-year-old patient to the hospital in Moulmein. As she returned, she was kidnapped three miles from Kamarweit. The kidnappers delivered a ransom note demanding 10,000 kyats and 10 grams of gold. Realizing the inability of her friends to meet the demand, Miss Maxville wrote: "I know that you neither have money nor gold. You do not need to redeem me. Do not worry about me for God is with me." The letter was delivered to her ex-coworkers at the Moulmein Mission Hospital.

Miss Maxville was bound with an iron chain to a post of a hut in a rice paddy field at Kamarchine Village. But she was so well revered by the nationals that a dozen men determined to free her. Thus U Pu, U Pe, U Jalee, U Ta, U Guh, U. A. Ti, U Kon Ka Lu, U Aung Sein, U Hline, U Pan Taine, U. A Du Karen, and U Pa Lay (the U is mister in the native tongue) discovered her location and cut the post with a saw to free the victim. They then transported Miss Maxville in an ox cart to Mudon. However, the effort of the men to rescue her was discovered, and the kidnappers ambushed the party. Miss Maxville was shot down with a machine gun but lived through the attack and was taken to the clinic in Mudon where she opened her eyes in the presence of the Lord in glory. Thus Miss Maxville gave her life for the Mons, whom she loved so dearly.

In loving memory of her heroic rescuers and Miss Maxville, the nationals erected a monument in Kamarweit, a town between Moulmein and Amherst.

The prayers of a post Civil War mother in Cape Town, Mississippi, led not only to a life of faithful service, but also to the crown of glory that will never fade away.

DLC

February 27

Patriotic Preachers

Scripture: 1 John 4:17

As I write this devotional entry, it is apparent that America is in need of pastors who are loyal to the Word of God and faithful to our God-given Republic. It is heart-rending to hear of men of the cloth who are unwilling to voice an opinion for fear that they might be politically incorrect. The prophets of old censured God's people, but they excoriated God's enemies as well. As one reads of the early days of our Republic, it is heartening to know that Baptist pastors were willing to put their very lives on the line for truth.

I invite your attention to the life of Samuel Stillman who was born on February 27, 1737. His first eleven years were spent in Philadelphia, and then he was sent by his parents to Charleston, South Carolina. In that city he came under the ministry of Reverend Oliver Hart. In his youth he saw himself as a sinner, repented, and trusted Christ as Savior. Soon he was baptized, and almost immediately felt an urge to prepare to preach. Following his classical studies, he entered into theological training under the tutelage of his pastor. He preached his first sermon on February 17, 1758, and a year later he was ordained. Soon after his ordination, he took charge of a church on James' Island, near Charleston. During that pastorate he returned to Philadelphia and married. The

College of Philadelphia conferred upon him an A. M. degree, and in 1761, Harvard University did the same.

He returned to James' Island, but his health began to fail, and he resigned and moved to New Jersey. The Baptist church at Bordentown, New Jersey requested his services, and he labored there for two years. In 1763 the pastor of Second Baptist Church of Boston, Mr. Bound, suffered a stroke, and the congregation asked Stillman to come to assist their pastor. A year later the First Baptist Church of Boston was without a pastor, as Pastor Condy had resigned, and Reverend Stillman was asked to accept that pastoral office. He was installed as pastor on January 9, 1765, and he spent the remainder of his life serving the Lord there. Boston became a hot-bed of revolutionary activities, and Pastor Stillman was in the very middle of it.

The Reverend Dr. Magoon produced an interesting account of those days, and I should like to share portions of it here.

> This distinguished patriot ... was born in Philadelphia. ...He removed to Boston and remained there until his death in 1806, the universally admired pastor of the First Baptist Church. He was small of stature, but great of soul. His courtesy was proverbial, his accomplishments diversified; his piety undisputed by all, and his patriotic preaching unexcelled. He was explicit and bold in avowing his own peculiar views, but was exceedingly forbearing toward those who were conscientiously opposed to them.
>
> ...Standing in the presence of armed foes, he preached with a power that commanded respect, even when he could not create compunction. When the British took possession of Boston, and desecrated its sacred edifices, some of the more skillful of their number, who had recoiled under Stillman's patriotic appeals, illustrated their spite by drawing a charcoal line of the great divine on the plastered wall of his own pulpit, in all the freedom of expressive gesture and eloquent denunciation.
>
> It will not seem strange that Dr. Stillman's own church was habitually thronged, or that, whenever he visited other cities, his instructions were sought

with avidity by the most exalted minds. John Adams wrote to his wife- 'Philadelphia, August 4, 1776. "Went this morning to the Baptist meeting in hopes of hearing Mr. Stillman preach, but was disappointed. He was there, but another gentleman preached."[1]

Not only did John Adams feel at home in the First Baptist Church, but others such as Governor John Hancock and General Henry Knox attended services often. How America today needs preachers who are unafraid to preach with conviction and confidence!

Samuel Stillman's last words were these: "God's government is infinitely perfect." With that statement he entered into the reality of the Lord's very presence on March 12, 1807.

DLC

---

[1]Joseph Belcher, *The Religious Denominations in the United States* (Philadelphia: John E. Potter, 1856), 188-189.

February 28

Lest We Forget

Scripture: Hebrews 6:10

It is easy to forget Baptist leaders of the past, particularly when they were not well known other than in their original locality. Reverend Joseph Reese was such a man.

Little is known of Joseph's family except that he was born in 1732 to Evan and Sarah Reese from Wales. The Reese family immigrated to Duck Creek, Kent County, in what is now Delaware. In 1745 his parents moved the family into the area of South Carolina known in those days as the Congarees. They were among the first pioneers to settle permanently in the area. The parents lived only twelve more years, dying within thirty days of each other in November of 1757.

In 1753 Joseph married Ann Reynolds. When Morgan Edwards, the Baptist historian visited the area in 1771, he reported that there were six children in the Reese family. Between 1771 and 1792, God blessed them with three more children. Only one of the children did not live to maturity. According to Joseph's will, he married a widow named Sarah after the death of Ann.

Joseph Reese was reared in the Anglican Church. In 1760 he was converted through the ministry of the famous Separatist Baptist preacher, Philip Mulkey. At that time Mr. Mulkey was pastoring the Fairforest Baptist church and itinerating all through the Midlands of South Carolina. Daniel Marshall, another Separatist Baptist preacher, also ministered throughout that region. After Reese and Marshall saw thirty-two people converted, they founded the Congaree Baptist Church in 1765. Joseph Reese became the first pastor. John Newton, who was helping him at Congaree, and Reese were ordained on February 28, 1768. Oliver Hart and Evan Pugh, who were Regular Baptist preachers performed the ordination. Hart pastored the Charleston Baptist Church and Pugh pastored the Cashaway Baptist Church in Mount Pleasant. The Sandy Creek Baptist Association censored Reese and Newton for obtaining ordination at the hands of the Regular Baptists.[1]

Pastor Reese served the Congaree church during most of his pastoral ministry except for some time spent in Lawson's Fork, which today is in the area of Boiling Springs, South Carolina. Because of his patriotism during the Revolutionary War, Reese was forced to leave the Congarees. He was instrumental in starting almost all of the Baptist churches in the Midlands. One of the highlights of his ministry was the conversion of Richard Furman in one of his evangelistic meetings in the High Hills of Santee area. Furman became Mr. Baptist of South Carolina and exercised his gifts nationally.[2]

Pastor Reese was an outstanding influence for Christ in the Congarees. He served as a chaplain in the Revolutionary War under Captain Goodwyn's unit. His son, Ephraim Timothy Reese, also served in the War. Joseph served in the Second General Assembly in the House of Representatives from the Richmond District from 1776 to 1778.

The Baptist historian, David Benedict, states that during the last years of his life Pastor Reese was in poor health. "He (Reese) was very infirm about ten years before his death, and during the last two of them, [was] one of the most afflicted of men . . . . When publick worship was supposed at the place of worship nearest to him, about three miles distant, he was several times carried there on his bed, lying down during the services; and if he found himself able, which he sometimes did, would sit up at the conclusion of worship, and address a few words to the congregation in the style of conversation and advice, by which they were generally melted into tears. His last attendance at the church was about twelve months before his death; at which time, in great pain and weakened, he administered the Lord's Supper . . . ."[3]

Reese's death occurred in his sixty-third year on March 5, 1795, in Richland County, South Carolina. It was said of him that he was a man of good understanding and warm affections. His piety was never called into question. Though limited in his education, he had common sense and experiential knowledge. He had natural eloquence and a command of the passions of those who listened to him. In spite of opposition, Reese had great success in the ministry.

May God give us more men like Joseph Reese, who, though unknown today, are known on high and whose works do follow them.

DCB

---

[1]Morgan Edwards, *Materials Towards a History of the Baptists* (Danielsville, GA: Heritage Papers, 1984), 2:145-146.

[2]Leah Townsend, *South Carolina Baptists 1670-1805* (Baltimore: Genealogical Publishing Co., 1978), 129-157.

[3]David Benedict, *A General History of the Baptist Denomination* (Gallatin, TN: Church History Research, 1985), 2:365.

February 29

A Faithful Tennessee Volunteer

Scripture: Psalm 37:3-7; 23; 30-31

Interesting variations of names in America often make difficult the tracing of ones ancestry. However, F. C. Lewallen, faithful Baptist preacher in Tennessee in the nineteenth century, has roots easily traced. F. C. Lewallen was born on February 29, 1832, to Samuel and Katharine

Llewellyn. The change in the spelling of the name apparently was merely meant to simplify it. The Llewellyn's family came from staunch Welch roots. In fact, as one researches the history of the Baptists in Wales, one reads that the Blaenau Baptist Church in the county of Monmouth was constituted in 1660. The church . . . suffered much by bitter persecutions. At that time, they were obliged to meet to worship God in the fields, the woods, and the rocks of the mountains, like many of their brethren. Sometimes, however, they ventured to meet in some private houses. They often met at the house of Nest Llewellyn. Though she was frequently dragged before the higher powers, to answer for her crimes, yet she was not at all daunted, but Lydia-like she invited the disciples of Christ to her house. She neither feared their threats and frowns, nor courted their smiles, let the consequences be what they may. Then continuing on in the account of the Welch Baptists, one reads of Moses Llewellyn who was baptized in 1699 and began to preach in 1701. He died in 1745.[1]

F. C. Lewallen's father was born in 1805, and died in 1870. His mother, Katharine Llewellyn, was born in 1809, and she lived until 1883. Tracing the family during the sixty-year interval from the time of Moses Llewellyn's death and the date of Samuel Llewellyn's birth is not our purpose just now, but the genealogy would surely prove interesting.

F. C. Lewallen was raised on a farm in the beautiful foothills of the Great Smoky Mountains. He was blessed with the opportunity of obtaining a sound educational background during his youth. In 1854 he married Miss Margaret Ann Smith, and the couple had three children. It is interesting to note that F. C. was teaching school during the time of the Civil War. Tennessee was a border state, but with the beginning of hostilities, in June 1861, the citizens voted by an overwhelming majority in favor of separation from the Union. Tennessee was the last of the eleven states to leave the Union. From 1862 to 1865, Tennessee was under the military governorship of Andrew Johnson. However in 1866, Tennessee was reinstated to its position in the Union, and thus escaped the harsh congressional program of military reconstruction applied to the other states of the Confederacy.

It was during this period that F. C. Lewallen came under conviction, and on September 8, 1866, he was gloriously converted. He united with the Bethel Baptist Church in Anderson

County. He was then thirty-four years of age. During the next four years, the congregation observed F. C. Lewallen's ability to handle the Word of God. This resulted in his being ordained into the gospel ministry. His ministry began when he was thirty-eight, but the Lord granted his servant a rich ministry. The population had been deeply divided, and animosities existed. But in such a crisis, Reverend Lewallen served faithfully as pastor of the Clinton Baptist Church.

Reverend and Mrs. Lewallen provided a godly atmosphere during difficult days for their three children, and their offspring grew to honor the Lord. Their daughter married a Baptist preacher who served as pastor in Williamsburg, Kentucky. Reverend Lewallen has been described as a strong preacher and an able defender of the faith; he ranked among the strong preachers and able leaders of the Clinton Association, and served many of her best churches as pastor. He left an untarnished record as a Christian man and a gospel minister.[2]

Regardless of the political circumstances in which we find ourselves, our faithfulness will always be rewarded by our Lord.

DLC

---

[1]J. Davis, *History of the Welch Baptists* (Pittsburgh: D. M. Hogan, 1835), 119-120.

[2]J. J. Burnett, *Sketches of Tennessee's Pioneer Baptist Preachers* (Nashville, TN: Marshall & Bruce Company, 1919), 331-332.

March 1

Baptists and the Lone Star Republic

Scripture: Psalm 144:1-2

The Texas Revolution was an amazing contest that featured unbelievably unequal numbers. The Mexican population at that time numbered in the millions, while Texans could be counted in the thousands. Mexico's organized army should have swamped the few hundred Texan volunteers, but, in the end, Texas won the great conflict. Texas was colonized to Mexico under the 1824 Mexican Democratic Constitution, but Texas was trampled under Mexico's feet. Santa Anna, whom the Texas colonists had supported, violated the Constitution and established himself as supreme ruler. Texan colonists, with many citizens of Mexico, remained loyal to the Constitution and democracy. Forced submission to Santa Anna's dictatorship was attempted, but the Texans fought under and for the Mexican Constitution of 1824.

A General Consultation was held on November 3, 1835, where 55 delegates were present as a Declaration of Independence was voted down by a vote of 35 to 15, and the Colonists determined to remain loyal to Mexico.[1] A number of small battles were fought beginning at Gonzalez. San Antonio was captured by the Mexicans, but it was recaptured by the Texans, and most of the Mexican army was captured too. A generous liberation was offered the Mexican troops with the promise they would never return to fight in Texas. However, after their release, Santa Anna reorganized his troops and planned to return and conquer Texas. The Texans realized that they could not rely on Mexican Constitutionalists for help, and thus determined to fight for total freedom, freedom from bondage, revolutions and religion.

A general convention was called, and it met on March 1, 1836 in Washington, Texas. Churches, except Catholic churches, had been forbidden by law, and no schools had yet been built. So they met in a blacksmith shop owned by a Baptist, N. T. Byars. Blacksmithing was suspended; the area was cleared, and benches prepared for the first great Texas convention. Judge

Richard Ellis, a Baptist farmer, was chosen to preside over the session. The following day Texas independence was declared, and governmental organization was begun. General Sam Houston was selected as the commander-in-chief of Texan armies. General Houston appointed Mr. Byars as armorer and blacksmith for his quickly gathering army.

Simultaneously with the general convention, Santa Anna with his 10,000 soldiers was besieging San Antonio and the Alamo. Four days after the signing of the declaration of Texas independence, the Alamo fell and 182 courageous men were slain. It has been averred that 1,600 Mexican troops were lost at that battle as well.[2] Thirteen days after the fall of the Alamo, Fannin and 350 Texans were surrounded by 1,500 Mexican troops. The Texans fought bravely, but in time Fannin surrendered his men as prisoners of war. However, the Mexican commander ordered the prisoners slain. Eighty-two somehow escaped.

Just twenty-five days after the horrible massacre of those Texan troops, the Battle of San Jacinto was fought. The Texans, led by General Houston, were spurred on by the battle cry, "Remember the Alamo." The main battle lasted only thirty minutes as 750 Texans took on 1500 Mexican troops. In about thirty minutes half of the Mexican troops were dead and the remainder captured. Santa Anna was a prisoner, and Texas was free. A new state had been born, and it must be noted that the leaders in obtaining freedom for the Lone Star State were Baptist men.

Judge Richard Ellis was from a prominent Virginia Baptist family that provided preachers for Virginia and Texas. N. T. Byars, the blacksmith, in time was appointed the first Texas Baptist missionary, and became a church planter. General Sam Houston became a great Baptist nobleman. We observe again the fact that these men were not desirous of planting a state church, but sought political and religious freedom for all the citizenry.

We doff our hats to past heroes, and pledge ourselves anew to the preservation of soul liberty and total religious freedom which our Baptist forefathers have sought from New England all the way to Texas. Thank God for our glorious history.

DLC

---

[1]J. M. Carroll, *A History of Texas Baptists* (Dallas, TX: Baptist Standard Publishing Co., 1923), 54-55.

[2]Ibid., 57.

March 2

Verifying our Historical Roots

Scripture: 2 Timothy 4:1-5

While ministering in the State of Illinois, a member of the local congregation informed me that several years previously a Baptist historian had been in the area and sought to discover the burial site of Jacob Knapp, famed Baptist evangelist of another era. In time, he had been successful in his effort. Reverend Knapp was the subject of our entry in Volume One of this set for the date of August 27. I had quoted a contemporary of Mr. Knapp as saying: It is quite certain that no man in America ever equaled him in the number of his meetings, and in the extent of the territory they covered. Another had written that it has been estimated that Elder Knapp preached 16,000 sermons; that one hundred thousand persons were converted under his labors . . . and . . . among the converts of his meetings two hundred fifty persons entered the ministry. At any rate, the article and the historian's concern had stirred the interest of one of the church members, and in the course of time he had come upon information that led to the cemetery and grave site of that once well-known preacher.

In my first volume I mentioned Elder Knapp's homegoing on March 2, 1874. His funeral was conducted on the following Lord's Day and lasted from 1 p.m. until sunset. Jacob Knapp was a man of honor, but an American trait is soon to forget our heroes, both in the spiritual and political realms. As the 21st century dawned, it seemed as though no one knew or cared where Elder Knapp had been buried.

Needless to say, I was thrilled to visit Elder Knapp's burial site; and accompanied by my wife and host pastor, we made our way to the Greenwood cemetery at the corner of Main and Auburn in Rockford, Illinois. At that time, we rededicated ourselves to the task of worldwide evangelism until the Lord calls or comes. What a blessing to pause there and realize that we serve the God Who is the same yesterday, today, and forever. Our Lord is still calling out a people for His name, and He is still looking for those who will stand in the gap in these closing days of the dispensation of grace.

It is needful, as the Scripture says, that we call to remembrance the faithfulness of our God through His servants in days gone by. It is personally gratifying to know that through these volumes of Baptist history, the Lord has kindled a concern in the hearts of readers to attempt to revive interest among Baptists concerning their past. For instance, as Pastor Jeff Faggart of North Carolina read historical accounts of Baptist leaders who suffered for Christ in the Commonwealth of Virginia, God stirred his heart to preserve the memory of these leaders of former days. Inasmuch as my friend Dr. E. Wayne Thompson is an unquestioned authority of Baptist history in Virginia, I asked him to write with me. His accounts of our Baptist forefathers in Virginia are most graphic, and the Lord used several of those presentations to catch the attention of Pastor Faggart. In the course of time, Pastor Faggart established **The Baptist History Preservation Society**. This worthy society sponsors tours and reestablishes meaningful Baptist historical markers across America. If you would be interested in accompanying an exciting tour sponsored by this society, let me recommend that you contact Pastor Faggart at Harvest Baptist Church in Rockwell, North Carolina. May I also ask that if you know of important historical markers that need restoration, or if you know of long-forgotten sites of interest to our heritage, that you contact Pastor Faggart.

Almost simultaneously Pastor James Beller of Missouri was so stimulated as he read the first volumes of this set that he sought to rediscover our history in New England history that has been revised and distorted by revisionists. Following months of painstaking research, Pastor Beller wrote a newly published volume of American history that accurately portrays the vibrant history of godly men. The book is entitled *America in Crimson Red*. The volume should become a classic in classrooms across our land, but liberal educators will do their best to ignore it.

Thank God, there is a ground swell of renewed interest in our Baptist history, and we invite your personal participation.

DLC

March 3

The Reward for Faithfulness

Scripture: 1 Corinthians 4:2

Florida! The land of the sun with palm trees and tropical breezes! A tourist's paradise! The vacationland of America! But it hasn't always been that way. As far as the Baptist message is concerned, Florida was pioneered by sacrificing, trail blazers without air conditioning and modern means of conveyance. Those early preachers were surely not snow birds as they made their way to Florida. They became the Lord's vanguard to penetrate the unevangelized territory and plant the Gospel message everywhere they went.

Among the first Baptist preachers to enter Florida was an interesting fellow who served the Lord faithfully for a number of years before his wife finally acknowledged the truth and participated with him in obedience to the Lord's command. The story unfolds like this.

H. Z. Ardis was born on August 8, 1811, in Edgefield District, South Carolina, into a Presbyterian family. His father died when the lad was only six, but his caring mother saw to it that her children received the best education possible at that time. As a teenager, H. Z. made a profession of faith and united with others in constituting a Presbyterian church on Beach Island, South Carolina.

He married happily in 1832, but the birth of a daughter the following year created a crisis for the young father and the entire family. He was urged to have the child baptized, but he was insistent on first studying the subject of baptism in the Word of God. In the course of time, he determined that the New Testament taught no such doctrine or practice. In fact, his study led him to submit himself to the ordinance of believer's immersion, and he became a Baptist. He was baptized on September 26, 1834.[1] He suddenly found himself at odds with his dear mother, his wife, his mother-in-law, brothers, and sisters. It is never easy when one's convictions place him or her at odds with family members. Pressures are brought to bear that seem impossible, but like the Apostle Peter of old, a child of God must come to the position where he must obey God rather than man!

Rather than despairing, H. Z. immediately began to conduct prayer meetings, and soon he was exhorting sinners to come to Christ. On Sunday, January 18, 1835, by request of the Union Baptist Church, Barnwell District, South Carolina, he was ordained to the Baptist ministry. Though his wife refused believer's immersion, he served that congregation for nine years as pastor, and simultaneously he assisted other churches in South Carolina as his schedule allowed. In the meantime, H. Z.'s brother had come to the understanding of believer's immersion and had followed the Lord in baptism. He moved to Louisiana and became involved in the Baptist ministry there.

In 1845, H. Z. was overcome by poor health. This led him to move to Florida, and in January of 1845, he became pastor of the Baptist church in Madison. Florida actually became a state three months later on March 3, 1845. H. Z. served the Lord there faithfully for the next twenty-one years. During his tenure of service, he once again supplied other churches in the area, and he became a leader among the Baptists. Five years after assuming the pastorate at Madison, H. Z. experienced the thrill of immersing his wife. She had refused believer's immersion until that time. Can you imagine the joy that must have flooded his heart on that occasion?

In 1871, H. Z. joined his brother in the work of God in Louisiana. He was enabled of the Lord to continue an active ministry until his death on July 11, 1881. His name has never appeared in *Who's Who in America*, but H. Z. Ardis was a faithful man of God. Building upon the foundation he laid in Florida, other faithful men have been able to successfully hold forth the Word of God. May faithfulness be our trademark as we serve the Lord where He has placed us.

DLC

[1]John Leonidas Rosser, *A History of Florida Baptists* (Nashville, TN: Broadman Press, 1949), 13.

March 4

The Heroine of Burma

Scripture: Hebrews 13:5-6

It had been a long, hot trip from Yangon, Burma's capital, up to Amherst, but the four preachers who gathered at the grave site that day in March of 2004 were rewarded for their efforts. Two Americans and two Burman men had made the trip-all intent on finding the place where the remains of Ann Judson had been laid to rest. Ann had originally been buried under a Hopia tree near the waters of a Bay in the Indian Ocean, but with the incursion of the waters, it had been necessary to disinter her body and bury it a bit further inland. They were still in sight of the ocean, and they stood there in silence as they thought of the faithfulness of their Heroine—Ann of Ava—and her years of devoted service. A national had written: Though Ann's thirteen years in Burma exceeded the average for those early days, her death, when prospects looked so promising, was a great loss to the growing church.[1]

Thirteen years . . . but, it must have seemed an eternity crowded into that short period of time. Adoniram and Ann were two and a half years away from home before they received their first letter from the homeland! Can you imagine how those days must have dragged on? The account reads as follows: "No word from home had yet reached them and they had been absent a year and a half. As famished as the starving people they saw about them, were they when at last, a whole year later, two years and a half after leaving America, the first home letter was laid in their hands!"[2] And if that were not burden enough, finally ". . . after three years of waiting, came the assurance that the Baptist churches of America had accepted Mr. and Mrs. Judson as their first missionaries and assumed responsibility for their support. A burden also was lifted from the English missionaries at Serampore, who all this time had been supplying funds for the two Americans, according to their generous promise, but out of meager resources."[3]

Through it all, Ann had shown great confidence in the Lord of Heaven. On August 8, 1813, she wrote the following: "Exposed to robbers by night and invaders by day, yet we both unite in saying we never were happier, never more contented in any situation, than at present. We feel that this is the post to which God hath appointed us; that we are in the path of duty; and in a situation, which, of all others, presents the most extensive field of usefulness."[4]

But the trials were not over. After losing her first born to the hand of the death angel, as the tears fell, Ann wrote to a friend, "God is the same when He afflicts as when He is merciful; just as worthy of our entire trust and confidence now as when He entrusted us with the precious little gift."[5]

It is impossible to measure the grief experienced by Ann through the twenty-one month imprisonment of her Adoniram. She must have seemed ubiquitous to the guards. She was ever present, begging, cajoling, to provide special care for her beloved!

But when the hour of her departure from this life came, Ann's mate was away serving the Lord. On the sixth of October, 1826, as the dusk was settling upon that scene, Ann's spirit soared into the brightness of an eternal dawn. Some weeks later her broken-hearted husband returned. Part of what he wrote to Ann's mother follows: "O, with what meekness, and patience, and magnanimity and Christian fortitude she bore those sufferings! And can I wish they had been less? Can I sacrilegiously wish to rob her crown of a single gem? Much she saw and suffered of the evil of this evil world, and eminently was she qualified to relish and enjoy the pure and holy rest into which has entered."

Those four preachers can never forget Ann Judson and her life of sacrifice. Can you?

DLC

---

[1]Maung Shwe Wa, *Burma Baptist Chronicle* (Rangoon: Burma Baptist Convention, 1963), 56.

[2]Ethel Daniels Hubbard, *Ann of Ava* (New Hampshire: Ayer Company, 1941), 87.

[3]Ibid., 101.

[4]Ibid., 88.

[5]Ibid., 108-109.

March 5

Father and Son: Divided but United

Scripture: Proverbs 22:28

The Civil War was devastating to our nation. It caused division not only of North and South, but also division of the border states of Tennessee and Kentucky, and division in churches, as groups within local assemblies polarized. But even more crippling was the division of families, as parents and offspring disagreed, and siblings found themselves physically warring on opposite sides of the conflagration.

James Madison Pendleton, one of the leading Baptist preachers of Kentucky, and his son, John Malcolm Pendleton, stood on opposite sides of the war. The father, well-known pastor and subject of our entry, advocated abolition, while his son had such strong convictions on the other side, that he joined the Confederate army. The two shared the love and respect of father/son, but disagreed completely philosophically. Tragically, John Malcolm Pendleton was killed during the Civil War, and once again that terrible nation-rending struggle cost America severely. We will never understand the heartbreak experienced by the father when word was received of the death of his son. What horrendous days of great sorrow they must have been.

But consider the life of James M. Pendleton. He had been born in Spotsylvania County, Virginia, on November 20, 1811. At the time of his birth, James Madison served as President. The little son was named for the President. The Pendleton family moved to Kentucky when the baby was a year old. Having trusted Christ as Savior in the loving environment of his home, J. M. Pendleton was baptized on April 11, 1829. He began to preach immediately, and was trained at a seminary in Hopkinsville. He was ordained on November 1, 1833, and served two churches as pastor. On March 13, 1838, J. M. married Miss Catherine Garnett, and they made their home in Bowling Green, Kentucky. For the next twenty years the man of God served the Baptist church there. J. M. Pendleton was the first pastor in Kentucky to give himself full-time to ministry without working a side-job to supplement his salary.

During his pastorate in Bowling Green, the pastor invited J. R. Graves for evangelistic meetings. Good success was experienced in the meetings, and during the time together, Pastor Pendleton firmed up his convictions concerning association and cooperation in ministry with pedobaptists. He logically concluded that if obedience begins with believer's immersion, Baptist pastors ought not to open their pulpits to non-baptized believers who had not obeyed the Lord's command. He wrote his views in a booklet entitled *An Ancient Landmark Reset*. Aberrations of this position, in time, have led to much confusion; however, the original statement is the logical consequence of believing the Word of God literally and applying its principles.

On January 1, 1857, Pendleton left Bowling Green and moved to Murfreesboro, Tennessee, to teach preacher boys at Union University. When Union troops captured Murfreesboro in 1862, J. M. Pendleton, in sympathy with the Northern cause, moved to Hamilton, Ohio, where he served as pastor for a short period. His last pastorate was the Upland Baptist Church in Pennsylvania, and while there, he assisted in founding Crozer Theological Seminary.

Pendleton was an excellent writer, and his *Baptist Church Manual* was used for years by many Baptist churches as their guide. On his seventy-ninth birthday, Pendleton began to write a volume entitled *Reminiscences of a Long Life,* and he completed the task within two months. The life of the man of God terminated on March 5, 1891[1], and his funeral was conducted by T. T. Eaton of Louisville, Kentucky. He was buried in the Fairview Cemetery in Bowling Green.

It saddens the author to think that the mind and labors of J. M. Pendleton have been so misread as to make him appear an extremist. No doubt, some who have assumed the name "Landmarkers" have built faulty structures upon the solid foundation that J. M. Pendleton laid. But this man of God deserves a place of honor among our heroes of the faith who dared apply the principles of the Word of God to our pathway, enabling us to declare that the Bible is our only rule of faith and practice.

DLC

[1]Leo T. Crismon and Harold Stephens, *Encyclopedia of Southern Baptists* (Nashville, TN: Broadman Press, 1958), 2:1082.

March 6

Just Like Paul

Scripture: 2 Corinthians 11:23-28

It was a hot, sunny day the sixth day of March 2004, when we came upon the site of the awful Oung-pen-la prison (now spelled Aungpinle) in Burma. In the entry for March 4 we mentioned visiting the burial site of Ann Judson. We rejoiced in thinking of valiant Ann as she faithfully beat a path to the prison in Ava during the agonizing months when Adoniram was held there. But one day, unannounced, her beloved had been taken from the prison in Ava and forced to march twelve miles to Oung-pen-la. It had been rumored that there the prisoners would be burned to death. However, the prisoners were in such tragic health that they were unable to endure the entire march. They had to be transported in a solid-wheeled ox cart for the last four grueling miles. Surely it was only the grace of God and tender care of Ann that allowed Adoniram to abide such suffering.

Learning of her husband's removal, Ann was at first horrified; but then the resilient, audacious Ann set out to find her husband. She traveled with a Bengali servant, two little Burmese girls, and little baby Maria in her arms. Eight miles in a Burman ox cart is not enjoyable, but Ann, though exhausted and sick, endured it. She was temporarily crushed when, arriving at Amarapoora where she thought her husband had been taken, she discovered that Adoniram had actually been removed to Oung-pen-la. That was another four tedious miles away. The ox cart driver refused to move another inch, but Ann was undaunted and secured the service of a second ox cart owner. Ultimately she completed the journey, but she had no housing. She persisted and persuaded a jailer to allow her and the children to sleep in his paddy bin. That became her home for six months. During that time little Maria succumbed to smallpox, and Ann's own health gave way. For two months Ann herself hovered between life and death.

The fact that Adoniram was needed to interpret a peace settlement between the Burmese and British gained him his initial freedom, but in time, the actual site of the awful Aung-pen-la prison was lost. The story of its rediscovery is of interest.

In 1902 Edward, the son of Adoniram, purposed to find the prison site and mark it for posterity. Traveling to Burma, he entered into extensive research and was enabled to determine the very place of the prison. He purchased the 2.58-acre plot and donated it for the construction of a church that would honor his father's memory. The Judson Memorial Baptist Church was constructed in 1905, and the congregation began with sixteen members. Interestingly, American missionaries had entered the village in 1892 and purchased a Buddhist temple, where they opened a mission school. Of course, evangelism quickly ensued throughout the region.

During the Second World War, the British confiscated the church building and used it to house military personnel. With that exception, the building has always been used as a Baptist church. At its centennial celebration, the congregation averaged just over one hundred in attendance. In a personal interview the current pastor, Saw Seelah, assured me that he believes and preaches the good news of the Gospel. As a result, nearby residences hear the Gospel, come under conviction, and are saved. Baptisms are held twice a year. Interestingly, Pastor Seelah's father served as pastor from 1975 to 1997. Upon his death, the current pastor was called to succeed his father. Burma boasts a population of more than 46 million, and it is a country formed from many different tribes. Over 125 languages are spoken. In the Aungpinle church alone, six tribal backgrounds gather as one in God's family. The church is located on 54th Street, Chunmyathazi Township, Aungpinle, Mandalay, Burma. It might be helpful to know that Aungbinle Village is located on the Mandalay-Maymyo highway east of the City of Mandalay.

Surely we do not worship relics or old sites, important as they might be. But we do well to pause to meditate on the sacrifices of another generation to deliver the ageless message of grace. We have so many helpful tools in our day, but I fear we lack the consecration and determination to let the whole world know that Jesus Christ is the ONLY Savior of men.

DLC

March 7

He Had a Baptist Bible

Scripture: Acts 2:41-47

Today we consider the life of a man who exercised profound influence in his lifetime and whose life is largely forgotten today. Oliver Willis Van Osdel was born to godly Methodist parents on October 30, 1846, in the village of Middlebush, near Poughkeepsie, New York. His father was a blacksmith and served the Lord until his death. The family moved to Illinois in 1854.

Oliver's parents raised him and his five siblings in a Christian atmosphere. John H. Wilson states, "His was rather the experience of a young child, by means of instruction and example, being directed to the Savior in such a real way as to be able to recall no time when he did not have his faith in Christ as his Savior and Lord."[1] After finishing high school, Van Osdel enlisted in the Union Army, serving in Georgia from February 1865 until January 1866.

Van Osdel intended to prepare for a career in the law but sensed God's call to the ministry. This led him to an examination of his own beliefs. Though Methodist by heritage, He had decided that New Testament truth was most accurately taught by the people who called themselves Baptists.[2] Thus on March 7, 1869, Oliver Willis Van Osdel was baptized by immersion and joined the Baptist church of Yorkville, Illinois. That night he preached his first sermon. When Van Osdel's family pressed him about his decision to become a Baptist, *he replied flatly that he had a Baptist Bible.* [Emphasis mine.][3]

Van Osdel attended the old Chicago Baptist Theological Seminary, and in 1871 he married Harriet Wood, who was also a member of the church in Yorkville. In 1874 he assumed the pastorate of the Community Baptist Church in Warrenville, Illinois. He was ordained to the ministry on April 30, 1874.

The next thirty-five years were eventful. Van Osdel held a number of pastorates during this period. He pastored churches in Aledo and Rock Island, Illinois, before returning to Chicago in 1881 to complete his seminary training. He graduated with his B.D. degree in 1884. Subsequent pastorates took him to Ottawa, Kansas; El Paso, Texas; Galesburg, Illinois; Grand Rapids, Michigan; and Spokane, Washington. These pastorates were characterized by God's blessings. In each ministry people were saved, and in several of the ministries (Aledo, Ottawa, Galesburg, and Spokane) the growth was significant. In most of the churches, Van Osdel led the congregation to build new, much needed facilities. His time in two of the ministries (El Paso and Grand Rapids) was brief because the congregations did not have the vision to build as their pastor felt they needed to.

Van Osdel developed some strong convictions and the courage to stand by them during his years of ministry. He faced opposition from several fronts throughout these years and stood firmly for the Gospel, for the truth of God's Word, and against unbelief.

In 1909 something unusual happened to Van Osdel. He was called to return to Grand Rapids to pastor the church he had formerly led, the Wealthy Street Baptist Church. At age sixty-two, he began a ministry that would span twenty-five years! We will consider that significant part of his life and ministry in another entry.

This brief survey challenges us. We speak with kindness and respect toward our non-Baptist friends, but we, with the subject of today's consideration, affirm that we hold our Baptist distinctives because they are clearly taught in Scripture. Let us never be afraid to affirm and practice what Scripture teaches. With Van Osdel, let us invest our energies in winning lost men to Christ. Man's only hope for salvation is in Christ. We have the responsibility to take the message of Christ and His cross to them. Whether you are a pastor or a lay person, work actively to witness to and win lost people to Christ.

FJM

---

[1]Cited in Kevin Thomas Bauder, "*Biography of O. W. Van Osdel*" (unpublished Th.M. Thesis, Denver Baptist Theological Seminary, 1983), 1. I am indebted to Dr. Bauder for the use of this thesis, from which all the information in this entry is taken.

[2]Bauder, 3.

[3]Bauder, 3.

March 8

Down the Sawdust Trail

Scripture: Hebrews 13

Many Southern evangelists of the 20th century patterned their preaching style after Billy Sunday, the flamboyant baseball evangelist. Billy Kelly from Olive Springs, Tennessee, born on April 17, 1932, was one of those. He was an interesting personality whose big frame peaked at 350 pounds or more. Not only was he athletic, playing football and baseball at the Young High School in Knoxville, but he was musically talented, and well known for his fiddle playing and singing with a country band on radio and other places of entertainment.

Billy Kelly was saved on May 16, 1950, at the University of Tennessee in an area-wide revival meeting. He was influential, and people were interested in the testimony he gave at the First Baptist Church on the following Sunday morning. Southern Baptist pastors mentored him, and he was soon called to preach. Billy was ordained on his twenty-third birthday. He enrolled at Carson Newman College in East Tennessee, but dropped out due to finances. Soon thereafter he was drafted into the army and stationed in Fayetteville, North Carolina. While there, Billy started a church. After gaining experience as a pastor, Billy entered the field of evangelism, and he preached literally to thousands of people. One wonders just how many were saved under his powerful preaching.[1]

Billy married Dorothy Frost on September 6, 1953. Dot's dad stipulated that she finish college and he financed her education. This paid off, because Dot home-schooled their son while traveling with Billy for eleven years. Later God blessed the Kelly's with a daughter, and these two children produced five grandchildren.

Billy's first acquaintance with old time fundamentalism was when he met Dr. Harold Sightler at a preachers' prayer meeting where everyone prayed at the same time. This informal type of praying was new to him.

Brother Billy, as he was called, was known as Mr. Camp Meeting and directed the Greer Baptist Camp Meeting in Greer,

South Carolina, for twenty-two consecutive years. He preached, led singing, played the piano, sang special numbers, and was responsible for the grounds. Almost single-handedly, he built a new tabernacle.

Billy was a very animated, popular speaker and turned down as many as 300 preaching requests a year. One special event in his ministry was portraying a bootlegger in the film *Sheffey* produced by Unusual Films.

Evangelists have a repertoire of sermons called "sugar sticks" that they preach regularly. Some have catchy titles to attract the attention of the audience and to help people remember the sermons. One of Brother Billy's famous sermons was *When Lefty Let Fatty Have It*, speaking of Ehud, the left-handed judge of Israel who thrust the dagger into the fat belly of Eglon, king of Moab found in Judges 3. When he held a meeting for Pastor Bud Hunter, he was asked to play ping-pong. Always competitive, he accepted the challenge and proceeded to beat everyone. The pastor's wife, Esther, offered to play a game with Billy. Regarding Esther's less than five-foot frame and 100 pounds, he was certain of another victory over this left-handed player. Things got exciting when Esther passed him by two points. Trailing by two points he never caught up and the little lady won. He was deflated and became more so when Esther said, "Maybe this is another case of Lefty letting Fatty have it!"

Recognized for his work in evangelism, Billy was awarded the Honorary Doctor of Divinity degrees in 1987 from Tabernacle Baptist College in Greenville, South Carolina, and in 1992 from Trinity Baptist College in Jacksonville, Florida.

He met his Lord on April 1, 1997. It is estimated that 500 preachers attended his funeral on April 4 at Tabernacle Baptist Church in Greenville, South Carolina, where he and Dot became members in February of 1961.[2]

Not every evangelist is as flamboyant, dynamic, and musical as Billy Kelly was. God uses differing personalities in different ways. The important thing is that we be faithful in our message and service to the Savior. May He find us faithful.

DCB

---

[1] *Billy Kelly, 1932-1997*, Old Paths Radio Program article, n.d.

[2] Telephone interview with Dot Kelly by Bettye Baughan, August 11, 2004.

March 9

Unknown, But Not Forgotten

Scripture: Proverbs 15:13a; 15:15b

The basis of America's greatness surely has been caused by the preaching of the glorious Gospel. But the magnificent impact of the Gospel has not primarily been produced by a few brilliant preachers, but rather by a multitude of faithful ministers who have labored in out-of-the-way places. These have served forgotten and unknown, but it has been through their efforts that our nation, in days gone by, became the great bastion of freedom.

William Hickle was just such a preacher. He was born in Virginia on March 9, 1807, and his Lord called him home on June 23, 1891. His parents moved early to Tennessee. As a lad William Hickle had trusted Christ as his Savior at the Little Flat Creek Baptist Church, and he was baptized on August 19, 1826. With no formal training, the youth was licensed to preach, and in June the next year, young twenty-year old William Hickle was ordained. On June 7, 1827, William married Miss Nancy Rutherford, and his ministerial life of service began. Through the years, God blessed William and Nancy with eleven children, and William preached and plowed faithfully. His farm land was not too productive, but he worked to provide for his family, and, at the same time, He labored in the Word of God. Tragically, his churches paid him meagerly, but he was obeying the call of God, and not the call of man.

During the next sixty years, William Hickle pastored twenty-seven churches, and not infrequently, he served five or six of them simultaneously. During that sixty year period, the man of God served as evangelist for protracted meetings, missionary of the association, and moderator of the Association for twelve years, and then he served as clerk for ten. When the Northern Association became infiltrated and over-run with an anti-missionary spirit caused by Antinomianism, he led the way in the formation of the Northern Association of United Baptists that maintained great missionary emphasis. Until the year of his death, Elder Hickle served the Cedar Ford and Prospect Baptist churches as their pastor.

William Hickle enjoyed robust health, and he possessed a jovial spirit. He was used of God in "turning many to righteousness", and was known for his good natured humor. "He preached so well when in the pulpit, and was of such a jovial and joking disposition when out of the pulpit, that not a few of his friends and admirers said, 'When he was in the pulpit, you would think he never ought to be out, and when he was out, you would think he ought never to be in.'"[1]

It is said that Reverend Hickle possessed a powerful set of lungs, and he could preach and sing for weeks without getting hoarse in the least. Just a week before his homegoing, after having been confined to bed for seven weeks, he sang with delight, *Jesus, Lover of my Soul*, and *Nearer My God, to Thee*.

In his younger days, Brother Hickle preached a protracted meeting at the Lyon's Creek Baptist Church. Among those in attendance was a godly Methodist brother who was known for his shouting. The man's name was Trent, and he was accustomed to shout in Methodist meetings when the spirit moved him. As Brother Hickle was preaching on some glorious truth, the elderly Methodist brother was getting more and more blessed. He finally called out, "Hold on, Brother Hickle, hold on! I don't want to interrupt you! But I can't stand any more!"

Throughout his lifetime Reverend Hickle was paid little, but he gave himself fully to the ministry. Someone commented, "Uncle Billy Hickle did more as a preacher and received less pay that any man in Tennessee."[2] Be that as it may, America owes much to such men of God who were willing to spend and be spent for the glory of our Savior. And today, though the conditions differ, we would honor faithful men of God whose names may never be known broadly, but who willingly serve in the center of His will.

DLC

---

[1]J. J. Burnett, *Sketches of Tennessee's Pioneer Baptist Preachers* (Nashville, TN: Marshall & Bruce Coming, 1919), 223.

[2]Ibid., 224.

March 10

The Land of the Free

Scripture: Psalm 86:11

Back in 1898, Charles F. James observed, "There has been manifested at various times and on various occasions a disposition to rewrite the history . . . , and to rob our Baptist fathers of the peculiar honor which has ever been claimed for them, that of being the foremost, most zealous, and most consistent and unwavering champions of soul liberty."[1]

If Mr. James were living today, he would realize how successful the revisionists have been. At this point in our national history, it seems impossible to most that anyone has ever been discriminated due to his or her faith. It is politically correct to be continually bombarded with reminders of past racial inequities. In fact, at times the news media even features mini-series concerning injustices to ethnic groups in bygone days. This has resulted in some believing that reparations are due to the progeny of both those who suffered racial or ethnic wrongs. But religiously, Americans have arrived at the place where they proudly hold their collective heads high in the assumption that in the area of religion, America has ever been the land of the free.

But, has it? Secular historians consent to the racial and ethnic distortions, but revisionists either ignore or belie the religious torts. I should like to introduce two historians of the early days of our history. Both men were Baptist preachers during the foundational days of our republic. Doubtless Isaac Backus is the better known of the two. He wrote the engrossing volume entitled, *Church History of New England from 1620-1804.* The second, John Comer, is not as identifiable, even among Baptists. It is true that his life was not too long. He was born August 1, 1704, and after a rich ministry, he passed into the presence of his Lord on May 23, 1734. John Comer had purposed to write a Baptist history, but the brevity of his life kept him from it. However, his diary has been preserved, and it is a treasure trove as it presents a miniature portraiture of life in early America.

An early entry into Backus' diary informs us that Philip Tabor, pastor of the Baptist church on the borders of Tiverton and Dartmouth[2], was imprisoned on May 25, 1723, and he was detained for thirteen months. And why? He refused to pay the tax that was assessed by the town for the support of the minister of the standing order. In fact, not until King George became aware of the situation were Elder Tabor and others released from jail.

On his diary entry for March 3, 1729, Comer recorded the following: "A number of Baptists, Churchmen, and Quakers, in all 30 persons, belonging to the township of Rehoboth [M], were committed to Bristol jail, by reason of their refusing to pay the ministers' rate. On March 10 he wrote, "I went to visit the prisoners at Bristol with Mr. Stephen Gorton. Upon the request of the prisoners I preached this day in the old prison at Bristol, from Psalm 86:11. Sundry of the town attended the meeting."[3]

In a previous volume, I have quoted an entire letter from Mrs. Elizabeth Backus addressed to her son telling of her imprisonment for refusing to pay the tax for the support of the standing order pastor in 1752. Mrs. Backus was fifty-four years of age at the time. She was arrested on a dark, rainy night and incarcerated for two full weeks before being released. In the letter she also reported that Isaac Backus' brother, Samuel, was imprisoned with the same accusation for twenty-one days.

We thank the Lord for our national religious freedom, but as one has said, the condition upon which God hath given liberty is eternal vigilance. Let us be ever alert to governmental intrusions, and let us use our freedom to defend our freedom.

DLC

---

[1]Charles F. James, *Documentary History of the Struggle for Religious Liberty in Virginia* (New York: Da Capo Press, 1971), Preface.

[2]Isaac Backus, *Your Baptist Heritage* (Little Rock: The Challenge Press, 1976), 104.

[3]John Comer, *The Diary of John Comer* (Providence: The Rhode Island Historical Society, 1893), 62.

March 11

Freedom is Not Cheap

Scripture: Matthew 25:35-40

It is unfortunate that an accurate, faithful history of the early days of American colonization has not been available to school children in America. Historians, given to the revision of our actual history, have obliterated a true picture of the religious scene in those days. Volume eight of the Collections of the Rhode Island Historical Society featured *The Diary of John Comer*, but it has long since been out of print.

John Comer (1704-1734), had purposed to write a history of Baptists in America, but his early death made that an impossibility. It has been said of him, "Mr. Comer was the most remarkable young man in the Baptist history of New England, and his early death was a calamity to the churches in that section of the country, suffering at the time so severely from Puritan persecutions, and needing so much his unusual talents . . . ."[1]

As we have already observed, in his diary dated March 3, 1729, he wrote "A number of Baptists, Churchmen, and Quakers, in all 30 persons, belonging to ye township of Rehoboth, were committed to Bristol jail, by reason of their refusing to pay ye ministers' rate." On March 10 and 11, 1729, he recorded the following: "I went to visit ye prisoners at Bristol with Mr. Stephen Gorton. Upon ye request of ye prisoners I preached this day in ye old prison at Bristol, from Psalm 86:11. Sundry of ye town attended ye meeting."[2]

In his *History of New England Baptists*, Isaac Backus provides more details of the occasion. The two State Church (Congregational) pastors who were to be supported by general tax revenue, were John Greenwood and David Turner.

There were twenty-eight Baptists, two Quakers and two Episcopalians who were "...seized and imprisoned at Bristol, by Jonathan Bosworth and Jacob Ormsbee, constables of Rehoboth . . . . Following Mr. Comer's visit there, inasmuch as no other way appeared of deliverance from a nauseous place which had injured their health, but paying said taxes and costs, this was soon after done by their friends."[3]

In the course of time, the state church finally allowed Baptists and others to obtain a certificate granting them tax exemption from the state church taxation. However, the system was open to many abuses. Often town constables or parish tax collectors would simply refuse to accept the certificates. At such time the protesting Baptists would be taken to jail, or their cows, horses, or household goods would be sold at auction to pay the tax. During that period in American history many Baptists stubbornly refused to pay the tax, and literally hundreds of Baptists were jailed.

Mr. Backus served as the Agent of the Warren Association of Baptist churches, and he led the way in seeking litigation to obtain freedom from that obnoxious taxation. Unfortunately, though Mr. Backus lived through all the stages of the Revolution, he did not live long enough to see the state church concept completely abolished. He died on November 20, 1806, and Massachusetts maintained the state church concept until 1833.

How we ought to thank the Lord for the freedom we experience in America at the beginning of the twenty-first century. It is ours today because our faithful forefathers were willing to pay a great price to obtain it. May we not allow soul liberty and religious freedom to be lost for our future posterity. We often sing, *God Bless America*, but we should be praying that revival will again be experienced upon our shores. We need to petition the Lord of Heaven, that, until Jesus Christ comes, America might continue to experience the freedom to preach, to witness and to send missionaries around the world with the gospel message.

DLC

---

[1]William Cathcart, *The Baptist Enclyclopedia* (Philadelphia: Louis H. Everts, 1881), 2:255.

[2]C. Edwin Barrows, Editor, *The Diary of John Comer* (Rhode Island Historical Society, 1893), 62.

[3]Isaac Backus, *A History of New England* (Newton, MA: Backus Historical Society), 1871), 1:519.

March 12

God Writes the Final Chapter

Scripture: Isaiah 46:1-13

Many times the end is significantly different than the beginning. A good start does not guarantee a good ending; nor does a poor beginning always necessitate a bad conclusion. God frequently changes a deficient beginning into a conclusion which glorifies Himself. The city of Pownal, Vermont, and one of its pastors, Caleb Nichols, are both good examples of God at work in the lives of His people and churches.

Pownal lies in the southwest corner of Vermont. Dutch people from the State of New York first settled there. In 1764, Benjamin Garner, a Baptist minister from West Greenwich, Rhode Island, traveled into the region and preached to the settlers. The following year he and his family moved into town. It was not until 1772, however, that Garner found five Baptists besides himself. They united and soon formed a church. The next year Pownal was visited with a terrible sickness; as is often the case in times of distress, many in the community turned to God. The church in that year increased to sixty members.[1] Garner made high claims to godliness, but his practice did not match his profession. There was a sin, unnamed by any who have written about him, which plagued him. He had been accused of this sin while in Rhode Island; the accusation was repeated in Pownal. The accusation threw Garner into disgrace and the new church into embarrassment and confusion. All of this took place just after the growth of the church. For eight years the church struggled in a miserable condition.

In the winter of 1781, however, God began to bless. Francis Bennet came from Foster, Rhode Island. He preached and ministered among the people, and the church began to grow in strength and vitality. In 1788, Caleb Nichols, another Baptist pastor from Rhode Island, came to Pownal to become the pastor of the church. He served there for many years with the clear blessing of God. God took the problems that had developed in this church and turned them into blessings under Nichols' ministry.

Nichols is himself an example of God completely changing a man for His own glory. Nichols was born in Exeter, Rhode Island, on March 12, 1743. He was a selfish and thoughtless young man, interested primarily in playing his violin and enjoying his worldly friends. At the age of twenty-four, however, he trusted Christ as his Savior and was soon baptized. Not long after his baptism he began to preach and was soon ordained as pastor in Coventry, Rhode Island. Under Nichols' ministry, this church prospered, and in less than ten years it increased to 350 members.[2]

In 1788 he moved to Pownal. Under his ministry the church grew and prospered. The year after he arrived, a revival broke out. In 1793, God blessed with another revival, and about seventy were added to the church that year.

John Leland wrote the following concerning the character of Caleb Nichols: "Elder Nichols moved into Pownal in 1788, bringing with him not only fair paper credentials, but what far exceeds, a heart flowing with love to God and men; and now, instead of using his violin to captivate the thoughtless throng, he is engaged with successful zeal in sounding the gospel trumpet. His life and conversation are exemplary; his preaching is spiritual and animating, pretty full of the musical *New-Light* tone. But his gift in prayer is his great excellency; for he not only prays as if he was softly climbing Jacob's ladder to the portals of heaven, but his expressions are so doctrinal, that a good sermon may be heard in one of his prayers."[3]

This worthy minister finished his earthly ministry in 1804. God took a church through the depths of tribulation and brought it out with blessings from above. God also took a young man, filled with himself and his sin, and turned him into a blessed servant.

LRO

---

[1] David Benedict, *A General History of the Baptist Denomination in America* (Boston: Lincoln and Edmands, 1813), 337.

[2] Ibid., 338.

[3] Ibid.

March 13

Early Baptists in America

Scripture: Matthew 10:16-17

The debate continues among Baptist historians as to whether the Baptist church in Providence or Newport, Rhode Island, is the oldest. Perhaps we will never know definitively, but in 1639 it is apparent that an attempt was made to establish a Baptist church at Weymouth, a town located a few miles southeast from Boston. The effort proved in vain due to the strong arguments of interposing magistrates.

John Smith, John Spur, Richard Sylvester, Ambrose Morton, Thomas Mackpeace, and Robert Lenthal, were the principal promoters of this design. They were all arraigned before the General Court at Boston, March 13, 1639, where they were treated according to the order of the day; Smith, who was probably the greatest transgressor, was fined twenty pounds, and committed during the pleasure of the Court. Sylvester was fined twenty shillings and disfranchised. Morton was fined ten pounds, and counseled to go to Mr. Mather for instruction. Mackpeace had probably no money; he was not fined, but had a modest hint of banishment, unless he reformed. Lenthal it seems compromised the matter with the court for the present; consented to appear before it at the next session; was enjoined to acknowledge his fault, and so on. How matters finally terminated with him I do not find; but it is certain he soon after went to Mr. Clark's settlement on Rhode Island, and began to preach there before the first church in Newport was formed.[1]

The indomitable Baptists did not surrender their desire to worship the Lord according to the dictates of their hearts. Governor John Winthrop wrote that the Anabaptists increased and spread in Massachusetts. The Baptist growth was a continual agitation and caused fearful response in the minds of the rulers of this colony. The gradual growth of Baptist sentiment was doubtless the means of leading the General Court to pass the following act for the suppression of what they considered an obnoxious sect:

> Forasmuch as experience hath plentifully and often proved, that since the first rising of the Anabaptists, about one hundred years since, they have been the incendiaries of commonwealths, and the infectors of persons in main matters of religion, and the troublers of churches in all places where they have been, and that they, who have held the baptizing of infants unlawful, have usually held other errors or heresies therewith, though they have (as other heretics used to do) concealed the same, till they spied out a fit advantage and opportunity to vent them, by way of question or scruple; and whereas divers of this kind have, since our coming into New England, appeared, amongst ourselves, some whereof (as others before them), denied the ordinance of magistracy, and the lawfulness of making war, and others the lawfulness of magistrates, and their inspection into any breach of the first table; which opinions, if they should be connived at by us, are like to be increased amongst us, and so must necessarily bring guilt upon us, infection and trouble to the churches, and hazard to the whole commonwealth; it is ordered and agreed that if any person or persons, within this jurisdiction, shall either openly condemn or oppose the baptizing of infants, or go about secretly to seduce others from the approbation or use thereof, or shall purposely depart the congregation at the ministration of the ordinance, or shall deny the ordinance of magistracy, or their lawful right and authority to make war, or to punish the outward breaches of the first table, and shall appear to the court willfully and obstinately to continue therein after due time and means of conviction, every such person or persons shall be *sentenced to banishment.*[2]

This was the first law made against the Baptists in Massachusetts. It was passed November 13, 1644. It will be remembered that just seven years later Obadiah Holmes was beaten severely for daring to worship in Massachusetts as a Baptist. How we ought to thank God for the freedom of religion our Baptist forefathers championed for us in America.

DLC

---

[1]David Benedict, *A General History of the Baptist Denomination in America* (Boston: Lincoln & Edmands, 1813), 1:356.

[2]Ibid., 1:359-360.

March 14

A Versatile Christian Educator

Scripture: 1 Corinthians 2:2

Robert Ryland was blessed in being born into a godly home on March 14, 1805, at Farmington in the old Commonwealth of Virginia. Of his life he wrote: "In my father's family morning and evening worship, consisting of reading, singing, and prayer, was from early infancy a uniform habit. It was also his constant practice to attend public worship with all his family when his church was open. His house was the common resort for preachers, whose discourse in the private circle often turned upon spiritual topics."[1]

Living in such an environment, Robert's salvation experience was without great fanfare. Upon hearing the testimonies of others who had agonized in coming to Christ, young Mr. Ryland was concerned that he had not experienced the same emotional turmoil. But in the course of studying God's Word, he became satisfied that the Spirit of God works differently in every life. He expressed it well in saying, "I mourned because I could not mourn." Having settled that issue, he was soon baptized and united with the church in 1824.

On December 23, 1826, two years later, he graduated from Columbian College and entered the ministry as his life's work.

Regarding his call he said, "When I began to cherish the hope of divine mercy, the thought of preaching occurred to me and I shook it off as a vile presumption. It came back again and again as affording the highest and holiest pleasure if I were only fit for the work, but I could not venture...I concluded to give myself to study, so as to qualify myself as far as possible for the ministry, to make it the subject of constant prayer for divine guidance, and to submit the final question of my life work to the decision of the church and the rulings of Providence."[2]

His first pastorate was a Baptist church of nineteen members in Lynchburg, Virginia, whose building was unsightly and incommodious, and located on the extreme western verge of the town as far off from the residents as it could possibly get. The newly-formed congregation was actually a split from the First Church. His first sermon was from Paul's text: "For I determined not to know anything among you save Jesus Christ and Him crucified." The desire to fulfill that goal seemed to control his entire life. The congregation sat around the walls leaving the middle of the room vacant, and as he surveyed the situation he concluded that there was only one direction in which the work of God there could go! It was surely bound to get better!

Slowly the congregation increased. Prayer meetings were held nightly in private homes. Songs became more tender, the petitions more earnest, and finally, sinners were heard to sob and cry for mercy. Early in August the pastor baptized the first of many converts.

After six years in the pastorate Pastor Ryland resigned to take charge of the Virginia Baptist Seminary. The student body was comprised wholly of ministerial candidates. Dr. Ryland organized the school well and served as president for thirty-four years. It will be noted that he led the school through the difficult days of the Civil War. While still serving the college, Dr. Ryland assumed the pastorate of the First African Baptist Church in Richmond. At the time, Virginia Law forbade a black church unless it had a white pastor. The congregation had about one thousand members. Dr. Ryland determined that his preaching would be instructive, dwelling on distinctive doctrines and precepts of Christianity. He wrote a catechism of fifty-two lessons, which produced spiritual knowledge for the benefit of the whole congregation. In 1865 he resigned that pastorate believing the emancipated black people would prefer a pastor of their own race. He had enjoyed a long and blessed pastorate from October 1, 1841, to July 1, 1865.

Dr. Ryland lived through the century serving in various capacities. His death occurred on April 23, 1899. It was fitting that his funeral was conducted at Richmond College, where he was also buried.

EGC

---

[1]George Braxton Taylor, *Virginia Baptist Ministers,* Fourth Series, (Lynchburg, VA: J. B. Bell Company, 1913) 348.

[2]Ibid., 349.

March 15

Remember, Repent, or Ruin

Scripture: Revelation 2:1-12

It is heart-breaking to meditate upon a church whose glory exists only in past memories. But such is the case of the First Baptist Church of Hopewell, New Jersey. Organized on April 23, 1715, with fifteen constituents, the congregation met for the first thirty-two years in the private homes of its members. In 1747, property was given the church by John Hart, the only Baptist signatory of our national Constitution. Reverend Isaac Eaton assumed the pastorate on April 17, 1874. He was ordained on November 29, 1748, and the blessings of God were attendant upon his ministry until he was called home on July 4, 1772, in his forty-seventh year. Morgan Edwards is quoted as saying, "There have been remarkable revivals in this church. In 1747, fifty-five were baptized; in 1764, one hundred and five united with the church." These figures might not seem impressive in our day, but when one remembers that Hopewell was but a village in a rural area, it is apparent that the church was baskinq in the spiritual blessings of heaven.

Perhaps the most important historical significance attached to this church is the fact that Reverend Eaton, in

1756, established the first Baptist school in America aimed at training young men for the ministry. Many of the leading Baptist ministers looked back upon Hopewell as their Alma Mater in ministerial training. John Gano, outstanding leader, and one of six Baptist chaplains in the Revolutionary War, was trained at Hopewell. Hezekiah Smith, outstanding missionary-minded pastor and Revolutionary chaplain looked back upon Hopewell as the source of his training. James Manning, founder and original president of Brown University, was trained by Reverend Eaton at Hopewell. It can well be said that the Baptist Church at Hopewell had a great deal to do with the growth of the Baptist cause in our land.

It will be remembered that the most meaningful conveyance in that day was the horse and buggy. For the convenience of the ladies in mounting and dismounting their carriages or horses, across the street from the church there stood a Amounting block. This consisted of a huge stone six feet long and four feet wide. It stood about three feet high and the top of the stone was reached by steps at the rear of the stone.

On Sunday, April 23, 1775, news of the Battle of Lexington reached Hopewell while the congregation was in the morning worship service. As the people began to exit the building, Joab Houghton, a member of the church, mounted the block and began an oration that would challenge every male member of the church. He inspired the men with love of liberty and desire for independence. He closed his news-release thus: "Men of New Jersey, the Red Coats are murdering our brethren of New England. Who follows me to Boston? Every man answered, "I." Mr. Houghton was chosen leader of the party of men who left for the scene of the war. On October 19, 1776, Mr. Houghton was made a captain, and on March 15, 1777, he was made Lieutenant Colonel.[1]

How thrilling to stand on what historically we consider hallowed ground. But how pathetic to realize that damnable heresy can destroy the actual life of a church once vibrant with gospel truth. In the course of time Reverend John Boggs assumed the pastorate. At first he wrote the Associational annual letter, and in it challenged churches to sustain missions, but in a short time he embraced hyper-Calvinism which led to Antinomianism[2] and the death of the Hopewell Church. After sixty-five years of a glorious history, the vital life-blood of the church was sapped, and the Lord removed His candlestick.

How essential that local assemblies consider well the words of the Savior to the church of the Ephesians. In essence our Lord said: Remember; repent; or else I will remove thy candlestick. We are reminded that a productive present is better than an honored history. What glory is our wonderful Savior receiving today from your local church?

DLC

[1]Thomas S. Griffits, *A History of Baptists in New Jersey* (Highttown, NJ: Barr Press Publishing Company, 1904), 69.

[2]Ibid., 71.

March 16

Despise Not Thy Youth

Scripture: Acts 19:20

The name of Thomas Hume, Sr. is little known in Baptist circles today, and it would be impossible to do justice to his life in such a brief entry. However, I should like to focus attention on a short synopsis of his life. Thomas Hume was born March 16, 1812, into the home of a Presbyterian pastor. While Thomas was a youth, his father passed away while preaching! Thomas matured, receiving a fair education and some background in business. When he was eighteen he made a profession of faith, but delayed public confession that he might study the Scriptural demands of church membership. Amazingly, his newly-formed convictions forced him to unite with the Baptists, though they were very weak in the area.

Feeling a call to the ministry, Thomas entered the newly-established Virginia Baptist Seminary. As a student, he gave two Sundays a month to supplying churches in Chesterfield County, Virginia. It came as a complete surprise to him when he was called by a little Baptist church in Portsmouth to become their pastor. Dr. Joseph Schoolfield, a successful physician, had moved from Baltimore to Portsmouth, and he wrote the young theological student and explained the call. Thomas Hume demurred. He explained that he wished to better prepare himself academically for such a challenge. However, the congregation would not take "No" for an answer, and the doctor invited Mr. Hume to live in his home. The doctor possessed a good theological library, and doubtless, that was a lure to the young man ultimately to accept the call.

On the day of his twenty-first birthday, March 17, 1833, he was welcomed as new pastor. The church had been established on September 7, 1789, but it had experienced many trials. Under previous pastors the work had progressed and then retrogressed. Mr. Hume entered into the work with compassion for people and a passion for work. The environment was not too favorable. The Episcopal Church was strong and drew the people of society. Methodism had been introduced in 1772, and its church was aggressive and advancing. In fact, the Methodist pastor, Dr. Waller, made light of the young Baptist preacher. As a controversialist he wrote in the town newspaper that "the young preacher might do well to tarry at Jericho till his beard be grown."[1] But the young pastor won the day. Soon the street rhyme was heard:

While Waller at home was studying his Greek,
Hume took the converts down into the creek

At one time we are reminded in the Scripture that ". . . mightily grew the word of God and prevailed," and such could be said about the ministry of Pastor Hume in Portsmouth. The church soon numbered 650, and the church historian records that the pastor conducted at least 800 baptisms during his ministry there.

In 1835, the young pastor married Miss Mary Anne Gregory, and for twenty-five years she served faithfully at her husband's side. Eight children were born into the warm atmosphere of their loving home, and hospitality became the keyword in their lives. Living in a seaport town, visitors were many.

Reverend Hume's preacher son wrote that his father's notes indicated that he dealt with the fundamental elements of Biblical truth, and addressed himself to Christian experience. His old volumes of Andrew Fuller show that he compared his moderate theology with the strong meat of Gills' *Body of Divinity*, and sought to be judicious and discriminating in his statement of doctrine.

This man of God endured many trials such as the outbreak of Yellow Fever in 1855, his wife's death, the tragedies of the Civil War with three of his sons absent in the Confederate Army, and the death of his only daughter in 1866. Through it all, he found the blessedness of prayer and the presence of the Lord to be real. This choice servant was called home on March 16, 1875, at the completion of sixty-three years of a faithful life.

Let us pray for young Bible college and seminary students in our day. These are our leaders for tomorrow.

DLC

---

[1]George Braxton Taylor, *Virginia Baptist Ministers*, Third Series (Lynchburg, VA: J. P. Bell Company), 190.

March 17

Baptists and the Land of the Free

Scripture: John 8:32

What an important date March 17, 1644, is for American freedom. It was on that date that Roger Williams obtained a free and absolute charter, entitled "The Incorporation of Providence Plantation, in the Narragansett Bay, in New-England."[1] The influence of our godly Baptist forefathers created in Rhode Island the only one of the thirteen original colonies that featured total religious freedom! Nine of the thirteen colonies maintained a State church, and others such as Pennsylvania and Maryland offered partial religious freedom, but only Rhode Island granted complete religious liberty.

It has been pointed out that though Baptists have been persecuted by many wherever they have existed, they have never persecuted others. When laying the cornerstone of the great Metropolitan Tabernacle in London, Mr. Spurgeon stated: "Persecuted alike by Romanists and Protestants of almost every sect, yet there has never existed a Government holding Baptist principles which persecuted others; nor, I believe, any body of Baptists ever held it to be right to put the consciences of others under the control of man. We have ever been ready to suffer, as our martyrologies will prove, but we are not ready to accept any help from the State, to prostitute the purity of the Bride of Christ to any alliance with Government, and we will never make the Church, although the Queen, the despot over the consciences of men."

It is apparent that Rhode Island never became what might have been expected for Baptist strength, and this is well explained by a current Baptist historian: ". . . Rhode Island Baptists never quite lived up to early expectations. They formed the first Baptist church in America . . . located their first college there thinking that the state would be predominately Baptist. Perhaps their extreme diversity hampered [Baptist] growth for Rhode Island. Baptists included Regular, General, Six-Principle, Seventh-Day, and Separates. For a time the Separate churches out numbered the Regulars, but their reluctance to participate in associations and the tendency of Regular Baptists to reclaim some of the Separate members hampered their witness."[2]

Be that as it may, historically Baptists have always held to the principle of voluntarism, and as a result, they would rather provide total religious freedom than to dictate the religious persuasion of another. Baptists have ever championed a free church in a free state.

This is clearly witnessed by the fact that the Quakers found freedom in Rhode Island. In 1656, "the Massachusetts, Plymouth, Hartford, and New-Haven colonies, pressed them [Rhode Island residents] to relinquish this point, [total religious freedom], and unite with them in crushing and driving the Quakers from New England, and preventing any more from coming hither: they nobly answered—"We shall strictly adhere to the foundation principles on which this colony was first settled"— wherefore, the persecuted Quakers found protection in this asylum of safety while persecution and destruction followed them elsewhere."[3]

At the unveiling of the statue of Roger Williams at the United States Capitol in 1872, Rhode Island Senator William Sprague observed that Roger Williams "successfully vindicated the right of private judgment in matters of conscience, and effected a moral and political revolution in all governments of the civilized world." Rhode

Island became home to the first Jewish synagogue in America as well as being a sanctuary for the Quakers. Rhode Island set a pattern of religious freedom for all America, as it became a safe harbor in a vast sea of tyranny and oppression.

Religious freedom does not mean that Baptists agree with all religious persuasions, but because of soul liberty, as Roger Williams expressed it, Baptists believe that every man must give account personally to the God of Heaven. The term "soul liberty," I believe, ought better be set forth as "soul responsibility." Baptists believe that every individual stands personally before God and has spiritual accountability before the Lord. How we thank God that after the successful experiment of religious freedom in Rhode Island, this principle has been adopted by our entire Nation.

DLC

---

[1] Richard Knight, *History of the General or Six Principle Baptists in Europe and America* (New York: Arno Press, 1980), 246.

[2] Leon H. McBeth, *The Baptist Heritage* (Nashville: Broadman Press, 1987), 206.

[3] Knight, 247.

March 18

A Common Layman With A Godly Influence

Scripture: Psalm 78:1-7

Our story begins in East Prussia, March 29, 1858. Friedrich Moritz was born to Henry and Wilhelmina Moritz, one of seven children born into the home of these believing German Baptists. Henrietta Krakel was born nearby on May 5 of the same year to Friedrich and Henrietta Krakel. She was the first of two children born to her parents, who were also Christians. Both families were members of a German Baptist church near Barmen, East Prussia. Much of the story is lost in obscurity, but we do know that these children came to know Christ in their young years. Reverend Haupt, a German Baptist pastor, baptized them.

These years were momentous years in Europe. Garibaldi unified Italy in 1861, and Bismark unified Germany in 1871. This was also a spiritually momentous time, for in 1867, when these children were just nine years old, German Baptist preachers went from East Prussia to Russia. People came to faith in Christ through their ministry and followed the Lord in baptism. The first Baptist churches in Russia were established at that time.[1]

Friedrich and Henrietta's parents determined to seek a better life in the United States and came to America in May 1883. Friedrich could not come at that time because he was serving in Kaiser Wilhelm's army. After his discharge he followed in October of the same year. On April 10, 1884, Friedrich and Henrietta, who had grown to love each other, were married in Pekin, Illinois. For all their lives they faithfully served the Lord Who had saved them, and Whom they loved.

Nine children were born to this union, one of whom died six weeks after her birth. Seven of the children were girls and two were boys. The record is that all nine of the Moritz children received Christ as their Savior and are in Heaven today. The family faithfully served the Lord in the old State Park Baptist Church, a German Baptist assembly in Peoria, Illinois. We learn something of the atmosphere of the home from the conversion of one of the children. Emma was the second oldest, born in 1887. About two years before her death she told me how she came to know the Lord. Each evening after supper Friedrich Moritz would get his German Bible and read to the children, who would move from the table to the floor of the dining room for this exercise. Emma told me that one evening as her father read the Scriptures, the Holy Spirit convicted her of her lost condition. The young girl, twelve or thirteen at the time, began to weep. Friedrich asked her what was bothering her, and she told him that she needed to be saved. This simple German farmer led his daughter to pray and receive Christ right then and there.

On July 26, 1901, the last of the nine children was born to Friedrich and Henrietta. The father stood over Walter's crib that summer day and prayed that God would save his boy and call him to preach. Walter grew up to be an ironworker. He, too, knew Christ and faithfully served the Lord for all of his eighty six years. As Walter's son, I often wonder if God called me to preach one generation later in answer to my grandfather's prayers.

On Saturday evening, March 18, 1933, Friedrich Moritz ate supper and then reviewed his Sunday school lesson in preparation to teach his adult class the next day. But God had other plans, and that evening a heart attack ushered this faithful layman into the presence of the Lord Whom he loved and served.

The story of my grandfather's life is simple and unremarkable in the great flow of human history, but his testimony is an encouragement to us as we seek to serve the Lord. His parents knew the Lord and served Him. He, with his wife, served the Lord until his dying day. All nine of their children knew the Lord. His grandchildren, and now his great grandchildren are saved and living for Christ. As Psalm 78:6 and 7 declare, we can live in obedience to God so that our children and generations beyond them can know the Lord. We cannot propagate a godly heritage, but we can, by obedience to God, perpetuate that heritage.

FJM

---

[1]Alexander de Chalandeau, *The Christians in the U.S.S.R.* (Chicago: Harper and Company, 1978), 2.

March 19

A Quiet but Successful Ministry

Scripture: Philippians 1:21

When looking at Baptist growth in Virginia, we often marvel at the sufferings and privations of early Baptist preachers. Forty-four were incarcerated for preaching without validation from the state church, but many of the preachers were unscathed by the attacks of the unruly mobs and the militia. Such a man was Benjamin Watkins.

Benjamin Watkins was born into an Episcopalian home on July 5, 1755. That was the very year that Shubael Stearns and Daniel Marshall began the work of the separate or new light Baptists that would have such an impact upon Virginia. The lad's father died during his infancy, but his mother instilled in her son's mind very high moral standards. The lad abided by those rules and was known for his fine demeanor. An emptiness filled his heart, however, until age 19 when he was pointed to Jesus Christ, the only Savior of sinners. He trusted the Savior, but postponed his baptism until September 22, 1776.[1]

Mr. Watkins was filled with peace and joy and could not hold his peace. He began preaching in 1783, and he was ordained on March 19, 1786. For the first few years he supplemented his living by teaching school, but in 1790 he became a full-time traveling preacher of the Gospel. His unique style in the pulpit set him apart. He might well have been considered a bit eccentric. He never sought to amuse as he spoke with great earnestness.

Elder Watkins was known for his desire literally to owe no man any thing. He was peculiarly scrupulous in all his transactions. His testimony in this regard was always above reproach. His piety was but a reflection of his Christ-like mind. As a father of ten children, he sought to establish an environment that would point his children early to Christ. He loved the fellowship of God's children, and he was known for his godly influence that promoted sweet harmony in the churches.

It will be observed that the modern-day mission movement came into being during the early days of Elder Watkins' ministry. Many Baptist preachers looked with suspicion, and some viewed the new movement with disdain. This was particularly true of those who had imbibed strong Calvinistic tendencies and were fearful that some non-elect might respond to the Gospel. However, Elder Watkins looked upon the scene with a thrilling anticipation. He said, "The beams of truth have begun to dawn on almost every land; and the Lord is adding to the church daily such as shall be saved."[2]

God willed that Elder Watkins should live a full life of years, and he continued to labor in the ministry until just a few days prior to his home going. He preached twice on the Sunday before his death, and his last sermon was founded on the prayer of the publican, "God be merciful to me a sinner." His preaching was always with evangelistic fervor, and he anticipated an ingathering of souls such as had been experienced early in his life through the preaching of Samuel Harris and the separate Baptists in Virginia.

The Wednesday before his death, he was too weak to attend the meeting at the house of God, and the saints gathered in his home. On Thursday and Friday he grew continually weaker, and he sensed that his home-going was near. He was perfectly resigned to God's will in the matter, and a sweet assurance surrounded him as he knew he would soon be with the Lord. On the Lord's Day, July 17, 1831, the Lord's call came, and God's servant triumphantly went home. He was 76 years old.

Elder Watkins had not suffered for his faith, but he had been faithful. During the forty-eight years of his ministry, the man of God had preached more than six thousand sermons, which averages to one hundred and thirty-two messages every year. Our sovereign God does not call all of His servants to suffer, but He does call each to be faithful. May that be the epithet that marks our lives.

DLC

---

[1]James B. Taylor, *Virginia Baptist Ministers* (Richard: Yale & Wyatt, 1838), 1: 234.

[2]Ibid., 236.

March 20

Caring for God's Servants

Scripture: Hebrews 13:7,17-18

As Baptists, we treasure the truth of the autonomy of each local Baptist church. There is no human authority that supersedes spiritual decisions made by the membership of a local congregation. No political or ecclesiastical government has the jurisdiction to override spiritual choices made by local churches. Throughout the years, however, Baptist churches have voluntarily united in fellowships and associations in an effort to accomplish together what an individual congregation might not be able to perform singly.

This Day in Baptist History III

In the seventeenth century, the Abingdon Association of Baptist churches gathered in Tetsworth, England on the 20th, 21st and 22nd of the 3rd month 1657[1] to consider matters of mutual concern in the associated local churches.

One of the matters to be considered was remuneration and support of pastors in the various local churches. The minutes are of specific interest:

> It hath bene for some time sadly observed by us that there hath appeared a great neglect in the churches in taking care to provide a maintenance for the comfortable supply of a (spiritual) ministerie, according to what the rule doth require, which hath brought some to pinching povertie, run others upon desperate temptations and occasioned some to fall into sinfull disorders to the dishonour of their high and holy calling. And, we feare, made the work of the ministrie not onely uncomfortable to the teachers but unprofitable to the hearers. We shall not name particular persons now instance particular cases, supposing they cannot be unknowne unto you. Onely in generall we have this account to give you, that as the conditions of severall nearer to us which we have had some knowledge of, doth call for reliefe and assistance, so also we have lately received an account from our brother Abraham Chayer of the poore and low condition of severall brethren employed in the worke of the ministrie in the westerne churches which, although modestly and sparingly expressed by our brother yet, from what was said, we could not but gather that their want is very great. And the want of a comfortable supply for themselves and their families is a great discouragement to them in the work of the Lord and an obstruction to the propagation of the Gospell among the churches and to the world. . . .
>
> And because we find in the apostolike times the churches did hold an association together in their contributions that so it

> might be done by an equalitie and not some eased whiles others are burdened we thought it our dutie to commend it unto you and desire you to commend it to the severall churches to which you belong. . . .
>
> We shall not use many arguments to excite you to a worke [of] this nature. Onely we shall desire you would consider two things (i) your duty (ii) the necessite of the case....

I have no idea what response the individual churches of the Abingdon Association had to the request of the association members, but the problem of the pastors' financial remuneration has continued until this day. Though it is told jokingly, it is suggested that a deacon once prayed concerning his pastor in the following manner. "Lord, you keep him humble, and we'll keep him poor."

Pastors have many demands upon them. Society expects them to dress as though they were business men. They must have reliable transportation that will not fail them in visitation both to homes and hospitals. Their tools are not available on sale at the local hardware store, for their tools form an expensive library. They must be well read if they are to lead well! The pastor entertains missionaries, evangelists, and itinerant Bible teachers, and usually such expenses come from his own budget. The perks known in business are unknown in the pastorate, and even the annual cost of living that is expected today in the union shop and business office is often unknown in the ministry. By the way, a godly man is not hired; rather, he is called. I have observed that when God's people lovingly care for their pastor's financial needs, he usually reciprocates with service that is beyond cost. How is your pastor being cared for?

DLC

[1]H. Leon McBeth, *A Sourcebook For Baptist Heritage* (Nashville, TN: Broadman Press, 1990), 63.

March 21

Taxation Without Representation

Scripture: Acts 22:25-30

Had one the resources to research the subject fully, the old court records of New England would reveal the names of many Baptists who were constrained to pay taxes for the support of another denomination. Nathanael Green was ordained as the pastor of the Baptist Church in Charlton, Massachusetts on October 12, 1763. That congregation experienced many trials through the years, and at times spiritual depression was known. Yet again, great spiritual revival was experienced as well. When mention is made of the fact that Elder Green served until his death on March 21, 1791, it is apparent that the church endured the period of the Revolutionary War. The pastor is spoken of as being exemplary, "until he fell asleep in Jesus . . . ."[1] But the public court record declares that Elder Green was arrested and taken to Worcester to be imprisoned.

Why would an exemplary man be arrested and jailed? The reason is simple. The Baptist pastor objected to and refused to pay taxes for the support of the pastor of the Established state church. It is true that the man of God spent only six hours in the jail before paying his fine and being released, but the record reveals the following: "Mr. Green was arrested for ministers' rates (church taxes), and taken to Worcester to be imprisoned. By the advice of Colonel Chandler, he paid the fine and was released, after having been in custody six hours."

The constable gave the following receipt: "Leicester, February 13, 1769. This day I made distraint upon Mr. Nathanael Green's body, of Leicester, for his rate which he was rated in the year 1767, and received of said Nathanael Green, seventeen shillings, nine pence, one farthing, so much being in full for his province rate; and also of said Nathanael Green, three shillings, nine pence, one farthing, being in full for his town and county rates for the year 1767: I say, received by me. Benjamin Bond, Constable for the year 1767."

The Scriptures teach us that believers are not to go to court against brethren, but the purpose of the law is to protect citizens against unscrupulous actions. As a result, Elder Green took court action against the assessors for damages. The lower court gave judgment in his favor, and allowed him forty shillings and the costs involved in the suit. The assessors, unwilling to set a precedent that would take the power of church taxes from them, appealed to the superior court. Once again the case was won by Elder Green, and the man of God was allowed all the money he had expended in the law and all costs involved as well.

This action surely pointed up the fact that the Baptists were beginning to gain some respect in the society. Just a few years previously in 1752, the Baptists had become so desperate that they raised the money to send one of their men, Mr. John Proctor, to England to protest the actions of Massachusetts. Before leaving for England, Mr. Proctor made one last appeal to the Assembly in Boston in May 1754. He stated the case clearly, and some of the governing body desired to take the Baptist petitioner into custody. The newly appointed governor from England, Governor Shirley, convinced them otherwise, and he appointed a committee to confer with the Baptists. Though the matter was not fully resolved, the committee attempted to assuage the anguish of the Baptists, and this continued until the actual time of the Revolutionary War.

Thank God that America is the Land of the free, but our freedom has been won at great cost. It is incumbent on us to preserve our freedom for posterity that the Gospel of Jesus Christ might have free course. Thank God for heroes of the past, but let us determine to be faithful citizens for the present, that our progeny of the future might give forth the Gospel without fear or favor.

DLC

[1]Isaac Backus, *A History of New England* (Newton, MA: Backus Historical Society, 1871), 2:459-460.

March 22

Discipline's Sweet Result

Scripture: 1 Corinthians 5:1-5

Discipline is one of the apparent missing ingredients in twenty-first century Baptist churches. There are those who believe that the late twentieth century witnessed a spirit of legalism among Bible-believing Baptists, but as the pendulum usually swings from extreme to extreme, today we seem to be headed toward the awful error of license. Of course the biblical position is that of liberty. Legalism demands rules and regulations; license insists on one's rights as one does as he pleases, but liberty calls upon believers to walk responsibly before the Lord.

The early Baptist churches in America believed it was a privilege for one to be a member of the congregation, and thus the membership policed itself. While reading of the early churches in Tennessee, some interesting matters of discipline bring this whole issue into focus. The purpose of discipline was always that it might be corrective. The Sinking Creek Baptist Church was a branch of the historic Buffalo Ridge Baptist Church. Thus the deacons from Buffalo Ridge had the oversight of the Sinking Creek Church. On November 1, 1789, ". . . a brother was cited to the church for giting Drunk and Swearing and geting angry." In December following he was excluded "for giting Drunk and profain Swaring and wanting to fight." At the same meeting another man was excluded "for abscenting him Self from the Church and Refuseing to hear the Church."[1]

On April 18, 1795, a member was disciplined for "Dancing at Sundry times and places. He admitted his guilt, and was Suspended from Communion with us." In the following month he was excluded from the church for not attending the business meetings and because he "had been dancing since last meeting." Then in April of 1798 a committee was appointed to confront a prominent member "in Regard of Leting his Darter go to the Dansing School."[2]

It is well that we fully understand that discipline was not a matter of the congregation venting its anger upon individual members. Several factors were involved. Saints realized that a pure testimony was essential if the work of God was to go forward. They understood too that when public sin was allowed to become the norm, the entire level of the spirituality of the congregation would suffer. But, first and foremost, it was the desire of the congregations to restore the failing member.

In July of 1800, one of the members of Sinking Creek was declared "out of fellowship" because he was found "Gilty of fiting and intends to fite again." Another man was guilty of slandering and was excluded on March 20, 1802.

Buffalo Ridge was in one of the areas most severely impacted by the heresies of Alexander Campbell and the Church of Christ. Members were disciplined out of the church when it was discovered that they had been contaminated by those heresies.

Thankfully, many who had been enticed to believe in baptismal regeneration were returned to biblical truth by the convicting power of the Holy Spirit. Upon confessing their error to the church, they were restored with joy. The record of March 22, 1828, states that the church restored Polly Grissom to membership.[3] Surely this lady had been deceived, but when her eyes were opened to truth, she repented, returned, and was restored.

The case of church discipline at Corinth (1 Corinthians 5) resulted in restoration (2 Corinthians 2). It is well that "all things be done decently and in order," and this calls for loving discipline that leads the offending party back to full restoration and the joy of the Lord. We must not be legalists to statutes, nor should be caught up in the modern error of license to sin, but we should live in the lovely law of liberty in the Lord. This position brings freedom to do what we ought to do.

DLC

---

[1]O. W. Taylor, *Early Tennessee Baptists* (Nashville: Tennessee Baptist Convention, 1957), 212.

[2]Taylor, 213.

[3]Taylor, 218.

March 23

A Cloud Without Rain

Scripture: 2 Peter 2

In speaking of false teachers, Peter says they will be brought into bondage by what overcomes them. Many are overtaken by their own intelligence. Ironically, while many people will compromise truth for the pleasures of popularity, friendship, and love, *others* so overtaken by their own intelligence will forsake these pleasures for the sake of error! Thus did one Crawford Howell Toy who was born on this day in 1836.

Baptists must not forget Crawford Howell Toy. There are few events in history that illustrate how heart-breaking division can be even when there is not the slightest taint of personal animosities, conflicting ambitions, or private affections, but when it comes wholly from doctrinal persuasion like the account of Toy's resignation from a Southern Baptist Seminary and his move to Harvard. C. H. Toy continued in his apostasy against the powerful, natural incentives that God had so graciously provided for faithfulness, because he had become the bond slave of his own intelligence. God had provided C. H. Toy with an outstanding education, a towering intellect, intimate friendship with the leading men of God in his era, and a romance with a godly woman destined to become a missionary hero. However, Toy's life is the account of a man who will live long in the memory of Baptists as one beloved and admired, but who had submitted his soul to a powerful genius that was unrestrained by Spirit-endowed faith in the unadulterated Word of God. Consequently, Toy's genius led him away from the pure and undefiled doctrine that comes from the Scripture, away from his closest friends, and into unrecoverable apostasy. Toy would ultimately become Unitarian.

Consider the charmed and exciting life that God had given to Toy. He received a superb education at the University of Virginia and then fought valiantly for the Confederacy during the Civil War under the direct leadership of Robert E. Lee. He was wounded and captured by the Union forces and biographers tell us that he utilized his captivity as a time to study Hebrew, a language in which he would later become a foremost authority. After the war he studied in Europe, and likely it was there that he began to drink the poison of liberalism. Not only did God provide C. H. Toy with education and excitement, but Toy became well acquainted with great men and women of God. He had the blessed privilege of boarding with the great man of God, John A. Broadus. He taught, fell in love with, and ultimately became engaged to the charming and intelligent missionary heroine, Charlotte (Lottie) Moon. Surely, no one had more opportunity than did Toy to interact with godly people.

C. H. Toy was an intellectual giant. To this day it is not difficult to find articles and writings by this celebrated professor from Harvard. Yet in the zenith of his career among outstanding Bible preachers and professors he would imbibe Darwinism and shipwreck his faith. (What a sad irony that the very same Darwinism that godly Baptists steadfastly resisted in spite of the nearly overwhelming pressure of the intelligentsia is now being increasingly regarded by secular intelligentsia as simply a theory and, in fact, not science at all. God has made a fool out of Toy.)

In this day, as in Toy's day, we must not forget that the truths of God are held in the heart of man by the miracle of grace and Divine illumination. While we must encourage education, we must remember the old Baptist catechism that reminds us that the Spirit of God *only* bearing witness by and with the Scriptures in our hearts, is able fully to persuade us that the Bible is the Word of God.[1] Thus, David could say, "You have more understanding than all my teachers." And likewise, Toy's humble, former student, Lottie Moon, would prove wiser than her teacher by declining his hand in marriage for the sake of truth.[2]

One moving account of C. H. Toy's life that demonstrates a genuine love and biblical separation is the poignant event that occurred at the train station when Toy was prepared to leave Louisville for his new post at Harvard. The saintly Dr. Boyce put his left arm around Toy's shoulders, lifted his right arm out before him, and cried, "Oh, Toy, I would freely give that arm to be cut off if you could be where you were five years ago, and stay there."[3] Pray that God would give us men, educated men, that can learn, but that can also *stay*.

RPB

[1] Keach's Catechism

[2]See Volume 1, 537.

[3]L. Rush & Tom J. Nettles, *Baptists and the Bible* (Nashville: Broadman, 1999), 216.

March 24

A Premier Evangelist

Scripture: Psalm 40:8-10

Fred Brown was born to Calvin and Sarah Nations Brown in Birmingham, Alabama, on August 23, 1909, the third son among nine children. Life was not easy for the Browns, but they were a closely knit family. Those were days when, particularly in the South, the Gospel was preached faithfully in all the major denominations. It was in a protracted meeting in an old-fashioned Presbyterian church that Fred, as a seven-year-old, realized his need of salvation as he heard a message on Hell. As he put it: "Hell was so real I could smell the fumes from the pit and hear the screams of the dying; and I could see myself and the worm, and the fire there is not quenched." As a lad, Fred trusted Jesus Christ as his Savior.

As Fred matured, it was apparent that he was athletically gifted. Upon graduation from high school, Fred was offered a football scholarship at Birmingham Southern College. He refused the scholarship, opting to enter into the labor force, and he was hired as a clerk in a department store. However, the Lord of the Harvest had other plans for the youth.

As he continued to attend church services, the Lord began speaking to him about Christian service. Fred was now nineteen, and it was imperative that if he was indeed to serve the Lord, a decision would have to be made soon. In 1928 Fred surrendered to God's call to preach, and he prayed under a tree near his home, affirming his willingness to follow the Lord's leading.

Shortly thereafter, Fred entered Bob Jones College in Panama City, Florida. The college was in its infancy, but there could not have been a better school of the prophets for the young man. Dr. Bob Jones, Sr., a great evangelist, was the President. Fred's classmates each made names for themselves in the ministry of the Word of God. Among those classmates were Monroe Parker and Jimmy Johnson, both great servants of God. The "preacher boys" delighted in holding revival meetings throughout the area. It will be remembered that the Great Depression struck in 1929, and it was very difficult for the students to pay their bills, but it was a great time to learn to trust wholly in the Lord.

An interesting development took place when Fred Brown and Jimmy Johnson were placed on trial by the Methodist Church for preaching the Gospel without an official commission from the Methodist Church. They were defended in court by Bob Jones, Sr.

It was in 1934 that Fred Brown and Jimmy Johnson were invited to preach the Gospel in Ireland. They made their first evangelistic trip overseas at that time, and the blessing of God was evident. That would be the first of many such trips for Evangelist Brown, for throughout his lifetime he preached the Gospel in twenty foreign lands. Preaching was Fred's priority. He never wrote books, led tours to the Bible lands, or sold tapes. His passion was to preach the Word, and God blessed him with a unique ministry.

While in college, Fred met and fell in love with Donella Cochran. They were married on August 7, 1938, and left at once for a one-year honeymoon/evangelistic tour in Ireland. The success of their meetings was heralded abroad, and doors of evangelism began to open for Reverend Brown across America. In the sixty-one years following his college graduation, Fred preached in almost every state of the Union. Rather than seeking city-wide meetings, the man of God determined that the Lord would have him center his efforts in evangelizing through local churches. He made his home base the Highland Park Baptist Church in Chattanooga, Tennessee. In 1955, Dr. Fred Brown received the honorary doctor of divinity degree from Tennessee Temple University, and he served as an active member of the Board of Trustees of that institution. Mrs. Donella Brown was at Dr. Brown's side throughout his ministry, but during the last five years of her life, she chaired the Department of Music at the University. For many years she also coordinated the music program of Highland Park Baptist Church.

Tragically, after a three-year struggle with cancer, the Lord took Mrs. Brown home on March 24, 1983. The Lord granted Dr. Brown several additional years to serve Him, and he passed into the presence of his Lord on September 6, 1992.

DLC

March 25

A Faithful Pioneer Preacher

Scripture: Psalm 92:1-15

Jonathan Mulkey was one of the early pioneer Baptist preachers in Tennessee. Upon making one's way to the old Buffalo Ridge Cemetery near Gray, Tennessee, it is rewarding to find the burial site of this stalwart servant. A modern-day preacher feels insignificant as he pauses to realize the sacrifice of such men of sterling character. The writing incised on his tombstone in the old cemetery is still quite readable. It states, "In Memory of JONATHAN MULKEY, SEN. BORN OCT 16, 1752 - DEPARTED THIS LIFE SEP. 5, 1826, AFTER HAVING BEEN A PREACHER OF THE BAPTIST ORDER MORE THAN FIFTY YEARS."

Jonathan's father, Philip Mulkey, was a very successful preacher among the Separate Baptists in the Carolinas. Philip had been baptized by Shubal Stearns on Christmas of 1756, and led in establishing the Baptist witness in South Carolina. However, Philip had fallen into sin, and done irreparable harm to his testimony. His son, Jonathan married Miss Nancy Howard, daughter of Obadiah Howard of North Carolina. In time the couple made their way westward into Tennessee. A historian reports that Jonathan Mulkey and a companion, trying to cross the North Fork, were overtaken by the Indians. The companion was scalped and left for dead while Mulkey was slightly wounded by a bullet. Mr. Mulkey jumped into the river, swam across and made his way to Eatons. To his great surprise, he found that his scalpless companion had gone by a shorter route to the fort and was waiting for him.[1]

Jonathan Mulkey served the Buffalo Ridge Baptist Church as pastor for forty-two years, and during that same interval of time, he pastored the Sinking Creek Baptist Church for thirty-one years. On March 25, 1786, Pastor Mulkey, along with Isaac

Barton, constituted the French Broad River Baptist Church which is now the First Baptist Church of Dandridge, Tennessee. Working with William Reno, Pastor Mulkey also assisted in the founding of the Big Pigeon Baptist Church in Cocke County.

It has been pointed out that the churches where Jonathan Mulkey ministered grew in spirituality, doctrinal stability and practical service. Godliness, consecration, and spirituality seemed to characterize Jonathan Mulkey, and this spiritual maturity was caught, practiced, and exhibited by his people as well. Jonathan Mulkey was possessed of a missionary spirit, and he constantly kept the cause of missionaries before his congregations and the Holston Association, of which he served for eight terms as moderator.

An interesting insight into this pioneer Baptist preacher has been found in a manuscript of one of his relatives. It seems that when Pastor Mulkey became elderly and was crippled by disease, he trained his horse to kneel like a camel so he could mount and dismount and travel about preaching the Word of God. When he no longer could stand to preach, his congregation gave him a large armchair that sat behind a table upon which his Bible was held. Thinking of this arrangement, it is not difficult to transport ourselves in mind to the scene. We observe the elderly man of God mounting his kneeling horse and riding to the church house. Then the horse would kneel that the servant of Christ might dismount and painstakingly make his way into God's house. We see him in our mind's eye as he makes his way slowly up the aisle to the armchair behind the table. And there he opens the bread of life and feeds the church family that he loves so well. How the hearts of his people must have been stirred at such a sight.

On August 23, 1826, when Jonathan Mulkey prepared his will, he was too weak to sign his name. Rather he simply made the mark of an X. Then, on September 5, 1826, the tired, old servant of the Lord closed his eyes on earth and was gathered to his people in glory.

May we purpose in our hearts so to live that we might also have an abundant entrance into our home above.

DLC

---

[1]O. W. Taylor, *Early Tennessee Baptists* (Nashville: Tennessee Baptist Convention, 1957), 66.

March 26

A Lengthy Pastorate

Scripture: Acts 20:36-38

It is apparent that the apostle Paul's ministries were rather short, but it must be remembered that the great apostle was primarily a church planter. He spent eight months ministering in the church at Corinth, but after three years as pastor in Ephesus, many tears were shed when he left. In reading Baptist history, it is apparent that lengthy pastorates have been the most fruitful, and the stability of those churches has led to producing evangelists, missionaries and pastors.

We look today at the ministry of Joshua Brown Hutson. He was born in Pittsylvania County, Virginia to Methodist parents. Soon after Joshua's conversion, he was immersed on February 3, 1858, and it was said that he was the first Baptist in the Hutson family. He was educated in the country schools, but before he could get to college, the Civil War broke out, making additional training impossible. Following the Civil War, the Byrne Street Baptist Church in Petersburg licensed him to preach February 7, 1869. Almost two years later, the same church approved of his efforts and ordained him on December 14, 1871.

He began his ministry in a rural pastorate. During that ministry he was invited to conduct special services at the Belvidere Baptist Church in Richmond. The Belvidere church had been organized during the Civil War to minister to soldiers. Sixty-seven charter members had organized the church on May 6, 1865, but with the conclusion of the war, the congregation relocated and became known as the Pine Street Baptist Church. Reverend Hutson married Miss Leonora J. Baugh on March 26, 1874.

Soon following the special meetings, the pastor of Pine Street Church resigned and moved, and Reverend Hutson was invited to assume the pastorate. At that time the church had one hundred sixty-two members, but through the faithful ministry of Reverend Hutson, the membership grew steadily. By 1890 the membership had grown to 1,110, and by the time of his retirement there were 1,901 members. During his lengthy ministry he had baptized 2,799 people, an average of one per Sunday. He had made 50,605 pastoral calls, married 1,764 couples and conducted 2,202 funerals. He had pastored the Pine Street Baptist Church for forty-five years and six months.

When asked by a gentleman on the street how long his sermons were, he answered that on hot Sundays they were nineteen or twenty minutes, or sometimes twenty-five or twenty-seven minutes in length. He was then asked why his people had kept him so long. He reply was classic as he suggested that it was because he had kept them (his sermons) so short! At his death, the *Richmond News-Leader* said: "In some strange way Dr. Hutson learned to know each recruit to his congregation — and to know him in his home and family life. . . . In more than 500 homes in Richmond Dr. Hutson was for years a regular visitor; and of perhaps five times as many people he was an intimate counselor. . . . Although honors and titles came to him, he always remained to his flock, 'Brother Hutson.' He could not have a loftier title."[1]

The *Religious Herald* wrote: "He made no attempt at rhetorical display or display of any sort. He was content to take some theme of doctrinal or practical value or some historical or biographical incident and from it bring to his people useful and valuable lessons of warning, comfort or courage. . . . His conscience was so clear and his trust so simple that he became to his brethren a model of patience and self-command."[2]

What we have been told explains why on the fortieth anniversary of his ministry at the Pine Street Church, the congregation presented the pastor and his wife a generous gift of love. It has well been said that "A home going pastor makes church going people." May I suggest that if you are a pew-packing member, you ought to encourage the man of God who serves you, and if you are a Bible-preaching pastor, you ought to love each member of your flock who uphold you. Such a combination makes for a healthy and growing witness for Christ.

DLC

[1]George Braxton Taylor, *Virginia Baptist Ministers* (Lynchburg, VA: J. P. Bell Company, 1935), 6:118.

[2]Ibid., 119.

March 27

A Two-Fold Baptist

Scripture: 2 Timothy 4:2

The Baptists in Virginia entered into the nineteenth century with a new slate of leaders with vision that impelled them onward. Among those leaders was Pastor Edward Baptist, Sr. Along with others, he helped open the way with a gigantic thrust of home and foreign missions. This philosophy included promoting ministerial education and challenging youth to look on the fields of the world. Simultaneously, these men were determined to minister to the Indians of Virginia and to tribes that were moving westward. They realized there were multitudes in the West without evangelical preaching and the word of salvation. As a result, Baptists of Virginia were among the early supporters of the American Bible Society when it was organized in 1816. Our forefathers desired to make the circulation of the Bible a prominent part of ministry by placing a Bible in every destitute home in the state. Along with these efforts, Reverend Baptist was also elected to a committee to initiate a program of education for the improvement of the ministry.[1] In these various roles, Pastor Edward Baptist, Sr. became one of the leading Baptist pastors of Virginia.

When God blessed Edward Sr. and his wife, Eliza, with a son, on March 27, 1828, it was only normal that the baby should be named Edward Baptist, Jr. In time the man of God also passed along his burden and philosophy to young Edward. Being reared in such an environment, young Edward trusted Christ as his Savior at an early age and was baptized by immersion, making him a Baptist by both name and conviction. When little Edward was just eight years old, the family moved to Alabama.

At about twenty-four years of age Edward, too, was ordained into the gospel ministry. He spent several years ministering in Alabama in strategic churches, where he served with honor.

In 1856 Edward, the son, returned to Virginia accepting a call to a church in Spottsylvania County. He served the rest of his life pastoring a number of churches in the same county as a circuit-riding pastor. By 1893 his unusual pastorate involved four churches. They were Goshen with a membership of 76; Mine Road, with 142; Mount Hermon, with 126; and Rhoadesville, with 129. On Saturday before the first Sunday of the month and on the first Sunday of the month, he preached at Mount Hermon. On the second Sunday and the Saturday preceding it, he ministered at Mine Road Church. On the third Sunday he spoke at Goshen and the fourth Sunday at Rhoadesville. Once every quarter he would minister on Saturday before the fourth Sunday at Rhoadesville. The total membership was 473. During 1893, he baptized fifty-eight converts into the fellowship of the four churches. Certainly he was faithful in season and out of season and enjoyed a most unusual ministry.

During many physical problems, Reverend Baptist was ministered to in his own home by family members. On January 29, 1896, he departed this world and entered into the presence of our Lord Jesus Christ. The following is taken from his obituary written by Dr. L. J. Haley: "Elder Baptist was a man of stern and upright religious and moral character. He was a true and unselfish friend, kind and gentle in his family, a friend and generous neighbor, a loyal and patriotic citizen, an able and eloquent preacher of the gospel, a faithful and loving pastor, and a man and Christian, who in all the relations and responsibilities of life earnestly and conscientiously strove to do his duty and to make himself useful and helpful to his fellow-man. He was a man of extraordinary power and ability in the pulpit. I think I can truthfully say that some of the finest specimens of pulpit oratory I ever listened to came from the lips of E. G. Baptist."[2]

Are we Baptists by conviction, as was Pastor Baptist, or are we Baptists in name and perhaps by convenience? May we determine to live faithfully for God in season and out of season to glorify Him.

EGC

[1]William Latane Lumpkin, *The Portsmouth Baptist Association, 1791-1991*, (Clawrenceville, VA: Edmonds Printing Company, 1991), 28

[2]George Braxton Taylor, *Virginia Baptist Ministers, Volume Four*, (Lynchburg, VA: J. P. Bell Company, 1913), 291

March 28

Honey, Listen to Daddy

Scripture: 1 Kings 2:1-3

If you knew you were going to die a death of martyrdom, what legacy of words would you leave to your only daughter who was still very young? We shall discover what one of our forefathers wrote in this historical devotional. But first, let me paint the verbal background. Jan Wouters van Kuijck was in Dordrecht, Holland at the time of his apprehension. He had been moving family from place to place in his effort to avoid arrest, for he was considered a heretic for his belief that salvation was a personal matter of faith in the Lord Jesus Christ alone. Perhaps someone had served as an informer, but somehow the bailiff learned where Jan was residing and he and his men came to arrest him. The bailiff hammered on the door, and Jan realized that his flight would merely end in the capture of his entire family. Thus when he met the bailiff at the door and was asked, "Does Jan van Kuijck live here?" he replied in a booming voice that he was their man. Of course, he took that action to enable his wife and children the opportunity to flee. Fortunately she and the children successfully escaped. Jan was tortured and scourged in the prison. Finally he was burned at the stake for his faith on March 28, 1572.

During his imprisonment, Jan wrote a dozen letters that have been preserved. Eleven were written to family and friends and smuggled from the prison. The twelfth was written to his captors presenting clearly an account of his faith and a warning to them of judgment. He concluded that letter with this classic statement: "I confess one Lord, one faith, one God, one Father of all, who is above all, and in all believers. I believe only what the holy Scriptures say, and not what men say."[1]

Fearing his testimony, Jan's mouth was gagged before he was taken to the place of execution. Somehow he managed to get rid of the gag. A fellow believer managed to press close to him on the way to the stake and urged Jan to bravery. At that, Jan pulled open his shirt and showed him his body bloody from the scourging, and said, "I already bear in my body the marks of the Lord Jesus." As the fire was kindled he looked over those assembled and cried, "Adieu and farewell, my dear brethren and sisters, I herewith commend you to the Lord, to the Lord Who shed His blood for us."

What a hero! But what about his instruction to his young daughter? He wrote as follows: When you come to years of understanding "Diligently search . . . the holy Scriptures and you will find that we must follow Christ Jesus and obey Him unto the end; and you will also truly find the little flock who follow Christ. And this is the sign: They lead a penitent life; they avoid that which is evil, and delight in doing what is good; they hunger and thirst after righteousness; they are not conformed to the world; they crucify their sinful flesh more and more every day, to die unto sin which wars in their members; they strive and seek after that which is honest and of good report; they do evil to no one; they pray for their enemies; . . . their words are yea that is yea, and nay that is nay; their word is their seal; they are sorry that they do not constantly live more holily, for which reason they often sigh and weep. Let not this however be the only sign by which you may know who follows Christ; but [they are] also these, namely who bear the cross of Christ, for He says: 'If any man will come after me, let him deny himself, and take up his cross, and follow me' (Luke 9:23)."

As I read that verbal description given by Jan to his young daughter of the true followers of Christ, I ask myself, "Could she recognize me as a follower of the Lamb?" And, "Would my church home fit that description?" May we determine to live faithfully in prosperity even as our forefathers did in persecution.

DLC

---

[1]John Christian Wenger, *Even Unto Death* (Richmond, VA: John Knox Press, 1961), 99.

March 29

A Reminder of Past Blessings

Scripture: Proverbs 22:28

While ministering recently in Nova Scotia and New Brunswick, I was disheartened to see many empty church buildings, places where once the Gospel was preached. While talking with some believers, I was given an autobiographical sketch by Isaiah Wallace, a man whom God greatly used in that very area in days gone by. The material had been printed in *The Christian Messenger* of March 29, 1871.

Isaiah Wallace was born in Hopewell, New Brunswick, on January 17, 1797, the first-born child of James and Catharine Wallace. Early in life he trusted the Lord Jesus Christ as his Savior, and publicly declared that fact in baptism. As he arrived at the age of maturity, God the Holy Spirit burdened him to preach, and he exercised his gifts in public as opportunity offered. During the course of his ministry he served in various capacities as pastor, agent for the Baptist college at Acadia, and as evangelist. Everywhere he ministered he experienced the hand of the Lord upon him, and the Baptist work greatly expanded throughout both Nova Scotia and New Brunswick.

In reading his account of the Lord's dealing in his life, I could not help but pause to pray that the Lord would once again awaken that physically beautiful but spiritually destitute portion of North America.

Along Reverend Wallace's pathway there were many interesting anecdotes, but room allows for only two. As he ministered in New Harbour, Seal Harbour, and Tor Bay, he reported the following day's work: "My last Lord's Day, during this tour, was a busy and eventful one. I began the day at Isaac's Harbour with a baptism, followed by a sermon, the giving of the hand of fellowship, the observance of the Lord's Supper, and an affectionate farewell. After taking a hasty meal we got into a whaleboat and started for Seal Harbour, and there in the afternoon went through exactly the same process. At the close of the afternoon service we found the wind blowing a gale, so that it was impossible to proceed to my next appointment at New Harbour, eight miles distant, by whaler, and as there was then no carriage road I was compelled to walk there. On reaching New Harbour I found the people assembled in large numbers in their place of worship waiting anxiously for my arrival. After a few minutes rest I proceeded to baptize the six candidates in readiness and then preached, gave the hand of fellowship, observed the Lord's Supper, said farewell, and then proceeded to cross the river to my lodgings at 11 o'clock at night, pretty well tired out. That was indeed a busy and eventful day. In company with Deacon Cunningham I proceeded the next day to Guysborough, and then to New Glasgow."[1]

Often in his evangelistic crusades, Reverend Wallace preached three times a day, and multitudes were saved. When possible, he insisted on having the local area pastors baptize the converts soon after their conversion.

At another time while ministering in the northern portions of New Brunswick, his meetings resulted in the establishing of the Campbellton Baptist Church. A lady of high social standing requested baptism.

She had belonged to another communion and her friends advised her to pause, as she would surely endanger her health by going into the water. They also remonstrated with her husband, and intimated that he should prevent his wife taking a step that would imperil her life. Whereupon the husband came to me to ask if I knew of any, whom I had baptized, taking cold in their baptism, and I answered "No," and then he continued, "Did you ever hear of anyone taking cold in their baptism?" and I answered, "Yes – Reverend T. S. Harding told me that he had baptized a thousand people and he never knew of but one taking cold, and she was a hypocrite." "All right," said the husband, "My wife is no hypocrite," and she joyfully made her profession without the slightest bodily harm.[2]

God is no respecter of persons. Let us pray that Nova Scotia and New Brunswick shall again know the power of God and that darkened churches may be revived and become again the light of the world in Canada.

DLC

[1]Isaiah Wallace, *Autobiographical Skeetch - Reminiscences of Revival Work* (Halifax, NS: Press of John Burgoyne, n.d.), 31.

[2]Ibid., 343-35.

March 30

Down and Out or Up and At Em?

Scripture: Psalm 111

Discouragement is one of Satan's chief tools in defeating God's servants. I must admit that there have been times when the words of Brewster Higley's familiar song, *Home on the Range* (1873) were most appealing to me. The words of that relaxing western song follow:

Oh, give me a home where the buffalo roam,
Where the deer and the antelope play,
Where seldom is heard a discouraging word
And the skies are not cloudy all day.

That third line is so inviting. ***Where seldom is heard a discouraging word*** . . . . Every preacher knows the sickening disappointment of an apparent failure in the pulpit, a snide remark by a member, or a bit of ridicule from the world. But we must ever remind ourselves that failure is only experienced when we do not rise from despair, yield to the Holy Spirit and realize that we are only the messenger, and our disappointment is often God's appointment.

I could not but realize this as I read an account of a missionary report from Rev. A. B. Earle in the state of New York in 1838. The account is as follows. He has ". . . labored faithfully for two years as missionary pastor at Mohawk, Auriesville, Fultonville, Fonda, and vicinity; at the close, he says, 'I do not know of but one person that has given evidence of a new birth since I began my missionary labors.'"[1]

Surely that missionary, Rev. A. B. Earle must have felt down trodden. Was it really worth it all? Could he have missed the will of God? Did the Lord have something else in mind for His servant? I am sure I might have responded that way. But then the reporter/author continued by saying, "And yet afterward this man became a noted evangelist, and was instrumental in bringing thousands to confess Christ as their Savior."[2]

You can imagine my pleasure when I read for the first time an up-date on the life of Rev. A. E. Earle. I am delighted to share the account with you from a blessed volume of my dear friend, Reverend James Beller. He writes, "Absolom Backus Earle was born in 1812 in Charlton, New York. He was converted at the age of 16 and began preaching the Gospel at age 18. He was ordained at Amsterdam, New York when he was 21. He pastored at Amsterdam for five years, and then resigned to enter the field of evangelism. For 58 years he held revivals, city-wide campaigns, and protracted meetings in every state of the Union and Canada. It is estimated he conducted nearly 1,000 protracted meetings, and traveled over 350,000 miles. He had nearly 160,000 conversions, and 400 called to the Gospel ministry. Earle also was the author of several books. He died at Newton, Massachusetts, on March 30, 1895, at the age of 83."[3]

It is wonderful to know that the Lord can take His children out from a pit of despair and elevate them to a place of prominence. However, we must understand that it is God's glory that is most important in the light of eternity. Whether the Master Craftsman opts to use us as a vessel of honor or as a lowly vessel of service, all that really matters is our faithfulness. Once we have done our best in prayerful and studious preparation, and when we have labored that our delivery shall be as sharp as possible, we must be pleased to rest in the Lord, just thankful that we are privileged to be servants of the most High God. When we can assume that position in honesty, discouragement is minimized and the joy of the Lord becomes our portion.

Let me urge you to pray for God's messenger whom you call Pastor. Encourage him lest Satan gain an advantage through discouragement.

DLC

[1]Charles Wesley Brooks, *A Century of Missions in The Empire State* (Philadelphia: American Baptist Publication Society, 1909), 129.

[2]Ibid., 129.

[3]James R. Beller, *America In Crimson Red* (Arnold, MO: Prairie Fire Press, 2004), 425.

March 31

Women in the Church

Scripture: 1 Corinthians 11:1-16

Women have always been a significant part of God's work, both in the Old Testament and in the New Testament church's work and ministry. In the Old Testament, we find women like Deborah, Esther, Ruth, and others whom God used in mighty ways. In the days of Christ, a number of women were active among His disciples. Throughout the early days of the church, as recorded in the Book of Acts, many women were busy servants in the ministries of these early churches; women like Priscilla, Phoebe, and others. There is no evidence of women pastors or leaders in the New Testament, and those who would contend for the validity of women in places of leadership are arguing a position contrary to the New Testament. Nevertheless, the church would be much poorer without the influence and work of her women.

Early in the history of the Philadelphia churches, the women of those churches apparently were not involved in the business meetings. The minutes of the church meetings include the names of the men who were present at each business meeting, but no ladies are mentioned as attending. On March 13, 1764, a new phase of church polity was introduced to the churches of Philadelphia. On that date, on behalf of some of the sisters, the following question was propounded: "Whether women have a right to vote in church affairs?" On March 31, an answer was returned, with due honor to the sisters, as follows: "That the rights of Christians are not subject to our determinations, nor to the determinations of any church or state upon earth. We could easily answer that, in civil affairs, they have no such right; but whether they have or have not in the church, can only be determined by the Gospel, to which we refer them. But, if, upon inquiry, no such grant of right can be found in the Gospel, and if voting shall appear to be a mere custom, we see no necessity for breaking it except the custom should, at any time, be stretched to subvert the subordination which the Gospel hath established in all the churches of the saints: "I suffer not a woman to usurp authority, but command that she be in subjection, as also saith the law" (1 Timothy 2:11-12; 1 Corinthians 14:34-35). Nor do we know that this church, or any of us, have done anything to deprive the sisters of such a practice, be it a right, or be it a custom only, except a neglect on a late occasion be deemed such, which we justify not. On the contrary, if the sisters do attend our meetings of business, we propose that their suffrage or disapprobation shall have their proper influence; and, in case they do not attend statedly, we purpose to invite them when anything is to be transacted which touches the interest of their souls."[1]

The argument was scriptural, not political. The churches recognized that in the political affairs of their day, women were not allowed to vote, but in the church secular standards held no weight. They recognized that the women had been, by neglect and not by design, deprived of their right to vote. They quickly and humbly recognized their error and declared their willingness to include the women in the vote of the church. This message was transmitted to the women, and on May 5, a communication was received from the women in reply, and it was decided that the sisters should have and exercise their right to vote.[2]

There is no specific teaching in the church on whether or not women should have the privilege of the vote. Some interpret 1 Corinthians 14:34 as a prohibition against women speaking in any way in the church. The churches in Philadelphia viewed this interpretation to be unacceptable. There being no denial of the vote for women in the New Testament, the Philadelphia churches decided in favor of the women. They recognized that the priesthood of the believer extended to all believers, whether they be men or women.

LRO

[1] David Spencer, *Early Baptists of Philadelphia* (Philadelphia: William Syckelmoore, 1877), 93

[2]Ibid., 94.

April 1

Great Advice!

Scripture: Ephesians 4:29-32

Dr. Henry H. Savage, who pastored the First Baptist Church of Pontiac, Michigan, for thirty-eight years, was considered by many to be a "pastor's pastor." Henry Savage was an engineer when God called him to preach. He had earned his Master's Degree at the University of Colorado in 1910, but when the Lord called him, he enrolled in and completed the one-year Bible course at Moody Bible Institute in Chicago. From Chicago he went to northern Wisconsin and pastored the Baptist church in Barren. While serving in Wisconsin the bachelor-preacher met and married a church organist, Miss Bessie Jensen. From Barren, Pastor Savage moved to Baraboo, Wisconsin, to assume the pastorate there. It was from Baraboo that Pastor Savage was called in 1924 to pastor the First Baptist Church of Pontiac, Michigan.

His practical, innovative ministry transformed First Baptist Church into a leading fundamental citadel of the North. The church experienced continued growth under his ministry. On March 2, 1926, a radio ministry was begun, and the morning worship services were broadcast over the 50,000-watt radio station, WJR. Soon after, a second regular radio ministry was introduced. It was known as the "Happy Half Hour of Heaven and Home." The program's popularity was revealed as up to 500 letters were received weekly in the church office in response.

In 1937 Pastor Savage led in purchasing the Lake Harbor Conference Grounds near Muskegon, Michigan, for summer conferences. The conference center became known as Maranatha Bible and Missionary Conference. It was on that very conference grounds that this writer was regenerated in August of 1945.

Being a man of vision, Pastor Savage reached throughout the Pontiac area and planted twenty Sunday schools. The pastor encouraged his members who lived in those neighborhoods to help in the Sunday schools nearest them, and twelve independent churches came into being in the Pontiac area as a result of that effort.

The attendance of First Baptist continued to swell, and on April 1, 1950, construction began on a lovely new edifice to adequately house the congregation. Just over a year later the new building was dedicated, and became the hub of ministries around the world. Dr. Savage led the congregation in a missionary vision, and all three of his children ended up serving the Lord in South America. During Dr. Savage's ministry at First Baptist Church one hundred and twenty left the church to enter into full-time ministries around the world.

Dr. Savage's ministry extended to serving as a professor in a local Bible college and in being a regular speaker in pastors' conferences. One of the greatest lessons ever taught the present writer was learned in such a pastor's conference. About sixty pastors had gathered for fellowship and challenge in the early 1960s. As Dr. Savage closed one of his speaking sessions, he opened the meeting for questions. As a young preacher I asked: "Dr. Savage. How is it that you have had three children, and all of them have ended up on the mission field?" The man of God was getting up in years, and he smiled and reflected, and then he answered. "Brother Cummins, years ago Bessie and I decided we would never talk of church problems before our children. They would grow up thinking that First Baptist Church was perfect. We would never complain of members or talk of problems in their presence." Then he paused. Finally, with a smile, he concluded by saying: "And you know, they had already graduated from Bible college and were on the way to the mission field before they found out otherwise."

I scurried home and told my wife what I had learned. I pledged to her that rather than being a griping father-pastor who shared his problems before his children, I would follow Dr. Savage's plan. How I thank the Lord for that little bit of advice that proved to be a blessing in my life as well.

Dr. Savage died of cancer in 1967. His funeral was conduced on December 5, 1967, and the filled house of God spoke volumes of God's faithful servant.

Pastor, if you are reading this devotional page, let me urge you to follow Dr. Savage's advice. It will do wonders in your home, and it may well be blessed of God in producing ministers or missionaries from your offspring.

DLC

April 2

An Amazing Missionary

Scripture: Matthew 18:6

Though in volume one of this set (February 11; October 12) I have mentioned the life and ministry of Isaac McCoy, in recently reading his intriguing volume, *History of Baptist Indian Missions*, I have felt constrained to revisit the sacrificial life of that great hero of the faith. With his wife and seven small children, Isaac McCoy entered the wilderness that he might preach Christ to the American Indians. Isaac and Christiana had thirteen children in all, and they raised their family in the most primitive conditions. The privations that the family suffered were almost beyond description. Isaac refused to arm himself, even though from time to time his life was threatened. The Triennial Board failed to support him as they promised, and yet he persevered trial after trial to the glory of our Savior.

As I read of his traveling experiences, I was somehow caught up in the very scene. For instance, he wrote: "On the 1st of April we left Thomas (a mission station), to return to Carey (yet another mission station). In a storm, our horses attempted to escape from camp, and occasioned an unpleasant jaunt in the night to recover them. On the following night, they caused us to make another brief nocturnal tour in the woods, at a time when repose would have been more acceptable."[1] Isaac McCoy lived many times without food, shelter, or rest!

Amidst all the trials the man of God faced, one's heart is crushed when reading the account of the attempted murder of his nine-year-old daughter. He wrote,

> When about five miles from home, I received the distressing intelligence that, two days before, a Potawatomi Indian had almost murdered one of our little daughters, about nine years of age. She and two of our Indian girls, larger than she, went on an errand about two hundred yards from the house, and the greater part of the way in full view of the

house, when three Indians appeared at a little distance from them, one of whom made toward the largest Indian girl. The children fled for their lives. Our daughter being the least, and being more affected by fright than the others, and accidentally falling as she ascended the river bank, was left in the rear, and fell into the hands of the savage. He choked her until she was on the point of expiring. The Indian girls alarmed the family. Her distressed mother, and many others, hastened to her relief. Mr. Edmund Liston, a young man hired to labor, and Mungosa, one of our Miamie lads, first reached the place of our horrid scene, which was just as the child apparently was struggling in the agonies of death, and still in the grasp of the monster. He fled, and they pursued him, while the other two Indians followed close in their rear. Liston soon overtook him, and knocked him down with a club, and beat him severely. Mungosa, on coming up, drew his knife, and would have dispatched him, but was prevented by Liston.

The mother, and many others of the family, reached the child before she could breathe. The blood was issuing from her neck, mouth and nose, with a considerable quantity of sand and earth in her mouth. The feelings of her mother can be more easily conceived than described. The design of the Indian was of the basest kind, but happily the child was not injured beyond what we mention in this place. Her neck was gashed with the monster's nails, and her lungs were injured by violent exertion for breath. Her eyes and face soon swelled frightfully. But she recovered.[2]

As I read those words, I could not question how dedicated I might be to the cause of giving the Indians the Gospel. But Isaac and Christiana were completely sold out to Christ, and remain they did. In 1824 Isaac's plan for Indian relocation to the West was tentatively accepted by the United States Secretary of War, and in 1830 the plan was ultimately approved by the Congress.

The volume mentioned above is available from the Particular Baptist Press at 2766 W. FR 178, Springfield, Missouri, 65810. Let me urge families to secure a copy and read it in devotions. It will strengthen the missionary fervor of those who carefully and prayerfully read it.

DLC

---

[1]Isaac McCoy, *History of Baptist Indian Missions*, (Springfield, MO: Particular Baptist Press, 2003), 329-330.

[2]McCoy, 125-126.

April 3

Born A Yankee - Raised A Mohawk

Scripture: Psalm 112:1-4

I am overwhelmed when I consider the productivity and power of the old Separatist Baptist preachers. Few of their number had the privilege of a solid education, but they were used of God in miraculous ways. Such a man was Abraham Marshall who was born to Daniel and Martha Marshall in Windsor, Connecticut, on April 23, 1748. Abraham was an infant when his parents undertook to minister among the Mohawk Indians. He was only seven when his parents moved to Sandy Creek, North Carolina, in 1755. This accounts for the fact that the lad had only forty days of formal education. His father, Daniel, in an itinerant ministry, founded churches throughout the Carolinas and Virginia. In 1771 Daniel became the premier Baptist pastor in Georgia, where he served for thirteen years. Until his death he continued establishing churches and training a multitude of young men who saturated the area with Baptist witnesses.

Soon after Daniel's death, Abraham became pastor of the Kiokee Baptist Church. Though having limited formal training, Abraham was blessed of God with a keen mind. His diary reveals an amazing grasp of the English language. He was also gifted with a voice that compelled folk to listen. When some lack of social grace became apparent to Abraham, he would often feign to apologize by saying, "I was born a Yankee, and raised a Mohawk."[1] The truth, however, is that Abraham Marshall was a most balanced pastor. He dearly loved his people, and, according to his contemporaries, he possessed an intuitive understanding of human nature that allowed him to minister to their needs. His sense of humor was winsome, and he was dearly loved, in turn, by his congregation. This accounts for the fact that, though he surrendered members to assist in planting churches, the membership of the Kiokee flock grew consistently, making two building programs necessary during his tenure of service. Abraham's son, Jabez, claimed that Abraham baptized, married, and buried about six thousand people. Judge C. C. Pittman of Cartersville, Georgia, opined in the *Augusta* (Ga.) *Chronicle*, that Abraham led in the organization of thirty-nine churches.[2] Along with his pastoral abilities, Abraham Marshall was a unique evangelist. However, the account is best given in the light of this amazing fact: Abraham Marshall served as a bachelor-pastor during the first seven years of his ministry at Kiokee!

Soon after becoming pastor, Abraham mounted his horse and rode 1100 miles back to Connecticut to care for his deceased father's business. During that journey he preached at every opportunity, and the trip produced great spiritual fruit. Conversions on the trip were counted in the hundreds, and as he returned homeward, he was greeted by many converts with tears and expressions of joy. His audiences ranged up to 3500, and he addressed 1500 at the State house in Connecticut. The crowds were such that on one occasion as he arose to speak in Simsbury, the galleries collapsed. Fortunately no one was injured. Undaunted, Abraham went into the fields, mounted a wagon, "lifted up his voice like a trumpet, and sounded the alarm in God's holy mount."[3]

In 1792 our bachelor-pastor set out again for Connecticut, but this time he was determined to seek for a wife. Led of the Holy Spirit, Abraham stopped in Virginia at the home of John Waller, Separatist Baptist preacher of note. It was love at first sight as Abraham met Ann Waller. Abraham was early into his journey, but he determined to stop on his return trip and propose marriage to the lovely lady. Thus on April 3 he fell to his knees to propose, and on that very evening, they were wed. Soon thereafter the couple mounted their steeds for a honeymoon of 500 miles back to Kiokee.

Ann served admirably as the first lady of Kiokee until her death on November 14, 1815. Abraham continued on in his ministry until his call upward came on August 15, 1819. Their son Jabez was called as pastor, and faithfully ministered as until his home-going in 1832. Let us thank God for faithful men as we realize it is not education but dedication that often makes the difference.

DLC

[1]Robert G. Gardner, *A History of the Georgia Baptist Association* (Atlanta, GA: Baptist Historical Society, 1988), 93.

[2]James Donovan Mosteller, *A History of the Kiokee Baptist Church in Georgia* (Ann Arbor, MI: Edwards Brothers, Inc., 1952), 149.

[3]Ibid., 154.

April 4

A Breach of Promise

Scripture: 1 Corinthians 6:1-5

In the early days of our Republic, church membership was of great importance. Local churches provided fellowship, and they influenced the moral fiber of entire communities. An interesting illustration is found in a case of a charge of "breach of promise." The matter was adjudicated by a combined committee of the Bethel Baptist and French Broad Baptist Churches in Tennessee. The case involved the honor of two sister churches, and the combined committee served as judge and jury, ultimately rendering a verdict that could not be appealed.

A brother of the French Broad Church had a daughter who was "courted" by a member of the Bethel Church. The suitor visited the family often, and paid particular attention to the daughter in question. The girl's parents encouraged the arrangement. The courtship went along smoothly for some time, but finally it came to a standstill, and was then broken off. The father of the young lady approached the membership of the Bethel Church with his complaints.

With due deliberation, Bethel "agreed on a plan," which was consented to by the father and the supposed suitor. The matter was referred to a committee of six brethren (each church selecting three). A date was set for the hearing and for the deliberation. Both congregations agreed that the "action of the committee shall be final."

Following the meeting, the report of the joint committee was recorded as follows:

State of Tennessee, Jefferson County, 4th of April, 1822: We, Richard Wood, Thomas Hill, Elijah Rogers, Joseph White, Charles Kelly, and Lewis Reneau, chosen by the joint choice of Bethel and French Broad churches to hear and determine a matter of controversy subsisting between Brethren ________ and ________ having convened and taken upon ourselves the final decision of said matter in dispute: Whereupon (the distressed brother) came forward and charged Brother __________ with having for a considerable time paid addresses to one of his daughters, under forms and circumstances that authorized him and his family to believe that he intended to marry her, and having expressly solicited his daughter to give her consent to join him in the matrimonial contract, and after having obtained sufficient encouragement, both from her, himself and his family, and after so far succeeding in gaining the approbation and consent of his said daughter, himself and family, abandoning his suit and treating his said daughter, himself and family with entire inattention and contempt: To which charges so made as aforesaid to the Brother _________ was evasive in his reply, neither admitting nor denying the fact of his telling the said daughter directly and positively that it was his wish to marry her, but admitted of having for some time visited the family, paid particular attention to the daughter, talked to her about marriage, and was well treated by the family: Whereupon the accuser read a copy of a letter by him sent to the accused relative to said subject, and one sent by the accused in reply, and a third from the accuser, rejoining the said reply. After the reading of which said letters several witnesses were introduced and gave evidence against the accused. After hearing of which and having retired to consider the said charges and having considered the whole of the testimony, are of the opinion: First, That the brother bringing the charges erred in his mode of dealing with the accused, in deviating from the rules laid down in the 18th chapter of

Matthew, (we) do determine that he receive a public reproof, and that Brother Rogers deliver it. Second, We are unanimously of the opinion that the accused is guilty to the full extent of the charges exhibited against him, and for such his offence in willfully, wickedly, falsely, maliciously and deceitfully imposing himself on Brother __________, his family, and particularly on his said daughter, by pretending a wish to marry her without having any such intention, he (ought to be) and is hereby excommunicated from the fellowship of the church. Signed by the committee."[1]

It is well to read our Savior's words in Matthew 18:17.

DLC

[1]J. J. Burnett, *Sketches of Tennessee's Pioneer Baptist Preachers* (Nashville: Press of Marshall & Bruce Company, 1919), 561-562.

April 5

He Put Away Sin Once

Scripture: Hebrews 9:26

Variations among Baptists always amaze the general public. Baptists cannot be "cloned" due to several important distinctives. On a personal level, "Individual Soul Responsibility" means that every believer is responsible before the Lord. He is a priest before God. Collectively the autonomy of each local church allows for difference in local church polity. These distinctives have been blessed of God in keeping many Baptists from succumbing to the incursions of liberalism. In this entry we shall consider the amazing conversion of Benjamin Randall, founder of Freewill Baptists.

Benjamin Randall was born on February 7, 1749, and reared in New Hampshire on a small island at the entrance of the Portsmouth harbor named New Castle. His father was a sea captain, and the families were members of the Congregational church. As a lad, Benjamin seemed to possess strong religious impressions. At the age of nine he accompanied his father to sea, but the Godlessness of crews was repugnant to his nature. The youth requested apprenticeship to a sailmaker in Portsmouth, and his wish was granted. Educational opportunities were limited, but young Benjamin made the most of every opportunity. Upon reaching his twenty-first birthday, he returned to New Castle to set up an independent shop.

During 1770 George Whitefield was scheduled to preach at Portsmouth. By this time the great English evangelist had about worn out his welcome in America. The leaders of the Congregational church wearied of his insistence on a regenerate ministry, and the Godless had become more hardened against his preaching. Young Benjamin had calloused himself against attending the meetings, but somehow he seemed compelled to go. He attended, and the Holy Spirit moved mightily upon his heart. But the searching truths and stirring appeals only steeled his heart the more. It was on Friday night, the last time he went to hear Whitefield, and on the following Sunday his own minister was to preach at Portsmouth. Sunday, September 30 dawned and what a day to remember. Whitefield was called into the presence of His Lord that morning, and at noon Randall heard a stranger riding through the streets calling out in a subdued tone: "Mr. Whitefield is dead. He died in Newburyport at 6 o'clock this morning."[1]

The words struck like thunder. The young man thought, "Whitefield is now in heaven, but I am on the road to hell. He was a man of God, yet I reviled him, and spoke reproachfully of him. He taught me the way to heaven, but I regarded it not. O that I could hear his voice once again! But ah, never, no never shall I hear it again, till, in the judgment of the great day, it will be 'a swift witness' against me."

For days his agitated mind caused him great distress. The preaching of Whitefield sounded in his ears, and was often brought to his remembrance. He knew that God was just, and he must suffer the consequences for his refusal to receive God's mercy and grace. For days agony of soul gripped Mr. Randall until God brought to his mind the words of Hebrews 9:26: "But now, once in the end of the world, hath He appeared to put away sin by the sacrifice of Himself." Could it be that Christ had died for him? On October 15, 1770, God's grace won, and he put his complete trust in the finished work of Christ upon Calvary's cross.

Benjamin Randall could not remain silent, and he could not be at home with the Congregationalists. After studying passages such as John baptized in Enon, "because there was much water there," and "Jesus, when He was baptized, went up straightway out of the water," he chose to follow the Lord in believer's immersion. The Lord then burdened him to preach, but he felt inadequate. But again God's grace overwhelmed him and placed such a burden on him that he could not remain silent. As he began to preach, the blessings of heaven fell upon his ministry. He was ordained on the fifth day of April, 1780, and became one of the many whom the Lord raised up through His servant George Whitefield.

This author does not agree with all the tenets of the Freewill Baptists, but he praises the Lord for the sure mercies of his Savior and rejoices in knowing that someday he will rejoice around the Lamb's throne with Benjamin Randall.

DLC

---

[1]I. D. Stewart, *The History of the Freewill Baptists* (Dover: Freewill Baptist Printing Establishment, 1862), 1:34.

April 6

The Hammer and Sickle Against Truth

Scripture: Ezekiel 38 and 39

The persecution of Baptists in Russia has been a perpetual problem since the New Testament form of worship was introduced there. Whether opposed by the Russian Orthodox Church or the Communistic regime made little difference. Spiritual truth has been rejected by both the liturgical priesthood and the Leninist politicians. With either group in ascendancy, Gospel truth that set individuals free to follow the God of Heaven was considered a dread enemy. The Russian Orthodox Church and the civil government alternated, and at times collaborated, in the effort to restrict the spread of Baptist witness. From the time that the German Baptist, Johann Gerhard Oncken, penetrated Russia with truth until the rise of communism, persecution of Baptists has been general.

In the April 6, 1874 issue of *The Quarterly Reporter*, one reads the following excerpts in a letter addressed to Reverend Oncken:

A considerable religious awakening took place about fifteen years ago, through study of the Scriptures, in several villages in the neighborhood of Odessa, chiefly through the instrumentality of Michael Ratuschus and Alexander Kopustjan. Those who were unable to read assembled together . . . and listened with the greatest eagerness to the reading of the New Testament. The consequence was that they soon became aware of many of the errors of the Greek Church, and spread their new discovery far and wide. Having in this way attracted the attention of the Russian priesthood, they were denounced to the authorities, and a course of imprisonment, corporal punishment, and abuse of every kind was set in operation against them. These severe measures however, only had the effect of driving the people more and more from the church to which they had hitherto belonged, and of which they had been constant adherents . . . .

In the year 1866 the Bible was extensively circulated in Elizabethgrad, Lubonirke, and the surrounding district in the province of Kherson. At one place, a Russian named Ivan Kjaboschapka, bought a Testament, and a number of people were led to meet together to hear the gospel. But no sooner did this come to the knowledge of the clergy than the most stringent measures of repression were instantly set on foot. By their orders these people were severely beaten, imprisoned, and persecuted in every conceivable way. While Ivan was so cruelly flogged that the ground was covered with his blood, a priest who was looking on exclaimed, "Beat him to death: he is a son of Satan!" and told the others that they had better have taken [to] horse-stealing than to be engaged in such an affair. . . .

A great awakening took place about four years ago among the Russians in several villages in the neighborhood of Nicholaiof, also in the province of Kherson. After suffering a great deal of persecution from the priests and the authorities, a number of these people were attacked by a brutal mob while assembled at a prayer meeting on the 2nd of January,

> 1872, and were dragged to prison through the miry roads, in the presence of some of the local authorities and the priests. Five men and one woman in particular were thrown down and beaten with rods at intervals during the whole day in so cruel a way that their bodies were almost stripped of the flesh. . . . In the village of Bastanka some of the people received as many as 150 strokes of the rod. . .These sufferers ventured to address the emperor, and sent three petitions to him, in which they gave a full description of the barbarous treatment to which they had been subjected, and begged that they might be permitted to live in peace according to the dictates of God's Word; but all their efforts were in vain, no reply was received, and the meetings are still strictly prohibited. . . .[1]

Russian hatred of God's earthly people, Israel, and God's heavenly people, the saved, has assured the judgement of our Lord upon that land. It is true that communism's new approach, seeming to allow some religious freedom, has provided a brief respite to suffering saints. However, prophecy portrays the rebirth of Russia's rebellion against truth. The leaders of the land will mobilize against Jerusalem. But Messiah, Himself, shall crush that opposition. Today, however, we need to pray for our brethren who stand true to the Lord within the borders of that land so entrenched in atheism.

DLC

[1]H. Leon McBeth, *A Sourcebook for Baptist Heritage* (Nashville, TN: Broadman Press, 1990), 357.

April 7

Purifying Intimacy

Scripture: Colossians 1:19

Cornelius Tyree was born into a spiritual divided home in Amherst County, Virginia, September 14, 1814. His mother was a member of a Methodist church, while his father did not become a believer until later in life and then united with a Baptist church. In adulthood Cornelius wrote: "Among the earliest things I remember was my mother having me sprinkled by an aged Methodist preacher, who prayed that I might be 'as Cornelius of old.'" As he matured, Cornelius was led to seek the Lord. Upon trusting Christ he began to search the New Testament for light. He wrote, "The third chapter of Matthew taught me to be a Baptist. I learned there that Christ was immersed, and that he was immersed as the pattern for his people."

When God called him to preach, he entered William and Mary College and completed his training at Columbian College in Washington, D.C. While in the nation's capital, he would often attend debates in Congress, where he heard Clay, Webster, and Calhoun deliver their finest speeches. This aided him in the study and acquisition of the art of public speaking.

In September 1839, he was ordained to the ministry and did missionary work in Rockbridge County, where he established new churches and experienced the joy of having a new house of worship built.

Because he had determined to defend believer's immersion, he advertised in the local newspaper that on a given Sunday he would show that immersion was necessary to Bible Baptism and that believers only were proper subjects. Following that service the congregation voted to publish the sermon. Later he wrote a book entitled *The Living Epistle; or The Moral Power of a Religious Life* which became very popular. He also authored another interesting volume entitled *The Glorious Sufficiency of Christ.*

His love for the Lord was revealed in a diary in which he periodically made entries. One special note was from August 19, 1890. "Various things have hindered me from being as devotional of late as I might and ought to have been. I have been absorbed in preparing for and attending to the details of the recent meeting of the Valley Association and have allowed myself to lose the habit and spirit of devotion. In no sense can I afford this. Many personal and relative reasons urge me to resume the habits of devotion and, God helping me, I will attain unto and maintain a joyful and purifying intimacy with my Divine Father and Saviour."[1]

Pastor Tyree followed the Apostle Paul's admonition to Timothy: "Take heed unto thyself, and unto the doctrine; continue in them: for in doing this thou shalt both save thyself, and them that hear thee." Our need today in America is for pastors who have that same concern for their own purity and doctrinal soundness.

Pastor Tyree's faithful ministry brought many tributes of honor to the man of God. For example, Dr. W.E. Hatcher said: "Dr. Tyree was a great preacher. He was a student, and many of his sermons were works of art made in moments of his best inspiration and improved by preaching under the happiest spiritual excitement, recast from time to time so as to include all the best thought they called forth from year to year. As a revivalist he had widespread and honorable success. His sermons were short, clear as sunlight, richly evangelical, tersely and compactly constructed and admirably adapted to produce immediate effect. His voice was solemn, impressive and authoritative; his manner was full of candor and dignity; his denunciations of sin were startling and eloquent, and his exhortations were well-nigh irresistible. Thousands were led to Christ by his preaching."[2]

On Wednesday, December 23, 1891, Cornelius Tyree passed into the presence of His Lord. His funeral was conducted on Christmas morning, and it caused a uniquely different spirit in that community. Instead of the joy and celebration, a spirit of silence reigned throughout the area. A long procession followed the Christian warrior to the beautiful East Hill Cemetery. May our lives be characterized by devotional sincerity and doctrinal purity.

EGC

---

[1]George Braxton Taylor, *Virginia Baptist Ministers,* Fourth Series, (Lynchburg, VA: J. P. Bell Company, 1913), 132

[2]Ibid., 133

April 8

An Evangelistic Pastor

Scripture: Proverbs 29:1

In Fayetteville, North Carolina, on February 25, 1901, a son was born to the John Christopher Cowell family. The baby was named after his father. From his father the boy inherited a cheerful optimism. From his mother he learned gracious manners. As he grew, school was only endured, for young John was intrigued with fishing and hunting. He finished high school at age seventeen, but America was soon plunged into the First World War, and area lands were being surveyed for establishing Fort Bragg. No better surveyor's guide could be found than a youth who had spent much time hunting there. John was offered what seemed "big money" to serve in that capacity. Being too young to join the military, he could help the cause and even be paid well for it.

One job followed another, but finally an accounting position opened in a local bank. John had money in his pocket, and with the exuberance of youth, his heart was bent on pleasure. He was excellent on the dance floor or with a billiard cue in hand. At twenty-one the future looked bright. John lost interest in church, and learned the twin evils of tobacco and social drinking.

In April of 1923 the Ham-Ramsay evangelistic team erected a huge tabernacle in Fayetteville. The music was inspiring and the preaching dynamic. The meetings became the talk of the town. John was not interested, but when he broke his wrist in an accident, it was impossible to work. Time dragged, and he decided to attend the meetings one night. He returned, and was invited to join the choir. He did, but now the Holy Spirit began to convict him. On April 8, Mordecai Ham preached from Proverbs 29:1, and the Holy Spirit broke John's heart. He could hardly wait for the invitation. He was probably saved before the invitation began. John's life was transformed. He gathered old friends and gave a glorious witness of new life in Christ.

John possessed an insatiable desire to follow Christ. He revealed such zeal that Dr. Ham asked him to accompany him to work with youth. John consented, but he had an earnest desire to study God's Word formally. After assisting in campaigns in Sumpter, South Carolina, and Decatur, Alabama, Dr. Ham assisted John in attending Moody Bible Institute. He enrolled in the fall. John spent one year there, took a heavy schedule, and preached in Christian services at every opportunity. With no money to return to school, he spent the next year saturating his mind with Bible. He read the Old Testament through every three months, and the New Testament every ten days.[1] Along with extended Bible reading, John applied the study principles he had learned so well.

Beginning in 1925 and through the early days of 1937, the Lord opened many doors for evangelism. Through 1931 his meetings were in North Carolina, but then doors began to open as far west as Texas. Converts were many, and their endurance proved the reality of regeneration. John conducted over a hundred revival campaigns during that period. To read the success of John's ministry during that period is thrilling, but in the fall of 1936, John accepted an invitation for meetings in Central Baptist Church, Decatur, Alabama. The campaign was to open on the first Sunday in January, but before that time the pastor resigned the church and moved. John immediately offered to cancel, but the people, remembering him from the Ham-Ramsay meetings, called him to be their pastor. This shocked John, for he was an evangelist and had never been a pastor. It was a difficult decision, but John accepted.

The *Decatur Daily* announced his call and acceptance on February 15, 1937. John and his wife moved into the parsonage, and the next twelve years were days of heaven on earth. The services were geared to evangelism. A large campaign-type choir was formed. A radio ministry was begun that broadcast the entire morning service. The membership was trained in soul-winning, and both pastor and people were commissioned to reach the city. Pastor Cowell preached the necessity of "separated living," calling for repentance and a closer walk with the Lord.

Cowell preached extensively against both liquor and Hollywood. As a result, the adjacent counties of Limestone and Lauderdale became "dry" counties. After two years, John could say, "I don't have a deacon or a Sunday school worker or a choir member who dances, plays cards, or even attends the moving picture shows anymore."[2] The pastor gave Sunday morning services to expository preaching to nurture young Christians. He inaugurated the Radio School of the Bible, a thirty minute Bible study via radio five days a week. From time to time he brought outstanding Bible teachers – men such as Harry Rimmer, Wm. L. Pettingill, W. B. Riley, Wm. Ward Ayer, and Bob Jones, Sr. He urged his young people to attend sound Bible institutes and colleges. Twenty-three young people attended Moody Bible Institute in 1941, while another dozen studied at Bob Jones College. The pastor was assisted by Homer Britton, a graduate of Moody, and then, following him, Elmer Piper from Bob Jones College. Pastor Cowell was indeed growing a shepherd's heart as he ministered to his flock.

But then it happened. He had just closed special meetings in Birmingham, Alabama, when he suffered a severe heart attack. Six years previously he had endured such an attack, but his strength had returned, and he was able to take on a full schedule. Mother's Day of 1944 would be special, and somehow he made his way back home. His people expected him on Mother's Day, and he wanted to preach. And he did! On Monday his wife and mother-in-law insisted that he remain in bed. But about 9:30 a severe attack forced a cry from his lips. Three doctors and a nurse attended him, but all in vain. The date was May 15, 1944, and John C. Cowell, Jr. went home to be with His Lord. Greetings were sent from Ma Sunday, Mordecai Ham, Hyman Appleman, and Vance Havner.

Let us pray that God shall raise up a host of evangelist/pastors to step up and call Christians to repent and turn from our modern-day compromises.

DLC

---

[1]Walter R. Alexander, *All Out For God* (Chicago: Moody Press, 1946), 41.

[2]Ibid., 71.

April 9

A Baptist in Gomorrah

Scripture: Acts 5:29

A Baptist in Gomorrah is the appropriate title selected by James J. Kilpatrick, syndicated news columnist, as he wrote concerning the case of Benjamin Endres, Indiana State Trooper and deacon of Community Baptist Church in South Bend, Indiana. Mr. Endres had joined the Indiana State Police in November of 1991. He determined to be a good representative of the Lord of grace while he served in the field of governmental law. All went well in that effort until March of 2000 when he was assigned to work as a Gaming Commission agent at the Blue Chip Casino in Michigan City, Indiana. According to Indiana's procedures of law enforcement, such gaming agents must function in part as ombudsmen or facilitators. Among other tasks, they may be assigned full-time to investigate gamblers' complaints, certify gambling revenue, and conduct licensing investigations for the casinos and their employees. Furthermore, a gaming agent receives a bonus, which is paid directly from the gambling proceeds.

When this assignment created a dilemma for him, Deacon Endres, with a tender conscience toward His Lord, determined, in the words of Peter that he "...ought to obey God rather than men." As a believer sensitive to God's Word, Deacon Endres knew that gambling was sinful, and therefore he could not assist others in participating in such a practice. As a result of his biblically-based conviction, Officer Endres requested an alternative assignment. His legitimate request was refused by his superior officers, and when Officer Endres refused to report to the casino for duty, he was fired. The charge brought against him was insubordination!

A court case ensued under Title VII of the Civil Rights Act of 1964, which makes it unlawful to discharge any employee "because of such individual's religion." The case was heard in the District Court, and Deacon Endres won the case. However, the decision was appealed, and in the summer of 2003 the 7th U. S. Circuit Court reversed the decision and entered final judgment in favor of the State Police. Three judges of the 7th U. S. Circuit Court panel, however, dissented. Speaking for the three, Judge Kenneth F. Ripple said: "Time and time again, we profess that, in interpreting a statute, we begin with the plain wording of the statute. Unless there is an ambiguity, we apply the explicit command of Congress. No one suggests that Congress has left any doubt as to what it expects in this situation. Unfortunately, however, our current decisional behavior does not follow the course of our rhetoric. In future cases, judges, attorneys, and litigants will have to accept the reality that they must observe not what we say, but what we do."

I must agree with Judge Ripple and comment that in the majority decision of the panel of judges in the 7th U. S. Circuit Court we observe the same convoluted logic evidenced among the United States Superior Court Jurists as they refuse to observe the "original intent" of the first amendment.

Mr. Kilpatrick expressed doubt that the Supreme Court would grant a review to Officer Endres. This case places in focus the truth that our once grand Republic, which in the past offered soul liberty and religious freedom to all citizens, has been skewed to the point that Bible believing Christians are a minority to be ignored. Christianity and the Bible are not to be allowed in our schools, but, of course, we must not infuriate the followers of Islam, Buddhism, and Hinduism, and thus these religions must be presented to young minds.

If Deacon Endres' case is not heard by the Supreme Court,what will the outcome be for other sincere, born-again Christians who already serve in law enforcement agencies? Will all sincere Christian believers be disenfranchised from participation in State and local police units?

We behold again that there is a difference between an opinion and a conviction. An opinion is a view that we hold, while a conviction is that principle that holds us! It may well cost Deacon Endres because he is a man of conviction. It has cost saints through the years. It cost Joseph, Daniel, John, and Paul, but, thank God, they were "more than conquerors" through God's grace. May we determine by God's grace that we will obey God rather than men, for it will be worth it all when we see our Lord.

DLC

April 10

The Chair of Evangelism

Scripture: 2 Timothy 4:1-5

Lee Rutland Scarborough was born in Colfax, Louisiana, on July 4, 1870. He was the son of George Washington and Martha Elizabeth (Rutland) Scarborough, and grew to maturity in a pastor's ranch home in West Texas. A family altar was a regular feature in that home. Lee was the eighth of nine children. During his youth Lee's father conducted many revival meetings in brush arbors and in the open air. Lee was taught the meaning of hard labor for it was a regular part of the family life.

Lee graduated from Baylor University in 1892 with a Bachelor of Arts degree, and invested the next three years of his life selling books and teaching school in order to earn money to study law at Yale University. At Yale, where he earned his second Bachelor of Arts degree, Lee was a Phi Beta Kappa student. But during his years at Yale, the Lord burdened his heart concerning the ministry. He returned to his native state and became pastor of the First Baptist Church of Cameron in 1896, and he was in constant demand as a pastor-evangelist. He served there until 1901, and at that time accepted the call to pastor First Baptist Church of Abilene. In 1900 the pastor married Miss Neppie Warren of Abilene. Scarborough attended Southern Baptist Seminary in 1899-1900, but he returned to Abilene before obtaining a degree. In time two honorary doctorates were bestowed upon him.

In 1908, Dr. B. H. Carroll prevailed upon Lee Scarborough to join the faculty of Southwestern Baptist Theological Seminary for a unique experiment. Dr. Carroll was desirous of beginning a department of evangelism, the first ever started in a theological seminary. No one was better equipped to fulfill this desire. Dr. Lee Scarborough had an evangelist's heart, and from 1908 until his retirement in 1942, he occupied what became known as the "Chair of Fire." He shared his zeal, commitment, and expertise with more than 8,000 students throughout the years. When Dr. Carroll was called home in 1914, Dr. Scarborough was chosen as president of the seminary. He became an excellent administrator, and during his twenty-eight-year tenure established a strong financial base for the institution. However his interest lay in evangelism, and he conducted hundreds of successful evangelistic campaigns. He was always available to the students, and he built within them a love for an evangelistic ministry. He wrote fourteen books, nine of which centered on evangelism. His book, *With Christ After the Lost,* has been used of the Lord to stir the hearts of many pastors to reach the lost for Christ. We, who are fundamentalists, look with displeasure upon Dr. Scarborough's ecumenical assistance to the liberal Baptist World Alliance, but we thank God for the emphasis on evangelism that he provided. Dr. Scarborough was called home to be with his Lord on April 10, 1945.

In these days, many fundamental Baptist Bible colleges and seminaries seem to be interested in "academic excellence" even to the exclusion of evangelism. As a result, professors are sometimes chosen only because they possess degrees from accredited schools. Surely the Lord places no premium on ignorance! But there must be "balance" in the training and ministry of young men who will lead the fundamental Baptist movement into this new century. Twenty and thirty years ago the popular "seminars" for pastors' fellowships centered on evangelism. At that time, expository preaching was ridiculed. The pendulum had swung to an extreme position. But in these early days of the twenty-first century the pendulum has swung in the opposite direction. Now most such preaching conferences major on expository preaching. We do well to remind ourselves that Greek and Hebrew words have only a limited number of meanings. It is possible to go deeper and deeper and to come up dryer and dryer than ever before! May we come anew to the realization that the pastor's study of God's Word is meant to edify believers, challenging them, not merely to thrill at the exposition, but to go forth in evangelism. Information is not an end in itself, it is meant to inspire God's children to impact the world with the glorious gospel.

Pray that our Bible colleges and seminaries might major again in preparing young people to serve at home and around the world in soul-saving ministries.

DLC

April 11

Martyrs A Plenty

Scripture: 2 Corinthians 4:8-11

From the days of King Edward through the reign of King James II, it is common to find accounts of Baptist martyrs. One of the early martyrs was Mrs. Prest, whom Mr. Fox acknowledged as an Anabaptist. The last of the Baptist martyrs at the hand of British royalty was Edward Wightman, who was burned at the stake on April 11, 1612. The account of his death is found in volume one of this set.

Almost all the Baptist martyrs were accused of heresy for denying the Roman doctrine of transubstantiation. Mrs. Prest resided near Launceston, in Cornwall, and is a great case in point. A Bishop questioned her and portions of the conversation follow:

> **Bishop.** "Thou foolish woman, I hear say that thou hast spoken certain words against the most blessed sacrament . . . the body of Christ. . . Wilt thou talk of so high mysteries? Keep to thy work. . . . It is no woman-matter, to be grated about while carding and spinning. If it be as I am informed, thou art worthy to be burned."
>
> **Mrs. Prest.** "My lord, I trust your lordship will hear me speak . . . . I will rather die than (to) worship that foul idol, which, with your mass, you make a god."
>
> **Bishop.** "Dare you say that the sacrament of the altar is a foul idol"
>
> **Mrs. Prest.** "Yea, truly: there never was such an idol as your sacrament is made by your priests; and commanded to be worshiped of all men, with many fantastic fooleries. . . . Christ did command it to be eaten and drank in remembrance of his most blessed death for our redemption."
>
> **Bishop.** "Alas! poor woman, thou art deceived.

Mrs. Prest. "If you will give me leave, I will declare a reason why I will not worship the sacrament."

Bishop. ". . . Say on."

Mrs. Prest. ". . . I will lose this poor life of mine for (it)."

Bishop. "Then you will die a martyr, goodwife?"

Mrs. Prest. "Indeed: if denying to worship that *bready* god be my martyrdom, I will suffer it with all my heart."

Bishop. "Say thy mind."

Mrs. Prest. " I will demand of you, whether you can deny your own creed, which says that Christ perpetually sits at the right hand of his Father, both body and soul, till he come again? Or whether he be there as our Advocate, and intercedes for us with God his Father? If it be so, he is not here on earth in a piece of bread. If he be not here; and if he do not dwell in temples made with hands, why do we seek him here? If he did offer his body once for all, why make you a new offering? If, with one offering, he made all perfect, why do you, with a false offering, make all imperfect? If he be to be worshiped in spirit and truth, why do you worship a piece of bread? If he be eaten and drank in faith and truth, and if his flesh be not profitable to be among us, why do you say that you seek his body and flesh, and that it is profitable for the body and soul? Alas! I am a poor woman! but rather than I would do as you do, I would live no longer. I have said, sir."

Mrs. Prest's clear, lucid testimony seemed to drive the Bishop to despair. She said: "God's own body will not be so handled, nor kept in prison in boxes and cups. Let it be your god; it shall not me mine. My Saviour sits at the right hand of God, and doth pray for me."

She was imprisoned, (but) they could not change her mind or faith. At last, her persecutors having exhausted all their powers of argument to shake her constancy, but in vain, brought her before the court; and railing at her as an Anabaptist, delivered her . . . to the civil magistrate, who sent her from one prison to another, and endeavored

> to persuade her to recant. . . . She responded, "Yet with my death I am content to be a witness of Christ's death. I pray you make no more delay with me; my heart is fixed, and I will never turn to their superstitions. . . ."
>
> The sentence read, she was . . . delivered to the sheriff; and in the midst of an immense crowd of spectators was led to the place of execution, outside . . . the walls of . . . Exeter. . . . While being tied to the stake, . . . her last prayer was, "God be merciful to me, a sinner." She died, exhibiting a most noble example of faith and constancy. . . . [1]

May God give us grace to be "living sacrifices" in this twenty-first century for the glory of His Name.

DLC

---

[1]J. Newton Brown, *Memorials of Baptist Martyrs* (Philadelphia: American Baptist Publication Society, 1854), 288-296.

April 12

Baptist Camp Meetings

Scripture: Deuteronomy 23:14

Conditions on the frontier were deplorable because most settlers were determined to keep God out of their lives and to profane the Sabbath. Desperate conditions demanded a new approach to confront the problem. Credit must be given to the Presbyterians for the innovation of beginning the camp meeting movement. The first camp meeting in modern-day Christendom, according to Mr. Smith of Logan County, Kentucky, was held at Gasper River in July 1799. The preachers were James McGready, William Hodge, and William McGee, all Presbyterians. Soon Methodists joined the Presbyterians in the endeavor, but the Baptists declined. The reason for the Baptists' response was that a communion service was planned, and Baptists realized that the Lord's Table has been given to local churches to administer[1]. However, people came from as far away as one hundred miles, sleeping in their wagons or under temporary shelters formed of bed covers. Revival began, and according to the records, forty-five people were saved. Encouraged by this, camp meetings were held all over the Green River country, and a large part of Middle and East Tennessee. Emotional excesses were reported with responses such as twitching, jerking, dancing, falling, and barking. This caused further disinterest on the part of Baptists.

Once assured that such extravagances were not necessary, camp meetings became an important part of the Baptists' revivalism and evangelism for many years, but of course, the ordinances are not practiced at Baptist camp meetings. John Taylor, who lived from 1752 to April 12, 1835, was perhaps the first Baptist preacher who could be classified as a "camp meeting" preacher. Someone has said, "The camp meeting is an island of stability in an unsettled, sinful world."[2] For the most part, the procedure does not change. As preachers, singers, and attendees' age and move off the scene, others take their places. The campgrounds become a place where friends renew acquaintance in fellowship and refresh souls through the preaching of God's Word and singing of the old hymns of Zion. It is a blessed refuge from the world. People anticipate its approach with excitement, and they sigh when the last amen is said. When participants leave, their handshakes are firmer and hearts are fuller.

Much has been accomplished at camp meetings. An interesting research project would be an effort to discover how many have surrendered for God's service during the days of such intense preaching. Only eternity will reveal the numbers who have been saved, called to preach, or serve as missionaries. The Camp Meeting is a time of revival for many.

Prayer is an important player in the success of a camp meeting. Without intercessory efforts, not much would be accomplished. Before the first public prayer is offered, many petitions have already been offered to God beseeching the Lord's blessings.

Camp meetings are usually held in an informal, relaxed atmosphere reminding us of days gone by when our forefathers preached every Lord's Day in buildings without the comforts of our modern day facilities. Preachers from all corners of the country enjoy the spirit of the camp meetings when God is working. An example of a successful camp meeting is the Greer

Baptist Camp Meeting, which began in 1947 in Pelham, South Carolina, in a brush arbor with sawdust on the ground. Year after year the meeting has been held and has become an annual highlight that still exists. Many churches across America put up tents in the summer for these old-fashioned camp meetings. It is sometimes easier to get visitors to attend such an informal service than a regular church service.

It may sound "old fashioned" to many twenty-first century Christians, but there is something wholesome and blessed as saints gather in such relaxed circumstances to sing God's praises. It has been the privilege of the present author to preach in several camp meetings over the years, and what a blessing they have been! Let me urge you to seek out such an event, and let the Lord speak to your heart at such a place. Oh, may the Lord continue to allow these oasis in the summer time to continue where God's people get together for singing, preaching, fine food, and great fellowship.

DCB

---

[1]*David Bendict,* A General History of the Baptist Denomination *(Boston: Lincoln & Edmands, 1813), 2:253.*

[2]James H. Sightler, *50 years of the Greer Baptist Campmeeting.* July 4, 1997.

April 13

The First German Bible an Anabaptist Work

Scripture: 1 Corinthians 10:1-13

The first translation of the complete Bible from the original Hebrew and Greek was given to the Germans by the Anabaptists, not by Luther. "The fact is by no means yet sufficiently recognized, that the first complete Bible translation of the Reformation which we possess, namely, the so-called Worms Bible, of the year 1529, had its origin from the Baptists."[1] This first gift to Germany of the full Bible translated directly from the originals was by Ludwig Hetzer and Hans Denck, two Anabaptists who were accomplished scholars and thoroughly versed in Hebrew and Greek. Denck had received the degree of Master at the University of Basel, under and with Erasmus. Hetzer was an alumnus of Basel and also of the University of Paris. The book was published at Worms, and is hence known as the Worms Bible.

Hetzer and Denck first made and published a translation of the Prophets of the Old Testament. The introduction to their first edition of the Prophets is dated April 13, 1527. This translation was the foundation on which both the Swiss and the Lutheran translations of the Prophets were built, but without due acknowledgment. At the time of its publication, the approval of the Denck-Hetzer edition was unlimited and universal. Within three years, 13 separate editions appeared.

Even Luther, in a private letter found in his published correspondence, written on May 4, 1527, less than a month after the Prophets was published, wrote: "The Worms translation of the Prophets is not to be despised. The authors have shown industry; yet no one can accomplish everything. All the late reviews I have been able to see give to the work unlimited praise." This was Luther's private opinion of the work; but he was a relentless enemy of the Anabaptists and was in full sympathy with their persecution. Therefore, for the public he wrote: "I hold that no false prophet and factious spirit can truly translate, as appears clearly in the translations of the Prophets, done at Worms."[2] Nevertheless Luther, in his translation, used liberally the Worms translation, many passages agreeing word-for-word.

In 1529 Protestants in Zurich published a translation of the Prophets. In their introduction, they denounced the Worms translation in the harshest terms, not based on its merit or demerit, but solely because it emanated from the Baptists. They said: "Who is there who would not be shocked and horrified by the translation that has been issued by those who are the ringleaders of the sect and rabble that causes us to-day more trouble than the papacy ever has."

After the publication of the Prophets, Hetzer and Denck completed the translation of the whole Bible. In the meantime, Luther was working at his translation of the Old Testament and used in it expressions and sentences taken word for word from the Worms Bible.

The Anabaptists were suffering under a merciless persecution by Catholics, Lutherans, and Reformers alike. Denck, suffering with tuberculosis and under a decree of banishment and outlawry, died in hiding in Basel, in 1529, a little before the complete Bible came from the press. Hetzer was arrested, condemned as a heretic, and beheaded the same year at Constance. Everything emanating from the Anabaptists was under the ban. Every possible effort was made to suppress this "heretic bible." Printing offices, places where the book was for sale, private houses, and individuals were searched, and all copies found were destroyed. As of the early 20th century, only three known copies had survived. One copy in the New York Public Library is of the first edition, a folio volume, heavily bound, printed in old German black-faced letter.

Luther's translation of the New Testament appeared in 1522; his translation of the Old Testament and the complete Bible appeared first in 1534. The Worms Bible was published in 1529. Thus the full Bible was put into German by the Baptists five years before Luther's Bible appeared.

LRO

---

[1] Ludwig Keller, The Reformation and the Older Reform Parties, 432. Quoted in J. W. Porter, The World's Debt to the Baptists (Louisville: Baptist Book Concern, 1914), 139.

[2] Porter, 139a.

April 14

That Annual Fateful Day

Scripture: 2 Corinthians 9:6-11

Today is a fearful, frightening, fateful day to many Americans. They look upon this day as "Income Tax Report deadline eve!" It is not necessary to remind many Americans of the date, for hosts have been dreading the arrival of the morrow for several weeks. April 15 is perhaps the most unpopular day of the year! Accountants and tax consultants have been working around the clock, and post offices will remain open tomorrow until midnight to accommodate lethargic citizens who must get their tax reports postmarked before the deadline. Many genuine Bible-believing Christians are part of the number who face the urgency of the moment.

It surely is well that those who profess Christ set a faithful pattern in the matter of stewardship. Faithful stewardship to the Lord takes much of the burden out of this season. The Bible would have us understand that every believer ought to tithe. This is a Divine principle that predated the giving of the Mosaic Law, continued under the provisions of the law, superceded the law, and exists in this dispensation of Grace. As the temple was the storehouse in the Old Testament, and saints were to take their tithes to the "storehouse," so the local church is the storehouse of God in this dispensation. Of course, real stewardship is not merely the giving of the tithe, but it begins at that point. Our National government recognizes the principle of tithing, and provides for it both in the short and long forms of income tax recording.

Over and above the tithe, every child of God ought to learn the privilege of giving love offerings. The only quotation of our Lord during the days of His incarnation that are not found in the gospel accounts, are recorded in Acts 20:35. Paul quotes the Giver of every good gift as saying, "It is more blessed to give than to receive."

The New Testament uses a human analogy namely, the steward's relationship to his master for underscoring this personal responsibility. As such, the individual believer is a steward of His Master's goods to invest them in the best interests of his Master.

Again, the Apostle Paul used an interesting analogy as he wrote the saints in the Church at Corinth. He spoke of the Law of the Harvest as he wrote in 2 Corinthians 9:6-11. Chapters 8 and 9 of 2 Corinthians both relate to the matter of stewardship. The Holy Spirit directs His servant concerning the matter of "giving" in chapter 8, and then in chapter 9, He redirects Paul to use the word "sow." The words are used interchangeably. In chapter 9 Paul explains the *Law of the Harvest* in three ways. First there is the *law of likeness*. One reaps what one sows. This principle is true physically as well as spiritually. If one sows discord or hate, he will reap a whirlwind of despair.

Secondly, Paul sets forth the *law of multiplication*. The principle in nature is clear. If one plants an apple seed, he surely does not expect to receive one apple in return. The principle would have us understand the truth that one cannot outgive God. We always reap more than we sow.

Thirdly, the Apostle would have us understand the *law of time*. One always reaps after he has sown. This is true physically as some seeds mature to harvest in sixty days and some take much longer, but it is also true spiritually. To the Galatians Paul wrote: "Be not deceived; God is not mocked for whatsoever a man soweth, that shall he also reap. . . . And let us not be weary in well doing for in due season we shall reap, if we faint not."

I trust as you look out upon April 15 you will have peace of heart and will be able to claim with a pure heart that which is deductible because of your faithful stewardship to the local church where you worship and labor. And rather than complain for having made enough that causes taxes to be needful, thank God for His abundant health and strength that has caused you to be so blessed. Let us render unto Caesar the things that are Caesar's; and unto God the things that are God's.

DLC

April 15

God's Providence in War

Scripture: Psalm 91

The Civil War was America's bloodiest conflict. It claimed the lives of two percent of the nation's population. The holocaust cost nearly 1,100,000 casualties and claimed more than 620,000 lives. The campaigning armies left destruction and total devastation in their wake. This was particularly true in the Southern states that bore the brunt of the fighting. It is estimated that the total number of wartime clashes was in excess of 10,000. Many of these were large-scale encounters that resulted in staggering losses for both sides. Engagements such as Gettysburg, Shiloh, the Wilderness, and Chickamauga are ranked among the great battles of military history. Their sites bear witness to this day of the courage and tenacity with which the Federal and Confederate soldiers fought for their beliefs.

Not only was our Republic torn asunder, but in the so-called "border states" of Tennessee and Kentucky, families were divided in their loyalties. However, in the face of such massive destruction, the God of Heaven undertook. Most present-day Americans do not realize that great evangelistic efforts were mounted during that nation-tearing war to present the Gospel to the soldiers. This was true both in the North and the South. Several intriguing volumes have been written concerning evangelism at the front lines. The books mesmerize the reader, and transport him vicariously into the camp meetings.

"But with the opening of the Civil War, an organized evangelism was set in operation and prosecuted throughout, under Dr. M. T. Sumner, the corresponding secretary of the Domestic Mission Board.... To show how thoroughly the heart of the great denomination was enlisted in this work, on the suspension of the exercises of the Southern Baptist Theological Seminary, at the outbreak of the war, much of the time of men like Boyce, Broadus, and others was devoted to the hardships of camp life, preaching to the troops, holding prayer meetings, and equaling to the full the work of evangelization.... As a result of the unprecedented movement of army evangelization, revivals in the armies were frequent, and thousands of rugged veterans were baptized in the streams of Virginia and the West.... After the close of the war, it was estimated that not less than 150,000 men were converted by this timely movement."[1]

Early in the conflict, Reverend I. T. Tichenor became chaplain of Alabama's seventeenth regiment. The commanding officer was General Thomas Watts. The chaplain became known by the men as "the fighting parson." At the Battle of Shiloh, his courage carried him suddenly into the ranks, and with his musket in hand, he rushed to the front and urged his soldiers to follow him. Later he wrote to the General as follows: "Camp Watts, Near Corinth, April 15, 1862. My Dear Friend: Enclosed I send you a copy of a petition to the Secretary of War, asking that the two flags, taken in the great battle of Shiloh by our regiment, may be transferred to Governor Shorter, to be placed in the Capitol at Montgomery."[2] To be sure, the chaplains were heroes.

But another consideration is of great importance. Born again soldiers who lost their lives in the various battles were prepared for eternity. Upon breathing their last on earth, they were ushered into the presence of the Savior. But what of the living? At the war's conclusion, Southern troops returned to their devastated homeland. As we have observed, the primary fighting had taken place in the South. Sherman's "March to the Sea" featured a burnt ground policy. Southern troops returned home to a major task of reconstruction. It would have been overwhelming apart from the fact that a large proportion of the men returned home as new-born children of God. These were empowered of God to persevere and rebuild the old South into a new South with a spiritual foundation. We thank God for over-ruling in the tragedy of war and are reminded again of the truth of Romans 8:28.

DLC

---

[1]B. F. Riley, *A Memorial History of the Baptists of Alabama* (Philadelphia: The Judson Press, 1923), 152, 154.

[2]Ibid., 153.

April 16

The Fruit of Compromise

Scripture: Genesis 19:14

The name of Dr. Peter Bainbridge should have gone down in Kentucky Baptist history as one of the distinguished leaders. Peter was saved in his youth, and baptized by Reverend Joseph Reese on December 11, 1784. His training in theology was excellent, and he was ordained six years later on April 4, 1790, by Reverend Edmund Botsford. Peter seemed to have everything! He possessed a good mind, was articulate, speaking with resonant authority. He was trained in theology and medicine, serving both as pastor and physician. With all these gifts, he married into wealth. Eleanor McIntosh was the only daughter of General Alexander McIntosh. Her father brought his wealth to America from Scotland and had been commissioned a General in the American Revolution. Eleanor was his heiress and had been reared in polished society. She was not only rich, but beautiful and talented.

After their marriage Peter practiced medicine and preached in South Carolina, Maryland, New York, and finally in Kentucky. God blessed the marriage of Peter and

Eleanor with six children who lived to maturity. Tragically Peter could not handle money, and by poor investments, he lost a large portion of Eleanor's estate. As a physician, he could amass money quite rapidly, but he never handled it well. Furthermore, though Peter doubtless loved the Lord and His Word, he did not hold firmly to standards of separation. For instance, believing that music and dancing, under prudent restraints, were not inconsistent with purity of heart, he allowed his daughters to attend dancing parties, and to dance. He was too loving to say, "No." The end was not the result he desired.

Peter was censured by the Elkhorn Association in Kentucky in 1798,[1] but far worse than that, his daughters did not follow His Lord. As old age approached, on April 16, 1819, Peter wrote the following to one of his daughters: "My dear Ruthy, I want you to get religion - an interest in the blessed Jesus. Lord! How can I bear the thought of your being left behind? O, that God would enlighten your mind, and pour His pardoning love into your soul, that we may all, at last ... meet in a better world, never to part again! ...I have just composed some verses which are enclosed. They have flowed from the affectionate feelings of a father's heart. I wish you to read them with attention, and consider them as a tribute of my warmest regard for your happiness and immortal glory.

My daughter dear, though far away,
Receive a father's tender lay,
And while you tread this earthly sod,
Seek Christ, the Lord, and peace with God.

This portion fair, my daughter dear,

Will do you good when death is near;
'Twill make you happy when you die,
To God and Christ 'twill bring you nigh.

O Though now you roam in distant clime,
Mark well the gospel's holy line,
'Twill guide you to your journey's end,
And Christ, the Lord, will be your friend.

Oh! Do make Heaven your only care,
And seek the Lord by humble prayer.
Sit down, my dear, and count the cost,
Lest your immortal soul be lost.

Oh! Fly to Christ - to Jesus fly,
And on His dying rely.
Oh! Venture now your soul to God;
Oh! Venture on redeeming blood.

This blood can cleanse from foulest stain,
Revive the dead and raise the slain;
Can joy, and love, and peace impart,
And fill with hope the mourner's heart

Now let a parent's feeling love
Invite your mind to look above,.
Above the fading joys of time,
For joys sublimed in glory's clime.

When nature fails, and life doth end,
The Lord Himself will be your friend
Then, done with sorrow, sin and pain,
With Christ, the Lord, you'll ever reign."

In our day, some well-meaning fundamental pastors have failed to hold the line on Bible standards. They have adopted the music of the world in their churches and attempted to cater to the world. These doubtless love the Lord and His Word, but they do not realize that their failure in holding to right standards will be visited upon the next generation! May God give us pastors who are willing to be as narrow minded as God's Word!

DLC

[1]J. H. Spencer, *A History of Kentucky Baptists* (Gallatin, TN: Church History Research & Archives, 1984), 2:115-116.

April 17

Honoring Our Past History and Heroes

Scripture: Genesis 35:19-20

The birth of the American Baptist Historical Society came about in 1853, and it was doubtless organized at the instigation of the famed missionary, John Mason Peck. After a devastating fire had destroyed an extensive collection of his books and memorabilia on November 18, 1852,[1] John Mason Peck personally realized the need. Having served as the famed Baptist missionary to our nation's West, Peck had written extensively, and he had obtained many precious books that would have made an unusually rich treasure trove of Baptist history. However, that horrendous fire deprived us of material that has never been replaced. On April 17, 1843, John Mason Peck was appointed as the corresponding secretary of the American Baptist Publication Society, and in the course of time he called for the establishment of a historical society where valuable historic data could be gathered and shared.

Others, too, had been advocating the establishment of such an organization. In those days Sewell S. Cutting, of the University of Rochester, edited *The Christian Review.* In the January 1851 issue of the magazine he wrote the following sobering evaluation of the lack of interest Baptists had shown concerning their heritage. "No Christian denomination has been so indifferent to its history as our own. Our fathers have been left to sleep in dishonored graves. The labors they performed—the sufferings they endured—the heroic characters they bore—have alike been forgotten. The books which, amid penury and toil, they wrote in defense of their persecuted faith, are almost wholly unknown to those who now possess the noble heritage of religious freedom and Christian truth which they bequeathed. It is time for the honor of our name, as a Christian people, that this indifference were broken up, and that we begin to study for ourselves, and to teach our children the lives and deeds of the founders and fathers of our churches. We hail therefore with delight any discussion which shall make our brethren acquainted with the early history of their own denomination, or lead them to linger in pious reverence around the graves of those who, amid obloquy and contempt, first taught the faith we cherish, and first established the institutions of religion and learning to which we are so largely indebted."

At the time of its birth, the American Baptist Historical Society was considered a branch of the Publication Society. However, within ten years the value of the preservation of historical records was recognized for its importance, and the Historical Society was separated from the Publication Society. Today the largest collection of Baptist historic materials in the world exists in the facility of the Historic Society of Rochester, New York. In conjunction with this vast collection, the Samuel Colgate Baptist Historical Collection is also available.

Having used the extensive library of the Historic Society, I am personally indebted. I surely recommend that every Baptist pastor take the time to visit the collection in Rochester. However, the first sentence of Sewall Cutting's article was not addressed properly until recent date. After mentioning our history in the words, "No Christian denomination has been so indifferent to its history as our own," he immediately mentioned the burial sites of many heroic Baptist stalwarts that had been left to the ravages of time. I am thankful for the birth of The Baptist History Preservation Society. Born through the vision of a pastor and the congregation of the Harvest Baptist Church in Rockwell, North Carolina, a firm commitment is now underway to restore gravesites and place enduring markers on many of the graves of undaunted heroes of our faith. Already many long-forgotten gravesites have been rediscovered and restored. I have been particularly gratified to be informed that this concern for such a glorious project was born as a result of reading the first two volumes of this work.

If you would care to know more about this effort, write to The Society at: 640 Rimertown Road, Rockwell, North Carolina, 28138.

DLC

---

[1]Rufus Babcock, Editor, *Memoir of John Mason Peck*: (Carbondale, IL: Southern Illinois University Press, 1965), 349.

April 18

A Teenager In Prison

Scripture: Psalm 34:4

"But he's just a kid!" Surely those words could have been said of Joseph in Egypt, or of Daniel, Shadrach, Meshach, and Abednego in Babylon. But they might also have been said of Andrei Yudintsev, teenager in the Russian gulag!

Andrei was eighteen when he and his friend, Vladimir Timchuk, were arrested during the Thanksgiving service at their Baptist church. The lads thought they might spend a short time in the local jail or be fined, but soon they discovered they were going to be "tried" and the mandatory "guilty" finding would confine them for years in prison.

In handcuffs, Andrei approached the people's court in Khartsyzsk. He observed many church members present to encourage him, but they were not allowed into the courtroom. False witnesses had been summoned, and though they disagreed among themselves, the judge accepted their witness as factual. Andrei and Vladimir realized it was the court's duty to convict and sentence them. And so it would be. They were given prison terms of three and a half years. Following a brief incarceration in the local prison, the two were transported to different prison camps. On April 18, 1982, Andrei arrived in his camp where he worked as a welder.[1] For two years, he had no Christian fellowship, but one day he was told that a fellow believer had been brought in. He rejoiced to meet Pavel Zinchenko and to discover that they had many mutual friends. The men continually encouraged each other, and it caused the burdens of prison life to be almost tolerable.

In the course of time, a third believer, Vladimir Vlasenko from Nikolaev, was also transferred into their camp. Vladimir had suffered severely for his faith in former camps, but his captors had not been able to break his spirit. Vladimir was thrilled to discover that Andrei and Pavel had a New Testament, and he read late into the nights.

The Lord granted the men a quiet room just before New Year's Day of 1985, and they used it to refresh themselves spiritually.

Surely that time was providential, for soon pressures began to mount. Pavel was sent to do hard labor, and Vladimir was punished continually for things for which he was not guilty. Andrei's New Testament was confiscated, and when he protested that the Book was not forbidden, he was committed to an isolation cell. Pavel too was given a seven-day sentence in isolation.

During the time Andrei was in isolation, Pavel and Vladimir were taken from the camp to be assigned elsewhere. This was a severe trial of faith for Andrei, but miraculously his New Testament was returned. He never discovered who had done it, but the first third of the Testament had been removed as well as the last third. Apparently, some communist jailers had confiscated those sections for their own use.

The last six months of confinement found Andrei working as a carpenter. He discovered as he became absorbed in his work, that time seemed to pass quickly.

Several days before his release from prison, Andrei's mother and a young brother visited him. For several years Andrei's father, Vasily Yudintsev, had been serving the Lord while in hiding. Mrs. Yudintsev was in tears as she reported to her son that his father had been discovered and arrested just weeks before. This was a blow to Andrei, for he had envisioned his meeting with his father upon his own release from prison, but now his father had been sentenced to seven years in bonds.

Andrei reported: "At first it might seem that this was a waste of my youth, but when it was over, nothing remained except gratitude to the Lord and gladness. David says in Psalm 33, 'For our heart shall rejoice in Him, because we have trusted in His holy name.'"

"He's just a kid?" Of Andrei we can say, he became a man, and a special kind of man, a man of God! God's ways are not our ways, and surely His ways are past finding out, but Andrei's life is a source of encouragement. May our lives prove to be benedictions too!

DLC

---

[1]George Vins, Compiler, *Let the Waters Roar* (Grand Rapids, MI: Baker Book House, 1989), 22.

April 19

"Protracted Meetings"

Scripture: 2 Chronicles 7:14

The "Great Awakening" was an amazing movement of God's Holy Spirit of which it has been written, "There are few instances in history of transformations of religious life so profound and so widespread during so short a period."[1] Though the movement was experienced primarily in New England, in the course of time, through the ministry of the Separate Baptists, the so-called "Bible Belt" in the Southern states of America was the primary benefactor. However, there is no doubt that the "Great Awakening" left its impact in Baptist churches throughout America.

As a youngster, I was raised in a congregation that believed in evangelistic campaigns that were usually denoted as "Revival meetings." At times my home church held meetings that lasted for six weeks. When I began in the ministry (in the 1950s), the usual time frame for such meetings was for fifteen days. However, even then I was asked to preach meetings that lasted three weeks. I have watched helplessly as the norm has fallen from two weeks to eight days to four days, and even to "week-end" revivals. I cannot help thinking that Baptists in America are the great losers for this neglect.

There can be no doubt that one of the gifts to the church is the service of evangelists. Such men have been so used of God. Recently I was reading the history of the First Baptist Church of Cape May, New Jersey. One chapter dealt with "Revivals," and I found some statistics of interest. First Baptist Church of Cape May has never been large. Morgan Edwards reported that there were about 90 families in the congregation on April 19, 1790, "whereof 63 persons are baptized and in the communion which is here administered every other month."[2] In reading of the church, I discovered the periods of growth in that work that came during "revival meetings." The first such services were called "protracted meetings," and they were usually held during the winter months when farmhands and fishermen experienced an idle season.

This Day in Baptist History III

I believe that one of the secrets of success in these evangelist outreaches was the fact that they usually began with an appointed day for fasting and prayer. At times cottage prayer meetings were held prior to the meetings as well. In 1838 the meetings resulted in the baptism of 51 converts. In 1839, sixty-eight were baptized and united with the church. In 1849 another 29 converts were saved, baptized, and added to the church. With the infiltration of German rationalism, revivalism as such began to wane, and today it is tragic to report that many churches are pleased to merely maintain their membership.

We could well ask why such evangelism has waned. The answers surely would be many. Modernism that undercuts faith in the inerrant Word of God has had a toll. Materialism and the quest for the "American dream" on the part of many believers is certainly to be considered. Television and America's mania for sports must also be cited. We could add indifference, apathy, lethargy, and the list could continue *ad infinitum*.

What is the answer? The answer summarized in one word is "REVIVAL." If God's people are right with the Lord, they will become committed to the salvation of the lost. The time involved will become inconsequential. Plans will be changed and schedules rearranged if we truly put God first. Tragically even the Lord's Day has ceased to be a holy day and has become merely a holiday.

The answer is best found in our text of Scripture. "If My people, which are called by My name, shall humble themselves, and pray, and seek my face, and turn from their wicked ways; then will I hear from heaven, and will forgive their sin, and will heal their land." The answer is simple. The question is: are we willing to pay the price?

DLC

---

[1]A. H. Newman, *A History of the Baptist Churches in the United States* (New York: Charles Scribner's Sons, 1915), 242.

[2]Morgan Edwards, *Materials Towards A History of the Baptists* (Danielsville, GA: Heritage Papers, 1984), 1, 91.

April 20

The Danger of Extremism

Scripture: 2 Peter 1:10

For years Thomas Collier was a Particular Baptist serving as a successful evangelist/church planter in the west of England. Collier's labors were so blessed of the Lord that he was referred to as the Baptist "Apostle of the West." One faithful historian wrote: "Mr. Thomas Collier, a man of great moderation and usefulness; one who lived in those times, when preaching the gospel was attended with very severe trials.... He was imprisoned at Portsmith...."[1] Only two letters remain of his writing, and the one is dated April 20, 1646. It is apparent that at that early date, Mr. Collier became concerned about a growing emphasis he saw among Baptists that would cripple evangelism. In 1691, prior to the life of John Gill (1696-1771), Collier witnessed the tendency toward the growth of Antinomianism in England.

Though Baptists are not a "creedal" people, one must observe that our forefathers were surely a confessional people. H. Leon McBeth explains the difference. A confession *affirms* what a group of Baptists believe, whereas a creed *prescribes* what members of a group must believe. Confessions *include* while creeds *exclude*. Our Baptist forefathers were careful to emphasize that confessions were only human statements.[2] Both Particular Baptists and General Baptists provided confessions of faith.

Unfortunately there is a tendency to read Confessions of Faith with a dogmatism that springs from a hermeneutic of eisegesis. That is, the reader reads into the text what he wants it to say. For the Particular Baptist the Baptist historian Joseph Ivimey said: "such a system tended to lull persons to sleep in sinful security."[3] For the General Baptist the dangers lie in becoming Arian and Socinian in one's interpretation of Scripture.

Seeing the apparent dangers, in 1691 Collier issued a Short Confession or a Brief Narrative of Faith. This was an attempt to moderate Baptist theology to serve both groups of Baptists. When one considers the timing, it must have been a response to the General Assembly reaffirmations of the Second London Confession in 1689. The General Baptists would have been encouraged by the declaration that salvation was for all who believe, along with the freedom for all to believe. He also presented the position that one might apostatize and lose salvation. For the Particulars, Collier emphasized the inevitability of God's will coming to pass and the fact that only God can give a person the will to believe.

Unfortunately Collier's attempt to come to a central consensus did not work. It could not work. The pendulum always moves from side to side. Consequently antinomianism settled in and evangelistic fervor died. Antinomianism may be defined: As "the belief that the moral law is not binding on Christians who are 'under grace.' . . . Any consistent Calvinistic theology must make faith a consequence and not a condition of election. By making man's depravity total and the divine grace irresistible, it denies the freedom of the human will.... By its doctrine of their final perseverance, it teaches that the elect can never forfeit divine grace, however great and grievous the sins into which they fall. In the eighteenth century, however, many Particular Baptists became hyper-Calvinists and supralapsarians. The supralapsarians taught that God decreed the salvation of some and passed by others to their damnation after the fall of Adam. The supralapsarians placed the divine decree of election and reprobation before the fall of man and the creation of the world. For them the fall of man was decreed as a consequence of the double decree of election and reprobation. This scheme made God the author of evil and maintained that men were virtually called into existence by the will of God in order to be saved or in order to be damned."[4]

What we believe determines how we behave. England today is spiritually dead as a result of the hyper-Calvinism that predominated in the course of time. May America not follow suit.

DLC

---

[1]Thomas Crosby, *The History of the English Baptists* (London: John Robinson, 1740), 3:51-52.

[2]H. Leon McBeth, The Baptist Heritage (Nashville, TN: Broadman Press, 1987), 66.

[3]Joseph Ivimey, *A History of the English Baptists* (London: Printed for the Author, 1811), 3:55

[4]A. C. Underwood, *A History of the English Baptists* (London: The Baptist Union of Great Britain and Ireland, 1970), 133-134.

April 21

Fundamental Baptist Fellowship

Scripture: Romans 16:17-27

Fundamentalism as a definable and specific movement began in the battles between Bible-believers and modernists in the major denominations of North America. One of the great battlefields was the Northern Baptist Convention. As modernism grew in strength, the fundamentalists realized that unless they were able to gain administrative control over the denomination, they would lose the Convention to the modernists. Therefore, they decided to hold pre-Convention meetings to determine a strategy to end the modernist stranglehold.

The following letter, adopted on April 21, 1920, is the invitation to the first of these pre-Convention meetings. The spirit of the letter is instructive to us today.

> *To All Baptists within the Bounds of the Northern Convention*
>
> Greeting:
>
> We view with increasing alarm the havoc which rationalism is working in our churches as evidenced by the drift upon the part of many of our ministers from the fundamentals of our holy faith. The teaching in many of our educational institutions is proving disastrous to the faith of the young men and women who are to be the leaders of the future. A wide-spread and growing worldliness has crept into the churches, a worldliness which has robbed us of power and brought upon us open shame.
>
> We believe that there rests upon us as Baptists an immediate and urgent duty to restate, reaffirm, and reemphasize the fundamentals of our

New Testament faith. Beyond all doubt the vast majority of our Baptist people are as loyal as were our fathers to our Baptist principles and our Baptist policy, but this loyalty will not long continue unless something is done to stay the rising tide of liberalism and rationalism and to preserve our principles in their simplicity and purity.

Therefore, acting upon our own initiative as your brethren, we issue this call for a conference on "The Fundamentals of Our Baptist Faith," to be held in the Delaware Avenue Church, Buffalo, from 7 p.m., Monday, June 21, to 9.30 p.m., Tuesday, June 22. These dates immediately precede the meeting of the Northern Baptist Convention.

All Baptists within the bounds of the Northern Convention are invited to attend this conference. Let increasing prayer be made for the guidance and favor of God.

Adopted April 21, 1920.

Your brethren in Christ. . . .

We . . . are assured that some of our treasured historic fundamentals of the faith are in jeopardy. The situation in our schools and seminaries is critical. . . .

We are, we believe, justly concerned at the presence in our schools of the radical, scientific attitude of mind toward the Bible, of the materialistic evolutionary theory of life and the extreme propaganda in behalf of the gospel of social betterment in substitution for the gospel of individual regeneration. . . .

We are equally distressed, and justly so, at the growing tendency on the part of some ministers and laymen to advocate openly the practical abandonment of the historic ordinances of the church and the creation of an open church-membership. . . .

The Conference is called frankly and openly in the interest of the conservative interpretation of our historic position and principles. . . . Orthodoxy, like the virtue of a woman, need not be, indeed cannot be, defined, but when once lost leaves an ineradicable

> taint upon those who have departed therefrom. Therefore we would seek to save our Baptist family from the disastrous results of a departure from the faith once for all delivered to the saints. . . .
>
> Therefore, in formally opening this Conference, I voice the earnest prayer and constant desire of the men who have called it and of the Brooklyn Committee who have arranged for it, that we may here abide in the bonds of unity in Christ our Lord, and that the results of our Conference may be to His glory, the furtherance of His Gospel in the earth, and the further establishment of those great truths, dear to our fathers, and to us as dear as life itself.[1]

Sadly, this conference and following similar conferences failed to save the Convention. Liberals maintained their control of the denomination and its educational institutions. The fundamentalists eventually had little choice but to compromise thoroughly their own position or to separate completely from the Convention. The result was the beginning of two separatist organizations, the General Association of Regular Baptist Churches and later the Conservative Baptist Association of America.

LRO

[1] *Baptist Fundamentals: Being Addresses Delivered at the Pre-Convention Conference at Buffalo June 21 and 22, 1920* (Philadelphia: Judson Press, 1920), 3-11.

April 22

From The Bar of Justice to the Court of Grace

Scripture: 1 Timothy 4:1-16

Richard Fuller was born at Beaufort, South Carolina, on April 22, 1804. He entered Harvard College, but health problems forced him to leave in his junior year. He then studied law and rose to eminence in his profession. However, it was not until 1831 that he was converted.[1] He was busily engaged in his law profession, when Beaufort was visited by Rev. Daniel Barker, the celebrated revivalist.

During those meetings, some of the most prominent and intellectual individuals of the place were brought to salvation and the dedication of their lives to the cause of Christ. One of these was Richard Fuller. He said of his conversion: "My soul ran over with love and joy and praise; for days I could neither eat nor sleep."[2]

He had been up to this time a member of the Episcopal Church, but with his salvation he began to give himself entirely to the work of Christ among the Baptists. He had previously been "baptized" by the rector of the Episcopal Church. He realized his conversion had taken place when he was 27 years of age, and he had become thoroughly convinced that believers' baptism alone was scriptural. Therefore, he was biblically baptized by the Rev. Wyer, then pastor of the Baptist church in Savannah, Georgia.[3] He joined the Baptist church in Beaufort and was soon chosen as its pastor. He was ordained in 1832 and served in the church for 15 years. When he became the pastor, the church was weak; but under his faithful care, it increased to about 200 white members and 2,400 black members. His zeal was so great that he preached for weeks in various parts of the South, and great numbers were won to Christ.

In 1847 he left Beaufort and became the pastor of the Seventh Baptist Church in Baltimore, a church which numbered but 87 members at that time. Under his ministry it grew to about 1,200. A few years later, he and several members left Seventh Baptist and established the Eutaw Place Baptist Church. He remained pastor for five years, and after much suffering, he was called to his reward on high on October 20, 1876.

Dr. Fuller was best known as a preacher. His focus in the pulpit was the Word of God, and it was obvious that he walked with its Author continually. He did not bring to his people the kind of idle speculation which was common in his day, but instead his sermons were filled with the Word and with the evidence of his own spiritual devotion. His sermons evidenced careful study of the languages. He wrote out his sermons in the study but usually preached without notes.

He preached with a majestic personal presence, bordering on the imperial. He recognized the necessity of a powerful pulpit presence, yet he did not rely upon his own abilities in the pulpit.

He cultivated his voice and pulpit presence, framing their management on the best of rules and using them with consummate skill. Having a message from the Man of Calvary, he wished to deliver it as an accomplished pleader with men for Jesus' sake. Armitage says of his preaching: "The writer once heard him when he showed himself to be a perfect master in the art of oratory, by denouncing the tricks of the orator in preaching. He wove one of the most fresh, vivid, and finished pieces of oratorical denunciation against dependence on pulpit oratorical effect that man could put together. Under this spell he held his audience in breathlessness, and when they found a free breathing place men grew pale and nodded to their neighbors with a look which plainly said: 'What a horrible thing it is to be eloquent in the pulpit!' The doctor did not intend to soar to the third heavens on the winds of inspired invective against pulpit eloquence, but he did, whether he intended it or not, and when we all returned to the earth with him, every man of us was ready to subscribe to the new litany: 'From false doctrine, heresy, and *eloquence*, good Lord deliver us!'"[4]

LRO

[1]Thomas Armitage, *A History of the Baptists* (New York: Bryan, Taylor, and Co., 1890), 760.

[2]Ibid., 760.

[3]William Cathcart, *The Baptist Encyclopedia* (Philadelphia: Louis H. Everts, 1883), 423-424.

[4]Armitage, 761.

April 23

Did the Baptist Movement Begin in 1641?

Scripture: Matthew 16:13-19

The premise of the authors of these devotional, historical volumes has been that history vindicates the succession of Baptist principles from the days of the New Testament. In other words, Baptists did not spring from the Reformation. They preceded it, and the New Testament principles that we call distinctives have long endured. Verification of this position has been discovered time and again even in cursory reading of church histories. For instance, I will base this entry on quotations from a Brethren source.

"In the report of the Council of the Archbishop of Cologne about the 'Anabaptist movement,' to the Emperor Charles V, it is said that the Anabaptists call themselves 'true Christians,' that they desire community of goods, 'which has been the way of Anabaptists for more than a thousand years, as the old histories and imperial laws testify.' At the dissolution of the Parliament at Speyer it was stated [of] the 'new sect of the Anabaptists' . . . . 'It is a fact that for more than twelve centuries baptism in the way taught and described in the New Testament had been made an offence against the law, punishable by death.'"[1]

The full report of the Council was presented to Emperor Charles V, and on April 23, 1529, the Decree of the Emperor against the Anabaptists was issued. In the decree one reads language such as the following: ". . .yet do we find daily that, contrary to the promulgated common law and also to our mandate issued, *such ancient sect of the Anabaptists condemned and forbidden many hundred of years ago* (italics provided) more and more advances and spreads." The decree called for the following penalty: ". . .that all and every Anabaptist and re-baptized man or woman of intelligent age shall be sentenced and executed by fire, sword, or the like . . ."[2] When reading this decree, it is apparent that the so-called "anabaptists" did not spring from the Reformation. They long preceded it.

Two other interesting points should be made. How was baptism practiced? "In 1463, in the mountains of Reichenau, and again in 1467 at Lhota, there were general gatherings of brethren, at which many persons of rank and influence were present, where they considered afresh the principles of the Church. One of the first things they did was to baptize those present, for the baptism of believers by immersion was common to the Waldenses and to most of the brethren in different parts, though it had been interrupted by pressure of persecution."[3]

Thus it is acknowledged that immersion of believers was practiced among the so-called Aanabaptists. Finally, we are constantly shocked to learn that professed Baptist historians are teaching in our Bible colleges and seminaries that the Baptist churches actually only came into existence in 1641. This teaching is just more than a hundred years old, and it has long been repudiated by careful scholars. Broadbent comments: "There are records of 'Congregations' in England in 1555 and Baptist churches are known to have existed in the reign of Queen Elizabeth, before 1589. Both those called Independents or Congregationalists and those called Baptists were independent churches of believers, differing in this, that the Baptists practiced the baptism of believers only, while the Independents baptized infants one of whose parents (or whose guardian) was a believer."[4]

Bible-believing Baptists need to thank God for perpetuity of truth. Ours is not a modern day movement, but one that is built in and bounded by God's precious infallible Word.

DLC

---

[1]E. H. Broadbent, *The Pilgrim Church* (London: Pickering & Inglis, 1935), 154.

[2]Johannes Warns, *Baptism - Studies in the Original Christian Baptism* (London: The Paternoster Press, 1957), 134.

[3]Broadbent, 130.

[4]Broadbent, 239.

April 24

Shipwrecked!

Scripture: 1 Corinthians 4

Sometimes we despair at the difficulties we face in our efforts to serve God. We wonder why the highest and noblest of all human work would be impeded by wrecks, trouble, and near disaster. It confuses us that the Omnipotent God whom we serve has not only withheld a guarantee of perfect safety, but providentially clutters our pilgrimage with pain, setbacks, and frightening walks through the Valley of the Shadow of Death. It is beyond the human capacity to grasp the full reason for providential obstacles, but history has shown that it is often the lot of God's ambassadors to suffer shipwreck, whether literal or figurative, on their way to greater ministry.

Consider the case of James Voller who set sail from England with his family to become the pastor of the Bathurst Street Baptist Church in Sydney, Australia. The earliest known Baptist worship service in Australia had been conducted on April 24, 1831, but now the James Voller family were on their way to minister in the Bathurst Baptist Church. Their ship was highly anticipated by the congregation who had bright hopes for their new pastor, but a dark shadow was cast over them when word came that their pastor's ship was lost at sea. The Voller's ship, the *Meridian*, had been run aground on the uninhabited island of Amsterdam in the Indian Sea. The family who just hours before had been casually enjoying tea and fellowship were now huddled together despairing even of life as the angry waves beat their vessel. "Ours was the stern cabin on the lee side of the ship," says Voller. "The scene frightened us beyond all description. Crashing timbers, the tumult of the elements, and the wild darkness of the night, combined to induce moods of common terror and despair. With destruction appearing inevitable, we gathered our little ones around us and, amid mutual embraces, took our last farewells."[1]

Shortly thereafter they were forced to abandon ship and clung to the rocks at the bottom of cliffs that seemed impossible to scale. They were cold, wet, hungry, and almost naked. But God caused some of the *Meridian's* shipment to break open in front of them and the group was thus providentially supplied with warm clothing and food. One sailor courageously climbed the cliff and threw down ropes by which they were able to hoist everyone up to dry land, an effort that took almost two days to accomplish because of the difficulty of the terrain. After several days when the crew and passengers thought all was lost, God heard the cries of His ambassadors and caused an American whaling ship to see their smoke signals and launch a daring rescue.

On this day in 1854, James Voller preached his first message at his new church. Such was the excitement of the shipwreck and rescue that national papers carried the story and many came to hear the new Baptist preacher speak. A large sum of money was collected to help the pastor's family re-settle and recover what had been lost at sea.

James Voller was a Baptist man of conviction who took the pastorate of a church that had lost some of its Baptist distinctives.[2] Many of its members were not baptized by immersion and there was some reticence among the membership to proclaim with conviction and enthusiasm the distinctives that make a church Baptist. Voller would change that. He arrived in Australia at the age of forty. Forty-eight years later, when he entered his reward, he left behind him many Baptist churches and a strong Baptist association, the first in Australia.

We do not always know the reason for shipwreck. It seems ruinous, cataclysmic. We cry out, O, Lord! I want to serve you, and I'm on a mission that is noble. Now I find myself in complete despair. But the obstacles we face in our ministry are all integral pieces of a puzzle God is putting together for his glorious work, which more often than not far exceeds our wildest dreams and reaches beyond the limitations of our own lives. Thus, God allows his children, his missionaries to face life and death situations, to endure hardship, sometimes without relief. While one of the reasons is certainly the personal sanctification of His servants, another great effect is often discovered over time: that of motivating more servants into the ministry. James Voller was tested at the outset of a wonderful ministry. In the darkest moment of despair, he cried out to God Who rescued him and confirmed his faith in a God who saves to the uttermost, even from shipwreck.

RPB

[1] Craig Skinner, *Spurgeon and Son, The Forgotten Story of Thomas Spurgeon and His Famous Father, Charles Haddon Spurgeon* (Grand Rapids, MI: Kregel, 1999), 12.

[2] H. Leon McBeth, *The Baptist Heritage, Four Centuries of Baptist Witness* (Nashville: Broadman Press, 1987), 324.

April 25

An Exciting Missionary Adventure

Scripture: 2 Corinthians 11:23-28

The die was cast on April 25, 1844, when Richard Fuller, prominent pastor from Charleston, South Carolina, presented a resolution at the Triennial Convention to restrict its action to missions and not to become involved in the problem of slavery.[1] From 1814 until 1845, missionary efforts had been primarily made through the Triennial Convention, but in 1845 the split between North and South occurred. However, Baptist associations in various states had formed small, independent mission agencies as well, and our entry deals with one of those today. Our subject was sent as a missionary by a Georgia association to serve the Lord in Africa.

Richard Henry Stone was born in Culpeper County, Virginia on July 17, 1837. Desirous of a good education, he studied at Kemper's University at Gordonsville, and then transferred to the University of Virginia. After finishing his schooling, he moved to his uncle's home in Georgia and began teaching. He was baptized on June 28, 1856, and united with the Salem Baptist Church in Culpeper County. On October 22, 1858, Richard married Miss Susan Gaines Broadus, and answering the call of the Baptists in Georgia for a missionary to Africa, the couple sailed out of Baltimore on November 4. They were three months on the journey, and landed at Lagos. They disciplined themselves to learn the Ijaye language, but with failing health, the couple was forced to return to the States.

Mr. Stone then joined the Confederate army, and served as a chaplain with the 49th Georgia, Benning's Brigade. In 1867, with the completion of the war, Mr. Stone returned to Africa and Lagos for two years.

He wrote:

> We went out in the Colonization Ship "M. C. Stevens" and touched at Sierra Leone, Cape Mount, Monrovia, and Cape Palmas, passing a month in Liberia.... and onto Lagos. . . Here we were compelled to land by crossing a most dangerous bar, swarming with sharks, but got safely through and were made comfortable by Brother J. M. Harden, our colored missionary, stationed at that point especially to receive missionaries and forward them to the interior. . . . He forwarded me by canoe to Abbeokuta . . . . We found Abbeokuta very different from Lagos. . . . Abbeokuta had no marks of civilization anywhere . . . situated amidst isolated granite cliffs and surrounded by vast, beautiful palm-dotted plains of grass and jungle. . . .

> We proceeded by land to Ijaye. This town was surrounded by a dense forest . . . the lair of hyenas, leopards and other wild beasts, which howled and prowled about the streets all night. But this forest and the outside jungle furnished the people with the greatest abundance of the largest and best game. We lived mostly on game, milk, and butter, but all kinds of provisions were very abundant, of the best quality and exceedingly cheap . . . I lived here two years.... In 1860 I was captured by a party of Ibadans and taken to their town and tried for my life on the charge of being a spy. . . . Having escaped my captors I reached Ijaye in time to see a large army approach and attack it. Every five days there was a pitched battle. . . . The town was taken and completely destroyed. . . . When all was lost, I came down to Abbeokuta, bringing what children we had left and all our effects.... We established a flourishing school of 70 children and a church of 30 converts .... This is a sad and joyful period of my missionary life . . . But I was compelled to return to this country [America] in 1869. . . On the painful and perilous journey mentioned above I reached that place (Ogbomishaw) in the night after a ride of sixty miles that day; I was in great danger from wild beasts and was also sick, hungry and distressed. . . . I spent the whole of the next day in Brother Clarke's deserted house. . . . and in wandering about the premises and in prayer. In one corner in the tangled grass was a grave that I found to be Sister Reid's grave.[2]

The last twenty years of Mr. Stone's life were spent in Virginia and Kentucky where he supported his family by teaching. Mr. Stone died on October 7, 1894, and he was buried in the Fairview Cemetery in Culpeper.

The pioneering days of missions is over, but the need is greater than ever for those who will go with the Gospel to Africa. Would you be willing to say, "Here am I, Lord, send me?"

DLC

---

[1]William R. Estep, *Whole Gospel Whole World* (Nashville, TN: Broadman & Holman Press, 1994), 53.

[2]George Braxton Taylor, *Virginia Baptist Ministers* (Lynchburg, VA: J. P. Bell Company, 1935), 6:24-25.

April 26

The General's Right Hand Man

Scripture: Romans 15:5-7

Prior to the Civil War there were few black Baptist preachers in the North or the South. But it is a thrill to read of the exploits of those few that existed. In our previous volume, we have examined the outstanding ministry of John Jasper in Richmond, Virginia. Throughout the Southland the Lord of the harvest was calling choice black preachers to declare His truth.

In his interesting book entitled *History of the Negro Baptists of North Carolina*, the author, J. A. Whitted, lists several. "Uncle" Harry Cowan was a slave to Thomas L. Cowan. On one occasion Mr. Cowan was present for a funeral where his servant was to preach, and he was shocked at Uncle Harry's grasp of the Scripture. This resulted in the master granting "privilege papers" allowing Uncle Harry to preach, marry, and baptize anywhere on his four plantations. Actual legal papers were drawn up by an attorney and they read as follows: "This is to certify that whosoever is interested about my man Harry he has the privilege to preach and marry also; to baptize any one who makes a profession of faith."[1]

In time Uncle Harry's success caused his master to extend this privilege of preaching wherever his slave had "protection." The blessing of God was attendant upon this choice servant of the Lord, and literally thousands of both races heard him gladly. His ministry extended from before the Civil War, during that awful conflict, and following it as well. In fact, during the Civil War, Uncle Harry served as Confederate General, Joseph Johnston's body servant. He preached every night during the war, with the exception of May 2, 1863, when General Stonewall

Jackson fell in battle. He served General Johnston faithfully until the General's surrender on April 26, 1865.

Following the war, Uncle Harry Cowan was a leader greatly respected. It is estimated that during his ministry, he baptized eight thousand converts.

At Louisburg, North Carolina, everyone knew "Dr. Lewis Perry." In actuality, Lewis Perry was the body servant of Dr. Willie Perry, but he was given permission to conduct prayer meetings and preach in Louisburg. People of both races attended his preaching, and many came to Christ through his faithful presentation of the Gospel. He conducted revival meetings in both the Baptist and Methodist churches. During that period of time, Lewis Perry was a member of the white Baptist church, and invariably he was called upon to close the church meetings in prayer. Whenever a slave applied for church membership, he or she had first to obtain the permission of "Dr. Perry."

Another outstanding example before us is that of Reverend Thomas Parker. It is believed that he baptized four thousand converts during his ministry. Simultaneously he pastored four of the largest Baptist churches in the Kenansville Association, and he served as the moderator of the Association for thirty years.

The honor goes to Abraham Marshall for establishing the first Negro Baptist church in Georgia. David Benedict describes it as follows: "In one of his excursions down the country, in the suburbs of Savannah, not far from where once stood Whitefield's famous orphan house, Mr. M., in one day, baptized forty persons of color, formed them, with others previously baptized, into a church, and ordained Andrew Bryan as their pastor. This was in 1788. Thus arose the first African Baptist church in Savannah which soon became a distinguished community of this people. Bryan lived to the age of ninety in this pastoral station. He was succeeded by his nephew, Andrew Marshall, who held this pastorship with good reputation to old age."[2]

The Gospel fits all people, rich and poor, black and white, and large and small. Let us pray that our Lord will raise up men of every background in this day who will preach the Word in season and out of season.

DLC

[1]J. A. Whitted, *A History of the Negro Baptists of North Carolina* (Raleigh: Edwards & Broughton Printing Co., 1908), 10.

[2]David Benedict, *Fifty Years Among the Baptists* (New York: Sheldon & Company, 1860), 53

April 27

America: A Vital Mission Field

Scripture: Mark 1:38

Several historic dates of interest to Baptists in America are essential to understanding the ongoing of the Baptist witness. The Triennial Convention, which became the arm of foreign missions for Baptist churches, was established on May 18, 1814. As the Baptist cause proliferated in America, it soon became apparent that Baptist literature must be supplied for both the home and foreign ministries. Thus it was that the Baptist General Tract Society (which ultimately became known as the Baptist Publication Society) was formed on February 25, 1824. Long before the formation of the Triennial Convention when Baptists became interested in missions across seas, there was an interest in the ministry among the American Indians and in the expanding borders to the West. Thus home mission work had been established in 1807 as the Baptist Missionary Society of Massachusetts sent Reverend John Mason Peck to what was then the far West of the nation.

It is this thrust of ministry that will command our attention in this entry. John Mason Peck and Dr. Jonathan Going championed the desire for participation of all Baptists in America in the cause of reaching into the West. These men envisioned the planting of Bible-believing Baptist churches from coast to coast. Thus, the American Baptist Home Mission Society was formed on April 27, 1832.

"The object of the society was, 'The preaching of the gospel to every creature in our country,' which object was so well expressed in its grand motto: 'North America for Christ.'"[1]

"During the first year 50 missionaries were employed for longer or shorter periods-6 in New York, 12 in Ohio, 5 in Indiana, 3 in Michigan, 9 in Illinois, 7 in Missouri, 2 in New Jersey, and 1 each in Pennsylvania, Kentucky, Tennessee, Arkansas, Mississippi, and Lower Canada. In the second year 80 missionaries were engaged and Upper Canada and Louisiana were added to the fields. The third year shows an increase of missionaries to 96."[2]

"...By the end of the decade, the society's efforts had reaped nearly 11,000 converts on the frontier and established 400 churches pastored by 142 ministers. In addition, many benevolent societies, Sunday schools, and Bible classes also had been established. Peck and the Home Mission Society had laid the groundwork for a vast home missionary enterprise that eventually would embrace the entire continent.[3]"

As we enter the twenty-first century, it is apparent that there is once again a great need for church planting of fundamental, independent Baptist churches in our once great republic. Even as I write these lines I am aware of the frightful statistics that there are an estimated 195 million unchurched people in the United States. According to the *Journal of Church Growth*, during a ten-year period from the mid 1980s to the 1990s, the United States population has increased 11.4% while church membership has declined by 9.5%. It is reported that North America is the only continent where Christianity is not growing. Church attendance has declined approximately 10% over the last seven years. According to the American Society for Church Growth, there is a net loss of forty-eight churches per week or nearly seven churches per day. Researcher George Barna reported at the beginning of 2003 that the United States is the world's third-largest unchurched nation, whose unchurched population exceeds 195 million.

We must learn the lesson that the secret of growth is not merely addition. Our churches must multiply. It is essential that fundamental Baptists reseed America. Unfortunately there are some sizeable cities in our land without a strong, fundamental Baptist witness. Why not encourage your church family to consider "mothering" a church in an area of need? Pray for revival in America.

DLC

---

[1]Rev. Richard R. Cook, *The Story of the Baptists in All Ages and Countries* (Baltimore: H. M. Wharton & Co, 1886), 363.

[2]Albert Henry Newman, *A History of the Baptist Churches in the United States* (Philadelphia, American Baptist Publication Society, 1915), 422.

[3]Anne Devereaux Jordan and J. M. Stifle, *The Baptists* (New York, Hippocrene Books, 1990), 78.

April 28

Evangelize or Fossilize

Scripture: John 5:24; 2 Timothy 4:5

From our twenty-first century vantage point, it is difficult to appreciate the extreme poverty of the old South in the days following the Civil War. The land had been ravaged, and the future looked bleak. Into that atmosphere T. T. Martin was born on April 28, 1862, in Smith County, Mississippi. His father served both as a preacher and a college professor. The family, though surrounded by the privations of war, knew the assurance of the Lord's care.

In his youth the lad desired to become a lawyer. In time he graduated from Mississippi College, where his father taught mathematics. While preparing for his chosen career, T. T. Martin experienced a growing burden to preach. Following intense self-examination, he surrendered to the leading of the Holy Spirit and devoted himself to prepare for the ministry. To support himself, he served as professor of Natural Science at Baylor Belton College in Texas from 1886 to 1888.

In 1888 our subject was ordained and enrolled in Southern Baptist Seminary in Louisville, Kentucky. His pastoral ministry began in 1890 in the Baptist church in Glenview, Kentucky. God's call then took him to the two-mile-high city of Leadville, Colorado, where he pastored from 1891 through 1893. In 1894 he ministered in a Baptist church in Canon City, Colorado. He then accepted the invitation to return to Glenview, Kentucky, and served there in 1895 and 1896. While finishing his Th. M. degree, T. T. Martin pastored the Baptist church in Beattyville, Kentucky.

Being challenged by the missionary vision of his day, Reverend Martin applied to serve as a foreign missionary. However, as he awaited appointment, he was stricken with a life-threatening case of food poisoning. He was advised to return to Colorado as perhaps his only chance of recovery. Thus from 1897 until 1900, he pastored the Baptist church in Cripple Creek, Colorado. There he preached in mining camps and in the open air. As he did so, he recovered his health and developed an unusual strength of voice that served him well during the duration of his ministry. His ministry majored in the clear-cut preaching of the Gospel, and many were won to saving faith in Jesus Christ. Thus, in 1900 a new door was opened to evangelism, and T. T. Martin began a full-time evangelistic ministry. The protracted meetings ran from fifteen to twenty-one days, and the man of God preached twice daily and four times each Lord's Day. His schedule often kept him on the road for six months at a time.

Early in the twentieth century, Reverend Martin began to use large tents to accommodate his crowds. As his schedule filled, and as the crowds grew, the evangelist determined upon a new course of service. He originated a system of using two tents. One tent would be sent ahead with a song-leader and evangelist to begin meetings. When T. T. Martin closed his current meeting, he would ship the tent that he had been using to a third location. He would then move to the second tent while the evangelist and song-leader that had been there would move to the new location.

As demands for his services continued to proliferate, T. T. Martin organized a corps of gospel singers and evangelists. He booked these men throughout the country. This group was named the Blue Mountain Evangelists, and he chose choice men whose singing and preaching was Christ-centered.

Somehow, midst his strenuous schedule of evangelism, T. T. Martin authored a number of books. His was a unique ministry, for his scholarship made him a teacher/expositor as well as a great evangelist. He continued in his active ministry until the last few months of his life, entering the presence of his Lord on May 23, 1939.[1] His grave marker in Gloster, Mississippi, bears only the dates of his birth and death along with three Scripture texts (John 3:16, Acts 16:31, John 5:24) which formed the basis of his ministry.

Let us pray for the waning gift of evangelism. How we need those whom God will raise up to serve in evangelism in the twenty-first century.

DLC

[1]T. T. Martin, *God's Plan With Men* (Orlando, FL: Daniels Publishing Co., 1978), Forward.

April 29

From Ritualism to Reality in Christ

Scripture: John 14:6; Acts 4:12

From the time of his youth, William Baskett purposed to know God. William was born in 1741 in Goochland County, Virginia. Because of their limited means, his parents were unable to provide William with great educational opportunities. We know little of his maturing years until he turned twenty, and at that time he married Miss Mary Pace.

As a youth, William envisioned the blessings of sincere Christianity, and he regularly attended public worship services. In the course of time, because of his sincerity, he was allowed to participate in the Communion service of the established state church. From the time they were married, William and Mary established a family altar, and both morning and evening they united in the reading of the Bible and prayers. As their family grew during the first seven years of their marriage, though they had no assurance of salvation, they were continually faithful in observing the family altar.

Baptist preachers began visiting the area about that time, and the citizenry openly discussed the new doctrines that were being heard in the neighborhood. The first Baptist preacher to visit the area was John Corbley. Mostly out of curiosity, William Bassett went to hear the Baptist. He returned home late, but Mrs. Bassett refused to serve supper until she heard the report of her husband concerning the meeting. In a short time William and Mary both went to hear Mr. Corbley and to witness a baptismal service. They were both greatly impressed, and according to Mr. Bassett's testimony, follow that, he was scarcely able to follow his plough, and his wife frequently found him engaged in prayer.

With great anxiety as to what God required for salvation, Mr. Bassett journeyed three miles on a dark and rainy night to ask the preacher of the established church how one could know he was saved. The preacher replied that for his own part, he felt a comfortable hope while he kept the commandments, but only during such a time. The established preacher, because of William's continued questioning, charged William with being deranged, and of course, this brought no satisfaction to the Basketts.[1]

By this time William saw himself as a guilty, undone sinner. Great conviction gripped his heart and he continually examined God's Word. Finally one night God brought the Scripture to mind: "He that trusts in the Lord shall never be confounded." At that moment he trusted Jesus Christ as his Savior and threw himself on the Lord's grace. He found immediate peace with God. In the mean time Elijah Craig and David Thompson, faithful Baptist preachers, had entered the area, and the Basketts were immersed upon their profession of faith. Soon a small congregation was gathered, and Philip Webber was called as pastor. The work of God grew, and in 1788 a revival in the area brought significant growth to the local church. When Pastor Webber accepted a call to Kentucky, the congregation called upon William Baskett to assume the pastorate of the Lyle's Baptist Church. His faithfulness and zeal as a pastor, and his conduct in his personal life were exemplary during the twenty-one years of his ministry there.

The amazing event, however, of the home going of the Basketts is thought provoking. On April 21, 1815, his life partner fell asleep in Jesus. A week later on April 29, 1815, he preached his last sermon from the words: "We have no continuing city, but seek one to come." On the following day, William's tranquil spirit took flight to Glory. A joint memorial service was conducted on June 24, 1815, and a vast concourse of admirers and friends attended to pay their last respects for the godly couple who had come to know the Lord Jesus Christ confidently as their perfect Savior from sin.

If you are seeking eternal life in ritual or religion, let me assure you that you will never find it there. But the Lord Jesus Christ is no respecter or persons. As He saved the Basketts He will save you immediately if you will trust Him alone as your Savior.

DLC

[1]James B. Taylor, *Lives of Virginia Baptist Preachers* (Richmond: Yale & Wyatt, 1838), 90.

April 30

Who Will Go?

Scripture: 1 Samuel 17:29; Psalm 32:7

The work among the Karens in Burma is a thrilling account of missionary sacrifice and faithfulness. George Dana Boardman and his wife were appointed by the Triennial Convention on April 30, 1823, in Washington, D.C., and they pioneered that rapidly expanding ministry. God's blessing rested heavily upon their efforts. By 1910 the work among the Karens had grown to 50,000 members in 774 churches. All but 92 of those churches were self-supporting.

In touring among the churches, the missionaries often looked away to a range of mountains where a notorious savage tribe existed. The missionaries wondered how they might reach the wild tribes who were known as Brecs. Living by plunders and known to be fond of uncooked meat and blood, the tribes were greatly feared.

At an annual assembly of the Karen churches, the matter of evangelizing Brecs was discussed, but none volunteered to go. During the appeal, one of the national Karen evangelists bowed his head, evidently in prayer. Finally he stood, and almost as though talking to himself, he said, "I am sorry for the poor Brecs, who know nothing of God, or his law to men. I am very unhappy because no one goes to them with the great tidings. If my church will give me leave, I will go."

He was accepted, but some argued that he ought not to go alone. The national responded, "Yes, if God sends me, He will take care of me." Still they persisted, telling him that he did not know the way. But the man of God responded, "God delivered me from the mouth of a bear, and also from death when, crossing a swift stream . . . He also saved me from the mouth of a tiger. He will be with me in this work, no matter how difficult."[1]

Committing his family to the care of the local church and taking a testament and hymnbook, he began the journey.

Others escorted him until he reached the boundary of the English territory. Then he pushed on alone. The second day, he reached a mountain where he could look down on the smoke of distant villages. He continued down the mountainside.

Late in the afternoon, he neared a village. Unbeknownst to him, this was the most wicked of all of the Brec villages. He seemed to be spotted by a number of men simultaneously. Thinking him to be the advance of an attacking group, they seized their spears and knives, and soon surrounded the Karen evangelist. Anger was written on their faces, but the national evangelist stood quietly. He asked, "Do men of war go about in the daytime alone and unarmed?" Then pulling out his Bible and hymnbook, he said, "This is the white book of which our ancestors have told us from ancient days. It speaks. Listen." Then he read, and after that he began to sing. The evangelist was a sweet singer, and the men were fascinated with his fine voice. But the man of God was singing for his very life. The love of God flooded his heart for these savage people, and soon his music calmed the angry hearts of those wild men.

After the men put their spears down, the evangelist boldly announced his message of salvation. He told them how the Lord had sent him to deliver that particular message. As he spoke, it was evident that he was gaining the confidence of the people. The reception was so great among the Brecs that the national evangelist remained some time proclaiming the gospel. However, his concern for his own family was such that he left the Brecs, promising to return.

In a few short years a church was established in the village. Then other villages responded, and churches and even schools were formed. All of this was the result of a fearless national who was willing, if necessary, to give his own life for the ongoing of the gospel. What are we willing to do to reach those around us who are in heathen darkness?

DLC

---

[1]Alonzo Bunker, *Fifty Missionary Stories* (New York: Fleming H. Revell Company, 1903), 173.

May 1

British and Colonial Baptists United

Scripture: Ephesians 4:1-16

During the Revolutionary War, Baptists on both sides of the Atlantic were united with a single purpose. This amazing truth has shocked some, but a careful consideration reveals the reason for this unanimity of agreement. It is true that for almost one hundred years the Baptists in Great Britain had a semblance of freedom, but they lived in continual fear that the situation was only temporary. As long as the established State Church existed, certain limitations would be experienced. The Edict of Toleration in 1689 did not grant total religious freedom. Baptist church buildings had to be designated as chapels, tabernacles, or with some other name. And that restriction would continue until early into the twentieth century. Thus Baptists of England looked upon the American Revolution, and considered that an American victory might bring about the relaxation of such restrictions, and provide for a wider and permanent freedom.

Dr. John Rippon, of London, in a letter written to President James Manning, of Rhode Island College, on May 1, 1784, stated it thus: "I believe all of our Baptist ministers in town, except two, and most of our brethren in the country were on the side of the Americans in the late dispute. . . . We wept when the thirsty plains drank the blood of our departed heroes, and the shout of a king was among us when your well fought battles were crowned with victory; and to this hour we believe that the independence of America will, for a while, secure the liberty of this country, but if that continent had been reduced, Britain would not have long been free."[1]

When Robert Hall was a small boy he heard John Ryland, Jr. (later the president of Bristol Baptist College) say the following to his father, Dr. John Ryland, Sr.: "If I were Washington I would summon all the American officers, they should form a circle around me, and I would address them, and we would offer a libation in our own blood, and I would order one of them to bring a lancet and a punch bowl, and we would bare our arms and be bled; and when the bowl was full, when we all had been bled, I would call on every man to consecrate himself to the work by dipping his sword into the bowl and entering into a solemn covenant engagement by oath, one to another, and we would swear by Him that sits upon the throne and liveth forever and ever, that we would never sheathe our swords while there was an English soldier in arms remaining in America."[2]

What was the common denominator that caused both Colonial Baptists in America and their counterparts in Great Britain to share the desire for victory together? The answer is simple. Prior to the Revolutionary War, Baptists in both the Colonies and in England did not know complete freedom. This might be illustrated as well during the Second World War concerning Bible believing Baptists who lived in Germany under the reign of Hitler. Of course they could not fly an American flag. They could not publicly sing, "God Bless America," but in their hearts they were desirous of experiencing the freedom they knew existed in America. This has been true throughout the years of history since our Republic has existed. Prior to the Revolutionary War, no denomination in America was as determined to stand for freedom as were the Baptists. Congregationalism established the State church in Massachusetts. The Pilgrim offspring were intent on building a theocracy. The religious control of the colonies of New England was theirs. Episcopalians prospered through the State-Church concept as the clergy was supported, and property and buildings provided by taxes in Virginia, the Carolinas, and Georgia. Methodism was an offspring of the Episcopal system and considered a cousin. Presbyterianism flourished under the teaching of Calvinism that called for a State church. Primarily these denominations, though each was desirous of more, were not strongly adverse to the status quo. But Baptists had the most to gain with the establishment of a Republic and total religious freedom. Our forefathers sought this freedom not only for themselves, but for all.

United Baptists of both the Colonies and Great Britain longed for the free exercise of soul liberty and religious freedom. Let us determine to maintain that freedom for all until our Lord returns.

DLC

---

[1] John T. Christian, *A History of the Baptists* (Nashville, TN: Broadman Press, 1926), 228.

[2] Ibid.

Simple in Style - Solemn in Manner

Scripture: Colossians 3:1-17

James Barnett Taylor was ordained for the gospel ministry on May 2, 1826, at Sandy Creek Church in Virginia. He had been born in the village of Barton-upon-Humber, England, on March 19, 1804. His father brought his family to America the next year, and they settled in the city of New York. At the age of 13, young Taylor was baptized and united with the First Baptist Church of New York City. That same year the family moved to Virginia. At the age of 16, he began to preach, and in 1824 the local church provided him with a license. Soon afterward he was appointed by the General Baptist Association of Virginia to serve as a missionary.

In 1826 he became pastor of the Second Baptist Church of Richmond, Virginia, where he served for sixteen years. During that time he organized Sunday schools and Bible societies and promoted the cause of education. Six hundred and sixty members were added to the church, three new churches were organized, and upwards of a dozen of the men in his church entered the ministry. In 1838 he traveled as an agent of the Virginia Baptist General Association. In 1839 he was elected chaplain of the University of Virginia. In 1840 he became pastor of the Third Baptist Church (later known as Grace Baptist Church) in Richmond. In 1844 he traveled south to encourage the churches to increase their support of missions. He collected large sums of money for the American Baptist Missionary Societies.

When the Southern Baptist Convention was organized just prior to the Civil War, Taylor became its corresponding secretary; he held the position until his death 26 years later. During those years, he traveled constantly, preached three times on most Sundays, addressed letters of encouragement to missionaries, edited several journals, and accomplished far more than his contemporaries knew. During the Civil War, he ministered in camps and hospitals and served as Confederate post-chaplain three years.

At the close of the war the mission societies of the Southern Baptist Convention were in difficult straits, with a debt of more than $10,000. Taylor immediately began encouraging the churches to give toward liquidating the debt. At the same time, he renewed the missions work of the Southern Baptists that had suffered during the War. He was also greatly interested in the welfare of the Negroes and was appointed to work with the secretary of the Freedmen's Bureau. His last sermons were preached in Alexandria to Negro congregations. This servant ministered faithfully in a very difficult time and died on December 22, 1871.

Taylor was a preacher, simple in style and solemn in manner. Taylor was a pastor, able to serve comfortably among his people and among the community in general. As a writer, Taylor edited the *Religious Herald*, the *Southern Baptist Missionary Journal,* and *Home and Foreign Journal*. He wrote the *Life of Lot Cary*, the *Life of Luther Rice*, and two volumes of the *Lives of Virginia Baptist Ministers*, an extremely valuable work for those interested in the history of the Baptists in this country. He also began the *History of Virginia Baptists*, although he did not live to complete it. In addition to all these literary, pastoral, and official labors as secretary of the missionary board, he wrote, as editor of the *Foreign Mission Journal*, articles that would fill many volumes. Dr. Poindexter, who was associated with him for some time as one of the secretaries of the board, said of him, illustrating the pressure of his labors, "He was at the same time corresponding secretary, financial manager, general traveling agent, and editor of the board."

In his various areas of ministry, Taylor quietly and perseveringly accomplished the high and holy purposes to which God had called him. He was never physically strong, but few men have left a more abiding impression on the Baptist churches than James Barnett Taylor.

LRO

William Cathcart, *The Baptist Encyclopedia* (Philadelphia: Louis H. Everts, 1883), 1134-1135.

May 3

Spurgeon: Calvinist or Biblicist?

Scripture: John 5:40; 6:37-40

Little could Reverend Cantlow realize the spiritual and historical significance of the baptismal service on May 3, 1850, when he immersed the teenager, Charles Haddon Spurgeon in Isleham, England. The teenaged lad had walked seven miles from New Market to Isleham because he had become firmly convinced that believer's immersion was an ordinance of the Lord and not a sacrament. Desiring to serve, the young man made himself available to the Lord. Though he had received limited formal education, within a year he was called to the pastorate of the small Baptist church in Waterbeach, England. Quickly his fame spread to London, and on April 28, 1854, he accepted the call to pastor the New Park Street Chapel where famed Baptist predecessors had served. Charles Spurgeon was still a teen, but soon his name would be known throughout Great Britain, and he would be addressing thousands of people every Lord's Day. Such a spiritual phenomenon was amazing.

Charles Haddon Spurgeon was soon targeted for criticism by the press in London. He was made the subject of political cartoonists, and the general Christian public examined his doctrine closely. There can be no doubt that the youth had been greatly influenced by the theology of his grandfather, a Congregational pastor. The youth became keenly appreciative of his Puritan heritage and its accompanying Calvinistic theology. During all his ministry his theology was closely examined by both Calvinists and Arminian theologians. He was attacked by the Hyper-

Calvinists and accused of being Arminian in doctrine. Simultaneously he was assailed by the Arminian theologians and accused of being Hyper-Calvinistic. In reality, though Mr. Spurgeon used many Calvinistic terms, it is apparent that he did not embrace the complete Calvinistic grid. He surely preached the whole counsel of God, even when it did not conform to human logic.

Lewis A. Drummond, in a rather recent volume, wrote, "Spurgeon did not think the preaching of Calvinism stood synonymous with the preaching of the Gospel. He said, I believe most firmly in the doctrines commonly called Calvinist, and I hold them to be very fraught with comfort for God's people; but if any man shall say that the preaching of these is the whole preaching of Gospel, I am at issue with him. Brethren, you may preach these doctrines as long as you like, and yet fail to preach the Gospel; and I will go further, and affirm that some who have even denied those truths, to our own grief, have nevertheless been Gospel preachers for all that, and God has saved souls by their ministry . . . preach Christ, young men, if you want to win souls."[1] Drummond continued: "Of course, there were those who would not criticize Spurgeon for his paradoxical stance. To the contrary, they commended him. Fullerton said, Spurgeon's great contribution lay in his ability to cling to two concurrent truths without diminishing the significance of either."

Moreover, Spurgeon had a very practical reason for holding truth in tension. He felt this to be the best way to evangelize people. As an evangelist he would unhesitatingly employ any scriptural approach that he could use to bring others to faith in Jesus Christ.

As Spurgeon grew older, he shifted some of his emphasis in theology. In his early days at New Park Street, he declared very forcefully his essential orthodox Calvinism. But later in life, as his doctrinal position became widely known, he preached less vociferously on these issues. His doctrinal emphasis moved more to the fundamentals of the faith concerning the person and work of Christ, the substitutionary atonement, and similar central doctrines. This speaks highly of the man. He matured as a Christian; he matured as a theologian. He must be evaluated in that light.

However, some of Spurgeon's contemporaries seem to lose their basic theological moorings. He said, "We used to debate on particular and general redemption, but now men question whether there is any redemption at all worthy of the name."[2]

Preacher friend, in Spurgeon's words let me urge you to preach Christ if you want to save souls.

DLC

---

[1] Lewis A. Drumond, *Spurgeon: Prince of Preachers* (Grand Rapids, MI: Kregel Publications, 1992), 657.

[2] Ibid., 660.

Don't Take Freedom for Granted

Scripture: 1 Timothy 2:1-8

Around the world in this twenty-first century, obedient followers of Christ are forced to meet secretly to worship. These saints are in constant danger, if discovered, of being fined, imprisoned, and perhaps martyred. Their clandestine meetings must be carefully guarded, for continually they are hunted and hounded by godless authorities. Western hemisphere believers became aware of suffering Russian counterparts during the long and hideous days of Russian Communism.

In Great Britain, prior to the Edict of Toleration in 1689, Baptist believers found themselves in the same condition. We are greatly indebted to notes of Edward Terrill, of the Bristol Baptist congregation in Bristol, England. He recorded a running log of that assembly during those fright-filled days. Mr. Terrill died in 1685 or 1686. During that period from 1640 to 1648, several pastors of that daring flock were arrested, imprisoned, and martyred. The record for 1682 is similar to the experience of other years.

> 1682. *Jan. 29.* The Church met at four different places. Many of them went in the afternoon on Durdham Down, and got into a cave of a rock toward

Clifton, where Brother Thomas Whinnell preached to them.

March 12. Met in the fields by Barton Hundred, and Mr. Samuel Buttall of Plymouth preached in the fore-part of the day, and Brother Whinnell in the evening. It was thought there were near a thousand persons in the morning.

March 19. Met in the lanes beyond Baptist Mills.

April 13. Met in the rain in a lane.

April 20. A day of prayer, from nine to five in the evening, at Mr. Jackson's over the Down, in peace."

May 4. Information was brought to a petty session for Gloucestershire, against brother Jennings, for preaching in the lanes, and a warrant granted for levying five pounds, or else goods, or person.

June 11. Brother Fownes being come from London, but not daring to come into the city because of the Corporation Act, met with us, and preached in Kingswood, near Scruze Hole, under a tree, and endured the rain.

July 2. Our pastor preached in another place in the wood. Our friends took much pains in the rain, because many informers were ordered out to search; and we were in peace, though there were near twenty men and boys in search.

July 16. Brother Fownes first, and Brother Whinnell after, preached under a tree, it being very rainy.

August 20. Met above Scruze Hole, in our old place, and heard Brother Fownes preach twice in peace. Brother Terrill had caused a workman to make banks on the side of the hill to sit down on, several of them like a gallery; and there we met also on the 27th, in peace. On both days we sang a psalm in the open woods.

On the 7th of December we met for our lecture at Mr. Shuter's on Redcliffe Hill, in peace, taking a great deal of care in going and coming, the women wearing neither white aprons nor pattens.[1]

This Day in Baptist History III

Danger lurks in many parts of the world for those who will worship the Lord God in truth. In many places in Southeastern Asia, faithful children of God worship in the face of hatred and malice. Radical Hinduism, radical Buddhism and the jihad of Islam have much in common. Bible Christianity is detested by each of these groups, and martyrdoms have been experienced at the hands of each. It is apparent that Satan realizes that his days are short, and he is stirring up a vicious, violent, malevolent spirit among his dupes. It has been suggested that there were more martyrdoms in the last half of the twentieth century than during any other like period of church history.

In an effort to be politically correct, many American politicians refuse to identify the victims of jihad in Africa as being martyred by Islam. But make no mistake about it, these are terrible days for believers in many parts of the world. Will the true Church go through the Tribulation Period? NO! But real believers have suffered greatly elsewhere, and America may not be immune. Pray for revival in our land while freedom remains.

DLC

---

[1] J. M. Cramp, (1871; 2003). *Baptist History: From the Foundation of the Christian Church to the Close of the Eighteenth Century* (Page 308). Roger Williams Heritage Archives.

Sunday Evening Services

Scripture: John 20:19; Acts 20:7-12

In the early days of my ministry, I can well remember preaching on Sunday evenings to standing-room-only crowds. Surrounding liberal congregations met only on Sunday mornings, and our evening services were attractive to many conservatives in the liberal churches. We discovered it was easier to get the unsaved out on Sunday evenings, and we used that meeting primarily for the purpose of evangelism. How I looked forward to the gatherings each Sunday night. In the golden days, a youth ministry was conducted an hour before the evening service, and one could always depend on the enthusiasm of the young people to spark the evening service. The Sunday evening meeting was a bit more relaxed, and the hymn singing was always a rich blessing.

But then television came along, and crowds began to deteriorate. Television surely made the general populace mindful of being entertained. This resulted in many pastors, with a desire to maintain a good Sunday evening attendance, opting to show Christian films. More and more the service became entertainment-centered, and the distinctiveness that it once held was lost. The car manufacturers produced comfortable and dependable transportation, and Sundays became more and more a day for relaxation and travel. All of these factors entered into the scenario, and tragically, Sunday evening services in the average fundamental Baptist church today is but a shell of what it once was.

I have heard folk suggest that there is no biblical warrant for Sunday evening gatherings. But the passages that are listed in this devotional tell of our Lord meeting with His disciples on Sunday night following the resurrection, and the Savior showed Himself alive with many infallible proofs. And Paul certainly gathered the saints together in Troas. In fact, he had a standing-room-only crowd, and one poor fellow even went to sleep on that great preacher!

But I was interested in observing that in the Baptist petition to the House of Burgesses of Virginia, on May 5, 1774, the Baptists wanted the privilege of having evening meetings. The record reads, "A petition of sundry persons of the community of Christians called Baptists . . . was presented to the House and read, setting forth that the toleration proposed by the bill ordered at the last session of the General Assembly to be printed and published not admitting public worship, except in the daytime, is inconsistent with the laws of England, as well as the practice and usage of the primitive churches, and even of the English church itself; that the night season may sometimes be better spared by the petitioners from the necessary duties of their callings; and that they wish for no indulgences which may disturb the peace of government; and therefore praying the House to take their case into consideration, and to grant them suitable redress."[1]

This Day in Baptist History III

Many Baptist pastors are afraid to invite evangelists to conduct series of meetings today, because the saints of God have adopted the habit of being only Sunday morning attendees. It is an embarrassment to the pastor to invite an evangelist and have 500 in the morning service, and then only 65 present on Sunday evening, and lesser numbers present on the weeknights. The result has been that many pastors have just given up on evangelism.

Beloved, these things ought not to be. Surely Sunday is still the Lord's Day, and those who are spiritual and have interest in God's Word and God's work should be willing to surrender the full day to the Lord. Baptist congregations are seemingly filled with morning glories, but God has not told us to be flower children. We are to be lights in the world, and light shines brightest at night.

Let me challenge you to shock your pastor and determine that you are going to become faithful in the evening, as well as in the morning.

DLC

---

[1] Charles F. James, *Documentary History of the Struggle for Religious Liberty in Virginia* (New York: Da Capo Press, 1971), 38.

Bring the Books

Scripture: 2 Timothy 4:13

Books were very important in the life and ministry of the Prince of Preachers, Charles Haddon Spurgeon. His dear wife, Susannah Thompson Spurgeon, became an invalid at age thirty-three, but yet she illustrates his love of books. Though an invalid through much of her lifetime, she headed up a unique ministry of providing books for rural preachers across the English countryside and missionaries around the world. Mr. Spurgeon had a personal library of 12,000 volumes. We know that from early on in his ministry he cultivated the habit of reading six books per week. As his multiplied ministries began to expand, he established a Colportage ministry. On May 5 and 6, 1878, the Annual Conference of the Colporteurs was held at the Metropolitan Tabernacle in London. At that time, sixty-one men were employed in distributing gratuitously and by sale Christian literature throughout the countryside of Great Britain.[1] During that reporting period, those men had distributed 160,000 tracts, had visited 500,000 families, and sold 84,147 Christian books and 239,758 periodicals. Needless to say, they also distributed by sale a large number of Bibles. We would have to conclude that Mr. Spurgeon apparently believed in the ancient adage, The pen is mightier than the sword. Twenty-first century Christians would do well to follow suit and distribute gospel tracts and literature far and wide.

However, my concern in our devotional today is to emphasize our own personal reading. Mr. Spurgeon's personal library consisted of 12,000 volumes, and he treasured and knew his books. I fear that in this modern day, the distraction of television and social schedules keep the average believer from reading as he ought. Books are readily available, and it is essential that one be selective in choosing what volumes to purchase. Much that is being written today is but spiritual froth. It is possible for a sincere believer to be sidetracked by being absorbed with frivolous material and not be spiritually nurtured at all.

Following the death of Mr. Spurgeon, it became necessary for his wife and son to sell a portion of his library. Thankfully for Americans, 5,103 of his 12,000 volume library was purchased by the William Jewel College in Liberty, Missouri. The books were actually purchased in 1905, and the five thousand books cost £500, which was the equivalent in that day to about $2,500 American dollars. The books arrived in the States in 1906, and a beautiful replica of Mr. Spurgeon's study was built in the Curry library of the college to house the volumes.

This author has had the privilege of visiting the library and handling many of the priceless volumes contained therein. Mr. Spurgeon had written his brief evaluation of the various books on the fly leafs within the covers. In fact, it is apparent that his notes in the various tomes were used in preparing the volume, *Commenting on the Commentaries* which was published under Mr. Spurgeon's name. The volumes must be protected, and thus they are kept in locked bookcases with wire mesh sealing them away from careless hands. However, the archivist has been known to open a case that visitors might examine several volumes.

During my first visit there, I purchased a mimeographed bibliography of the 5,103 volumes. More recently a printed form of the bibliography has been made available and can be purchased from the library. Tours are allowed of the library, but special arrangements must be made in advance. If you plan to be in that area, I suggest you write to the Charles H. Spurgeon Library at 500 College Hill in Liberty, Missouri 64068-1896 for an appointment to view the thrilling display. Why not ask your pastor to recommend several good Bible study books that you might use to begin a personal habit of reading?

While visiting the Spurgeon Library at William Jewel College, it is well also to stop by the college chapel to behold an artists's rendition of the immersion by the noted Baptist preacher, John Gano, of General George Washington. Those who have admired the ministry of Charles Spurgeon would surely find the time on campus rewarding.

DLC

---

[1] *The Sword and the Trowel*, May 1878, 316.

May 7

A Model for Preachers

Scripture: 2 Timothy 2:1-2; 3:10-11

Elsewhere in this volume we consider the life of Dr. Monroe Parker as an evangelist and as a missionary leader. A review of his life would be greatly diminished without consideration of his work as an educator.

In 1937 Monroe Parker returned to Cleveland, Tennessee, where he joined the faculty of Bob Jones College. During his first year, he taught Survey of the Bible and Bible Prophecy. He also assumed leadership of the Practical Instruction for Preachers class. He first taught the class in Dr. Bob Jones, Sr.'s absence and later assumed full teaching responsibility for it. His title was Director of Religious Activities, and he organized many of the student ministry activities and all extension services. He also found time to complete his M.A. degree in 1944 and the Ph.D. in 1947.

These years saw the advent of World War II. As professors left for military service, Dr. Parker assumed more and more responsibilities at the college. Many young men were saved during the war, and God called them to preach. After being discharged from military service, many enrolled in Bob Jones College. The preachers' class at Bob Jones expanded rapidly in these years and in the post war years. Eventually Dr. Parker taught a thousand men who were training for the ministry. Many of those men are still faithfully preaching after many years. As the college grew, and his responsibilities increased, he was given the additional title of Assistant to the President.

At this time a great sorrow entered Dr. Parker's life. On December 30, 1946, his wife Harriet was killed in an automobile accident between Birmingham, Alabama, and Atlanta, Georgia. But he continued his ministry as an evangelist and on the faculty at Bob Jones. And God led a second wife into his life, and on January 5, 1948, he married Marjorie Parker. God blessed them with their two children, John and Penny.

In 1949 Dr. Parker left Bob Jones University to become a full-time evangelist again. In 1954 he was called to the pastorate of Grace Baptist Church in Decatur, Alabama. The church grew and prospered greatly under his ministry, but God had further plans for Dr. Parker.

On February 1, 1958, Dr. Parker assumed his responsibilities as President of Pillsbury Conservative Baptist Bible College. Just a few more than 100 students were enrolled in the fledgling school, which had opened the previous fall. During his eight years as president, Pillsbury grew to an enrollment of more than 500.

I am glad God led Dr. Parker to Pillsbury, because God led me there also. He became leader, teacher, role model, friend, and confidant. Many of us who graduated from Pillsbury are still in the ministry. We are inspired by his example and warmed by the memories of our time under his ministry.

Dr. Parker's ministry at Pillsbury was marked by fruitfulness in his evangelistic work, dramatic growth and expansion in the college, and years of decisive leadership.

This Day in Baptist History III

In 1957 Harold John Ockenga announced the movement known as New Evangelicalism to the world. Pillsbury was part of the Conservative Baptist movement, and the struggle over New Evangelicalism raged within that movement. The decline was dramatic over a decade. In 1953 the Conservative Baptist Association of America had adopted its Portland Manifesto on biblical separation. Just ten years later the same association refused to reaffirm it! Many men, too numerous to name here, stood for biblical principles. Dr. Parker was one of the leaders in that biblical battle, and he was constantly at the front lines of the conflict. We who knew him in those days saw his dynamic personality, his strong convictions, his keen mind, and his resolve to be loyal to God and His Word. We saw that military bearing combined with a Spirit-controlled life, a tender heart, a gracious spirit, and unfailing ethical conduct even in the heat of the controversy. We knew, as one of our texts for today says, his doctrine and his manner of life. The honorary Doctor of Laws was presented him on May 7, 1988 by Maranatha Baptist Bible College in Wisconsin.

Monroe Parker was highly effective in training preachers for God's service because he was a biblical model of what a preacher of the Gospel should be.

FJM

May 8

Not Many, But Thankfully, Some

Scripture: 1 Corinthians 1:26

Our entry opens on May 8, 1660, when King Charles the Second was proclaimed King of England. With the Commonwealth's demise, he actually arrived in England on May 23, 1660. He was known as the "Merry Monarch," and some religious toleration dotted the political horizon during his rule. Charles had numerous mistresses and illegitimate children, and he loved racing and gambling. However, even at that, several interesting Baptists came to the fore, during his reign.

Mr. John Gosnold had been a minister of the established church, and during the civil unrest, he made the Scriptures the center of his thinking. The *Dictionary of National Biog-*

raphy Volume 22 informs us that John Gosnold had been educated at the Charterhouse, from which he proceeded to Pembroke Hall, Cambridge. After taking religious orders, he became chaplain to Lord Grey. Following his conversion to Baptist convictions, he was chosen pastor of a Baptist congregation at the Barbican in London. He was one of the ministers who submitted an appeal to the king. His preaching was very popular, and he drew visitors from every denomination. His audience was usually composed of three thousand, and among them very often six or seven clergymen in their gowns, sat in a convenient place, under a large gallery, where they were seen by few.[1]

With that background, let me introduce Carolus Maria Du Veil, a man who had been born into a Jewish home in Mentz, France. He was educated in Judaism, but as he began comparing the prophetical books of the Old Testament with the New, he was convinced in his heart that Jesus was indeed the promised Messiah! When he embraced Christianity, his father was incensed, and attempted to kill Carolus with a sword. As a result, Carolus joined the Roman Catholic church, and obtained great preferential treatment. In 1672 he published a commentary on Matthew and Mark and gained the reputation of having a polemic mind. As a result, Carolus was appointed to write against the French Protestants. In his effort to refute them, it was necessary to read their writings. Doing so, he discovered that truth was on their side, and thus he fled from France to Holland. In a short time, he traveled on to England. There he gained the patronage of several Episcopal bishops and dignitaries. In 1679 he published an exposition of the Song of Solomon, and in 1680 he wrote on the minor prophets. Through these works, he became quite well known and the bishop of London sought his friendship. That friendship procured for Carolus the use of the bishop's library. There he discovered writings of the English Baptists, and being an honest inquirer, he discovered that the Biblical hermeneutics of the Baptists caused him to realize that they were in agreement with the Word of God.

At that time Carolus Maria Du Veil sought an interview with Reverend John Gosnold. In the course of time Carolus was immersed by the Baptist pastor, and became a member of the Baptist church. In 1684 he published a study on the Book of Acts in which he vindicated his newly discovered principles.

For a short time Carolus Du Veil served as pastor of the Baptist Church on Grace Street, but his inability to speak the English fluently rendered his preaching unintelligible to his English audience. He entered into the practice of medicine during the last years of his life, and when he could no longer work, his Baptist friends raised an annuity in his behalf that met his needs.[2]

In his summation of the life of Carolus Du Veil, Crosby wrote, "He was a grave, judicious divine, a good chronologist, a great historian, a skillful grammarian, and such a pious good man, as brought honour to the cause in which he was embarked."[3]

Thankfully the Scripture does not say, not ***any*** wise men after the flesh, not ***any*** mighty, not ***any*** noble are called. Our Lord is able to use ***any*** who will surrender to His will and obey His Word. God places no premium on ignorance. The most important factor for service is the total acceptance of God's Word by faith. May we be found in that group.

DLC

---

[1] Thomas Crosby, *The History of the English Baptists* (London: By the Author, 1740), 3:62.

[2] Richard Knight, *History of the General or Six Principle Baptists* (Providence: Smith and Parmenter, 1827), 209-210.

[3] Crosby, 4:259.

America's Rare Baptist Tory

Scripture: 1 Thessalonians 4:13-18

During the Revolutionary War, only one Baptist preacher in America stood with the English! That man was Morgan Edwards, who had been born in Wales on this date in 1722. Morgan Edwards grew to maturity in the British Isles. He began preaching in 1738, and served several small congregations in England for seven years. While pastoring those charges, he entered Bristol College in 1742 and remained until graduation in 1744. It will be remembered that Bristol College was the first established Baptist college in Great

Britain. He was ordained to the Baptist ministry on June 1, 1757, and served for nine years as pastor in Cork, Ireland.

In May of 1761 Morgan Edwards emigrated to America and became pastor of the Baptist church in Philadelphia. He served the church well, but resigned that charge in 1770, and never again served in a pastoral capacity. Morgan Edwards was very scholarly, and though he was a strong preacher, it seems that his ministry might have been better directed to a classroom. In the next years he traveled widely as preacher and lecturer.

It is apparent that during the Pre-Revolutionary War period, Baptists were strong advocates of freedom. Baptists were weary of paying taxes to support established churches in the various colonies. Of course, Pennsylvania did not have a state-church, but Baptists realized that as long as the colonies were subservient under the control of another nation, freedom could not be fully experienced. On the other hand, Morgan Edwards was a loyal son of Great Britain. Thus, when the Revolutionary War began, Reverend Edwards proved to be the only Baptist minister in the country, with one other possible exception, who held to the Tory persuasion and sympathized with the mother county. Edwards was never jailed during the Revolutionary War, but his travel was curtailed, and he was limited to traveling in the area of Philadelphia. His was not an easy life, for he experienced significant tragedies in life. He outlived two wives and most of his children. One historian describes Edwards as a man of versatility, being both a capable leader for many years and a historian of some importance. In temperament he was eccentric and choleric but "with all of his varied gifts, he was always evangelistic in spirit."[1]

A careful look at the life of Morgan Edwards reveals strong characteristics. To him, more than to anyone else, is due the credit of founding Rhode Island College, now Brown University. Besides being the principal mover in the enterprise, he was active in securing funds for the permanent support of the institution, and was one of its fellows from 1764 until 1789. His efforts were surely recognized as he was honored with the degree of A. M. from Rhode Island College in 1769.

More importantly, Reverend Edwards was the first Baptist in America to attempt a history of his denomination in this country. In pursuing that effort, he traveled from New Hampshire to Georgia eagerly collecting all available materials. Besides various published discourses, he was the author of *Materials Toward a History of the Baptists of Pennsylvania* (1772), and *Materials Toward a History of the Baptists in Jersey* (1792). He also left a large body of manuscript records, which have proved of great value to subsequent writers. In recent days his *Materials Toward a History of the Baptists* has been reprinted, and those interested in Baptist history are greatly indebted to his laborious search of information.

However, it is interesting to notice that Morgan Edwards had a keen understanding of Bible prophecy. While a student at Bristol College, he submitted an essay in a class of Bible prophecy. The essay was later published in Philadelphia in a fifty-six page work. Though published in Philadelphia in 1788, Reverend Edwards published it as written during his college days of the 1740s. In it Morgan reveals faith in the Pre-tribulation coming of the Lord Jesus Christ to receive His own, before the millennial reign of Christ. Morgan died on January 28, 1795, not having experienced the rapture. However, his article proves that the pre-tribulation rapture is not a new interpretation of twentieth century saints, but is the doctrine that has endured among Bible-believers from the times of the New Testament.

May we live today, not looking for signs, but listening for the shout!

DLC

---

[1] Robert G. Torbet, *A History of the Baptists* (Philadelphia: The Judson Press, 1950), 243-244.

May 10

Why Tarriest Thou?

Scripture: Isaiah 51:9a

At the close of the Triennial Convention in May of 1814, Richard Furman on his way home to Charleston, S.C., stopped in the nation's capitol. He happened to meet an acquaintance who was in the company of Mr. James Monroe, then a member of the Presidential Cabinet. As they were introduced, Colonel Monroe asked, "May I enquire if you were once of the High Hills of

Santee?" The High Hills of Santee was a Baptist Church in South Carolina where a group of dissenters called a meeting to discuss religious liberty. The young pastor was a zealous advocate and became an outstanding spokesman for the movement. Thus when Reverend Furman answered in the affirmative, Mr. Monroe said, "And you were the young preacher who fled for protection to the American camp, on account of the reward which Lord Cornwallis had offered for your head?" Upon acknowledging the truthfulness of that statement, their conversation became quite lengthy. Colonel Monroe related to distinguished bystanders the circumstances to which he had alluded.

It seems that young Furman was not only a warm-hearted Baptist preacher, but an ardent advocate of the Revolutionary War. Everywhere, on stumps, and in barns, as well as in pulpits, he preached resistance to Britain. When Lord Cornwallis was told of the impact the young Baptist preacher was having, he offered £1000 for his head. Realizing that the Tories were on his tracks, the youthful preacher fled to the American camp, and he did not return until after the conclusion of the War. By his prayers and eloquent appeals, he encouraged and stimulated the colonists to throw off the chains of British tyranny insomuch that it was reported that Cornwallis had remarked that, he "feared the prayers of that godly youth more than the armies of Sumpter and Marion."[1]

Colonel Monroe insisted that Reverend Furman preach in the Hall of Congress. The preacher did his best to decline. He disclaimed his talents as a Court preacher. All the elite, including the President and Cabinet Ministers, would be present, for Colonel Monroe had circulated the early efforts and eloquence of the young preacher. Furman chose for his text, Acts 22:16, "And now, why tarriest thou? Arise and be baptized." He enjoyed great freedom as he spoke, and his voice rang out as in days of old. His earnestness caught the imagination of his audience and everything built as with a grand crescendo. Catching the spirit of the hour, he rose to the grand climax of his presentation. His clear stentorian voice rang out, "And now, why tarriest thou? Arise! And be baptized." At the word "ARISE," several of his august audience seemed electrified and rose from their seats, as if alarmed at their past sinful hesitation.

This Mr. Monroe, or as we identified him Colonel Monroe, was none other than the man who soon after became leader of the United States – President James Monroe. From that day onward President Monroe always retained the highest veneration of Reverend Richard Furman.

Following the Revolutionary War, Reverend Furman returned to South Carolina and contributed greatly to the constitutional change, which ended the established church (i.e. state/church) in South Carolina. While serving as a delegate to the South Carolina constitutional convention in 1790, he obtained the passage of measures that discontinued the special privileges of the Episcopal Church and granted the right of incorporation to all denominations.[2]

We have come full circle in American history. Men of God must speak up and boldly declare truth. The First Amendment was never meant to isolate our land from morality that is based upon God's Word. The so-called Wall of Separation was a guarantee that the nation would never establish a national statewide church. There is a movement abroad in the land that would silence the voices of preachers concerning moral issues such as abortion, homosexuality, and pornography. Let us pray that our pastors shall not succumb to the pressures of the politically correct advocates. Pastor, speak up for truth regardless of the cost!

DLC

[1] James Belcher, *The Religious Denominations in the United States* (Philadelphia: John E. Potter, 1856), 185-186.

[2] Winston C. Babb, *Encyclopedia of Southern Baptists* (Nashville, TN: Broadman Press, 1958), 1:519.

No Idle Man, This Man

Scripture: Proverbs 4:23

Dr. Harold Bennett Sightler, an old fashioned fundamentalist, was probably best known for his radio broadcast, *The Bright Spot Hour*, which began in 1943. Harold was born to Horace and Pauline Bennett Horace Sightler on May 15, 1914. The Sightler home was a god-fearing, Bible-believing, Baptist family in St. George, South Carolina. Young Harold had the early blessing of seeing Christianity practiced. In September 1924, the family moved to Greenville where Harold spent the remainder of his life. The family united with the East Park Baptist Church.[1]

Harold was saved and baptized at age twelve and began tithing from his paper route. In 1932 he began working after school as a stock boy for a local wholesale grocer. For eleven years the hard hours of labor helped shape Harold's life and taught him to use time wisely. He had wanted to be a physician but had no money for college.

On May 11, 1935, Harold Sightler and Helen Grace Vaughn were married. After the birth of their first child, they dedicated their lives to God, and soon the Lord began dealing with Harold about preaching. Harold thought he must be mistaken because he was timid and shy, but God's calling enables. In March of 1940, he preached his first sermon at East Park. True to his call he was willing to preach anywhere—street corners, jails, cottage prayer meetings, prison camps, brush arbors, or old buildings. His first revival was in the yard of Mrs. Wardlaw.

Following the Lord's leading in 1941, he bought a 20' by 40' tent in which to hold meetings. He made the seats and personally helped pitch the tent. In 1942 the East Park Church ordained him. He entered Furman University with the help of Pastor Lee and the Greenville Baptist Association and graduated in 1946 with a degree in Greek. In 1943, while at Furman, he began his radio program. While in college he worked at the wholesale grocers and pastored Mauldin and Pelham Baptist churches. Only eternity will reveal the many souls who were saved and encouraged to live for Christ through his preaching.

Concerned for souls, Brother Harold in 1946 called for a week of prayer at Pelham Baptist Church that God might save sinners. These nightly meetings went on for five months, and a revival of old time power broke out. Many were saved both at the church and through the radio program. The first of the Greer Baptist Camp Meetings was held in a brush arbor at Pelham in 1947. With the help of Percy Ray, the Camp Meetings became an annual event.

As a result of the revival Brother Sightler began holding meetings in other churches. While he was away at a meeting in 1951, a drunken driver struck his family's car, claiming the life of his daughter, Carolyn. At this lowest point in his life, and with a broken heart, he was comforted by an old mountain preacher,J. Harv Stanbury. He was encouraged by God and kept to his duty and to the old paths.

In 1952 he organized Tabernacle Baptist Church in Greenville. The church had a miraculous growth to a membership of over 3,000. The congregation has sent out many pastors and missionaries. One part of Tabernacle's missions around the world is a mission church in the Kentucky coalfields. The mission budget reached $1,000 a day.

Tabernacle Christian School began on September 6, 1960, with seventy-three students from nursery to fourth grade. By 1966 all grades were included. A most rewarding outreach has been Tabernacle Children's Home, established on August 1, 1962. In 1963 Tabernacle Baptist Bible Institute began training men and women for God's service. It became Tabernacle Baptist Bible College in 1975. Dr. Sightler taught Baptist History from Orchard's *Concise History of the Baptists* and *The Trail of Blood*. These books reveal that the Baptists were never part of the Roman Catholic Church and thus did not come from the Reformation.

Brother Sightler was granted an honorary doctorate in 1964 by Tennessee Temple. In 1982 the Helen V. Sightler Retirement Center was built for housing the church's widows. We honor the memory of Dr. Sightler who evangelized, pastored, authored, and administered many ministries. He surely was a champion of old-time faith. He was found faithful until the Lord called His servant home on September 27, 1995.[2]

DCB

---

[1] Harold B. Sightler, *The Story of My Life,* 31.

[2] James Sightler, *Personal Recollections of Dr. Harold B. Sightler's Early Ministry and the Heritage of Tabernacle Baptist Church.*

May 12

Revive Thy Word, O Lord

Scripture: Isaiah 59:1-2

The beautiful scenery of Nova Scotia was negated for me on a recent trip as I saw a multitude of old church buildings, now boarded up by indifference. What a needy mission field exists in that part of our continent. I could not help meditating upon our current spiritual situation in America as fundamental Baptist churches seem to be on the wane due to apathy and spiritual lethargy. Once Nova Scotia experienced the power of God in refreshing revival. Souls were saved, churches were alive and growing, and additional churches were being established. As the twenty-first century has dawned, all indications in Nova Scotia reveal a great spiritual decline and dearth.

Revival had swept across Nova Scotia early in the nineteenth century. For instance, Israel Potter wrote the editor of the Baptist Missionary Magazine, Dr. Thomas Baldwin in Boston, as follows:

> Clements, Annapolis county, Nova Scotia, May 12, 1810,
>
> Dear and Rev. Sir,
>
> In the beginning of March last, a most powerful reformation began in the lower part of this town, which seemed to pervade the minds of old and young, and many, we hope, were brought to the knowledge of the truth. About ten days after, the good work made its appearance in the middle of the town. The people assembled from every quarter, and it seemed that it might be truly said, that God was passing through the place in a very powerful manner. The glorious work has since spread through every part of the town, and some of all ages have been made to bow to the mild sceptre of the Redeemer.
>
> The ordinance of baptism has been administered for five Sabbaths successively. Forty-five have been admitted to the sacred rite, and a church has been constituted upon the Gospel plan, consisting of sixty five members, to which we expect further additions. If I should say that two hundred have been hopefully converted to the Lord in this town since the reformation commenced, I think I should not exceed the truth. The good work is still spreading eastward very rapidly, and looks likely to spread through the province.

This Day in Baptist History III

The opposition has been great, and many oaths have been sworn even in the time of divine service. But the Lord has triumphed gloriously over the horse and his rider, and blessed be His name.

At Round-hill I understand there is a number to be baptized to-day. The province of Nova Scotia has been highly favoured with the gospel. We beg an interest in your prayers, that the Lord would give us strength to contend earnestly for the faith that was once delivered to the saints.

Your unworthy friend,
Israel Potter.[1]

"Surely the Lords hand is not shortened, that it cannot save; neither His ear heavy, that it cannot hear: BUT your iniquities have separated between you and your God, and your sins have hid His face from you, that He will not hear" (Isaiah 59:1-2). There is a tremendous need for a great awakening in America and Canada! The spiritual indifference among God's people, which has been caused by materialism, selfishness and pride, has darkened our minds. Saints today feel they are doing God a favor by attending a Sunday morning service. To provide spiritual salve for the consciences of believers who plan a Sunday morning round of golf, hireling religion leaders have scheduled Saturday evening services.

How long has it been since you have cried out to God for forgiveness for your own torpid attitude? Are you as spiritually minded today as you were in former times? If not, it is high time to awake out of sleep and observe the spiritual indifference that is choking our churches. Righteousness is waning, and we are in such a state of spiritual coma that we fail to recognize it. Rather than being the Lord's Day, Sunday has become another holiday. Let us put off the works of darkness and adorn ourselves in the armor light as we seek the Lord for revival in our own lives, in our churches, and in our nation.

DLC

---

[1] David Benedict, *A General History of the Baptist Denomination in America* (Boston: Lincoln & Edmands, 1813), 1:302-303.

May 13

It Hasn't Always Been "The Land of the Free"

Scripture: Romans 13:10-14

Historians have done great service in providing an exposure of the vile treatment of Baptists in the early days of the Commonwealth of Virginia at the hands of the State Church there. But we still await a complete exposition of the severe treatment given Baptists by the State Church in Massachusetts. Small notations in various sources have made us aware of that history. We have read of the persecution of William Witter, Obadiah Holmes, Thomas Painter, Dr. John Clarke, John Crandall, Henry Dunster, Thomas Gould, William Turner, John Farnum, and a host of others, but still the public awaits a definitive history of the cruelty doled out to the non-conformists of those days. Perhaps someone reading this volume will be challenged to research and write such an intriguing and helpful volume.

Be that as it may, Massachusetts, from its earliest days targeted the Baptists as enemies of the colony's goal. From the beginning, the pilgrims planned to establish a theocracy. Every citizen would be a Christian and a member of the state church. The Reformers had similar goals in their areas of government. Both the Reformers and the Pilgrims sought to accomplish that goal through infant baptism. Of course, it soon became apparent that infant baptism did not assure one's salvation. That heretical sacrament had been invented by the Roman Catholic Church because of its belief in baptismal regeneration. The Pilgrims did not believe that salvation came through one's baptism; nonetheless they felt it might somehow assure that one would become a Christian. No such reality existed, and soon the state churches were composed of more unbelievers than genuine Christians. Ritual soon replaced reality, and only the Great Awakening ever reversed the situation, and that correction was temporary. However, the church fathers of the state church were determined not to allow any dissent to rear its head.

This Day in Baptist History III

From the earliest day, laws were enacted against the Baptists. Fines for refusing to pay the clergy tax, imprisonment for refusing to attend public services of the state church, and public whippings for daring to hold their own meetings, were meted out regularly to Baptist citizens of Massachusetts.

Petitions were often presented to the government urging the tightening of anti-Baptist legislation. For instance, on May 13, 1646, a petition from Roxbury, Dorchester, and other points was submitted, urging that the laws against the Baptists be strengthened. It read: "At the prevaylinge of errors and heresies is noted by our Saviour in the gospel, and elsewhere in Scripture, as a forerunner of God's judgments, and in as much as the errors of the Anabaptists, where they do prevayle, are not a little dangerous to church and commonwealth, as the lamatable tumults in Germany, when the said errors were grown into a height, did too manifestlie witnesse, and such good laws or order are enacted amongst us, against such persons having alreadie bene, as we are informed, a special meanes of discouraging multitudes of erroneous persons from comminge over into this countrie, which wee account noe small mercie of God unto us, and one sweet and wholesome fruite of the sayd lawes, it is therefore our humble petition to this honorable court, that such lawes or orders as are in force amongst us against Anabaptists or other erroneous persons, whereby to restraine the spreadinge and divulginge of their errors amongst people here, may not be abrogated and taken away, nor any waise weakened, but may still be continued."[1]

America is indeed The Land of the Free, but it is that only because our Baptist forefathers were willing to pay the price in leading the way to secure that freedom. Today Baptists are often referred to as Bigoted Baptists, but in reality it has been our Baptist forefathers in America who have insisted on soul liberty and total religious freedom! For additional information on this subject, let me recommend the book *America in Crimson Red* written by my friend, Reverend James R. Beller. Through much tedious research, Brother Beller has attempted to restore much of the history of our Land that revisionists have removed through the years.

May God stir our hearts to use our freedom to maintain it for all our citizenry.

DLC

[1] John T. Christian, *A History of the Baptists* (Nashville, TN: Broadman Press, 1926), 2:56.

May 14

Preaching Experiences in Early America

Scripture: Proverbs 29:22

John Leland was born on May 14, 1754, about forty miles west of Boston. We have looked with wonder at the fruitful life our Lord gave him in the early days of our Republic. In 1787, when he was thirty-three years of age, he doubtless reached the zenith of success in his ministry. A visit from the old Separate Baptist leader, Colonel Samuel Harris, had stirred his heart. He reported that through Harris' ministry he caught the spirit of prayer, and the Lord gave him renewed confidence that He was going to work mightily to meet the spiritual needs of those in Orange County, Virginia.

A dancing school had been established in his neighborhood, and it had a spiritually debilitating influence. At the conclusion of a Sunday morning preaching service, Elder Leland announced that he had opened a dancing school and would fiddle the tune while the angels sang, if they would dance repentance on their knees. His audacity caught the congregation by surprise, and soon crowds began to mount to hear the man of God. Solemnity, sobs, and sighs characterized the audiences, and these gave way to tears of repentance. As a result, Elder Leland began working in a twenty-mile area bordered by Orange, Culpeper, Spottsylvania, and Louise counties. When the work languished in one neighborhood, it would break out in power in another. There seemed to be a continual experiencing of heavenly blessing from October 1787, until March 1789. During that period, Leland baptized about 400. In fact, 300 were baptized in 1788 alone.

Of course, Satan was not pleased. In the southern part of that area, an irate man took his gun and made it known that he was going to shoot the man of God. It seems he had given his consent for his wife to be baptized, and the meeting was scheduled. The man, however, had changed his mind, and the threat of murder was real. The service began, and John Leland entered the water with the lady. An alarm was sounded that the man was coming with his gun. A detachment of men went to meet the irate husband in an effort to pacify him. Knowing the circumstances, Elder Leland baptized the candidate without hesitancy. Fortunately, the irate husband never did accomplish his goal.

At another time, a lady invited the Elder to preach at her home on a certain evening. When he arrived at the gate, her son, who was a Captain in the militia, met the preacher and demanded that he not comply with his mother's wishes. John Leland asked the young man if he thought he was right in making such an injunction. The Captain said, "No. I know I am wrong, and I expect to be damned for it; but I have said it, and shall abide by my word." The husband also came to the gate and insisted the preacher continue with their plans. John Leland entered the house and the people began to gather.

With that the young Captain withdrew, but he did so with threats. As the service began, the Captain rushed into the house like a wild man. He drew his sword out of the scabbard, and exclaimed, "Let me kill the damned rascal!"[1] As he made a stroke at the man of God, he slipped and the sword point hit his own knee, and he was quickly subdued. Actually what had happened was that Mrs. Leland, seeing the intent of the young Captain, had clasped her arms within his elbow, and thus the blow was caused to miss its mark. Furthermore, she held his arm, making him powerless until the men disarmed him. Taking a lantern, those who had gathered went out into the yard, and Leland preached as though nothing had happened.

We must admire the holy boldness that John Leland exhibited. At the same time, we cannot help but wonder if such audacity might not be called for in face of the great apathy in much Christian service today.

DLC

---

[1] J. B. McInturff, Editor, *The Old Paths* (New Market, VA: Henkel & Company, 1891), 146.

May 15

Victorious Martyrs

Scripture: Matthew 5:10-12

An interesting account of Anabaptist martyrdom appears in an ancient history of England as follows: "...On Easter-day, April 3rd, was disclosed a congregation of Dutch Anabaptists without Aldgate in London, whereof seven-and-twenty were taken and imprisoned .... Next month, May 15, one Dutchman and ten women were condemned...."[1]

Again, I would remind our readers that It is a prejudiced and false representation which many writers allow themselves to make when they stigmatize the Anabaptists as "numerous licentious and fanatical sectaries, whose excesses afforded a plausible pretext for punishing"; or impute to them "the wild excesses of the Communists at Munster." Thomas Munzer, . . . was never an Anabaptist. He remained in the Romish Church, and received its sacrament at his beheading.[2]

In relating additional facts concerning the severe treatment of the accused Anabaptists listed above, another author wrote, "Their meeting, though conducted in quietude, was detected, and a constable and his aids, addressing them as devils, demanded which of them was teacher. Twenty-seven of their names were at his command recorded, and he took seven of them to the magistrate, charging the rest to remain, and, soon returning, drove them with cruelty to the jail. After a few days they were all arraigned before the queen's commission, and told that they must renounce their belief and practice, on penalty of banishment or death. Remaining firm, they were remanded to prison.

During some three months they were repeatedly brought before the inquisitors, and subjected to every means of securing their recantations; but only meek and faithful responses were elicited. Finally the larger part of them were doomed to banishment; but five of the men were told that they could escape burning only by signing the Articles of the State Church. They were again thrust into a horrible prison, in separate cells, and given a month to face their fate. One of them died from the rigors of their treatment. Of two of the others we have no record; but the remaining two had their death warrant signed by Elizabeth . . . and they went together to be burned alive. For several days they were tantalized by preparations for the burning and then deferring it; but on the fatal hour they went forth serenely . . . . Together they were bound to the same stake, and while a church preacher hurled at them his accusations, and thrust before them his Articles for them to acknowledge, they affirmed their faith in God's mercy through Jesus Christ, and rose triumphant over the last enemy."[3]

Interestingly, Dr. Haskell, whom I have just quoted, continued by averring that Baptist churches existed in Great Britain long before the time of the Reformation. He wrote, "A stone has been exhumed in the Baptist churchyard at Cheshire inscribed with the date 1357. The records show the death of a pastor of the church in 1594, but it is not known how long previously the church had existed. Soon after the close of Elizabeth's reign, records of other churches appear. Under James I their persecutions continued, and drove them to secluded resorts."[4]

George Bancroft, famed American historian, wrote as follows: "The Baptist party, whose trophy from the first was freedom of conscience, unlimited freedom of mind, was trodden under foot with foul reproaches and most arrogant scorn, and its history is written in the blood of myriads of the German peasantry; but its principles, safe in their immortality, escaped with Roger Williams to Providence, and his colony is the witness that naturally the paths of the Baptists are paths of freedom."

Our Baptist forebears were ever the hunted and hounded, but they never sought to impose a creed by coercion. One of the distinguishing factors of our Baptist forebears was ever the principle of voluntarism. Let us determine faithfully to present the Gospel that our neighbors might be able to respond voluntarily to changeless truth.

DLC

---

[1] Thomas Fuller, *The Church History of Britain from the Birth of Jesus Christ until the year MDCXLVIII*, (London, England: Thomas Tegg and Son, 1837), 2:506.

[2] Samuel Haskell, *Heroes and Hierarchs* (Published for the Michigan Baptist Convention, 1895), 99.

[3] Ibid., 111-112.

[4] Ibid., 113.

May 16

Faithful Unto Death

Scripture: Revelation 2:9-11

The opposition of both Rome and the Reformers to our Anabaptist forefathers has been evidenced time and again in these volumes. Yet one is continually appalled in considering the undying hatred that the religionists of Christendom exhibited when dealing with these believers who wanted simply to follow the commandments of the Lord. In his *Reply to False Accusations* of 1552, Menno Simons wrote, "All Christians are commanded to love their enemies, to do good unto those who abuse and persecute them, to give the mantle when the cloak is taken, the other cheek when one is struck . . . . O beloved reader, our weapons are not swords and spears, but patience, silence, and hope, and the Word of God . . . . True Christians do not know vengeance, no matter how they are mistreated . . . . They do not cry, 'Vengeance, vengeance,' as does the world; but with Christ they supplicate and pray, 'Father, forgive them; for they know not what they do.'"[1]

An outstanding example of such response to persecutors is that demonstrated by Dirk Willems of Asperen in Holland. Having escaped from prison in the middle of the winter, Dirk Willems was pursued by a company of Anabaptist hunters.[2] Upon discovering that officers were about to arrest him in his home, he fled out the back door. The officers were soon in hot pursuit, and Dirk Willems hazarded fleeing on a frozen dyke. His bid was successful, but the officer who was closest in the chase fell through the thin ice, and he was about to perish in the icy water. What action would Dirk take? Would he flee considering his own life, or would be turn back and save the life of the drowning officer? There was no question in the mind of Dirk Willems. He returned and saved the life of his enemy. Surely we might expect that this heroic action would be rewarded by some act of kindness.

It was not to be. Dirk Williams was arrested by the officer, and the Catholic judges passed sentence on him on May 16, 1569.[3] The sentence rendered was that Dirk Willems was to be burned at the stake as an Anabaptist heretic! On the day appointed for the fulfillment of his sentence, a strong wind blew, and the man of God was consigned to suffer a slow death. Seventy times he was heard to cry out, "O my Lord; O my God." Finally, the bailiff had a mite of mercy on Dirk Willems, and he called out, "Dispatch the man with a quick death."

Studies of the number of martyrs in Belgium and the Netherlands have shown that no less than 1,500 Anabaptists were killed, possibly as many as 2,500, from the early days of the movement to the death of the last martyr in 1574.[4] George Huntston Williams estimated that "Persecutions of the Anabaptists in the southern Netherlands (Belgium) had been especially severe from the outset, because of their greater proximity to Brussels, the seat of the Spanish administration for the Low Countries." He further stated, "In the period covered by our narrative the number of Belgium martyrs was about three thousand, of whom the majority were Anabaptists. . .by the end of our period some fifty thousand dissidents had been driven from the Hapsburg Netherlands (mainly Flanders), the majority of them Anabaptists."[5]

Our Baptist forebears championed freedom for this Republic. They paid a heavy price to secure it, and still in this twenty-first century, America boasts that it is the land of the free. However, it is apparent in modern day America that soul liberty and religious freedom are under attack. May we who are followers of the Lamb do everything we possibly can to preserve this freedom for all mankind. But may we so walk in obedience to our Lord that if open persecution is experienced, we might be enabled by His grace to be faithful even unto death.

DLC

---

[1] Menno Simons, *The Complete Writings*. Trans. Leonard Verduin, ed. John C. Wenger, (Scottdale, PA: Herald Press, 1956), 555.

[2] Cornelius J. Dyck, *An Introduction to Mennonite History* (Scottdale, PA: Herald Press, 1976), 86.

[3] John Christian Wegner, *Even Unto Death* (Richmond, VA: John Knox Press, 1961), 101.

[4] Dyke, 86.

[5] George Huntston Williams, *The Radical Reformation* (Kirksville, MO: Truman State University Press, 2000), 1178.

May 17

Our Mandate: Missions

Scripture: 2 Corinthians 8:1-7

The Baptists of Kentucky were sorely attacked by two anti-missionary forces that would have destroyed all vision had it not been for stalwarts of the faith who dared to withstand them. The leaven of Alexander Campbell and his distorted doctrinal delusions, and the Antinomianism of Daniel Parker with his two-seeds-in-the-spirit concept, threatened to sidetrack all evangelism. One of the men who assisted in delivering Kentucky from the narrow prejudices of both of these systems was William C. Buck. Possessed of great physical endurance, he traveled on horseback regardless of weather and urged believers with the call of missions. With undying courage, he preached in churches or the open air, presenting the biblical standard and calling people to obedience.

William Buck was born on August 23, 1790, in Virginia. He lacked educational opportunities, but he had a strong natural intellect and used every opportunity to read broadly. Early in life he had come to personal faith in Christ, and it was apparent that God had called him to preach. He was ordained in October of 1815, and ministered in his native state. In 1820, he moved to Kentucky and settled in Union county where he pastored a small congregation. Soon he founded a second church, and gave leadership to a third near Princeton. There was no other Baptist preacher within thirty miles, and a large proportion of the population was Roman Catholic.

In 1836 he moved to Louisville to assume the pastorate of the First Baptist Church. In two years time the congregation had grown to well over five hundred. It was then that, with the approval of his church family, Reverend Buck accepted the call of the General Association of Baptists in Kentucky to serve as their General Agent. His purpose was two-fold. He would seek to encourage churches to provide their pastors with a livable salary, and he would present the cause of world-wide missions.

His diary provides rich insights into the ministry that was given him. As he traveled and preached, he received offerings for the General Association and for missions. A brief of some of his comments reveal the indifference that in the beginning he faced: "Prospects here were at the first very discouraging; but whatever their prejudices might have been, like the noble Bereans, they came out to hear for themselves; and, by the evening, the clouds began to dissipate. Twice we met them again, on Saturday; and on Sabbath morning, the house, though large, could not contain near all the people. Every cloud was now gone, a bright heaven canopied the church, and harmony prevailed the entire rank and file of the host. I met them again in the afternoon, and obtained individual pledges to the amount of $400 for their pastor, and donations in cash for the General Association of $48.10, and for the China Mission, $22.75. The prospects are bright."[1] Again he wrote:"On Friday, the 17th day of May, 1839, I arrived at home, after an absence of 31 days. I averaged at least three hours pulpit labor each day while absent, traveled about 210 miles, and collected in case for the General Association $77.41, for pastorates $1,671.50, for the China Mission $272.89, and for the *Banner* $28.50, making a total of $2,050.30."[2]

Of course he met with much opposition, but he persisted in presenting the challenge that strengthened the Baptist ministry in Kentucky and produced great spiritual results.

In 1841, believing that he could better reach the churches with the pen, Reverend Buck took the editorial charge of the *Baptist Banner and Western Pioneer*. He edited this paper for nine years. In 1850, he moved to Alabama and continued laboring for ten years, both with tongue and pen. He published a volume entitled the *Philosophy of Religion*, and was editing a religious paper at the beginning of the Civil War. Following that, the man of God moved to Texas where he lived out his remaining days. He died on May 18, 1872, in Waco, Texas.

Once again we need missionary statesmen in our churches to warn believers of the danger of materialism that threatens to sidetrack our efforts to fulfill the Great Commission. Let us pray for missions.

DLC

[1] J. H. Spencer, *A History of Kentucky Baptists* (Cincinnati: By the author, 1885), 2:173.

[2] Ibid., 2:176.

May 18

A Friend to Preachers

Scripture: 2 Timothy 4:7

J. William Kanoy was born on November 26, 1928, in Jamestown, North Carolina. He was converted while a teen-ager on June 3, 1945, and called into the ministry one year later. Our subject took his undergraduate work at Piedmont Bible College in Winston-Salem, North Carolina, and in time he earned three additional degrees. Later in life he was granted an honorary Doctor of Divinity degree as well.

Pastor Lanoy established the Bible Baptist Church in Greensboro, North Carolina, with twelve charter members in 1967. A few months later this small congregation moved to the basement of one of the members. As the congregation grew, it sought a permanent location. After much prayer, an old Methodist church was purchased along with the fel-lowship building and parsonage. An additional house and parking lot were added to the church campus. On Mothers Day of 1969 the church moved into its new facilities and changed its name to Church Street Baptist Church. There the congregation experienced blessed times of renewing and growth as God's presence was manifest.

Church Street Baptist Church became the home of Greens-boro Bible Institute, a four-year institute organized to train pastors, teachers, and Christian laymen. Primarily the Institute was founded to serve the black community. Pastor Kanoy, who established the school, also served as president. Brother Bill, as he was affectionately called, loved the black people and desired to help them in their ministries. In time the institute became known as Greens-boro Bible College, and the first class was graduated in April of 1972.

Pastor Kanoy was active in revival work and conducted many revivals throughout his lifetime. He was a favorite speaker at the ever-popular camp meetings in the Carolinas. During such times, if a particular song blessed him, he would take the music home for his church choir to learn. He loved the Church Street Baptist choir and he showed great emotion as he was blessed of the Lord when they sang.

A gifted speaker, Bill was also a pastor's pastor. He loved preachers and helped them in various ways. He formed a preachers' group insurance plan designed to help them to afford good health care. Among the twenty-five books he authored, one finds both commentaries on various Bible books, sermon outline booklets, and volumes dealing with various Bible subjects. These books have been especially helpful to young preachers. He was a favorite speaker in many Bible conferences, and that ministry carried him into many states of the nation, along with several foreign countries.

Brother Bill's wife of forty-nine years accompanied him on many of his preaching tours, and she served as bookkeeper for the institute as well. The Kanoys were blessed of God with a family of three children.

As has already been noted, Brother Kanoy was a friend of pastors. He supported local revival meetings in area churches. Often he would encourage fellow pastors by taking large numbers of his own congregation to attend the special meetings in sister churches. His counsel was often sought by fellow pastors. His love of young people was a hallmark of his life. Many preachers who serve in the ministry to this day remember fondly the encouragement Brother Bill gave them during their teen years.

Dr. Kanoy was not only a charismatic personality to the world without, but he possessed a pastor's heart and truly loved his church family. This was witnessed as he faithfully visited the bereaved, sick, and shut-ins, and served those needing counsel. He was much loved by those who saw the real man who loved God and whose greatest thrill was to preach God's Word and see people come to Christ for salvation and then go out to serve. Simultaneously he was a man of God in the home, always taking time for his children.

Dr. Kanoy was promoted to Glory on May 18, 1995. We may say of him, that he truly kept the faith, fought a good fight, and finished the course. May we follow his example.

DCB

May 19

Winning the Wild West

Scripture: Isaiah 40:31; 43:2

America owes a great deal to pioneering Baptist missionaries who aided in establishing law and order as our national population extended its borders westward. To be sure, many in the general population who extended our western frontier were adventurers whose social standards were not of the highest character. Baptist missionaries were willing to forego the luxuries of having a stationary home and serving a stable congregation that they might minister to a mobile mixture of mankind who greatly needed spiritual enlightenment.

One such home missionary was Reverend Jacob Bower who labored in Illinois. His report under the date of June 11, 1833 included the following:

> I have spent much time and laboured incessantly to get the people to throw away their prejudices against missions, and to begin to do a little for the good cause: but they have gone far off, and it will require a tedious time for them to return. It is like putting different kinds of metal into a crucible over a slow fire: they are a long time warming, and then a long time heating, before they will melt and run together. A Missionary must be possessed of a good share of patience and fortitude. Three churches have united in an Association: the last article of its constitution is in these words. "Each church and member shall be left free to act according to their views of duty on the subject of Missions, Societies, Temperance measures, &c. and that the supporting, or not supporting either of these, shall be no bar to fellowship." We are a

feeble band and few in number. I have recently made a tour in Pike County, a thinly settled region, where in 16 days, I preached 27 times. Sometimes I would ride 8 or 10 miles and meet about a dozen hearers, who in general seemed to be thirsting for the waters of life. . . .

The cause of Missions within the range of my travels is not flattering. I have not been able to do much in the field for some time back. The Cholera, that dreadful scourge, has visited Illinois; many towns have been almost evacuated. It was found necessary to suspend our preaching, except twice on Saturday and Sabbath.

Some people love much in word and in tongue, but not in deed and in truth. They say, 'We like to hear you preach; we are fond of you; come and preach for us,' but only mention their duty, that the labourer is worthy of his hire, and they will be offended, and say, money-hunter, beggar, missionary, &c. Under these circumstances, the poor missionary must wear out his clothes, his horse and saddle, his body, lungs, and voice, and spend his whole living, and get no help from those who pretend to love him so well. These things are very discouraging . . . . Since May 19, I have rode 372 miles, preached 42 sermons, and baptized one and there are 4 hopeful converts, making in all since the date of my commission, 1247 miles, 191 sermons and 43 baptized. Sunday Schools suffer greatly for want of competent superintendents and teachers.

Feb. 24, 1834. After noticing the severe winter as interrupting active operations, he says, "Meetings have been full, and I think I may venture to say that there is a good state of feeling among my hearers in several places, which is truly encouraging to my heart. The good cause is evidently gaining ground, though its progress is slow; it is like the morning dawn; darkness imperceptibly withdraws, and the light approaches. Opposers [sic] are not so saucy and violent as they were two years ago: it will be a great work to get professors properly into their duty. In 81 days, I have ridden 634

> miles, preached 75 times, baptized one, and aided in the ordination of one preacher. I have cheering prospects of communicating to you some good news in my next. I have sat down and wept with a mixture of sorrow and joy, when thinking over the distressing situation of Zion in Illinois, and now God has remembered her in mercy.[1]

Our missionary heroes served not only overseas, but helped tremendously in establishing the United States of America in biblical truth that historically has made our nation great. Thank God for such men.

DLC

[1]H. Leon McBeth, *A Sourcebook For Baptist Heritage* (Nashville, TN: Broadman Press, 1990), 225-226.

May 20

A Champion of Regenerate Churches

Scripture: Philippians 1:1-11

Abraham Booth was born in Blackwell, Derbyshire, England, on May 20, 1734. At the age of ten he was saved under the preaching of New Connection Baptists. At the age of twenty-one he was baptized into a General Baptist Church. He was encouraged to preach and soon became pastor of a church at Kirby-Woodhouse. As a General Baptist, he was a bitter enemy of personal election and particular redemption.[1] However, in the next few years his views began to change. When he was thirty-three years old, he published his *Reign of Grace*, a defense of the Calvinist position. He never lost his evangelistic fervor, however. He stated in *Reign of Grace*, "Complete provision is made for the certain salvation of every sinner, however unworthy, who feels his want, and applies to Christ. The Gospel is not preached to sinners, nor are they encouraged to believe in Jesus, under the formal notion of their not being elected. No: these tidings of heavenly mercy are addressed to sinners, considered as ready to perish."[2] This combination of Calvinism and evangelism was published a year before John Gill's *Body of Divinity*. While Gill refused to evangelize the lost, Booth called upon them to repent. As a result of the printing of this work, he moved to London and was ordained pastor of the Prescott Street Particular Baptist Church on February 16, 1769.

He had little formal education, yet he was an excellent author, producing eight significant works. Perhaps because of his own lack of education, he was instrumental in the founding of Stepney College. Even though he lacked education, he was a careful student of the Scriptures. One of his more important works was *Pedobaptism Examined*. This was the result of a tremendous amount of research and his objections were never fully answered. In this book he quoted eighty Pedobaptist writers who conceded that the original meaning of the Greek verb *baptizo* is "to dip or to immerse."[3] He also published a book entitled *An Apology for Baptists*. In this book Booth defended his denomination from the all too common accusation that Baptists lay an undue stress on the ordinance of baptism. It was a defense of those who became known as Strict Baptists and marked the division between those Baptists who insisted upon immersion as a condition of church membership and communion and those who held that immersion is left to the individual conscience as a matter of obedience and is not a prerequisite to church fellowship.[4] Booth feared that if the Lord's Supper were extended to the unbaptized, it would undoubtedly lead to the admission of the unbaptized to church membership and perhaps also to the admission of the unregenerate to church membership. This would undercut his concept that the church consists of visible saints.[5]

Booth was also involved in the practical application of his theology to the culture in which he lived. He was a heroic advocate of freedom for the slaves of England. He was one of the first in England to declare that the traffic in men and women was sinful and shameful. Baptists were involved in the petitions to Parliament in favour of the abolition of the slave trade. One petition reads, "Nor can your petitioners help observing with sorrow that a slave trade is a dishonour to humanity, a disgrace to our national character, utterly inconsistent with the sound policy of commercial states, and a perpetual scandal to the profession of Christianity."[6] Most of the prominent Baptist ministers stood out as the advocates of freedom for the colored races, though it required more than common courage to oppose the vested interests and the prejudice which united in favor of slavery.

After thirty-seven years as pastor of the Prescott Street Particular Baptist Church, Abraham Booth died in 1806 at the age of seventy-three.

LRO

---

[1] William Cathcart, *The Baptist Encyclopedia* (Philadelphia: Louis H. Everts, 1883), 246.

[2] W. T. Whitley, *Calvinism and Evangelism in England* (London: Kingsgate, n.d.), 35.

[3] David Benedict, *A General History of the Baptist Denomination in America* (Boston: Lincoln & Edmands, 1813), 76.

[4] John C. Carlile, *The Story of the English Baptists* (London: James Clarke & Co., 1905), 171-172.

[5] H. Leon McBeth, *The Baptist Heritage* (Nashville: Broadman, 1987), 196.

[6] Ibid.

May 21

When Did Baptists Begin?

Scripture: Matthew 16:13-18

The fact that Baptist history is well hidden in antiquity has caused great consternation among certain scholars. Throughout the past years and until the turn of the nineteenth century, the majority of historians held to what we refer to as the Spiritual Kinship Principle theory. This is not to be confused with the Successionist theory that calls for a chain-link approach to Baptist history and seeks to identify the historical record of lineal church descent, which admittedly is both impossible and unnecessary. Rather this position substantiates the fact that Baptist distinctives or Baptist principles such as those found in Matthew 16:18, Ephesians 3:21, and 1 Timothy 3:15-16 have been continuously in existence.

In the course of time Leopold von Ranke led in formulating what has become known as the scientific school of Baptist history. The efforts of using principles of historical research and critical methodology led Dr. William

Heth Whitsitt, then the president of Southern Baptist Seminary, to declare that Baptists did not exist before 1641. Dr. Whitsitt set forth his views first in unsigned articles that appeared as encyclopedia articles, and then in a little book entitled *A Question in Baptist History*, which was published in 1896. He held that Richard Blunt received baptism from John Batten in Holland, and actually reintroduced immersion to England in 1641. He came to the conclusion that there had been no immersion anywhere in Holland until 1620 when John Geesteranus became the first of the Collegians to submit to it.

Immediately his views provoked a storm of controversy that was primarily led by the famed Dr. B. H. Carroll. The position was soundly repudiated as well by John T. Christian and by many other reputable Baptist historians. The negative response grew to a crescendo through Baptist circles in America. The ground swell became so great that Dr. Whitsitt was forced to resign the presidency of Southern Baptist Seminary. The May 21, 1896 issue of the *Texas Baptist Standard* pretty well summarized the feelings of Bible-believing Baptists through out America. On page 49 the editor wrote: "...a higher critic in Baptist history is not as bad as a higher critic in theology, but he is too bad to be sustained in his work of weakening the backbone of our young Baptist ministry. . . we shall never cooperate with the seminary until Dr. Whitsitt resigns or does all in his power to heal the wounds he has given the denomination."

However, the position that Dr. Whitsitt popularized has through the years became the "academic" standard for many modernistic Baptists. In 1950 Robert Torbet, liberal Baptist historian of the American Baptists, confused both the positions of those who hold to the Successionist theory and those who hold to the Spiritual Kinship-Principle theory. And since that time there has been a rebirth in Dr. Whitsitt's position making Baptist history to begin in the days of the Reformation. Not only have liberal Baptist historians, colleges and seminaries bought in to this position, but tragically many professed fundamental educational institutions have followed suit.

It is not our intention to impugn the motives of those who hold to Whitsitt's theory, but several concessions must logically follow if such a position is substantiated. First, one must admit that for years, Rome, with its Papal edicts, was indeed the true church of Jesus Christ. Secondly, it is then necessary to acknowledge that Baptists sprang from the Reformation, and thus Reformed theology is the cradle of Baptist doctrine. I presume that many espouse the second position. Such postitions are unconscionable to this author. I agree with the great Charles Haddon Spurgeon. When laying the cornerstone of the great Metropolitan Tabernacle, Mr. Spurgeon said it well. "We did not commence our existence at the reformation; we were reformers before Luther or Calvin were born; we never came from the church of Rome, for we were never in it, but we have an unbroken line up to the apostles themselves. We have always existed from the very days of Christ, and our principles, sometimes veiled and forgotten, like a river which may travel underground for a little season, have always had honest and holy adherents."[1]

I do not apologize for the name or history of those who have stood for truth through the years. I am thankful for such an heritage.

DLC

[1]Charles H. Spurgeon, *Metropolitan Tabernacle Publications* (Pasadena, TX: Pilgrim Publications, 1973 reprint), 225.

May 22

The Red-Eyed Monster

Scripture: Proverbs 20:1; 22:6

Liquor is a terrible enemy! That was the graphic lesson Washington Bryan Crumpton learned one day in a little town ten miles south of Montgomery, Alabama. A prominent citizen, whose brother was a drunkard, saw two barrels of whiskey rolled from a wagon to the stoop in front of the village store. With an axe he burst them open and poured their contents on the ground paying the merchant for the whiskey.

It would be several weeks before more could be gotten up from Mobile, and during that time his brother would be sober.[1]

Washington Crumpton had been born at Camden, Alabama, on February 24, 1842. When he was but a lad his parents had moved to the little town mentioned above, and the boy was educated in the common community schools of his day. When the lad was eleven his family moved to Pineapple, Alabama, and soon after that, his mother passed away. His father broke up housekeeping, and young Crumpton was shifted among various relatives. Of course, he was expected to work in the fields for his keep.

An older brother had gone to California with the early forty-niners in search of gold, and young Crumpton decided he too would move westward. One can only imagine the excitement experienced by a teenager on such a trek, and in his old age, Mr. Crumpton enjoyed regaling company with many of the tales. However, soon after his arrival in California, the Civil War broke out. With anti-Southern attitudes prevailing in California, young Crumpton opted to return home and join the Confederate forces. Once again, can you imagine that lad traveling alone over the uncharted trails back home? Again, in old age Mr. Crumpton enjoyed relating some of those adventures too.

Arriving home, he united with the troops and saw service in the armies of northern Mississippi. He was at the siege of Vicksburg on May 22, 1862. He was taken prisoner and sent to Mobile, where, after treatment, he was part of a prisoner exchange. He then joined Company H, 37th Mississippi Infantry. He was in the dreadful battles about Atlanta, Georgia, in May of 1864, and was slightly wounded. He marched with Hood in Tennessee, and was in the Battle of Franklin, and was wounded again fighting at Nashville. The last gun was heard by him at Columbus, Georgia.

Following the war he returned to Alabama, got right with God, and was called to preach. He studied at Georgetown, Kentucky, and was ordained on November 30, 1870. He married in 1872 and began a fruitful ministry in Meridian, Mississippi. But he loved the country, and so in time he returned to a rural setting to minister the Word of God among people of the soil. He always demanded that his churches grant him a Sunday free per month to minister to struggling rural churches that were pastorless. He never forgot the lesson learned in childhood as he watched the citizen dispatch the liquor with an axe, and he was strong for prohibition.

When Alabama Baptists organized their State Board of Missions, W. B. Crumpton was made their State Evangelist. In time he was asked to serve as Secretary of Alabama's Missionary Board, and he operated in that post for twenty-eight years. Knowing the importance of Christian literature, W. B. Crumpton organized the Alabama Baptist Bible and Colportage Board. Interestingly, throughout his experience as an executive leader in the State of Alabama, W. B. Crumpton pastored a small country church where he felt so much at home. I have sought in vain to find a copy of his book, *The Adventures of Two Alabama Boys*. W. B. Crumpton was called to his heavenly home from Montgomery, Alabama, on March 9, 1926.

We learn many lessons from the life of W. B. Crumpton, but let us reinforce the important truth that graphic lessons taught in the tender years of youth are often life-abiding. Take time to train your children in paths of righteousness.

DLC

---

[1] B. J. W. Graham, *Baptist Biography* (Atlanta, GA: Index Printing Company, 1920), 2:87.

May 23

A Baptist Epaphroditus

Scripture: Philippians 2:25-30

John Comer was born August 1, 1704, in Boston and died May 23, 1734.[1] His brief years were characterized by his strong convictions, kindly spirit, and significant usefulness in the Lord's work.

Comer's parents were Presbyterian.[2] Young Comer came to Christ in 1721. He was a student at Yale and fled to Cambridge in an attempt to escape a smallpox epidemic.[3] God used this crisis in his life to bring about his salvation. Apparently he and his parents became convinced that the immersion of believers is the scriptural form of baptism by reading Joseph Stennett's *Treatise on Baptism*.[4] He was baptized in the First Baptist Church of Boston on January 31, 1725.[5] Elisha Callender was pastor of the church and also Comer's uncle.[6]

It cost one to be a Baptist in those Massachusetts colonial days. Baptist pastor Obadiah Holmes had been whipped for preaching in the colony on September 6, 1651.[7] On March 3, 1729, a group of 32 people from Rehoboth were jailed for refusing to pay the tax that supported the established church. Twenty-eight of these were Baptists.[8] To follow the Lord in believer's baptism required conviction and courage since persecution of Baptists was widespread throughout the colonies.

Comer began his preaching ministry in Swansea, Massachusetts, in May of 1725. In November of that year he became co-pastor of the First Baptist Church in Newport, Rhode Island. Later he preached in the Second Baptist Church of the same city. In 1732 he became pastor of the Baptist Church in Rehoboth, Massachusetts.[9] Backus called him "an excellent preacher of the gospel."[10] We are told that he was used in bringing a revival of doctrine and practical religion in Newport, and that he exhibited a firm regard for what he believed to be the truth, tempered by a kind and Christian spirit."[11]

In addition to his obvious usefulness during his lifetime, John Comer also possessed a keen attention to detail for which we rejoice. This attention to detail resulted in a two volume handwritten diary. Isaac Backus, the first historian of Baptists in America, and Morgan Edwards drew heavily on his work in their historical research.[12] I have had the privilege of reading in Comer's diary, where he recorded the history of those early Baptists in intricate detail. We are indebted to Comer for providing a record and source for later historians.

Comer must have loved the Lord with great devotion. Willmarth tells us: "His ability, piety, and wisdom marked him out for high usefulness and leadership among the New England Baptists, who were then a feeble folk, struggling with opposition and persecution. But in his zeal he taxed his physical powers too severely, contracted consumption, and died joyfully at Rehoboth, May 23, 1734, when not quite thirty years of age."[13]

Comer's life challenges us in much the same way as the biblical Epaphroditus who was Paul's "brother, and companion in labor, and fellow soldier..." (Phil. 2:25).

Comer came to Christ in a definite conversion experience. He labored diligently in the Lord's work and stood firmly for the truth of the Bible in the face of opposition and persecution. Like Epaphroditus, he gladly used his days in the service of his Lord without regard for his own wellbeing (Phil. 2:30).

We enjoy the privilege to worship and serve the Lord in liberty. We stand in the lengthened shadow of those who paid a price to perpetuate our New Testament faith. Let us determine to serve our God without reservation. Let us live and proclaim the Gospel to a lost world. May we be willing to stand for the faith in the face of opposition, and may we be willing to serve Christ without regard for our lives.

FJM

---

[1] James W. Willmarth, "Introduction" in C. Edwin Barrows, ed. *The Diary of John Comer* (RhodeIsland Historical Society, 1893), 7-8.

[2] Thomas Armitage, *The History of the Baptists* (Watertown, WI: Maranatha Baptist Press, 1976 reprint), II:665.

[3] James Beller, *America in Crimson Red* (Arnold, MO: Prairie Fire Press, 2004), 93.

[4] Thomas Armitage, (II:665) and Beller (93) agree that this is how young Comer came to his Baptist convictions. Armitage informs us that his parents also became Baptists.

[5] Willmarth, 7.

[6] Armitage, II:665.

[7] Ibid., 688.

[8] C. Edwin Barrows, Editor, *The Diary of John Comer* (Rhode Island Historical Society, 1893), 62.

[9] Beller, 94-95.

[10] Willmarth, 7.

[11] Ibid., 7-8.

[12] Armitage, II:665.

[13] Willmarth, 8.

May 24

Multiplying the Word of God

Scripture: 2 Timothy 2:1-4

The persecution our forefathers experienced in old England actually was used of God in purifying them. On May 24, 1689, soon after William and Mary were seated on the throne, a Toleration Act was passed without much difficulty. Compulsory attendance at the Church of England was abolished. The State Church was still privileged but could no longer persecute.[1] One might have expected a great spiritual revival to follow, but a cold fog of indifference settled upon England, and many dissenters were overcome by spiritual lethargy. Perhaps the many trials had wearied them and weakened their resolve. However, the Deists made great strides at that time. Presbyterians were greatly affected by the denial of Christ's deity, and liberalism had permeated many churches.

The Norfolk area seemed to have been somewhat exempt from the spiritual stupor among the Baptists. In 1717 Richard Culley established a church with 120 who had seceded from a General Baptist Church, and this congregation became a strong influence for righteousness. In 1741 Edward Trivett succeeded to the pastorate, and for the next fifty years he maintained a strong witness for the Savior throughout the area.

Baptist congregations in those days faced tremendous difficulty in securing pastors. There were few institutions of higher learning established to produce preachers. The Bristol Baptist College had been founded in 1679, ten years before the Edict of Toleration, but primarily young men for the ministry were of necessity trained by local pastors. Edward Trivett specialized in such a situation. His ministry of fifty years was particularly notable for the ministers he trained, and illustrates the theory and practice of ministerial supply and training.[2] As young men from the congregation expressed an interest in preaching, they would be given the opportunity of speaking on lesser occasions than on the Lord's Day. If the congregation sensed that the young man was indeed gifted, he would be encouraged by the church family to preach in the area. But there was the realization that the call of the Holy Spirit and a natural speaking ability were insufficient for the work of the ministry. It was then that Pastor Trivett would begin to instruct the potential pastoral leader in the Word of God. Pastors who had the capacity, would also teach such students the Greek and Hebrew languages, thus allowing them to study the Scriptures in the original tongues. The training was only complete when the vocation was finally confirmed by the receipt of a call from some congregation in need of a pastor. Usually a call followed a time of probationary service which often extended to several years.

When a call was given and accepted, an ordination would be planned, and two or more pastors would meet with the candidate, question him, and make a recommendation to the local church.

During his ministry, Pastor Trivett trained his own son Zenas Trivett and his son-in-law, Thomas Purdy. They became pastors in turn at Langham in Essex and Rye in Sussex. In 1754 William Cole was sent to become the first pastor in Yarmouth, and that church became very influential, sending many into the ministry. Cole was succeeded by Jabez Browne, whom Pastor Trivett had trained. John Webster Morris went out to pastor at Clipstone in Northamptonshire, and he became an early supporter of the Baptist Missionary Society. Robert Denham settled in the pastorate at East Dereham, and John Ewing in Great Ellingham. Charles Farmery founded the church in Diss, and that ministry was greatly used of God by planting other local churches in many areas. Thus Edward Trivett, though never famous, was used of God in having a great impact upon the area.

Our missionaries around the world use this system of training workers today. Growth is really experienced more beneficially by multiplication than by addition as additional churches are planted. May the Lord teach us this truth again in the twenty-first century in America.

DLC

---

[1] A. C. Underwood, *A History of the English Baptists* (London: The Baptist Union of Great Britain and Ireland, 1970), 116.

[2] Charles Boardman Jewson, *The Baptists in Norfolk* (London: The Carey Kingsgate Press Limited, 1957), 51.

May 25

The Fruits of Liberalism

Scripture: Matthew 7:20

Since October 2, 1792, Baptists have taken the Great Commission of our Lord seriously. With William Carey and Andrew Fuller leading the way, generation after generation responded, and missionaries circled the globe with the Gospel. By 1900 the American Baptist Missionary Union (formerly the Triennial Convention) had 474 missionaries serving around the world. But, it must be remembered, that from the very date of the organization of the Northern Baptist Convention, German Rationalism became very evident among the leadership of the Baptists in the Convention. Liberalism saw no need for the preaching of the Gospel, and the missionary outreach of the Northern Baptist Convention began to wane. On May 25, 1920, The Board of Managers of the Foreign Society, meeting in Boston, appointed Cecil G. Fielder, a modernist, to missionary service.[1] This practice continued and proliferated, and by 1982 the missionary family of the Northern Baptist Convention had dwindled to 203.[2] That trend has continued, for in the 2001-2003 *Mission Handbook* (18th edition) *U. S. and Canadian Christian Ministries Overseas report*, the same agency reported that they were down to only 120 full-time missionaries.[3]

The Northern Baptist Convention (from 1908) changed its name in 1950 to the American Baptist Convention, and then in 1972, the name was changed again to The American Baptist Churches in the U. S. A. But regardless of the name, decline in the number of churches, membership, and Sunday School enrollments has been experienced in the liberalizing organization. In 1928 there were 8,292 churches that formed the convention, whereas in 1982 the number had fallen to 5,703. Even more pronounced was the Sunday school enrollment. It fell from 1,139,613 in 1928 down to 417,134 by the end of 1982.[4]

Wherever liberalism has taken root, the result has been the same. For instance, in Great Britain the Baptist cause has suffered since the days of the Down Grade Controversy in the 1880s. Mr. Spurgeon left the Baptist Union because the Union refused to acknowledge and deal with the liberalism of that day. Mr. Spurgeon was ridiculed for his separatist position, but history has vindicated that dear man of God. From that time on, the refusal to accept the authority of Scripture, the downplaying of the person of Christ, and a hesitancy to clearly declare the message of redemption has splintered the Baptist cause in Great Britain. Though numbers may not always prove the point, L. G. Champion reported the following statistics: In 1921 there were 3,068 churches in the Baptist Union with a total membership of 442,000; in 1981 there were 2,058 churches with a total membership of 170,000. This is a 57% decline in membership. In 1921, Sunday schools had 518,000 scholars; in 1981, 157,000, a decline of 70%.[5]

In truth, liberalism has almost always taken over existing colleges, seminaries, churches, and man-made organizations. Rarely has liberalism ever built on its own foundation. Liberalism is the result of the second spiritual law of thermal dynamics and it always leads to entropy. It is a repudiation of truth, and tragically, because of sinful man's inherent propensity to sin, its seeds lie within the spiritual as well as the secular world.

The need in the twenty-first century is for our churches, colleges, seminaries, and mission agencies to continue lashed to the rock of ages, God's Word. Only as we stand upon the inerrant, infallible, inspired, integral Word of God is it possible for man to steer a straight course that brings glory to our Savior. May we reaffirm today our total trust and obedience to God's Word.

DLC

---

[1] Chester E. Tulga, *The Foreign Missions Controversy in the Northern Baptist Convention* (Chicago: Conservative Baptist Fellowship, 1950), 14.

[2] *Annual Report,* American Missionary Union (ABMU), Detroit, 1900, 215; *Year Book,* ABC, 1982, 135.

[3] *Mission Handbook*, Billy Graham Center, 2000, 90.

[4] *Annual*, NBC, 1928, 27; *Directory*, ABC, 1983, 100.

[5] L. G. Champion, *Baptist Church Life in the Twentieth Century: Some Personal Reflections*, in Clements, 4.

May 26

Preaching and Politics

Scripture: James 1:20

The history of Bible believing Baptist missions is in sharp contrast with the efforts of other such movements in Christendom. Believing that we must major in the message of Redemption, Baptists have ever emphasized the spiritual rather than the social and political. Andrew Fuller, one of the founders of the modern-day missionary movement, early recognized this principle. It is reported that BMS (British Missionary Society) missionaries who gave voice to overtly democratic sentiments on the field soon felt the weight of Fuller's reproof. Jacob Grigg, one of two Bristol-trained missionaries sent to establish a mission in Sierra Leone in 1795, was the first such offender. When in October 1796 John Ryland received a letter from Zachary Macaulay, the Evangelical governor of the colony, complaining that Grigg had conducted himself with great impropriety, Fuller was quick to recognize that there was great danger of the African Mission being utterly destroyed through Grigg's imprudence.[1]

In 1797 the mission committee had expressed suspicions that John Fountain, who had applied to serve in India, also had strong political persuasions. In the course of his service, such tendencies became evident. Andrew Fuller realized that the mission to India was in danger of being expelled through the political power of the East India Company. The situation was so tense that Mr. Fountain was warned by the Mission Committee that if he continued to enter into the political arena, he would be recalled from India.

On May 26, 1802, the Massachusetts Baptist Missionary Society was formed in the First Baptist Church of Boston, Massachusetts. This was the first Baptist missionary society in America. On the fifteenth of September of 1802, a letter was framed by the committee and sent to the newly appointed missionaries who were designated to carry the gospel westward into our expanding nation. The third paragraph reads as follows: "The Committee most strenuously recommends that you solicitously avoid all interference and allusions to those political topics which divide the opinions and too much irritate the passions of our fellow citizens. Subjects of this description are not merely irrelevant to the spiritual purposes of missionary exertion, but manifestly subversive to all reasonable prospect of success, since their inevitable tendency is to excite disunion, division, and that asperity of feelings which stand directly opposed to the meekness and gentleness of the Christian temper. We are persuaded that you feel the propriety of this suggestion, and that you are convinced that 'the wrath of man worketh not the righteousness of God.'"[2]

Tragically, in the name of the Lord Jesus Christ many so-called missionaries have been sent into the world with the political aspirations of perfecting social order and building a utopia through political means. Bible-believing Baptist missionaries go armed with the life-transforming truth of regeneration by faith in the shed blood of the Savior. The politically oriented missionary is desirous of putting a new suit on an old sinner. Bible-believing Baptist missionaries seek to put a spiritually resurrected man into the suit.

Having alluded to the attitude of Bible-believing Baptist missionaries on political issues, it must be pointed out that these same stalwarts of the faith have always taken a stand on moral matters. This is true among Godly Baptist pastors in America as well. Abortion, euthanasia, and homosexuality are not political subjects. They are moral issues. Of course, the true child of God will not break civil law to protest, but he will declare the entire counsel of God, and preach the necessity for mankind to repent. With current day political correctness, our own once great Republic may seek to still the voice of its Christian conscience. Without becoming politically oriented, fundamental Baptists at home and abroad will stand for truth.

Regardless of political correctness, peer pressure, or coercion, may we who treasure the name of Christ and the historic Baptist position stand gallant for truth.

DLC

[1]Brian Stanley, *The History of the Baptist Missionary Society 1792-1992* (Edinburgh: T & T Clark, 1992), 23-24.

[2]W. H. Eaton, *Historical Sketch of the Massachusetts Baptist Missionary Society and Convention* 1802-1902 (Boston, MA: Baptist Convention, 1903), 14-15.

May 27

"Glory! Glory!"

Scripture: John 17

As is often the case, the birth of their first son, James Ellison on April 29, 1778, caused his parents to became deeply concerned for spiritual matters. Wanting to provide spiritual reality for their offspring, the parents united with the Baptist church. Though they now had a spiritual foundation, poverty reigned, and education was limited. Thus James Ellison matured in a loving home, but with a background that provided little else. When he was eighteen, James married Miss Mary Calloway.

James now considered his own spiritual condition. Though having heard the Word of God preached, he recognized himself as lost in sin. Determined to correct the flaw by his own efforts, a family altar was established. Faithfully he led in family worship, and the couple attended the local church regularly. But, his spiritual interest cooled, and to all outward appearances, James became more wicked than previously. Thankfully the gentle wooing of the Holy Spirit and the claims of Christ upon his heart brought him to repentance and faith in the Savior. James Ellison was born again in 1800, was baptized, and united with the Indian Creek Baptist Church near Greenbriar, Virginia.

For the next eight years James Ellison became grounded in the Word of God. When it became apparent that he possessed gifts of leadership, he was asked to lead groups in worship. In time, he was licensed by the congregation to preach, and his spiritual appetite grew insatiable to thoroughly know God's Word. He secured theological books, and saturated his mind in the Divine revelation. In 1808 when thirty years of age, James Ellison was ordained into the Gospel ministry. His first charge was his home church. After faithfully serving that flock, Elder Ellison moved toward Fayette, Virginia, and for many years was one of the most active ministers in the Greenbriar Association. His theology was a careful blend of Divine sovereignty and human responsibility. He was a personal soul winner, and he was uncompromising in his promotion of missions. He found great joy in preaching on prophecy and the glories awaiting the children of God.

In May of 1834 he determined to attend the General Association which was to convene at Richmond. Taking his son he left home planning to preach to several congregations along the way where previously he had ministered. Along the way he attended the Strawberry Associational meeting, and then shared in a protracted meeting at Deep Run near to Richmond. Becoming ill, he did not arrive at the General Association meeting until the second day of sessions. Though not fully recovered, he pushed himself to attend every session of the General Association. Because of commitments previously made to preach on the way home, he left before the consummation of the sessions. The next morning while traveling, James Ellison became hoarse, and was unable to preach until the next Lord's Day. Two days later he was too sick to travel. They stopped at a friend's house between Liberty and Fincastle, Virginia.

In a couple of days it became apparent to his son and friends that his condition was serious. He too realized his condition and confided that he believed this was his last journey. His mind was clear, but his whole concentration seemed to center on the need for revival in the churches. On the morning of May 21, 1834, his conversation majored on the glories of the gospel, and the duty of believers to send it into all the world. That evening he meditated on the love of David and Jonathan, and his mind was uncommonly lucid. The Lord's Day fell on May 22, and, being unable to attend services, he asked his son to read the seventeenth chapter of John aloud. He fed upon and delighted in the Lords prayer for His own.

His condition continually and slowly worsened, and on the evening of May 27, . . . after lying for some time as though in a deep sleep, he opened his eyes; with a smile, he raised his feeble emaciated hands toward heaven, and exclaimed, "Glory!, Glory!" and soon after repeated,

All my capacious powers can wish,
In Thee doth richly meet,
Not to my eyes is life so dear,
Nor friendship half so sweet.[1]

In the wee hours of the following morning, with his journey run, James Ellison enjoyed an abundant entrance into heaven above. May we so live in constant readiness for His coming or our home-going.

DLC

[1]James B. Taylor, *Lives of Virginia Baptist Ministers* (Richmond: Yale & Wyatt, 1838), 360.

May 28

Humility or Timidity?

Scripture: Micah 6:8

Andrew Broadus was born in Caroline County, Virginia, on November 4, 1770. His father, John, was a schoolteacher and supplemented his living by farming. Andrew was the youngest of a dozen children. Though educational opportunities were limited in the community, there can be little doubt that his father gave special attention to his children's educational needs. It is said that young Andrew had an insatiable appetite for knowledge, and with a retentive mind he absorbed all the literature he could obtain. The well- respected J. B. Jeter claimed that when candles were scarce young Andrew would stretch out on his stomach before the fireplace and read using the dim light provided by the log on the fire.

John Broadus was a member of the Episcopalian church, and he forbade Andrew to attend services conducted by Baptist preachers. However, when Andrew was eighteen years old, under the influence of Theoderic Noel, a Baptist preacher, on May 28, 1789, the youth was baptized and became a member of the Upper King and Queen Baptist Church. The Lord burdened Andrew's heart concerning preaching, and he, along with another young man, preached at the home of one of the church members. The other youth was R. B. Semple, who became known as the historian of the Baptists of Virginia. Andrew's ministry became very acceptable, and he was ordained on October 16, 1791 by his home church. His first pastoral responsibility included three rather rural churches including the Burrus Baptist Church, whose founder was one of the imprisoned preachers of Virginia. During that pastorate, to supplement his salary, the youthful pastor taught school, and he gave himself to close study as well.

Following his initial ministerial experience, he became pastor of five Baptist churches B Upper Zion, Beulah, Mangohic, Salem, and Upper King and Queen. He invested most of the remainder of his life ministering to the Salem and Upper King and Queen. These were rural ministries, but knowledge of his ability was heralded far and wide. In the course of time he was invited to candidate in the First Baptist Churches of Boston, Philadelphia, Baltimore, and New York, along with the influential Sansom Street Baptist Church in Philadelphia. None of these seemed to have attraction for the man of God. He did accept an invitation from the First Baptist Church of Richmond, but his tenure there was short, and soon he returned to minister at the churches of his first love in the country.

J. B. Jeter, noted contemporary leader of his day, was convinced that his friend, the competent man of God, preferred the small, country churches because of an innate timidity. At times Reverend Broadus lost his flow of language in the presence of strangers. It is apparent that his finest preaching was not done in large assemblies, but before his own people. On one occasion he was assigned to preach at a meeting of the Dover Association. The preliminaries were completed, and the audience settled down to enjoy a spiritual feast, but when the man of God stood to speak he came to a sudden pause and said, "The circumstances of the case, I mean my case, make it necessary to excuse myself from proceeding with the discussion." His biographer added, "The thought had probably seized him that the expectations of the people could not be met; or he had recognized in the congregation some one whose criticism he dreaded; or the wind and roar of the ocean had disturbed his nervous system; whatever it was, a serious surprise and regret were felt by all."[1]

Andrew Broadus was a gifted writer, and early in his ministerial career he penned a reply to Thomas Paine's attack on Christianity entitled *The Age of Reason and Revelation*.

His work entitled *A Bible History, with Occasional Notes to Explain and Illustrate Difficult Passages* has been considered a valuable contribution to Christian literature.

An interesting illustration of Broadus' humility is seen in the fact that he refused an honorary doctorate from Columbian College, as he doubted the wisdom of ministers accepting such outward adornments. Knowing my own need of humility, I prefer to honor Andrew Broadus for his humility rather than his timidity. May the Lord give us humble men for the hour in which we live.

DLC

[1] William Cathcart, *The Baptist Encyclopaedia* (Philadelphia: Louis H. Everts, 1881), 1:139.

May 29

Religious Taxation

Scripture: Matthew 10:23a

The name John Gano stands out in the annals of Baptist history in America. He was ordained by the Hopewell Church in New Jersey on May 29, 1754. Soon thereafter Elder Gano married Miss Sarah Stites, daughter of the mayor of Elizabethtown, New Jersey. To gain experience preaching, he traveled southward into the Carolinas. Upon preaching in North Carolina, Gano learned of settlers who had moved to the Yadkin Valley from New Jersey. Thus, the area was known as the Jersey Settlement. Between 1755 and 1757 the man of God visited the Jersey Settlement several times. The small congregation at Jersey Settlement pled with Elder Gano to become their pastor. He grappled with the Will of God, and finally accepted their invitation.

His move to North Carolina from New Jersey entailed a five-month trip. This was managed with a two horse wagon for furnishings and a small four-wheel vehicle that conveyed his wife and young son. The latter cart was drawn by one horse. On November 15, 1757, the Gano family completed the difficult journey. In a short time the church was stabilized and great strides were made in the work of God. A second child, David, was born to the couple on November 11, 1758. However, Indian raids in the area caused unrest. Mrs. Gano urged her husband to take her back to New England. As the situation deteriorated, and many residents of the country moved eastward, in 1760 the preacher returned to New Jersey with his family. In his own words he said, "I resigned my commission and left this place, and under the protection of a kind providence arrived safely at my father-in-law's at Elizabethtown."[1]

But the purpose of this entry is to reveal the lack of freedom that Baptists experienced in the early days of America. North Carolina had a state church, and this resulted in a vestry tax. The Vestry Act provided tax money "in order that the clergy may have a decent and comfortable maintenance and support, without being obliged to follow any other employment than that of their holy function to the extent of an annual salary of eighty pounds, Proclamation Money." The Acts also provided that every minister should have a Certificate from the Bishop of London, certifying that he had " ...been duly Ordained, conform to Ye Doctrine and Discipline of Ye Church of England and of a good Life and Conversation."

Freedom loving Baptists did not believe in paying taxes to support ministers of the Church of England. A protest arose against the Vestries Tax. About seven hundred people . . . met and formulated a set of Articles, one of which demanded that the Vestries be abolished and that each denomination pay its own ministers. The meeting was held near Salisbury, perhaps at Jersey Settlement. John Gano, who held strong convictions about the necessity of religious freedom and separation of church and state, was a natural leader in such a movement. The officials in government referred to the protesting group as a "mob."[2]

Needless to say, the Governor detested the Baptists, and soon his militia was sent from the capital at New Bern, North Carolina, to deal severely with them. We do not have the time to deal fully with the matter, but every community in North Carolina where Baptists were present in considerable numbers soon came to regard (Governor) Tryon and his entire administration as avowed enemies ready to deprive them of every civil and religious right.[3]

This persecution and ultimate exodus of the Baptists from the area concluded in God's glory for in its final result it was much like the persecutions that drove the early Christians from Jerusalem. These Baptists went preaching Baptist principles and establishing Baptist churches on the new frontiers in Tennessee, South Carolina, and Georgia.[4]

May we thank God for religious freedom, and may we honor the memory of our Baptist forefathers who paid the price to obtain such liberty.

DLC

---

[1] Garland A. Hendricks, *Saints and Sinners at Jersey Settlement* (Charlotte: The Delmar Company, 1988), 20.

[2] Ibid., 15-16.

[3] George Washington Paschal, *History of North Carolina Baptists* (Raleigh: North Carolina State Convention, 1930), I:347.

[4] Ibid., I:381.

May 30

A Brief but Successful Ministry

Scripture: Isaiah 6:1-8

George Pearcy, early Baptist missionary to China, was born on June 23, 1813. The lad matured in a fine Christian home, and professed Christ as Savior while still a teen. However, he struggled to obtain an education. He saved his money and finally studied at Richmond College. Then he went to what was Columbian College from 1836 to 1843. From the dates, you will observe that Mr. Pearcy was thirty years old when finally graduating from college. Mr. Pearcy then became an instructor in the Botetourt Springs Male and Female Institute, having charge of the Male Department there.

Two years later, in May of 1845, the Southern Baptist Convention was organized in Augusta, Georgia. On November 3, 1845, Pearcy appeared before the Foreign Board, and after being examined, he was accepted for missionary service in China. To better prepare himself for such service, Mr. Pearcy pursued a study of medicine for a year at the Richmond Medical College. On May 30, 1846, he married Miss Frances Patrick Miller. A thrilling commissioning service was held on June 15, 1846, in the Second Baptist Church of Richmond, Virginia, for George and Frances Pearcy and Rev. and Mrs. S. C. Clopton, who were accompanying them to the field. A week later on June 22, the two missionary couples sailed on the *Cahota* for China.

The ship reached Canton in only four months, and the two families shared living quarters in perfect harmony. The life of pioneer missionaries in those days was not always peaceful. During trouble between the English and the Chinese, the rabble threatened to burn the factories, and actually entered into gunfire with the English troops. The merchants quickly relocated their wares to safety. Thousands of Chinese left with their families and property. It was decided that Mr. Clopton would take the women to Hong Kong, and Mr. Pearcy would remain to protect their property.

Sickness and death soon invaded the four. Mr. Clopton suddenly died, and, from the very outset, Mr. Pearcy's health had been declining. But leaving China did not seem to be an option for Mr. Pearcy, and in an effort to overcome his failing health, two trips were made to Shanghai. On both of those trips the couple encountered great storms. The first was said to have been the worst typhoon that had visited China for fifty years. All hope of their ship was gone, and the fact that they survived seemed miraculous. A hundred vessels and a thousand lives were lost at that time. Finally the mission transferred Mr. and Mrs. Pearcy to Shanghai permanently. Here, as they labored for five years, Mr. Pearcy accomplished one of his greatest works. He originated the phonetic system of reading and writing Chinese. Later, another missionary, Dr. T. P. Crawford, perfected the program.

Mr. Pearcy's health continued to degenerate, but he was unwilling to obey the doctor's command: "I order you home."[1] However, when Mrs. Pearcy's health began to decline, there was nothing else that could be done. When they were about to sail, Mr. Pearcy was seized with Asiatic cholera, and for a day and night he lay as though dead. The doctor did everything he could, and finally there were favorable results. During that period the patient, unbeknownst to the others, had been conscious and was in fear of being buried alive. On January 8, 1855, the two sailed for America.

Their ship landed in Boston, and gradually both husband and wife responded, and their health was renewed. The Board,however, determined that he could not return to the field, and he became an agent for the foreign mission board.

Faithfully he stirred the hearts of others for the fields white unto harvest. His successful recruiting continued until the Lord called him home on July 24, 1871.

China today boasts 1.2 billion people. They refuse to allow American missionaries to enter their land, but the seed has been planted, and house churches are evangelizing with great success. Why not pray just now for the national believers in China?

DLC

---

[1]George Braxton Taylor, *Virginia Baptist Ministers,* Third Series (Lynchburg, VA: J. P. Bell Company, 1912), 135.

May 31

A Real Student of the Word

Scripture: 2 Timothy 2:15

Porter Cleveland was born in Burlington, Hartford County, Connecticut, on May 31, 1797. His occupation as a peddler brought him to Virginia. His early acquaintances in Virginia were not overly impressed by him or sure of his character or success.

As unusual as it may seem, he was saved as the result of his own preaching. He was prompted by some ungodly friends to preach a mock sermon. However, as a result, his heart was touched and moved, and he was converted. He immediately joined the Pine Grove Baptist Church. The day after his baptism he preached his first sermon as a Christian. A short time later he was ordained and began his public ministry, which lasted for fifty-four years. A number of men who sat on his ordination council were well-known and successful pastors of his day.

Brother Cleveland pastored churches in Nelson and Fluvanna counties, as well as Albemarle. In addition, he was also a home missionary for the General Association, ministering in Augusta and Rochingham for several years. His ministry included a seventeen-year pastorate at Mount Ed.

Not only was he a faithful preacher, but he was of the family that gave our nation one of our presidents,Grover

Cleveland. He was loved not only by his church members but also by his neighbors and the members of churches of other denominations. Porter was zealous, devoted, and active in preaching the Gospel for the conversion of sinners and also for the edification of the people of God.

From the beginning of his ministry until the end, he was a genuine student of the Word of God as admonished by 2 Timothy 2:15. As a serious student, he accumulated a library that contained the best works of theology of his day and practical duties for the Christian life.

An interesting incident revealed he made good use of his library. Rev. Lyons, a Methodist minister, came to his neighborhood and after a sensational announcement preached on baptism. After closing, he asked if anyone wished to speak. Pastor Cleveland arose and said he would reply on a certain day. At the appointed time, Pastor Cleveland spoke for four hours to a large crowd. Mr. Lyons arose and questioned the accuracy of Pastor Cleveland's quotations. Pastor Coleman and Pastor Goss, two Disciple preachers, arose and showed the books which they had brought with them and proved that Pastor Cleveland's words were both true and accurate.

In regard to his religious convictions, he was firm and definite yet charitable and tolerant of all who differed with him. He was a strong advocate of temperance and was eager to do away with the terrible evils, misery, and ruin attending the manufacturing, sale, and drinking of intoxicating liquors. During the Civil War, someone tried to buy his apples to make brandy, but he refused to sell them. He replied he would let them rot before he would sell them for that purpose. He continued by saying that he had been opposed to intemperance for forty years and was not about to change now.

At the time of his death he was pastor of Mountain Plain Church, Albemarle County, Virginia. He passed away at the age of seventy-eight years and twenty-six days.

Porter Cleveland is a splendid role model for us today. He was a great student of the Word. He labored at studying to know and to understand the Bible. He had a balanced thrust of giving the Gospel to the lost and of feeding the saints that they might grow in grace and become mature Christians. Also, he was an example in practical Christian living. He would not bow to pressures of society but stood firm. He allowed God to mold and develop the new character that he received in conversion and to become strong in biblical convictions.

Hebrews 13:8 tells us "Jesus Christ is the same yesterday, today and forever." We have the same opportunities as Porter Cleveland. Let's follow this man of God as we remember this day in Baptist history.[1]

EGC

---

[1] George Braxton Taylor, *Virginia Baptist Ministers*, (Lynchburg, VA: J. P. Bell, 1912), 214-216.

June 1

Another Hero of the Faith

Scripture: Acts 4:31-33

When Elder Noah Alden baptized John Leland on June 1, 1774, in Northbridge, Massachusetts, he could little envision the unique ministry God would grant the young convert. John Leland became an outstanding Baptist leader during the early days of our American Republic. Mention has been made previously of his influence in drafting the first amendment to our national constitution, but John Leland was first and foremost a preacher of the grace of God! On September 30, 1776, he married Sallie Devine of Hopkinton, Massachusetts, and immediately the couple made arrangements to move to Virginia. His first residence in Virginia was at Culpeper, but his ability in the pulpit opened continual doors of ministerial opportunity. The man of God spent most of that year in evangelism, and his travels took him as far south as the Pedee River in South Carolina.

Early in 1778, the Lelands moved to Orange County, and the majority of his ministerial service was invested there. With inexhaustible energy, John Leland was soon preaching twelve to fourteen times each week. In the spring of the following year, he arranged for a string of meetings that would cover about 120 miles. His experiences along the way read like fiction. At a small crossing known as North Garden, Mrs. Bailey informed him that she desired to be baptized, but her husband threatened to whip her within an inch of her life and kill the man that should baptize her. The man had once seen John Leland and, somehow, had approved of the Baptist preacher. He had told his wife that if John Leland should come that way, he could baptize her. The man of God asked the lady if she was willing to suffer even if her husband should change his mind. She responded, "Yes, if I am whipped, my Savior had long furrows ploughed upon His back." "Well," responded Leland, "if you will venture your back, I will venture my head." Thus the baptism was accomplished, and early the next day, John Leland continued on his itinerant course. Later, however, he heard that Mrs. Bailey had indeed been whipped, but he commented, ". . . The head of John the Baptist is not taken off yet."[1]

In October of 1779, John Leland came to a crossroad in his ministry. He felt he had not been as tender to God's leading as he should have been. He cried out to God to give him a new burden for souls. A definite change took place in his ministry. From November 1779, to July 1780, he baptized 130. This was a refreshment to his ministry and a turning point in his evangelism.

At another time, when he was preaching in York, Virginia, Mrs. Robert Howard, wife of Captain Robert Howard, responded to the invitation and desired to be baptized. The Captain was a vestryman in the state church, and he strenuously opposed his wife's being immersed. However she persisted and was baptized by John Leland. When her husband learned what had happened, he took his carriage whip, threatening to whip the preacher out of the country. His sister stopped him and said: "Brother Bobby, Mr. Leland is a large man, and will be too much for you." "I know it," said the Captain, "but he will not fight." At that, Mrs. Howard spoke up and said, "Perhaps he may; he goes well armed; and if he should wound you in the heart, you would fall before him." "Ah," said the Captain, "I know nothing about this heart work." "I wish you may, my dear," said his wife.

The Captain gave up the idea of whipping Elder Leland, and afterward he listened to the preaching, fell under conviction, and was genuinely saved and followed the Lord in believer's immersion. A real transformation of his life took place, and in the course of time he accompanied Elder Leland in his preaching journeys.

Let us pray that the Lord of the Harvest will again raise up special servants whom He has prepared for the desperate needs of America today.

DLC

---

[1]J. B. McInturff, Editor, *The Old Paths* (New Market, VA: Henkel & Co., 1891), 95.

June 2

The Candy Bomber

Scripture: Hebrews 4:12

When Army pilot Major Ron Brooks was reactivated during the Vietnamese War, he and his wife, Barbara, were given assurance by the Lord of Ron's safe return. The Major and his wife had been high-school sweethearts since his graduation from South Charleston High School on June 2, 1953, and they had already gone through many trials together. Now they prayed unitedly that the Lord would grant him spiritual fruit during his tour of duty. The Lord answered, and as he personally witnessed, the opportunity of teaching spiritually starved soldiers expanded his outreach. Still, the Major thought there must be something else that he could do.

After being shot down in enemy territory, he was delivered by the hand of God. But that experience stimulated the Major to somehow do more in proclaiming the gospel. In time, Major Brooks was promoted to the position of headquarters commandant. This assured time for his evening Bible studies, and they became more fruitful than ever. More than 350 men trusted Christ as Savior in one year.

Still his heart cried out for expanded service. Each Saturday the Major filled his pockets with hard candy, and driving into local villages, he distributed it. Children thronged his jeep, but he felt frustration in being unable to witness to them. The Major wrote his wife, his pastor, and close friends explaining his frustration. There was almost immediate response. His pastor sent him boxes of the wonderful tract, *God's Simple Plan of Salvation* in Vietnamese. A friend sent along a wooden, hand-cranked record player with a stack of records of Bible reading and preaching in Vietnamese. His wife sent him hundreds of pounds of hard candy.

Thus equipped, he returned to the villages, and set up shop with the record player. He gave out the candy and the tracts. Now a brilliant idea emerged. Why not "bomb" the adjacent villages with bags containing several pieces of candy and a copy of the gospel tract? The idea was perfected, and as the Major returned from his flying missions, he would veer ten to fifteen miles, begin a slow, lazy circle, and toss out his "candy bombs" to villagers below. A United Press International reporter, doubtless thinking this was the act of a super patriot, wrote up the exploit. He titled his article, "The Candy Bomber."

But did his efforts pay off? Three years later on his second tour of duty, Major Brooks had a new assignment. He was responsible for the refueling and rearming of equipment on nineteen air fields. Frequently he negotiated with village and provincial chiefs. At such times he was treated as an honored guest, and given the seat of honor at the chief's right hand. On one occasion, a village chief said, "Major Brooks, I understand you are a Christian." "Yes, I am," the Major replied. "Good," said the chief. "We have a Christian in our village. He is our music teacher. I've invited him to sit beside you during lunch today, at the second seat of honor." As they ate, the young man confided in the Major, "Sir, they think I'm their music teacher, but really, I'm a missionary." The Major's curiosity was piqued, and he asked him how he had come to know Jesus Christ as his Savior. "That's a very interesting story," he began. "Three years ago I was a student at the University of Saigon, studying in the conservatory of music. I went home one week-end to visit family. While at home, my little brother ran into the house and said he had found a brown paper bag with candy inside. At the bottom of the bag was a piece of paper. I must have stuck the paper in one of my books, because when I returned to Saigon, there it was. The paper talked about a God who had a Son who loved me and died for my sins. I had never heard a story like that before, and I couldn't understand it." The young man then told how a missionary in Saigon had explained what the tract meant and had led him to Christ.

The Major was thrilled as the truth flooded his mind. He could have shouted for joy in the realization that "All things work together for good to them that love

God, to them who are the called according to His purpose." Friends, God's Word always brings results. Have you witnessed for Christ today? Have you given anyone a gospel tract? Read our text of the day again. It is still truth.

Upon returning from Vietnam, Ron and Barbara Brooks went to Germany as missionaries. In time Dr. Brooks was asked to serve Baptist World Mission as a Field Director. He is still giving out God's Word.

DLC

June 3

The Missionary Foundation

Scripture: Matthew 9:35-38

Often we have alluded to the sermon by William Carey before the Northamptonshire Baptist Association on May 6, 1792, as being one of the major building blocks that led to the establishment of the first modern-day mission agency. At other times reference has been made to the action by the pastors of the Northamptonshire Baptist Association October 2, 1792, as being the cornerstone of the mission agency's founding. But in actuality the Holy Spirit had been moving on the hearts of several individuals in preparation for the great event.

In a Brief Statement of the Baptist Missions in the East, the following account was presented.

> This undertaking had its origin amongst the churches of the Northamptonshire and Leicestershire Association. On June 3rd, 1784, at the Association at Nottingham, it was agreed to hold a prayer-meeting for the general spread of the gospel on the evening of the first Monday in every month. In this prayer-meeting Christians of other connexions, denominations, and countries soon united, and continue to unite to this day.
>
> About three years after this, Mr. Carey was ordained pastor of the church at Moulton, and

> joined the Association. His mind from an early period seems to have been impressed with the state of the heathen world. In reference to this object he made himself acquainted with the geography, population, and religion of the various nations of the earth; and with the labours of Christians, both of early and later ages, in propagating the gospel. He also acquired some considerable knowledge of the learned languages. The subject having occupied so much of his attention, he would often converse upon it with other ministers. At length, after having been seven years engaged in praying for the spread of the gospel, some began to feel with Mr. Carey, that they ought to do something else as well as pray. Two sermons by Mr. Sutcliff and Mr. Fuller, the one on *Jealousy for the Lord of Hosts*, and the other on *The pernicious influence of delay*, made some impression. These were printed and followed by Mr. Carey's *Inquiry into the obligations of Christians to use means for the conversion of the heathen*. A very impressive sermon was also preached by Mr. Carey at the Nottingham Association on *Zion's enlargement*: and a pungent Circular Letter, written on *Godly Zeal*, by Mr. Ryland. The result was, that on October 2nd, the same year (1792) a Society was formed at Kettering *for the propagation of the gospel among the heathen*; and John Ryland, Reynold Hogg, William Carey, John Sutcliff, and Andrew Fuller, chosen as a Committee to carry the object into execution.[1]

The interesting article continues with notes of interest concerning the first modern-day mission society, but it is well to point out that the entire effort emerged from the faithful prayers of God's people as they designated one night a month for the purpose of prayer. As we have entered into the twenty-first century, one cannot help but be distressed while considering the stirring realization that while the world population is greatly proliferating, the army of faithful missionaries is in numerical decline. Tragically, most fundamental Baptist mission agencies are experiencing more retirements from their missionary numbers than they are receiving applicants from young people interested in investing their lives in an effort to reach the growing multitudes of heathen around the world.

Mission agencies have determined to advertise in Christian and secular periodicals in an attempt to interest young people to invest their lives in the Gospel. Some mission agencies have established teams of "missionary recruiters," to confront youth head on in an effort to stem the tide. I am not evaluating these programs, but we might do well to obey the Lord and repeat the effort of our British brethren in 1784 and "Pray the Lord of the harvest that He would send forth laborers into His harvest." Parents, have you prayed that prayer for your own children? Grandparents, have you prayed such a prayer for your grandchildren? This would be a good time to begin such praying.

DLC

---

[1]*The First Annual Report of The Baptist Board of Foreign Missions for the United States* (Philadelphia: William Fry, Printer, 1815), 42-43.

June 4

Baptists are not Protestants!

Scripture: Mark 1:1-11

It is incongruous that fundamental Baptist Bible colleges in the twenty-first century have fallen into the error of declaring that Baptist churches came into being in 1641! Those who follow this error would have us believe that Baptists sprang from the Reformation. It would seem that these might have a hidden agenda. Let us reaffirm that in doctrine and practice, our forefathers preceded the Reformers. To be sure, fundamental Baptists protest more than all of the Protestants, but our Baptist heritage precedes the Reformation! The teaching that would suggest Baptist beginnings in 1641 was unknown until the very ending of the nineteenth century. That deceitful teaching led to the resignation of Dr. William Heth Whitsitt from the presidency of Southern Baptist Theological Seminary. Let us consider several quotations that totally obliterate the erroneous assumption of a Reformation beginning for Baptists.

> Dr. W. H. King, London, who made an extensive investigation of the pamphlets in the British Museum, says: "I have carefully examined the titles of the pamphlets in the first three volumes of this catalogue, more than 7,000 in number, and have read every pamphlet which has seemed by its title to refer to the subject of baptism, or the opinions and practices of the Baptists, with this result: that I can affirm, with the most unhesitating confidence, that in these volumes there is not a sentence or a hint from which it can be inferred that the Baptists generally, or any section of them, or even any individual Baptist, held any other opinion than that immersion is the only true and Scriptural method of baptism, either before the year1641 or after it. It must be remembered that these are the earliest pamphlets, and cover the period from the year 1640 to 1646 (*The Western Recorder*, June 4, 1896)."
>
> Dr. George C. Lorimer, who gave much attention to Baptist history, said in an address September 14, 1896, before the students of Newton Theological Institution: "I insist that …our Baptist churches and their action on the world's progress should not be ignored. As a rule they do not receive the recognition they deserve. Dr. Dexter in his *True Story of John Smyth* has, let us believe unintentionally, put them in an entirely false light; and his representation that Edward Barber originated the practice of immersion in England, and that before the publication of his book (1641) the Baptists poured and sprinkled, is, to put it mildly, incorrect. I have just returned from the British Museum, where I went over the documents which are supposed to substantiate such a view, and I solemnly declare that no such evidence exists."
>
> Dr. Joseph Angus, former President of Regents Park College, London, . . . says: "During

this period, very little is said about immersion, and the silence of the writers on the mode is said to be deeply significant. But it is overlooked that in that age immersion was the generally accepted mode of baptism in England. The Prayer Book has all along ordered the child 'to be dipped warily' in the water. The practice of dipping was familiar in the days of Henry V111, and both Edward V1, and Queen Elizabeth were dipped in their childhood. In that century it was not necessary to lecture on the meaning of the word, or to insist on the mode of baptizing, which is still described in the English service as 'dipping.' . . . That there was no such delay in forming Baptist churches as our American friends have supposed, is proved by the dates of the formation of a number of them. Churches were formed, chapels built and doctrines defended long before 1641, and others, down to the end of the century, owing probably to the discussions of that year(*The Western Recorder*, October 22, 1896)."[1]

With Baptists of old, such as Charles Haddon Spurgeon, the present writer acknowledges that he is confident that truth is eternal. Baptist distinctives, which are New Testament principles, have never ceased since our Lord established His Church. As the local church is the "pillar and ground of the truth," those principles have long endured. The gates of hell have not prevailed against it!

DLC

[1] John T. Christian, *A History of the Baptists* (Texarkana: American Baptist Association, 1922), 298-299.

June 5

A Well-Known Country Preacher

Scripture: 2 Corinthians 4:5-7

It was on Big Hurricane Creek in the hill country of West Virginia on June 5, 1901, that the proud father, Richard Lakin, heard the doctor announce, "It's a boy!" Life in the hills of West Virginia was not easy, but the prospect of having a son to ultimately assist with chores certainly must have been pleasing to Richard and Mary Elizabeth, parents of Bascom Ray Lakin. Every aspect of farming in that day called for strenuous labor, and the Lakin's situation was no different.

We know little of the early life of the lad who later in life was called by his initials "B. R." His first educational experience was received in a one-room school building located on Queen's Creek, far back in the hills of West Virginia. His teacher was School Master Jake Dawson. There B.R. learned the basic skills of education.[1] Mountaineers soon learned the value of a dollar, for one labored from daylight to dark for little compensation. During his teen years, he was able to gain employment with a timber-cutting company. It was at this formative stage in life that the Lord began stirring his heart with conviction. Bascom was invited to evangelistic meetings by another youth, Ben Cornutte. He welcomed the invitation as a bit of diversion from his work-a-day world, and that evening he made his way to the church house. That night the preacher, Reverend J. C. Simpkins, hammered away on eternal truths and the necessity of being prepared for eternity. As the preacher declared such truths, conviction came upon Bascom. He felt that the sermon was being delivered just for him. The preacher was no novice to the sinful nature of mankind. Indeed, he was a nephew of the legendary "Devil Anse" Hatfield, one of the principle figures of the infamous nineteenth century Hatfield-McCoy feud between two families on the West Virginia/Kentucky border. The feud had resulted in death to many. Thus the preacher was no citified lecturer sent to deliver a theological discourse. He knew the sinfulness of men, and he preached with fervor! But it was not the power of the preacher, but the conviction of the Holy Spirit that caused eighteen year old Bascom Lakin to bow at an old-fashioned altar and receive the Lord Jesus Christ as his Savior.

A few days later, Bascom Lakin was baptized in the Big Hurricane Creek by Reverend Simpkins. As was so often the case in Appalachia, young Bascom soon thereafter began to preach! His unique personality shone through his preaching, and he declared all the truth he knew with conviction. His first pastorate was the Evangel Baptist Church located at Greenbriar Creek. That was the beginning of what would become a famed ministry. He became a familiar figure as a circuit-riding preacher as he rode a mule to many country churches near the forks of the Big Sandy River. The Big Hurricane Baptist Church called for an ordination council on May 28, 1921, and the twenty-year-old pastor was ordained. His desire to better understand God's Word led Bascom to enter Moody Bible Institute in Chicago.

His preaching began to bring notoriety, and in time he received a call from E. Howard Cadle of Indianapolis, Indiana, asking him to come to the Cadle Tabernacle and assist Dr. Cadle in that ministry. He accepted the call, and following Mr. Cadle's death, Reverend Lakin became pastor. During the next fourteen years of service in Indianapolis, the services were broadcast nationwide, and he was preaching to thousands of people each Sunday. The preacher from the hills of West Virginia was honored by Bob Jones University when he was granted an honorary doctorate.

In the early 1950's, Dr. Lakin began a thirty year itinerant ministry that found him preaching in some of the largest churches in America. It is estimated that he was used of God in over 100,000 professions of Christ as Savior. After more than sixty-five years of preaching, B. R. Lakin was called home to be with His Lord on March 15, 1984.

It is wonderful as one preaches the Gospel, to look over the audience and wonder what plans God the Holy Spirit has for those who hear and heed the Word. May our churches produce young preachers who love and preach the Word in this twenty-first century.

DLC

---

[1]Wm. K. McComas, *50 Years of Plowing, Planting and Watering* (Newton, KS: United Printing, Inc., 1973), 6.

June 6

"Give me Liberty, or Give me Death"

Scripture: Luke 9:54-56

Patrick Henry, a lover of freedom, was born on May 29, 1736, in Hanover County, Virginia. Henry suffered failures as a storekeeper, and a farmer, but success finally came after his admission to the Virginia bar in 1760. Historians remember him for his impassioned pleading in the Parson's Cause in 1783. This was a case in which he defended the right of the colony to fix the price of the tobacco by which the clergy were paid. This he did in spite of a contrary ruling from London. From that point on, Patrick Henry's oratory assured him of a commanding influence in all the actions of legislatures. He entered the House of Burgesses in 1765. After the passage of the Stamp Act (1765) he introduced a set of radical resolutions denouncing the British Parliament's usurpation of powers vested in the colonial legislature. The British claimed they alone had power to tax. The famous conclusion of one of his speeches revealed his keen mind. With passion he said: "Caesar had his Brutus-Charles the first his Cromwell-and George III-may he profit from their example." That statement assured his popularity among the colonists.

Lord Dunmore, the British Governor of Virginia, dissolved the legislature following the closing of the port of Boston in 1774. Henry called for a rump session of the legislature to meet in Williamsburg. That session invited the other colonies to send delegates to a Continental Congress. Of course, Henry was a member of the Continental Congress, and he was a leading voice as he advocated strong measures of resistance.

Americans best remember Patrick Henry for his famous statement in the Virginia assembly in Richmond on March 23, 1775. He pled with the colonists to arm, exclaiming: "Give me liberty, or give me death." Soon he actually led the militia of Hanover to force Governor Dunmore to surrender munitions belonging to the colony.

During the Revolutionary War he remained in the legislature, working toward and urging independence. He helped to draft the first state constitution. He was elected governor in 1776, and served until 1779. He supported the war effort, and again served as governor from 1784 to 1786. Patrick Henry recognized the danger of centralized government, and championed the cause of state's rights. But, in time, fearing lest the radicalism of the French Revolution would infect our young nation, he ultimately turned to support the Federalist party. Just prior to his death on this date in 1799, Patrick Henry was elected again to the state legislature as a Federalist.

"But," you wonder, "why is Patrick Henry, an Episcopalian, featured in a 'Baptist' historical tome?" The answer is simple. Patrick Henry was a sincere and generous friend of the Baptists. A letter from Judge Spencer to William Wirt, Henry's biographer, states that, "Mr. [Edmund Pendleton], on the bench of Caroline court, justified the imprisonment of several Baptist preachers, who were defended by Mr. Henry, on the heinous charge of worshiping God according to the dictates of their own consciences.[1]

A portion of Mr. Henry's defense of the Baptists follow: "May it please your worships. I think I heard read by the prosecutor, as I entered the house, the paper I now hold in my hand. If I rightly understood, the king's attorney has framed an indictment for the purpose of arraigning, and punishing by imprisonment, these three inoffensive persons before the bar of this Court for a crime of great magnitude,-as disturbers of the peace. May it please the Court, what did I hear read? Did I hear it distinctly,-or was it a mistake of my own? Did I hear an expression, as of a crime, that these men, whom your worships are about to try for a misdemeanor, are charged with,-with-what?- Then in a low, solemn, heavy tone he continued-'preaching the gospel of the Son of God?' Pausing amid profound silence, he waved the paper three times round his head, then raising his eyes and hands to heaven, with peculiar and impressive energy, he exclaimed-'Great God!' A burst of feeling from the audience followed this exclamation." Needless to say, the three Baptist preachers were dismissed from the Court.[2]

Let us thank God for friends He has provided for our cause through the years.

DLC

---

[1]Garnett Ryland, *The Baptists of Virginia 1699-1926* (Richmond, VA: The Virginia Baptist Board of Missions and Education, 1955), 76.

[2]Lewis Peyton Little, *Imprisoned Preachers and Religious Liberty in Virginia* (Lynchburg, VA: J. P. Bell Co., 1938), 107.

June 7

A Baptist Warrior

Scripture: Psalm 18

He was a cool-headed warrior and an outstanding rifleman. He was also a committed Baptist. Waverly Wray was an American soldier who participated in one of the most glorious eras of our American history, the liberation of Europe. On June 6, 1944, our soldiers began the largest amphibious assault ever attempted. Lt. Waverly Wray, an officer in the 505th Parachute Infantry Regiment, had jumped into the scene of war just prior to the historic landings and now, not more than thirty hours later, on June 7, he sensed a German counter-attack forming. Wray was already a decorated veteran of several campaigns, but he would be most remember for his June 7 reconnaissance trip that would place him in the permanent memory of military lore and earn for him one of America's highest honors.

While scouting out the land he came upon a group of eight German soldiers who were busily studying a map. He shouted at them to surrender, but while one German reached for his pistol, another from over one hundred yards away began to fire at him with a machine gun. Wray calmly disposed of all eight men then went back to the Command Post with bullet holes in his uniform and his ear half gone, blood soaking his shirt. When his commander saw him he commented on how close the Germans had gotten to the scout, to which Wray responded, grinning, "Yes, but not as close as I got to them." Indeed. The next day it was discovered that Wray had disrupted a counter-offensive that would have cost many American lives. They found all eight bodies shot in the head, some over one hundreds yards away from where Wray fired. Wray insisted on burying his victims, for while he was a soldier doing his duty, he was also a Christian with a profound respect for life. Even his mortal enemies would get the dignity of a painless death and a decent burial. Several months later after repeated displays of bravery and courage, Waverly Wray was finally struck in the head by an enemy sharp shooter.

Wray's marksmanship was legendary. And so was his bravery. He would face the withering fire of the opposition with a calm that astounded his brothers-in-arms. Once while hunkered down behind some defense barricades waiting for the US artillery to cease fire, he turned to his sergeant and said, "John, I wish that artillery would stop so we can go in after them!" The sergeant muttered an expletive and said that he thought the artillery was doing well enough! The same sergeant exclaimed to a ranking officer, "Aren't you glad Waverly is on our side!"

Waverly was not only on our side, but he was distinctly on the Lord's side. His story is fascinating. However, what is more interesting is that Wray was not only a courageous soldier on the European battlefields, but he was an outstanding soldier in the toughest battle of all -- life. He was respectfully called "Deacon" because he lived a separated life among the troops. He did not swear, drink, or womanize. In fact, he sent half his pay back to his Mississippi church to aid in its building project. The fact that secular history remembers this aspect of the Baptist warrior's life suggests that Wray is a true Baptist hero and demonstrates to all of us that Baptists can have a significant impact in this world not only with the Bible but, if duty and country call, with a gun.

Soldiering is a noble profession when the soldier and the country he serves fight for a just cause. It is an ungrounded, misguided sense of morality that attempts to shame men and women in uniform who have accepted the horrible business of killing for our country when necessary. God is not ashamed to be identified with men who put their lives on the line to eliminate warriors of evil ambitions. The one man in the Bible who was said to be a man after God's own heart, David (1 Samuel 13:14), recorded in a Psalm that God, "teacheth my hands to war" (Psalm 18:34). God is not ashamed of this profession, nor is He ashamed to be the Helper of the valiant believers who serve Him this way. Therefore, we should thank God for our soldiers and ask Him to instruct them in *both* their professions: soldiers for their country and for Christ.

RPB

June 8

The Revision of History

Scripture: 2 Samuel 11:1-17

What an interesting text we have chosen. Someone has well said that although God cannot alter the past, historians can. In Israel's history, David attempted to cover up his sin by providing for the possibility that Bathsheba's illegitimate son might not have been spurious. Had David's plan worked, it could be claimed that the baby was the actual son of Uriah. When his efforts failed, David reverted to murder. In our day with American history, truth is often revised simply with the pen by a professed chronicler. But in Burma, at least in the matter of cruelty to Baptist missionaries, the revision of history is accomplished with a bulldozer! Let me explain.

Two weeks after British troops had taken Rangoon, Adoniram Judson was arrested as a spy. Prior to that time the capital had been moved to Ava where Adoniram and Ann were living. A dozen Burmese men burst into Judson's small home, and an official bore a black book. With him was a man who bore a circle tattooed on each cheek. Such men were known as "Spotted Faces"-- criminals who had been appointed as executioners/jailers. The Spotted Faces lived outside of Burmese society and married among themselves. Often their crime was branded into their foreheads. They enjoyed inflicting punishment on those committed to their keeping in the jails.

The Spotted Face threw Adoniram to the floor and quickly trussed his victim. As Ann protested, the Spotted Face dragged Adoniram out of the house--the others following, while Ann was being restrained. Adoniram was taken to the palace courtyard and there consigned to the dreaded *Let-may-yoon Prison*. His windowless cell was approximately 30 by 40 feet. All the prisoners were in ankle chains, making walking impossible. A long horizontal bamboo pole, suspended by pulleys, hung from the ceiling. A block and tackle arrangement at the ends allowed it to raised or lowered. During the nights, the pole was lowered and passed between the fettered legs of prisoners. Then, secured again at the ends, the pole was hoisted with the aid of block and tackle. Ultimately only the prisoner's shoulders and heads rested on the floor.

The prison was two miles from the Judson's home, but Ann beat a pathway by continued visits. Every day Ann also contacted officials and members of the royal family, seeking relief for her husband. She argued that Adoniram and Dr. Price were Americans and had nothing to do with the war with British troops. She interceded, implored, and entreated until permission was finally given to vacate her small house and build a one room dwelling on the prison ground. In fact, when Adoniram's health broke, it was feared that he could not long endure such continued treatment, and he was allowed to crawl to the one-room hut for meals with Ann. On one such occasion, as the Judsons were eating, Ann was summoned to appear immediately at the governor's. She hurried, thinking there was some fast-breaking news. The governor occupied her in a lengthy discussion of no importance. But while she was meeting there, a servant came running, her face pale with terror. "The white prisoners have all been carried away," she gasped.

We shall consider the outcome in another entry, but for over two years, the *Ava Let-ma Yoon Prison* had been Judson's home. In following years a huge monument was placed at that site. Incised upon that monument in both English and Burmese were the following words:

JUDSON MEMORIAL SITE OF AVA LET-MA YOON PRISON

Today that monument is no longer to be found. In traveling to Ava one discovers that the old city has been destroyed. Only an ancient heathen tower remains. What happened to the monument? It was apparently too large and permanent to be destroyed, but memories of that place had to be eradicated. Thus bulldozers were ordered in, and the topography of the area was changed. The monument was buried near the site.

How do we know this to be the case? An elderly Christian gentleman in Mandalay "happened" to have a picture of the monument. Making it available to the author, copies were made. The trees in the background of the picture make it possible to pinpoint the very location where God's grace was so displayed.

The pictures enable those stones to cry out! The history of Judson's suffering may be obliterated, but the reminder of God's grace in that terrible place cannot be destroyed!

DLC

June 9

Serving Whether Bond or Free

Scripture: 1 Corinthians 7:20-24

Prior to the Civil War, many Baptist churches in the South had a majority of black members. To be sure, these could not serve as pastors or deacons, and for the most part, they were segregated in their seating. Most church buildings provided a gallery to house slaves. When the Civil War concluded, many black members of predominately white Baptist churches determined to build a heritage of their own. Often white members offered financial assistance to make such a program viable. On June 9, 1865, black members of three white churches in Charleston, South Carolina, withdrew from those churches to form the Morris Street Baptist Church of that city.[1] The first pastor of the church, Reverend Jacob Legare, laid a solid foundation and served that congregation for more than twenty years. During his tenure as pastor, this man of God baptized more than three thousand who had made profession of their faith in Christ. Reverend Legare emphasized missions, and contributions to the cause of state, home, and foreign missions grew continually. The Morris Street church became the "mother" church of several other flourishing black Baptist churches in Charleston. From the Morris Street church, an entire congregation was organized and sent to Africa as a full-blown church. More than a dozen young men were sent out to preach the Gospel, and several of them became outstanding in their own right.

Following Reverend Legare's ministry, the Lord provided Reverend John L. Dart to serve the congregation. Reverend Dart was born March 10, 1854. His parents, William and Susan Dart, had purchased their freedom prior to the Civil War, and they were apparently successful in business. Young John was sent to a private school when he was six. Following the Civil War, public schools were opened to all, and for a time, young John

studied there. In 1872 he graduated as the valedictorian of the Avery Normal Institute. William Dart was a deacon and Susan a consistent Christian. The testimony of his parents and the strength of the pulpit ministry brought young John to salvation when he was 17 years old.

At the age of 18, John taught school for a year, and in 1873 he entered Atlanta University. When 21, John was licensed to preach, and partly supported himself through college by preaching and teaching during the next few years. When 25 years of age, John entered Newton Theological Seminary and graduated with honors. He was the only black student in the seminary. Surely the Lord was preparing His servant for a place of leadership. He was ordained following his seminary training, and for two years he taught in the public schools of Washington, D. C. After that, he labored in the pastorate of the Congdon Street Baptist Church in Providence, Rhode Island, and then supplied the pulpit of the Union Baptist Church of Augusta, Georgia. Great revival ensued, and the man of God was invited at that time to assume the pastorate of the Morris Street Baptist Church in Charleston. After a year of service there, Reverend Dart was married to Miss Julia A. Pierce of Washington, D.C. God's blessing rested upon His servant, and in four years of ministry in Charleston, over 500 were added to the membership.

During the time of that pastorate, Reverend Dart wrote a controversial pamphlet entitled *The Immersion Issue*, which consisted of extracts from his sermons on baptism. Several Methodist preachers had declared sprinkling to be scriptural baptism, and Reverend Dart challenged them to debate the issue. Of course, his challenge was never accepted.

Our sovereign God overruled the tragedy of slavery in America. He also overcame the bitterness the Civil War produced in American society, and His work of evangelizing all men to His own glory is thrilling to behold. This is merely one such case in a series of glorious victories our Lord has accomplished when believers, regardless of race, have sought to serve the King of Kings and the Lord of Lords.

DLC

---

[1]A. W. Pegues, *Our Baptist Ministers and Schools* (Cincinnati, OH: Lyons Brothers Publishing Co., 1891), 147.

June 10

The Martyrdom of a Teenager

Scripture: Acts 7:55-60

In the year 1535, Charles V received a memorandum from the Council of the Archbishop of Cologne. In that note he was told to suppress the Anabaptists because they, ("as [has] been the nature of the Anabaptists throughout the ages, even as the old histories on imperial law over a thousand years testify"[1]) were attempting to reinstate a community of goods. One must note that though many today want to present Anabaptists as existing only during the days of the Reformation, authors of Roman Catholicism mention their presence throughout the history of Christendom.

Be that as it may, on June 10, 1535, Charles V viewed the growth of the Anabaptist movement as a threat to Romanism. He issued a special decree that anyone who baptized others and refused to recant would be put to death by fire, and any who would not recant or had helped provide hospitality to the Anabaptists would be beheaded or, in the case of women, would be drowned.[2]

Anabaptism was growing rapidly in the Netherlands in the 1530s. Anabaptists flooded the area from Switzerland. Many congregations were being formed, and some were sizeable. There was a joy in the lives of the communicants. It was apparent to the Roman clergy that the challengers to Romanism had to be exterminated. Scores of Anabaptists were burned at the stake, decapitated, or drowned for their witness. At that time a young fifteen-year-old lad became aware of this strange movement. He had heard it discussed in his home, but he became aware of it when he actually attended a public burning. He was caught up in amazement as he watched the victim, who was chained to a pillar and incinerated. He listened to his witness of Christ and observed a peace that seemed supernatural.

Fifteen-year-old Cornelis Aertz de Man left the city square, but he could not dispel the scene or that witness from his mind. In time he heard of a meeting of Anabaptists held in a home and he attended. Hearing the Word of God, he soon came to the conclusion that these people had spiritual truth and reality. In a matter of weeks he trusted Christ as Savior, and

the group leader personally discipled the young man. Cornelis requested believer's baptism, and he united with the group.

His family saw the difference and became concerned for his and their safety. They could not deny his transformation, but they cautioned Cornelis that his boldness would be observed by the authorities.

By the late 1540s large numbers of Anabaptists were being arrested and executed. For two years Cornelis had been a faithful follower of the Savior, but in a raid in early 1549 he was arrested. His captors thought that a youthful lad would easily recant, but they did not know Cornelis. He endured interrogation, answering with a humble but assuring confidence in Scripture. When asked what he believed, Cornelis responded: "I believe that Jesus Christ is the true, living Son of God, and that there is no other salvation either in heaven or on earth, either under it or above it."[3] All efforts were useless in causing him to recant.

Gradually his torture grew more severe. He was locked in a filthy jail cell and was undernourished. His one hand and foot were placed in stocks. In time he was hung by his hands with a heavy stone tied to his feet. He was then elevated and allowed to hang until he fainted. He was then placed in the rack and stretched until the excruciating pain was almost more than he could bear. But he would not recant. Finally, when it became apparent that he could not be broken, it was determined he must die. On August 13, 1552, Cornelis was taken to the marketplace of Kulenburgh. He was tied to the stake, and while preparations were made to burn him, he prayed. Looking over the crowd, he saw a fellow believer, and a smile broke upon his face. The flames soon rose, and Cornelis opened his eyes to the smile of the Savior's face.

He was only seventeen, but he was a stalwart of the faith for Christ. Surely ours is a rich heritage forged by young and old who have been willing to stand for truth in a wicked and perverse world.

DLC

---

[1]Leonard Verduin, *The Anatomy of a Hybrid* (Grand Rapids, MI: William B. Eerdmans Publishing Company, 1976), 153.

[2]Myron S. Augsburger, *Faithful Unto Death* (Waco, TX: Word Books, 1978), 10.

[3]Ibid., 13.

June 11

How to Handle Persecution

Scripture: James 2:14-20

The complete independence of every Baptist church is a New Testament tenet that has protected local congregations from being absorbed by cross-currents of doctrine. However, to assure continuity and uniformity of truth, when Baptist churches began rapidly to proliferate in the Commonwealth of Virginia, a "General Association" was established to serve as a clearing house in assisting local churches by responding to questions of doctrine, organization, practice and discipline. In 1774, Samuel Harris was serving as moderator and John Waller as clerk when letters were received from preachers confined in prison. Of particular interest was the letter from David Tinsley, who was then in Chesterfield jail. "The hearts of their brethren were affected at their sufferings, in consequence of which, it was agreed to raise contributions for their aid." It was "agreed to set apart the second and third Saturdays in June, as public fast days, in behalf of our poor blind persecutors, and for the releasement of our brethren."[1]

David Tinsley was the seventh Baptist preacher to be imprisoned in Chesterfield. He was pastor in the adjoining county of Cumberland, and he had been convicted on February 4, 1774, by the county court "of having assembled and preached to the people at sundry times and places in the County as a Baptist preacher." "This was in the depth of winter. His condition appears to have been painful in the extreme. Not content with sundering him from his friends and placing him in a dungeon, other attempts were made to annoy and distress him. The suffocating effects of burning tobacco and red pepper were applied to the door and window of his cell." His confinement lasted four months and sixteen days. He preached through the barred window while "all around the jail the crowded assembly would stand; some weeping and others rejoicing, as they received the word of truth."[2]

At the time of his imprisonment, David Tinsley was pastor of the Powhaton Church. During his ministry there, many had been saved and added to the membership, and some were called into the ministry, but in 1774 "he was clutched by the iron hand of persecution and immured in Chesterfield prison."[3]

I invite you now to divert your attention from the historic jail scene, and consider some practical aspects of what we should learn from the past. The General Association of Baptists in Virginia entered into a two-fold effort in behalf of their suffering members. First, they determined to assist their brethren financially. That is, they realized that the need existed to give material assistance, and they set out to do that. Then, they set two Saturdays in June of 1774 as days of fasting and prayer that the Lord might undertake in the lives of their persecutors.

That is another way of saying, they did what they could, and they committed the rest to the Lord. It would have been just so many words to pray that the Lord would meet the material needs of their friends when they had the ability to address those needs. However, they were not in a position to adjust the thinking of their persecutors, and they submitted that problem to the Lord.

Persecution and even martyrdom is very prevalent in our modern-day world. This problem will doubtless increase, and when it is possible, we need to do what we can to alleviate the suffering of those who stand for Christ. Islam is on the move in Africa (and elsewhere) and militant Hinduism has been very active in India. Where it is possible, we need to assist suffering Christians.

In addition, we can pray for the persecutors! And this we must do. Our God is not the Great "I Was." He is the Great "I Am," and He is able to do exceeding abundantly above all we ask or think. Let us pray for Divine intervention in these days.

DLC

---

[1]Garnett Ryland, *The Baptists of Virginia 1699-1926* (Richmond, VA: The Virginia Baptist Board of Missions and Education, 1955), 86-87.

[2]James B. Taylor, *Virginia Baptist Ministers* (Richmond: Yale & Wyatt, 1840), 2:101.

[3]Robert Baylor Semple, *History of the Baptists in Virginia* (Lafayette, TN: Church History Research and Archives, 1976), 264.

June 12

Fundamental Statesman/Editor

Scripture: Jeremiah 15:16; 23:29

With the mind of an attorney and precision of a surgeon, for twenty-four years, Noel Smith served as editor of the *Baptist Bible Tribune*. He used words like a scalpel cutting away the superfluous and applying Divine principles to American religious and political life. Surely he was the leading statesman in America for the cause of fundamental Baptists.

Noel Smith was born in Greenvale, Tennessee, on August 7, 1900. When but a child his family moved to Murfreesboro. He was converted at the age of fifteen in the Presbyterian Sunday school. Following the death of his mother, he left home and became a Railway Express Agent, working out of Nashville. In 1918 while living in Chattanooga, Smith attended the meetings of Billy Sunday, and at that time the Lord transformed his life. Immediately he became thrilled with the things of God. His Bible seemed to come alive, and he read voluminously the works of outstanding Godly men. God's Word was like a fire in his heart, and he began holding meetings throughout the South. He preached whenever and wherever the possibility presented itself.

In the Fall of 1930, Smith resigned his job with the railroad and was ordained by the Second Baptist Church of Clarkville, Tennessee. During the depths of the depression, Noel Smith married Miss Mattie Linda Stuart, a convert whom he had baptized in Dixon, Tennessee. She was a school teacher, but in those days, teachers were not allowed to be married. As a consequence, Mrs. Smith lost her employment, and the couple lived on Smith's meager love offerings.

In 1935, after having suffered the loss of two children at birth, the Lord blessed Noel and Linda with a son, Charles Stuart Smith. During ensuing years, Reverend Smith served as an evangelist in small Southern Baptist churches in Kentucky and Tennessee. However when the Southern Baptist Convention elected Louis D. Newton as its President, Reverend Smith broke with the Convention. Newton's liberal views of Communism incensed Noel Smith, and he felt it would be compromising to serve under that banner.

Independent Baptists were almost unknown in the South, but Reverend Smith was invited to speak to a group of independent Baptists in Texas. As a result of his addresses, several doors of opportunity opened to him for continued evangelism. In time Dr. J. Frank Norris invited him to teach at the Bible Baptist Seminary in Fort Worth. Reverend Smith was reluctant, wanting to return to the place of his roots in Clarksville, Tennessee. However, he finally agreed, and in the winter of 1947 the Smiths moved to Fort Worth. For the next years he taught and edited Norris' paper: *The Fundamentalist.*

In 1950 a division took place in the World Fundamental Baptist Fellowship, and the Baptist Bible Fellowship was born. Smith played an important role in the founding of the new group. In one exciting afternoon pastors met and formed the Baptist Bible Fellowship, voted to establish a new college - the Baptist Bible College, and decided to establish a Fellowship paper called the *Baptist Bible Tribune*. The organization headquarters would be centered in Springfield, Missouri. Eleven issues of the *Baptist Bible Tribune* had already gone to press when the college opened its doors in September, 1950. The early direction of the Baptist Bible Fellowship was charted by Dr. Noel Smith. He was tireless in his work as editor, and his wife served faithfully at his side.

Tragedy stuck in 1953 with the home-going of Mattie. Noel Smith was inconsolable. He wrote of his heartbreak in the June 12, 1953, *Tribune*, and the faculty were concerned lest he suffer a nervous breakdown. A further blow was experienced when Charles left for the Navy. The man of God was alone. But God heals all, and Noel Smith continued as Editor and also went back into evangelism. While preaching in Knoxville the following summer, Smith met Willadean Bowerman who was pianist for his meetings. To make a long story short, they fell in love and married on November 20, 1954, in Knoxville. For twelve blessed years Willadean stood at his side encouraging the man of God. On January 12, 1974, the Lord took His unusual servant. Philosopher, writer, editor, evangelist -- he was all of this and more. His students often commented that the most important thing he taught them was "COMMON SENSE." May the Lord raise up a host of such leaders in this twenty-first century.

DLC

June 13

An Unsung Hero

Scripture: 1 Timothy 3:8-13

The power of the Great Awakening was greatly experienced in Connecticut. In 1740 eighty new members were added to the church in Groton, the home of Joseph and Priscilla Breed. In North Stonington the church grew by 104 new converts. The indifference of the Congregational churches to the young converts produced through the revival led to the organization of the New Lights or, as they were also called, the Separates. (These are not to be confused with the Pilgrim's Separatism of the previous century.) This new movement became a unique denomination of almost one hundred churches.[1]

About 1753 Joseph and Priscilla Breed became associated with Daniel and Martha Marshall, and the two families ultimately decided to enter into missionary work among the Mohawk Indians in New York. The Mohawks were allied with four other tribes that formed the Iroquois nation. During this period the English, French, and Spanish were engaged in periodic battles as they sought to control the entire territory. The English governed lands on the eastern seashore east of the Appalachians. The French dominated most of Canada and the territory west of the Appalachians all the way to the Mississippi River. The Spanish regulated the territory of Florida. In 1754 the conflict between the French and English grew into the French and Indian War, and the Breeds and Marshalls decided that they could not continue to minister safely. Thus the families made their way South into northern Virginia. A faithful historian opines that they must have been surprised to find a Baptist church there (near Winchester, Virginia). The pastor of the church was Samuel Heaton, and, in the course of time, both the Breeds and Marshalls were baptized by immersion.[2]

Both of the men had been converted under the revival preaching of George Whitefield, and they too had learned to preach for a verdict. Much has been written concerning the fact that as Daniel Marshall began preaching in the area of Mill Creek some criticized him for his enthusiasm. Apparently some complained about him to the Philadelphia Association, accusing him of disorder, but when Benjamin Miller was sent to examine the matter, he could but thrill at such heart warming ministry. Soon Mr. Marshall's brother-in-law Shubal Stearns joined the two families. Through a letter received by Reverend Stearns on June 13, 1755, they were all challenged as to the spiritual need in North Carolina. This resulted in the entire group of sixteen moving to Sandy Creek, North Carolina. The amazing story of the establishing of what is called "The Bible Belt" is clearly set forth in this and the two preceding volumes in this set.

Shubal Stearns became pastor of what became a rapidly growing congregation. Both Daniel Marshall and Joseph Breed were chosen as assistants. Much has been written concerning the ministry of Daniel Marshall, but what of Joseph Breed? One of the early converts of Sandy Creek was Phillip Mulkey, a young man whom Shubal Stearns baptized on Christmas of 1756. Shortly thereafter, Phillip Mulkey joined with the Breeds and others to establish a church at Deep River, North Carolina. In 1759 the Mulkeys, Breeds, and several others left Deep River and moved into South Carolina.

A faithful historian presents the background. "The original thirteen of the migrating church moved on in December to Fairforest, a tract in the fork between Fairforest Creek and Tyger River. Mulkey continued as pastor of the Fairforest people at least through 1776. By 1772 the church ministered to three hundred families . . . (and) had four branches."[3] (i.e. "daughter churches")

It is believed that the Breeds, after their continual moving, finally settled down at Fairforest for the remainder of their lives. Joseph Breed was not a leader such as Shubal Stearns or Daniel Marshall, but he was what every Christian ought to be. He was a faithful follower and witness in the labors of love. We are not all called to be a Peter or Paul, but Joseph Breed is a great example for each of us.

DLC

---

[1]C. C. Goen, *Revivalism and Separatism in New England, 1740-1800* (Middletown: Wesleyan University Press, 1987), Introduction, XXVII.

[2]William L. Lumpkin, *Baptist Foundations in the South* (Nashville, TN: Broadman Press, 1961), 27.

[3]Ibid., 52.

June 14

A Missionary's Burden For His Family

Scripture: Ephesians 6:4

Many books chronicle the work of great missionaries. A book recently published produces, for the public, records from the journal and letters of William Carey.[1] *The Journal and Selected Letters of William Carey* merits study by anyone interested in the life of the man who pioneered the modern missions movement.

Carey kept his journal only "from June 13, 1793 to June 14, 1795, recording the trip to India and the first days on the field."[2] From the journal and letters to friends, family, and associates back in England, we gain an insight into the heart of the man. Much can be said of the trials on the field, of the preaching of the Gospel, the missionary's burden for the Indians in their idolatry, and his indefatigable work of translating the Scriptures into Bengali.

Carey's journal also shows us a father's tender heart for his children. On April 20, 1794, Carey wrote: "Began the day with uncomfortable expectations, and heart breaking views of Wretchedness, Pride, and unmortified Affections within, and Confusing appearance without, yet notwithstanding, I enjoyed a very Comfortable Day; I had much pleasure in instructing my Family, and found my soul drawn out in desires for the salvation of my Children. Blessed be God for this Day."[3]

Years later, on February 7, 1816, Carey still reflected a father's concern for his children. He wrote to his son Jabez: "Give my love to Eliza, in which your mother joins very heartily; we very frequently think and converse of you both and I trust your steadfast adherence to the cause of our dear Redeemer will occasion us always to converse about you with joy. Not so Felix. The thought of him rends my heart."[4] He rejoiced in one son's walk with God and grieved over another's waywardness.

This account should grip the heart of every Christian father. God directly charges *fathers* with the responsibility for training children in the ways of God. *Fathers* are responsible for rearing their children "in the nurture and admonition of the Lord" (Eph. 6:4). It is our responsibility to provide for our children training and teaching in the ways of the Lord. It is not enough to provide for the material needs of our families. We must nourish their hearts in the ways of God as surely as we provide food for their bodies. That task is not given primarily to mothers, though they have a great influence on children, as Lois and Eunice influenced Timothy (2 Tim. 1:5). As important as the local church is, its ministry can never replace the responsibility of fathers to nourish, train, and teach their children. Christian education is available to Christian families in various forms today. Yet a Christian school or a Christian curriculum can never do for our children what God has instructed fathers to do. Churches and institutions can have a good and profound influence on young lives, and we thank God for them. But fathers must take the lead in the instruction and training of their children. We must provide a spiritual heritage for our children. Christian father, are you providing spiritual training for your children? Is your concern, like Carey's, for the salvation of your children?

I cannot close this entry without a challenge to fathers who are also ministers. Carey, called from England to India, from the pastorate to missionary service, had a greater priority than his vocational service. That great priority was for the salvation of his children. How tragic to invest our lives in the salvation of others and to lose our own children! Preacher, remember that part of your qualification for ministry in a local church is effective leadership in your home (1 Tim. 3:4, 5). Let us give ourselves to the work to which God has called us, but let us invest our lives in the salvation and growth of the children God has given to us as His heritage (Ps. 127:3).

FJM

---

[1]Terry G. Carter, Editor, *The Journal and Selected Letters of William Carey* (Macon, GA: Smyth and Helwys, 2000).

[2]Carter, 4.

[3]Carter, 26.

[4]Carter, 283.

June 15

All Things Work Together for Good

Scripture: Acts 8:1-4

It is interesting to observe that our God is sovereign in all His dealings. As human beings we often do not know the purpose of our Lord, but we accept all things as from His hand. In Acts 8, persecution led to the expansion of the gospel. With that in mind, it is interesting to read the following: "At the New London, Conn., Baptist Association, 1849, the Rev. A. V. Dimock furnished the following account of persecution in Connecticut .... My great-grandfather, Shubael Dimock, and his son Daniel, were bitterly persecuted for preaching the Gospel "contrary to the law," and their property wasted by repeated fines. But this did not satisfy their persecutors, nor close the mouths of these men.

"Just as Shubael closed his sermon at a school-house in Mansfield, a sheriff arrested him upon a warrant to commit him to Windham jail. His offence was as follows: 'The said Shubael Dimock has been convicted of preaching in a school-house in Mansfield, and under an oak tree in Ashford.' He was required to walk before the officer to prison. But he replied, 'I have no call there, neither can I voluntarily go, since I have said, God willing, I will preach this evening in Ashford under the oak tree.' The officer urged that it was his duty to commit him to jail. 'Well, then,' said the prisoner, 'If you have a duty to perform, you must attend to it; I shall not resist.' He was at length set upon a horse and directed to guide it to Windham. Even this he refused to do, and the sheriff was compelled to mount the horse behind, and with his arms around him to guide the horse to the prison. Here he lay confined nine months, still proclaiming the truth as he had opportunity, for he declared that it was impossible to prevent his preaching unless they cut out his tongue.

"Soon after his release he removed with his family to the province of Nova Scotia, which had just fallen into the hands of the English, where he found a wider door of usefulness opened, and a more productive field of labor."[1]

The remainder of Shubael's life and that of his son Daniel, were spent in Nova Scotia, Canada, and they continued in the ministry of the Word of God. In the course of time, revival broke out under the ministry of Henry Alline, and the work of the Lord progressed throughout Nova Scotia and New Brunswick. However with the death of Henry Alline doctrinal aberrations became prevalent. ". . . Excesses developed in some quarters. A kind of antinomianism reared its head, extending even to immorality. Recurring from time to time since the sixteenth century, this doctrinal deviation suggests that the Christian, freed of guilt, unfettered by the Law and resting safe in 'eternal security' may wander from the pathway with some impunity. According to this view there is a dichotomy between spirit and flesh, and all wrongdoing may conveniently be blamed on the latter. This was a perverted Calvinism, which threatened the widespread spiritual quickening."[2]

These conditions led Baptist pastors to the realization that an association could provide a standard and promote Godliness. As a result, discussions were held on June 15, 1798, and the first Baptist association in all of Canada came into being on June 23 and 24, 1800. Joseph Dimock, then pastoring the Baptist church in Chester, was a leading voice in the work of God.

As the twenty-first century has opened, we view growing persecution around the world. It has well been said, that though we do not know the future, we know Who holds the future. Though that might seem like a trite cliché, many of those who know the power of God realize the truth in the statement as we watch our Lord work out His will. When persecution comes, let us trust Him as did Job when he said, "Though He slay me, yet will I trust in Him."

DLC

---

[1]Joseph Belcher, *The Religious Denominations in the United States* (Philadelphia: John E. Potter, 1856), 176-177.

[2]Henry A. Renfree, *Heritage & Horizon* (Mississauga, Ontario: Canadian Baptist Federation, 1988), 52.

June 16

Pastoral Appreciation

Scripture: 1 Thessalonians 5:12-13

William A. Baynham was born into a wealthy, southern, cultured family, which provided many wonderful opportunities. His educational advantages are apparent when one considers the fact that he received his M. D. degree at only twenty-one years of age. Following that, he spent two years in hospitals and schools in Philadelphia where he interned. Then, with a bright future, he returned to Essex County, Virginia to practice medicine. However, he soon gave up his medical practice, for he had inherited a large plantation along with many slaves. He needed to invest his time in superintending his land. He was inclined to free his slaves, but friends persuaded him otherwise. Throughout his entire life, William Baynham regretted that decision.

During the summer of 1834, he was aroused by the Spirit of God to think upon spiritual things. A short time later, in response to the preaching of Pastor Broaddus, William was converted at a meeting in Essex County. It is reported that for months after his conversion, whenever he heard the name of Jesus, he would cry. Immediately upon conversion, he joined an Episcopal church, but after a careful study of the New Testament, he sought immersion and joined the ranks of the Baptists. When he returned home, William Baynham joined the Enon Baptist Church in Essex County and became a very active member. Before long he began occasionally to preach, and the results were very pleasing. At the encouragement of the congregation, Mr. Baynham was ordained to the gospel ministry in September of 1841. In January 1842 he was called to pastor the Enon church, and he remained the pastor there until his death. As was the custom in those days, he also became pastor of the Upper Zion Church in Caroline County and, until the Lord called him home, he maintained that pastorate as well. He pastored Enon Baptist Church for forty-three years and the Upper Zion Baptist Church for thirty-three years.

In 1880 *The Religious Herald*, a Virginia Baptist paper, published letters from pastors who had served lengthy pastorates. Each one wrote on the causes of their long pastorate. Pastor William A. Baynham submitted the following: "The real ground of my continuance for so long a period as pastor of my two churches has been our strong mutual love. . . . In my position as pastor I have endeavored to be one with my charge. I have tried to show myself the friend. I have visited them freely, familiarly, and much. The children have had a good share of attention. In affliction I have been prompt and attentive, ready to render personal assistance as necessary. One rule has been unvaried with me: not only not to neglect the poor, but to show them all kindness and attention. My social relations I choose for myself-my kindness and affection for my church members is rendered to all without caste distinction. . . . I never scold . . . I avoid repeating what I hear in families. . . . My habit is daily to pray for all my flock and for many individually. . . . I have a list made of three classes: 1. Families; 2. Those who are Christians- names of the same; 3. Unconverted- named personally. Instead of going over them by name in prayer the paper is presented before God, each class separately. In addition, special cases named. . . . Another item for friends, enemies, acquaintances, neighbors, relations, members of my churches, and servants I have had."[1]

During his fruitful ministry, the preachers of the Rappahannock Association of Virginia titled him: *Beloved John*.[2]

June 16, 1887, at seventy-four years of age, he started out to make a promised visit. On the journey he was overcome with either heat or a heart attack. He fell down in the foot of his buggy and there he died. Dr. H. M. Wharton described the event: "The angels met him on the road and bore him up to the realms of bliss."

As we remember Pastor Baynham, we do well to ask ourselves whether we have been guilty of taking our pastor for granted. Have we failed to express our appreciation to him? Are we aware of his difficult tasks, discouragements, and disappointments as our undershepherd? Are we part of the solution or the problem? Those are good questions for each of us to ponder.

EGC

[1]George Braxton Taylor, *Virginia Ministers*, Fourth Series, (Lynchburg, VA: J. P. Bell Company, 1913), 32.

[2]Ibid., 33.

June 17

No Drones in the Hive

Scripture: John 4:35

The twentieth century phenomenon in America of the "super church" has not proved to be the blessing that might have been expected. Simultaneously with the popularity of "church attendance," the standards of righteousness have fallen. Church has become a place of entertainment rather than worship, and the divorce rate among "church attenders" parrots the divorce rate among unbelievers. Commitment is not evidenced with a life change, and all lines of demarcation between worldliness and holiness seem to have been destroyed. The establishment of churches has been the genius of the Gospel since the days of our Lord. But those congregations to be established were meant to be centers of evangelism to the lost and sanctuaries of holiness for the saints.

It is always exciting to read historically of the work of the Holy Spirit in saving the lost and establishing such churches intended to impact the world. Such an account is to be found in Torrington in North Devon, England. Before a Baptist testimony existed in the ancient town, Mr. Charles Veysey frequently visited from Barnstaple on the Lord's Day, and he preached to anyone who would listen. In 1818 Reverend G. C. Smith, who was a Baptist missionary to the military, narrowly escaped being burned to death while preaching in the market-place of the town. Such was the opposition as the citizenry attacked him eager for his life. God graciously preserved His servant from that attack.

The following year a Christian man from Bath, England moved to Torrington, and seeing the tremendous need, urged a godly gentleman, Mr. Pulsford, to move to the town and attempt to reach souls for Christ. Mr. Pulsford was a man of prayer. He was earnest, persevering, and courageous in his labors for Christ. Mr. Pulsford accepted the challenge as from the Lord, and on June 25, 1820, a church was formed. On that occasion he baptized six in the river Torridge, and with sixteen that he had previously baptized, the church was formally recognized by the Baptist congregation in Collumpton. On December 13, Mr. Pulsford was ordained, and began an itinerant work of evangelism to the surrounding towns. Because of his outreach, the congregation determined to call Mr. Veysey to assist in the work of God.

On March 18, 1829, the foundation was laid for a larger facility in which to worship, and the Lord blessed with a congregation that soon saw the fields of the world ripe unto harvest. On June 17, 1829, Mr. Veysey resigned as co-pastor, and it became necessary to organize the laymen to assist Pastor Pulsford. The pastor preached that that it was the duty of every church member to witness for Jesus. He would have no drones in the hive, but all were to make honey.

Soon he organized his laymen to care for the ministry in ten towns adjoining Torrington. Every two weeks a special meeting was held and the "preacher boys" would take turns sharpening their ability in the Word of God and the pulpit. Pastor Pulsford continually reminded his congregation saying, "I will not rock the cradle for the devil," and by that he meant he would not lull a Christian to sleep. Through his effort to stimulate his members to reach out into the adjacent towns, in the course time, five men entered into full-time ministry for the Savior.

The historian has written: Thus during a ministry of twenty years, Mr. Pulsford honourably fulfilled its varied duties. No man ever accomplished so much for the North of Devon. Restless in his "works of faith and labours of love," he preached in upwards of fifty different places, and generations yet unborn will revere his memory. The church over which he presided was missionary in its character.[1] Huge church buildings have become spiritual mausoleums. Oh, to be sure, they provide entertainment on Saturday evenings and Sunday mornings, and they have exercise classes, hobby clubs, reading societies, and single's hang-outs during the week. But as far as seeing a world in need of Christ , it is the last thing on the agenda. Oh that the Lord would raise up evangelistic cells in local churches that would reach out and herald the life-changing message of the gospel. Pray that American believers shall realize the need to "reseed" before Bible Christianity "recedes" in our Republic.

DLC

---

[1]D. Thompson, *A Book of Remembrance* (Watertown, WI: Roger Williams Heritage Archives, 1885; 2003), 31.

June 18

The Pillar of Truth

Scripture: 1 Timothy 3:16

The godly influence of a local Baptist church cannot be measured. On June 18,1781,[1] the Severns Valley Baptist Church was established near Elizabethtown, Kentucky. That church was used of God the Holy Spirit through the years in impacting the area with the Gospel. Many from the membership were sent out as ambassadors of Christ. Many times during plodding periods of discouragement, I am sure that many members grow weary, wondering if indeed anything is being accomplished in the work of God. Every church knows periods of barrenness, but one must see the overall picture to understand the working of God.

Visit Severns Valley Church with me twenty years after its formation. To be sure there had been times of refreshing, but there had also been periods of spiritual depression. During such periods, saints are depressed. Youth in the area seem unconcerned for matters spiritual. Isaac Hodgen was surely a case in point in the history of the Severns Valley Church. He had been born in 1780, about a year prior to the church's establishment. He had obtained what education he could secure in the neighborhood schools, but he was not interested in the academic. Rather he was a daring, reckless youth, and a ringleader of all the area young men. He exhibited a bold spirit of wickedness. His was more than a spirit of indifference to spiritual matters . . . it was one of contempt!

During the great revival of 1800-1803, Isaac Hodgen came under deep conviction, and he was genuinely converted under the ministry of Joshua Morris. In a very short time he was overcome with the unquenchable desire to preach the Gospel. In 1804, he was licensed to preach by the Nolin Baptist Church, a sister church three miles from the Severns Valley Church. He moved to Green County and united with the Mt. Gilead Baptist Church, and in 1805, he was ordained into the ministry.

Isaac Hodgen was surely gifted as an evangelist, and his entire efforts were directed at pointing men to Christ. However, due to the scarcity of pastors, from time to time he took the oversight of several churches, preaching whenever he was traveling with the gospel. He willingly served local churches in the pastoral position, but his great work was as a traveling evangelist. He traveled many thousand miles in an itinerant ministry. In fact, he became a co-laborer with Jeremiah Vardeman, William C. Warfield, and William and Walter Warder. The five men were raised up of God and endowed with pulpit power. Surely it was providential that the Lord called such workers just at the time when the Commonwealth of Kentucky was growing so rapidly.

In 1817, Mr. Hedgen and William Warder traveled as far east as Philadelphia, and then through several counties of Virginia preaching almost every night. Of course, they traveled these many miles on horseback. It has been estimated that at least 600 converts were baptized in Virginia alone during that journey.

Mr. Hodgen has been described as a large man with a commanding appearance. His preaching brought a thundering conviction to the hearts of his hearers. It is said that his eloquence flowed from an overwhelming compassion for perishing souls.

In 1836, the Lord of the Harvest was pleased to take his eminent servant unto Himself. In fact, of these five evangelists, four of the men were called home in what we would consider mid-life.

However, my consideration is of the Severns Valley Baptist Church. Doubtless that membership did not know of the spiritual victories that were being won through the ministry of one of their former members. Churches often go through seasons of spiritual drought. We surely do well at such times to examine our lives to see if there is a personal reason for the barren season. But we also do well to consider the blessings of the Lord through those whom He has called from our number to serve in evangelism at home and abroad. Our responsibility is to faithfulness, and as we are faithful, He will produce the fruitfulness.

DLC

---

[1]J. H. Spencer, *A History of Kentucky Baptists* (Cincinnati: J. R. Baumes, 1885), 20.

June 19

Another Forgotten Hero

Scripture: 2 Corinthians 11:27-28

It was almost twilight when we discovered the grave site of a forgotten Baptist hero. That spot had been dear to the heart of God's servant. He called it ". . . the most peaceful spot on earth." In deep meditation, I reflected upon the life of Reverend Luther Rice, champion of the cause of Baptist missions. Several entries in our first two volumes saluted his great achievements, but that intrepid advocate of missions has been almost totally forgotten by the present generation. Immediately upon the formation of the Triennial Convention by American Baptists on May 18, 1814, Adoniram and Ann Judson were appointed for missionary service. However it was deemed advisable that someone should serve as an agent to stir missionary interest among the Baptists of America. Who could fulfill that role better than Reverend Luther Rice? He had just returned from India, and he knew the need. He was a fine pulpiteer, and being a bachelor, he was free to travel. Thus Luther Rice was prevailed upon by a multitude of pastors to serve in that capacity.

Even before the formation of the Triennial Convention, Mr. Rice had traveled extensively to create interest in the challenging new venture for Baptists in America. Returning to America from India to arrange Baptist support for himself and the Judsons, Luther Rice had traveled extensively. On September 29, 1813, he began his first Southern tour of Baptist churches. He traveled to New York City, Philadelphia, Baltimore, Washington, D.C., Richmond, Savannah, and most of the prominent towns of South Carolina and Georgia.[1]

With unflagging effort, Luther Rice was determined to share the his spiritual burden for India and all the heathen world. It was only natural therefore, that the Baptist pastors urged him to become their agent for missionary recruitment. Rice and the leadership of the Triennial Convention envisioned this assignment as being temporary, but Rice entered into the labors with total abandonment of his own needs.

Taylor, in another account of his life, provides an extensive quotation from an early report from Reverend Rice. The quote follows: "Since the date of my letter of the 19th of June, 1816, I have travelled 6,000 miles--in populous and in dreary portions of country--through wildernesses and over rivers--across mountains and valleys--in heat and cold--by day and by night--in weariness, and painfulness, and fastings, and loneliness; but not a moment has been lost for want of health; no painful calamity has fallen to my lot; no peril has closed upon me; nor has fear been permitted to prey on my spirits; nor ever inquietude to disturb my peace. Indeed, constantly has the favorable countenance of society towards the great object of the mission animated my hopes, while thousands of condescending personal attentions and benefits to myself and the cause, have awakened emotions, which it is alike impossible to conceal, or to find terms sufficiently delicate and expressive to declare; and the fact, that although so large a portion of the whole time has been unavoidably taken up in passing from place to place, I have, besides many other aids and liberalities, received for the missionary project, in cash and subscription, more than $4,000, which could not fail to create a confidence of success in the general concern, which nothing but a reverse, most unlikely to occur, can possibly destroy."[2] During his journeys some of the finest missionaries of Baptist mission history were recruited.

At its eighteenth anniversary in 1832, the Triennial Society reported seventy-two missionaries serving the Lord on foreign strands. Three years later that number had grown to 112 missionaries. Primarily this was the direct fruit of the lonely ministry of the Lord's "missionary salesman" among the Baptists of America.

Many today know nothing of the sacrifices that Mr. Rice made for the ongoing of the task of worldwide evangelism. We would honor his memory today, and roll up our sleeves to complete the task as the Lord of the Harvest opens doors of opportunity.

DLC

---

[1]James B. Taylor, *Memoir of Rev. Luther Rice* (Nashville, TN: Broadman Press, n.d.), 132-133.

[2]James B. Taylor, *Lives of Virginia Baptist Ministers* (Richmond: Yale & Wyatt, 1838), Series 1, 435.

June 20

Taxation Without Representation

Scripture: Leviticus 25:10

When Baptists were finally allowed to exist in the young American Colonies, they found themselves forced to pay taxes to support the established or "state" church. A Baptist church was formed at Gorham, near to Casco Bay, Massachusetts on June 20, 1768. Joseph Moody was called as pastor, but soon the tax assessors visited him and commanded the parish tax for the support of the Congregational state church. They demanded approximately six dollars, and being unable and unwilling to pay, the assessors confiscated his horse in 1771. He petitioned the Assembly at Boston for the return of his horse, but his request was refused.

About the same time eighteen men, members of the Baptist society in Warwick, were seized for failure to pay a parish tax. It was in the dead of winter, and the men were transported forty miles and cast into the Northampton jail. On February 15, 1775, the agent of the Warren Baptist

Association, Reverend Isaac Backus, presented their case before the Legislature in Boston. His request for relief was ignored and then refused by the Legislature.

Attempts were made to write editorials in the *Massachusetts Gazette*, but unsigned letters from the leaders of the pedobaptists (infant sprinklers) made light of the situation and by innuendo suggested that perhaps the eighteen men were guilty of counterfeiting. In time, as the case came to light, the assessors of Warwick published a vindication for their actions in a Boston newspaper. The date was April 7, 1775, and they said: "We apprehend that every body politic have a right to choose their religion, and to enact laws for its support, and that they ought so to do; and since Congregationalism is the choice of the people of this province, the religion which our forefathers had in view to establish in coming over to this country, we think there is good reason why dissenters from us should pay to the support of it; *especially since it is one condition upon which they receive and hold their lands.*"[1] The italicized words were totally untrue.

Be that as it may, it is interesting to notice that these actions were performed against our Baptist forefathers just prior to the opening of the Revolutionary War. Is it any wonder why Baptists provided leaders in the Revolution? By the same principle that our national government wanted relief and freedom from "taxation without representation" politically from Great Britain, our Baptist forefathers sought freedom from the religious domination of the established church.

"In 1775 the Baptists of Virginia met in regular session in their General Association. "This was," says their historian Robert Semple, "a very favorable season for the Baptists. Having been much ground under the British laws, or at least by the interpretation of them in Virginia, they were, to a man, favorable to any revolution by which they could obtain freedom of religion. They had known from experience, that toleration was not a sufficient check, having been imprisoned at a time when the law was considered by many as being in force. It was therefore resolved at this session, to circulate petitions to the Virginia Convention or General Assembly, throughout the State, in order to obtain signatures. The prayer of these was, that the church establishment should be abolished, and religion left to stand upon its own merits; and, that all religious societies should be protected in the peaceable enjoyment of their own religious principles."[2]

This was true not only of the Baptists of Virginia, but of Baptists throughout our nation. I must point out that Baptists have always championed religious freedom. The inscription cast onto the Liberty Bell says it well. Quoting from Leviticus 25:10 it reads: **"Proclaim liberty through all the land and to all the inhabitants thereof."**

DLC

---

[1] Isaac Backus, *A History of the Baptists in New England* (Newton: Backus Historical Society, 1871), 2:181.

[2] John T. Christian, *A History of the Baptists* (Texarkana: American Baptist Association, 1922), 1:383.

June 21

Oklahoma's First Baptist Church

Scripture: Psalm 33:12-22

Baptists of America owe a great debt of gratitude to Isaac McCoy, the champion of Indian missions in our land. Born in June of 1784, he was called into the presence of his Lord on June 21, 1846, after a life that was fully dedicated to serving American Indians and reaching them with the glorious Gospel. His sixty-two year life formed an amazing panorama of sacrifice.

But our real interest in this entry centers about a full-blooded Creek (Muscogee) Indian who was responsible for the first Baptist church's birth in Oklahoma. John Davis was that unique man. He had been led to Christ by Lee Compere in Alabama, and had been educated in the Withington Mission at Tucheebachee. There he answered God's call to preach. Davis was the first Baptist preacher licensed to the gospel ministry in what is now Oklahoma.[1] Isaac McCoy had traveled to Georgia, Alabama, and Mississippi to assist in the "Trail of Tears" during that tragic relocation of the original Americans to the Indian territory. The American Baptist Society had sent a lone missionary David Lewis to the Ebenezer Station. The station was located three miles north of the Arkansas River and fifteen miles west of Fort Gibson, in what is today Oklahoma.

There on September 9, 1832, Isaac McCoy constituted the Muscogee Baptist Church, Ebenezer Station, Indian Territory. John Davis soon translated the Gospel of John and part of Matthew into the Creek language. But let me share McCoy's own account: "I enjoyed a blessed season in Arkansas [now Oklahoma] with our excellent missionary brethren, Davis and Lewis. They are both men of good sense, and ardent piety; and are devoted to their labours of love, in teaching sinners the way to heaven. I had written Mr. Lewis twice, but neither of my communications had reached him. He was in a land of strangers, and penniless, without knowing when I would arrive to afford him relief. Nevertheless, he went to work with Mr. Davis. They preached among the Creeks, and visited from house to house; and before I reached them, they had fixed upon a day for the constitution of a Baptist church. In this constitution, I had the happiness of assisting, on the 9th instant. The church consisted of Rev. Mr. Lewis and wife, missionaries, John Davis, Creek Indian and missionary, and three black men, (Quash, Bob and Ned,) slaves to the Creeks, who had been baptized on the east of the Mississippi. The church took the name of the Muscogee Baptist church. Mr. Lewis preached in the forenoon, and I preached at another place in the afternoon; and bro. Davis, besides interpreting, prayed, and exhorted, in both Indian and English. This was a good day to us all. We had not artifice employed to occasion excitement of feelings; nevertheless, we retired from our meeting place, not only with solemn countenances, but many faces, both black and red, were suffused with tears, and every heart seemed to be filled."[2]

In his 1836 report, McCoy related that the membership of the Muscogee Baptist Church consisted of eighteen Native (Indian) church members; fifty-eight Black church members, and four White church members for a total of eighty members. The church continued to grow, and soon it boasted a membership of 300.[3] That tremendous growth was attributable in large measure to the work of John Davis.

How unfortunate that, though John Davis has served under appointment of the American Baptist Board of Foreign Missions, the society ignored his work referring to him only as a "native preacher." The society also snubbed Isaac McCoy, and in time its attitude caused him to resign from the agency and form another society to better serve the needs of the people.

One of the sad marks on Baptists (and others as well) is the poor efforts made in the evangelization of the aborigines of our land. As the Lord reminds you, pray for the hardy souls who in our day are attempting still to take the Gospel of the Son of God to the American Indians.

DLC

---

[1] J. M. Gaskin, *Baptist Milestones in Oklahoma* (Oklahoma City: Good Printing Company, 1966), 17.

[2] Isaac McCoy, *The Annual Register of Indian Affairs* (Springfield: Particular Baptist Press, 1998), 325.

[3] George M. Ella and Isaac McCoy, *Apostle of the Western Trail* (Springfield: Particular Baptist Press, 2003), 375.

June 22

Missions Before William Carey

Scripture: Acts 1:8

William Carey is called the "Father of Missions." We understand what that statement means. Indeed William Carey and Andrew Fuller must be considered the fathers of the modern day missionary movement. But missions existed long before 1792. We pay tribute to the Moravians and their great sacrificial ministries. As we think of the American Indians, we must acknowledge Roger Williams, the first missionary to the American aborigines. And we cannot forget David Brainerd, who undertook that ministry on April 1, 1743. What a life of commitment was his! His journal for June 22, 1745 states: "About noon rode to the Indians again, and next night preached to them. Found my body much strengthened, and was enabled to speak with abundant plainness and warmth. Their number, which at first consisted of seven or eight persons, was now increased to nearly thirty. There was not only a solemn attention among them, but some considerable impression, it was apparent, was made upon their minds by divine truth. This was indeed a sweet afternoon to me. While riding, before I came to the Indians, my spirits were refreshed, and my soul was enabled to cry to God incessantly, for many miles together."[1]

But even prior to that time we must consider another large group of missionaries. Roland Bainton quotes page 67 of Hans Kasdorf's *The Anabaptist Approach to Mission* as follows: "Every member of the group was regarded as a missionary. Men and women left their homes to go on evangelistic tours. The established churches, whether Catholic or Protestant were aghast at these ministers of both sexes insinuating themselves into town and farm."[2]

The cost of obedience paid by the Anabaptists to the Great Commission was high indeed. Over 2,000 martyrs of the movement are known by name. Undoubtedly there were many, many more. Hans Kasdorf in the same volume cites one authority who estimates that 4,000 to 5,000 "men, women, and children fell prey to water, fire, and the sword."

On page 67 of his interesting volume, Dr. W. R. Estep quotes Capito, a leading minister of the Reformed Church in Strassburg, as saying: "I frankly confess that in most [Anabaptists] there is in evidence piety and consecration and indeed a zeal which is beyond any suspicion of insincerity. For what earthly advantage could they hope to win by enduring exile, torture and unspeakable punishment of the flesh."[3]

And on pages 72 and 73, Dr. Estep again cites Franz Agricola, a Roman Catholic theologian: "As concerns their outward public life they are irreproachable. No lying, deception, swearing, strife, harsh language, no intemperate eating and drinking, no outward personal display, is found among them, but patience, humility, uprightness, neatness, honesty, temperance, straightforwardness in such measure that one would suppose that they had the Holy Spirit of God."[4]

What a stellar reputation the Anabaptists had. It would be wonderful if real Holy Ghost revival fell on our churches today. Anabaptists practiced following in the footsteps of Christ, and each was expected to live out the truth in his or her daily lifestyle. Such a life called for self denial, sacrifice, and moral integrity. That attitude gave the Anabaptists the determination and courage to suffer for their faith as did the Savior.

Saints of the twenty-first century could surely learn much from sixteenth century Anabaptists. Those sixteenth century saints challenge our pragmatism with inspiring biblical idealism. Some in our day discount the example of the New Testament church, rationalizing that it was a unique period. Surely the first century and sixteenth century both had unique features, but our Lord has never rescinded His marching orders of the Great Commission! The willingness of the saints of the Apostolic age and the Anabaptist saints of the sixteenth century form an indictment on a church so often committed to comfort and ease. The Anabaptist legacy demands that we be willing to confront the world and to row against the cultural currents of our day. What are you doing for the cause dearest to our Savior's heart?

DLC

---

[1] *David Brainerd's Personal Testimony* (Grand Rapids, MI: Baker Book House, 1979), 63.

[2] Roland H. Bainton, *The Reformation of the Sixteenth Century* (Boston: Beacon Press, 1952), 101.

[3] William R. Estep, *The Anabaptist Story* (Nashville, TN: Broadman Press, 1963), 67.

[4] Ibid., 67-68.

June 23

A Man Sent From God

Scripture: Psalm 91

"There was a man sent from God, whose name was John" (John 1:6). John Monroe Parker was born June 23, 1909, in Thomasville, Alabama. His parents, Jacob and Lucy Parker, named him after John Parker, a paternal uncle who was a

Baptist preacher, and Monroe, a maternal uncle who died in infancy. He was always known by his middle name. Before he reached school age, Parker's parents moved the family to Texas. When he was thirteen, his parents returned to Thomasville, Alabama, and in 1925 the family moved to Birmingham. There the robust young man, an outstanding athlete, finished high school and entered college.

Monroe's parents were godly people, and they provided a godly atmosphere in the home. Monroe made a profession of faith at eight years of age and was baptized in Edgewood, Texas. He records that though he gave intellectual assent to the truths of Christianity, "I was a sinner and I knew it."[1] Many of us remember Monroe Parker's statement about his early college years as a lost church member. He used to say, "I helped make the twenties roar."[2]

Under conviction because of his sin, young Parker determined to reform. He quit all his bad habits but still was not saved. In this condition he agreed to teach a class of junior boys in a Methodist church in Birmingham. Through his parent's prayers and counsel, and after hearing Evangelist Bob Shuler preach, he fell under conviction of sin one Sunday morning while teaching his Sunday school class. He trusted Christ on the spot, made his profession of faith public that morning, and joined the Methodist church. The next Thursday night God brought Bob Jones, Sr., to Birmingham, and Monroe Parker heard him preach. That fall, in September 1928, he enrolled in Bob Jones College, which was then in Florida.

Thus began the Christian life of an evangelist whom God used greatly. During that first year in college, the Lord called Parker to preach. After some struggle, he surrendered to God's will. He began preaching immediately. He graduated from Bob Jones College in 1931 and returned for graduate work in the fall. After completing one year of graduate studies, he launched into full-time evangelistic work.

The years 1932-1937 were marked by great usefulness in the Lord's work. In 1933 he married his first wife, Harriette. He preached in evangelistic meetings across the country, and many were saved. The story of his great campaign in Bevier, Kentucky, is too long to recite here, but it is a testimony to God's power.[3]

The year 1934 saw a life-changing event in Dr. Parker's life. He spent most of his childhood years in the Methodist denomination, and he ministered during his first six years as a Methodist. Seeing the encroachments of modernism among the Methodists and becoming convinced of the Baptist distinctives, he was ordained as a Baptist preacher on December 2, 1934. He preached for sixty-five years, sixty of those years as a convicted Baptist.

Parker's ministry led him into diverse endeavors. He served for twelve years at Bob Jones University. He later served for eight years as president of Pillsbury Baptist Bible College. He was instrumental in the founding of Baptist World Mission and served as its general director for twenty-five years. He served briefly as pastor of Grace Baptist Church in Decatur, Alabama. Other entries will reflect on his work as an educator and mission leader.

Dr. Monroe Parker's life is a testimony to the grace and power of God. The Holy Spirit convicted him of his sin and drew him to Christ. The authority of Scripture led him to Baptist convictions. He dedicated his life to the service of the Lord, and God greatly used him.

In whatever else he did, and in every ministry to which God led him, Monroe Parker was first and always a fervent evangelist. He was consumed by a passion to tell lost people about his Savior, to lead them to Christ, and to train and assist others as they preached the glorious Gospel in the United States and around the world. May God help us to work consistently for the salvation of lost souls.

FJM

---

[1]Monroe Parker, *Through Sunshine and Shadows, My First 77 Years* (Murfreesboro, TN: Sword of the Lord Publishers, 1987), 58.

[2]Ibid., 136-142.

[3]Ibid., 54.

June 24

From Sincereity to Reality

Scripture: Psalm 112:6b; Proverbs 10:7a

Can you imagine a father so desirous of doing right that for seven years he conducted family devotions morning and evening with his family and yet did not know the Lord? Such a man is the focus of our consideration today. William Baskett was born in October 1741 into a religious but poor family in the Commonwealth of Virginia. His parents were members of the state church, and he was raised in the Church of England. We know little of his youth, but because of his manner of life, we assume that his parents were faithful to their religious understanding. At the age of twenty, William Baskett married Miss Mary Pace. The next thirty years of marriage produced thirteen children, eight sons and five daughters.

After seven years of faithful family devotions, William Baskett was challenged by the Baptist preachers who began visiting his neighborhood. When his curiosity became intent, the young father decided to go and hear a Baptist preach. This was his first experience of hearing any but preachers of the state church. The preacher was John Corbley. William Baskett was sufficiently impressed to return. This time he was accompanied by his wife, and for the first time they observed believer's immersion, as Elder Corley administered the ordinance of baptism.

Conviction settled in William's mind, and he was greatly concerned about salvation. He traveled three miles on a dark, rainy night to hear a state church preacher. Mr. Baskett asked the preacher if it were possible to obtain assurance of one's acceptance by God. The preacher replied that he personally had found satisfaction only in keeping the commandments. When Mr. Baskett persisted in questioning him, the preacher accused him of being deranged! The next months brought great anxiety, but ultimately he experienced full assurance. The lines from a letter he wrote shortly before his death summarize it well. ". . . I saw myself a guilty, undone sinner; and, during eight months, was without comfort. At length, one night, at midnight, on my bended knees, imploring divine mercy through Christ, and throwing myself at the disposal of sovereign grace, my mind was turned to the words, 'He that trusts in the Lord shall never be confounded.' I saw that 'God was, in Christ, reconciling the world unto Himself not imputing their trespasses unto them.'"[1] A complete transformation immediately took place in his life.

Soon after this event, the Basketts were baptized, along with several others, by Elder Elijah Craig. William Baskett became an outstanding witness, and soon many others came to know Christ personally. In 1774 a church was formed with eighteen men and thirty-two ladies. Elder William Webber became pastor and served for five years. When Elder Webber moved to Kentucky five years later, William Baskett was called to be pastor.

The man of God served the Lisles Baptist Church from 1779 until 1815. The work grew greatly under his direction. His faithfulness and zeal were exemplary. On April 21, 1815, his dear wife passed into the Lord's presence. The following Lord's Day, God's servant brought the last message of his life. His text was: "We have no continuing city, but we seek one to come"(Heb. 13:14). On April 30 his own tranquil spirit escaped this state of trial and entered Heaven. He had lived to see the blessing of God spiritually in the salvation of multitudes. During that period, the Lord blessed His servant materially, and he possessed large parcels of land. His children all married well and became testimonies of their faithful parents.

A memorial service was held for the Basketts on June 24, 1815, with two pastors speaking. Elder Hiter chose for his text Philippians 1:21: "For me to live is Christ, and to die is gain." Elder Purrington used 2 Kings 2:12 as background for his remarks. The Scripture reads: "My Father, my Father, the chariot of Israel, and the horsemen thereof." The service attracted multitudes and manifested the high veneration which Elder and Mrs. Baskett had inspired.

Famous? No. Faithful? Yes. May we be found faithful!

DLC

---

[1]James B. Taylor, *Lives of Virginia Baptist Ministers* (Richmond: Yale & Wyatt, 1838), 90.

June 25

Baptists by Conviction

Scripture: Hebrews 11:35-38

The first Russian Baptist (and the founder of the Russian Baptist movement) was saved and baptized in 1867 in the city of Tiflis. The man was Nikita Isaevitch Voronin. At the Baptist World Alliance in Toronto on June 25, 1928, Ivanov-Klyshnikov, secretary of the Baptist Union of the U. S. S. R., reported as follows: "During the sixty years of its existence in Russia our brotherhood has achieved wonderful results with which can be compared the achievements of no other religious movement. We can boldly state, that already in 1905 . . . among the so-called sects in Russia, the Baptists were the foremost in point of numbers, the firmest in defense of the purity of their teaching, the bravest during the heavy recession of the Tzarist regime and the most ardent in zeal of spirit and soul in the great work! And that is what we are now!"[1]

Fundamental Baptists in America never became part of the Baptist World Alliance. It had become apparent to fundamental Baptists that the liberalism introduced by German rationalism had saturated much of Christendom, and the principle of separation prevented such an amalgamation. However, national Baptist groups around the world had been unwittingly drawn into the vortex of that ecumenical movement. It is intriguing to realize that at that time Nikolai Odintsov was president of the Federated Union of Baptists in the Soviet Union, and it was he who headed the twenty-eight member delegation from the Soviet Union to the Fourth World Congress in Toronto. Nikolai Odintsov (his name is set forth phonetically in the minutes of the Congress and is spelled Adinzoff) was born in 1870, just three years after Nikita Voronin had been immersed. We know little of Nikolai Odintsov's life, but he must have been a powerful preacher!

In 1917 the Bolsheviks had come into power in Russia, and on October 23, 1927, Joseph Stalin had tightened his control of the communistic leadership. Early in his administration, he realized that he could use the churches to control the multitudes. It is apparent that Odintsov was a thorn in the flesh to the Russian authorities, for shortly after he returned to Russia from Toronto, he was arrested. Alexandra, his wife, was allowed one last visit to see her husband in a Siberian prison in 1937. Following World War II, other believers testified that Reverend Odintsov had died as he was eaten alive by guard dogs while being transported between prison camps.[2]

Why did Baptists in Russia suffer so extremely at the hands of the Communist leadership? The answer is simple. In the course of time, Baptists were coerced into federating with other so-called evangelical churches that they might be controlled. The ultimatum was simple: either submit or suffer. The new group was known as the All-Union Council of Evangelical Christians-Baptists. The leaders of this group, in order to escape persecution and gain governmental recognition, compromised biblical principles. Baptists who submitted to this council had to "register" their churches and were brought under the control of the government.

Thank God, Bible-believing Russian Baptists believed there was a cause worth dying for! These refused to submit to government control. Believing in soul-liberty, these stalwarts of the faith became known as the Council of Evangelical Baptist Churches. Such congregations were forced to meet in private homes, apartments, forests--wherever they could assemble to worship and serve the Lord. Their elected leaders were targeted by the proletariat politicians, and many of the preachers were imprisoned or martyred. These heroes of the faith, believing the Bible, acted on principle. For this they suffered tremendously at the hands of the Russian communist regime.

We thank God for the freedom the Lord has given us in the United States of America. The question that we must face is this: If we were confronted by the same choices, is our faith sufficiently based in God's Word to enable us to suffer unto death?

DLC

---

[1]W. T. Whitley, Editor, *Fourth Baptist World Congress* (Toronto: Stewart Printing Service, n.d.), 75.

[2]Georgi Vins, compiler, *Let the Waters Roar* (Grand Rapids, MI: Baker Book House, 1989), 263-264.

June 26

A Useful and Worthy Life

Scripture: 2 Timothy 4:6-8

The Commonwealth of Virginia provided some of the finest Baptist leadership in the westward movement of America's population. A parallel with the persecution and dispersion of the saints from Jerusalem pictured in Acts 8 was surely duplicated in the early days of our Republic. Many Baptist saints fled westward from Virginia and North Carolina due to severe persecution. They fled the ignominy heaped upon them by the Gentry, but most of all from the incarceration called for by the state church. As a result, Baptist churches were generously planted in newly developing areas.

Thirty-year-old John Borum and his father, Richard, moved from Virginia in 1805 and settled their families in Tennessee. John had been born on December 15, 1775, and early in life he had been born again by faith in the blood of the Lamb. From that time, John had been active in serving the Lord, but he did not enter the ministry until later in life. On April 4, 1807, he united with the Round Lick Baptist Church in Smith County, Tennessee. He was soon active in the work of God, and before long he surrendered to his God-given burden and began preaching. Not only did he have great influence in his home church, but in a short time he impacted many congregations in the surrounding area. His ordination was called for and accomplished by the Round Lick Church on August 5, 1810.

John began preaching near Big Spring, Tennessee, and the converts there were developed into a branch of the Round Lick Church. On Saturday before the fourth Sunday in July 1820, he and Thomas Durham, the pastor of the Round Lick Church, constituted this branch into an independent church. Elder John Borum became the pastor and served that congregation for twenty-four years, through the remainder of his life. He preached to the hearts of his hearers, and it has been said that "few were ever able to sit under his ministry and restrain their tears."[1]

John Borum had married Miss Elizabeth Bratten in 1813. The union was blessed with seven sons and three daughters. John was a strong disciplinarian, and this had much to do in shaping the lives of his children. One of his sons, William, followed his father in the ministry, and he also had a grandson who became a Baptist preacher.

Like so many of his fellow ministers, John Borum's ministry was invested primarily in his neighborhood. There was no media coverage of his preaching, and transportation systems were not available to whisk him across the land. But those who knew him, loved and appreciated his ministry. His congregation was part of the Salem Association, and in the Annual Meeting following his death, the Salem Association presented a touching tribute to his ministry. It read in part: "No man, perhaps, ever gave greater evidence of love to God and the souls of men, than Elder John Borum. But he is gone to enjoy that rest that remains to the people of God, while his usefulness and worth live, and are cherished in the memory of all who were acquainted with him."[2]

John Borum passed into the presence of his Lord on June 26, 1844. The memorial service was conducted by Elders E. W. Haile and E. B. Haynie in the old Cedar Creek meeting house in the presence of a vast throng of sorrowing friends. The Scriptures read included a passage from Psalm 23 and the Bible reference for today's reading.

His body was laid to rest under a mulberry tree near his home to await the coming of our Lord Jesus Christ at the rapture. The multitudes may never hear our names, and our lives may impact only those about us, but may we be found faithful in our service to our blessed Lord.

DLC

[1]J. H. Grime, *History of Middle Tennessee Baptists* (Nashville, TN: Baptist and Reflector, 1902), 162.

[2]Ibid., 162.

June 27

Important Firsts

Scripture: Acts 2:46-47

While visiting Myanmar (Burma),I was amazed in reading a copy of *The Sesquicentennial Pictorial of Baptist Work in Burma 1813-1963*, to discover that "Since the arrival of the Judsons in 1813 there have been 794 of the fraternal workers from abroad who have served Christ . . .here in this land." How glorious to realize that though Satan has done everything possible to obliterate that witness for Christ, the gospel still shines forth in the land of pagodas. I always thrill to learn the "firsts" in a ministry, and I found record of many of the "firsts" in Burma.

On April 4, 1819, Adoniram Judson preached his first message in Burma.[1] The message was delivered in his zayat (a thatched hut) to a group of fifteen adults. The first convert was Moung Nau. He listened to Mr. Judson intently, and in time experienced conviction for his sin As Mr. Judson worked with him, Moung Nau professed his faith in Christ Jesus as Savior. On June 27, 1819, Moung Nau was immersed as the first Burman convert to be baptized.[2] What a thrilling day that must have been for the Judsons. It is interesting that the Moung Nau New Memorial Baptist Church exists to this very day (2004) in Yangon, Burma.

The growth in the ministry among the Burmans was slow, but the fourth convert, Moung Shwe Bay, showed evidence that he was qualified for ministry. Mr. Judson was impressed with Moung Shwe Bay's humility and persevering spirit. Thus it was that Moung Shwe Bay was appointed as the first Burmese Evangelist, and he became a very fruitful worker in the Moulmein-Amherst District. The first Burman to be ordained was U Tha Aye. The date of his ordination was January 4, 1829, and U Tha Aye became the faithful pastor of the Baptist Church in Rangoon, serving there during dangerous years between the first and second Anglo-Burmese wars.

Successful missionary service is not merely evangelism, but it is soul-winning that leads to discipleship and finally to the establishing of a local church. But even that falls short of the real goal. Successful missionary service is the witnessing of an indigenous church. That is to say, the church is to be self-supporting, self-governing, and self-propagating. U Tha Aye had a very fruitful ministry in Moulmein, but he left there on January 11, 1829, to return to the church in Rangoon. U Tha Aye had become indispensable to the work in Burma, and Mr. Judson wrote of him: "We love him like a brother missionary-a humble, conscientious, faithful servant of the Lord Jesus. During his visit he has endeared himself to all of us; and we should gladly retain him here were he not so evidently called to another part of the vineyard."

Back in Rangoon, Pastor U Tha Aye divided his time between Rangoon and the surrounding villages. One inquirer after another was assisted by the pastor so that the little Rangoon church grew almost as rapidly as that in Moulmein where the missionaries were working. It was in Rangoon that the first indigenous Baptist church became a reality in Burma. Of course, an indigenous church is an autonomous assembly. The Burman church historian stated the wisdom of this system well when he wrote: "The genius of the Baptist system of independent churches was most evident during those war years. Not being used to central control, the churches were able, in many cases, to carry on and remain in contact with neighboring churches."[3] How important is this principle!

We could continue with the "firsts," but it is thrilling to think of the conclusion of Judson's ministry there. The work started so slowly, but "There were at Judson's death seven thousand Burmese and Karen Christians; and . . . reckoning from the birth hour of our foreign missions, and so including even the fruitless, formative years, (it) has organized a church on the mission-fields for every three weeks, and baptized a convert every three hours, day and night."[4]

May we be intent on presenting the Gospel "first" yet to untold millions.

DLC

---

[1]Maung Shwe Wa, *Burma Baptist Chronicle* (Rangoon: Board of Publications Burma Baptist Convention, 1963), 1:15.

[2]Francis Wayland, *A Memoir of the Life and Labors of the Rev. Adoniram Judson* (New York: Sheldon & Company, 1860), 1:211.

[3]Maung Shwe Wa, 1:261.

[4]James L. Hill, *The Immortal Seven* (Philadelphia: American Baptist Publication Society, 1913), 28.

June 28

A Dramatic Conversion - A Clear Call

Scripture: Psalm 40

Richard Volley Clearwaters was born June 28, 1900, in Wilmot, Kansas, the fourth child of Guy and Hannah Clearwaters. Before he was a year old, the family moved to Oklahoma. His parents knew Christ and served Him faithfully. Family devotions were held regularly in the home. When only five, he sensed early pangs of conviction of sin,[1] but he was not saved for fifteen years. In 1907 the family moved to Spokane, Washington.

Clearwaters claimed that he was the poorest student of his mother's eight children. He detested school and barely passed grade school. When only 15, he ran away to Canada and lived the life of a prodigal. He said: "I really wanted to live for the world, the flesh and the devil."[2] For five years he roamed from job to job across Canada. He severely injured his hand in the rollers of a paper mill. Providentially, a nurse who cared for him knew his mother and wrote to her. Mrs. Clearwaters wrote her son urging him to come home, concluding with the words: "The way of the transgressor is hard." While at home for what he intended to be a short visit, Richard's brother Weldon was killed in a farm accident. God used this tragedy to again bring deep conviction.

Conviction and emotional depression continued from June 1920 until December of 1921. A Holiness Methodist preacher visited the area to conduct a two-week revival in the Methodist church. Though no one was saved during the meeting, the folks decided to extend the meeting another week. On December 10, 1921, R. V. Clearwaters responded to the invitation and was gloriously converted. God delivered him from his old habits and vocabulary.

Shortly thereafter he heard his mother singing as she prepared breakfast. In his own words: "She was singing,

'The Ninety and Nine.' She had a clear natural soprano voice. She came to the last verse, 'I will go to the desert to find my sheep.' The Lord spoke to me in that verse. 'Will you go?' and I without hesitation said 'Yes.' My call was that simple and that sudden-as clear and as positive as my salvation experience."[3]

Six weeks later Clearwaters, with only one year of high schooling, found himself in Chicago, enrolling at the Moody Bible Institute. The man who called himself the dullest of his mother's eight children completed Moody, earned Th.G., Th.B., and B.D. degrees at Northern Baptist Seminary, a B.A. degree at Kalamazoo College, and a master's degree at the University of Chicago, but his money was depleted six weeks before earning his Ph.D. in New Testament at the University of Chicago! Truly the dullest of his mother's children? We who knew him marveled at his intellectual brilliance, combined with a fervent love of God and knowledge of the Word of God. God's saving grace and call to the ministry awakened the slumbering intellect in him.

His academic experience at the liberal Kalamazoo College and University of Chicago hardened his convictions that the Bible is God's Word and is authoritative for life and faith.

Clearwaters began preaching while pursuing his education. While at Moody, he pastored in Wilton Center, Illinois. When he moved to Kalamazoo, Michigan, he pastored the First Baptist Church of Lawton and was then called to the Bethel Baptist Church of Kalamazoo. There he met Florence Welch, whom he married on April 17, 1935.

The same year, Pastor Clearwaters was called to pastor the Calvary Baptist Church of Cedar Rapids, Iowa. The next four and a half years were marked by the blessing of God. People were saved, the church grew, and the mortgage was paid off. These were glorious years of ministry, but his story had only begun.

R. V. Clearwaters' life is a testimony to God's rich mercy and saving grace to those who surrender to Him. His convictions, grounded in the Word of God, formed in a Bible Institute, and hardened in liberal schools, enabled him to serve God effectively for many years.

FJM

[1]Richard V. Clearwaters, *On The Upward Road* (Minneapolis: Nystrom Publishing, 1991), 5.

[2]Ibid., 14.

[3]Ibid., 24.

June 29

Obedience Brings Blessing

Scripture: Acts 5:29; 1 Samuel 15:22b

A. J. Gordon, graduated from Brown University in 1860, and was ordained on June 29th of that year. He became well known as an author, missionary statesman, and educator, but he was ever and always a pastor. In 1869 he became pastor of the Clarendon Street Baptist Church in Boston. It was there that the following story unfolded. Dr. Gordon told of a lady who sought his counsel continually about uniting with the church. She longed to unite and gave an outstanding testimony, but her husband repeatedly threatened her if she professed her faith in baptism and joined the church. She knew what her duty was before the Lord, but for several years she put it off. Her husband was a violent man, and whenever she approached the subject of making a public profession of her faith by baptism, he flew into a fit of uncontrollable rage.

The timid lady battled this problem throughout that period, but she had no peace of mind. As the spiritual battle raged, she ultimately determined that, regardless of the outcome, she must obey the Lord. Accordingly, she presented herself for membership in the church. She was examined, and the deacons recommended her for membership following her baptism. The congregation concurred, and a date was set for the ordinance. But now the battle really began to intensify. Her husband was incensed upon hearing the news, and he made her life miserable as the date neared. On Saturday night before the date of baptism, he padlocked his wife's clothes, so she had nothing to wear. But the resolute lady was determined, and so wrapping herself in a sheet, she made her way to a Christian neighbor's house and there obtained the necessary clothing. Needless to say, she had no plans to return home until after the baptism had been accomplished.

As the service began, Dr. Gordon observed the husband seated in the rear of the auditorium. He wondered what to expect, but the service progressed regularly. The hymns were sung. The congregation rejoiced in the prayer of dedication for those who were to be baptized. One by one as the candidates were buried in the water, Dr. Gordon intoned the words, "Buried with Him in baptism . . . and raised to walk in newness of life." No interruption transpired, and the pastor rejoiced in the Lord's care.

At the conclusion of the baptismal service, the congregation was dismissed, and Dr. Gordon went to change clothes. As he exited, he discovered that everyone was gone except the husband who had been so irate! The man was still sitting in the rear of the auditorium alone. What did it mean? The pastor drew near the man, and as gently as possible expressed his pleasure at seeing the man in church. As he did so, the man with great emotion said, almost in a whisper, "What must I do to be saved?" Then with uncontrollable feeling, he confessed his sin against his wife and God. He bowed with the pastor alone in the pew and cried for mercy. Of course the Lord wonderfully saved him, and in a few weeks, he too was baptized and united with the church. Faithfulness became the watchword of that couple until, five years later, they moved away. Years passed, and Dr. Gordon was informed of the death of that gentleman. Attending the funeral, the pastor rejoiced again in the thought of that wonderful event twenty years earlier. Dr. Gordon wrote that as he looked into the casket, and circumstances of that man's religious history flooded his mind, he instinctively asked himself, what, but the power of the Holy Spirit could have accomplished such a sudden, unexpected, and enduring transformation. The lesson became obvious to him: "We ought to obey God rather than men."

He concluded the account by stating: "This 'ought' carries a blessing, as well as an obligation. This wife's domestic happiness, for all her subsequent life, lay wrapped up in her surrender to this divine 'ought.'"[1]

Perhaps this lesson is needed in your life today.

DLC

[1]J. B. McInturff, Editor, *The Old Paths* (New Market, VA: Henkel & Co., 1893), 214-215.

June 30

The Use of Influence

Scripture: Hebrews 6:10

Influence is immeasurable. When all God's children get to heaven they will begin to unravel with unspeakable joy and surprise the intermingling details of lives and influence which cooperated together without earthly recognition to fulfill the purpose of God. Some of God's children will likely be surprised to discover how the faintest hue of influence flowing from them so indelibly and permanently marked others' lives. Some of God's choicest servants were so influenced that their ministries were thereafter uniquely colored for their place in the spectrum of God's work. Did the godly cook at the boarding school know that her influence would be permanently etched into the ministry of Charles Haddon Spurgeon? Did the apprentice know that his faithful witness would sway the young man next to him named William Carey who would become the father of modern-day missions? They probably did not know how powerful their influence was.

On June 30, 1775 the leader of the Bristol Baptist College, Caleb Evans, decided to sit down at his desk and exert some influence on a young and disheartened pastor! The young pastor he had in mind was John Sutcliff who had trained in Bristol under the tutelage of Evans. John Sutcliff had had a rough time of it in the early months of his pastoral ministry. He did not preach well, even though he was a brilliant student, and his first pastorate was abruptly terminated when after only four months the opposition within his church became so intense he knew that he could not stay. He was paralyzed by discouragement when the first invitations to speak at the Baptist church of Olney in Northhamptonshire first began to arrive. In fact, Sutcliff ignored the appeals! He simply did not believe he could do it. But Caleb Evans, sensing an urgency from the

Spirit of God to save a soldier of Christ for future warfare, mustered all the arguments and influence he could gather, and penned a letter to the timorous Sutcliff. The letter was almost aggressive saying, essentially, "if you do not at least visit the Olney church, I will be personally offended!"

The effort that Caleb Evans put into his letter is actually quite intense. One historian states, "This letter well illustrates the way in which Caleb Evans, like his father, unashamedly sought to be a father in God to those whom he had taught. It is a forceful letter, but it appears that it was the very thing that Sutcliff needed. If Evans' words and tone had been any less commanding, Sutcliff might have given way to his natural diffidence and the door to Olney would have been left to shut once and for all. As it was, he received Evans' letter on 3 July and three days later he had written to Mary Andrews seeking to arrange a time when he could visit Olney."[1]

Baptists will be forever grateful for the effort of influence that was spent on June 30, 1775. It was clearly used by God to move John Sutcliff into the region where he would become one of the four visionary pastors who, lifting up their eyes, saw the fields white unto harvest. He, along with Andrew Fuller, John Ryland, Jr., and William Carey would begin to pray earnestly for the cause of missions. They would become the founders of the first missionary society, and Sutcliff would become one of Carey's most faithful supporters. Writing from India, Carey would say to Sutcliff, "I think I should be wanting in friendship if I neglected to write to you, especially considering the ties of Christian affection by which I am bound to you."[2]

Do you think Caleb Evans' time that summer afternoon, the postage for the letter, and the effort to exert his influence was a waste? Do you think that God did not notice Evans' contribution? Do you really believe that God did not providentially mingle the life and character of Caleb Evans' into the life and character of John Sutcliff so that at the critical moment foreseen by God the influence of the one would direct the other? Oh, my friends, surely God has designed the ministry of influence! You may not be on center-stage in the ministry of God, but you may have just the right amount of influence to help one of God's servants just when he needs it most. Perhaps one day you will write a letter that will affect a man who will affect the world.

RPB

---

[1]Michael A.G. Haykin, *One Heart and One Soul, John Sutcliff of Olney, his friends and his times* (Durham, England: Evangelical Press, 1994), 98.

[2]Ibid., 236.

July 1

Preach/Teach the Word

Scripture: Ephesians 4:11-13

A generation ago, the name of W. Graham Scroggie was a byword among all those who loved the study of God's Word. Dr. Scroggie's unique ability to dissect a passage of Scripture and present its message succinctly was his trademark for many years.

William Graham Scroggie was born in 1877 at Great Malvery, England, to Scottish parents. His father was an evangelist, but was unable to afford higher education for his children. William's mind, however, was saturated in Bible truths as he grew to manhood in a Brethren home. Upon coming to maturity, he entered first into the business world for a brief time, but at the age of nineteen, matriculated in Spurgeon's College to prepare for the Baptist ministry. He was actually welcomed into the student body by Charles Haddon Spurgeon himself.

The world might look askance at his resume, for Scroggie was asked to resign his first two pastorates. The first congregation objected to his opposition to modernism, and the second thought he was legalistic in denouncing worldliness. Rather than leading to despair, these efforts drove William Scroggie to a deeper study of God's Word. During the next two difficult years, his only income was occasional gifts, but he laid a foundation that allowed him to excel in exposition.

For seventeen years he pastored the Charlotte Baptist Chapel in Edinburgh, Scotland. He first preached at the chapel on May 7, 1916, and the congregation voted to extend a call to him to become their pastor on May 12, 1916. Responding to their call on July 1, 1916, the newly- chosen pastor set forth one condition. He made it clear that he would not accept the call to do "social pastoral visitation." In essence he told them he would confine his pastoral work to the sick and sorrowing, and that he was not essentially an evangelist or pastor, but a Bible teacher. He desired to major in his pulpit and writing ministry.

The congregation agreed, and his ministry began in October 1916. "...From the first service it was evident that God was going to do a great work through His servant. The services were crowded to capacity with the aisles filled with campstools. People were packed in the vestry, on the communion platform, on the pulpit steps and even in the pulpit leaving the preacher just room to stand . . . . He had an analytical mind and was a master of English. He reigned like a Prince in the pulpit . . . . All felt that here was a man who had come straight from the Presence of God and bore in his heart and upon his lips the Word of the Living God."[1] The congregation was delighted when on July 1, 1927, the University of Edinburgh conferred the Doctor of Divinity degree upon their pastor.

Terminating his Edinburgh pastorate on October 1, 1933, the next four years found him traveling and preaching extensively in South Africa, Australia, New Zealand, the United States, Canada, and Great Britain. From 1938 to 1944, Dr. Scroggie again entered into pastoral service, ministering in Spurgeon's Tabernacle in London. The reader will observe that the period of time mentioned covered the dreadful days of the Second World War. During the London blitz, the Scroggies were bombed out of three houses, and the historic church was also greatly damaged. Dr. Scroggie was heroic as he ministered to the physical needs of his congregation during those days.

Increasing ill-health forced him to retire from the active pulpit ministry in 1944. He then used his available strength in completing his literary work and lecturing in the Spurgeon College until 1952. His health became such that he could no longer minister, and the Lord took him home in 1959.

In all, Dr. Scroggie wrote in excess of twenty valuable volumes of Bible research and exposition.

God gifts every one of His servants in a different way. Today would be a grand time for you to pray for the man of God who serves as your shepherd and breaks the bread of life faithfully to you.

DLC

---

[1]William Whyte, *Revival in Rose Street* (Edinburgh, Scotland: Lindsay & Co. Ltd., n.d.), 45.

July 2

"Sing"cerely

Scripture: Galatians 2:20

Music has been a vital part of the Baptist worship service since Benjamin Keach reintroduced congregational music to the Baptist churches in Great Britain following the Edict of Toleration. Down through the years, songwriters have written many wonderful songs to sing for various occasions, such as worship services, evangelistic services, children's services, camp meetings, youth activities, and mission conferences.

One of the great spiritual composers of the 20th century was Alfred B. Smith. He loved to sing and teach. He especially appreciated the histories of the songs and songwriters. Dr. Smith often visited Ambassador Baptist College in Shelby, North Carolina. He would sit in the music classes of Dr. Don Scovill. He would sing whatever came to mind and then lecture on that particular song. Students loved him and enjoyed watching him enjoy music. Everyone was fascinated by his easy style as the music flowed from within.

Alfred Smith was born in Wortendyke, New Jersey, on November 8, 1916. He was the only child of Barney and Carrie Junta Smith, immigrants from Holland. His first recollection of music was that of listening to the Bergen County Concert Orchestra, comprised of Dutch-speaking relatives. He began playing the violin before he was nine and later soloed with the New York Symphony Orchestra. He studied at the Julliard School of Music as a teenager and played at Carnegie Hall when he was only thirteen years at age under the direction of Walter Damrosh.[1]

Often called the "Dean of Gospel Music," Dr. Smith was an authority on church music. He was a composer, gospel soloist, song leader, lecturer, recording artist, and publisher. He performed on national radio and television. His sacred concerts were the same in the little white New England churches as in the large auditorium of Bob Jones University. Many churches of all sizes across America were privileged to have Dr. Smith challenge their people to better serve the Lord in song. He obviously loved the work God had called him to do.

In 1941 Smith published his first chorus book, "Singspiration," which became a best seller. Other books followed: the *Favorite Series* of solos, duets, etc. and the *Action Series* for boys and girls. He founded "Singspiration Publishing Company" in 1943. His first hymnbook, *Inspiring Hymns,* was a favorite. He pioneered the sacred recording field. Al Smith's *Treasury of Hymn Histories* is a compilation of authentic, inspiring, and often unknown stories behind the writing of over 115 favorite hymns and gospel songs. It is estimated that over 100 million of his songbooks have been sold.

For God So Loved the World, one of Mr. Smith's all-time favorites songs, has been translated into hundreds of languages all over the world. He is especially remembered for *Surely Goodness and Mercy*, *My Father Planned it All*, and *His Banner Over Me Is Love*. These, along with many others, are standards in our church services.[2] Smith dedicated himself to composing, publishing, and recording God honoring Christian music. Much of today's so-called Christian music has drifted from its moorings of scriptural standards. All of Smith's songs emphasized Bible doctrine and centered in the Lord Jesus Christ.

Smith graduated from Moody Bible Institute in Chicago, Illinois, in 1941, and Wheaton College in Wheaton, Illinois, in 1943. Smith's first wife, Catherine, died in the summer of 1960 leaving him with two teenagers-Barbara and Gordon. He remarried on July 2, 1966, and the day after the wedding, he and his new wife, Nancy Lee Wilbur, moved to the Montrose Bible Conference in Montrose, Pennsylvania. They made their home there for several years. His marriage to Nancy produced four children-Becky, twins David and Sarah, and Jonathan.

Among his many honors was an honorary Music Doctorate from John Brown University in Siloam Springs, Arkansas.[3] Alfred B. Smith used the salutation of "Sing"cerely and Galatians 2:20. He coined the word "singspiration" and used the term for the after-church song time with the youth.

Al Smith was buried in Montrose, Pennsylvania. I have no doubt that Brother Smith has found his place in the choir and has been singing with the heavenly chorus since his home going August 9, 2001.[4]

DCB

[1] *The Greenville News*, August 10, 2001.

[2] Al Smith, *Treasury of Hymn Histories* (Greenville: Better Music Publications, Inc., 1985).

[3] Telephone interview with Nancy Smith by Bettye Baughan, September 5, 2004.

[4] Telephone interview with David Smith by Bettye Baughan, July 23, 2004.

July 3

A Preacher and a Pastor

Scripture: Ecclesiastes 12:9-12

On this date the *Perry Journal* in Michigan carried an article that was far more momentous than could ever be known. The struggling Baptist church in the village of Perry, with only seven members, called Howard Frederic Sugden to be their pastor.[1] Thus began a pastoral ministry that would span almost sixty years and influence unknown thousands for Heaven.

Howard Sugden was born April 4, 1907, in Mayville, Michigan. The second of five children, Howard grew up on a farm. He was converted to Christ at the age of nineteen in an evangelistic crusade in the local Baptist church. Lucile Miller moved to Mayville to teach school in 1927. Soon Howard and Lucile fell in love and were married on December 21, 1928.

In 1927 Howard sensed the Lord working in his life for the ministry and spent a couple of months at Moody Bible Institute. He struggled with the program there. God continued to call the young man, and the newlyweds spent two years in Johnson Bible College in Tennessee. The Lord used this experience to shape Howard's ministry, for he worked in the college library while a student. He fell in love with books and with study. Throughout the rest of his ministry, the Sugdens would complete their college degrees at the Winona Lake School of Theology, and Howard would do some graduate work.

Sugden's ministry began inauspiciously in Perry. In just a couple of years, the church grew from seven members to more than 100, and eventually grew to 150. In 1935 he was called to the Ganson Street Baptist Church in Jackson, Michigan. By 1951 attendance had reached 1000. After a struggle with the Michigan Baptist Convention (part of the Northern Baptist Convention), Sugden led the church to leave that organization. He was a true independent Baptist for the duration of his ministry. From 1951 to 1954 Pastor Sugden ministered in the Central Baptist Church of London, Ontario, Canada. In 1954 he was called to the pastorate at South Baptist Church in Lansing, Michigan, where he would enjoy the blessings of God for thirty-five years of fruitful ministry. Each of his ministries began in a church that was struggling, and each ministry was marked by the evident blessing of God and by dynamic growth.

Our scripture for today aptly describes some of Sugden's strengths. He was a studious preacher. He was gifted as an orator and a dynamic pulpiteer because he came to the pulpit with something to say. He loved to preach the Word of God, and he gave himself to diligent study of the Book in preparation for his pulpit ministry. His library would eventually number 15,000 volumes! Therein lies a great lesson and challenge for preachers today. There is no place in the ministry for a lazy preacher. Sugden normally gave himself to uninterrupted study from 6:00 a.m. until noon each day. We who preach the Word of God must love it, study it to know it experientially, and study it with much prayer to preach it to our people.

Sugden distinguished his ministry by another great strength. He was a great pastor. He called on his people incessantly. He gave himself to personal evangelism and led many to Christ. The children in his churches loved him. For years at South Baptist he visited the children's Sunday school departments each Sunday before teaching his own Sunday school class.

Sugden was also greatly used in Bible conferences. He preached at summer Bible conferences in Canada and the United States and in several Christian colleges. Sugden was also a friend of preachers. He regularly made time to meet with struggling pastors or to encourage them by telephone. Many men gave testimony that God used him to encourage them in their own difficulties.

In Howard Sudgen's life we have the record of a man who gave himself to the ministry of preaching the Word, ministering to his people, and encouraging pastors. In many ways he was a model for preachers. His diligent ministry of the

Word and his compassionate ministry to his people should encourage and challenge another generation of preachers.

FJM

[1] Don Denyes, *For the Love of Preaching: The Life Story of Howard F. Sugden* (Lansing, MI: Wellington House Publishers, 2004), 44, 54 n. 3.

July 4

The Chair of Fire

Scripture: 2 Timothy 2:2; 4:5

Lee R. Scarborough was one of the most versatile evangelists ever to minister in America. His success surely was attributable to the love and faithfulness of his parents George Washington and Mary Elizabeth Scarborough. Lee was the eighth of nine children, and was born on July 4, 1870 in Louisiana. His father served as a soldier in the Civil War, and following the war became a faithful Baptist pastor. When Lee was only three weeks old, his mother, though physically weak, crawled to his cradle and prayed that the baby would grow up to be a preacher. There can be no doubt that the warm-hearted spiritual environment of his home had a lasting impact upon Lee's life. Family devotions was a regular part of his home life, and this doubtlessly contributed to the great emphasis on the Christian family that characterized his later ministry.

When Lee was four years old the family moved to a farm near Waco, Texas. In 1896 the family relocated to the pioneer section of West Texas where Lee grew to maturity on a farm-ranch. It was during this period that Lee's father conducted many revival meetings in brush arbors, log school houses, and under trees. During this interval, Lee learned the value of labor.[1]

His varied academic background included earning degrees from Baylor University in Waco, Texas, in 1892 and from Yale in 1896. While at Yale he was a Phi Beta Kappa student. Honorary doctoral degrees were also conferred upon him from Baylor and Union University in Jackson, Tennessee.

Lee's father was honored to witness the beginning of his son's ministry. As Lee was preaching his first sermon, his father took a seat in one of the front rows in the auditorium. During the course of the sermon, a woman seated just in front of his father whispered to the lady at her side: "He's surpassing his father, isn't he?" Lee's father exhibited no jealousy as he leaned forward and said, "He ought to beat me, he is standing on my shoulders!"

Ordained in 1896 Lee Scarborough served as pastor of the First Baptist Church in Cameron, Texas, from 1896-1901. During his pastorate in the First Baptist Church of Abilene, Texas, from 1901-1908, Lee Scarborough was in constant demand as an evangelist. In all, Dr. Scarborough served in the role of pastor for a period of twelve years. On June 1, 1908, the 37-year-old Scarborough accepted the position as professor of evangelism at Southwestern Theological Seminary. B. H. Carroll, president of the seminary, referred to Scarborough's chair of evangelism as the *"Chair of Fire."* Through the years that followed more than 6,000 students thrilled at the challenge of evangelism as they were instructed by the man of God. Upon the death of Dr. B. H. Carroll in 1915, Dr. Scarborough was elected president of Southwestern Seminary. He served in the dual capacity as president and professor of evangelism until his retirement on August 1, 1942.

I have mentioned the versatility of Lee Scarborough. Through his lifetime of illustrious service, he served as pastor, evangelist, seminary president, and author. Among his other responsibilities at the seminary, Dr. Scarborough annually participated in from eight to fourteen evangelistic campaigns. During his lifetime he authored no less than sixteen books. Many of his books are worthy of continual perusal, but two of the volumes are unusually outstanding. *With Christ After the Lost*, was written in 1919, and *Endued to Win*, was written in 1922. Both of these tomes were used as text books as Dr. Scarborough taught from the *Chair of Fire*. These volumes still stir one's heart.

The death of the man of God took place in Amarillo, Texas on April 10, 1945, and his remains were buried in the Rose Hill Cemetery in Fort Worth. The rare combination of talents that God granted Lee Scarborough is not often seen. However, it would be well if every fundamental seminary throughout our land had a seat of evangelism that we might refer to as the *Chair of Fire*.

DLC

[1]Franklin M. Segler, *Encyclopedia of Southern Baptists* (Nashville, TN: Broadman Press, 1958), 2:1186.

A Quiet but Successful Ministry

Scripture: Luke 18:13

When looking at Baptist growth in Virginia, we often marvel at the sufferings and privations of early Baptist preachers. Forty-four were incarcerated for preaching without validation from the state church, but many of the preachers were unscathed by the attacks of the unruly mobs and the militia. Such a man was Benjamin Watkins.

Benjamin Watkins was born into an Episcopalian home on July 5, 1755. It was the very year Shubael Stearns and Daniel Marshall began the work of the separate, or new light Baptists that would have such an impact upon Virginia. The lad's father died during his infancy, but his mother instilled in her son's mind very high moral standards. The lad abided by those rules and was known for his fine demeanor. An emptiness filled his heart, however, until at age 19 he was pointed to Jesus Christ, the only Savior of sinners. He trusted the Savior but postponed his baptism until September 22, 1776.[1]

Mr. Watkins was filled with peace and joy and could not hold his peace. He began preaching in 1783, and he was ordained on March 19, 1786. For the first few years he supplemented his living by teaching school, but in 1790 he became a full-time traveling preacher of the Gospel. His unique style in the pulpit set him apart. He might well have been considered a bit eccentric. He never sought to amuse as he spoke with great earnestness.

Elder Watkins was known for his desire literally to "owe no man any thing." He was peculiarly scrupulous in all his transactions. His testimony in this regard was always above reproach. His piety was but a reflection of his Christ-like mind. As a father of ten children, he sought to establish an environment that would point his children early to Christ. He loved the fellowship of God's children, and he was known for his godly influence that promoted sweet harmony in the churches.

It will be observed that the modern-day mission movement came into being during the early days of Elder Watkins' ministry. Many Baptist preachers looked with suspicion, and some viewed the new movement with disdain. This was particularly true of those who had imbibed strong Calvinistic tendencies and were fearful that some non-elect might respond to the Gospel. However, Elder Watkins looked upon the scene with a thrilling anticipation. He said, "The beams of truth have begun to dawn on almost every land; and the Lord is adding to the church daily such as shall be saved."[2]

God willed that Elder Watkins should live a full life of years, and he continued to labor in the ministry until just a few days prior to his home going. He preached twice on the Sunday before his death, and his last sermon was founded on the prayer of the publican, "God be merciful to me a sinner." His preaching was always with evangelistic fervor, and he anticipated an ingathering of souls such as had been experienced early in his life through the preaching of Samuel Harris and the separate Baptists in Virginia.

The Wednesday before his death he was too weak to attend the meeting at the house of God, and the saints gathered in his home. On Thursday and Friday he grew continually weaker, and he sensed that his homegoing was near. He was perfectly resigned to God's will in the matter, and a sweet assurance surrounded him as he knew he would soon be with the Lord. On the Lord's Day, July 17, 1831, the Lord's call came, and God's servant triumphantly went home. He was 76 years old.

Elder Watkins had not suffered for his faith, but he had been faithful. During the forty-eight years of his ministry, the man of God had preached more than six thousand sermons, which averages one hundred and thirty-two messages every year. Our sovereign God does not call all of His servants to suffer, but He does call each to be faithful. May that be the epithet that marks our lives.

DLC

---

[1] James B. Taylor, *Virginia Baptist Ministers* (Richard: Yale & Wyatt, 1838), 1:234.

[2] Ibid., 236.

July 6

Ebenzer Kinnersley - Baptist Against Whitefield

Scripture: Acts 15:30-41

Ebenezer Kinnersley was born in Gloucester, England, November 30, 1711. Three years later his father moved to America and settled near the Pennypack Church, the early Baptist church near Philadelphia. On September 6, 1735, young Kinnersley was baptized and became a member of that church. In 1743, he was ordained to the work of the gospel ministry. Although Ebenezer was ordained, because of health problems and his interest in science, he never became the pastor of a church.

Kinnersley was well known to the scientific community. He was associated with Benjamin Franklin and worked with him in the development of his theories on electricity. The discoveries he and Franklin made astounded the scholars of Europe. "The Philadelphia experiments" on "electric fire," as it was then termed, became well known, and Franklin and Kinnersley became famous in Europe and America. In 1751 Kinnersley began to deliver lectures on "The Newly Discovered Electrical Fire." In September of 1751, he went to Boston to deliver his lectures in Faneuil Hall. While there, he suggested that houses and barns might be protected from lightning with what is today called a "lightning rod." This was months before Franklin flew his kite in the famous lightning storm. Kinnersley also proved that heat could be produced by electricity. In this country at that time, he was better known than Franklin.[1]

We are more interested in Ebenezer Kinnersley for his spiritual insights, however. The Great Awakening was taking place, and many Baptists joined in the revival. Kinnersley was one of the few Baptists in Philadelphia who had doubts regarding the character of the preaching that had been introduced by Whitefield. This kind of preaching was different than anything the Baptists had heard before.

On the 6th of July, 1740, he entered a solemn protest against Whitefield's revivalism in the pulpit of the Pennypack

Church. There was a strong reaction to Kinnersley's arguments. The tension his sermon created was so great that he was forbidden by the church to join them in the Lord's Supper. As a result, according to David Spencer, Kinnersley left the church and for some time attended the Episcopal church in Philadelphia, the church of which his wife was a member.[2] David Benedict rejects this, however. He insists that Kinnersley merely waited for his wife outside the Episcopal church but never attended services there.[3] Whichever story is true, Kinnersley was a Baptist at heart, and the difference between himself and his church was soon settled, and he returned to service there.

A few years later a number of the members in the Pennypack Church requested permission to begin a separate church in Philadelphia proper. Many of these people had been meeting separately from the Pennypack Church since 1698, although they considered themselves to be true members of the Pennypack Church. The request was initiated in 1746 because of a legacy which had been left to the branch in Philadelphia. Was this legacy to be reserved for the Philadelphia branch of the Pennypack Church or should a portion of this inheritance also be given to the Pennypack body? There was no division or jealousy at all between the two bodies, but there was a concern that the purpose of the gift could be perverted. Therefore, letters of dismissal were granted by Pennypack on May 3, and the branch in Philadelphia, consisting of fifty-six members, was formally constituted on May 15, 1746. Kinnersley was one of the charter members and remained connected with it until his death in Lower Dublin on the 4th of July, 1778.

Although he was ordained, Ebenezer Kinnersley was never the pastor of a church. Today he would be considered a layman. But what a church member he was! He was faithful to his church, faithful to his convictions, and faithful to the Lord.

LRO

---

[1] James Grant Wilson and John Fiske, Editors, *"Ebenezer Kinnersley," Appleton's Cyclopedia of American Biography* (New York: D. Appleton and Company, 1887-1889).

[2] David Spencer, *Early Baptists of Philadelphia* (Philadelphia: William Syckelmoore, 1877), 68-72.

[3] David Benedict, *A General History of the Baptist Denomination in America, and other Parts of the World* (Boston: Lincoln & Edmands, 1813), 587-588.

July 7

A Judson Legacy

Scripture: John 4:35

Extenuating circumstances kept early Baptists in America from lifting up their eyes to behold the mission fields of the world. Persecution and poverty filled the lives of our forefathers, and they entered into the missionary field primarily in meeting the needs of the developing westward shift of our population, and in ministering to the American Indians. Actually our Baptist forefathers were forced to enter into the arena of foreign missions when Adoniram and Ann Judson became convicted Baptists. As the Judsons were on their way to serve the Lord in India under the sponsorship of the Congregational church, the Judsons, while aboard ship, became Baptists in heart. Soon after they arrived in Calcutta, India, they were immersed by William Ward, Baptist missionary from England. Baptists in America were thrust into the arena of foreign missions as it became necessary to support the Judsons in their quest to serve the Lord overseas. Thus, in 1814, the Triennial Convention, a Baptist foreign mission agency, was formed in Philadelphia, Pennsylvania. The growth of the missionary cause among Baptists is thrilling. Though the Baptist constituency in America was not comprised of the affluent citizenry of the day, the response to the missionary vision was instantaneous. Not only was money given, but year by year young people answered the call of God as the cause of missions was made better known.

In May of 1835, the Triennial Convention met at the First Baptist Church in Richmond, Virginia.[1] Representatives from nineteen states listened to the thrilling reports of what was being accomplished around the world. Twenty-five mission stations were in operation, and 112 missionaries were involved in preaching God's Word.

With the meetings being held in Virginia, it is only natural that local young people would respond. Their hearts were touched by the reports, and as preachers declared the need, the Holy Spirit made real the call. The Virginia Foreign Missionary Society undertook to provide the expenses for three young couples from Virginia. William Mylne had been born in Scotland, and moved to Virginia in his early youth. Mylne was appointed for service in Liberia. He married Miss Elizabeth Davis in June of 1835, and the Second Baptist Church of Richmond served as the sending church for this couple. The Mylne's sailed on July 7, 1835. Tragically, within a month of landing on the field, both suffered severe cases of malaria, and Elizabeth passed into the presence of the Lord on September 16. William Mylne recovered and continued to minister until ever declining health forced his return to Virginia in 1838. He served pastorates in the Goshen Association of Virginia until his death.

On September 7, 1835, Robert Dunlavy Davenport and Jehu Lewis Shuck were appointed for service in Siam and China. Before leaving for their respective fields of service, both young men married young ladies who had been students of the Richmond Classical and English school. Robert Davenport married Miss Mary Frances Greenhow Roper, and Lewis Shuck married Miss Henrietta Hall. A combined commissioning service was held for the couples in the First Baptist Church of Richmond on September 22, 1835. The couples actually sailed together from Boston. Their ship arrived in Singapore on March 31, 1836, and the couples went their separate ways at that point.[2]

The Davenports were enabled of the Lord to serve for nine years in Siam, and Reverend Davenport gave outstanding service both in a printing and preaching ministry. Unfortunately, his health ultimately necessitated their return to America in 1845.

The Shucks remained six months in Singapore and then settled in Macao. There they ministered for six years before moving on to Hong Kong where they experienced a rich ministry. Henrietta conducted schools in both cities, and she gained the honor of being "The First American Female Missionary in China." She died on her field of service in 1844.

Let us pray God that once again young people in America will be stirred to carry the Gospel into the uttermost part of the world.

DLC

---

[1] Evelyn Wingo Thompson, *Luther Rice Believer in Tomorrow* (Nashville, TN: Broadman Press, 1967), 196.

[2] Garnett Ryland, *The Baptists of Virginia 1699-1926* (Richmond, VA: The Virginia Baptist Board of Missions and Education, 1955), 272.

July 8

The Patriotic Professor

Scripture: Ephesians 4:11; 1 Timothy 3:2

Students from Indiana Baptist College (now Heritage Baptist University) in Indianapolis, Indiana, knew that if they passed Dr. Forster's Bible Doctrine's class, they would pass any ordination council. Dr. Forster was a superb Bible teacher instilling a love of Bible truths to college students. Pastors could always recognize Dr. Forster's students because they were well versed in Bible doctrines.

William Emil Forster, Jr. was born on April 18, 1924, in Indianapolis, Indiana, to William and Agnes Mundale Forster. He was saved as a teenager in 1941 in a Sunday evening service at Broadway Baptist Church in Indianapolis. Later in the month he was immersed upon his profession of faith. On June 8, 1942, he enlisted in the United States Navy, and having served faithfully throughout World War II, he was honorably discharged on December 14, 1945.

William was Radioman 1C-V-6 USNR for Lieutenant Sabby on the Long Slow Target 309, the most reliable ship the Navy ever had. Bill, as the crewmen called him, received a bronze star in recognition of his heroic action in battle. When the LST 309 was fired upon, Lt. Sabby, without protocol, called to Bill, "Reverse engine!" Lieutenant Forster relayed the order; the engine was reversed immediately. This quick response caused an enemy shell to fall short of its target, and hit and destroy an enemy ship. Thus the LST 309 was saved. This, and other outstanding events in Bill's military life provided him with the assurance that he was called of God to preach. During his years in the military, Bill took advantage of opportunities to preach to his fellow servicemen and won many to Christ.

Following the completion of the war, Bill entered Bob Jones College at Cleveland, Tennessee. He married Margaret Shreve on December 24, 1946, at Broadway Baptist Church where they had first met. Margaret had graduated from a Seventh Day Adventist Academy, and her first exposure to the Gospel was reading John 3:16 on the wall of the Baptist church when her academy used the building for a Christmas program. She was saved at the age of fifteen and became a member of Broadway. Together she and Bill served the Lord for almost 50 years. In October 1947, Bill and Margaret had returned to Bob Jones University, but this time it was to the new campus at Greenville, South Carolina. Bill completed his education, earning a Bachelor of Arts in 1949 when he was ordained in June of that year. He earned a Bachelor of Divinity in 1951. He was later awarded an honorary Doctor of Divinity from Indiana Baptist College.

The Forsters moved back to Indianapolis, and started the Shelbyville Baptist Temple in June 1951. After establishing he work, he remained there for 18 months. In his early ministry he was involved in helping to start several local churches. Dr. Forster, following the leading of the Lord, began Bible classes with three couples plus the group from Shelbyville. From this group, Bill founded the Berean Bible Institute (later changed to Indiana Baptist College). Dr. Ford Porter opened his church and the institute met in those facilities. Dr. Forster was a teacher and evangelist, traveling the world sharing the Gospel. He and his good friend and co-worker, Dr. Clinton Branine, were invited as guests of the Israeli government to visit Israel the week of July 8, 1993. This was one of nine trips Dr. Forster took to the Holy Land.

In his busy ministry he preached in 680 churches. At Indiana Baptist College/Heritage Baptist University, he was honored on November 10, 1995, when the campus chapel was given his name. He taught his last class at Heritage University in October of 1995. After a teaching career of forty one years, the college lost a passionate, compassionate, soul-winning professor who was much loved by his students and faculty.

Before his death, he was able to complete his textbook on Bible Doctrines. He went home to be with his Lord on January 6, 1996, and was buried on January 9, 1996, with military honors. Hundreds of pastors and friends joined his widow on that cold, bitter day to pay their final respects to one of God's choice servants. It behooves us to follow his godly example.[1]

DCB

[1] Telephone interview with Mrs. Margaret Forster by Bettye Baughan on August 28, 2004.

July 9

Give of Thy Sons

Scripture: 1 Samuel 1:19-2:11

Christian parents often find it difficult to accept the call of God upon their offspring for missionary service. Many times twentieth and twenty-first century believers set a personal goal for their sons and daughters desiring them to excel in business, sports, or a profession. Upon hearing that God the Holy Spirit has called their children to Christian service, particularly to missionary service abroad, these parents have a difficult time in acquiescing and accepting the will of God. Doubtless the materialism of society has permeated their thinking.

Apparently that was the case in the nineteenth century as well, for when the Lord burdened the heart of Mr. George Hough to partner with Adoniram Judson in missionary service in what ended up to be Burma, his in-laws protested. As a result, Mrs. Hough wrote with a view to reconcile their minds to her going. She most tenderly addressed them as follows: "I can anticipate your feelings in parting with one of your children probably for life, and I feel all that reluctance, which an affectionate child would feel for kind parents, when I leave you for a distant country. My husband has long been desirous of going to India, [He ultimately ended up in Burma] and he feels confident that he can be more useful in the cause of Christ there, than in any other place. He is professedly engaged in that cause, to promote which ought to be the subject of all Christians. They ought to be willing to make sacrifices, to endure hardships, and to forsake all for Christ's sake and the gospel's.

"You, my dear mother, professing to be a follower of Jesus, to feel interested in His cause, let me ask, if you do not wish to promote it, if you do not desire to see that day, when the gospel shall be preached to every nation under heaven? How would you feel if deprived of your Bible and the preaching of the gospel? Would you not be willing to go even to India [Burma] for the enjoyment of such a blessing? And if salvation depends upon knowing and believing in Christ, and if there is greater joy in a well grounded hope and faith in the gospel, than in all the pleasures of the world, is it not of great importance, that the heathen should taste of these joys? I know you will say that it is of importance that the gospel should be preached to them, and why not my husband endure the hardships incident to a missionary life, as well others? Why should not I go to India [Burma] as well as other women, and share with my husband the trials and comforts of a life devoted to the cause of truth? I hope you and all other Christians will pray for us, that we faint not in the day of trial."[1]

It is surely not easy for godly parents to bid farewell to their offspring and see them leave American shores for service abroad. There is a hesitancy in the realization that the joys of "spoiling" grandchildren will be forfeited, and there is a lingering question concerning health care. These reactions may be considered "normal," but those of us who know the Lord in reality are assured that the most blessed place in the life of the believer is in the center of God's will. He has revealed Himself sufficient for every need. He has promised His presence in every situation whether it be for physical protection or material supply.

Needless to say, the George Houghs were appointed for missionary service, and ended up in Burma. In the course of time Mr. Hough endured many of the trials that befell Mr. Judson including suffering in miserable Burman jails. His contribution to the ministry was primarily in the area of printing the literature that was so greatly used of God in spreading the gospel message. The Lord called his servant home on July 9, 1859[2], from Maulmain, Burma.

Dear Christian parent, our attitude ought to be that of Mr. Spurgeon when informed by his son that God was calling him into Christian service. Mr. Spurgeon is reported to have responded: "Son, if God is calling you to be a missionary, don't stoop to become the king of England!" May we obey the words of the great hymn: "Give of thy sons (children) to bear the message glorious."

DLC

---

[1] *The First Annual Report of The Baptist Board of Foreign Missions for the United States* (Philadelphia: William Fry, 1815), 28-29.

[2] *The Missionary Jubilee* (New York: Sheldon and Company, 1865), 251.

July 10

Don't Forget our Jerusalem

Scripture: Acts 1:8a

Edmund Botsford was characteristic of many of the pioneering Baptist preachers who were used of God in laying a great foundation for spiritual growth in the early days of our Republic. He was converted under the preaching of Reverend Oliver Hart of Charleston, South Carolina, and almost immediately he became a serious student of the Word of God. On March 14, 1773, the Baptist Church of Charleston ordained him, and Edmund Botsford became a tireless itinerating evangelist, sowing the Word and planting churches under the authorization of his ordaining church.

During 1773 and 1774 his labors resulted in the baptism of many throughout South Carolina. On one occasion he said: "In the month of August, 1773, I rode 650 miles (by horse), preached forty-two sermons, baptized twenty-one persons, and administered the Lord's Supper twice. Indeed, I traveled so much this year that some used to call me the '*flying preacher*.'"[1] After arriving in an area on July 10, 1773, and clearly declaring the Gospel, "the following incident occurred on the 16th of July, in that year, at Stephen's Creek, South Carolina. Several candidates came forward for baptism; but one, a Mrs. Clecker, 'did not know that her husband would permit her to be baptized.' 'Is he present in the congregation?' asked Mr. Botsford.

'Yes, sir.'

'Mr. Clecker, please come to the table!'exclaimed the preacher. Mr. Clecker came forward, and proved to be a little German. 'I have reason to hope, Mr. Clecker,' said Mr. Botsford, 'that your wife is a believer in Christ, and she desires to be baptized by immersion, but not without your consent. Have you any objection to make, sir?'

'No. No! Got forpit I should hinter my vife! She was one goot vife.'

Nevertheless, the little man was enraged at being thus summoned and publicly interrogated: and while the preparations were going on, he vented his wrath privately in swearing and abusing Mr. Botsford.

'Vat! Ax me pefore all de peeble if he might tip my wife!'

Of this, however, Mr. Botsford was ignorant. Coming up from the water, after the administration of baptism was all over, and passing through an orchard, he saw the little German, by himself, and leaning against a tree, apparently in trouble.

'Mr. Clecker, what is the matter?' asked Mr. Botsford. 'O, sir, I shall go to de tivel, and my vife to hevin. I am a boor lost sinner. I can't be forgifen. I fear de ground will open and let me down to de hell, for I cursed and svore you vas good for notting. Lord, have mercy on me!'

Afterwards he found peace in believing, and Mr. Botsford had the satisfaction of baptizing him in September of 1773."[2]

A great debt is owed the faithful pioneering preachers who faithfully proclaimed the message of redemption and were used of God in transforming the wild frontiers into fruitful communities of civility. These unheralded giants of the faith preached faithfully without fear, favor or fame.

Early American historians often repeated the imaginary story of the Baptist and Methodist itinerants vying to get to a new territory to preach Christ.

This Day in Baptist History III

A Baptist was determined to reach a settlement first, and so he took the first seat in the front car of the first train over the new track. When he jumped off at the end of the road, he found that a Methodist had ridden in on the cowcatcher.[3]

Of course the roles of the Baptist and Methodist would be reversed if the one relating the incident happened to be a Baptist.

In this day, when there is such a need to sow America down anew with the Gospel, it would be wonderful if God would again raise up young men of vision for the task. Let us thank God for men such as Edmund Botsford, and let us ask the Lord to burden others for such a task today.

DLC

---

[1] Samuel Boykin, *History of the Baptist Denomination in Georgia* (Atlanta, GA: Jas. P. Harrison & Co., 1881), 20.

[2] Ibid., 20-21.

[3] Reuben Post Halleck, *History of our Country* (New York: American Book Company, 1923), 364.

July 11

"All Your Needs"

Scripture: Philippians 4:19

The name "Stennett" was often synonymous with a "Baptist preacher" in old England (Vol. 1:225). Joseph Stennett married a lady in Wales and served the Abergavenny Baptist Church faithfully for years. The Lord called him home on July 11, 1713.[1] In this entry we will focus on a poor coal miner who was a member of the Abergavenny church. The miner was a faithful man, and his knowledge of the Scriptures amazed his pastor, but he was simply known as Caleb. He lived seven miles from the church, but he and his family were always present unless the weather made the trip impossible.

One winter the weather had become harsh, and Caleb was unable to get to the meetings. As the severe weather continued, Pastor Stennett became concerned for his welfare. However, no sooner was there a break in the weather, than the pastor saw Caleb in the audience. As the meeting concluded, he made his way to him. His first question was how Caleb and his family had endured the weather. Caleb responded, "Never better in my life. We not only had necessaries, but lived upon dainties during the whole time . . . ." Pastor Stennett asked to know the particulars. Caleb explained that one night after the bad weather had begun, they ate their last provisions. There was no food for the next day. However as Caleb prayed and reminded God of His promises, the Lord gave them peace of heart. They retired in peace. Before daybreak Caleb heard a knock at the door. Upon answering, he discovered a man with a wagon. Being assured that he was at Caleb's home, the deliveryman requested Caleb's assistance in unloading. Caleb asked what it was, and the man said, "Provisions." When Caleb asked who had sent it, the man replied that he believed God had sent it! When the wagon was unloaded, Caleb and his wife discovered bread, flour, oatmeal, butter, cheese, both salted and fresh meat and much more.

The pastor was greatly impressed. Throughout his visitation he sought to discover the benefactor. Two years later he was visiting in the home of Dr. Talbot in Hereford. Mrs. Talbot was a faithful church member. Her husband, a medical doctor, though a man of moral character, was basically an infidel. When Pastor Stennett visited in the home, he was received with great politeness. Often, because of the distance involved, the pastor would spend a night. One evening as they were visiting, the pastor spoke of the power of prayer. In explaining the doctrine, he mentioned Caleb's experience. "Caleb! I shall never forget him as long as I live," said the doctor. "Do you know him?" asked pastor. "I had but little knowledge of him, but by your description I know he must be the same man."

Dr. Talbot related the following events. In the summer prior to the harsh winter, he had been riding horseback in the country. While riding, he observed a number of people assembled in a barn. His curiosity got the best of him, and he rode up to the barn door. To his surprise, there was a man preaching to a large gathering. While he was waiting during the preaching, he noticed one poor man who had a Bible and looked up every reference mentioned. Following the service, the doctor entered into conversation with the poor gentleman, and he was pleased to discover that the gentleman was very intelligent. The doctor asked of his employment, his family, and his name. With his curiosity satisfied, the doctor rode home.

He thought nothing more of the occasion. However, after the severe weather had set in, in the middle of the night the doctor thought he heard a voice saying, "Send provisions to Caleb." He was startled, but concluded it was only a dream. After a while, he heard the same words again only louder and stronger. He awakened his wife, but she assured him it was just a dream. He attempted to sleep again, but he could not. At last he heard the voice powerfully saying, "Get up and send provisions to Caleb." He could resist no longer. He arose, called his servant, bid him to bring his horse, and then they loaded a wagon of whatever he could find. He instructed his servant to take the provision to Caleb. "Caleb?" said the servant, "What Caleb, sir?" "I know very little of him," said the doctor, "but his name is Caleb; he is a collier, and lives among the hills; let the horse go, and you will be sure to find him." The servant seemed under the same influence as his master, which accounts for his telling Caleb, "God sent it, I believe."[2]

Thank God we serve the same God Who is able to meet all our needs. Make your requests known unto Him, and then rest in assurance.

DLC

---

[1] Thomas Crosby, *The History of the English Baptists* (London: Published by Author, 1740) IV:326.

[2] J. B. McInturff, *The Old Paths* (Woodstock, VA: W. N. Grabill, 1897), 118.

July 12

Living With Eternity in View

Scripture: 2 Corinthians 5:1-8

Anabaptists found themselves continually in the pincers movement of persecution from Rome and the Reformers. Neander points out that Constantine led the attack against the Donatists by interpreting Luke 14:23 to authorize persecution. Neander wrote: ". . . the theory expressed. . . that men were authorized and bound to employ force, and compel men to participate in the supper; -that is, to enter into communion with the universal visible church, out of whose pale salvation was not to be obtained."[1] Interestingly, John Calvin followed Constantine at that point. Thomas Aquinas concluded that the Anabaptists caused division, and should be "avoided." He then concluded that the best way to "avoid" such an one was by means of execution!

An interesting case in point is that of Algerius of Naples. The lad was born into a family of luxury, and thus was enabled to attend an excellent school. His family desired a position of respect for their son, and his early life was full of promise. Algerius had been born at a strategic time when the fruit of Luther's challenge of Rome had fully matured, and many were discussing the doctrinal differences. Students found it interesting that both Luther and Rome claimed authority through Augustine. Doubtless the controversy stimulated the minds of many students, and Algerius was no exception.

During his academic training, Algerius met another student whom he found interesting. The young man spoke of a personal knowledge of and relation to Jesus Christ. He spoke boldly of his faith, and Algerius was attracted to what he was hearing. A Bible study ensued, and in the course of time, Algerius too came to know the Lord Jesus Christ as his personal Savior. His life was transformed, and his interest in God's Word allowed him no time for gala activities. He began faithful attendance with a little congregation that met in a humble home for Bible study. It was not long before Algerius requested believer's baptism. His faith grew, and, being very articulate, his testimony became known throughout the campus.

Soon his testimony was made known to members of the Inquisition, and he was arrested. To dissuade him from continuing with the Anabaptists, in prison he was forced to witness tortures of both criminals and Anabaptists. From prison he wrote compelling letters telling of his experiences. The Inquisition leadership were anxious that Algerius be salvaged for the Roman church. Therefore he was continually interrogated by priests, and he was questioned before the entire city senate. But that was to no avail. In time it was thought a visit with the Pope would suffice to change his views, and he was transported to Rome. Pope Paul IV did his best to persuade young Algerius by recounting the power of Rome, but again failure resulted. As a last resort, the Capuchin monks were called in, but the reality of Christ could not be overcome. Ultimately it was determined that Algerius must die.

Taken to the stake, he was stripped to his waist and boiling oil was poured over his head and body. Those that gathered were immune from sympathy, but that sight brought them to silence. They watched as the fire was lit and ignited the flowing oil. It was but a matter of a few minutes, and Algerius left that scene to open his eyes in glory.

He had penned a letter that lives on! It is too long to quote, but he signed it as follows: "Written in the most delightful pleasure garden of the prison, called Leonia, the 12th day of July A. D. 1557."[2] These few lines are but a "delightful" sample. "Here on earth I have "no continuing city" or place of rest. My home and country are in heaven. I seek the new city of Jerusalem, which I see before me, which comes to meet me. In fact, I am already on the way to it; there is my sweet home, my riches, my parents, and my friends, my pleasure and my honor. I have no fear that I shall miss them.

"All these earthy things are only shadows; they are all transient, and a vanity of vanities to those who miss the hope and essence of eternal life."

May the Lord give us in our day such bold conviction and blessed certitude.

DLC

---

[1] Augustin Neander, *History of the Christian Religion and Church*, (Boston: Crocker & Brewster, 1872), 2:248-249.

[2] Myron S. Augsburger, *Faithful Unto Death* (Waco, TX: Word Books, 1978), 30.

July 13

From One Generation to the Next

Scripture: Psalm 102:28; 145:1-4

How wonderful to own the diary or memoir of a godly forebear! To read the personal testimony of a believing grandparent or saintly great-grandparent surely is a great thrill. Missionary Al Bonikowsky, who serves the Lord in Europe, has a copy of the memoir of his grandfather, Reverend Emil Bonikowsky. Emil Joseph Bonikowsky was born in Wolynian, Poland, on May 24, 1881. Emil's godly Baptist parents (Al Bonikowsky's great-grandparents) were descendants of the German settlers that the ruler, Catherine the Great (1729-1796), persuaded to emigrate to Russia from Germany to assist in the developing of Russia's rich farm land. The gospel message has been faithfully presented from generation to generation in the family, and now Al Bonikowsky's son, Andy, is also serving the Lord in Spain.

Formal education was almost unknown in the days of Emil Bonikowsky, but with self-effort and parental encouragement, he learned the rudiments of reading, writing, and math. Emil was a weaver by trade, but he was conscripted during the Russian-Japanese war, and served as the Czar's private bodyguard in Petersburg from 1902 to 1906.

When he was thirteen Emil entered his apprenticeship as a weaver and operated a handloom in a shop thirty miles from home. The work schedule was grueling as he labored from six in the morning until ten at night. During his three-year apprenticeship, he received room and board and was paid the equivalent of two and a half cents per week.

When nineteen, Emil made public profession of faith and was baptized on July 13, 1900. In 1902 Emil was drafted into the military, and the next four years found him fulfilling that responsibility as he was assigned to service in Petersburg. He soon learned that military life in Russia at the time was much akin to slavery. He had little fellowship with other Christians, but remained true to his Lord through the trying experience.

On July 10, 1907, the young man took Miss Maria Zozmann to wife, and as the custom was, the couple began housekeeping in two rooms in the home of the bride's parents. The young couple was faithful to the house of God, and soon the church leaders observed the hand of God upon Emil. He was urged to enter into Bible training, which was primarily through correspondence. In the course of time, Emil proved himself faithful in handling the Word of God and was ordained on September 17, 1912.

An itinerant ministry took the young preacher to the colony of Mogeinitze in Poland where he was strengthened in his resolve to serve the Lord. He visited the site of the first Baptist church established in Poland and stood in awe at the memory of the ministry of Gottfried Alf, who had suffered greatly for the sake of the gospel. Surely the Lord allowed this experience to prepare the man of God for exile in Siberia. As soon as World War I had begun, the Russian government interned all citizens of Germany, and the Bonikowskys were sent by train some three thousand miles to the village of Fjedorofka. A few believers were found, and Reverend Bonikowsky exercised his gifts as he evangelized among the lost and encouraged the saints.

At the conclusion of the war, a call was extended to the man of God to pastor in Vosnesensk, near Orenburg, a large Cossack city on the Ural River. This was on the border between Europe and Asiastic Russia. Four small branch works extended from the main ministry, and once or twice a year the pastor traveled by horse and buggy to minister in those works. The round trip entailed 190 miles.

The concluding years of ministry found Brother Bonikowsky in the Ukraine. The man of God wrote concerning "remarkable spiritual movements and awakenings," and rejoiced in the privilege of baptizing those who had put their trust in the Savior. But the political pressure of the Bolsheviks became continually worse. In April of 1926, Stalin ordered that no children could attend Sunday school or belong to any church organization. Communism's persecution began in earnest. We do not have the space to tell of Brother Bonikowsky's emigration to Canada, but his obituary reads, "He passed away peacefully on October 20, 1967 in Medicine Hat (Alberta, Canada) with a vision of Glory at the age of 86." May we each determine to leave such a heritage for our descendants.

DLC

July 14

Friends of Those who Stand for Truth

Scripture: Proverbs 22:28

It has been interesting to receive "feed back" from some who protested any mention of Anabaptists in our first two volumes. Once again I want to affirm that the authors of these volumes do not claim a "direct link" between modern-day Baptists and our heroes of biblical principles in earlier centuries, those who were erroneously called "Anabaptists."

One of the four leading Anabaptist scholars of the twentieth century was Dr. William R. Estep, author of *The Anabaptist Story*. Dr. Estep passed into the presence of the Lord on July 14, 2000, and funeral services were conducted in the Gambrell Street Baptist Church in Fort Worth, Texas, on July 21, 2000. Dr. Estep wrote or edited twenty-one volumes in all, but the above mentioned volume and *Renaissance and Reformation,* deal most closely with the sixteenth century Anabaptists.

Dr. Estep was born in Kentucky on February 12, 1920, and when he was ten years of age, he accepted Christ as his Savior. His mother died during his youth, and young William was raised by relatives. Upon graduating from Berea College in Kentucky, he married Edna Alice McDowell in 1942. While serving churches in Kentucky, Oklahoma, and Texas, he acquired a masters and doctor of theology degree. From 1954 until his retirement in 1990, Dr. Estep taught at Southwestern Baptist Theological Seminary in Fort Worth, Texas. Dr. Estep has been considered, as reported in his obituary, "one of the most prominent church historians in Southern Baptist life, whose work threw a spotlight on Baptist origins and church-state issues . . . ."

At the time of Dr. Estep's death, Dr. James Leo Garrett, distinguished emeritus professor of Theology at Southwestern said: "It was in the study of the 16th-century Anabaptists and their influence on the development of Baptist history that Estep made his most significant contribution." Dr. Garrett went on to explain: "He was always probing the Anabaptist side of the story. He helped to broaden understanding of Baptist origins." Dr. Estep had said: "Without Anabaptists, we'd be hard pressed to know who we are or what we believe as Baptists."

And just what did Dr. Estep claim for the Anabaptists? The distinguished historian was on the campus of Oklahoma Baptist University Monday, February 15, 1999, delivering the Gaskin Lectures, designed to preserve and promote the study of Baptist history and heritage. He delivered two lectures: "An Anabaptist Ancestry" and "Calvinism and Baptist Beginnings."

This Day in Baptist History III

The two streams, Anabaptism and Calvinism, "help Baptists to understand themselves and the tensions that have frequently characterized Baptist life through the centuries and into the present generation," Estep said, including "tensions created by the contemporary resurgence of Calvinism."

The (Anabaptist) movement spread to England and then to Amsterdam when English immigrants fled there to avoid persecution. These English Anabaptists stood for seven distinctives:

(1) The priority of New Testament over Old Testament, interpreted through an understanding of Christ.

(2) The necessity of the new birth for salvation and as a prerequisite to baptism.

(3) Believers' baptism with the corresponding rejection of infant baptism.

(4) Discipleship viewed as the essence of Christianity.

(5) The church as a fellowship of baptized believers for the primary purpose of obeying the Great Commission (to make disciples).

(6) The observance of the Lord's Supper to remember the sacrifice of Christ and as a communion of believers.

(7) Religious freedom and separation of church and state.

Anabaptists made central to the whole movement a lifestyle of discipleship based upon the example and teachings of Jesus Christ. For thousands, this meant that when one became an Anabaptist through believers' baptism, one was signing his own death warrant. "The heritage that some of us take so lightly was paid for by blood," Estep emphasized, citing specific examples of Anabaptists who were drowned, burned at the stake, or otherwise executed for their beliefs.

The authors of these Baptist devotional volumes claim succession only of truth, but we confess, we find eternal truth in the above mentioned distinctives. We cannot help but notice that these truths parallel what Independent Baptists champion in our day.

DLC

July 15

From Darkness to Light

Scripture: John 9:1-25

It was June 6, 1944, and the young soldier was aboard the *S. S. Colombie*, a French freighter converted as a troop carrier. America was embroiled in World War II, and Billy Renstrom was on his way to Europe with the 133rd Combat Engineer Battalion. The ship sailed from New York harbor. Some of those soldiers were catching what would prove to be their first and last glimpse of the Statue of Liberty.

Billy Renstrom was the youngest of twelve children born to Swedish parents who had emigrated to America. In his youth, Billy had heard the gospel preached, and at the age of fifteen he had trusted Christ as Savior. He was immersed and united with the Struthers Baptist Tabernacle in Struthers, Ohio. He was a high-school student on that fateful day of December 7, 1941, when Pearl Harbor was attacked. Soon his life would change drastically. His mother passed away suddenly in 1942. With determination, he decided to continue in athletics. He became the captain of his high school football team.

In July of 1943 Billy received his draft notice and reported to the armory in Akron, Ohio for his physical and induction into the army. Following training, he boarded the ship in New York and was soon on his way to the battlefield, landing first in Ireland. Billy gained the rank of Corporal. On D-Day, June 6, 1944, Allied Forces invaded the shores of France. It was on July 15, 1944, that the 133rd Combat Engineer Battalion landed on the Omaha Beachhead.[1]

Billy's squad was given various assignments such as repairing highways to enable rapid troop deployment. One task of his squadron was the discovery and destruction of enemy land mines. This was a dangerous assignment, but the date of November 28, 1944, could never be forgotten by the young soldier. While performing his duty, Billy was struck with shrapnel from a land mine explosion. Immediately he lost total vision in one eye, and suffered serious injury to his other eye. Of course, other wounds were sustained, but the injuries to the eyes would plague him throughout his life.

He was evacuated to military hospitals and finally transported back to the States. When it was determined that the medics had done all that they could, it was apparent that he would be blind for life. This was devastating to Billy. Self-pity in time was replaced by bitterness. Billy wanted to become a recluse. However a friend insisted Billy attend revival services with him. That very night God the Holy Spirit brought conviction and restoration to Billy, and his life began to change.

Wanting to know more of God's Word, the evangelist recommended home Bible study, but Billy desired to attend Bible College. He enrolled in the Western Bible Institute in Denver. The G.I. Bill enabled him to avail himself of the training. In time Billy began singing in a quartet and many doors were opened for Christian service. Billy fell in love with the pianist, Miss Ruby Harwood, daughter of the Institute President. Ruby accepted his proposal of marriage, and, following graduation, Billy and Ruby married, and he served as a pastor.

Dr. Bill Rice, evangelist and director of the Bill Rice Ranch in Tennessee, invited Billy Renstrom to join his team as soloist in evangelistic campaigns. The Renstroms accepted the invitation, and moved to Tennessee. While having minor surgery on his eye, Billy's ophthalmologist expressed hope that something could be done to restore partial sight. Following additional examinations by experts at the Veteran's Hospital, surgery was performed, and God granted the miracle of renewed vision to His servant. After thirty-one years of darkness, Billy Renstrom could see.

May we learn that nothing lies outside the power of God except that which lies outside His will. We do not question the power of God, though at times we do not understand His purpose. May we learn to trust as did Job, when he said: "Though he slay me, yet will I trust in Him."

DLC

---

[1] Billy Renstrom, *Darkness is Light* (Murfreesboro, TN: Bill Rice Ranch, Inc, 1976), 19.

July 16

Liberty's Limitations

Scripture: 1 Corinthians 8:9-13

Religious freedom in America is foundational to our republic! We are reminded that the Baptists who formed Rhode Island introduced such liberty in our land. Often we honor the memory of Roger Williams, but for some Rhode Island historians, Dr. John Clarke has been undeservedly overshadowed by Roger Williams, as a defender of religious liberty, an upholder of democracy, a founder of the Baptist faith, and a guiding force toward unification of the bay settlements. It was Clarke who obtained the important charter from King Charles II in 1663. It is Clarke's definition of religious liberty, not Williams's, that is engraved in letters a foot high under the marble dome of the state capitol today.[1]

On July 8, 1663, through the efforts of Dr. John Clarke, King Charles II granted Rhode Island its charter which stated, "no person within the said colonye at any tyme hereafter shall bee any wise molested, punished, disquieted or called in question for any difference in opinions in matters of religion which doe not actually disturb the civil peace of our sayd colonye; but that . . . freely and full ye have and enjoy his and their own judgments and consciences in matters of religious concernments."[2]

That pattern of religious freedom continued in Rhode Island, and Quakers, Jews, and Catholics were allowed freedom there. The historian observed that the Colony . . . "would probably have tolerated Moslems, had any come."[3] It is interesting to observe that not only Baptists, but Quakers were abused in the Bay Colony. In fact, in the course of time, four Quakers were put to death in Massachusetts for daring to preach their doctrines. Massachusetts persuaded Plymouth and Connecticut to enact severe laws against Quakers, and repeatedly they urged Rhode Island to do the same. Rhode Island's legislature responded to their request on October 13, 1657, saying that, while it found Quaker doctrines strange, "we have no law among us whereby to punish any."[4]

Thus Rhode Island stood firm in its position of overall freedom. On May 4, 1776, the general assembly of Rhode Island voted to abrogate its allegiance to the king. On July 4, 1784, Rhode Island's two representatives to the Continental Congress signed the Declaration of Independence with no qualms. In its session from July 16 to July 20, 1784, Rhode Island's General Assembly discussed the ramifications of the actions of the colonies in separating from Great Britain, and on July 18, 1784, they altered their charter replacing the word *colony* with the word *state*. On July 20, 1784, they pledged to support the said General Congress with their lives and fortunes. We thank God for these lovers of freedom.

Today our nation faces a serious threat! Within our borders those espousing an entirely different religion have flooded our population. These meet covertly in mosques and are instructed therein under the guise of religious freedom in the methods of terrorism. I have been asked, "Do you still believe in religious freedom? And the answer is "Yes, absolutely!" But, we need to understand that religious freedom has limitations. Someone has well said, "**Liberty is not the power to do what we want. It is the power to do what we ought!**"

Our forefathers realized that liberty must have limitations! They carefully worded their declaration and stated, "**Noe person within the said colonye at any tyme hereafter shall bee any wise molested, punished, disquieted or called in question for any difference in opinions in matters of religion which doe not actually disturb the civil peace of our sayd colonye....**" We would concur with the statement that the most stringent protection of free speech cannot protect a man in falsely shouting ***fire*** in a theater and causing a panic. By the same token, religious freedom must not protect individuals who advocate violence and terror in the name of their god. May we urge our civil authorities to deport any and all within our borders who would use the cloak of religious freedom to destroy our nation!

DLC

[1] William G. McLoughlin, *Rhode Island a Bicentennial History* (New York: W. W. Norton & Co., 1978), 23.

[2] Ibid., 38.

[3] Ibid., 34.

[4] Ibid., 36.

July 17

The Bigotry of Empty Religion

Scripture: Acts 14:19; 16:19-25

As Isaac Backus, the intrepid Baptist historian of New England, was on one of his regular preaching tours in 1782, Mr. Richard Lee used the opportunity of visiting the revered man of God. Their paths crossed at the home of Mr. Lambert on July 17, 1782. Mr. Lee was a lay preacher, and he wanted to share the blessings and burdens of his ministry with Mr. Backus.

Mr. Lee related the blessings of God upon his ministry throughout the area during the past year, and spoke of the evident tokens of the Lord's presence in the meetings. It seemed providential to enter into Hingham, Massachusetts, a town that had been impenetrable to the Baptists for forty years. As Mr. Lee had gone to preach there on May 28, 1782, he was confronted by Captain Theophilus Wilder, a member of the established church, along with a mob. They seized Mr. Lee, and with great violence, escorted him to the town limits.

Actually two affidavits signed by six witnesses relate the following details of the riot:

> Richard Lee was invited to preach at David Farrar's home in Hingham on 28 May 1782. Just before he began, a mob assembled at the door of the house led by Wilder and Nathaniel Dammon of the Standing church. They ordered him not to preach, and when he persisted, "Capt. Wilder then said, 'Men come in'; upon which a number came in, and Zechariah Whiting, being stripped to his shirt sleeves, by Wilder's order, seized Mr. Lee by his left arm and collar, and twitched him away with great violence,

> and others taking hold with him hauled Mr. Lee along clear out of town, cursing and swearing most terribly." They knocked his Bible from his hand and clapped their hands over his mouth when he tried to speak, "And one of them cast soft cow dung in Mr. Lee's face; then they presented Prince Wilder, a large Negro man, and said, 'There is your disputer,' and some said, 'Here he is as black as hell!' And Captain Wilder shook a long club over Mr. Lee's head, and swore that if he ever came into that town again he would take him and tie him up and whip him thirty stripes. Mr. Lee said, that is not so much as they whipped Paul. 'What, damn you, said one, do you compare yourself to Paul!'"

Upon hearing this account, Mr. Backus insisted that Mr. Lee accompany him the following day to the meeting of the Warren Association in Boston. The men of the Warren Association encouraged Mr. Lee to prosecute Mr. Wilder and the men of the mob.

Thus Mr. Lee used what legal protection that was offered him, and he prosecuted the rioters. "The grand jury found a true bill against five of them; four were arraigned on 12 Oct. and pleaded not guilty. Considerable obstacles were placed in the way of the Baptists, and Robert Treat Paine, who was counsel for the rioters, obtained several adjournments. Finally, in May 1783, the rioters settled out of court, paying all the costs but no damages."[1]

If you will observe the date, it will be clear to you that the events described above took place after the Revolutionary War. They transpired when America had gained its independence. However, it is interesting to notice that Massachusetts continued with a State, or established church, until 1833. Our Baptist forefathers led the way in insisting upon the First Amendment to our Constitution out of fear that the state would impose a national church upon America.

Unfortunately, in this day the Supreme Court of the land is no longer interested in the principle of "original intent" in the interpretation of the Constitution. In the twenty-first century everything is based upon "precedent," even though the so-called "precedent," which liberalism established, contradicts the actual meaning of the First

Amendment. America's new-found state religion is humanism. Freedom cannot long endure under such a religious-philosophy. But while freedom continues to exist in America, we must use every means of presenting the glorious Gospel of the Savior to those about us.

DLC

---

[1] Issac Backus, *The Diary of Isaac Backus* (Providence: Brown University Press, 1979), 2:1104-1105.

July 18

God Blesses Obedience

Scripture: Romans 6:1-6

The Gum Spring Baptist Church in North Carolina was constituted on this date in 1829 by the Separate Baptists of that area. Shubal Stearns and Daniel Marshall had entered the State in 1755, and rapid growth of the Baptist cause through revival had swept the entire region. In 1771 Governor Tryon's troops had routed the Regulators, and many Baptists left the State by moving westward into Tennessee and Kentucky. However, a residue had remained in North Carolina, and the work of the ministry had continued, though at a slower pace. The two prime movers in the establishment of the Gum Spring Church, Elders Hezekiah Harmon and Isaac Kirby, ministered previously in the New Hope Mountain Church, but for various reasons, it had dissolved.

Elder Harmon assumed the leadership in the formation of the new congregation, and the blessings of God were manifest in a number of periods of revival. The church family grew considerably.

The account of the conviction, conversion, and baptism of the man who became the first deacon of the congregation is interesting. During an exciting revival in 1802, the wife of William Drake was gloriously converted. Upon her profession of faith she was baptized and received into the membership of the New Hope Mountain Baptist Church. This action enraged Mr. Drake. Not understanding the significance of baptism, and fearing the water, he thought such an action ridiculous and dangerous. Prior to his wife's baptism, he avowed that if the pastor of the church, Elder Hicks, drowned his wife, he would shoot the pastor. When the baptism took place, Mr. Drake appeared on the scene in a state of great mental agitation. He followed his wife into the water to quite a depth without seeming to be conscious of what he was doing. Mrs. Drake was baptized, and the Lord honored her obedience, using it to bring great conviction to the heart of her husband. He returned home in great agony of heart and mind and retired to bed. He was unable to get up for several weeks. He feared he was going to die.

At Mr. Drake's request Elder Hicks was asked to conduct services and preach at the Drake's home. After the preaching Mr. Drake called upon the Lord to save him. He then said to the pastor, "You must baptize me." Elder Hicks assured him that he would do so the next morning. "No!," said Mr. Drake, "it must be now!" The pastor consented, and some of the men carried torches while others carried Mr. Drake as they made their way down to the Haw River. The pastor entered the water, and the men carried Mr. Drake out to him. The pastor then immersed Mr. Drake, and when he came up out of the water, he was well. He walked home, happy in the love of Christ, and free from any bodily or mental affliction.[1]

In the course of time Mr. Drake's growth in grace caused him to be selected as a deacon of the New Hope Mountain Church, and with its dissolution and the establishing of the Gum Spring Church, he became the first deacon there.

There is no magical formula that brings physical cures in the waters of baptism, but the important principle throughout Scripture is that obedience is better than sacrifice! One is not saved by being baptized. The Lord Jesus did not become the Son of God in the waters of the Jordan as John baptized Him. His Divine Sonship was declared by the Heavenly Father when He was immersed. It has been pointed out that only in the waters of baptism can we perfectly follow an action of our Savior. With that in mind, have you been obedient to the Lord by professing your faith in Him through baptism? If not, in the words of Scripture: "What doth hinder (you) to be baptized?"

DLC

[1] George W. Purefoy, *A History of the Sandy Creek Baptist Association* (New York: Sheldon & Co., 1859), 283-284.

July 19

"Protracted Meetings"

Scripture: Ephesians 4:11-16

Today we shall spotlight Alfred Taylor, one of the early "evangelists" of Baptists in America. Alfred Taylor was the son of Reverend Joseph Taylor. His father was a native of North Carolina, and in early life had made profession of faith in a Methodist church. His growth in grace was so great that in time he was ordained as a Methodist preacher. However, in his reading of the Word of God he became convinced of believer's immersion, and in September of 1804, John and his wife were baptized. Having moved to Warren County, Kentucky, he entered into the ministry with the Baptists, and served the Providence Baptist Church there until he moved in 1811 to Butler County where he served another church as pastor until 1837.

Alfred was born in Warren County on July 19, 1808, and he accompanied his parents to Butler County while but a lad. Though being reared in a Godly environment, while still a youth, Alfred lived a wicked life. Oh how wonderful is the grace of God that seeks the sinner! The Holy Spirit did His work, and Alfred wrote in his journal: "I was enabled in my 22nd year, October, 1829, to trust in Him whose blood speaketh better things than that of Abel, in whom believing, I was enabled to rejoice with joy unspeakable and full of glory."[1] His opportunities of gaining an education were very limited, and at the age of twenty he could still not read. But possessing a strong and logical mind, he was encouraged to study under the tutelage of two outstanding men, and being an earnest student, in time he made rapid educational progress.

In November of 1829 Alfred was baptized into the membership of the Sandy Creek Church in Butler County, and soon he began preaching. Though awkward in his early attempts to declare God's Word, he was licensed to preach on May 21, 1831. After three years of efforts, he was ordained in May of 1834 and called to pastor the Pond River church. He married in 1835 and moved the next year to Ohio County to pastor the Beaver Dam church.

His ability to declare God's Word clearly, and the power of the Holy Spirit upon his ministry opened many doors to Alfred Taylor. He seemed gifted particularly in declaring the Gospel in such a manner that the Holy Spirit fastened the Word to the hearts of unsaved and brought them to repentance. About this time the brethren were considering the propriety of holding what were termed "protracted meetings." This was a series of evangelistic preaching that later became known by the general term "revival" or "evangelistic" meetings. Alfred Taylor concluded that this was a means that God would bless. He entered into such efforts, and the blessings of the Lord surely were manifested as many came to Christ. By this time he had developed as a preacher to such a degree that he had few peers who were his equal.

The evangelist was not of robust health, but he labored tirelessly. Dr. J. S. Coleman stated, "He baptized over 800 persons."[2] In time his physical condition deteriorated so greatly that it was necessary for him to withdraw from preaching for a period. But as soon as his condition improved, he went back to the pulpit. In the fall of 1865, with the assistance of one of his sons, he went to conduct a funeral and then remained for a "protracted" series of evangelistic meetings. Arriving at the home of a friend, he was so weak it was necessary for those present to assist him to bed. His condition continued to worsen until his Lord called him home on October 9, 1865.

The man of God was not only successful as a pulpiteer, but his faithfulness of life led three of his sons to follow him into the ministry as well.

One cannot read God's Word seriously without realizing that the gift of evangelism is still a viable ministry. We need to pray for faithful evangelists who traverse our nation in local churches stirring the hearts of God's people and reaching the lost for Christ.

DLC

---

[1] J. H. Spencer, *A History of Kentucky Baptists* (Printed by the Author, 1886), 1:406.

[2] James R. Beller, *America in Crimson Red* (Arnold, MO: Prairie Fire Press, 2004), 421.

July 20

A Pastor With a Missionary-Heart

Scripture: Matthew 9:35-38

When the Lord of the Harvest burdened the hearts of His children about the world in need of Christ, He selected four unique Baptist pastors. Their names belong on any listing of a Baptist Hall of Fame. I refer to William Carey, Andrew Fuller, John Ryland, Jr., and John Sutcliff. Each has his hallowed place in the modern-day mission movement. However, though less well-known than the others, Samuel Pearce, pastor of the Cannon Street Baptist Church in Birmingham, England also demands special attention.

Samuel Pearce was born on July 20, 1766. Following his conversion in 1782, he was baptized on his seventeenth birthday, July 20, 1783. Almost immediately, young Mr. Pearce gained a passion for the souls of the lost. He studied for the ministry in Bristol College from 1786 to 1789. On June 28, 1790, following fifteen months as supply pastor, Mr. Pearce was called to pastor the Cannon St. Baptist Church. He was ordained in August 1790. On February 2, 1791, he married Miss Sarah Hopkins. During that same month, Reverend Pearce met William Carey for the first time.

Though not a member of the Northampton Association, Pearce determined to attend the May 1792 meeting when he learned that a decision was to be made concerning establishing the first modern-day missionary agency. From the inception of the movement, Samuel Pearce became a vital part of the Baptist Missionary Society. At the first scheduled meeting of the society, gloom fell upon the founders as they realized the financial commitment that would be called for to make the effort a success. At that time Samuel Pearce, though not a member of the Association or Society, came to their rescue with a gift of £70.

From the very start Samuel Pearce longed to join William Carey in service for Christ in India. This desire was not at first voiced to others, but he shared his desire with his reluctant wife. His diary records his tenderness of heart. We have room for only a few entries. In his entry of October 15, 1794 he wrote: "Birmingham, fifty thousand people, and ten evangelical ministers. Hindustan twice as many millions with not ten preachers. Why this disproportion? I must go, if others go not."[1]

On October 24: "Reaching home, the sight of my wife replaced my load. She had been for some time much discouraged at the thought of our going. I kept silent. But, noting my uneasiness, she said, 'Don't be any more anxious on my account. You are taking the right course. When you consult the ministers, represent your obstacles as justly as your inducements; then, if they advise your going, though the parting from my friends will be almost more than I can bear, I will make myself as happy as I can, and God can make me happy anywhere.' For me that was peace, joy, gratitude, rapture."[2]

Pearce communicated this to William Carey, and in time he shared his burden with others. The Cannon St. congregation met to discuss the issue, and Pastor Pearce informed them that he would consider their opinion, but he could not bind himself by any decision they reached. The membership resolved to urge him not to leave them. As a result, it was decided to ask board members of the mission for their recommendation.

On November 5 he recorded these words: *"One thing have resolved. If I cannot go abroad, I will do all I can to serve the Mission at home."*[3]

The board met in Northampton on November 12, 1794, and in consideration of Andrew Fuller's physical condition, and the need for Pearce's leadership in the event of Fuller's becoming incapacitated, the men gave their unanimous decision. Occupying as he did "a post very important to the prosperity of the Mission itself," they urged his continuance therein "for the present."[4] Samuel Pearce acquiesced in the matter, but true to his pledge, he did all in his power to serve the cause of missions until his death on October 10, 1799. May God give us a multitude of missionary-minded pastors in fundamental Baptist churches today that the cause of Christ may go forward around the world.

DLC

---

[1] S. Pearce Carey, *Samuel Pearce, The Baptist Brainerd* (London: The Carey Press, n.d.), 160.

[2] Ibid., 163.

[3] Ibid., 169.

[4] Ibid., 171.

July 21

Franklin's Godly Heritage

Scripture: Deuteronomy 6:18

We honor William Carey as the "Father of Missions," but in reality we must acknowledge him as the "Father of Modern-day Missions." For years prior to 1792 and the establishing of the Baptist Missionary Union in Great Britain, followers of the Savior were heralding the Gospel in all parts of the world. An interesting book entitled *Two Thousand Years of Missions Before Carey* was written at the outset of the twentieth century to honor the memory of many of these. The account of missionary activity among the Moravians around the world in the eighteenth century is surely thrilling.

Coming to our own continent, the ministry among the American Indians by Roger Williams, Henry Dunster (first president of Harvard College), and John Eliot was outstanding. "The Mayhew Family, five successive generations of them, did an ideal work for the Indians in Martha's Vineyard and Nantucket Islands during one hundred and sixty years (1646-1806)."[1]

While reading the account of the Thomas Mayhew family, I was amazed when my eyes fell upon the following: "Associated with the Mayhews in mission work for the Indians was Peter Foulger, grandfather of Benjamin Franklin. Being an ardent Baptist, Foulger introduced his distinctive views among the Indians. By 1694 a Baptist church was in existence on Martha's Vineyard and another on Nantucket."[2]

Peter Foulger was a schoolmaster rather than a preacher; and through his influence the elder Mr. Mayhew embraced Baptist convictions and united with the Baptist church in Newport, Rhode Island where Dr. John Clark pastored. I discovered that the Foulgers had their roots in Fouges, a town in Normandy, France. Peter Foulger's parents eventually moved to the county of Norfolk, England. When eighteen years of age, Peter crossed the Atlantic with his father, John, and they settled in Massachusetts. Along with teaching school, Peter practiced surveying. His ability allowed him to assist in laying out the Island of Nantucket, and on July 4, 1663, he was granted one half share of the land, or half as much as one of the twenty purchasers. In time Peter married Miss Mary Morrill. To this union a daughter, Abiah, was born. It was she who became the mother of the American patriarch, Benjamin Franklin.[3]

Because of his ability to speak the Indian language, Peter Foulger played an important part in the negotiations between the purchasers and the Indians. As a result, he was chosen "clira"of the Courts on July 21, 1673.

Peter Foulger opposed the religious intolerance in Massachusetts, and in 1676 this led him to write a book entitled *A Looking Glass for the Times*. Years later, Benjamin Franklin described it as a defense of liberty of conscience in "homespun verse, written with a good deal of decent plainness and manly freedom."

Though Peter's illustrious grandson never publicly professed faith in the Savior, one cannot help but wonder if the convictions of his old Baptist grandfather did not form the inspiration for Franklin's statement at the formation of the Constitution. The eighty-one-year-old Franklin addressed the chairman and said: "I have lived, Sir, a long time, and the longer I live, the more convincing proofs I see of this truth-that God governs in the affairs of men. And if a sparrow cannot fall to the ground without His notice, is it probable that an empire can rise without His aid? We have been assured, Sir, in the sacred writings, that 'except the Lord build the house they labor in vain that build it.' I firmly believe this; and I also believe that without His concurring aid we shall succeed in this political building no better than the builders of Babel. . . .

"I, therefore, beg leave to move that, henceforth, prayers imploring the assistance of Heaven, and its blessings on our deliberations, be held in this assembly every morning we proceed to business, and that one or more of the clergy in this city be requested to officiate in that service."[4]

May we who are grandparents live not only to instill our standards in our offspring, but may we be intent in seeing them come to personal saving faith in our Lord Jesus Christ.

DLC

[1] Lemuel Call Barnes, *Two Thousand Years of Missions Before Carey* (Philadelphia: American Baptist Publication Society, 1900), 410.

[2] Ibid., 411.

[3] David Benedict, *A General History of the Baptist Denomination in America* (New York: Lewis Colby and Company, 1848), 414.

[4] Benjamin Weiss, *God in American History* (Grand Rapids, MI: Zondervan Publishing House, 1966), 38-39.

July 22

Honoring Those who Were Faithful Unto Death

Scripture: Revelation 2:9-10

As Mr. Spurgeon said when laying the cornerstone of the great Metropolitan Tabernacle in London, in 1861, "We [Baptists] ...did not commence our existence at the Reformation; we were reformers before Luther or Calvin were born; we never came out of the Church of Rome, for we were never in it, but we have an unbroken line up to the apostles themselves. . . .Our principles, sometimes veiled and forgotten, like a river which may travel under ground for a season, have always had honest and holy adherents. [We have been] persecuted alike by Romanists and Protestants of almost every sect . . . ."[1]

It is interesting to note that in the middle of the sixteenth century, "the influence of John Calvin had begun to be felt in English affairs. His books had appeared in translations in England. He was responsible in large measure for the demon of hate and fierce hostility which the Baptists of England had to encounter. He advised that 'Anabaptists and reactionists should alike be put to death' (Froude, *History of England*, V. 99). He wrote a letter to Lord Protector Somerset; the translation was probably made by Archbishop Cranmer (*Calvin to the Protector*, MSS. Domestic Edward V1, V. 1548), to the effect: 'These altoqether deserve to be well punished by the sword, seeing that they do conspire against God, who had set him in his royal seat.'"[2]

Again in writing to Henry V111, Calvin recommended that the Anabaptists be burned as an example to other Englishmen, for he wrote: "It is far better that two or three be burned than thousands perish in hell."[3]

Of course, each of the primary Protestant Reformers despised the Baptists of their day. Ulrich Zwingli was guilty of the martyrdom of Felix Manx, along with many others. Franklin H. Littell wrote of Mr. Luther as follows: "His attitude to Anabaptism was molded by a succession of unfortunate events, and he turned from toleration through banishment to the death penalty for sedition and for 'blasphemy' (a term which in practice was largely equated with what hitherto had been called heresy."[4]

Therefore we should not be shocked to read of the martyrdoms of Anne Askew (1546), Joan of Kent (1549), Joan Boucher (1550), or of the Baptist surgeon, George van Pare. The list continues onward growing in momentum throughout the reigns of Kings and Queens, regardless as to whether they were adherents to the Church of England or the Church of Rome. This martyrdom persisted until the time of the Edict of Toleration in 1689.

For instance, we read: "Two noble men were carried to Newgate and burnt at Smithfield, July 22nd, 1575. One was a man of years with a wife and nine children; the other was a young man who had been married only a few years."[5] While leading a tour group in England, we visited Smithfield in London. I tried to picture in my mind's eye the above scene.

I was reminded of an illustration used by Mr. Spurgeon in one of his sermons. He told of a group of people trudging wearily along the road toward London. They were stopped by a constable and asked where they were going. They responded that they were on their way to Smithfield. When asked the purpose of their journey, their spokesman replied, "We are going to see our pastor burned that we might learn how to die for Jesus Christ."

Let us pause to thank God for our forefathers who dared to die for the cause of the Gospel, and let us ask the Lord to give us grace to at least give ourselves in bold witness in these days when we can freely preach the glorious Gospel.

DLC

[1] Charles Haddon Spurgeon, *Metropolitan Tabernacle Pulpit* (Pasadena, TX: Pilgrim Publications, 1969), 7:225.

[2] John T. Christian, *A History of the Baptists* (Texarkana: American Baptist Association, 1922), 1:198-199.

[3] William Estep, *Renaissance and Reformation* (Grand Rapids, MI: Eerdmans Publishing Company, 1986), 241.

[4] Franklin H. Littell, *The Origins of Sectarian Protestantism* (New York: The Macmillan Company, 1964), 11.

[5] Christian, 1:210.

July 23

To Die is Gain

Scripture: Proverbs 27:17

The Dutch city of Nijmegen had achieved some fame for its linen weaving industry, and many of the laboring class were employed there for manual labor. This environment allowed expected travel in the region, and to such areas Anabaptists were attracted. History reveals that as early as the 1530s several Anabaptists had suffered martyrdom there, and thus the truth of God's Word was known throughout the district.

Jan Block was a wealthy celebrity in the town and needed neither occupation nor profession, for he was independently wealthy. This resulted in a lifestyle that was given to frivolity. Jan and a friend, Symon van Maren, spent a great deal of time visiting the taverns and drinking together. Symon too was aware of the Anabaptists, for martyrs had given their lives in his home town of Hertogenbosch. In fact, Symon had heard the Anabaptists preach, and he had fallen under conviction. Perhaps his move to Nijmegen was an attempt to escape that burden. Be that as it may, Symon became a friend of Jan Block, and the two enjoyed each other's fellowship.

Try as he might to shake conviction, Symon could not forget the faithful witness of those who knew the Lord. In time he repented and trusted Christ as his Savior. What a difference this made in the relationship of Jan and Symon. No longer would the young believer frequent the drinking hole with Jan. A deep sense of peace came upon Symon, and he could not help but urge his friend Jan to at least read the Word of God. Being impressed with the change in Symon's life, Jan in time consented. As he read, conviction also fell upon him. He compared the emptiness in his own life with the fulfillment in the life of Symon. He soon sought out the leadership of the Anabaptists, and came to personal, life-transforming faith in the Son of God. He too sought baptism, and now everything changed for Jan Block as well. He could not keep silent. He experienced what Jeremiah spoke of when he said: "Thy words were found, and I did eat them; and thy Word was unto me the joy and rejoicing of mine heart." The transformation of his life was apparent, and friends began to ask him of the change. Soon his testimony became known by the authorities, and almost immediately they sought to arrest Jan. He was a popular figure in town, and his influence must not be allowed to contaminate others! However, Jan escaped, but the authorities confiscated his estate, and offered a reward for his capture.

Jan went to a small village and sought menial employment, but the potential employer refused to hire him for fear of being arrested for complicity with a heretic. After seeking unsuccessfully to obtain work, Jan was forced to return to Nijmengen, hoping to find labor in an unobtrusive position. However, the bounty that had been placed on his head led a traitor to acknowledge his return. His landlady attempted to hide Jan when the bailiff arrived, but the traitor persisted until Jan was discovered in hiding.

He was imprisoned and ultimately tried. The authorities did not want to condemn Jan to death, for some had been his close friends. One such lord, a former confidant, tried his best to convert Jan to Catholicism. However, Jan chided him, reminding him that when Jan was living a wild life of dissipation, they were not interested in his conversion. But now that he had found reality and was living a useful life, they were attempting to persuade him away from truth. Of course, they could not entice him away from the reality in Christ.

The sentence of burning at the stake was pronounced. But on July 23, 1569,[1] as he was being led from the prison, it seemed as though he himself was in charge. Van Braght claims that his conduct was as though he were going to a festival or wedding feast.[2] As the executioner bound him, and lit the fire, some of his judges wept to see him die. There was no hesitation on the part of Jan Block as the Lord walked with him through the ordeal.

May we be characterized by a transformed life so that all around might know that we are children of God and followers of the Lamb.

DLC

---

[1] Myron S. Augsburger, *Faithful Unto Death* (Waco, TX: Word Books, 1978), 110.

[2] Thieleman J. Van Braught, *The Martyr's Mirror* (Scottsdale, PA: Herald Press, 1950), 894.

July 24

Confronting the King With Truth

Scripture: Acts 5:29-32

James Stuart became King of Scots on July 24, 1567, at the age of thirteen months, after his mother Mary, Queen of Scots was forced to abdicate. She fled to England, where she was imprisoned for the next nineteen years. His father, Lord Darnley, was assassinated under mysterious circumstances shortly after James was born. Though his mother was Catholic, James was raised as a member of the Scottish protestant Kirk and educated by men with Presbyterian sympathies. James Stuart, on March 24, 1603, succeeded Elizabeth I as King James I of England and Ireland. Thus he served in that dual role until his death on March 27, 1625. This was known as the *Union of the Crowns*.

Though lacking the governmental skills of Queen Elizabeth I, the government of the kingdom was relatively stable during the years of his reign. However, James I experienced difficulties in meeting criticism from the parliament. His belief in the Divine Right of Kings made him unwilling to listen to any opposition to his diplomatic schemes.

James I chafed at the use of the Geneva Bible (1560), for it was annotated, and some of the comments were not favorable to his position on the Divine Right of Kings. In 1607, the King agreed to the labor of producing a new translation into English, and that translation, published in 1611, has been a blessing for many years. But King James was certainly no friend of our Baptist forefathers. In the first volume of this set, we mentioned the Baptist martyr Edward Wightman (April 1), and the year following the publication of the King James Version.

In 1614, Thomas Helwys, a daring Baptist, wrote the following letter to the King. It is a penned inscription in a book which Helwys authored entitled *The Mystery of Iniquity*. The Oxford University Library has a copy to this day. The letter reads,

> Heare o King, and dispise not ye counsell of ye poore, and let their complaints come before thee.
>
> The King is a mortall man, and not God therefore hath no power over ye immortall soules of his subjects, to make lawes and ordinances for them, and to set spiritual Lords over them.
>
> If the King have authority to make spirituall Lords and lawes, then he is an immortall God, and not a mortall man.
>
> O King, be not seduced to sin so against God, whome thou oughtest to obey, not against thy poore subjects who ought and will obey thee in all things with body life and goods, or else let their lives be taken from ye earth."
>
> God Save ye King
> Tho: Helwys.
>
> Spillefeild neare London

> One historian has said: "Spoken like a man! But what happened to such a rugged man who so dared to address such a King? He was jailed in Newgate prison and while there he died, probably in 1614, and certainly prior to 1616. What a debt Baptists,

> and others, owe to such a man! For let one mark it well! In this brief letter great principles are stated or implied. (a) A Christian should be loyal to civil authorities. (b) No King has authority over the consciences of men. This first principle of obedience to those in civil authority had been stated some eighty-five years prior to this time by H?bmaier, and it was this principle which caused Helwys to differ with the Anabaptists, Mennonites, and others. (c) Another principle implied here, is the principle of the separation of church and state, a principle to be clarified and expanded a bit later on by another Baptist, Roger Williams.
>
> Helwys, however, took a further step and, in his *A Short Declaration of the Mystery of Iniquity*, he made 'the first claim for freedom of worship to be published in the English language.[1]

Few Baptists even recognize the name of Thomas Helwys. But he and other courageous men of faith pioneered the way to provide our heritage of freedom. May we be faithful to our Lord and to these principles as we protect the freedom of worship and soul liberty for posterity.

DLC

---

[1] M. A. Huggins, *A History of North Carolina Baptists* (Raleigh: The General Board Baptist State Convention of North Carolina, 1967), 12.

July 25

"I Died at my Post"

Scripture: Nehemiah 7:2b

Any consideration of the founding of the first Baptist church in Chicago must begin with an acknowledgment of the importance of John Mason Peck. He was the forerunner of the Baptist ministry in the west. On this date John and Sally Peck said their farewells in Litchfield, Connecticut, and invaded the "wild west" with the Gospel. Their 1215 mile journey was completed December 1, 1817, as they entered St. Louis, Missouri. We have mentioned Peck doubtless shaped

Baptist life in Illinois more than any other has. He was a unique missionary-preacher of righteousness with a vision for the ongoing message of redemption.

In the early days of America's expansion to the west, Baptists were unable to supply a sufficient number of preachers. John Mason Peck pioneered the areas and knew the need well. In 1832 Peck led in establishing the American Baptist Home Mission Society to organize Baptist efforts in meeting the challenge. And that brings us to the city of Chicago.

A godly medical physician, Dr. John Temple, had moved to that spiritually needy field, and he, requested a friend to prevail upon Jonathan Going, Secretary of the American Baptist Home Mission Society, to send a missionary to Chicago. Dr. Temple promised financial assistance. A young student at Hamilton (later known as Colgate University), one Allen B. Freeman, had recently been appointed for service in Ohio. He was asked to change fields and go to Chicago. He was at first reluctant, but accepted the direction, and soon after was "convinced . . . that as to the place this [was] the most judicious appointment." Chicago at the time was a . . . wet prairie, as far as eye could reach . . . "a few scattered dwellings: . . . a small military post at the mouth of the river . . . . A trading post . . . three framed stores . . . and . . . a fourth commenced."[1]

Mr. Freeman arrived on the field in August of 1833, and almost immediately the construction of a small church building ensued. Sunday school classrooms were provided on the second floor and an auditorium utilized the first. On October 19, 1833, the church was organized with fifteen members. The service of Mr. Freeman was to extend only for a year and a half, but he was tireless in his efforts. In that brief period of time he was instrumental in establishing at least three churches.

Following a frigid winter, in April of 1834 Freeman submitted the following report: "Our Sunday School is flourishing. There being no Baptist Minister within a compass of 150 miles of me, while the country is filling up in an unparalleled manner with emigrants from all the East, and a large proportion favourable to Baptist views, who are inclined to religion at all, I could not confine my labours exclusively to Chicago. Since my last communication, I have preached 56 times, traveled into most of the settlements West, and South West of Chicago, within 50 miles."[2]

The roads were almost non-existent as Freeman rode horse-back fifty miles to the southwest to a place called Long Grove. There, early in December 1834, Mr. Freeman baptized a young man named David Matlock, who later became a faithful minister. As Mr. Freeman was returning home, his horse came up lame, and the youthful preacher waited two days hoping the horse would improve, but, rather than amending, it died. There being no public transportation, the twenty-seven-year-old-pastor set out to walk the eighteen miles home through the bitter winter weather. He arrived home with a severe cold which turned into terminal pneumonia. He died within ten days on December 15, 1834. His last words to his courageous wife were: "Tell my father I died at my post and in my Master's work."

With the growth of Chicago, the place of his burial has been lost to history. But in the north vestibule of the church building a tablet can be found with the following inscription:

In Memory of Allen B. Freeman.
Born 1806;
Founded this church October 19, 1833;
Died December 15, 1834. I die at my post and in my Master's service.[3]

Heroes of the faith such as Allen Freeman have made America a great nation.

DLC

---

1 Myron D. Dillow, *Harvesttime on the Prairie* (Franklin, TN: Providence House Publishers, 1996), 66-67.

2 Ibid., 67.

3 Justin A. Smith, *A History of the Baptists in the Western States* (Philadelphia: American Baptist Publication Society, 1896), 98.

July 26

From Disgrace to Grace

Scripture: 1 Corinthians 15:10

Born February 14, 1915, the sixth child of Mr. and Mrs. J. D. Greene, Oliver B., was a real live valentine to his parents. At the age of five, the lad almost died, but his godly mother sought the Lord. "You may have him, Lord," she prayed, " to use anywhere and in anyway you see fit. Just make him well."[1] The Lord intervened. However, ten years later, Oliver's rebellion drove Mrs. Greene to pray again. "Oh, dear God, how I do wish I had not prayed that night when Oliver was so sick that you would spare him. If you had taken him then, I know he would be with you now, but it seems that Oliver is going to hell in spite of all that anyone can do. If taking my life will cause him to be saved, then take me on." [2]

Oliver's sister, Sadie, also prayed fervently for her younger brother. He loved Sadie and his parents, but Oliver loved his sins more. Close calls did not deter him from evil. One night en route to steal from a local store, his car broke down. As he walked home, the proprietor stopped him and told him that he had been lying in wait armed for the thief, and was determined to kill him. Oliver sobered up temporarily but soon forgot those close calls. Surely Oliver escaped the penitentiary only by the grace of God.

One evening, in order to use the family car, Oliver had to take his sister to revival meetings. What happened that evening changed the world for the 20-year-old. He accepted God's payment for his sins that he thought too gross to be forgiven. The next morning when Sadie revealed what had happened at the tent the night before, her father did not believe it. Oliver's salvation was the talk of the town. He made restitution to everyone he had wronged.

Oliver accepted God's call to preach and bought a 40' by 60' tent for $375. He set it up in Greer, South Carolina, and began depending on God for his needs. How the Lord blessed! He was thrilled when God began using him in the salvation of the lost. His tents kept getting larger as he replaced worn-out ones. Over 200,000 professions of faith were recorded in his tent meetings, and it is estimated that more than 300 young men became preachers.

He attended a denominational school and became a popular student there. However, three months before graduation, though he was an excellent student, Oliver was asked to leave because he would not cooperate with the denominational program. He could not compromise his convictions.

Oliver preached church revivals and continued his tent ministry. The records of his meetings reveal that he preached over 9,000 times. The greatest number of recorded salvation decisions was 7,000 in a two-week meeting in Rocky Mount, North Carolina.

At its peak, his radio program, *The Gospel Hour*, was carried over 180 stations. On October 8, 1956, *The Gospel Hour* was officially incorporated into a non-profit ministry.[3] Oliver edited *The Gospel Hour News,* which was sent to 30,000 recipients a month. Using laymen's terms, he authored many pamphlets, sermon booklets, and commentaries that continue to be a blessing. His autobiography *From Disgrace to Grace* is the story of the black sheep of a respectable family before and after conversion.

Oliver married Ailene Collins on a Sunday morning during a revival meeting in Elberton, Georgia. Mrs. Greene was a godly example for women as she cared for her husband and children and made home a haven for Oliver. When home from meetings, Oliver greatly enjoyed his wife's fascinating qualities of flower gardening. Although he loved Jesus and looked forward to heaven, he also loved life and lived every moment to the fullest of his ability.

The Lord called His servant home on July 26, 1976. He never compromised his convictions, but remained true to the Lord who had saved him from disgrace. His sister never gave up on him, but fervently prayed for Oliver's salvation. May this be an encouragement to all of us to continue faithfully in praying for our lost loved ones.

DCB

---

[1] David B. Greene, *From Disgrace to Grace* (Greenville: The Gospel Hour, Inc., 1996), 13.

[2] Ibid., 14

[3] Ibid., 14

July 27

Little is Much When God is in it

Scripture: Matthew 25:21-23

As the American population expanded and extended westward, missionaries of the American Baptist Home Mission Society made the trek and attempted to plant Bible-believing Baptist churches all along the way. The North Pacific slope consisting of Orgeon, Washington, and Idaho presented unique problems. The population was quite sparse, but the Great Commission was not intended only for great metropolitan areas, but also for small towns and hamlets as well as rural areas. Wherever people settled, there was the need of evangelism, discipleship and church planting. Interestingly, though slavery never existed on the Pacific slope, a considerable portion of the population was originally from the South, and certain "Yankee" missionaries were at a decided disadvantage. But slowly inroads were made, spiritual advances developed, and churches were established.

The labor of love in eastern Washington and northern Idaho was closely associated with the work in eastern Oregon. Noah F. Lieuallen, Spencer Neil, and A. Land worked in Walla Walla County in the winter of 1867 and 1868. The first church in the region was formed in the "Blue Creek Schoolhouse," and it took the name of Friendship Baptist Church. Within a few years three other churches had been organized, but inasmuch as the population was quite transient, in time all of those works became extinct.

In 1873 Rev. William H. Pruett moved from the Willamette Valley, under the appointment of the American Baptist Home Mission Society, as the pioneer missionary from eastern Oregon, and settled at Western. In the course of his journeyings he visited Dayton, Washington, and there, on the fourth Sunday of July, 1873, he organized the Dayton Baptist Church, and thus began the permanent and continuous history of our work in eastern Washington. A house of worship was soon built, which, after some years was replaced by a substantial brick edifice in which the church now worships.[1]

May we be reminded in this account that the most important thing in the life of a believer is the will of God! In the sight of men, too often the size of the church that one pastors signifies the importance of that individual in the sight of God. Some have advocated that the mission budget of a church be determined by the professions of faith made through the ministry of each of the missionaries represented in the budget. How absurd! Our Lord is not willing that any should perish, and He is concerned for the less populated areas just as much as He cares for the vast megalopolises of our day. To be sure, we must be vitally interested in the population centers, but again, it is the will of God that each individual must be sought. I once read that Mr. Spurgeon reported the following: "A brother said to me, "I cannot do much with a hundred hearers," and I replied, 'You will find it hard work to give in a good account for even a hundred people.' And then the man of God added: 'I confess it very quietly, but I have often wished I had a little congregation, that I might watch over every soul in it; but now I am doomed to an everlasting dissatisfaction with my work, for what am I among so many?'"

Many pastors serve in rural ministries to this day. They are tucked away in areas that seemingly do not have great numerical potential. If they are faithful in the situation where the Lord has placed them, someday they will hear His wonderful words, "Well done, thou good and faithful servant." If the Lord is preparing them for work wherein there is more potential, He possesses their name, address and phone number, and He will direct them. Faith is exhibited not in distributing one's resume, but rather faith is living without scheming.

Faithful men in small fields often become distressed and oppressed, but they are greatly needed just where the Lord has put them. Today why not pray for missionaries and pastors who serve unknown and unheralded, but who serve sacrificially and selflessly? It should be the will of God we seek, nothing more, nothing less, and nothing else, and in His will He provides blessed contentment.

DLC

[1] A. H. Newman, *A Century of Baptist Achievement* (Philadelphia: American Baptist Publication Society, 1901), 106.

July 28

Giving Honor to Whom Honor is Due

Scripture: Romans 13:7

Pastor Kallam, known as B.W. to friends, was born Broadus Willard Kallam on July 28, 1917, to Thomas and Alice Kallam of Stoneville, North Carolina. He spent his childhood mostly in that farming area with his eight siblings. On October 9, 1937, he married Carrie Neil Tolbert. Together they reared three daughters: Lois, Deanie, and Wanda.

Brother Kallam was saved at the age of 31 under the ministry of Pastor Lamb of Community Baptist Church in Reidsville, North Carolina. Mrs. Kallam was saved at the same time; and soon thereafter both were baptized. Having received the call to preach Brother Kallam was ordained to the gospel ministry on October 24, 1954, at the Community Baptist Church where he was a member. Dr. Charles Stevens, pastor of Salem Baptist Church and president of Piedmont Bible College in Winston Salem, North Carolina, served on the ordination council.

Brother Kallam was a godly man. Although limited in education, he became a good pastor through dedication. He received some training at Piedmont Bible College, but most of his knowledge came from personal study as he served the Lord. Once ordained, B.W. became pastor of Wayside Baptist Church in Reidsville, North Carolina, and through personal soul winning and preaching, brought the small congregation of a dozen to approximately 300.[1]

On September 25, 1960, Pastor Kallam began pastoring the McLeansville Baptist Church in McLeansville, North Carolina, where he was used of the Lord to bring about revival. Under his leadership, this 60 member church grew to over 500. Many were assured of their salvation because of his Bible teaching on the doctrine of security. The church went through several building programs including an auditorium to seat approximately 500 people. My wife, Betty, was saved and baptized in this church, having been led to the Lord by Mrs. Kallam.

Brother Kallam's genuine interest in young people led to his ministry in the lives of "preacher boys," as he referred to them. These young men came from Bible college to his church for extension work. Many gained valuable experience under his pastoral leadership, and many men were called to preach under his ministry. For several years he also carried on a radio ministry which God used in the Piedmont area of North Carolina.

I had the privilege of holding numerous revival meetings for Brother Kallam and was a member of his church for several years. Brother Kallam officiated at our wedding and preached the funeral of our first child. Years later he participated in the wedding of our daughter at McLeansville Baptist Church.

Though little is known of Brother Kallam outside of the Carolinas, he was well-known among a great number of friends, and converts who were saved through his influence. His charismatic personality made him a favorite among preachers. He enjoyed attending revivals, preachers' fellowships, gospel singspirations, and services wherever the Word of God was expounded. He would take a carload or church busload of people to nearby meetings to hear great men of God. This was a social event for some young people of the church and a way to expose the unsaved to gospel preaching. Many young people were saved in revival meetings in his own church.

Brother Kallam's mate of 20 years went to be with the Lord on June 26, 1990. Mrs. Kallam was truly a servant of the Lord who led many to the Savior. She was a great help in her husband's work. Her sweet spirit and love for the Lord were an encouragement to the people of the church and she, too, was much loved. Brother Kallam continued his preaching ministry even after his retirement on October 13, 1985. In 1992, Brother Kallam married Ailene Simpson, a faithful member of his church.[2] She cared for him until his death on June 26, 1996.

May God raise up more men in our day who are as worthy of honor as Brother Kallam and who are as loath as he was to seek such recognition for themselves.

DCB

---

[1] Personal letter from Wanda Kallam Stewart, daughter of B.W. Kallam, to Bettye Baughan, dated May 17, 2004.

[2] Phone conversation with Faye Gaulden, Church Clerk at McLeansville Baptist Church, on June 5, 2004.

July 29

The Price of Freedom

Scripture: Isaiah 58:1-14

In 1572 the continent of Europe was ablaze with the fires of persecution; human bodies were lighting men everywhere to a better day. Protestant persecuted Catholic and Catholic persecuted Protestant, and both persecuted the Anabaptists. In no country was there more bloodshed than in Holland, under the inquisition of Philip II of Spain and Duke Alva (ruler of the Netherlands). Early in 1572 Henry II of England and Philip of Spain made a treaty to put all Netherland Protestants to death. At that time, William, the Prince of Orange, was only twenty-six, but he resolved to stir up the Protestant population of the Netherlands to throw off the Spanish yoke. There were several early victories, which aroused popular sympathy, but appeals for financial aid were met with very limited success. William had spent his fortune, sold his gold and jewels, and mortgaged his estates. He was at the end of his resources when a seemingly trivial circumstance gave him new courage.

Early on an April morning, William was walking near his headquarters at Dillenburg. Two strangers approached him and asked to speak with him. These two were Jacob Fredericks and Dirk Jans Cortenbosch, Dutch Anabaptist preachers. They had been visiting fellow Anabaptists on the Rhine, and on their return home they decided to see if there was some way they could serve the prince. They explained to him the principles of Anabaptism, and the prince asked them for a contribution of money. On May 5 he sent his secretary with a letter to his new friends pleading: "Let every one contribute. This is a time when even with small sums more can be effected than at other times with ampler funds. His lordship will ever be ready to reward them for such good and faithful service to the common cause and to their prince."[1]

Years of persecution had left the Anabaptists with little beside their patriotism; yet, on July 29, 1572, they brought their patriotic offering of a thousand florins to the prince at Remund. The prince had already faithfully kept his word. At a meeting of the Estates of Holland, on July 15, he had been declared governor in place of the Duke of Alva. Almost immediately he proclaimed that "the freedom of religion shall be guarded; every body shall exercise it freely in private or in public, in church or in chapel, without let or hindrance from any one."[2] When the Baptists made their offering to him out of their poverty and under the burden of a large number of widows and orphans left by thousands of their martyrs, he asked them: "Do you make no demand?" They answered, "Nothing but the friendship of your grace, if God grants to you the government of our Netherlands." He assured them of his sympathy for them and for all men, and he kept faith with them to the letter. No one understood the prince. Not even his nearest friends understood the reason for his views. They could understand freedom for Calvinism, but not a wide freedom of conscience for everyone.

The result of this long, dark struggle was that the radical principle of soul liberty for Christians found its way into the first compact of States since the foundation of Christianity. While this document was not a constitution, but only a compact, it became the foundation-stone of the Netherland Republic. The Netherlands soon became the refuge of the oppressed from most of the nations of Europe. In 1579 Article XIII of the Union of Utrecht declared: "Every one shall be free in the practice of his religious belief, and that, in accordance with the peace of Ghent, no one shall be held or examined on account of matters of religion." The Anabaptists flourished in the Netherlands. English Separatists also came to the Netherlands to enjoy its religious freedom. One group, under the leadership of John Smythe, Thomas Helwys, and John Murton, concluded that baptism was only for believers and became the founders of the modern Baptist movement. Baptists should ever be grateful for the liberty secured by William and for the contribution of two Anabaptist preachers in a time of need.

LRO

---

[1] Thomas Armitage, *A History of the Baptists* (New York: Bryan, Taylor, and Co., 1890), 417

[2] Ibid.

July 30

For Whom did Christ Die?

Scripture: 1 Timothy 2:6; 2 Peter 2:1; 1 John 2:2

Of course the Particular Baptist preachers would not baptize the twenty-five-year-old man. Oh, to be sure, he spoke of regeneration, but he had the audacity to believe that Christ had died for the sins of all mankind! Imagine that! The historian recounts that Dan Taylor "applied to several ministers of the Particular Baptist persuasion; but they all refused to baptize him....They disapproved of his sentiments respecting the extent of the death of Christ."[1]

Dan Taylor was born into the home of a coal miner near Halifax, England. At the age of five the lad began working in the coal mines. Though short of stature, the youth made up for it with an agile mind. He early learned to read, and often he would take a book with him into the coal mine to read at any spare moments. His parents were not greatly religious, but at the age of sixteen the young man was confirmed in the Church of England. However, in a short time the teenager began attending Methodist preaching wherever he could find it. He walked for miles to hear John Wesley. Feeling called to preach, young Mr. Taylor presented himself to the Methodists and was soon a lay preacher. His first sermon was delivered in September 1761, and he became quite well known among the Methodists. However, objecting to the strict discipline and the almost dictatorial leadership of John Wesley, he withdrew from that fellowship. He continued to preach, and in time gathered a small group of converts comprised mostly of the poor.

Through his study, in 1762 Taylor became convinced of believer's baptism, and it was at that time that he approached the Particular Baptists requesting such baptism. Though repudiated by those men, one of the pastors referred him to some General Baptists in Lincolnshire who concurred with his doctrine of the atonement. He set out to find the General Baptists on February 11, 1763, and after convincing them of his orthodoxy, he was immersed on February 16, 1763.

Some few of his new friends of the Leicestershire fellowship accompanied him back to his home, and his little flock was organized as a General Baptist church. On July 30 of that year, Dan Taylor was ordained and thus began the unusual impact that Dan Taylor would have on the Baptists of England.

Learning of the local Lincolnshire Baptist Association, Taylor led his congregation to affiliate with it. Soon, however, he became disillusioned. He did not find the warm evangelism that he had experienced among the Leicestershire fellowship. Furthermore he discovered that the doctrines of the Arians and Socinians were tolerated. He confronted the leadership, but found no satisfaction. As a result Taylor led his congregation to a position of separation. They professed a strong position concerning Christology. Congregational singing became a vital part of their worship. Needless to say, they were very evangelistic. This led to continual conflicts with the older General Baptists.

On June 6, 1770, the New Connection of General Baptists was formed, and Dan Taylor became the leading light. For the next forty-six years the intrepid leader was a dynamo. He published 45 pieces, from brief tracts to major works. In his diary he counted any day as wasted if he did not preach one or two sermons, visit different churches, and write several pages of some treatise. His schedule was continually teeming with activity.[2] Dan Taylor was the unquestioned leader among the New Connection. He was ever mindful of the doctrinal position of the preachers, and if he perceived that a pastor was approaching the dangers of Arian or Socinian views, he was prompt in confronting and reprimanding him.

Dan Taylor died in London on November 26, 1816. Like all man-made organizations, the New Connection ran its course, and the second law of spiritual thermodynamics overtook it. In 1891 the New Connection lost its identity as it merged with the Baptist Union of Great Britain. It was swallowed up with the liberalism that permeates the Baptist Union to this day. May the Lord raise up twenty-first century editions of Dan Taylor in Great Britain in our day.

DLC

---

[1] Adam Taylor, *Memoirs of the Rev. Dan Taylor* (London: T. Bore, 1818), 11-12.

[2] H. Leon McBeth, *The Baptist Heritage* (Nashville, TN: Broadman Press, 1987), 165.

July 31

Old Time Power

Scripture: 2 Corinthians 10:4

"Old time" Baptist preachers often found themselves threatened by irate husbands whose wives professed faith in Christ and/or desired to be baptized. Scenes of impending danger from wrathful mates have been graphically recorded in our histories. Such an example is found in the account of D. L. Mansfield's life, a nineteenth century Kentucky Baptist preacher.

D. L. Mansfield, oldest of eight sons, was born on June 18, 1797. His education was quite limited, but he was ambitious to learn. During his youth, he served on a surveying team, which took him into Missouri. Wanting to excel, he studied the art of surveying and was soon appointed a deputy. Upon returning to Kentucky, he married Miss Elizabeth Barnett on July 31, 1817.

As a young husband, he began to think seriously of life and fell under conviction for his sins. Through the preaching of John Berry, a "circuit riding" Cumberland Presbyterian minister, D. L. was saved. Interestingly he had gone to the meeting with the intention of intimidating the preacher, but left the service under great conviction. The arrows of God's Word penetrated his mind, and for ten days his soul agonized. As pressure mounted, he spent a day seeking the Lord's forgiveness, and the simplicity of salvation was finally realized. He praised the Lord for the reality of peace with God. Having been so impacted by the Cumberland Presbyterian preacher, it was only natural that he would affiliate with that denomination. However, he delayed that decision until he had time to read the New Testament. Upon completing that task, he became a convinced immersionist, and thus in August 1820, united with the Stony Point Baptist Church in Logan County.

The joy of the Lord was upon him, and soon he began declaring spiritual truth to those about him. The congregation was so impressed that they sent D. L. to Robert Anderson's academy at Glasgow to study for a year. In November of 1823, he was ordained and began preaching in connection with the Providence Baptist Church in Warren County. Two years later, he was asked to become pastor of that church, and served there through the remainder of his life.

D. L. Mansfield never lost his love of evangelism, and his appeals to sinners seemed irresistible. In the fall of 1832, a wonderful revival pervaded the churches in his area. This was before the time of protracted or extended evangelistic meetings. Most of the services were held in private homes. D. L. devoted himself to the work with great zeal. He preached day and night from house to house wherever invitations were extended. In a year's time, the young pastor had baptized about three hundred people.

Needless to say, everyone did not concur with either the message or manner of this spiritual movement. From time to time the fervent preacher met with violent opposition. "At the house of Simon Shaw, ... [T]he wife of Sandy Spillman, and two daughters of William Doors, came forward for prayer. The husband and father of these women became enraged, and threatened violence to the . . . preacher, vowing, at the same time, that they would have their women out of the house, if they had to drag them out. Mr. Mansfield replied in a conciliatory manner, that the moon would be up presently, and then they would come out. After some other threats of violence, the men withdrew. Next night, at the house of John Spillman, the outlaws were still more violent. . . . Knowing that the men were desperadoes, the friends of Mr. Mansfield. . . advised him to arm himself. . . . He replied, 'The weapons of our warfare are not carnal,' and added, 'I will pray for them.' The following night, while Mr. Mansfield was hitching his horse, [Mr.] Doors approached him, and began to confess his sins, and to beg him to pray for him and Spillman. On his way to the house, he found Spillman on his knees, praying for mercy. Both of the men, the wife, and the two daughters, were baptized a few days afterwards."[1]

Let us pray, "Lord, revive us again!"

DLC

[1] J. H. Spencer, *A History of Kentucky Baptists* (Gallatin, TN: Church History Research & Archives, 1984), 2:262-263.

August 1

Jamaica's Emancipator

Scripture: Exodus 5:1-23

It has often been remarked that when God is about to execute some great purpose, he prepares the appropriate individuals beforehand. One such individual was William Knibb. In the early nineteenth century, while doing missionary work in Jamaica, Knibb, an English Baptist missionary, was brought face to face with the horrors of slavery. His whole manhood revolted, and he vowed that he would not rest until freedom was granted to these slaves.

In 1810 at the age of seven, Knibb entered the Sunday school at Kettering, with which he was associated until he moved to Bristol to be apprenticed to a printer. Dr. John Ryland baptized him in 1822.

He followed his brother Thomas to Jamaica to engage in mission school work among the slaves. The authorities did all they could to restrict this missionary enterprise. The House of Assembly passed an act called "a consolidated slave law." It contained clauses restricting evangelical missions. As a result, a storm of persecution broke over Knibb and his colleagues. Knibb was thrown into prison and charged with inciting the slaves to rebellion. The Attorney General declared that there was no case against the missionary, and Knibb set out for England upon a holy crusade of freedom. He reached Liverpool in June 1832.

The Missionary Committee under which Knibbs served regarded slavery as a political question and required their representatives to be silent upon the subject. Knibb met with the committee and was advised to be prudent and temperate. He declared, "Myself, my wife, and my family are entirely dependent on the Baptist Mission. We have landed without a shilling, and may at once be reduced to penury. But, if it be necessary, I will take them by the hand and walk barefoot through the kingdom but I will make known to the Christians of England what their brethren in Jamaica are suffering."[1] At a public meeting in Spa Fields Chapel, where

Mr. Knibb was speaking, the secretary of the Missionary Society thought he was going a little too far and pulled his coattails as an admonition. The touch was understood. Knibb raised his voice and said, "Whatever be the consequences, I will speak. At the risk of my connection with the Society and all that I hold dear I will avow this. If the friends of missions will not hear me I will tell it to my God, nor will I desist till this greatest of curses is removed, and 'Glory to God in the highest' is inscribed on the British flag."[2] It was a dramatic moment. The audience caught the spirit of the hero who could not be silenced. The place rang with cheers.

All England rang with the eloquence of William Knibb. Churches and committees, timid at first, were carried along by the contagion of courage. When he returned to Jamaica, the slaves received him with great rejoicing. Before long the news came that on August 1, 1834, the children of slave families were to be regarded as free, and August 1, 1838, was to bring the complete liberation of the whole slave population. Knibb and an associate led 14,000 adult slaves and 5,000 children in a service of praise and thanksgiving. A mahogany coffin was made, and a grave was dug. In the coffin they packed the whips, the branding irons, and other badges of slavery. As the hour of freedom dawned, Knibb cried, "The monster is dying," and when the hour of twelve had struck, he exclaimed, "The monster is dead; let us bury him! The negro is free." The coffin was lowered into the ground. The winds of freedom were loosed, men and women cried with joy, and William Knibb saw the accomplishment of the work to which he had consecrated his life.[3]

Seven years later, after preaching, he returned to his house exhausted. It was whispered that he was ill, and a little later he was dead. Forty-two years is a short life as we count age, but for William Knibb it was long enough to accomplish a task so colossal that it seems impossible and to leave a record of heroism which time will neither obliterate nor dim.

LRO

---

[1] John C. Carlile, *The Story of the English Baptists* (London: James Clarke & Co., 1905), 206-207.

[2] Ibid., 207.

[3] Ibid., 208.

August 2

Baptist Camp Meetings

Scripture: 2 Chronicles 7:12-22

Though in the entry of April 2, credit was given to the Presbyterians for the origination of camp meetings in America, it is well that we point out that more recent research points to an early Baptist presence in such efforts. James Beller has noted that "Many historians mistakenly credit the Presbyterians and James McGready with the invention of the camp meeting during the Great Revival of the West in 1800, but the record clearly points 42 years earlier to the 'Apostle of the Backcountry' and his army of converts."[1] Mr. Beller credits Shubal Stearns and the Sandy Creek Baptist Association in North Carolina with the origination of the camp meeting.

Regardless of the origin of the camp meetings, they have been important to the Baptists for many years. The camp meeting is a rock, an island of stability in an unsettled, sinful world.[2] The format of the camp meetings has not changed. Preachers, singers, and attendees grow older and move off the scene and another generation takes their places. The camp meeting is a place where friends meet to renew acquaintances and refresh their souls from the preaching of God's Word and singing of the old hymns of Zion. Though the late 20th and early 21st centuries have seen a loss of attendance of camp meetings in general, where the practice has continued, the camp meeting has provided a blessed refuge from the world.

Much can be accomplished at camp meetings. It would be well to have a definitive study that would reveal how many people surrendered their lives for God's service during the days of intense preaching. Of course, only eternity will really provide the statistics as to how many have been born again and called to preach or serve the Lord on the mission fields of the world through such efforts. It is certain that the camp meeting is a revival of dedication for many.

The preparation for the meeting requires much physical labor. The building or tent, or whatever is being used to house the meeting, has to be prepared. The grounds have to be cleaned, grass mowed, sawdust laid, chairs set up, pulpit supplied, instruments placed, songbooks gathered, parking areas readied, restroom facilities provided, water and power turned on, letters sent, announcements published, phone calls made, and speakers and musicians scheduled. Preparing and operating the facilities take money. Those working behind the scenes are often overlooked, but God will remember them as they reap rewards for all eternity.

An example of a successful camp meeting is the Greer Baptist Camp Meeting, which began in 1947 in Pelham, South Carolina, in a brush arbor with sawdust on the ground. Year after year, with the help of Percy Ray, Odell Good, and Dan Norris, it became a yearly meeting, which still exists. For many years Evangelist Billy Kelly was the director of the camp.[3]

Churches across America put up tents in the summer for these old-fashioned camp meetings. Songwriters have felt impressed to put music to words for people to sing about the old camp meetings. Such a favorite is the *Old Camp Meetin' Time* by Ira F. Stanphill.

How often we have gathered at old camp meetin' time
And felt the Spirit movin', as voices sang in rhyme,
Our hearts were filled with heaven, as Jesus sent the flood
And sinners found salvation and cleansing in the blood.
I hear the bells a ringin', their signal strong and clear,
The meetin' time up yonder, is drawing very near,
I'm waiting now for Gabriel to blow his trumpet loud,
Then take my place up yonder, with that camp meetin' crowd.

It has been my privilege to preach in several camp meetings over the years. Trinity Baptist Church in Wilson, North Carolina celebrated its 30th year of camp meetings on August 2-6, 2004. May the Lord allow this oasis in the summer time to continue where God's people can gather for singing, fellowship, and old-time preaching of that blessed Book. And if you have never attended a good, old camp meeting, you might want to consider such an experience during a week of your vacation.

DCB

---

[1] James R. Beller, *America in Crimson Red* (Arnold, MO: Prairie Fire Press, 2004), 158-159.

[2] James H. Sightler, *50 years of the Greer Baptist Campmeeting*. July 4, 1997.

[3] Ibid.

August 3

Learning From History

Scripture: Psalm 78:1-8

John Asplund was born in Sweden, but being devoted in his early life to mercantile pursuits, he visited England, and for a short time was employed as a clerk. With an adventuresome spirit, he joined the British navy, and sailed to America. His personal interest in North Carolina caused him to desert when his ship was docked. However, in the overruling of providence, the Lord arranged that the youthful Swede "happened" to be in an area where the gospel was flourishing.

On August 3, 1769, the Kehukee Baptist Association had been formed with five area churches, and the association grew quite rapidly. The Baptists were expanding, and the preaching of Elder David Walsh in the Ballard's Bridge Baptist Church attracted Asplund. Previously the area had been known for its wickedness. "Burkitt in speaking of the section around Ballard's Bridge says, 'The small children were so well trained up in vice, that a small boy about nine or ten years of age had a pack of cards, and was challenging the whole company to play.'"[1] But the amazing grace of God transforms not only individuals but entire districts as well. In 1782, John Asplund was soundly converted and was baptized into the membership of the church. Following that, he moved to Southampton, Virginia. His ministerial gifts were recognized, and he was ordained and began ministering.

In 1785 he returned to Europe and visited England, Denmark, Finland, Lapland, and Germany. On returning to America, he traveled throughout the states collecting statistical information concerning Baptist churches. In 1791 Reverend Aslund published a small volume that contained many valuable facts. In the introduction of the work, he wrote:

> I have long been desirous, and have waited several years to see a publication of the nature of the following. And though I was sensible I could publish nothing of the kind without the fatigue and

expense of traveling over the greatest part of the continent, yet, at the request of many, I have been prevailed upon to make the tour of the Baptist churches to obtain the necessary information. With a view to this, I have travelled about 7,000 miles, in about eighteen months, chiefly on foot, and have visited about two hundred and fifteen churches, and fifteen associations. I am personally acquainted with two hundred and fifty ministers of our society, so that the Register may safely be depended upon in general, though after all, perhaps a few churches and ministers may be omitted. It is probable also, that the number of members in some churches may not be exact, as some do not associate while others who do, neglect to send forward their number, and some make conscience of numbering the people.

Having been brought up with a view to the business of merchandize, I have been accustomed to keeping accounts; and I now prefer accounts of souls with their faces set Zionward, to those which only respect money or trade. I have a natural turn for travelling, and I am convinced I could not better spend my time, than in itinerating to preach the gospel, and to collect materials which may assist the future historian; and though I have met with many discouragements from narrow-minded persons, whose illiberal souls are not concerned for the public welfare, I appeal to the searcher of hearts, that my principle design is to make the Baptists better acquainted with each other, that union may more generally obtain amongst them.

John Asplund, a Swede.

Southampton county, Va. July 14, 1791.[2]

In his history of Virginia Baptists, Semple concludes the story by recording the fact that John Asplund drowned in Maryland in 1807 as he attempted to swim across the Fishing Creek.

The Register has proved invaluable in discovering the early work of the Lord among Baptists in our land. Unfortunately, many modern-day Baptists have no interest in our past. We have a glorious past, and now let us rejoice in it and set our face toward an even more fruitful future.

DLC

[1] George Washington Pashchal, *History of North Carolina* (Raleigh: North Carolina State Convention, 1930), 1:527.

[2] John Asplund, *The Annual Register of the Baptist Denomination in North America* (Lafayette, TN: Church History and Research and Archives, 1979), Preface.

August 4

A Frontier Preacher

Scripture: Romans 11:29

If the Wild, Wild West was to be conquered, it surely would take a special breed of men, and George Webb Slaughter was well fitted for the peculiar work that he undertook. G. W., as he was called, was poverty stricken, and before entering Texas, he split rails for bread in Louisiana. G. W. was actually unpretentious, but his stocky frame had been toughened by hard labor, and he was ready for almost any kind of service. In 1831 G. W. joined a Methodist church in Texas, but upon hearing a Baptist preacher, he was challenged to study God's Word. In time he became a convicted Baptist.

When the war broke out between Texas and Mexico, G. W. Slaughter responded immediately. He soon became the trusted scout of Sam Houston. Houston sent him to Fannin and Travis with secret messages of the greatest importance, and though the undertaking was hazardous, it was executed bravely. A second time he was sent to bear a message to the ill-fated commander of the Alamo, but coming within sound of the booming cannon, he knew that the garrison was doomed. Rather than fleeing, he hid himself in a clump of woods on the edge of the prairie to await developments. On the day following the bombardment, he saw a man and woman approaching. The two proved to be Mrs. Dickenson, the heroine of the Alamo, and the negro servant of Colonel Travis. The two had been spared by Santa Anna to bear dispatches to Houston, telling of the total defeat of the Americans. G. W. directed the two safely to General Houston and received commendations for his bravery from the commander.[1]

At the cessation of hostilities, G. W. obtained a leave of absence to return home to be married. He and his wife obtained the first marriage license granted in the new Republic, and his marriage was the first after Texas obtained its independence. G. W. studied medicine and for years was the only physician in Palo Pinto County. But he could not get away from the call of God to preach. He delivered his first sermon on December 4, 1865, and it was the first sermon ever preached at Fort Davis, located at the Clear Fork, just across the line in Stephens County.

Historians report that during his voluntary evangelism he was equipped with a Texas pony, a lariat, coffeepot, rifle, a brace of six-shooters, and his Bible. Between the years of 1859 and 1871, he organized twenty-one Baptist churches and baptized 907 people. It is said that during his total ministry he actually baptized 2,509 people. He was fearless and was a western Boanerges thundering the anathemas of the Gospel into the ears of rough Texas pioneers.

In this twenty-first century, many preachers look forward to the leisure of retirement. They plan for the time when they can fish and loaf. Somehow they envision that as fulfillment. But amazingly, in 1878 when G. W. Slaughter was seventy years of age, he purposed to continue planting Baptist churches. On a high elevation within sight of his own residence, six miles north of the town of Palo Pinto, stood the Slaughter Valley Baptist Church, organized on August 4, 1877, with seventeen members. In the same month, [G. W.] organized the Elm Grove Baptist Church on August 4, 1877, with seventeen members.... [He founded] the Lake Creek Baptist Church, nine miles south of Palo Pinto, in November 1877, with eleven members. All of these churches added a third to their membership within a year of their organization dates.[2]

George Webb Slaughter passed away in 1895 having preached without compensation. The Lord had blessed him financially, and he had prospered in raising stock on the western plains. Though he had everything a nineteenth century Texan could have longed for, yet he gave himself to extensive missionary service.

Pastor friend and missionary friend, why are you considering retirement? What could be better than serving until the day of your home going? After all, God's call is without repentance.

DLC

---

[1] B. F. Riley, *History of the Baptists of Texas* (Dallas, TX: Published for the Author, 1907), 49.

[2] Zane Allen Maxon, *Frontiersmen of the Faith* (San Antonio, TX: The Naylor Company, 1970), 99-100.

August 5

A Sermon Blessed of God

Scripture: 2 Timothy 4:1-2

The three-room log cabin was already crowded with four children and their sharecropper parents, David and Sarah Lee, when Robert Green Lee was born on November 11, 1886. The old black nurse who attended the mother, lifted the little baby and exclaimed, "Praise Gawd! Glory be! The good Lawd done sont a preacher to dis here house. Yas, suh! Yes, ma'am! Dat's what He's done gone and done."[1] Thus R. G. Lee made his appearance into an amazingly humble lifestyle. Surely only in America could one rise from abject poverty to be known among Bible-believing Christians as one of the outstanding preachers of his day.

David was rather austere, but he and Sarah provided an environment that was anchored in God's Word. As a lad of twelve, R. G. Lee professed faith in the Savior and was baptized August 5, 1898. Almost immediately the youth sensed the call of God to preach. This became his all-consuming desire. While peers played, he studied. Perhaps because his father was not enthused at having a preacher-son, R. G. promised his father he would remain on the farm until he was 21. Educational opportunities were limited, but the youth made it to the eighth grade. He supplemented his studies by reading any book available.

Upon reaching the age of majority, he set out to obtain sufficient education to fulfill his dream. He discovered that our government needed workers for the Panama Canal construction. He applied, was accepted, and borrowed money to get to the job site. The travel was exciting, but R. G. had a single mind. His immediate goal accomplished, he returned home in 1908 to enter the preparatory school that would allow advancement. Discovering that his father had incurred additional indebtedness, he graciously cared for those expenses. After paying his metriculation fee, young Lee had thirty-six cents remaining.

Undaunted, he excelled in his studies. During his college career at Furman, he held evangelistic meetings in surrounding churches with God's evident blessing. Student pastorates, revival meetings, and the winning of the senior oration contest crowned his schedule.

At age thirty-one, R. G. Lee became pastor of the famed Bellevue Baptist Church of Memphis, Tennessee. From that pulpit the sharecropper's son became one of America's best-known preachers. Volumes could be written concerning his accomplishments, but I desire to focus on one sermon in Dr. Lee's repertoire. While serving First Baptist Church in Edgefield, South Carolina, the young pastor preached a never-dying sermon entitled "Pay Day-Some Day." This doubtless ranks as one of the most famous sermons ever preached. The message was presented as a brief sermon, but following the service, one of the church members approached the pastor and said: "You've got something there, my boy. Why don't you make a full-length sermon out of it? I think it is wonderful." That was the challenge the young pastor needed. He went home and worked on the message until two in the morning. Rather than a brief oration, the sermon became a message requiring an hour and fifteen minutes to deliver. The Lord blessed the message, and countless numbers of men and women came to trust Christ personally as Dr. Lee preached the sermon time and again.

Upon accepting the call to Bellevue Baptist Church, Dr. Lee set the precedence of preaching the message on the first Sunday of May each year. Because of his inability to fulfill all the requests to deliver the sermon, it was deemed wise to produce a film of the presentation and make it available to audiences far and near. It is estimated that over a million people have heard that amazing sermon. Surely we would agree with the evaluation of a dear man of God that said: "I do not see how anyone can listen to that message and not be saved."

Perhaps a young man whose heart has been burdened to preach the gospel is reading these lines. If that were the case, let me assure him that "God is not a respecter of persons," and He will use any willing vessel!

DLC

---

[1] E. Schuyler English, *Robert G. Lee, A Chosen Vessel* (Grand Rapids, MI: Zondervan Publishing House, 1949), 25.

August 6

From Infidelity to Assurance

Scripture: Psalm 14:1; 53:1

It is difficult to understand how a child reared in a fine Christian home could deny the faith and become an infidel. But such was the case of Jesse Babcock Worden, who was born on July 18, 1787, into the home of John and Elizabeth Worden. Jesse was the last of the family of nine children, and because no educational facility was available in Richmond, Rhode Island, when he was twelve years old he did not even know the alphabet. However, when it became possible for Jesse to attend a school for two months, he gained an insatiable desire to learn that led him to pursue every opportunity to expand his mind. By the time he was eighteen, he became a teacher! When he was sixteen his father had died, and this meant Jesse had to care for his own needs.

The young man moved for employment's sake, and there he met an infidel. Casually his new-found associate began to poison Jesse's mind, and soon Jesse became an avowed atheist.

About 1808 he moved to Otsego County, New York, and in 1812 was drafted into the sixteenth Regiment of the New York Militia. He marched to the Niagara frontier, and served as Sergeant Major and ultimately as Lieutenant. Following the war he returned home to enter the mercantile business. Settling in Sangerfield, Oneida County, New York, in December, 1813, he married Miss Hannah Norton, a fine Presbyterian lady. To that union five children were born. Jesse was a good husband and father, but, as a skeptic, he would have nothing to do with religion. However, in the back of his mind, Jesse could never forget his godly parental instruction from early days.

In the early 1840s revival swept the area, and the Baptists were forced to enlarge their building to accommodate new growth. The church family had a deadline, and men volunteered labor. Jesse had gone into town to instruct his employees, and preparing to return home, he stopped to see the construction at the Baptist church. He wondered why intelligent men would volunteer their time to construct a building for the God who did not exist. As he stood watching, the Holy Spirit convicted him that they were not doing this for a non-existent Deity, but for a living God! Nothing short of truth could cause men to so give themselves to such a project without human remuneration. Under conviction he staggered home to ask his wife's forgiveness for his cruelty when she had sought to worship. Conviction was heavy upon his heart, but in three day's time the Holy Spirit won, and Jesse came to full assurance of salvation. He and his wife were baptized in 1816 by Elder John Peck, and united with the Baptist church.

Jesse was transformed! He lost interest in business, and gave himself wholly to knowing the Scriptures. This led to witnessing, and in 1818 he began preaching. The following year he was ordained, and from that time Jesse Worden became a fruitful servant of God. He was distinguished for his great transparency of character. His ministry was greatly blessed of God in pastorates at Marcellus, New York, and Montrose and Jackson, Pennsylvania. He purposed to visit in the home of every one of his members at least quarterly. His was the honor of baptizing hundreds upon their professions of faith, and his ministry became known throughout the area. He enjoyed a fruitful evangelistic ministry.

Mrs. Worden passed away on July 4, 1849, in Jackson, Pennsylvania. It is pleasing to note that all five of the Worden children grew up to know and love their Lord, and were each active in the Baptist churches in their areas. Reverend Worden lived on for an additional six years, but his health began to wane. For the last two years of his life he could no longer serve as pastor, but two weeks before his death, on August 6, 1855, in his sixty-ninth year, he preached his last message. He urged listeners to "See that ye love one another with a pure heart, fervently." As death approached he assured those around him that he had no fears, but only a calm, clear, firm faith, the growth of many years.

How important that parents take time not only to instruct children in God's Word, but also to lead them to a personal relationship with the living God through His wonderful Son.

DLC

August 7

Making Melody in Your Heart to the Lord

Scripture: Ephesians 5:19-20

I enjoy picturing in my mind's eye the old circuit riding Baptist preachers who pioneered in the old South. As I think of Kentucky, Squire Boone, brother of Daniel Boone comes to mind. He ". . . may well have been the first Baptist preacher in Kentucky. He was first in Louisville, in Meade County, and the first to perform a Baptist marriage on August 7, 1776."[1]

Baptist preachers like Squire Boone must have been robust. They usually traveled in an itinerant ministry by horseback. Their trademark was a broad-brimmed, black hat that was useful in protecting them from both the sun and rain. Usually they journeyed with a leather pouch that protected their Bible and hymnbook. Streams and rivers presented no deterrent to their progress, for they and their horses would enter the stream or river at one bank and swim to the other. When the waterway could be crossed by wading, the preacher would remove the saddle and carry it above his head. These men were most versatile, for not only did they preach, but there was no piano or organ to assist in congregational singing. They would lead the congregational singing with the force of their voice. Rarely could one find a hymnal among a congregation, and thus these preachers were forced to lead the singing by "lining a hymn." It was interesting just how this was done. Hymn tunes were identified and known by church members. Modern-day hymnals until recent date retained the name of tunes such as "*Woodworth*," to which would be sung "*Just As I Am*" or "*God Calling Yet! Shall I Not Hear?*" The tune entitled "*Warwick*" provided the tune for the congregation to sing the words of "*Amazing Grace*" or perhaps the hymn titled "*Come, Let Us Join Our Cheerful Songs.*" Many times the congregation would know the tune but not the words, and the preacher would read or "scan" a line of a hymn, and the congregation would then sing the line of the hymn previously repeated by the preacher. Thus the congregation would sing the entire hymn, and the exercise of singing helped enthrone the message of grace in their hearts and minds.

"Occasionally amusing incidents occurred from this practice. One such embarrassing situation occurred when the pastor arose and said, 'My specks are bad and my eyes are dim: I can hardly see to read this hymn.' The congregation mistook the preacher's apology for poor vision and sang the apology as though it were a line of the hymn. The preacher announced again, 'I didn't mean that was a hymn—I merely meant my eyes were dim.' The congregation sang again. By this time the preacher was somewhat disgusted and said, 'If that's all you brethren know, I will take my hat and go.' The congregation sang this statement back to the preacher, still believing it was a part of the hymn."[2]

I cannot vouch for the accuracy of that supposed event. I do know, however, that often times present-day Baptist congregations sing stanzas of hymns by rote without thinking of the great doctrinal messages that are being presented. How we ought to thank God for the great hymns of the faith that reinforce the preaching from the pulpit. How tragic that many congregations have done away with their hymnals and have reverted to crooning meaningless so-called "praise songs" that major on the rhythm and minimize the message. With empty, vain repetition, certain words are intoned time and again, but the message is minimal and doctrine non-existent.

God's people have always been a singing people. Let us not surrender the great hymns of the faith that exalt our blessed Lord and Savior, Jesus Christ. We shall sing His praises throughout all eternity. Let us not fail to do so now.

DLC

---

[1] Leo Taylor Crismon, Editor, *Baptists in Kentucky, 1776-1976 - A Bicentennial Volume* (Middletown, KY: Kentucky Baptist Convention, 1975), 4.

[2] W. L. Winebarger, *A History of the Muhlenberg County Baptist Association in Kentucky* (Greenville, KY: The Western Recorder, 1966), 27.

August 8

An Ideal Pastor

Scripture: Hebrews 13:7, 16-17

One of the most difficult positions in the world to fill is that of pastor. The term, of course, refers to a "shepherd," and the fulfillment of this office calls for a man of God that will lead and feed, guard and guide the flock of God over which the Holy Spirit places him. He must be an expositor, expounder, exhorter, and evangelist all rolled up into one loving but firm personality. He must be humble and yet exert leadership that builds confidence and assurance of victory. No human being is adequate for the demands called for in this office, but when called of God, mortal men must, by the power of the Holy Spirit, enter into the task.

The subject in this entry came as close to being the epitome of the ideal pastor as I can imagine. I refer to George White McDaniel, who served the First Baptist Church of Richmond, Virginia, for almost twenty-three years.

Pastor McDaniel's parents were born in Sumter County, Alabama, his father, Francis Asbury McDaniel, on August 8, 1839, and his mother, Letitia, on February 19, 1835. They moved to Texas where George was raised on a plantation until he was thirteen. The family then moved to Navasota, Texas. Being interested in law, George entered college, and excelled in debating. He possessed an alert mind, and when called of God to preach, it seemed to be a natural fit. It was apparent that he believed profoundly the truth of God's Word. Even while in college he conducted several successful protracted meetings. Throughout his ministry he never allowed his power as an orator to cause him to neglect pulpit preparation. He became adept at the use of illustrations to illumine passages of God's Word.

His first pastorates were in Texas, but when he was thirty, he was invited to pastor the prestigious First Baptist Church of Richmond. There he invested twenty-three years of his life, and George McDaniel revealed the signs of an ideal pastor. He sought to know his people. When he assumed that pastorate there were 923 members. Before he left that charge there were 2,041 members, and the man of God knew each one. He was to be found at the doorways at the beginning and conclusion of the Sunday school hour that he might be available to his people. Without being ostentatious, he led his congregation in giving, as he and his wife contributed generously of their income. He was surely more interested in men and morals than in money. With his success, other churches sought him. ". . . One [church] . . . offered . . . him the best residence in their city, let him name his salary, allowed him the whole summer as vacation, and let him pick any automobile on the market . . . ."[1] He refused their call and surely could not be accused of being greedy!

After serving faithfully for eleven years, the man of God felt that the congregation had become satisfied and had grown indifferent. As a result, he resigned, saying: "My life is too short to spend it where I can secure no better cooperation." This resulted in an article in a periodical entitled *Pastors Whose Hearts Are Breaking*. First Baptist Church was aroused, and the resignation was withdrawn.[2]

The church members returned the pastor's love and care. Every year on the pastor's birthday, the church hosted a banquet in his honor. On the twentieth anniversary of his pastorate a special banquet was prepared, and on the silver wedding anniversary of Pastor and Mrs. McDaniel, the church family presented them with a silver tea service which was properly inscribed. In 1912 the church family insisted that Pastor and Mrs. McDaniel take a four-month leave of absence and travel throughout Europe. All expenses had been received by love-offerings for the couple.

Come to think of it, perhaps the loving people brought out the best in their pastor. By the way, how do you treat the man of God whom the Lord has provided you? The Lord called his servant home during his hey day of pulpit power, and his funeral service was conducted on August 20, 1927.

DLC

---

[1] George Braxton Taylor, *Virginia Baptist Ministers* (Lynchburg, VA: J. P. Bell Company, 1935), 225.

[2] Ibid., 225.

August 9

The Land of the Free

Scripture: Ezra 7:24

Ministers of the State Church in Connecticut were supported by levies upon all the citizenry, and their salaries were collected with all other taxes. From time to time Baptists visited Connecticut from Rhode Island, but it was not until 1704 that a few Baptists in the southeastern part of the colony petitioned the General Court for the privilege of holding religious meetings. Their request seemed to go unnoticed, and in time they invited Valentine Wightman from Rhode Island to become their leader. We have provided the history of the church in Groton, Connecticut, in volume one of this set. Somehow Pastor Wightman and his congregation were never as greatly persecuted as other Baptists in the colony, and in time a gradual relaxation of the clergy law allowed for an exemption from liability to distraint or imprisonment of those who refused to pay the minister's tax for the State Church.

Ebenezer Frothingham, of Middletown, Connecticut, reported that "Young Deacon Drake, of Windsor, now in Hartford prison for the ministers' rates and building their meeting-house, altho' he is a Baptist, is accounted a harmless, godly man; and he has pled the privilege of a Baptist through all the courts, and been at great expense, without relief, till at last the Assembly has given him a mark in his hand, and notwithstanding this, they have thrust him to prison for former rates, with several aggravations which I shall omit. But as to what the Constitution does to relieve the poor deacon, he may there die, and the cry of blood, blood, go up into the ears of a just God."[1]

Godly preachers were beaten at whipping posts in the town squares, and other persecutions were experienced. Nathan Jewett, of Lyme, a member of the Baptist church, was expelled from the Legislature because he was not of the Standing Order. In face of such opposition, the Baptist cause slowly made progress in the colony; however, the growth was not without a heavy price. When the minister's tax was to be collected for the State church pastors, dissenting laymen would discover that their cows or the contents of their corncribs could be seized and taken to the town post to be sold to cover the cost of their taxes. Such godly laymen considered themselves fortunate if they escaped the stocks or the jail. One of the old forms under which these iniquities were committed said in part:

> Levy.
>
> To Samuel Perkins, of Windham, in Windham County, a Collector of Society Taxes in the first Society in Windham:
>
> Greeting: By authority of the State of Connecticut, you are hereby commanded forthwith to levy and collect of the persons named in the foregoing list herewith committed to you, each one his several proportion as therein set down, of the sum total of such list, being a rate agreed upon by the inhabitants of said Society for the purpose of defraying the expenses of said Society, and to deliver and pay-over the sums which you shall collect to the Treasurer of said Society within sixty days next coming; and if any person shall neglect or refuse to pay the sum at which he is assessed; you are hereby commanded to distrain the goods, chattels, or lands of such person so refusing; and the same being disposed of as the law directs, return the overplus, if any, to the respective owners; and for want of such goods, chattels, or lands whereon to make distress, you are to take the body or bodies of the persons so refusing, and them commit to the keeper of the gaol in said County of Windham within the prison, who is hereby commanded to receive and safe keep them until they pay and satisfy the aforesaid sums at which they are respectively assessed, together with your fees, unless said assessment, or any part thereof, be legally abated. Dated at Windham, this 12th day of September, 1794.
>
> Jabez Clark, Just. Peace.

This Day in Baptist History III

Baptists continued to grow, and on August 9th, 1795, the State church in Middletown, Massachusetts passed the following: "When members of this Church shall renounce infant baptism and embrace the Baptist principles and practice baptism by immersion, they shall be considered by that act as withdrawing their fellowship from this Church, and we consider our covenant obligations with them as Church members dissolved."[2]

The victory of a free church in a free state was long coming in Connecticut, but thank God for our Baptist forefathers who were willing to pay the price for freedom. Let us determine to keep America free by instilling in our youth the long-forgotten history of this once great republic.

DLC

---

[1] Thomas Armitage, *A History of the Baptists* (New York: Bryan, Taylor & Co., 1890), 740-741.

[2] Thomas Armitage, *A History of the Baptists* (Watertown, WI: Baptist Heritage Press, 1988), 2:742.

August 10

A Martyr's Missive

Scripture: Matthew 10:28

It is difficult for us to imagine receiving a letter from one's imprisoned life partner who was waiting to die for his faith. Let me share portions of the epistle to his wife from Christian Langedul who was imprisoned in Antwerp.

> Know, my beloved wife, that yesterday . . . I had written you a letter, which I now send you. I could not send it then, for soon afterwards the margrave came . . . to torture us; hence I was not able to send the letter, for then all four of us were one after another severely tortured, so that we have now but little inclination to write; however, we cannot forbear; we must write to you.
>
> Cornelis the shoemaker was the first; then came Hans Symons, with whom also the captain went down into the torture chamber. Then thought I: "We

shall have a hard time of it; to satisfy him." My turn came next . . . When I came to the rack, where were the lords, the order was: 'Strip yourself, or tell where you live.' I looked distressed, as may be imagined. I then said: "Will you ask me nothing further then?" They were silent.

Then thought I: "'I see well enough what it means, it would not exempt me from the torture,' hence I undressed, and fully resigned myself to the Lord, to die. Then they racked me dreadfully, twisting off two cords, I believe, on my thighs and shins; they stretched me out, and poured much water into my body and my nose.... Then they released me, and asked: 'Will you not yet tell it?' They entreated me and again they spoke harshly to me; but I did not open my mouth, so firmly had God closed it."

Then they said: "'Go at him again, and this with a vengeance.' This they also did, and cried, 'Go on, go on, stretch him another foot.' Then thought I: 'You can only kill me.' And thus stretched out, with cords twisted around my head, chin, thighs, and shins, they left me lie, and said: 'Tell, tell.'"

They then talked with one another of my account which J. T. [his son-in-law] had written, of the linen, which amounted to six hundred and fifty-five pounds; and that it was so much cash and rebate. Then the margrave said: "He understands the French well," and I lay there in pain. Again I was asked: "Will you not tell it?" I did not open my mouth. Then they said: "Tell us where you live; your wife and children, at all events, are all gone away." In short, I said not a word. "What a dreadful thing," they said. Thus the Lord kept my lips, so that I did not open them; and they released me, when they had long tried to make me speak. . . .

I have not fully recovered yet from the torture, as may be imagined; but I trust it is all well; do not grieve too much about it.[1]

On August 10, 1567, Christian, along with Cornelis Claess, Mattheus de Vick, and Hans Symons, were arrested on suspicion of being Anabaptists. They each confessed their faith, which led to their cruel torture. After a month of confinement, they were sentenced to death. On September 13, 1567, the four were led to the great market place before the city hall. Each of the brave men reiterated their faith in the Lord Jesus Christ. Christian was taken first and affixed to a stake, and he called out to his brethren to contend valiantly for the truth.

The drums were beaten to drown out the messages of the believers, and one by one the executioner strangled them, and the fires were set to consume their bodies.[2] Oh, the blessed release as they entered into the presence of the Lord, Who doubtless stood to receive them even as He did the blessed deacon Stephen in Acts 7. Surely to be absent from the body was to be at home with their Lord!

DLC

[1] John Christian Wenger, *Even Unto Death* (Richmond, VA: John Knox Press, 1961), 108-109.

[2] Thieleman J. van Braght, *The Bloody Theater or Martyrs Mirror* (Scottdale, PA: Herald Press, 1950), 704.

August 11

A "Major" Evangelist

Scripture: Psalm 126:6

When William Evander Penn was born on August 11, 1832 in Rutherford County, Tennessee, his parents could never have envisioned what the Lord had in store for their little son. His early life was spent on the farm. He began his education at age ten and joined the Beachgrove Baptist Church on October 3, 1847. At the age of fifteen he was born again as the Holy Spirit brought great conviction upon his mind. In the fall of the same year, the teenager was baptized. Interestingly, the old preacher who was ministering when God the Holy Spirit did His work was known as "Uncle Jimmie." He was an obscure backwoods preacher, but oh, what America owes to such men!

William attended one term each at the Male Academy, Trenton, Tennessee, and Union University, Murfreesboro, Tennessee. He read law at the law firm of Williams and Wright and was admitted to the bar. Penn opened a law office in Lexington, Tennessee, about 1852. On April 30, 1856, he was married to Miss Corrilla Frances Sayle.

At the time of the Civil War, Captain Penn was assigned to Wilson's Regiment, Sixteenth Tennessee Cavalry in the Confederate Army, and was captured on February 18, 1864, in Hardiman County, Tennessee. A year later, when a prisoner exchange was arranged, Penn was repatriated on April 7. Upon returning to his unit, Penn was assigned to a regiment and promoted to major. With the completion of the war, Penn signed his own parole at Shreveport, Louisiana, on June 21, 1865.

The following year, he and his family moved to Jefferson, Texas, where he opened a law office. The war had ruined him financially, but he borrowed a copy of the *Digest Laws of Texas* and began work. In less than two weeks he was employed for a case that paid him $400 in gold, and from that time onward, as long as he practiced law, he had a lucrative practice.[1] Penn joined the Baptist Church at Jefferson, and was soon elected Sunday school superintendent. There were thirty-five in attendance at the Sunday School, but Penn threw himself into the task, and in two months' time the attendance was up to 400, the largest Sunday school in the town of 10,000. Major Penn entered into every opportunity with great enthusiasm.

Major Penn enjoyed singing, and that, coupled with his fervor made him a natural leader. While in attendance at a Sunday School Institute in Tyler, Texas in 1875, Reverend J. H. Stribbling, pastor at the Baptist church, asked Penn to remain over the weekend and address his congregation concerning the matter of soul-winning. He consented, and when the news was heralded that an attorney was to speak, crowds thronged the building. A revival broke out, and it continued for five weeks. Many were converted. That series of meetings changed the course of Major Penn's life. On December 4, 1880, the Broadway Baptist Church of Galveston formally ordained him. For the next twenty years he conducted phenomenal revivals throughout Texas[2] and in almost every Southern state along with evangelistic meetings in England and Scotland. His evangelistic campaigns had such an impact on the cause of Christ in Texas that he became known as the "Texas Evangelist," and the historian has said: "Not only did he win multitudes, but he encouraged them to exercise their individual gifts in soul-winning. Any analysis of the factors in Texas Baptist progress must include him and the movement he inaugurated."[3]

The Penns moved to Eureka Springs, Arkansas, about 1887. The evangelist's health began to fail about five years later. The Lord called His servant home on April 29, 1895, and his funeral was held on Saturday, May 1. One thousand in attendance at Eureka Springs, Arkansas, heard the pastor intone those appropriate words of our text for today: "He that goeth forth and weepeth, bearing precious seed, shall doubtless come again with rejoicing, bringing his sheaves with him"(Psalm 126:6). May we determine that though our gifts are small, we shall yield them all to the Lord that He might use us to the greatest possible extent.

DLC

---

[1]Ben M. Bogard, *Pillars of Orthodoxy, or Defenders of the Faith* (Louisville, KY: Baptist Book Concern, 1900), 120.

[2]L. R. Elliott, *Centennial Story of Texas Baptists* (Dallas, TX: Baptist General Convention of Texas, 1936), 51.

[3]Ibid.

August 12

Taxation Without Representation

Scripture: Acts 8:1-4

The first shot of the Revolutionary War actually took place in North Carolina on May 16, 1771, at the Battle of Alamance. The Separate Baptists in North Carolina, chaffed under the affliction of the unjust taxation placed upon them by Governor William Tryon, the British-appointed governor. The Baptists, along with other citizenry, had united in a group that became known as "The Regulators." These citizens objected to the oppressive misrule and extortion by the Governor. In September 1770, the Regulators addressed a letter to Judge Richard Henderson in the Hillsboro court in which they listed their complaints and demanded unprejudiced juries, and that all extortionate officers, lawyers, and clerks be brought to fair trials.

Three sets of taxes were being levied upon the citizenry prior to the War of the Regulators. A property tax and two poll taxes: one was for the general sale of goods, and the second was the parish tax for the support of the state church. When the Governor determined to build a castle for his own use in New Bern, North Carolina, more taxation was needed to pay the *15,000 silver sterling required for construction. In an empty claim, the Governor promised to "redress any real grievances," but this was an empty promise. In 1741 the "Marriage Act" was imposed, giving the church of England exclusive rights to perform marriages. This invalidated all "Baptist" marriages and essentially made the Baptists non-citizens.

The principle of "taxation without representation" was festering simultaneously in Massachusetts, and the citizenry in New England retaliated in what historians usually claim was the beginning of the Revolutionary War. However, in North Carolina the same principle preceded that in New England. When it became apparent that the Governor was organizing a militia to enforce his wishes westward into the North Carolina territory, the Regulators prepared for armed conflict. The Governor despised the Quakers and the dreaded Baptists. He knew that the Quakers were pacifists and they would not resist. Thus he pitted Presbyterians against the Baptists, and gathered a formidable army and demanded that the Regulators submit to his authority or be considered traitors.

The lines were drawn, and two thousand Regulators gathered to face the Governor's army of two thousand. A two-hour battle ensued. In all, eighteen lives were lost nine on each side. But the ill-prepared Regulators were routed, and William Tryon and his troops won the first battle of the Revolutionary War. The Governor believed that the Separatist Baptist preacher, Joseph Murphy had organized the Regulators, and he wanted his life. But Joseph Murphy could not be found. As a result, Tryon encamped on Sandy Creek in search of the Regulator leaders. His headquarters were located on the farm of Benjamin Merrill, a leader in the Baptist church at the Jersey Settlement. Merrill was captured, convicted as a traitor, and hanged publicly. His body was cut in pieces-quartered—and scattered. He was one of seven men so slain by Tryon for the resistance.

The Boston Gazette of August 12, 1771, gave the following report: "Merrill died in the most heroic manner, his children being around him at the place of his execution. He declared that he died at peace with his Maker and in the cause of his oppressed countrymen."[1]

William Tryon had accomplished his will. He had intimidated the Separate Baptists. This resulted in fifteen hundred Baptist families moving southward and westward into what would eventually become Tennessee. Rather than being a defeat, this proved to be a victory. Everywhere these Baptists went, they preached the Gospel, and we are reminded of the scene in Acts 8 where the persecuted saints went everywhere preaching Christ.

As for William Tryon, he had won the first battle, but in June of 1771 he went to New York to become the governor of that province. There he met defeat at the hands of General George Washington and the Continental Army.

We serve the God who rules all events. What appeared to be loss for the Separate Baptists resulted in an open door for the expansion of the Gospel westward. Let us accept whatever the Lord allows in our lives and determine that we will serve Him regardless of the circumstances. We do not know what the future holds, but we know Who holds the future.

DLC

---

[1] James R. Beller, *America in Crimson Red* (Arnold, MO: Prairie Free Press, 2004), 197.

August 13

A Strong but Quiet Man of God

Scripture: 2 Timothy 4

One of God's choice servants was laid to rest on May 12, 1971, at the foot of Jack's Mountain in the hills of Pennsylvania. His congregation at Saltillo, Pennsylvania, considered it an untimely death and still talk about "Brother Dick" with warmth and affection, but our loving Father had taken home one of His faithful servants.

Born on October 21, 1913, to Arthur and Mae Shickley Meyers, Dick was the oldest of seven children, Richard Meyers. Because he was extremely shy, everyone in his hometown was surprised when he entered Findlay College, a Church of God school, in Ohio in 1934. Gynieth Lucile Wilcox met his requirements for a wife: one who could sing, play piano, cook, and sew. They were married on June 8, 1936, while still in college and while Dick pastored a nearby Church of God. That same month Dick graduated *magna cum laude.*

While still in college, Dick and other students attended Calvary Baptist Church in Findlay, Ohio, and listened to Pastor Dunham expound the doctrines of the Second Coming and Prophetic Dispensationalism. This new revelation gave them an appetite for more of the truth of God's Word. Although they were forbidden to attend, they sat on the hoods and tops of their vehicles eagerly taking in the Word through opened church windows. This was the beginning of the questions Dick had concerning the Church of God movement where he had spent seven years.

As Dick preached the security of believers and tithing, he got into trouble with the church Eldership. He fought one battle after another because he would not follow their methodology. Dr. Kenneth Good, the town pharmacist in Saltillo, convinced Dick he had Baptist convictions. Thus it was that he left the Church of God and became pastor of the Baptist church in Saltillo. The congregation grew dramatically. As he continued his study of the Scriptures, he found himself at odds with the Northern Baptist Convention since he could not support their liberal program. Consequently, he took the bold step of pulling the church out of the Convention. The Convention sued Meyers three times, losing each case even on the State Supreme Court level. His life was threatened because of his stand against dancing, but he continued to preach his convictions. Finally, Attorney James Bennett persuaded Meyers to let the Convention have the property and to start over. The building was too small for the growing congregation anyway. The congregation and Pastor Meyers lost everything.

Soon Calvary Independent Baptist Church was in its new facilities. People began attending from three surrounding communities. Pastor Meyers, burdened for the people from these areas, organized churches there and a Sunday school in another town. All of these congregations were named Calvary Independent Baptist Church. He attracted great crowds of children and youth with Bible clubs. His radio program *Good Cheer Time* aired over six area Pennsylvania stations. His young convert's study was a key tool in the development of these ministries.

Meyers ministered in Bible camps, Bible conferences, and evangelistic services. He played several musical instruments, wrote choruses, and sang. He taught his daughters and other youth to play the piano. The Musical Meyers (family quartet) sang and played in the churches Meyers simultaneously pastored. He had a tremendous hospital visitation ministry. Patients beside those being visited would overhear and ask Brother Dick to talk to them. Seeing his quiet and discerning spirit, many looked to him for wisdom.

If Brother Dick were living today, he would be saddened to know that everything bearing his name (notes, tapes, music) was destroyed in a bonfire by a jealous pastor. Thankfully the original copies of most of this material is still safe with family members. His new-converts notes have been translated into many languages and are being used today on different mission fields.[1] When he became ill, his church family gave him an extended leave for healing. However, on May 8, 1971, His heavenly Father called him home. Galen Goshorn, one of the pallbearers, summed up the sentiments of many, "Brother Dick was just too good for this world." May our Lord raise up such godly men of vision to serve His children in the twenty-first century.

DCB

[1] Telephone interview with Lucile Meyers Safstrom by Bettye Baughan, August 17, 2004.

August 14

Legal Contract or Loving Call?

Scripture: 1 Timothy 5:17-18

In the eighteenth century great confusion reigned between some Baptist churches and their pastors. Often financial agreements had been made when a pastor was called, but those commitments were in actuality forgotten by the congregation. This resulted in difficulties with some congregations suggesting that the agreement had been made only with the pastor and deacons, and thus the congregation had no responsibility in the matter. In the course of time, a few pastors insisted on written contracts. A typical contract is that between the Salem church of New Jersey and Pastor Isaac Skillman which was drawn up and placed in the minutes of the First Baptist Church of Salem on December 12, 1791.

"Be it remembered that on the 16th day of November 1791 the following agreement was entered into between the Revd Mr. Isaak Skillman and the Baptist Church and Congregation . . . The said Mr. Skillman covenants and agrees to be the pastor or minister of the Church and Congregation, to execute all the duties that a minister ought to perform in a church, agreeably to the Baptist Confession of Faith, preaching all funerals that he may be called upon to preach for said Congregation, preaching two sermons a day in the summer season, visit the said congregation twice a year formally, and not leave or absent himself from the necessary services of said congregation. And said Congregation and their trustees doth covenant and agree to and with the said Mr. Skillman to pay him for his labours and services . . . the sum of one hundred and twenty five pounds per year to commence on the 14th day of August last. And further the said parties agree and promise each to the other that if any discontent on the part of the said Mr. Skillman, whereby he should wish to be dismissed from serving said Church and Congregation, and if any discontent should arise on the Church and Congregation's part that they should wish to have said Mr. Skillman dismissed from being their minister, in either case they may, if either of them see meet, call the ministers and some of the members from Cumberland and Wilmington Baptist churches to judge between them and their determinations shall be binding on each party."[1]

To this day in the twenty-first century some "Baptist" churches continue to enter into a binding contract with their pastor. However, among independent Baptist churches this practice is rarely experienced and is considered needless. Of course, congregations empower pulpit committees to make the financial stipulation known to any candidate for the pulpit of a local church. But as the pastor is expected to be ethical in all his dealings, it is not necessary for the congregation to draw up a listing of his responsibilities. Frankly, a pastor who expects to labor only forty hours a week is in reality a mere hireling. Study and prayerful sermon preparation, pastoral and evangelistic visitation, administration and oversight of the church staff, preparation for missions and evangelistic conferences, correspondence with the church's missionary family, weddings, and funerals, and a myriad of other responsibilities push the godly pastor to his limit in adequately serving his congregation. By the same token, as the pastor labors in behalf of a faithful congregation, it is expected that the congregation will insist that the pastor's needs be adequately cared for. It is said that on one occasion Queen Elizabeth requested a British businessman to serve a political appointment. He declined the offer stating that his family's financial needs demanded that he persist in his business. It is said that the Queen responded: "Sir, if you give oversight to our nation's needs, I can assure you that our citizenry will abundantly meet all your needs."

Such an attitude ought to be reflected by every Baptist congregation. Dare I ask the question? How is the pastoral staff in your local assembly being cared for?

DLC

---

[1] H. Leon McBeth, *A Sourcebook For Baptist Heritage* (Nashville, TN: Broadman Press, 1990), 158-159.

August 15

He was Guilty of Preaching!

Scripture: Jeremiah 38:4-6

Of the forty-three Baptist preachers who were imprisoned in Virginia, William Webber was the target of as much as, or perhaps more, persecution than any of the others. William Webber was not the typical spiritual leader. He was well versed in Scripture, but he was not a strong pulpiteer. He was remarkably plain, both in his dress and manners. To be sure, he was pleasant and cheerful, yet without levity. His education was minimal, yet he was greatly loved by the members of his church.

Webber had been born on August 15, 1747. He first heard Baptist preaching when he was twenty-two years old, and he experienced immediate conviction. About six months later he came to the full assurance of his salvation. He was baptized by John Waller in June of 1770, and began the task of exhorting immediately. Soon he was ordained, and, as so many of the Separate Baptists did during that period, he began preaching evangelistically as an itinerant.

He was first arrested in Chesterfield County, December 7, 1770, and imprisoned in the county jail until March 7, 1771. The charge, of course, was preaching without having a license from the state church. In August he was taken off a platform where he was preaching in Middlesex County, and put into prison. On that occasion he was confined forty-five days. He was actually bound for part of that sentence. In both jails, he and his fellow Baptist prisoners preached through the grates of the cells twice a week. Besides these imprisonments, he was often very roughly treated by the sons of Belial.[1]

On another occasion, Webber narrowly escaped being clubbed to death. A Baptist sympathizer grabbed the sheriff's stick as he was drawing back to strike.[2]

The jail at Middlesex was even below the standards of that day, and it swarmed with flies. "On September 10th they were allowed [to roam]the prison bounds, by which they were much relieved; yet they were frequently under the necessity of resorting to the jail to avoid the rage of the persecutors. The Lord daily opened the hearts of the people; the rich sent many presents-things calculated to nourish them in their sufferings and to alleviate their sorrows. William Webber fell sick.... The persecutors found that the imprisonment of the preachers tended rather to the furtherance of the Gospel. The Baptists preached regularly in prison; crowds attended; the preaching seemed to have double weight when coming from the jail...."[3]

Though not a great pulpiteer, William Webber was a very successful pastor. His chief ability was in the meetings of associations. He was elected moderator of the General Association as early as 1778. From that time, though there were many older and more experienced pastors, whenever he attended the meetings of the General Association, he was honored in chairing the meetings. He seemed to have composure as moderator that he lacked in the pulpit.

In 1799 he had a long sickness that threatened his life. Though he recovered, his constitution was so shaken that he was never able to travel extensively as before. When another physical attack was experienced, he had a relapse, and though he lingered, it was only a matter of time until he closed his eyes to this world and opened them in the land that is fairer than day. He was weary of the battle, and in his last illness he said to a preacher friend, "Brother Watkins, I never had so glorious a manifestation of the love of God in all my life, as I have had since my sickness. O, the love of God!"

The journey ended as William Webber entered the glory land on February 29, 1808. May we who know the Savior realize that the best is yet to be!

DLC

---

[1] David Benedict, *A General History of the Baptist Denomination* (Boston: Lincoln & Edmands, 1813), 399-400.

[2] James B. Beller, *America in Crimson Red* (Arnold, MO: Prairie Fire Press, 2004), 168.

[3] John T. Christian, *A History of the Baptists* (Nashville, TN: Broadman Press, 1926), 2:255.

August 16

Early Mob Violence in America

Scripture: Acts 19:29-34

It is thrilling to read of the inroads of Baptist influence in Virginia as the Separate Baptists, under the direction of Samuel Harris, penetrated the area with the Gospel. However, the Regular Baptists also made good progress in preaching God's Word. As we have mentioned previously, the Separates had ardor while the Regular Baptists featured order. The Separates were housed more often in the jails for they were perhaps more daring in preaching without authorization. In truth, the Regular Baptists had at an early date applied to the General Court and obtained licenses for specific places for preaching. The Separates were bold in insisting that no one had the authority to keep them from preaching. As David Benedict reported: "The Regulars were considered less enthusiastick than the Separates."[1]

The difference in attitude between the Regulars and Separates caused a preponderance of the forty-three imprisoned Baptist preachers to come from the ranks of the Separates. Only five of the forty-three jailed ministers are known to have been Regular Baptists. It is apparent that the Separate Baptist preachers became the primary target of the law officers of the land. However, this did not mean that the Regulars were not attacked. Their general opposition came primarily from the lawless mobs as anarchy and chaos ruled the land.

One of the leaders of the Regular Baptists was David Thomas. He was born on August 16, 1732,[2] in the London Tract, Pennsylvania. He was blessed in having a good educational background, and studied at the first Baptist training institution in all of America at Hopewell. There he trained under the famed Isaac Eaton. His academic accomplishments were so significant that Rhode Island College (now Brown University) granted him a Master of Arts degree. Along with his academic strengths, David Thomas was blessed as well with a strong and melodious voice, a compelling manner of speaking, expressive actions, and a heart filled with love to God and his fellow-men.

Mr. Thomas' first ministerial efforts were in the Millcreek Church in Berkley County, but in 1762 he moved to Fauquier County and became pastor of the Broadrun Baptist Church. However, Mr. Thomas was used of God in extending the Gospel by preaching throughout the whole countryside in the Northern Neck above Fredericksburg, Virginia. Though his reputation preceded him, and his fame spread abroad, Mr. Thomas suffered great abuse from outrageous mobs and malicious individuals. This was particularly true during the first few years of his ministry. Once he was pulled down, as he was preaching, and dragged out of doors in a barbarous manner. On another occasion someone attempted to shoot him, but a bystander wrenched the gun from his adversary, and prevented the act. But the gospel flourished and the Broadrun church in the course of a few years became the mother of five or six other congregations. These new churches too received terrible abuse from local mobs. The Chappawomsick church met violent opposition. One gang of forty was determined to destroy the work. They vented their rage in various ways. On one occasion they threw a live snake into the midst of the meeting, and yet again they threw a hornet's nest into the building. On another occasion they went to the meeting house with firearms, but fortunately they did not open fire. The gang leader died an agonizing death, and the gang mentality seemed to dissipate.

Through all these trials Mr. Thomas continued to travel and preach, and as his fame spread abroad, people would travel great distances to hear him declare Gospel truth. The man of God continued on in his ministry until he moved to Kentucky in 1796 and closed out his days in service there to the Lord.

Though the opposition is not physical, we still to this day battle against principalities and powers of spiritual darkness. May we be found faithful in representing the Lord of righteousness as evil times descend upon us once again.

DLC

---

[1] David Benedict, *A General History of the Baptist Denomination* (Boston: Lincoln & Edmands, 1813), 2:33.

[2] Ibid., 2:29.

August 17

Faithful to the End

Scripture: Psalm 37:23-25

We have looked several times at the life of the unique servant of the Lord, John Leland. His was such a fruitful life that much could be written of his service. When he was seventy-seven years old, he spoke of a gracious renewing of the Holy Spirit's work in his life. On July 11, 1831, he recorded the fact he had baptized ten; on July 17, four; July 24, two; July 31, four. Interestingly, he mentioned the fact that one of those baptized was 82 years old. It must have been some scene to see a seventy-seven-year-old administer baptism to an 82-year-old! Also, in his diary he wrote, "In the winter of 1800, I baptized one who was 90 years of age."[1]

John Leland continued on in his service, and he recorded the following: August 22, baptized one; September 4, baptized one; September 18, baptized two; October 2, baptized four; October 16, baptized three; October 23, baptized seven; October 30, baptized three, making a total of one thousand five hundred and fifteen.

On May 14, 1834, he recorded that he was 80 years old, but he was still unwilling to give up the call of God upon his life. He had traveled thirty miles to Chatham and had preached three times at the dedication of a new church building where he preached to 600 people. He wrote: "I now have several little preaching tours appointed; but my Maker only knows whether life and strength will be given me to fill them. It is now sixty years since I began to preach, but ah! how little I have done! and how imperfect that little!"[2]

Let me add just a few more lines from Leland's diary. "August 17, 1834. This day I baptized five, which are the first I have baptized since I was eighty years old. My baptismal list is now 1524.

"January 28, 1835. I have been preaching sixty years to convince men that human powers were too degenerate to effect a change of heart by self-exertion; and all the revivals of religion that I have seen have substantially accorded with that sentiment."[3]

Surely God's call is without repentance, and faithfulness is the greatest attribute a servant of the Lord can exhibit!

John Leland's diary went on to lament the profanation of the gospel that became evident during more than sixty-five years of his service to the Lord. I cannot help but wonder what his reaction would be to today's evident lessening of holy standards and godly living. The elder's life is surely a challenge to fundamental Baptists in this day when standards are degenerating. Separation is no longer popular, and the infiltration of compromise has been dangled before us as a tool that may open doors of evangelism. As a result, in many religious centers rapturous rhapsodies have been replaced by the world's raucous rhythms. Once, men entered the presence of God dressed in their best clothing that they might honor God's holy name. In the twenty-first century, there has been a marked reduction of the respect for Deity. In essence, He has been lowered to a level of the vernacular. Much of this has been brought about by transliterations of Scripture that profess to be literal translations. These actually cheapen one's view of a holy God! One result has been that informal grungy garb has become the accepted norm of attire in God's house! Tragically, moral standards have fallen right along with the music and dress standards, and even divorce is rampant in fundamental circles.

Our greatest need once again is for revival in America. Our hope is not in gaining control of the White House. It is rather in setting each of our houses in spiritual order. Our hope is only to be found in the Lord from Heaven! May God revive our hearts that we might live fully for Him.

DLC

---

[1] J. B. McInturff, editor, *The Old Paths* (New Market, VA: Henkel & Company, 1891), 229.

[2] Ibid., 230.

[3] Ibid., 231.

August 18

A Man of Integrity

Scripture: Psalm 20:7

He was seventeen years old when I first met him. The Second World War was on, and Harry Love, along with his older brother, Ken, had moved to the Detroit area for employment. They attended the local church in which I was raised, and it was there that we first met. I was a fourteen-year-old, and fast-pitch softball was the rage of the day. Our church participated in a softball league, and at fourteen I was too young to play, but I didn't miss a game. Harry, only three years my senior, pitched, and he could throw that ball! That was the first time our paths crossed, but it wouldn't be the last.

Harry had been born into a sizeable family on July 12, 1926, on the western side of Michigan. He had been led to Christ in a local Baptist church. In his teen years his athletic ability had been discovered. Sports became an issue in his life, for he battled the opportunity to play professional baseball or to answer the call of God to Christian service. The Lord won the contest, and Harry entered Moody Bible Institute in Chicago to study for the ministry. Preaching was his delight, and during his tenure as a student, he bought up every opportunity to proclaim the riches of Christ. Three great events soon occurred in quick succession. A month prior to his graduation, Harry married Miss Jeanette Lyster on November 17, 1949. His graduation took place on December 15, 1949, and on January 11, 1950, he was ordained to the gospel ministry.

When the Moline Congregational Church assured Harry that they desired to become a Baptist church, he accepted the call to pastor there on May 15, 1951. The church experienced the blessings of God, but during that pastorate his wife came down with polio. In those early days of service, Harry and Janetette endured the devastating trials so often used by the Lord to perfect His saints. Seeing the blessing of God upon God's man, the Rockford Baptist Church of Rockford, Michigan, called Reverend Love to be their pastor, and he assumed that pastorate on January 5, 1956.

In the course of time, the men of the association of churches, of which the Rockford church was a part, observed God's blessings upon Reverend Love's ministry. Needing a camping program and youth ministry in the association, they asked Reverend Love to join the association administration. He accepted that challenge and became associate director. He led the group in the purchase and development of a 600-acre camp in north central Michigan. On October 25, 1964, Harry became the General Director of the movement. Five years later Reverend Love was granted an honorary doctorate by a southern college. When apostasy crept into the national association to which the state association was loosely knit, Dr. Love led the state group to disaffiliate from the national organization. Thus on October 17, 1979, the Independent Fundamental Baptist Association of Michigan was formed, and Dr. Love served that organization as General Director until his retirement on August 18, 1998. In 1983 Dr. Love was invited to serve Baptist World Mission as a trustee. Through the years he served on various other boards, and his presence always assured that the board's proposals were well-thought-out.

I was privileged to work as Dr. Love's associate with the state association for several years, and he became my closest friend in the ministry. I prospered from his counsel. Faithfulness, consistency, and integrity marked him. He never lost the thrill of preaching, and he declared God's Word with power and conviction. He seemed never happier than when standing behind the sacred desk. Doctor Love never played politics to accomplish his purposes and goals. Though he was gracious in hearing all sides of an issue, one never had to question where he stood once a decision was made. He was resolute in conviction and maintained truth regardless of the cost. Harry was not only a great administrator, but he gained respect and admiration by his composure.

When he was promoted to glory on September 29, 1998, the large number of pastors who attended his funeral paid him a great tribute. The need of our churches today is for loyal, faithful, men of conviction who say what they mean and mean what they say. Let us pray for such leadership.

DLC

August 19

America's Religious Freedom

Scripture: Psalm 119:153-161

Baptists have always treasured the truth of local church autonomy. This doctrine, based upon Scripture, has kept Baptist churches from being swallowed up in apostasy. No hierarchy has been empowered to deliver the entire "denomination" to the liberal cause, for, in reality, there is no such thing as a "Baptist denomination." However, in the realization that there is wisdom in counsel, the Philadelphia Baptist Association was formed in 1707 to assist Baptist churches as they faced uncertain issues. No church was coerced to join, and the association could only render advice to local churches. As the association met, members discussed questions that were directed to them. They responded in order to strengthen those congregations that had written. Through the years, local associations were established, and they served locally in a similar capacity.

As the Philadelphia Association met on October 4-6, 1785, their minutes contain greetings from the Charleston and Ketockton Associations dated October 27, 1783 and August 19, 1785. But the greetings from the Warren Association are of special interest. "A letter from the Warren Association, held at Wrentham, State of Massachusetts, September 14, 1785, was delivered by their messenger, Brother Hezekiah Smith, and reads, "...It appears that in the neighborhood of Boston, several persons of unblemished reputation were imprisoned the winter past, by reason of their refusing to support a way of worship repugnant to the dictates of their own minds, though the constitution under which they live, equally secures their privileges with those who, repugnant to all sound policy, continue to persecute them."[1]

It is difficult to fully realize that at one time in the "Land of the free," citizens who refused to be part of the "established church" were persecuted. But such was the case. On October 6, 1807, at the centenary meeting of the Philadelphia Association, Dr. Samuel Jones delivered the "Century Sermon." In that message he stated: "Having been persecuted and oppressed, suffered imprisonment and alienation of property, it is but reasonable to expect, we should be very zealous of our religious liberty, which indeed is the case...." Then speaking of the Protestant Reformation, he said: "The reformation, which has been so much gloried in was but a poor piece of business, although it has been attended with valuable consequences. The reformers shook off the Papal yoke, but in the main retained its principles and spirit. They did not establish the right of free inquiry, liberty of conscience, and the Word of God as the only rule of faith and practice: but, on the other hand, opposed, restrained and suppressed every attempt to promote a thorough reformation. They were influenced by worldly motives, connected religion with worldly establishments, were the abettors of tyranny and oppression, and even of persecution by fire and the sword."[2]

I have been shocked to hear Baptists crediting American freedom of religion to the Reformers of the Reformation!

Such an assumption reveals a complete misunderstanding of history. Perhaps it is the result of the "brain washing" effects of revisionist historians, but soul liberty and freedom of religion are basically the result of our Baptist forefathers who willingly paid the severe price to obtain it for all. "Before the Declaration of Independence . . . the Baptists were alone in demanding the separation of church and state. The Presbyterians were simply demanding their rights under the Act of Tolerance and nothing more, while the Methodists were still nominally a part of the Anglican establishment, and seemed at first to favor its continuance."[3]

Liberal commentators often speak of "bigoted Baptists," but in truth, Baptists have ever sought religious freedom for one and all. The only one of the thirteen American colonies offering freedom of religion was Rhode Island, which was established by Baptists. Dr. Samuel Jones observed this very truth when he noted: "It has been often said, that all parties will persecute when they have the power. This may be admitted as a general rule; but I am bold in averring that the Baptists are an exception. They have had the power in Rhode Island, ...but not a single instance can be produced of their abuse of that power any where."[4]

Let us thank God for our freedom, and let us use our freedom to assure it until our Savior comes.

DLC

---

[1] A. D. Gillette, Editor, *Minutes of the Philadelphia Baptist Association 1707 to 1807*, (Springfield, MO: Particular Baptist Press, 2002), 205.

[2] Ibid., 460-461, 466-467.

[3] William Warren Sweet, *The Story of Religion in America* (New York: Harper and Row, 1950), 190.

[4] Gillette, 461-462.

August 20

Missions at all Costs

Scripture: 2 Corinthians 11:23-28

How we thrill in reading of the followers of Christ in the first century. Our Lord went up; the Holy Spirit came down; and the disciples went out. Our hearts thrill to read the accusation of their enemies in that century as they charged the believers with turning the world upside down. But in time, compromise entered the ranks of professing Christians, and soon true believers were forced to worship in secret. A false religious organization was forged between reigning politicians and religionists; a so-called state-church was established, and true believers were banished with persecution as their lot.

Those true believers endured throughout the years, and they rejoiced to ultimately see that which we know as the Reformation. They believed that freedom was right around the corner, but they were disillusioned when they soon discovered that the Reformers were also desirous of forming church/states with freedom granted only to those of their persuasion. In fact, the Reformers began to oppress the true believers as well, and our Anabaptist forefathers found themselves in the pincer movement between Rome and the Reformers.

Because of their doctrinal moorings, the Reformers had concluded that the Great Commission of our Lord was meant only for the apostles who had heard His actual words. The Reformer's concept of expansion of their ministries was centered in armed forces that practiced coercion by physical force. Expansion for the Reformers came as militarists conquered additional territory and superimposed their "faith" upon the population.

Our Baptist forefathers believed, however, in voluntarism that featured missions. "Thus there was formed in the crucible of suffering one of the most aggressive missionary movements in Christian history. The Anabaptists took the Great Commission seriously. They believed it was binding upon all true disciples of Christ in every age. And obey it they did. Into all Europe they went with their Bibles and tracts, their hymns and sermons—to preach, teach, live, suffer, and die for Christ's sake.

"Of all the Anabaptists, the Hutterites developed the most extensive missionary work. They took advantage of every lull in persecution to enlarge their scope of activity. One of the best known of their missionaries was Claus Felbinger. In his Confession of Faith he gave an admirable statement concerning the missionary motivation of the Hutterites.

"We have been asked by sundry people why we have come into the prince's land, [Bavaria] and draw people away. My answer is, we do not go only into this land, but into all lands, wherever our language is known, for where God opens a door for us and shows us zealous hearts that truly seek Him, hearts that are discontented with the godless life of the world and would gladly do what is right—there we go, for we have divine cause to do so. For heaven and earth are the Lord's, and all men are His; but we have given, surrendered, and sacrificed ourselves wholly to God. Where He sends and will use us, there we go, in obedience to His divine will, regardless of what we must suffer and endure."[1]

The hope of seeing lost sinners converted drove the Anabaptists all over Europe to spread the gospel. A conference of leaders was held at Augsburg in Swabia on August 20, 1527, and missionaries were sent out two by two to many areas of German-speaking Europe. Many of these servants of Christ were captured and martyred. The above mentioned conference became known as the **Martyr's Synod**. However, many were reached with the life-transforming Gospel. The concept of the necessity of a personal conversion to Christ stood in distinct contrast with the church-state system. To our forefathers, salvation had nothing to do with sacramental theology. They fully understood that salvation could not be attained; repentance and faith could only obtain it through the death, burial, and resurrection of the Son of God.

The day in which we live may well result again in martyrdom for those who will carry the message of redemption into the lands of religionists who worship heathen gods. May we be found faithful in this day regardless of the cost! Our Anabaptist forefathers lived with the full desire to bring glory to the Son of God by obedience to His will. May we do the same.

DLC

[1] W. R. Estep, *The Anabaptist Story* (Nashville, TN: Broadman Press, 1963), 188, 199.

August 21

The Land of the Free?

Scripture: Acts 16:25-34

On August 21, 1773, Nathaniel Saunders, who had been for five years pastor of Mountain Run in Orange (County), and William McClannahan, assistant to John Pickett at Carter's Run in Fauquier, were arrested in Culpeper County on a warrant issued that day, charging that they did "Teach & Preach Contrary to the Laws & Usages of the Kingdom of Great Britain, raising Sedition & Stirring up Strife amongst his Majestie's Liege People." ... On September 20, he [Saunders] was committed to jail on his refusal to give bond that he "neither teach, preach, nor exhort for one year except in his licensed meeting house."[1]

Soon thereafter Saunders received an encouraging letter from his mentor in the ministry, David Thomas. In that epistle Saunders was encouraged not to sacrifice his conscience to obtain peace!

We are reminded as we consider the forty-three incarcerated preachers in Virginia in those days, that not one of them ever compromised his faith to obtain freedom. In fact, it is thrilling to read of their exploits even while being imprisoned. Robert Boyle C. Howell (1801-1868), in 1857, wrote of

> A venerable gentleman, recently gone to his rest, some years ago said to his friend: – "I often heard, in my youth, the Baptist ministers preach from the windows of the Jail at Chesterfield Court House. The effects were sometimes most extraordi-

nary. On one occasion Webber was preaching; the heavy iron gratings partially concealed him; his appeals were most touching. A man that I did not know, came up and stood by my side. In a few minutes this man began to tremble violently; presently he fell upon his knees, and then upon his face; and there he lay during the service, praying audibly and agonizingly to God for mercy and salvation through Jesus Christ." This, he added, "was no unusual occurrence. Scores and fifties were often at the same time similarly exercised." Eleazer Clay, Sheriff of the county, the uncle and guardian of the distinguished statesman, Henry Clay, with reference to those who had professed religion at Chesterfield Jail, writes thus to his friend, Rev. John Williams of Amelia County: —

"We wish you to come down and baptize those who are now waiting for an opportunity. The Lord is now carrying on a glorious work in our country. The preaching at the prison is not attended in vain, for we hope that several are converted, while others are under great distress, and are made to cry out, 'What shall we do to be saved.'"[2]

How thrilling to realize that across Virginia many came to know Christ while listening to Baptist preachers declaring the Gospel through the jailhouse windows. It is amazing also to note the fact that as a result of "jailhouse" preaching, some local Baptist churches were born.

The solidarity of the Baptists is very notable. Among the Baptists were the Regular Baptists and the Separate Baptists. The Regulars were originally known as Particular Baptists, believing that Christ had died only for the elect. The Separatists did not hold tenaciously to the system of theology popularized by John Calvin. Yet the two groups served with a single heart as they faced the opposition of those who despised the Gospel. It is noteworthy that of the forty-three Baptist preachers who were imprisoned for preaching without licenses, thirty-five were identified as being Separate Baptists, and five were known as being Regular Baptists. Of the three arrested Baptist preachers, we are unaware of their affiliation.

It is interesting that persecution and opposition usually results in a united front as God's children stand against a common enemy. Because of their distinctives, Baptists have always had a far greater variance than other denominations. May we stand firm in our convictions in this day, but may we love those with whom we do not fully agree as we stand on the Word of God for truth that is eternal.

DLC

---

[1] Garnett Ryland, *The Baptists of Virginia 1699-1926* (Richmond, VA: The Virginia Baptist Board of Missions and Education, 1955), 80.

[2] Robert Boyle C. Howell, *The Early Baptists of Virginia* (Philadelphia: The Bible and Publication Society, 1857), 80-81.

August 22

Leader of Youth

Scripture: 1 Corinthians 15:58

Donald Edmund Nelson was born into the family of Arthur and Evelyn Miller Nelson in Yakima, Washington, on February 2, 1922. He was born again at sixteen while attending the Wisconsin Tabernacle in Milwaukee in 1938. Don attended Moody Bible Institute for one year. His grandmother wrote him expressing her joy in his studying for the ministry. His grandfather, a Holiness Methodist minister, was equally pleased.

On December 30, 1941, Don enlisted in the United States Army and served as a surgical technician. He volunteered for reassignment overseas, serving as a combat medic in the China, Burma, and India theater of operations with the 20th General Hospital Unit. He was awarded the Bronze Service Star and China War Medal for participation in China convoys over the Ledo-Burma Road. He completed his military service in January 1946.

To further his training for the ministry, he attended Northwestern College in Minneapolis, Minnesota. There he met Grace Sheppard, whom he called "Amazing Grace." They were married on Wednesday night during Bible school week on August 20, 1947. She was a godly wife and mother until her death on September 4, 2003. They continued their studies until graduation in 1949.

Don served the Lord as youth pastor of Fourth Baptist Church in Minneapolis from 1947 to 1950. After the death of one of his young people, he wrote:

Lord teach me now to live for Thee,
While in my youth my soul is free,
As yet unscarred with bitter shame,
For I could live this life in vain.
Lord, take my youth I now implore,
This life is thine for evermore,
And when I face the setting sun,
Lord may I hear Thy words, "Well done."

In 1951 Don and Grace joined TEAM-AVED and began a five-year ministry as missionaries in Japan. While there, Don realized he was Baptist by conviction. He left the Holiness Methodist/Non-denominational movement, and in December of 1955, they returned to Minnesota. Don was ordained at Fourth Baptist Church and again became the Youth Pastor under the leadership of Dr. Clearwaters. Those who sat under Don's ministry have often referred to the next eleven years as the "Glory Years".

The book he authored, *The Youth Program That Works*, has been used extensively by youth pastors throughout America. The principles have led to many souls being saved and young people dedicating their lives to full-time Christian service. The thrust of this system capitalized on Don's military background, and the program was unique.

Don wrote in his Bible, "I am a Youth Pastor. I am more than a teacher of religious education. I am more than a recreational director. I am a LEADER OF YOUTH. I must, by my life, make daily applications of the verse "For to me to live is Christ and to die is gain." It is imperative that I make a strong spiritual impact, exhibit personal integrity, have a strong competitive spirit, and exemplify good sportsmanship and champion fair play. I cannot be a quitter. I am training soldiers for Christ."

Hundreds of youth and young adults went through the Fourth Baptist youth program into full-time service worldwide.

After graduation from Pillsbury Baptist Bible College in 1966, Don pastored in Colorado. From 1971-1973, he taught at Piedmont Bible College in Winston-Salem, North Carolina, setting up their Christian service department. From 1973 to 1990 he pastored in Ft. Lauderdale, Florida. From 1990 to his home-going January 14, 2000, he ministered to many missionaries throughout the Caribbean Islands, Central and South America. His favorite word was *Courage*! His personal life challenged others for soul winning and service for the Lord.

Don always had a camera in hand. His Baptist film collection is housed in Pensacola Christian College, and his personal films are with his daughters. Don's final words to his wife, four daughters, grandchildren, and friends were from 1 Corinthians 15:58, "Therefore, my beloved brethren, be ye steadfast, immoveable, always abounding in the work of the Lord, forasmuch as ye know that your labor is not in vain in the Lord."[1]

DCB

[1] Telephone interview with Barbara Nelson Vallier by Bettye Baughan, September 8, 2004.

August 23

Not Many Mighty, But Some

Scripture: 1 Corinthians 1:26-29

Often as we think of the early days of the Baptist movement in America, we are led to the realization that our forefathers were not to be found among the high and mighty of society. It is apparent that most of the growth of the Baptists was to be found in the rural areas of the colonies. In speaking of the establishment of the First Baptist Church of Haverville, Massachusetts, Dr. David Benedict wrote: ". . . a Baptist church arose at the time . . . in the center of town; a rare occurrence in those days, when the denomination seldom made any efforts but in remote situations."[1] It should not shock us that the expansion of the Baptist ministry in the early days of America primarily attracted those in the lower economical strata of society.

However, there were surely exceptions to this rule. Before becoming the outstanding leader of the Baptists in Virginia, Samuel Harris "occupied several prominent stations in society such as, 'church warden, sheriff, justice of the peace, burgess for the county, colonel of the militia, captain of Mayo fort, and commissary for the fort and army.'"[2] Eleaszer Clay, uncle of Henry Clay the great American statesman, was another case in point. David Benedict claimed that "he was reputed worth 100 thousand dollars." Eleaszer Clay was Sheriff of Chesterfield county, Virginia, and when souls were saved by the proclamation of the Gospel through the jail grates by imprisoned Baptist preachers, Eleaszer Clay was concerned. He wrote to his friend, Rev. John Williams of Amelia County on July 21, 1773, as follows: "We wish you to come down and baptize those who are now waiting for an opportunity. The Lord is now carrying on a glorious work in our county. The preaching at the prison is not attended in vain, for we hope that several are converted, while others are under great distress, and are made to cry out, 'What shall we do to be saved.'"[3] "In the face of arrest John Williams and William Webber came into Chesterfield and on August 23, 1773, constituted Chesterfield Church with twenty members dismissed for that purpose from the church in Cumberland. . . . Eleaszer Clay . . . became its pastor."[4]

John Williams, himself, is another case in point. He had received a good education, and become a prominent citizen and served as Sheriff of Amelia County, Virginia. He was apparently saved under the preaching of Samuel Harris, and when the Meherrin Baptist Church was established, he was a charter member. Upon the resignation of Elder Jeremiah Walker, the founding pastor, John Williams became the pastor and served with great success. Under his ministry five or six branch churches were formed. In 1785 he moved to Charlotte, Virginia to become pastor of the Sandy Creek Baptist Church.

Reverend Williams became a proven leader. He was asked by his brethren on several occasions to represent them before the politicians of the commonwealth to present their case for the cause of religious liberty. He also became a patron among his brethren for the interests of education. Recognizing his ability, his peers asked Reverend Williams to write a history of the Baptist churches of Virginia. But after compiling a great deal of material, his health began to decline and he had to resign that challenge.

Following an accidental fall in 1793, Reverend Williams became a cripple. He persisted in preaching, though he had to be transported in a carriage. He actually preached while sitting in a chair. An attack of pleurisy early in the Spring of 1795 was more than he could endure, and on April 30, 1795, he fell asleep in Jesus.

Paul wrote that not many wise and noble are called, but he did not say "not any." Let us thank God for those whom the Lord has gifted along the way as they use their gifts for His glory.

DLC

---

[1] David Benedict, *A General History of the Baptist Denomination in America* (New York: Lewis Colby and Company, 1848), 402.

[2] James B. Taylor, *Lives of Virginia Baptist Ministers* (Richmond: Yale & Wyatt, 1838), 1:28.

[3] Ibid., 1:203-204.

[4] Garnett Ryland, *The Baptists of Virginia 1699-1926* (Richmond, VA: The Virginia Baptist Board of Missions and Education, 1955), 79.

August 24

A Brief But Wise Ministry

Scripture: Luke 1:1-4

Jacob Darden was born in Southampton, Virginia, on August 24, 1770. We know little concerning his early training with the exception that the records reveal he possessed a capricious spirit. When he reached the age of maturity he settled down and moved in the select circles of society. He imbibed the theology of deism, and continued in that realm until he was thirty-nine years of age. In privacy he approached the throne of God's grace, confessed his sin, and implored forgiveness in the name of Jesus Christ, Whom he had persecuted. God the Holy Spirit had performed the miracle of conviction and conversion in his life, and a genuine transformation of life took place. It was evident to all that he was a changed person. The Lord freed him from a tortured conscience, and soon he requested baptism at the hand of Elder John Bowers at the South Quay Baptist Church.

Recognizing the worth of a soul, and how close he had come to perdition, Mr. Darden soon began giving positive testimony as to God's grace. As he continued testifying, his witness soon developed into preaching, and shortly thereafter the congregation licensed him to preach. The Lord granted much fruit through his ministry, and on October 2, 1813, in his forty-third year, he was ordained to the gospel ministry.

The remainder of his life was spent in witness for Christ and service to mankind. His life was exemplary. He "ruled well his own household." He manifested an ardent spirit for the welfare of all men. He was deliberate in his decisions, and maintained a dignity seldom seen in his day. The result was that the citizenry gladly heard him. Solomon's words were surely applicable in his life: "When a man's ways please the Lord, he maketh even his enemies to be at peace with him."

Soon after he entered into his ministry, he became aware of a great weakness in his lungs. He discovered that he was spitting blood whenever he over-exerted himself. Thus he traveled but little, and seldom preached. However, during one of his extended efforts, a glorious revival was experienced. Tragically he could not continue long in the pulpit, and shortly he was ordered to bed. Knowing that God does all things well, His servant accepted trial from the hand of God. His entire dependence was upon the Lord Jesus Christ, and He knew that God makes no mistakes.

His physical condition continued to deteriorate, and about a week before his home going, an older preacher visited him. He invited the man of God into his room and asked him to close the door and take a bedside seat. When the gentleman was seated, Reverend Darden said: "Brother, I feel a great anxiety that young converts of the late revival should be instructed much in the leading doctrines of the gospel. I fear much that many young Christians may be led into error. I request that you will take much pains, in the spirit of meekness, to guard them against the heresies of the day; especially, the Unitarian and Socinian doctrine, which has already overthrown the faith of many. I expect this to be the last interview we shall have in time; I therefore make it as a dying request."

Two days before his heavenward journey, he said to a young believer, "Brother, I am glad to see you. I thought this morning I should have been gone before now; but I was resigned. I seem to be passing along pleasantly. I have had the presence of Jesus." After a few moments more, he said: "I have fought a good fight, and my trust is in the Redeemer for the crown of righteousness."[1]

It was October 28, 1827, when the Lord called His servant to His eternal rest.

One of the weaknesses of evangelism among fundamental Baptists has been the failure to properly disciple new converts. As much as we need evangelism, we need conservation in our efforts for Christ. May the Lord speak to some pastors' hearts as this reminder is given.

DLC

---

[1] James B. Taylor, *Lives of Virginia Baptist Ministers* (Richmond: Yale & Wyatt, 1838), 395.

August 25

A Multi-Talented Servant

Scripture: Matthew 6:25-34

From 1813 to 1815, Vermont had a unique circumstance—both its governor and its lieutenant governor were Baptists. The lieutenant governor was Aaron Leland. Leland was born in Holliston, Massa, May 28, 1761. He became a member of the Baptist church in Bellingham, Massachusetts, in 1785, and soon after was licensed by that church to preach. That same year he received a letter from fifteen people living in Chester, Massachusetts, none of whom were Baptists, requesting him to come and preach among them for a short time. He traveled to Chester a few months later. When he arrived, he found the situation so difficult and the prospect so unpromising, that he considered leaving town immediately. However after Leland was there a short time, the passage "The Lord hath much people in this city" captured his attention.[1]

Leland chose to remain in Chester. He ministered in the little church for more than a decade in peaceful harmony with the people and community. The church experienced a small increase, but nothing remarkable took place in those early years. However, in 1799 a revival began, which had a dramatic effect upon the church. This revival affected not only the Chester church, but it spread to several of the neighboring towns. At the end of this revival, Leland's church had become so large that the members decided to divide the congregation. On August 1, 1803, four churches were started in the towns of Andover, Grafton, Wethersfield, and Cavendish. Two of the new pastors had been deacons in the mother church.[2]

His fellow Baptists recognized Leland's administrative abilities. He was one of the Fellows of Middlebury College and received an honorary degree of Master of Arts from that institution in 1814 and another from Brown University in 1815.[3]

Leland served both the churches and the state. For nine years he was a representative in the General Assembly. He was Speaker of the House for three years, and he was on the governor's council for four years. For five years he was Lieutenant Governor of Vermont; for two of those years Rev. Ezra Butler, another Baptist, was governor. For eighteen years he was one of the assistant justices of the county court. He was asked to run for governor in 1828, but he feared this would take too much time away from the work of the ministry, so he declined. While he was Speaker of the House a proposition came before it calling for the separation of church and state. In the debate someone argued that Christianity could not survive without the support of the state. This stirred his spirit. He left his chair as Speaker and took part in the debate, "delivering one of the strongest speeches ever heard in Vermont in favor of religious liberty, the main strength of his position being that God had founded his Church upon a rock, and that the gates of hell should not prevail against her."[4]

Eventually he concluded that he was spending too much time in politics and too little time in spiritual pursuits. As a result, he gave up all his civil functions, except his position of circuit judge, which only occupied his attention a few weeks per year. He finished his life spending the majority of his time in ministry to his church.[5] On August 25, 1833, Aaron Leland, that bright light of early American Baptists, died and entered into his eternal reward.

Although he was an accomplished statesman, he was, first and foremost, a popular and effective preacher. He had a commanding preaching style; he was able to structure his sermons for the benefit of the people; his preaching voice was smooth and mellow; he was endowed with a great fervor of spirit; his preaching was clear, but impassioned, and he was able to carry with him the multitude irresistibly. How encouraging to find a man with such public abilities and political wisdom, who was popular with the masses, but who chose to seek first the kingdom of God.

LRO

---

[1] David Benedict, *A General History of the Baptist Denomination in America* (Boston: Lincoln & Edmands, 1813), 344.

[2] Ibid., 345.

[3] William Cathcart, *The Baptist Encyclopedia* (Philadelphia: Louis H. Everts. 1881), 1221.

[4] Thomas Armitage, *A History of the Baptists* (New York: Bryan, Taylor, and Co., 1890), 812.

[5] Benedict, 345.

August 26

Visiting A Hero in Prison

Scripture: 1 Corinthians 1:3-10

The emotional trauma of visiting one's father, son, or grandmother in a slave camp or Russian prison during the days of the communistic regime is beyond description. To discourage personal visits of family members, prisoners were usually transported to the far reaches of the U. S. S. R. Many time zones separated family members from the living martyrs who worked as slaves in the communistic penitentiaries. Georgi Vins knew the prison system well. His father, Peter Yakovlech Vins, had been shot to death on August 26, 1937, while in prison (Vol. 2:323). Between Georgi's two prison terms, his mother, sixty four year old, Lydia Vins, was imprisoned for a three-year term for assisting families of religious prisoners. Her grandchildren lovingly called Lydia "babushka." The Lord strengthened her resolve, and she was enabled to endure the rigors of prison life, finally being released on December 1, 1973. Georgi's wife, Nadia, and daughter, Natasha, along with the younger children, did all in their power to correspond and visit the inmates.

Of course, many of the letters from Georgi to his family were "lost," but graciously the Lord allowed some to penetrate the curtain of silence. The censors deleted references of a negative nature, but the unconquerable spirit of the victims became a continual source of encouragement to family members.

On October 5, 1968, Georgi wrote his wife: "Nadia, my dearest, I greet and hug you! How are you managing with the children all by yourself? I am constantly thinking about you. I always pray for you, the children, and our dear Babushka. Thank you for the family picture: the children are growing up, while you and I are getting older. Our hair is getting gray, and all this while we have been apart for years . . . But don't be discouraged: the Lord is with us! It is most important that we remain faithful to Him and to each other in sincere love. May the Lord protect you all. I am praying for a chance to see you. Please read 2 Cornthians 1:3-10 (especially verses, 3, 4, 5). With much love, Your Georgi"[1]

Brain washing efforts of the communistic regime were predictable. Public school education was mandatory, and beginning in the earliest grades, children were bombarded with atheistic philosophy. Pressure continued to mount on youth during the teen years. At times, the approach differed. Rather than ridicule, the maturing offspring of spiritual dissidents were informed that they would not be allowed to enter university classes if they persisted in believing the Bible and creationism. Natasha, being the oldest of the Vins children, was the first in the family to experience these efforts. But in the course of time, Peter, Lisa, and Jane also endured such ridicule. It is wonderful to realize that each member of the family was enabled to withstand the attacks of the enemy. How could it be? Doubtless there were several ingredients that merged with the grace of God to provide the victory. First, there were the faithful prayers and godly examples of Babushka, Georgi, and Nadia. Secondly, one must credit the saints of God in the local church who were willing to endure many privations. They repudiated the compromise of the "registered Baptists" and were willing to suffer the consequences. Regardless of the weather, saints met clandestinely, often in the dead of winter standing in the snow, worshiping for hours. The reality of personally knowing the Lord Jesus Christ could not be denied.

The deliverance God provided for the Vins family is amazing! In a prisoner exchange with the U. S. S. R., Georgi Vins was flown to America on April 27, 1979. His family was exiled on June 14. A new ministry was opened to His servant and his family. Georgi Vins continued in faithful service until his home going on January 11, 1998.[2]

May we determine that regardless of what the future holds, we will be true to our godly convictions until our Savior calls or comes!

DLC

[1] Natasha Vins, *Children of the Storm* (Greenville, SC: Bob Jones University Press, 2002), 26.

[2] Ibid., 134.

August 27

Does Baptism Really Matter?

Scripture: Acts 18:8

The story of the conversion of Adoniram and Ann Judson to Baptist convictions has been told before, but the following correspondence brings it into sharp focus. The first letter is from Ann to her parents. It was dated February 14, 1813, and sent from the Isle of France.

I will now, my dear parents and sisters, give you some account of our change of sentiment, relative to the subject of baptism. Mr. Judson's doubts commenced on our passage from America. While translating the New Testament, in which he was engaged, he used frequently to say that the Baptists were right in their mode of administering the ordinance. Knowing that he should meet the Baptists in Serampore, he felt impelled to attend to it more closely, to be able to defend his sentiments. After our arrival in Serampore, his mind for two or three weeks was much taken up with missionary inquiries and our difficulties with government, as to prevent his attending to the subject of baptism. But as we were awaiting the arrival of our brethren, and having nothing in particular to attend to, he again took up the subject. I tried to have him give it up, and rest satisfied with his old sentiments, and frequently told him, if he became a Baptist, I would not. He, however, said he felt it his duty to examine closely a subject on which he had so many doubts. After we removed to Calcutta, he found in the library of our chamber many books on both sides, which he determined to read candidly and prayerfully, and to hold fast, or embrace the truth, however mortifying, however great the sacrifice. I now commenced reading on the subject, with all my prejudices on the Pedobaptist side. We had with us Dr. Worcester's, Dr. Austin's, Peter Edward's, and other Pedobaptist writings. But after closely examining the subject for several weeks, we were constrained to acknowledge that the truth appeared to lie on the Baptists' side. It was extremely trying to reflect on the consequences of our becoming Baptists. We knew that it would wound and grieve our dear friends in America, that we should lose their approbation and esteem. We thought it probable that the commission would refuse to support us; and, what was more distressing than anything, we knew we must be separated from our missionary associates, and go alone to some heathen land. These things were very trying to us, and caused our hearts to bleed with anguish. We felt that we had no home in this world, and no friend but each other. Our friends at Serampore were extremely surprised when we wrote them a letter requesting baptism, as they had known nothing of our having had any doubts on the subject. We were baptized on the 6th of September, in the Baptist chapel in Calcutta. Mr. J. preached a sermon at Calcutta, on that subject, soon after which we were baptized and, in compliance with the request of a number who heard it, he has been preparing for the press. Brother Rice was baptized several weeks after we were. It was a very great relief to our minds to have him join us, as we expected to be entirely alone in a mission.

At the time of his decision to be baptized, on August 27, 1812, Adoniram Judson wrote to the Baptists missionaries,

Rev. Messrs. Carey, Marshman and Ward:

As you have been ignorant of the late exercises of my mind on the subject of baptism, the communication which I am about to make may occasion you some surprise.

It is about four months since I took the subject into serious and prayerful consideration. My inquiries commenced during my passage from America, and after much laborious research and painful trial, which I shall not now detail, have issued in entire conviction, that the immersion of a professing believer is the only Christian baptism.

In these exercises I have not been alone. Mrs. Judson has been engaged in a similar examination, and has come to the same conclusion. Feeling, therefore, that we are in an unbaptized state, we wish to profess our faith in Christ by being baptized in obedience to his sacred commands.

Adoniram Judson, Jr.

If it was essential for faithful missionaries such as the Judsons to follow the Lord in believer's immersion, is it not important for you? Have you been biblically baptized?

DLC

August 28

A Worshiper of Facts

Scripture: Acts 9

In the city of Rockford, Illinois, one can find a magnificent bust of a former pastor of the historic fundamental First Baptist Church, who is memorialized as a significant person in the city's history. To see this bust you must enter into the Unitarian church, the very temple of evil, where his memorial is prominently placed. For it is here where he is most appreciated.

This Day in Baptist History III

How did a Baptist pastor end up memorialized by a Unitarian church? The answer to this question is a vivid illustration of the Apostle's warning that false teachers could possibly spring from among us. It is the story of Dr. Thomas Kerr.

Dr. Thomas Kerr was a medical doctor. He was a Scottish immigrant with training from the Iowa State University and seven years of medical practice before theology and philosophy began to interest him. There is little to be found of his early life, but public records tell of a man who was remarkably intelligent. In 1860 he became the pastor of First Baptist Church in Rockford, Illinois. It seems that his ministry at First Baptist was appreciated, but Dr. Thomas Kerr desiring to expand his world resigned the Rockford pulpit to start a new life in Missouri. It was during this absence that the congregation of First Baptist began to realize how much they missed his brilliant messages, but it was also during this time that Thomas Kerr began to drink deeply from the writings of Darwin. After three years, Dr. Thomas Kerr responded to the call of his former church and returned to pastor in Rockford in 1869. However, as the Rockford Morning Star recalls it, Dr. Thomas Kerr began to "outgrow his environment." We do not concur with the wording of the secular paper that commended the open-mindedness of the apostate pastor. We would instead say that Dr. Thomas Kerr began to apostatize. The Rockford paper glowingly pictured Dr. Thomas Kerr as a "worshipper of facts" and celebrated his willingness to embrace other doctrine. Thankfully, stalwart members of First Baptist Church did not feel the same way.

On August 28, 1870, Dr. Thomas Kerr preached his resignation message in the sanctuary of First Baptist Church. It is a message filled with blasphemy. Forty-eight members of First Baptist Church left with Dr. Kerr to join a Unitarian group in order to form a new church. That fall they adopted bylaws, which, according to the records of the Unitarian church, "contained no fundamental dogmas or stated creed." Dr. Kerr's message is produced in pamphlet form by that evil group as a trophy of the triumph of humanism over historical Christianity. The false teachers who celebrate Kerr's life ignore the obvious irony: Kerr, the "worshipper of facts" sold his soul to a lie. Leading secular scientists today declare Darwinism as a theory, not a science.

George Whitefield incensed the clergy of his day when he dared to suggest that some of them, if not many of them, had not experienced the regenerating work of the Holy Spirit within their souls. They were mere professionals. They weren't even saved. This is possible even among Baptist churches. Men who have not had the saving power of God convert their souls will not have the keeping power of God to preserve their souls. It will be true of them as John said, "They went out from us, but they were not of us; for if they had been of us, they would no doubt have continued with us: but they went out, that they might be made manifest that they were not all of us" (1 John 2:19). This is also why Paul urged Timothy to be vigilant over his own soul. "Take heed unto thyself, and unto the doctrine; continue in them: for in doing this thou shalt both save thyself, and them that hear thee" (1 Timothy 4:16).

It was a difficult Lord's Day for First Baptist Church, but it was not a day of which to be ashamed. Their issues were not trivial, personal, or tainted by personal ambition. Vital truth was at stake. They survived. First Baptist Church continues to this day to preach the beloved Gospel for which it has suffered. Let's pray for the souls of our pastors.

RPB

August 29

Let Freedom Ring

Scripture: 2 Corinthians 3:17

Most Americans are amazed to discover that in the early days of this republic, religious intolerance was the accepted norm. In a sermon preached by N. L. Frothingham, Boston, August 29, 1830, he said: "Two hundred years ago there was no such thing as toleration. In practice it was unknown, save of a few mild spirits; and even in open theory it was derided and condemned."[1] Please observe that the two hundred years mentioned would take his hearers back to 1630 and the landing of the Pilgrims at Plymouth Rock.

Religious freedom was never planned for America, for the Pilgrims desired to plant a theocracy. It is safe to say that soul liberty and religious freedom might never have been experienced in America had it not been for our Baptist forefathers who were determined to assure such an environment as they established the little state of Rhode Island. The successful experiment in Rhode Island in time was adopted by every colony and finally by the entire nation. In speaking of the Baptists in Rhode Island, Gervinius, in the introduction to *The History of the Nineteenth Century*, wrote: "Here in a little state the fundamental principles of political and ecclesiastical liberty practically prevailed, before they were even taught in any of the schools of philosophy in Europe. But not only have these ideas and these forms of government maintained themselves, but precisely from this little state, have they extended themselves throughout the United States. They have conquered the aristocratic tendencies in Carolina and New York, the high church in Virginia, the theocracy in Massachusetts, and the monarchy in all America. They have given laws to a continent; and formidable through their moral influence, they lie at the bottom of all democratic movements that are now shaking the nations of Europe."

B. F. Riley in his book, *The Baptists in the Building of the Nation*, wrote, "On the western side of the capitol building, at Providence, [Rhode Island] cut in marble, one may read this inscription: 'That it is much on their hearts (if they may be permitted) to hold forth a lively experiment, that a more flourishing civil state may stand and best be maintained, and that among our English subjects, with a full liberty of religious concernments.' This is the language of Dr. John Clarke, the author of the Royal Charter, which he was able to obtain from Charles II."[2]

We would observe that Dr. John Clarke was founder-pastor of the Baptist church in Newport, Rhode Island.

Of the thirteen colonies, nine had a State/Church arrangement. Primarily in the northern tier of colonies, the State-Church was Congregational, while in Virginia, Georgia, and the Carolinas, the State/Church was the Church of England. Pennsylvania, having been founded by a Quaker, granted quite a bit of religious freedom. Maryland, though dominated by the Roman Church, was forced by political pressure to grant some religious freedom, but only Rhode

Island, founded by the Baptists, granted total religious freedom. As a result, the first Jewish Synagogue to be built in America was constructed in Rhode Island. When our national constitution was presented in 1787, it was sent to the individual states for ratification. The new constitution created a representative republic without the establishment of a national state-church. But liberty of conscience was still not assured, and thus Rhode Island along with Virginia would not vote to ratify until James Madison promised John Leland that he would propose a Bill of Rights, and the First Amendment would guarantee the fact that a national state-church would never be formed.[3]

Let us praise the Lord for those who have gone before us and established the freedom of religion and soul liberty that we have. And let us be ever alert to protect these freedoms for our posterity.

DLC

[1] John T. Christian, *A History of the Baptists* (Nashville, TN: Broadman Press, 1926), 2:20.

[2] B. F. Riley, *The Baptists in the Building of the Nation* (Watertown, WI: Roger Williams Heritage Archives, Maranatha Baptist College, n.d.), 50.

[3] James R. Beller, *America in Crimson Red* (Arnold, MO: Prairie Fire Press, 2004), 289.

August 30

Pioneering for Christ

Scripture: Romans 15:20

The expansion of the United States was greatly enhanced with the Louisiana Purchase in 1803. The purchase more than doubled the territory of our nation, and allowed for enlargement of the burgeoning population. The purchase was almost a gift from Napoleon who desired to avert the prospect of humiliation with the possible capture of the area by the British. The cost to America was about two cents per acre! But with the consummation of that purchase, the challenge of home missions in America greatly expanded.

Iowa was part of that purchase. On June 28, 1834, Congress made what is today Iowa a part of the Territory of Michigan. This was done to establish a more stable government. Twelve years later, December 28, 1846, the state of Iowa was formed with its present boundaries. In 1834, a young couple-William and Hepzibah Mathes-Manley-were united in marriage in Kentucky. Wanting to establish a homestead, they traveled to Iowa. In what is now Burlington, Iowa, they found four or five log huts. There they set up housekeeping in the unbroken wilderness. Across the river in Illinois was a Baptist preacher, Elder John Logan, and the young couple invited him to the new settlement to preach. Thus on October 19, 1834, John Logan preached the first sermon in Iowa. A few Baptists from Illinois had moved into the area, and the following day the first Baptist church in Iowa was formed. William and Hepzibah had carried the Articles of Faith from the Brush Creek Baptist Church in Green County, Kentucky. They were adopted and " . . . eleven people organized the Long Creek Baptist church. This later became the Danville church."[1]

The first Baptist minister known to have settled in Iowa was Elder Hezekiah Johnson. Born in the home of a Baptist preacher in Maryland on March 6, 1799, young Hezekiah soon came to know the Savior. His parents moved to Ohio when he was a teenager, and Hezekiah was licensed to preach in 1825. He married the following year, and was ordained in April of 1827.

The next seven years found him preaching in the Buckeye State, but he traveled and preached as far as Iowa. Hezekiah Johnson was commissioned as a missionary under the American Baptist Home Mission Society in 1838, and he made his way to Iowa, where, as we have noted, he became the first "settled" Baptist pastor. In 1845, Hezekiah Johnson and Ezra Fisher were asked by the Home Society to go to Oregon to pioneer that ministry. Hezekiah settled there in Oregon City, and established a church. He was one of the early Baptist preachers in that state as well. In the course of years, Reverend Johnson's health degenerated, and the Lord called him home on August 28, 1866.[2] A memorial service was held two days later on August 30.

How challenging to "pioneer" a work for Christ! That was the spirit of the early Baptists in America. Though they did not catch the burden of foreign missions until early in the nineteenth century, our Baptist forefathers in America saw the need of expanding to the West and they rose to accomplish that task. Make no mistake about it; they were in the religious vanguard of the day. For instance, consider the following quotation. "The first volume, now given to the public, deals with the Baptists because these groups *were the first to take an active interest in the frontier* situation as migrations moved westward when the territory between the Alleghenies and the Mississippi was settled"[3] (Italics not in original).

Unfortunately, numerical and financial expansion often produces apathy. Our Lord warned the Church at Laodicea against this very attitude in Revelation 3:17. With the receding spiritual impact of the Gospel today, it is time that fundamental Baptist churches in America re-seed the countryside with vibrant, victorious local congregations to reach others for Christ. Pray that your local church will gain such a vision today.

DLC

---

[1] G. P. Mitchell, *A Century of Iowa Baptist History* (Pella, IA: The Baptist Record, 1934), 18.

[2] C. H. Mattoon, *Baptist Annals of Oregon* (McMinnville, OR: Telephone Register Publishing Co., 1905), 1:47.

[3] William Warren Sweet, *Religion On The American Frontier* (New York: Cooper Square Publishers, Inc., 1964), VI.

August 31

You Cannot Hide From God

Scripture: Psalm 139:7-12

To Tidance Lane, born on August 31, 1724, goes the honor of establishing Tennessee's first Baptist church in 1779. Eighteen years later, Garner McConnico moved from Virginia to Tennessee, and he too made strides for the Baptists in the state. Consider his life.

This Day in Baptist History III

Following the Revolutionary War, an English Baptist preacher came to the area in Virginia where young Garner McConnico resided. Mrs. McConnico wanted to hear the preacher, and she insisted that her young son attend with her. Remembering treatment received from the British, the youngster wanted nothing to do with any Englishman! However, his mother insisted, and Garner accompanied her. Seeing a diminutive man stand to preach drew the boy's interest. By the sermon's end, the lad was standing near the old man in tears. From that time, Garner found no rest until he received the gift of salvation. Upon professing faith, he became a member of a Baptist church four miles west of the Lunenburg courthouse.

The boy matured into manhood and married Miss Mary Walker. Soon he was proclaiming the gospel, and the church licensed him. Hearing of the beauty of the Cumberland Valley in Tennessee, the young couple caught the "fever" and made their way toward the west. Young McConnico was, however, attempting to flee God's call to preach. For two years he was silent, but one day his horse strayed. As he sought the stray, Garner walked along a narrow path cut through tall cane. He spied a small, venerable-looking man approaching, and immediately he thought of the Apostle Paul. After the usual greetings, Garner asked the gentleman about the community. Then he asked, "Any Baptist preaching in it?" The elderly gentleman responded, "There will be Baptist preaching next Lord's Day." Garner asked, "Are you the preacher?" "I try to preach sometimes for want of a better preacher," he replied. The next Sunday, Garner was present to hear the old man who proved to be the well-known preacher, Elder Dillahunty. After the service, the Elder announced preaching the next Sunday at Richland Meeting House. Garner arose and said, "I will be there too." "And who are you?," asked the Elder. "The man you met in the canebreak." "A Baptist?" "Yes." "And a preacher?" "Why, yes, I have tried to preach a little." Now the secret was out.

When Sunday arrived, McConnico was present, and he tried to beg off of preaching. However, the old preacher would not allow it, and in time McConnico rose to preach. Before he had concluded the message, Elder Dillahunty threw his arms around Garner. He thanked God for sending young Timothy to the frontier to assist him.

In 1797, Elder McConnico moved to Franklin, Tennessee. There he lived and served the Big Harpeth Baptist Church for thirty-five years. Though not a classical scholar, he proved to be a diligent Bible student. Many professed Christ through his ministry, and many churches were founded through his instrumentality. His physical stature made him a leader of men, but his spiritual stature was greatly used of God.

McConnico lived during revival days. Among the so-called religious phenomena of that time was an exercise called the "jerks." People professing to be under the power of God's Spirit would "jerk" violently. Once as McConnico preached, someone in the audience began that gesticulation. McConnonico suddenly stopped. Then in a solemn voice he exclaimed, "In the name of the Lord, I command all unclean spirits to leave this place." Immediately the jerking stopped, and peace was restored.

McConnico's voice was rich and powerful. On one occasion when he went to preach, the river had flooded and he could not get over to where the crowd was gathered. He raised his hands and asked for silence. Then he lifted his voice a little above its usual pitch and preached his message with power. It was said that he had a voice like a trumpet.[1]

Perhaps God has called you, but you are fleeing His will. The happiest place is always the center of God's will. Obey Him today!

DLC

---

[1] J. J. Burnett, *Sketches of Tennessee's Pioneer Preachers* (Nashville, TN: Marshall & Bruce Company, 1919), 364.

September 1

Not Many Mighty, Not Many Wise

Scripture: 1 Corinthians 1:26

I believe had you known Reverend B. H. Farrington, you would agree with me that the Scripture verse I have cited applies to this man of God. Benjamin Harrison Farrington, who was named after President Benjamin Harrison, was born May 5, 1894, in Guilford County, North Carolina. His parents were Tilman Patrick Harrison and Martha A. Roberson Harrison. He had two sisters and four brothers.

Both of his parents were illiterate, and Farrington grew up without being able to read. He had little formal education. His mother was a godly woman who tried to instill good morals in her son, but his father was a heavy drinker. Early in his life he began to drink, following the footsteps of his father. He ran with the wrong crowd, wasted his money on booze, and also destroyed his health. Evil companions corrupted the good morals his mother had taught him. He became known as a king bootlegger.

In his sermon *From Blockade Still to the Pulpit*, Ben tells of a young man in the community who visited him and prayed for him regularly. Ben would avoid Richard O. Knuckles every chance he got, but God dealt with Ben's hard heart. When Ben could stand the conviction no longer, he sent for the preacher and, through the influence of Brother Knuckles, was saved at the age of 32. He was baptized and joined the Smith Grove Baptist Church, located in Guilford County. He now drank from God's fountain that never runs dry. Praise the Lord for godly preachers who will plead to God for the lost and seek them out.

Ben married Delia Ann Frazier on March 25, 1916. To this union were born six children, four girls and two boys. His oldest son was killed in World War II, one daughter died when she was two months old, and another daughter was killed in an automobile accident in Greensboro, North Carolina, in 1993. A son died in 2002. Two daughters are still living.

Benjamin was an electrician by trade. Having worked for several others in his youth, he eventually became self-employed. During the days he would work his job, and in the evenings he would hold services. He learned to read and write, studied the Bible, and began to carry on a ministry of revival preaching and church planting. He bought a tent for $150, loaded it in his Buick and began to hold meetings all around the Greensboro, Winston-Salem, and the High Point area in North Carolina. The first meeting was held in Smith Grove Baptist Church. His father and sister were saved in that meeting.

It was obvious that the power of God was on Ben. Everywhere he went souls were saved and churches were planted. He would set up his tent in an area, preach for several weeks, and organize a local Baptist church with the new converts. Many times he would take with him someone who wanted to pastor a church and leave that man there to establish the work; then he would move on to the next area. It is estimated that he was responsible for organizing between 21 and 30 Baptist churches. Many are still in existence today. Most of these churches are located in North Carolina and Virginia. As his ministry expanded, he had the privilege of preaching in other states. In fact, he was ministering in Florida when word came to him that his son was missing in action.

Though limited in training, this willing vessel was used in a great way. His ministry was not a long one, but it was productive. In 1965 he developed a kidney problem. After several years of battling this illness, the Lord called His servant home on September 1, 1969.

I never cease to be amazed how God takes men like B. H. Farrington, saves them, equips them, uses them in His service, and then takes them on to heaven. God help us to be faithful to the task He has given us until our time comes to go home to heaven.

DCB

---

[1]Recorded sermon by Rev. B.H. Farrington titled *From The Blockade Still to the Pulpit* (1954).

[2] Materials gathered from personal conversations and written material supplied by Rev. Farrington's daughter, Clara (Farrington) Long of Colfax, North Carolina.

September 2

A Faithful Servant of Christ

Scripture: Luke 16:1-13

Joshua Judson Myers was born July 20, 1846, in Orangeburg District, South Carolina. His father, Joshua, being a staunch Baptist, named his sons after Baptist ministers, and Joshua Judson was no exception, having been named after Adoniram Judson, the famous Baptist missionary to Burma. His brother Manly Furman Myers, was named after Basil Manly and Richard Furman, two outstanding Baptist leaders in the South. In his youth, Joshua attended local schools all close to his home.[1]

On June 7, 1864, while still a teenager, Joshua entered the Confederate Army. On that same day, unknown to him, his brother Gerard Joshua Myers died. It must have been a crushing day to his parents. Joshua was in Company I when the surrender took place at Appomattox, Virginia on April 9, 1865. In 1896 he attended his first reunion of Confederate veterans in Richmond, Virginia. He was asked to be the Chaplain at the Confederate veterans' reunion in 1917 in Washington, D.C. He accepted the invitation, but inasmuch as the Lord wanted him in Heaven prior to that appointment, he was not able to fill the appointment.

We surmise that before enlisting in the army Joshua probably knew the girl who would become his wife. She lived in the St. Matthews area of South Carolina where Joshua's grandparents lived, and from time to time he visited them. Joshua and Emily Rosalie Happoldt were married December 23, 1866, in St. Matthews. They lived with his parents initially, and then upon receiving a plot of land from his father, the couple built a beautiful home in Providence, South Carolina. They reared a family of five boys and four girls. The home place remained in the family until 1907.

Having been saved and wanting to serve the Lord, Joshua had a growing desire to preach. He was licensed in May of 1881 and ordained the following July by the famed High Hills of Santee Baptist Church. It will be remembered High Hills of Santee had been founded by Joseph Reese and was home church of the noted Richard Furman. Joshua was active in the ministry until 1917 when he retired because of failing health. His longest pastorates were at the Congaree Baptist Church and the Beulah Baptist Church located just out of Columbia. He was a faithful pastor, well beloved by his people. By trade he was a cabinetmaker. This helped to provide for the needs of his large family, but his main passion was preaching the Gospel.

Many of our early Baptist preachers worked to support their families so they could preach. Most churches in the South were too small to support a pastor, and financially the area had been impoverished during the Civil War.

Joshua Myers was a meticulous writer. He authored articles for several publications, kept detailed financial records, and wrote out all of his sermons in manuscript form. A number of his sermons have been preserved. The author of this article possesses three such sermons in his personal collection. It is said that when writing, if he made a mistake he would tear up the sheet and start over again.[2]

Joshua Judson Jud Myers entered the presence of the Lord February 14, 1917, at Congaree, Richland County, South Carolina. At the time of his death he was pastor emeritus of the Beulah Baptist Church. His funeral service was conducted in the First Baptist Church at Sumter. It was his wish to be buried there inasmuch as his daughter, Julia, had been buried there in 1899, and three of his children lived in the area. His good friend, Dr. Bristow, led the service along with Dr. Brunson and another Sumter minister. His grandsons were the pallbearers. His dear wife, Emily, died on September 2, 1928.

The dying words of the man of God were these: "Tell all the people to be faithful." May the Lord help us to heed those words in our day that we might finish the work He has for us to do.[3]

DCB

---

[1] William Cox Allen, *History of the Beulah Baptist Church* (Columbia: Vogue Press, 1962), 64.

[2] Personal correspondents with Mrs. Jean Myers Smith of Greer, South Carolina, who has written a history of the Myers family.

[3] *The State*, Columbia, SC, February 25, 1917.

September 3

Always Abounding

Scripture: 1 Corinthians 15:58

The Northern Neck, a peninsula lying between the Potomac and Rappahannock rivers, is one of the most historic sections of Virginia. George Washington, James Madison, John Monroe, and Robert E. Lee were all born there. Also, the first public association formed in America for resistance to the Stamp Act was organized on the 27th day of February 1766. Addison Hall was born, September 3, 1797, at Heathsville, the county seat of Northumberland and one of the counties of the Northern Neck.

The War of 1812 was especially difficult for the Northern Neck. As a result, little Addison only had thirty-three months of education. Although young, he volunteered to serve his country. Years later he received a land grant of 160 acres for this service.

On January 2, 1817, he married Miss Susan Edmonds. He went into partnership with his father in a department store and later he opened his own store. He also studied law by himself and was licensed to practice law. Hall was elected to the House of Delegates for five sessions.

Mr. Hall did not become a Christian until he was more than half way through his life. Although he had attended a Baptist church regularly, he had not been deeply moved. After a sermon by Rev. Samuel Lamkin, he publicly acknowledged concern and later received Christ as his Savior in a friend's room. A few weeks later, on October 19, 1819, he was baptized.

While serving in the Legislature, he met Rev. J. B. Jeter and hoped Rev. Jeter could become his pastor. Hall invited him to his home and church on a weekend. As a result, Rev. Jeter later became his pastor. The thoughts of the ministry began to pursue him. One Sunday Rev. Jeter was unexpectedly absent, so Mr. Hall preached to the congregation. After that, he preached often and was licensed by the church on June 20, 1829. Since a church was not available, he continued with his legal duties.

During the ministry of Dr. Jeter, a physician, Dr. W. H. Kirk, was led to the Lord at a camp meeting in Northumberland County. Later both Dr. Kirk and Addison Hall were ordained to the gospel ministry. Rev. Mr. Hall made a trip to the West, preaching as he had opportunity, attending the Baptist State Convention in Louisville and the Triennial Convention in Cincinnati.

Dr. Jeter, desiring to give greater opportunities to Rev. Mr. Hall and Dr. Kirk, resigned the churches in Morattico and Wicomico and moved to Richmond. The churches then called Pastor Hall, and a profitable arrangement was worked out to have Dr. Kirk as his associate. During the ministry of these men, the churches had great revivals, with hundreds added to the membership. They organized two new churches in Fairfield and Lebanon. The Wicomico church built a new building and changed the name to Coan. As a result, Mr. Hall became pastor of the Morattico and Lebanon churches and Dr. Kirk of Coan and Fairfield.

Dr. Jeter said of him, "He was not eminent as a preacher... but his ministry was distinguished by something better than the fluent verbiage which passes with most for eloquent preaching. He was a well-instructed theologian, a safe interpreter of Scripture, an earnest, laborious, faithful teacher of divine truth, a religious guide whom all trusted and loved."[1]

Numerous times Hall was asked to represent his county. He was a member of the Constitutional Convention, which was in session in Richmond for eight months, adjourning August 1, 1851. He was a member of the Virginia Convention in 1861. Like many others, he was opposed to separation from the Union, but when Virginia was threatened with invasion, he changed his mind. Some questioned the wisdom of a preacher holding public political positions. Yet it seemed necessary for him as he had 18 children. His oldest child, Henrietta, married Rev. J. Lewis Shuck, and she became the first woman missionary from America to China.[2]

Addison Hall was always abounding in the work of the Lord. Can this be said of us? He had planned to visit old Jerusalem, but before he could, he was called to the ***New Jerusalem***. He died on Sunday, April 2, 1871.

EGC

---

[1]George Braxton Taylor, *Virginia Baptist Ministers*, (Lynchburg, VA: J. P. Bell Company, 1912), 142.

[2]Ibid., 144.

September 4

Six Glorious Years

Scripture: Acts 11:24

God's sovereign providence was most evident in the life of Jeremiah Dale. He was born at Danvers, Massachusetts, in 1787. At eighteen years of age he accepted Jesus Christ as his Savior. During this time, ministry entered his mind, but his lack of education and his limited qualifications made that seem an impossibility. Being a wheelwright by trade, he pursued his business and was intent on serving the Lord as a layman.

In 1816 he moved to Zanesville, Ohio, and devoted himself to his trade. But a series of adverse events entered his life. Within two years of the move, his first wife and two children died. Before two more years had passed, his second wife also died. Then his commodious shop was completely consumed in flames. As though that was not enough, he remarried, but in time his third wife and another child had passed away. Job-like, Jeremiah Dale seriously sought to know the mind of the Lord in all of these vicissitudes. During this time, a Baptist church had been established in Zanesville under the care of Elder George C. Sedwick. Mr. Dale had been selected as a deacon, and feeling that the Lord had something more for him, Elder Sedwick began preparing him for ministry. Gradually the pastor called upon Mr. Dale to do more and more, until the deacon himself concluded that the Lord would indeed have him in the ministry. An ordination council was convened, and the thirty-eight-year-old candidate was ordained on May 8, 1825.

The next six years of the life of Reverend Dale read like a kaleidoscope. From that day onward Reverend Dale relinquished all worldly employment, and devoted himself and his faculties to the work of God. In June he took charge of Mount Zion and Bethesda Baptist churches in Virginia, and the next month he also began his labors in the Marietta Baptist Church in Ohio. From time to time he visited and ministered in the Parkersburg church in what is today West Virginia. At first he was traveling three hundred miles a month by horseback, but that soon increased to four hundred miles. It seemed that Jeremiah Dale realized he had but a short time to live, and was intent on doing everything possible in that period of time.

Early in 1831 Jeremiah's health declined, and he resigned his multiplied ministries and decided to return to his native area in Massachusetts. He arrived in Danvers near to Boston on July 14, 1831. After a few days he traveled to Gloucester to visit a brother. While in Gloucester he was induced by friends to preach three times on the Lord's Day, July 24. He returned to Danvers the next day intent on attending a series of revival meetings that were to begin on Tuesday, the 26. There he was asked to exhort the people, and on Tuesday and Wednesday he was able to do so. But his exertion doubtless hastened his weakening condition. On Thursday morning he was discharging blood from his lungs. Though medical assistance stanched the flow of blood, his physical condition declined rapidly from that time. This deterioration continued until September 4, 1831, when His Lord called him to his eternal rest.

In his last conversation with Pastor Barnaby, pastor of the Danvers church, he said, "I have no wish to live beyond my usefulness. It seems my labors are ended on earth and the time of my departure is at hand. I wish to go and to be with Christ; I feel perfectly resigned to the will of God, whether in life or death. His will is perfectly right. His sweet promises are my support and comfort. My faith is unshaken. I am a poor sinner, entirely dependent on the grace of God for salvation. I have felt I deserved hell; but His grace has comforted me. . . . I disclaim all merit. My whole dependence is on the blood and righteousness of the Lord Jesus Christ."[1]

It is said that Jeremiah Dale baptized new believers every Sunday during his six year ministry. His only living heir, a son, was a student for the ministry at the time of his father's death, and he assisted in the burial of his dad. A memorial service was conducted in Marietta, Ohio, for Jeremiah Dale on Sunday, October 23, 1831, and the text used was our text today: Acts 11:24. Oh that the Lord might be able to say that of my life, "For he was a good man and full of the Holy Ghost, and of faith, and much people were added unto the Lord."

DLC

[1]James B. Taylor, *Lives of Virginia Baptist Ministers* (Richmond: Yale & Wyatt, 1838), 409-410.

September 5

A New Baby Church

Scripture: Ephesians 5:23; Matthew 16:18

When the first worship service was held in the Shiloh area in 1717, no one had heard of Napoleon or George Washington. At the time, George I was King of England. Although England was growing stronger militarily, it was still a second-rate power. The population of North Carolina was about 30,000. There were more Tuscarora Indians living in the Albermarle than Englishmen.

As he traveled in the South, Rev. Paul Palmer made many missionary trips to eastern North Carolina. In time he developed a preaching center at the home of William Burgress in Pasquotank County, which is now known as Camden County. In Colonial times when a group of people wished to establish a church, they had to file a petition with the court. Such a document, which provided a list of the names of the early members of Shiloh Baptist Church, has been discovered among the old records in the Clerk of Court's office in Pasquotank County Court House at Elizabeth City, North Carolina. The document was dated September 5, 1729, and was addressed to the worshipful court of Pasquotank Precinct. In it, the court was petitioned to duly record the fact that "religious meetings were being held by people called Baptists in ye dwelling house of William Burgress on the North side of Pasquotank River at the head of Raymonds Creek." Reverend Palmer established the first existing Baptist Church in North Carolina in the home of William Burgess. Mr. Burgess was a Justice of the Peace, a member of the Provincial Assembly, and a prominent man in colonial affairs. Several persons, numbering about thirty, embraced the sentiments of the General Baptists and held their meetings in private houses in the neighborhood until 1736.

Rev. Paul Palmer, a native of Maryland, was baptized by Thomas Owens of Welch Tract, Delaware. He held many evangelistic meetings in New Jersey, Maryland, and Connecticut before traveling to North Carolina in the spring of 1720. While in Maryland, he preached in the home of Henry Sator, a Baptist layman, and nine people were saved and baptized. From this group of converts, the Chestnut Ridge Baptist Church, the oldest Baptist Church in Maryland, was organized.

Pastor Palmer was handsome, intelligent, and had a winsome personality that drew people to him. Governor Everard in 1729 wrote the Bishop in London: "When I first came here, there was[sic] no Dissenters but Quakers in the Government and now by the means of one Paul Palmer the Baptist teacher, he has gained hundreds."

In 1736 the saints who worshiped with Pastor William Burgess constructed their own church building. A second edifice was built after January 1758 on land belonging to John Burgess, son of William Burgess. Mr. John Burgess became the second pastor, and served the congregation until his death in 1763. Following John's death the church called Henry Abbott to be their pastor. He had come from England as a schoolteacher in the early part of 1760. The Burgesses built a schoolhouse soon after the church building was completed.

This church has also been influential in political affairs. Pastor Abbott served during the Revolution and was elected to the State Congress Meeting in 1776. He introduced Article 19 of the Bill of Rights, "That all men have a natural and inalienable right to worship Almighty God according to the dictates of their conscience." That sterling man of God served the congregation from about 1765 until his death in 1791.[1]

Genuine love for the Lord Jesus ought to be manifested by our faithfulness and love for our local church. The dear people of the Albermarle labored, suffered, and persevered to have their own local church. How much easier it is for us today and how grateful we should be for their example and memory.

EGC

[1]From history notes of the Shiloh Baptist Church, Shiloh, NC

September 6

An Unlikely Preacher

Scripture: 1 Corinthians 1:17-18

Can you imagine a timid, shy youth becoming a dauntless, daring preacher of righteousness? Such was the case of Absalom Waller, nephew of the famed Separate Baptist preacher, John Waller. The Holy Spirit had transformed "swearing Jack Waller" into a vessel for God's use, but could He transfigure a demure lad into a "preaching machine?"

Absalom was born in 1772. His parents were Baptists and reared their six children under the sound of the Gospel. Absalom was the oldest of the children, and when he was fourteen, he began to experience the Holy Spirit's convicting power. In 1786 he was soundly converted, baptized by his faithful uncle, and became a member of Waller's church in Spotsylvania. Somehow his pastor-uncle John, envisioned Absalom's brother, John, as becoming a preacher, but he could not imagine such a future for the timid lad, Absalom. However, John Leland, the noted Separatist Baptist preacher, was in special meetings at the Spotsylvania church, and he heard the two boys pray. He arose from his knees, and calling the pastor aside, he prophetically said, "Brother Waller, you are deceived in your impressions; John will never preach, but that little white-headed boy," pointing to Absalom, "will be the preacher in your flock."[1]

Absalom grew up with a singular desire to be a farmer, where, in the shades of obscurity, he could live a peaceful, serene life. However, the Lord had other plans. Though he lacked formal education and was self-admittedly unassertive, a sense of the call of God began to permeate his mind. A fire to preach began to burn within his heart, and the members of the church confirmed what Absalom was sensing, yet he hesitated. Finally, in July of 1793 the congregation unanimously proposed his ordination. Absalom spent that month in much prayer and fasting. In August he met the council and was ordained. He was only twenty-one, but it was reasoned that he would intern under his uncle in the work of God at Waller's church.

Before the year was over, the famed John Waller resigned the church that he might move to South Carolina. The Great Shepherd of the sheep had already arranged for a replacement. Absalom became pastor of three churches (Waller's, County Line, and Bethany), and for many years he served those congregations.

The work of God prospered under the young pastor's direction through the years. Continual growth occurred, and genuine revival seasons prevailed. To be sure there were times of spiritual barrenness, but more often, Absalom reflected on the joys of the ministry. The blessings of God in 1817-18 were amazing. During those two years, just prior to the association meeting on Saturday, September 6, 1817, Absalom had baptized more than 1500 persons. He wrote, "It would require the pen of an angel to describe the sensations of joy and gratitude which filled my own soul, when meeting the broken hearted sinner at a throne of mercy. . . . I had long since been watching the coming of the Master by fervent prayers, . . . and now to behold numbers upon their knees, crying out, 'What shall we do to be saved?' produced in my enraptured mind, a foretaste of those immortal pleasures which bloom in the paradise of God."[2]

God called his servant home in 1820. Some years before his death, he wrote the following lines: "O how near is the period when these active limbs will slumber in the grave, the land of silence, forever to rest. Forever did I say! No, death, cruel death, thou mayest triumph for a season and lock my bones in the prison of the grave, but Jesus will come, and will be thy plague, and thy destruction; I shall hear His voice, and come forth from thine iron domains, and feeling in an instant the springs of an immortal body, I shall rise to meet Him in the air."[3]

What joy it will be to see God's faithful rewarded at the Judgment Seat of Christ! "Even so, come, Lord Jesus."

DLC

---

[1]James B. Taylor, *Lives of Virginia Baptist Ministers* (Richmond: Yale & Wyatt, 1838), 249-250.

[2]Ibid., 257.

[3]Ibid., 263

September 7

Printing and Preaching the Gospel

Scripture: Jeremiah 45:5a

Paul Levin, the son of Swedish immigrants, was born in Rock Island, Illinois on October 13, 1914. He was the twelfth child born into the family. Paul's mother never became fluent in English, but she was a godly lady. When Paul was only four years of age his mother led him to a personal relationship by faith in the Savior. Because of his mother's efforts, little Paul was well grounded in God's Word. The lad launched his ministerial career immediately, as he "preached" with a piano stool for his pulpit! When he was sixteen, Paul was sent for one year to a Christian high school in Boone, Iowa. While there, a six-week revival broke out among the student body. During a cold winter night in 1930, Paul Levin surrendered his life for full-time service to Christ. He began preaching in local evangelistic campaigns soon after returning to his home. The Lord's blessings were apparent, and though he never attended Bible College, the Holy Spirit taught His servant in personal study, and directed and blessed.

Those were the days of the Great Depression, and the young evangelist just eked out a living, but the Lord proved Himself faithful. For transportation, Brother Levin drove an old Model T Ford. As God's servant learned to live by faith, he was sustained by the Lord. When only a nineteen year old evangelist, Paul invited the blind singer, Bob Findley, to join with him, and the two crossed the country preaching the Gospel for over forty years. Paul married in 1936, and his dear wife, Dorothy, became an inspiration throughout his ministry.

In his early days on the road, evangelistic meetings lasted from three weeks to a month. Campaigns were often held in empty store buildings or in tents. In the course of time, Levin and Findley became known to pastors, and the young men were invited for church revivals. Often times the team would be on the road for months at a time.

September

The Lord used his servant in many unique ways. After having written a couple of articles for a Christian magazine, Brother Levin was asked to put the material into tract form. In time the tracts became so popular that it led to the establishment of a tract ministry that would become worldwide. In the course of time, Paul wrote more than forty tracts with a circulation of over 230 million in more than seventy five languages. Perhaps the best known of his tract titles is "The New Birth." The booklet has been used of the Lord in the salvation of multitudes of men and women around the world.

Having been requested by a small radio station to produce recordings of music and messages for local use, the men gladly complied. Out of that effort, a permanent radio ministry entitled "Bible Tract Echoes" grew into a nationwide ministry.

After speaking in a youth camp in Nebraska on one occasion, that camp director recommended Dr. Levin to Bill Rice as a speaker for the youth ministry at the Bill Rice Ranch in Tennessee. Brother Levin accepted Rice's invitation, and for many years thereafter the evangelist was a featured speaker during youth weeks at the well-known Ranch. Through that ministry, literally thousands of young people were saved and called into Christian service. Levin had the unique ability in his preaching to minister in a personal manner though the audience was large.

Paul continued in evangelism following the death of Bob Findley, but he himself eventually succumbed to cancer. After a lengthy bout with the disease, the Lord graciously took his servant home on September 7, 1996.

His challenge toward the end of his life is a message needed in this day. He said, "I believe this a great hour of opportunity, and all evangelists, pastors and Christians of sound, separated churches ought to go all out in soul- winning, knocking on doors, extensive bus ministries, and forget all about why you can't see many people saved these days." Surely our God is not limited, and though these are the last days of the dispensation of grace, we are called upon to be faithful. Reaping always follows sowing!

DLC

September 8

Convicts of Conviction

Scripture: Acts 24:14-16

American Christians in the twenty-first century take religious freedom for granted, but nine of America's thirteen original colonies had a State/Church arrangement. In those colonies, every citizen was taxed to support the State church. The fact that you attended services of another denomination faithfully made no difference. Massachusetts with its Congregational state church, and Virginia with its Church of England state church were the most unrelenting in pursuit of those who refused to pay the tax, but other colonies utilized the same system. For instance, the laws of Connecticut were very stringent against all dissenters from the established religion. The authorities fell with special severity upon Baptists and Quakers, for those two groups constituted a large proportion of dissenters.

A case in point will illustrate the fact. Elder Philip Tabor was with others imprisoned May 25, 1723, in the common jail at New Bristol, where he remained for thirteen months for refusing to pay the tax assessed by the town for the support of the minister of the standing order (the State/Church). A petition on behalf of the prisoners, was presented to King George, and an order was finally granted for their release.[1]

An old law required each town to furnish itself with a pair of stocks where offenders could be secured. The modes of punishment were the whipping post, the stocks, the pillory, and jail. Baptists were acquainted with each mode of punishment as they led the way in refusing to pay the taxes to support the established state-church!

The Baptists of Connecticut petitioned the General Assembly requesting that a law be passed to abolish such taxes. The exact copy of the petition, utilizing the old English, that was sent by the Baptists to the General Assembly of Connecticut follows: "To the Honourable Genl

Assembly of ye Colony of Connecticut, to be convened at New Haven on ye second Thursday of October next. The humble Memorial of ye Genl Association of ye Baptist churches, convened at North Kingston, on ye 6th day of September, A. D. 1729, humbly showeth, That ye Honours' Petitioners having sundry Brethren of their Communion dwelling up and down in your Colony, they therefore do hereby humbly crave ye an Act of Assembly may be passed to free them from paying any taxes to any ministry except their own, and from building any meeting houses except for their own use, humbly hoping your Honours will consider they are utterly unable to maintain their own way of worship and to pay taxes to ye Presbyterians, and yet the gracious act of indulgence together with ye reasonableness of our request will be motive sufficient to move ye Honours to grant ye request of ye Honours' humble Memorialists. Signed in ye name and by ye order of the Sd Association. The petition was signed by four pastors and fourteen laymen."

I have been unable to discover the response of the "Genl Assembly of ye Colony of Connecticut," but I believe we can surmise that either the request was laughed off or totally ignored. After all, if others were not taxed to pay the parson and/or build churches, then the actual church members would have to care for those expenses!

We ought to thank God that our Baptist forefathers were willing to pay the price to secure the freedoms that all Americans now possess. Isaac Backus led the way among Baptists in New England, and John Leland championed our cause in Virginia, but many unsung heroes of our persuasion would rather go to jail than to surrender principle. To capitulate might have seemed for the time more judicious, but their willingness to stand upon conviction has provided freedom of religion and soul liberty for every American.

There are dangers today as we witness the Supreme Court manipulating the First Amendment. By using convoluted reasoning they interpret it to mean the very opposite of what was intended. In this twenty-first century those who love the Lord must make their presence felt and their voices heard to maintain freedom that the Gospel might be freely heralded around the world.

DLC

---

[1]C. Edwin Barrows, Editor, *The Diary of John Comer*, 1893, 68.

September 9

The Importance of Church Membership

Scripture: Acts 20:28; 1 Timothy 3:15-16

Church membership at one time was much more important among fundamental Baptists than it seems to be in the twenty-first century. As a case in point, we shall look at the record of the First Baptist Church of Boston. The church had been born in conflict, and many of the early members had been imprisoned for daring to establish such a witness in the Commonwealth of Massachusetts. But the years passed, and we read of the second law of thermodynamics as it entered the spiritual realm. "The 9th mo 1684 Mr. Dingley & his daughter Recevd as members to comunion by letter of Recomendation. . . . At A Church meeting September ye 13th 1685. It was Agreed upon that Brother Drinker upon consideration of his neglecting to officiate in his place for A long time & still prsisting in soe doeing should be discharged from ye work & office of A Decon and be Admonished to his duty as a member. .His admonition availed, for he was restored to his place as a member upon acknowledgment of his desertion and promise of Reforming. He did not long walk in fellowship with the church, but after two other admonitions, He was rejected for refusing to heare the Church according to the 18 Chap: Mathew: this was sollemly don 5th January 1695."

Many stirring and tender memories must have been in the minds of the church when this action was taken. He was the last of the constituent members then living. He had been a teacher and a deacon. He had been often in prison and had suffered much. He remained a faithful Christian through life, although outside the fellowship of this church. There is some slight evidence that he united with another Baptist church (Newberry), and that his irregularity in doing it without a previous dismission was the cause of excommunication: "24 march 1688 To the Church of Christ at Newberry: the Church of Christ at Boston: wishes ye Increase of grace & peace in Jesus Christ the Lord:

whereas we have considered ye condition of or Brother Edward Drinker & having weighed the circumstances thereof have thought fitt to suspend him from communion with us & Expect you should doe the same until he has given satisfaction according to the Rule of Christ; we thought fitt to signify to you. And so committing you to God & to the word of His grace we Rest: yrs. In ye fellowship of ye gospell 25th march 89. Isaack Hull, John Emblen in ye name of ye church.[1]

I fear that modern-day believers fail to realize the importance of the local church as it is set forth in the New Testament. Acts 20:28 is often quoted as having reference to some invisible body. But the reference is to the local church at Ephesus, to whom the elders were to minister, that God had purchased with His own blood. And when Paul wrote to Timothy instructing him of the qualifications for deacons, he was referring to a local church. In that assembly Paul wrote as to how Timothy was to behave himself (1 Timothy 3:14). Timothy was not instructed how to behave in some ethereal, invisible group that has never yet met. Rather it is to a local congregation to which Paul refers as being "the pillar and ground of truth" (1 Timothy 3:15).

Church discipline, for the most part, is tragically a thing of the past. Church membership in our day is but a badge of approval, and everyone is expected to join a church somewhere. We surely need to realize that the local church is not a paradise on earth to exhibit the finished product of salvation. The local church is rather a repair shop where imperfect saints are encouraging each other by offering accountability. If church membership is to be meaningful, it must entail a walk of Christian growth and obedience. Until the unregenerate see members of local churches walking this way, they will never appreciate God's institution upon the earth. Brethren, we ought to pray for our pastors, deacons, and church members that the local assembly of which we are members shall honor the Son of God.

DLC

---

[1]Nathan E. Wood, *The History of The First Baptist Church of Boston* (Salem, NH: Ayer Company Publishers, Inc., 1990), 192-193.

September 10

A Spiritual Dynamo

Scripture: Psalm 112

To say that Fred Barber was an unusual man is an understatement. He maintained a boyish disposition throughout the whole of his 70 years. Fred was the Pied Piper wherever he found children, or did they find him?

Fred was born on June 16, 1927, to Claude and Leora Meeker Barber. He grew up in Binghamton, New York. He enlisted in the United States Navy in 1945 before his high school graduation and returned home in 1947. Being in the Naval Reserves in 1950 he was recalled to service as an electrician during the Korean War. By this time he was married to Lindy Fairchild. After the Korean conflict, Fred returned home in 1952 and worked for IBM. At that time, Fred settled down into a comfortable life. Three children were born to the Barbers. Fred's parents were Methodists as were Lindy's. Fred's mother was a talented organist, but the Gospel was not presented to that congregation until a retired minister was sent to fill the pulpit. This theology was new to the members, and Fred was so interested he spent many hours at the parsonage learning from Pastor Dawson. When Fred asked Bible questions of a co-worker at his place of employment, the co-worker led him to the Lord. Fred was then 33 years old.

After Fred started a prayer meeting at the Methodist Church, people began to resent him. But he continued to grow as a Christian. When a liberal was sent to replace Pastor Dawson, Fred was furious and began attending a Baptist church. Soon the Baptist pastor, Reverend Gordon Hay, led Mrs. Barber to the Lord, and Fred then led their three sons, Bruce, Brian, and Scott, to the Lord at their family altar. All three of Fred's sons are in the ministry today!

Fred's heart burned for the Lord's work and he enrolled in a Practical Bible Training School's morning classes immediately. Working at night to support his family gave him little time for anything else. In the summers Fred worked at Camp El Rancho de Paz in Owego, New York. After graduation from the Practical Bible Training School in May 1966, Fred sought a pastorate. During the third summer at camp, he met Pastor Dick Meyers from Saltillo, Pennsylvania who was looking for someone to take the Calvary Independent Baptist Church he had started in McConnellsburg, Pennsylvania. I was privileged to hold evangelistic meetings there in 1968, and the old schoolhouse where they met was overrun with people sitting in the cloakrooms and standing outside. Fred pastored there for over seven years. During this time, the church built a nice brick building with wonderful facilities for the growing congregation. Fred acted as general contractor and was there at the site regularly during construction. The old schoolhouse still stands.

Following that ministry, the Lord led Brother Barber to the West Milford Baptist Church in West Milford, West Virginia. He ministered there for twelve years. He was involved in every aspect of the work. He directed the choir, and he and his wife provided special music. He had great appeal to young people. Each summer he took a busload of young people to the Bill Rice Ranch and rejoiced when spiritual decisions were made. Many were saved and are now serving the Lord in various ministries.

Fred was a disciplinarian, but children could see beyond that stern look. They loved him and were drawn to the tender hearted, energetic preacher. One day, our seven-year old son knocked on the parsonage door when we were in revival meetings in West Milford and asked Mrs. Barber, "May Pastor Barber come out to play?" The next scene found Torrey and Fred riding their bikes around the church parking lot.

Fred's once energetic body succumbed to an illness, which claimed his life, and he was laid to rest in Greenville, South Carolina, as he had worked at Bob Jones University the last few years of his life. He was called home by His heavenly Father on June 21, 1997. Many are the memories that people have of one who sacrificially invested his life in theirs and one who used his time to develop their spiritual well being. Fred's life was all about the needs of others.[1] O that the Lord would raise up a host of such godly men who would live their lives for others!

DCB

[1] Telephone interview with Lindy Barber Hay by Bettye Baughan, August 31, 2004.

September 11

Henry G. Weston - Baptist Educator

Scripture: John 21:15-19

Henry G. Weston was born on September 11, 1820 in Lynn, Massachusetts. His father, John Weston, was the first editor of the *Watchman*. Henry graduated from Brown University in 1840 and Newton Theological Institution in 1843. He was not an exceptional student, but he was known for his devotion to the study of Scripture.[1] When he developed the symptoms of consumption, the doctors gave him little hope for recovery, but suggested that he move to a drier climate where he could live more in the open-air. He moved to Kentucky, where he was ordained to the Baptist ministry at Frankfort. He then preached as a missionary for three years in Illinois and finally in 1846 became the pastor of the Baptist church in Peoria, where he developed a thriving ministry over the next thirteen years. In 1859 he and his wife took a vacation to New York City. He was invited to preach at the Oliver Street Baptist Church, which was without a pastor at the time. The church was immediately convinced that he was the man to assume the pulpit of their church; it took Weston several months to come to that conclusion. The church later moved to Madison Avenue and was renamed the Madison Avenue Baptist Church. He spent several years as the editor of the *Baptist Quarterly* and was also the president of the American Baptist Missionary Union.

Weston was one of the Baptist leaders who attempted to ensure that the American Bible Society in the 1880s would continue to support Bible translations that translated the Greek *baptizo* as "immerse." When the Society continued to refuse to do so, Weston (and numerous other Baptists) left the Society rather than compromise their Baptist convictions (See January 10). At about this same time, a number of Baptists undertook a new translation of the Bible into English. This new translation first appeared in 1865 and was revised in 1867. Weston took part in the revision of 1889.[2]

Weston is best known, however, for his work at Crozer Seminary. In 1868 Weston left Madison Avenue Baptist Church and became the president of Crozer. There were other seminaries in existence at that time, but Weston developed a unique two-fold purpose for Crozer. First, he wanted to provide a complete theological education to students who came directly out of college and could study the Scriptures in Greek and Hebrew. This would approximate the traditional seminary approach. Second, he desired to provide a quality education for men who were older and without a traditional college background. These men would have been unable to pursue a traditional seminary course of study. He wanted to help them develop a greater knowledge of the Scriptures and theology so they might be academically qualified, at least in a limited sense, for pastoral work. This dual approach to seminary education demanded a peculiar ability in the president of Crozer, and Weston was just this kind of man. Armitage described him as "a true scholar, a clear, sound and experienced theologian, broad in his views, simple in his habits, kind in his disposition, and devout in his piety."[3]

Weston was more than an accomplished academic, however. He was also a master in the pulpit. This combination of academic ability and preaching prowess combined to develop both the immature and the accomplished student. He was also a faithful church member. He regularly attended the services of the Upland Baptist Church whenever he was not preaching elsewhere. He was faithful to the evening services and the midweek Bible study, often preaching at those services. He had a pastor's heart, frequently visiting the sick, the grieving, and the poor with the pastor of his church.[4]

Weston often said of himself that he was the pet of Providence. He believed that God had ordered his life so differently and so much better than he could have planned it for himself. What a truth for all of us! And what a heart to have for God's people! Before Walter Calley, one of Weston's former students, accepted the pastorate of the Upland Baptist Church, Weston wrote to him quoting the words of Jesus, "Feed my lambs." He added, "No higher commission was ever given to men or angels than that of humble ministry to God's little ones."[5]

LRO

---

[1] *Henry Griggs Weston: In Remembrance* (American Baptist Publication Society, n.d.), 9.

[2] Henry Griggs Weston, *Appleton's Cyclopedia of American Biography,* ed. James Grant Wilson and John Fiske (New York: D. Appleton and Company, 1887-1889).

[3] Thomas Armitage, *A History of the Baptists* (New York: Bryan, Taylor, and Co., 1890), 878.

[4] Henry Griggs Weston: In Remembrance, 27.

[5] Ibid., 28.

September 12

"Mixed Communion?"

Scripture: 1 Corinthians 11:17-34

It is intriguing to realize that a few short years after the martyrdom of Edward Wightman in April 1611, a Baptist church, perhaps the first Particular Baptist Church of that era, was born. We do not know that the martyrdom of Wightman was used of the Lord to interest believers in the doctrine of baptism, but often the suffering of the saints caused others to rethink the whole matter of Baptist distinctives. It was so in the beating of Obadiah Holmes several years later in America. Doubtless, martyrdoms and persecutions of Baptists have caused many to research the religious cause that produced such a strong conviction.

The General Baptists (who believed in an unlimited atonement) increased rapidly, and fifteen years after Wightman's death, there were eleven General Baptist churches in England. They had increased to forty-seven churches in 1644. Armitage, in his book on Baptist History, points out that some claim that the first Particular Baptist Church (those who maintain a limited atonement) was established in Shrewsbury in 1627. But Dr. Armitage believed that, in essence, the first Particular Baptist church in England had been established by John Spilsbury in 1633.

In 1616 the first congregation of Independents (so the "Dissenters" were known) united in London under the pastoral leadership of Henry Jacob. He was succeeded by John Lathrop. In the course of time, a number of that group grew doctrinally to the point of rejecting infant baptism. By mutual consent they formed their church on September 12, 1633. John Spilsbury was chosen as the first pastor, and for some time after its formation, it was a Strict Communion congregation. By this we mean that the Lord's Table was given only to baptized believers. In his history of the

English Baptists, Crosby claims that most or all of these received a new baptism. The famed William Kiffin and others soon left another Independent congregation and united with Spilsbury's church. However, after a period of time, dissension divided the congregation over the matter of baptism. The charge of "mixed communion" was made, and Mr. Kiffin and others withdrew from the membership. By "mixed communion" we do not refer to the reception of unbaptized persons at the Lord's Table, but unimmersed preachers were being allowed to preach from the pulpit. A sweet fellowship continued between the membership of Spilsbury's church and the group who had left with Kiffin. The Particular Baptist churches in the area had soon grown to seven in number. Spilsbury and Kiffin remained in close fellowship, and in 1643 they signed a Calvinistic Confession of Faith together.

However, I would like to look again at the expression "mixed communion." Usually this expression is used in relation to the Lord's Table. Historically, Baptists have held three differing positions concerning participates at the Lord's Supper. Oftentime serious divisions have transpired because of one's understanding of the Communion Table. There are those who held to "Open Communion." Such believe that all true believers should be granted the privilege of participation at the Table of the Lord. That stance seemed to find its greatest adherents in Great Britain, and folk are often shocked to learn that this position was held by Charles Haddon Spurgeon. However, few fundamental Baptists in our day agree with such a practice. Secondly, there was a time when a majority of Baptists in the southern tier of states in America practiced what is known as "Closed Communion." This declaration maintains that the Lord's Table is to be taken only by members of the local church in which the ordinance is being administered. It seems that the majority of fundamental Baptists currently believe in what is called "Close Communion." By that expression is meant, that any "obedient" believers are invited to participate in the ordinance of remembrance. Obedience begins with believer's immersion, but it continues on into the practice of holiness in the life of the believer. Personalized judgment is called for at the Table but, of course, the local church reserves the right to refuse the ordinance to any who are under discipline or are walking in open rebellion.

This Day in Baptist History III

Having thought about the Lord's Table, we would do well, to reconsider "mixed communion" as it was meant by the Particular Baptists in old England. Those men were Baptists by conviction, and though they believed in soul liberty (soul responsibility), they were not about to open their pulpits to mere Protestants! Thank God for the principles that held those early Baptists, both Particular and General Baptists, who were Biblicists in their convictions.

DLC

September 13

A Missionary Pioneer and Bible Translator

Scripture: Romans 10:13-17

Compelling logic characterizes the thought of Paul's Epistle to the Romans. In Romans 10:13-17 Paul builds an unassailable case for the necessity of the Word of God for missionary enterprise. To be saved, one must call on Christ in faith, and faith comes only through the hearing of the Word. The work of Bible translation is indispensable to missions. Trying to build a church without the Bible is like trying to build a house without tools. Quality translation work requires much dedicated labor. We rightfully honor the labors of William Carey and Adoniram Judson as linguists and Bible translators. Numerous other missionaries also pioneered the work of Bible translation in various lands during the nineteenth century, the Great Century of missionary expansion.

John Taylor Jones was such a pioneering missionary. The son of Elisha and Persis Jones, he was born in New Ipswich, New Hampshire, on July 16, 1802. He joined the Congregational church in Ashby, Massachusetts, at age 15. After graduating from Amherst in 1825, he began to train for the ministry at Andover Seminary. During the course of his studies, his views on the mode and subject of baptism changed. He therefore decided it would be better to finish his training at Newton Seminary. In 1828 the

Reverend Doctor Malcom baptized him into the membership of the Federal Street Church in Boston. The Triennial Convention appointed him as a missionary to Burma, and he reached Moulmein, in February of 1831. Throwing himself immediately into the task of language acquisition, he was able to preach in both the Burmese and the Taling languages in a matter of months after his arrival.

The mission board believed that the time had arrived for an attempt to spread the Gospel to the Taling people in Siam (modern-day Thailand), and that Jones was the best person to do the job. He arrived in Bangkok in April of 1833. Jones realized that the first need for the Siamese was a Bible in their own language, and he began the work of translation. After many years of toil, he completed a translation of the New Testament in October of 1843. Besides his New Testament translation, he also published several Gospel tracts in Siamese, and *Brief Grammatical Notices of the Siamese Language* (in 1842) to help future missionaries learn the language and to further the work of Bible translation. Following the publication of the New Testament, Jones took two furloughs in the United States, the first being a brief one. The second furlough was longer, necessitated by his wife's health. In 1850 Columbian College honored him with the degree of Doctor of Divinity.[1] Returning to Siam, he continued his work of translation of books that would be of benefit to the national Christians. Following an attack of dysentery in the summer, the Lord called him home on September 13, 1851.

Missionaries contemporary with Jones had a very high regard for his labors, his character, and his example. Cathcart has the following to say about him: "'His great work, the translation of the New Testament into the Siamese language,' says Dr. Dean, 'compares favorably with the translation of the New Testament made in any of the Asiatic languages, including the life-work of such men as Carey, Marshman, Judson, and Morrison, and their worthy successors." He adds, 'I have met men on the missionary field who exhibited some stronger points of character, and some particular qualifications, or greater fitness for missionary usefulness, but, take him altogether, I have never seen his equal, and among more than a hundred men I have met among the heathen, I would select Dr. Jones as the model missionary.'"[2]

The need for skilled linguists to do the work of Bible translation is greater now than ever before, but not just for any kind of skilled linguists. The most important requirements for a competent Bible translator are a personal knowledge of its Author and a thorough education in sound theology. Let us pray that God will raise up more translators with the character, dedication, and skill of John Taylor Jones, who will lay the foundation for missionary work among unreached peoples in the years to come.

DRP

---

[1] Virtual American Biographies, www.famousamericans.net/johntaylorjones/

[2] William Cathcart, *The Baptist Encyclopedia*, 616.

September 14

Champions of Full Religious Freedom

Scripture: Luke 14:23

Most Americans are amazed to discover that of the thirteen original colonies only Pennsylvania, New Jersey, and Rhode Island were colonies that never knew a persecution.[1]

History confirms that freedom of conscience was not basic to the desire of the early founders of our republic. From the earliest days of American history, Baptists had petitioned those in authority for total freedom of religion for all Americans. When in September 1774, delegates from twelve provinces assembled in Congress at Philadelphia with a view to agreeing on united resistance to British control, it seemed propitious that the Baptists set forth their case again. Isaac Backus, Baptist pastor of note, was assigned by the members of the Warren Association (of Baptists) on September 14, 1774, to attend that meeting to see if something might be done to secure religious liberty. In Philadelphia, Backus was joined by Baptist leaders: James Manning, John Gano, Samuel Jones, William Rogers, and Morgan Edwards, and on October 14th, a meeting was arranged with the principal members of Congress. Thomas Cushing, Samuel Adams, John Adams, and R. T. Paine represented Massachusetts; while James Kinzie, of New Jersey, Stephen Hopkins, and Samuel Ward, of Rhode Island; and Joseph Galloway and Thomas Miflin, of Pennsylvania were also present. The grievances of the Baptists in Massachusetts were set before those men, but the contingent from Massachusetts sought to refute the charges. After a four-hour session the conference closed, and the Baptists had gained only small concessions. John Adams remarked that "the Baptists might as well expect a change in the solar system as to expect that the Massachusetts authorities would give up their establishment."[2]

We should thank God that our Baptist forefather persisted, for freedom of religion for all Americans was ultimately won through their efforts. Historian William Warren Sweet wrote of it in these words: "Religious freedom had triumphed in Virginia and was soon to spread throughout the nation, and a few years later in the form of the first amendment to the Federal Constitution was to become a part of the fundamental law of the land. At the time of the passage of the measure, Jefferson, its author, was in France, but so proud was he of his part in the memorable struggle that he asked that it be recorded on his gravestone: 'Thomas Jefferson, Author of the Declaration of Independence, of the Statute of Virginia for Religious Freedom, and Father of the University of Virginia.' But justice compels the admission that Jefferson's part in this accomplishment was not so great as was that of James Madison, nor were the contributions of either or both as important as was that of the humble people called Baptists."[3]

Baptists have always championed religious freedom. Let me illustrate the case. In 1651, Baptist Obadiah Holmes had been severely whipped in Boston for daring to preach in Massachusetts without a license. However, fourteen years later in 1665, Holmes was enabled to secure a large tract of land in East Jersey. In his patent of the land, Holmes guaranteed "Unto any and all who shall plant and inhabit any of the lands aforesaid, they shall have free liberty of conscience without any molestation or disturbance whatsoever in their way of worship."

Interestingly, a short time following Holmes acquisition of the land, a colony of Congregationalists from

Connecticut founded Newark, New Jersey. These resolved that, "None should be admitted freemen, or free Burgesses, save such as were members of one or the other of the Congregational Churches, and determined as a fundamental agreement and order that any who might differ in religious opinion from them and who would not keep their views to themselves should be compelled to leave the place."[4]

To be sure, America is the "land of the free," but religious freedom was won for all American citizens by Baptists who championed the cause of soul liberty!

DLC

---

[1]Thomas S. Griffiths, *A History of Baptists in New Jersey* (Hightstown, NJ: Barr Press Publishing Company, 1904), Introduction, X.

[2]Albert Henry Newman, *A History of the Baptist Churches in the United States* (Philadelphia: American Baptist Publication Society, 1915), 358.

[3]William Warren Sweet, *The Story of Religion in America* (New York, Harper & Row Publishers, 1950), 192-193.

[4]Griffiths, XI

September 15

A Missionary Leader

Scripture: Romans 15:18-21

Other entries in this volume chronicle the ministry of Dr. Monroe Parker as an evangelist and educator. The last twenty-five years of his life mark him as a missionary leader, and to that story we turn our attention.

The battle over New Evangelicalism was particularly contentious in the Conservative Baptist movement. Denver Seminary president Vernon Grounds was an early advocate for New Evangelicalism, and many within the movement capitulated to its compromises. This was especially true in the Conservative Baptist Foreign and Home Mission Society. The issue of inclusivism, or ecumenical evangelism, characterized much of the missionary work of these agencies.

This was a concern to Parker because as president of Pillsbury Baptist Bible College, he was seeing many students volunteer for missionary service. During a missions conference in early 1961, he asked how many students would be willing to go to the mission field if they knew God was calling them. More than one hundred of us stood! In the spring of the same year, Dr. Parker wrote a brief article in the *Pillsbury College Bulletin* entitled "Now Is the Time." In it he called for someone to form a new mission agency because Pillsbury was not going to train fundamentalist missionaries and then see them go to the field under a New Evangelical agency!

The full chain of events cannot be related here, but the result was that the Conservative Baptist Fellowship (earlier and again currently known as the Fundamental Baptist Fellowship) met in the Marquette Manor Baptist Church of Chicago on September 15, 1961. A statement of complaints against the Conservative Baptist mission agencies was read, a statement of purpose was proposed, and those assembled voted for the formation of a new mission agency to be called World Conservative Baptist Mission. In 1967, when all ties with the Conservative Baptists were severed, the name was changed to Baptist World Mission.

Dr. Parker was elected to the first Board of Directors of the agency and served in some capacity with it from its founding in 1961 until his death in 1994. He served on the committee that wrote the ministry's constitution.

Baptist World Mission struggled during its first eight years, and in November of 1969 Parker agreed to serve as general director with the condition that the office be moved from Chicago to Decatur, Alabama. From that time the mission began to grow. In 1969 just 14 missionaries were under appointment. By 1981 the roster had grown to 85.

In March 1981 Dr. Parker's second wife, Marjorie, passed away after a long illness. We who worked with Dr. Parker remember the great loneliness he endured. But he remained faithful to the Lord and never flagged in his evangelistic ministry or in his leadership of Baptist World Mission. On January 14, 1983, he married Ruby Whitley. God gave this wonderful helper to him. We who were closely associated with them believe that her presence and help in Dr. Parker's life prolonged his days on this earth and his effective service for the Lord.

This Day in Baptist History III

Baptist World Mission continued to grow under Dr. Parker's leadership. By 1994 the missionary family numbered 208. Dr. Parker's leadership not only produced growth in the ministry, but it also provided stability. His sane leadership and wise discernment steered the mission. Monroe Parker never wavered from his position as a Separatist, Baptist, and Fundamentalist. He had a great zeal for the Lord. He also had unusual wisdom and discernment and was able to avoid issues that would only be distractions from the task.

As age took its toll, Dr. Parker's health began to fail; but though his once strong body became increasingly frail, he continued to preach, provide wise counsel, and encourage all to whom he ministered. In June of 1994 he traveled to Alaska, where he preached his last sermon. He returned home from the trip greatly depleted in strength. On Sunday, July 14, 1994, just at the time for morning services in Decatur, Alabama, he quietly slipped away to a glorious entrance into Heaven (2 Peter 1:11).

His life stands as an encouragement to all who knew him. We are the richer for having been influenced by his life. We are also closer to the Lord because we followed one who followed Christ (1 Corinthians 11:1; 1 Thessalonians 1:6).

FJM

September 16

Separation or Infiltration?

Scripture: Amos 3:3; 2 Corinthians 6:14-17

Hosea Holcombe, born in South Carolina on July 20, 1780, became a pioneer historian of the work of Baptists in Alabama. He grew to maturity in South Carolina and married Miss Cassie Jackson, on June 7, 1802. He was ordained three years later on August 17, 1805, and served several churches as pastor in the years that followed in his native state.

In 1818 the couple moved westward to Jones Valley, Alabama, and in the next couple of years, Reverend Holcombe was instrumental in establishing several Baptist churches. He was chosen as moderator of the Ruhama Baptist Association, and in that role he lent his influence toward the establishment of the Convention of Baptists in the state of Alabama in 1922. He participated in organizing that association the following year and served on the committee to prepare the constitution for the organization. The man of God was chosen as one of fifteen domestic missionaries of the convention, and he served in the middle district of the state. From that time on until 1835 Reverend Holcombe served in various capacities. In 1835 the convention prevailed upon him to prepare a history of the Baptists of the state, and five years later the project was completed, and he presented the finished product to the convention. His book, *History of the Baptists in Alabama*, has been spoken of as being the first distinctly historical volume published in the state.

The interesting phenomenon of the Anti-missionary movement penetrated Alabama as it did in almost every state in the union. Several factors led to this movement. It was an extreme interpretation of Calvinism, that led to a rigid double predestination view. In other words, the leaders of the movement believed that individuals were elected either to salvation or damnation. The leaders, furthermore, claimed that they could find no justification for missionary societies and, they feared that the mission boards would become central in authority and remove the autonomy of local churches. Finally, most of this opposition was led by ministers who were uneducated, and these had a natural resentment to educated men of God. As a result of this thrust, in Kentucky, Tennessee, and Illinois, Luther Rice and John Mason Peck were at times met with prejudice, suspicion, and often, open hostility. Disciples of the anti-missionary group became active in almost all the states. In the face of this thrust, Hosea Holcombe determined that the best plan of operation was separation from such visionless religious leaders. As a result, he led in the organization of the Canaan Baptist Association on September 16, 1833.[1] The churches that comprised the new association were committed to the missionary program.

Holcombe died at his home in Jonesboro on July 31, 1841, after laboring for twenty-five years in building up the work of God in Alabama.

This Day in Baptist History III

A very important principle is set forth in our consideration today. The Lord calls His own to be a separate people. At times this truth calls for God's children to separate from unbelievers or even disorderly people. The needed separation is at times very painful. There are times when faithful believers must separate from family members and friends, but God calls us to obedience. He prefers our obedience rather than our sacrifice. Too often, modern-day Baptists adopt the Puritan philosophy of believing that an apostate or disobedient group or association can be reformed or purified.

Somehow, Hosea Holcombe learned the biblical principle and he established a precedent that is God-honoring. We do well to follow it. If we find ourselves in a local church, association, convention, or any other group that is apostate or is being led into a walk of disobedience, we must obey God and not man. After all, large numbers do not impress God. The group we must leave might well be numerically impressive, but God calls us to a walk of holiness, and at times the pathway can be lonely.

Be sure and read the Scripture references of the day carefully.

DLC

---

[1]Davis Woolley, *Encyclopedia of Southern Baptists* (Nashville, TN: Broadman Press, 1958), 1:629.

September 17

Picturesque Preacher and Friend of People

Scripture: Proverbs 18:24

Born on August 18, 1871, in the turbulent days of Reconstruction, John Philip Isenhower came up the hard way in rural Fairfield County, South Carolina, where he spent the majority of his life. His parents were John and Martha Stewart Isenhower. He managed through great sacrifice and perseverance to get an education at Furman Fitting School and Furman University in Greenville, South Carolina. Then in 1901 he graduated from Southern Baptist Seminary in Louisville, Kentucky.

Isenhower was licensed to preach the Gospel in September, 1892, and was ordained on September 17, 1896, by the Mt. Zion Baptist Church in Chester County, South Carolina. He pastored 38 years at the Rock Creek Baptist Church and worked 14 years as Rural Missionary for the State Mission Board. He was moderator of the Fairfield Baptist Association and spent most of his time in this area. As a circuit-riding preacher, he served several Baptist churches, some at the same time, when churches would meet once or twice a month. He pastored Congaree Baptist from 1900-1904, Beulah Baptist from 1902-1907, and Union Baptist during 1908-1909. Other pastorates were Sand Field, Asbury, Crooked Run, Mizpah, Little River, and Rock Creek. Through these years, from time to time, he supplemented his income as a farmer-dairyman.

Between 1927 and 1947 Isenhower served five terms as a representative from Fairfield County in the State Legislature. He was an outspoken advocate for his opinions concerning the issues of the day. Two of his major accomplishments are remembered. One of them was the passing of the bond issue for the paving of the roads in Fairfield County, which eventually got Fairfield and South Carolina out of the mud. That was a bold move for an ultra-conservative in the early 1900s, but it was vindicated. He was a voice for the people and they loved him and called him friend. The roads must have been a help to him as he rode a bicycle to his preaching engagements. People remember Isenhower for his picturesque and flamboyant style of campaigning. "Clad in the garb of yesteryear, he would mount the stump, beat the air with his arms, point the finger and relate down-to-earth anecdotes of the soil to illustrate his fairly modern theories."[1] Another of his many significant controversial accomplishments was that of supporting the building of a hospital in Fairfield County. Fairfield Memorial Hospital in Winnsboro was built with bond money as well.

Isenhower never married. He had few worldly goods, probably holding with the Biblical injunction that "the love of money is the root of all evil." But one of his few prized possessions was a library consisting of a collection of good books. He agreed with Sir William Osler who declared, "Money invested in a library gives much better returns than mining stock."[2]

On Isenhower's 90th birthday he received a card from President Dwight David Eisenhower. Although the spelling of the last name is different, the President and the preacher came from the same family tree, several generations back.

Isenhower lived a long and useful life both in the religious and secular world. He was a good example of leadership in both fields. After a brief illness, he died at the hospital that he helped to bring into existence, the Fairfield Memorial Hospital. His Fairfield friends paid their last respects to him at the Mt. Olivet Cemetery August 20, 1964, where he was buried on his 94th birthday. Buried with him was a vast knowledge of the history of the Fairfield Baptist Association. He made much of that history. Someone said that Pastor Isenhower set store by the simple fundamental and enduring virtues which probably has a message for us today, would we but listen. Perhaps some would catch some inspiration from the spirit of a man of the old school that believed in the law of change and progress, in charity, in worshiping his Creator, and in reading good books.[3]

DCB

---

[1] *The News and Herald*, September 3, 1964, Volume 120, No. 31.

[2] Ibid.

[3] Ibid.

September 18

A Faithful Son

Scripture: Proverbs 3:1-6

I am always thrilled when I read or hear of a son of a noted preacher who follows in his father's pathway. This is as it ought to be, but often it is not the case. Today's devotion centers around Francis Moore, son of the famed seventeenth century preacher, Jeremiah Moore, of Virginia. Francis' father had been assaulted by a mob, apprehended and carried before the magistrate, and on three occasions jailed for preaching the Gospel without a license from the state church. Francis Moore was born in Fairfax County, Virginia, on September 18, 1766. At an early age the grace of God was manifest in his conversion, and the youth was baptized by Elder David Thomas. Having been raised in a hot-bed of truth, young Francis began preaching early in life. After proving himself to the congregation, he was ordained at Zoar, Virginia.

On November 8, 1792, in Maryland, Francis took a faithful wife to himself, and the couple moved and settled permanently near Harper's Ferry, Virginia. As was the usual case, Pastor Moore served in multiple churches simultaneously. He was a man of industrious habits, and applied himself diligently to work as both a pastor and evangelist. He served in a different era than did his father, and was never in danger of being jailed, but he was greatly admired and beloved. His educational superiority came from his godly background, but he also disciplined himself to gain a solid English education. Francis Moore leaned heavily toward a Calvinistic theological position. However, inasmuch as he had been reared under the godly influence of his evangelistic father, Francis Moore possessed a generous, loving attitude toward those with whom he did not fully agree.

However, when Alexander Campbell came upon the scene, Francis Moore was one of the first to detect his doctrinal deviation. Even before Campbell's heresy was publicly evident, Pastor Moore in 1824 warned of the severe results of following his theology: "Many of the Baptist denomination are preparing to receive the most baneful heresies, as Mr. Campbell has commenced a crusade against benevolent operations (missions), and by the ridicule he is casting upon these efforts, he will induce many to follow him upon that ground, and having thus gained their confidence, a favorable opportunity will be furnished to lead them into the most dangerous errors. He has commenced a voyage on the ocean of speculation without helm or compass, and many will follow him to their sorrow. There is a desire on his part to be the inventor of new things, but mark it, he will revive some old exploded errors."[1]

Francis Moore exulted in the missionary efforts of William Carey and Adoniram Judson, and he was used of God to raise funds for missions abroad. At the same time he realized the need of extending spiritual work by planting additional preaching stations and churches throughout Virginia. He authored the constitution of the Domestic Mission society in the Ketocton Association.

This Day in Baptist History III

In October of 1831, while returning home from an ordination service, Pastor Moore suffered an attack of apoplexy, but after a few days of total rest, though plagued with debility, he began a long period of physical restoration. Finally he was able again to minister God's Word. Again on February 11, 1831, the man of God was overcome with another attack of apoplexy as he prepared to minister. As was his custom, on Saturday evening he went to the home of Robert Classet where he usually spent the night before ministering in the Pleasant Valley Baptist Church. After supper and family devotions, he went to his bedroom and prepared for a night of sleep. Once during the night he was heard to open the window and to close it again. But when he did not rise for breakfast, Mr. Classet went to his room to arouse him. When no response was given, he opened it only to discover Brother Moore in an almost comatose state. He remained in that condition until Tuesday morning when his disembodied spirit took its flight to Glory. On Wednesday, February 15, 1831, the sad processional, led by his wife and children, conveyed his body to interment.

Though not as well known as his illustrious father, Francis Moore's faithful life served to honor our blessed Savior. Regardless of our heritage, may we purpose in our hearts to live to the praise of our Savior's glory.

DLC

---

[1]James B. Taylor, *Lives of Virginia Baptist Ministers* (Richmond: Yale & Wyatt, 1838), 387-388.

September 19

The Disappearing Groom

Scripture: Psalm 129:2,4

Nothing was sacred to the Communist leadership of the Soviet Union at the height of its power. Followers of the Savior could be arrested at a wedding or funeral without impunity! Consider the case of Aleksei Kalyashin, twenty-six-year-old would-be groom. His wedding was scheduled for September 19, 1981. A week earlier he was arrested and whisked off to prison.

Aleksei was driven to the prison in Vladimir. As the prosecution prepared its case, an interrogator badgered Aleksei continually with the promise that a renunciation of his faith would grant freedom, and wedding plans could continue. The investigator always concluded with the reminder, "You're a young man. Why should you go to prison camp for three years instead of getting married? Think about it."[1]

Prior to trial, Aleksei was allowed a fifteen-minute visit from his finance. He told Nina, ". . .they're promising to sentence me to three years. We aren't talking about three days or three months. This is a long term. You shouldn't have to wait for me! I'm releasing you from your promise to marry me." Nina responded, "Alex, I love you, and I'll stand by my promise to be your wife for my whole life."

A multitude of church members gathered outside the court at Aleksei's trial, but they were not allowed entrance. Aleksei refused the court-appointed atheistic lawyers, defending himself. Upon the completion of the so-called trial, the judge withdrew to his chambers. Aleksei was led to a room and met a KGB agent who questioned him. The agent asked, "Aleksei, what's your opinion of Gennady Kryuchkov? Would you agree he's simply a vagrant preacher?" "No," Aleksei answered, "Pastor Kryuchkov is a minister of the Gospel, selected by the church, and respected by all believers. He's not a vagrant preacher." Following other questions, the KGB agent picked up the phone, called the judge, and dictated the sentence to be given.

Though Soviet law provided that prisoners be placed in a camp near their home, Aleksei was transported to a distant Siberian camp, in the Krasnoyarsky region. Conditions were oppressive. Survival was only made possible through his Bible, fellowship with another Christian prisoner, and letters that believers sent. Apparently, his captors realized that Aleksei and the fellow Christian were encouraging each other. When Aleksei was moved to camp Nizhni Ingash, with much harsher conditions, he discovered that the KGB were seeking evidence against him from fellow prisoners. He realized that the KGB was unwilling to release him. Two days before his scheduled release, a copy of the magazine, *Herald of Truth,* was found in Aleksei's belongings. Thus it did not surprise him when he was accused and transported to the prison in Krasnoyarsk for re-trial. He was put on death row. The cell had no mattress and the bed was made of iron. If a person attempted to lie down, he would have to lie on the cold metal without any protection. For a month Aleksei was confined there. Again many young people from the Krasnoyarsk Baptist Church arrived for his trial, but the assigned room was too small to accommodate them. However, the judge relented. The trial was moved to a larger room, and many Christian youth filled the facility. The verdict was already assured. The judge pronounced the sentence of two and a half additional years of imprisonment.

During his second term, Aleksei and Nina submitted an application to hold a wedding ceremony in the camp. Camp authorities attempted to block the move, but the Lord undertook. On June 10, 1985, Nina, accompanied by both sets of parents, along with evangelist Nikolai Kruchinin, were allowed into the prison camp, and Aleksei and Nina were married. But the persecution of Aleksei was not over. He was moved from prison to prison, and for five months prior to his release, the KGB agents repeatedly questioned him. But God sustained His servant.

Soon after release, Aleksei was ordained to the Gospel ministry in a solemn ceremony. He and Nina opened their home for the saints to use for prayer meetings, and from time to time Aleksei was fined for such activities. But encouraged by the grace of God, Aleksei Kalyashin has continued faithful to his heavenly calling. May God find us faithful!

DLC

---

[1]Georgi Vins, Compiler, *Let The Waters Roar* (Baker Book House, Grand Rapids, MI), 223.

September 20

Following in the Steps of a Giant

Scripture: 1 Corinthians 3:4-7

The happiness that was experienced by Pastor and Mrs. Spurgeon on the date of this entry can only be imagined. One author has written: "On September 20, 1856, twin sons were born to Mrs. Spurgeon at her home . . . and the joy of husband and wife knew no bounds. With what pride he gazed upon the babes, and how tenderly he comforted his wife and spoke of the new and happy responsibility which they now had to fulfill! The boys were named Charles and Thomas, and from the first there was a tacit understanding and desire that they should be devoted to the service of God."[1]

As the lads matured, both inherited the full voice of their father. From time to time, both of the young men ministered in the tabernacle, but Thomas, less robust than Charles, determined to follow the occupation of commercial illustrator. For reasons of health, Thomas immigrated to Australia when he was twenty years old. Though he was not ordained or trained in theology, he was called upon to preach because of his father's notoriety. Two years later, Thomas returned to London and at that time his father asked him to remain as his assistant. At that time, Pastor Spurgeon expressed the desire that Thomas would in time become his successor. However, poor health dictated that Thomas return to Australia, and he entered into an itinerant ministry before accepting the call to pastor in New Zealand.

The death of Charles Haddon Spurgeon precipitated serious trials for the leadership and congregation at the Tabernacle. James Spurgeon, brother of the great pastor, though not nearly as gifted, had served as co-pastor. History reveals that James was determined to assume the pastorate. The church family did not approve of such a move, and only when it was apparent that the congregation would split if James became pastor, did he remove himself from consideration. At the time of Mr. Spurgeon's death, the American, Dr. A. T. Pierson, had been filling the pulpit. His ministry was exceptional, but he had never been immersed, and therefore surely could not serve the congregation as pastor. He graciously removed himself from consideration, and following several months of agitation, Thomas Spurgeon was asked to assume the pastorate. It must be said that he did not seek the position, nor had he shared his father's private wish for him to be his successor.

Now we enter into mere conjecture, but it is speculation based upon historical reality. Imagine with me the pressure of ministering under the memory's shadow of such a pulpiteer as Charles H. Spurgeon? It must be remembered that Mr. Spurgeon had averaged 5,000 in attendance on Sunday mornings and Sunday evenings for 31 years. It is a well known fact that the first pastor to follow a man of God who has had a lengthy and fruitful ministry generally has a most difficult time. He is always being compared to the former pastor. I have experienced such a situation, and I know in fact that nothing the new pastor does is worthy of comparison to the former man of God. We must also acknowledge that Thomas did not possess the charisma that had belonged to his father. Yet, Thomas apparently had reasonable success as both preacher and pastor.

Let us also recall the burden that rested upon him as he sought to rebuild the Tabernacle following the disastrous fire of 1898. That in itself was a gigantic task, and yet the young pastor was used of God to accomplish the work.

Again, it must be pointed out that Thomas accomplished what he did without robust health. Thus it was in 1908 his health forced him to resign the pastorate. But his influence was continually felt as he headed up the Spurgeon College until his death in 1917. The Lord never gifts two of his servants identically, and yet as we pause to consider the ministry of Thomas Spurgeon we can but rejoice in his faithfulness in standing for truth in a difficult and trying day.

Today let me urge you to pray for pastors. Their's is a task often misunderstood and unrewarded. How we rejoice in the realization that there is a day coming when the Chief Shepherd shall reward all of His true undershepherds.

DLC

---

[1]Charles Ray, *Mrs. C. H. Spurgeon* (Pasadena: Pilgrim Publications, 1979), 40.

September 21

Exiled for Truth

Scripture: 1 Corinthians 15:58

"The first Baptist Church of Sweden was formed in Landa Parish, Halland, September 21, 1848. In the evening of that day four men and one woman were baptized in the waters of Vallervik, a bay of the Kattegat.... In a neighboring farm house, Borekulla, the homestead of one of the new converts, the small church was organized, and the ordinance of the Lord's supper was observed."[1]

The ordinance of baptism was administered by A. P. Foerster of Copenhagen, Denmark. The motivation for the establishing of this church was provided by Fredrik Olaus Nilsson, a sailor who had been converted in New York. In time he had been baptized in Germany by the famed Baptist leader, J. G. Oncken. Thus when A. P. Foerster made haste to return to Denmark, to escape persecution, Nilsson became the leader of the newly formed congregation.

The small church grew, and in December of 1848, four men were baptized by Nilsson in the Göta River, near Gothenburg. By April of 1849 the membership numbered thirty-five. The congregation requested that Nilsson make a journey to Hamburg, Germany that he might be ordained by the church pastored by J. G. Oncken, and this was accomplished in May of 1849.

Nilsson was aware that persecution doubtless awaited him, and immediately after the organization of the church, he wrote a letter to Doctor Sheward, pastor of the Baptist Mariners Church in New York City. In that letter he wrote, "Thus it has pleased the Lord to permit a church, built on New Testament principles, to be formed also in Sweden, the Spain of the North, religiously speaking, and now it depends on the Lord whether or not this church is to live and prosper. We are looking for persecution and trouble because of our faith. We have been planning to leave the country, but our conscience bids us remain here until we are driven off by the authorities. We do not know what the future may have in store for us, but we are determined to stand firm for the truth. And we feel, sometimes at least, that He will help us to remain firm in every trial."[2]

The congregation did not have to wait long until the persecution began. Baptist children were forcibly taken to the parish priest that he might christen them. The members were summoned to appear before the authorities of the state church to answer for their sins of omission. Nilsson was arrested and subjected to legal persecution. This ultimately resulted in his being banished from his country. On July 4, 1851, he left his sorrowing church family and went into exile. Religious liberty had been established in Copenhagen in 1849, and there he fled. In time he became pastor of a Baptist church there.

The persecution did not abate with the pastor's absence. Savage mobs broke out windows and doors. There was a prevailing sentiment often expressed that it did not cost more than eighteen shillings (the equivalent of ten cents) to kill a Baptist. When the mobs threatened the Baptists, the civil powers were not willing to provide protection. In cases, heavy fines were levied against these religious outcasts, and the membership began individually entertaining the idea of leaving Sweden. At their annual New Year meeting of 1853, the congregation agreed that as many as possible would emigrate to America. Twenty-one members left their homeland, and being joined by their former pastor, sought asylum in America, the land of the free.

As we worship without fear of persecution in America today, let us remember that such freedom does not exist at this time in many nations of the world. Bible Christians are suffering in many environments. Martyrdoms are still taking place in this day. Let us pray for suffering saints who do not have our liberty, and let us remain alert that America shall not lose the freedom of conscience that is so dear.

DLC

---

[1]J. O. Backlund, *Swedish Baptists in America* (Chicago, Conference Press, 1933), 23.

[2]Ibid., 24-25.

September 22

The Exception: Not The Rule

Scripture: Galatians 1:15-16, 24

Natural talents and Divinely given gifts to the children of men are amazing to observe. From time to time a young man, with limited educational background, but possessing a unique mind and persuasive abilities of speech seems to emerge from nowhere. When this occurs, one stands in awe at the exhibit of the blessing of God. Such a person was Abram Maer Poindexter. He was born on September 22, 1809, into the family of Pastor and Mrs. Richard Poindexter in Bertie County, North Carolina. Young Abram applied himself well to his early studies which would prepare him for college. We know comparatively little of his young life, but in 1831 he made a profession of faith and was baptized. The following year he was licensed to preach. During the next two years, young Poindexter studied under the tutelage of Reverend A. W. Clopton, a very useful minister in Charlotte County, Virginia. Without college training or a pastorate, two years later, Mr. Poindexter was ordained into the Gospel ministry in 1834.

In 1833, our subject entered Columbian College in Washington, D. C. While in his freshman year at Columbian College, Reverend Poindexter preached in various area Baptist churches, but poor health caused him to drop out of school after his first year, and he returned home. On May 25, 1837, the young preacher married Miss Eliza J. Craddock. His first pastorate was in Halifax County, Virginia, and there he became closely associated with Luther Rice. Mr. Rice, the catalyst among Baptists for both missions and ministerial education, thought highly of Reverend Poindexter. He considered the young man the most promising, young preacher he knew. Doubtless the association with, and interest of, Luther Rice had caused the young preacher to reciprocate the interest. He dedicated his time to assisting in the work of Columbian and Richmond Colleges, the Southern Baptist Theological Seminary in Greenville,

South Carolina, and the Foreign Mission Board. A tremendous tribute has been paid the gifted preacher, and we do well to consider the report: "From the very beginning of his ministry he displayed unusual talents, and was esteemed the most promising young minister of his time. As a preacher, Dr. Poindexter was deservedly held in very high regard, especially with large out-door assemblies, such as convene at Associational meetings. On such occasions his preaching was frequently distinguished by great fluency and power of speech, unusual vigor and depth of thought, a beautiful logical consecutiveness in the development of truth, and an earnestness and impetuosity of manner that swayed and moved the masses with resistless power. As a thinker he had but few equals. His intellect was clear, active, strong and original. His thoughts were pre-eminently his own. . . . As an extemporaneous debater he stood almost alone among disputants; and so accurate was his method, so precise his arguments, so correct his style, that a verbatim report of his remarks would rarely require the least revision for publication. . . . He was a man of deep convictions and intense feeling. His words were indeed the outer image of his inmost soul. He believed, and therefore he spoke; and when he spoke, men had no hesitation in saying, 'Here is a Christian man who will part with his life rather that with his convictions of right and duty.'"[1]

The man of God endured many trials in life. He lost two sons in the Civil War, and the rages of war swept away his estate. Several years later his beloved wife passed into the presence of the Lord on September 14, 1867. But the man of God continued to serve both in the capacity of an editor and writer of thoughtful articles for various Christian publications. The Lord called his servant home on May 7, 1872.

At the 1886 session of the General Association of Virginia, John A. Broadus said, "Poindexter was a Boanerges, a son of thunder, earnest, impetuous, resolute, resistless. . . . His utterances, always weighty, and powerful, were at times absolutely terrific and overwhelming."[2] Rarely does the Lord so gift a man that college and seminary are not needed. Let us continue to insist to our young men that this is the exception and not the rule. Let us encourage young preachers to prepare as much as possible for their greatest potential use in the hand of God the Holy Spirit.

DLC

---

[1]William Cathcart, *The Baptist Encyclopaedia* (Philadelphia: Louis H. Everts, 1881), 2:924.

[2]E. C. Routh, *Encyclopedia of Southern Baptists* (Nashville, TN: Broadman Press, 1958), 2:1093.

September 23

A Versatile and Generous Leader

Scripture: Mark 1:38

Jesse Mercer was born on December 16, 1769, into the home of Silas Mercer, who became a pioneer Baptist minister of Georgia. Silas had been raised as a staunch Episcopalian, and was still a faithful member of that denomination when Jesse was born. So Silas insisted that his first-born son, Jesse, be immersed in infancy by the Episcopalian minister. Silas Mercer had been well warned against the heretical Baptists, but through a long process of the Holy Spirit's leading, he ultimately embraced Baptist convictions, was himself immersed, and became a faithful Baptist preacher. Jesse's educational background was obtained through the tutelage of a Presbyterian minister who lived near his home. He studied as well for a year in Salem Academy, the first private Baptist school in Georgia.

During his early years Jesse was raised in the Episcopalian background, but when he was still quite young, his father became a convicted Baptist. During his teen-age years, Jesse endured a lengthy period of conviction, and it was not until he was seventeen that he was able to relate his Christian experience to the Phillips' Mill congregation. That was on July 7, 1787, and Jesse was baptized by his father, (probably on the following day,) being then in the eighteenth year of his age."[1]

When he was twenty, Jesse Mercer was ordained, and assumed his first ministerial charge, a church that had been founded by his father, Hutton's Fork Church (now Sardis). At the time of his father's death, Jesse returned to the family home in Wilkes County that he might administer the estate. His father had founded the Salem Academy, and Jesse became principal while he continued to serve the Sardis church as pastor. He also accepted calls to pastor his father's three churches: Phillips' Mill, Wheatley's Mill (later Bethesda), and Powelton. Jesse's pastorates became the center of much of the history of the Georgia Baptists.

Jesse had married Sabrina Chivers when he was nineteen, and the couple enjoyed nearly forty years of married life until her untimely death. Jesse had preached the convention sermon of the Triennial Convention in 1826, and while returning home through South Carolina, Mrs. Mercer became seriously ill, and passed away on September 23, 1826.[2] Jesse was now fifty-six years old, and he realized that he would have to slow his pace. On December 11, 1827, he married Mrs. Nancy Simons, a widow. He resigned his churches, moved to Washington, Georgia, and established a Baptist church there. He completed his ministry there, serving that pastorate until his death on September 6, 1841.

Throughout his ministry Jesse was convinced that an itinerant ministry was necessary to reach spiritually impoverished people in sparsely-settled areas. He preached to many congregations scattered throughout his section of the state. Wherever he traveled, he carried tracts and books of the American Tract Society. Throughout his ministry he was known as an ardent supporter of missions, Sunday schools, and temperance. He was well known for his support of missionary work among the slaves. Surely Jesse Mercer was not only a great preacher, but he was a successful businessman, and doubtless one of the most generous philanthropists of his day.

For years Jesse was the recognized leader of the Georgia Baptist Association and the Georgia Baptist Convention. His record is amazing, for he served as clerk of the association for twenty-one years, as moderator for twenty-three years, and as writer of its history. For nineteen years he served as president of the Georgia Baptist Convention. He greatly respected Luther Rice, and served as a trustee of Columbian College in Washington, D. C., when the college was organized. He was the first president of the board of trustees of Mercer University, which bears his name. Jesse believed in ministerial education, and he was a great benefactor through financial gifts to educational institutions.

Jesse Mercer was a man of the Book and Christian statesman for his day. Let us pray that the Lord shall provide renewed leadership for these closing days of grace.

DLC

---

[1]Charles D. Mallary, *Memoirs of Elder Jesse Mercer* (New York: Printed by John Gray, 1844), 25.

[2]Ibid., 102.

September 24

Preaching With Power

Scripture: Acts 4:8-13

The name of William Marshall is hardly known among Baptists today, and yet he was used of God in a most unusual way in Virginia and Kentucky. William Marshall was born in 1735, twenty years before the birth of his nephew, John Marshall, (September 24, 1755) who became Attorney General of the United States. During his youth, William was known as a fun-loving seeker after the amusements of his day. He was stately and tall, and was the pride of his circle of friends. When he was 33 years old, he was providentially brought under the influence of the Separate Baptists in Fauquier County, Virginia. He fell under deep conviction of sin, and for a time he despaired that he could ever be saved. But God, who is rich in mercy, gloriously saved William Marshall, and he immediately set out to share the Good News.

Being of a well-known family, crowds began to gather whenever he spoke. Some attended his preaching sessions out of curiosity. Some attended supposing he was deranged, but his preaching was with heavenly power. The historian states, "The word preached was not in vain, but was attended with the Holy Ghost, sent down from Heaven. One of the most remarkable seasons of the ingathering of souls which Virginia has ever known, resulted from his labors. The enemies of the truth were much enraged, and determined, if possible, to arrest the march of this new doctrine; they seized Mr. Marshall, and attempted to put him in prison, but his brother, Colonel Thomas Marshall, interfered, and succeeded in obtaining his release. He continued to preach . . . with unabated zeal and success. Among the seals to his ministry, were John Taylor and Joseph Redding, who afterwards became popular and useful laborers in the Lord's vineyard. . . . Thousands came to hear and see him. . . . The first baptism in the waters of the Shenandoah was performed by Elder Samuel Harris in 1770. At this time, as the result primarily of Marshall's labors, fifty-three went down into the liquid grave, and were thus buried with their adorable Lord in that ordinance."[1] William's brother, Colonel Thomas Marshall, was able to assist his brother, for he was a close friend of the man who would become our first president, George Washington.

William Marshall was surely not a doctrinal preacher. He had little time to study the deep things of the Word of God before he began preaching, but preach he did! His chief object was to warn men of the danger of living and dying in sin, and the necessity of turning to Jesus Christ by faith as the only Savior. The Virginia Baptist historian wrote that he was "a very zealous and successful preacher . . . of more warmth than wisdom, more grace than gifts."

For a short time, William Marshall settled down to a pastorate in Virginia, but in 1780 he moved to Kentucky and settled in what is now known as Shelby County. Early in his Kentucky ministry, he was injured in a fall from his horse, but this gave him time to read more thoroughly. His preaching became more doctrinally oriented, but he continued to preach with his old-time zeal. One of his contemporary preachers wrote, "It was interesting to see this old man assisted to the stand, and propped up by his friends, and to hear him pour forth the most delightful strains of gospel truth. His strong mind, deep research, and prayerful spirit, well qualified him to clear the subjects he discussed, of all ambiguity."

God's servant was called home at the age of seventy-eight, after he had labored for approximately forty years in the Gospel.

Great emphasis is being placed in the twenty-first century on exposition. Oh that the Lord would awaken anew the desire in the hearts of many young Baptist preachers to experience the thrill of evangelism. We surely need spiritual balance in this day. We need exposition, but we also need evangelism. We need information, but we must have inspiration. Pray for our young Baptist preachers in these days.

DLC

---

[1]James B. Taylor, *Lives of Virginia Baptist Ministers* (Richmond: Yale & Wyatt, 1838), 103-104.

September 25

He Read His Title Clearly

Scripture: 2 Timothy 2:1-4

It was almost evening when finally we found the long-sought church yard. In a short time the last rays of daylight would flee from the western skies, but we felt well rewarded as we stood and gazed upon the final resting place of the body of Luther Rice. Years have passed since the man of God was buried there. Time has begun the process of eroding the epitaph incised upon the cover of the vault. In part the engraving reads, "Perhaps no American has done more for the great missionary enterprise." It is thought the first American Foreign Mission, on which he went to India, associated with Judson and others, originated with him. His burial site had been chosen by Luther Rice on his death bed. In talking with Dr. J. C. Ready, physician and minister, he had said he wished to be buried in The Pine Pleasant churchyard, the most peaceful spot on earth.[1] How he loved to travel amidst the warmth of the Separate Baptists in the Southland. He enjoyed their simplicity of worship and warmth of heart.

His coronation had come on a golden autumn day – September 25, 1836. His traveling in behalf of missions and his beloved college was about over. He would soon experience the reality of his favorite hymn,

When I can read my title clear
To mansions in the skies,
I'll bid farewell to every fear
And wipe my weeping eyes.

He would awaken in the presence of his blessed Lord.

But what a life of sacrifice had been his! A terrible turmoil had raged in his mind. He was torn between two amazing opportunities. Adoniram and Ann Judson urged him to return to Burma and assist them. His heart was there, but American pastors begged him to remain Stateside and assist in organizing Baptist missions. After a long struggle he had determined God's Will, but the correspondence between Mr. Rice and the Judsons reveal a tenderness of heart that must have caused him much emotional agitation. Through his travels Luther Rice soon recognized the need for a trained ministry, and his heart was also large enough to envision a college to train preachers.

All of this came to mind as we stood in the twilight at his grave side. I thought too of the fact that he wore himself out in his service of the King. Luther Rice was an outstanding pulpiteer. Someone has described him as follows: "Above the ordinary height, robust, perfectly erect, of commanding presence, making a fine appearance in the pulpit, and having also the gift and temperament of a public speaker with talents of the very first order, sprightliness, pathos, and a vigorous, natural eloquence, always exceedingly felicitous and impressive, sometimes overpowering, he was often called 'the orator,' and as his pulpit efforts were highly attractive, he was ranked as one of the most interesting and effective speakers in the land."[2]

This man was not only a pulpiteer, but he was tireless in his efforts to support missions and Christian education. On August 26, 1816, he eclipsed John Wesley's horseback record as he rode ninety-three miles to keep a speaking appointment. In April 1818 he wrote Dr. Staughton that he had traveled 9,359 miles on horseback during that year.

But burning the candle at both ends caught up with the fifty-three year old Luther Rice. His travels took him again to South Carolina, and his health began to wane. Friends opened their home and hearts to the man of God, and it became apparent that death was imminent. Knowing what awaited him, he gave all that he possessed to the Columbian College that he loved so dearly. But all he had was a horse, sulky, and personal baggage. He owned no home for he had lived selflessly throughout his lifetime. But he would now depart for a heavenly home and read the title deed as he closed his eyes on earth's darkness only to open them in the eternal light of his enduring home.

We left the scene of Luther Rice's grave with a renewed determination to live wholly in dedication to the same Lord who motivated that great man of God. Friend, we need to often ask ourselves, "For what are we living?"

DLC

---

[1]Evelyn Wingo Thompson, *Luther Rice - Believer in Tomorrow* (Nashville, TN: Broadman Press, 1967), 200.

[2]James L. Hill, *The Immortal Seven* (Philadelphia: American Baptist Publication Society, 1913), 46

September 26

Meeting Christ Far From Home

Scripture: 2 Timothy 2:1-4

As we walked quietly through the British War Cemetery in Yangon, Myanmar (Burma), I could not help but think of the many Englishmen who had died in Burma from 1939 to 1945 during the Second World War. To be sure, I visited the grave sites of the three Americans who are also memorialized there. My three countrymen had joined the Canadian Royal Air Force and had given their lives in the Burman battles for freedom. But, as I walked through that hallowed area, my mind quickly moved back one hundred years to ancient Burma, and I was transfixed as I meditated again upon the multi-faceted ministry of Adoniram Judson.

In 1827 Sir Archibald Campbell, chief of the British troops in Burma, moved his military headquarters from Amherst to a newly-formed area known as Moulmein. The new city quickly grew, and it became the center of missionary activity. Sir Campbell, realizing the importance of the Gospel, had granted choice property to Mr. Judson for the work of God. In time, Baptist churches were established to reach the various tribes represented in the city population, and from time to time British soldiers would attend services. It became evident that a ministry must be established to reach these men with the Gospel. Adoniram Judson, though burdened with so many other tasks, invested enough time to establish a church for the military. In visiting Moulmein, I sat in a pew in the building that so-long ago housed those soldiers as a place of worship. It was thrilling to envision a godly

English mother praying for her son and then picturing that same dear lady as she opened a letter from her young soldier son in Burma. In my mind's eye I could almost see that dear mother exalt with ecstasy as she read of her son's conversion while serving in the military so far away!

On September 26, 1835, Adoniram completed his revision of the Old Testament. Ann was with the Lord, and Adoniram had remarried. Sarah Boardman Judson was now his faithful mate. As they continued in their labors among the Burmese, they witnessed to the English servicemen as well. As the Word of God was given, not only did the Spirit of God bring conviction and conversion among the Burmese, but service men were also saved. One such soldier was James Delaney, an artilleryman. In their association with him, both Adoniram and Sarah recognized that the good hand of God seemed to rest upon him for service to the Lord. When Delaney received his military discharge in 1834, the Judsons assisted in arranging for him to travel to America and enroll in the theological seminary in Hamilton, New York. Dear Sarah provided him with twenty-five dollars from her meager savings. In the course of time, he completed his studies and settled in the States, entering a pastorate in Appleton, Wisconsin. Other than for a period of time during the Civil War, when he served the Union troops as a chaplain, Reverend James Delaney served the Lord in Appleton through the remainder of his life.[1] He was fruit of the missionary dollars that had been sent to reach Burma for Christ!

The servicemen's church in Moulmein was first known as the 45th Regiment English Church, and morning and evening services were held each Sunday, with services also being conducted on Friday evenings.[2] The congregations were small, with ten to twenty soldiers gathering to hear the message of grace, but, thankfully, the Lord blessed, and lives were transformed. By the way, that work continues to this day and is known as the English Baptist Church.

As I sat in the pew in the building in which many English servicemen were led to Christ, I paused to thank God for the versatility of our Bible-believing missionaries as they faithfully share the good news with all who will hear. As our American troops are being called upon again to serve around the world, their hearts are often softened as they see a familiar face or hear their native tongue. Let us pray that many servicemen shall be reached with the Gospel by our missionaries as they continue faithful service.

DLC

---

[1]Courtney Anderson, *To the Golden Shore* (Boston: Little, Brown and Company, 1956), 419.

[2]Maung Shwe Wa, *Burma Baptist Chronicle* (Rangoon: Burma Baptist Convention, 1963), 63.

September 27

Either Commission or Omission

Scripture: Luke 10:30:37

A spirit of anti-missions is incongruous with the heart of the Savior and the reading of the book of Acts. Yet, early in the nineteenth century, a group of Baptist men arose protesting the missionary movement that had reappeared at the close of the eighteenth century with William Carey and Andrew Fuller in England. There can be no doubt that hyper-Calvinism had led some to an anti-missionary position. Others, who were also doubtless sincere, objected to any agency that could be considered para-church in nature. Those who were hyper-Calvinistic were fearful that the Gospel might be presented to some who were not elect. Those in the second group thought they were defending the biblical position of local church autonomy. Be that as it may, a sizeable number of Baptists particularly in Illinois, Indiana, and Kentucky flourished. Local churches and associations divided over the issue, and for a time the outcome seemed in doubt.

Georgia too experienced this anti-mission spirit. For instance, opposition to the missionary cause extended to the State General Association.

"The most violent anti-missionaries in the Association . . . were John Blackstone, James Gray, Jordan Smith, James Granade, and Claborn Bateman, who, for several years had been employed as an Association missionary."[1]

About 1825 the anti-missionary spirit peaked in the Hephzibah Association. Two years later, when Jordan Smith was moderator of the Association, he republished anti-missionary publications from a North Carolina association. These were answered anonymously, but the battle raged. Being unable to control the Hephzibah Association, the dissidents withdrew and formed the Canoochee Baptist Conference. In 1828 they accepted the name of the Canoochee Baptist Association, and the 6th article of their Constitution ran thus: "As the love of money is the root of all evil, and has produced so much distress among Christians, and we wishing to live in peace; therefore, this Association shall not engage in, nor in any wise encourage, any religious speculation, called the missionary, or by any other name, under pretense of supporting the gospel of Christ."[2]

In the course of time, the leaders of the anti-missionary movement passed from the scene as did that anti-missionary Association. However, as we have entered into the twenty-first century, I am concerned for churches that profess to be missionary minded, but who have little actual interest in the cause of world-wide evangelism. Lip service is given to the matter. To be sure, missionary conferences are held, but rather than producing young people interested in responding to the Great Commission, most congregations seem to be providing youth interested in responding to Great Commerce. Real disinterest is manifested in the fact that missionary giving has not continued to accelerate, but it is rather in eclipse. When a budget cut is necessitated in a local church accounting, the support of the newest missionary to have been taken on for support, is usually the first item to be cut.

Thank God for churches whose heart-beat is indeed missions at home and abroad. But in truth, it is apparent that the dominant generation of believers at the outset of this twenty-first century does not have the same ardor for missions as was known amidst the generations earlier in the twentieth century. To this author, this seems to be true even in the matter of those who pray for missionaries. I would remind you that missions is mandatory. We can boil down our Lord's challenge into two words. To all mankind He says, "COME," and to those who respond to that invitation and become His children, he says, "GO."

Most Bible-believers today would not dare deny the cause of missions, but it is so easy to relegate the missionary cause to an inferior position in our agenda. Surely the Lord of the Harvest blesses congregations that put the Great Commission first. The world population is proliferating, and the missionary arm is in decline. There is so little time and so much to do. May we determine that we will not be guilty of an anti-missionary spirit by simple neglect.

DLC

[1]Samuel Boynton, *History of the Baptist Denomination* in Georgia (Atlanta, GA: Jas. P. Harrison & Co, 1881), 164.

[2]Ibid., 165.

September 28

Hedging in the Sovereign God

Scripture: Psalm 78:41

The anti-mission influence of Hyper-Calvinists among Baptists in the middle of the nineteenth century was devastating. Accused of being antinomian, the charge struck a nerve in that group's thinking, and they sought to defend their position. The Particular Baptists of the Old School presented a unanimous statement that is enlightening. As they met on September 28, 1832, in the Black Rock meeting house in Baltimore, Maryland, they framed a statement censuring tract societies, Sunday schools, Mission societies, Bible colleges and seminaries, and protracted, or evangelistic, meetings. The statement begins as follows: "It constitutes a new era in the history of the Baptists, when those who would follow the Lord fully . . . are by Baptists charged with antinomianism, inertness, stupidity, &c., for refusing to go beyond the Word of God; but such is the case with us.

"We will notice severally the claims of the principal of these modern inventions, and state some of our objections to them for your candid consideration."

Tract Societies and Sunday Schools were attacked for not being Scriptural. They summarized the Tract Societies by saying, "If we were to admit that tracts may have occasionally been made instrumental by the Holy Ghost for imparting instruction or comfort to inquiring minds, it would by no means imply that tracts are an instituted means of salvation . . .

"[Concerning Sunday Schools they stated that Sunday Schools]. . . claim the honor of converting their tens of thousands; of leading the tender minds of children to the knowledge of Jesus; of being as properly the instituted means of bringing children to the knowledge of salvation, as is the preaching of the Gospel that of bringing adults to the same knowledge, &c. Such arrogant pretensions we feel bound to oppose. . . . Sunday Schools were never established by the apostles, nor commanded by Christ . . . ."

After considering the Bible Society, and also finding it fallacious in as much as it is ". . . foreign from anything which the gospel of Christ calls for. . .," they turned their attention to the subject of Missions.

"Previous to stating our objections to the mission plans, we will meet some of the false charges brought against us relative to this subject, by a simple and unequivocal declaration, that we do regard of the first importance the command given of Christ, . . . to "Go into all the world, and preach the gospel to every creature, . . . We also believe it to be the duty of individuals and churches to contribute according to their abilities, for the support, not only of their pastors, but also of those who go preaching the Gospel of Christ among the destitute. But we at the same time contend, that we have no right to depart from the order which the Master himself has seen fit to lay down, relative to the ministration of the Word. We therefore cannot fellowship with the plans for spreading the gospel, generally adopted at this day, under the name of Missions; because we consider those plans throughout a subversion of the order marked out in the New Testament. . . .

"Brethren, we cheerfully acknowledge that there have been some honorable exceptions to the character we have here drawn of the modern missionary, and some societies have existed under the name of Mission Societies which were in some important points exceptions from the above drawn sketch; but on a general scale we believe we have given a correct view of the mission plans and operations, and of the effects which have resulted from them, and our hearts really sicken at this state of things..."

After presenting their opposition to Bible colleges and seminaries, the statement closes with the following: "We now pass to the last item which we think it necessary particularly to notice, viz: four-days or protracted meetings . . . . Therefore, whenever circumstances call a congregation together from day to day, as at an association or the like, we would embrace the opportunity of preaching the Gospel to them from time to time. . . but to the principles and plans of protracted meetings, distinguishingly so called, we do decidedly object. The principle of these meetings we cannot fellowship. Regeneration, we believe, is exclusively the work of the Holy Ghost, performed by his divine power, at his own sovereign pleasure, according to the provisions of the everlasting covenant; but these meetings are got up for the purpose of inducing the Holy Spirit to regenerate multitudes who would otherwise not be converted, or to convert them themselves by the machinery of these meetings."[1]

How I praise the Lord that our faithful Baptist forefathers repudiated the extreme tendencies of those whose doctrine we have just read.

DLC

---

[1]H. Leon McBeth, *A Sourcebook For Baptist Heritage* (Nashville, TN: Broadman Press, 1990), 237-238.

September 29

Ignorance is Not Bliss!

Scripture: Romans 10:14-17

How interesting to read of the formation of the first Baptist church in central Canada. Elisha Andrews had been born on September 29, 1768[1], in Middletown, Connecticut. Having been saved and baptized, he worked in the church.

Elisha desired to be licensed to preach, but his home church questioned his call to preach. Thus he left the area and headed for Vermont. During his travels he was invited to preach in Granville, and the people there granted him a license. In 1793 Andrews took charge of the Baptist church in Fairfax, Vermont, and was ordained as an evangelist.

He traveled to Canada, and was providentially used of the Lord in assisting in establishing the first Baptist church in middle Canada. He provided the following account for *The Triennial Baptist Register*: ". . . We met at 9 o'clock in the morning, and spent the whole day in examining candidates for baptism; we heard and received thirty of all ages from 10 to 50 years. . . . Nearly all they knew had been taught them by the Holy Spirit, and they told a plain, unvarnished tale of the dealings of God with their souls; and I have seldom heard such a number of Christian experiences so highly satisfactory, and decidedly evidential of a real change of heart. The next day we repaired to the Lake, cut a hole in the ice, and fifteen of those happy and devoted disciples were . . . immersed. The baptism of the remaining fifteen was deferred until the next Monday . . . .

"Among those who were baptized, there was a family who were brought to the knowledge of the truth in an extraordinary way; indeed, in a manner which shows that God is wise in counsel, and wonderful in working. They were Low Dutch people, remarkably ignorant, and even profane in their common conversation. The eldest daughter, at about the age of fourteen, was employed as a hired maid, in the family of Mr. William Marsh, who was a pious and devout Baptist professor. Poor Mary was astonished to see the whole family, in the evening, . . . stand while Mr. Marsh talked ten or fifteen minutes. What it meant, or what it was for, she could not imagine. Nor could she devise to whom it was that Mr. Marsh addressed his conversation, as she could see no one to whom he could direct his speech. In the morning a similar scene occurred; and Mary became alarmed and uneasy, fearing there was something that portended evil to her, in this unaccountable proceeding. As the same scene took place every morning and evening, and she had in vain racked her invention to find out the meaning of it, she resolved to go home and ask her father. After stating her difficulty, and observing she did not like to live with Mr. William Marsh, she asked him to whom it was that Mr. Marsh talked? The old Dutchman, in his broken English, replied, *"I don't know, to de debil I subbose."* This answer did not quite satisfy Mary nor calm her apprehensions; she therefore plucked up her courage, and put the momentous question, . . . to Mr. Marsh himself. He asked her whether she knew that there was a God that made us, sustained us, and redeemed us; and that it was our duty to worship Him? She replied, that this was all new to her, that she had never heard anything of the kind before; she had indeed heard her father swear by God, but did not know what it meant. Mr. Marsh finding she could read a little, gave her a Bible, and encouraged her to pursue it. Being a girl of quick apprehension and bright intellect, she made surprising advances in knowledge.

"She soon became serious, and having obtained a hope in the mercy of God through Christ, she went again to her father, and told him that she knew what Mr. Marsh meant by talking as he did. In the most tender and most affectionate manner she expostulated with him for neglecting to tell her that there was a God, and teaching her to pray to Him. The poor old man replied that he had never prayed in his life, that he could not pray. "Then," said Mary, "will you allow me to pray?" "Yes, child", said he, "If you can pray you may." Mary immediately fell on her knees, and poured out her supplication for her father, her mother, her brother and sister. The old man, when relating the story, said that if she had been stabbing him through the heart with a knife, he could not have been in greater distress. The consequence was, that the whole family were converted, and Mary had the happiness of having them all accompany her into the Baptismal fount."[2]

Could there be heathens in your neighborhood who do not know Christ? How will they hear until YOU tell them?

DLC

---

[1]Stuart Ivison & Fred Rosser, *The Baptists in Upper and Lower Canada Before 1820* (Toronro: University of Toronto Press, 1956), 157.

[2]I. M. Allen, *The Triennial Baptist Register* (Philadelphia: Baptist General Tract Society, 1839), 290-291.

September 30

Great Baptist Educators

Scripture: 2 Timothy 2:1-2, 15

The first effort of educating Baptist pastors in America was that made by Reverend Isaac Eaton in Hopewell, New Jersey. Among his first graduates in his school was Dr. James Manning, who became the founder of the College in Rhode Island which ultimately became Brown University. Other outstanding men of God also served as presidents in the early days of Brown, men such as the Reverends Jonathan Maxcy, Asa Messer, and Dr. Francis Wayland, the last of whom passed away on September 30, 1865. From the very beginning, a solid academic education was provided, and the professors were true to the Word of God. This is witnessed in the first graduation as seven students in 1769 received the first Bachelor Degrees granted by the college.

"On Thursday, the seventh of this instance [1769], was celebrated at Warren the first commencement in the college of this colony; when the following young gentlemen commenced Bachelor of Arts; namely, Joseph Belton, Joseph Eaton, William Rogers, Richard Stites, Charles Thompson, James Mitchell Varnum and William Williams.

"About ten o'clock, A.M., the gentlemen concerned in conducting the affairs of the college, together with the candidates, went in procession to the meeting house.

"After they had taken their seats respectively, and the audience composed, the President introduced the business of the day with prayer; then followed a salutatory in Latin, pronounced with much spirit, by Mr. Stites, which produced him great applause from the learned part of the assembly. He spoke upon the advantages of liberty and learning, and their mutual dependence upon each other, concluding with proper salutations to the Chancellor of the college, Governor of the colony, etc., particularly expressing the gratitude of all the friends of the college to the Rev. Morgan Edwards, who has encountered many difficulties in going to Europe to collect donations for the institution, and has lately returned.

"To which succeeded a forensic dispute, in English, on the following thesis namely, "The Americans, in their present circumstances, cannot consistent with good policy, affect to become an Independent State." Mr. Varnum ingeniously defended it, by cogent arguments handsomely dressed, though he was subtly but delicately opposed by Mr. Williams, both of whom spoke with emphasis and propriety.

"As a conclusion to the exercises of the forenoon, the audience were agreeably entertained with an oration on benevolence, by Mr. Rogers; in which, among many other pertinent observations, he particularly noticed the necessity which that infant seminary stands in of the salutary effects of that truly Christian virtue.

"At three o'clock P. M., the audience being convened, a syllogistic dispute was introduced on the thesis: *Materia cogitate non potest,* Mr. Williams the respondent; Messieurs Belton, Eaton, Rogers, and Varnum the opponents, in the course of which dispute, the principal argument on both sides were produced toward settling the critical point.

"The degree of Bachelor of Arts was then conferred on the candidates. . . . A concise, pertinent, and solemn charge was then given to the Bachelors by the President, concluding with his paternal benediction . . . . The President concluded the exercises with prayer. The whole was conducted with a propriety and solemnity suitable to the occasion. The audience (consisting of the principal gentlemen and ladies of the colony), though large and crowded, behaved with the utmost decorum."

Since that time a host of Bible colleges have come into existence, and tragically, over the course of the years, the majority of those colleges have liberalized to the point of apostasy. Today there is a renewed interest in establishing strong, sound Bible colleges that will produce ministers and missionaries for a world in need. Let me urge you to pray for these institutions that, unlike their predecessors, they shall remain true to the Lord and strong in the faith. It is primarily true that as our colleges go, so our churches will follow in one short generation. Fundamentalism is suffering today because many of our schools have weakened their spiritual commitment to God's Word. May God grant us spiritual leadership that will produce faithful pulpiteers throughout our Land.

DLC

October 1

Revival in Alabama

Scripture: Psalm 85:7-13

As Alabama is now my home, I have sought to learn about the early Baptists in the state. I discovered that the first Baptists to enter our state came to northern Alabama near the very area where I live. However, many of these came because of the fertile country side and abundant springs of water. Worldly inducements attracted a large number of preachers to the area, but they seemed more interested in building their personal estates rather than establishing strong witnesses for the Savior.

About 1808 a few Baptist people made their way into the southern reaches of the state, and these seemed intent only on doing the will of God. In 1815 and 1816 the tide of emigration began to flow, and churches were formed in every part of the state.

Holcombe's *History of the Rise and Progress of the Baptists in Alabama* provides a good description of the buildings of worship. "Houses for the worship of God were scarce for several years after the writer came to this country in 1818; and many of those which were erected, were more like Indian wigwams than anything else; only they were more open and uncomfortable. It was common in those days, when the weather was favorable, for the minister to take his stand under some convenient shady bower, while the people would seat themselves around him on the ground. In many instances, large congregations would assemble; and they were far more attentive to the Word than they are at this time in many comfortable places. . . ."[1]

The work of God throughout America has progressed by means of revival preaching, and Mr. Holcombe gives an account of such services which became popular throughout the South.

"The first camp meeting, perhaps ever known in Alabama, was held with the church, where the writer has his membership. This meeting took place . . . the first of

October, 1831; it continued for five or six days, and twelve or fifteen families tented on the ground. Here the Lord bared His arm, and displayed His power in the salvation of many precious souls. The groans and cries of repenting sinners, the songs and prayers, the shouts and praises of Christians, formed an awful, and yet delightful harmony. At this meeting there commenced the greatest general revival ever known at that time in middle Alabama; it continued over twelve months; during which period there were near 500 baptized in three or four churches. One of the happiest seasons of the life of the author was the cold winter of 1831, and '32; during which he baptized over 150. From that time camp meetings became common among the Baptists in different parts of the State; yet some churches disapproved of the course. That there were extravagances at some of those meetings, we think few will deny; yet there was much good done."[2]

The author concluded, A number of the preachers did not approve of this kind of work; they thought it extravagant. Others fanned it as a fire from heaven. When the winnowing time came on, it was clearly demonstrated that there was much good wheat; notwithstanding, there was a considerable quantity of chaff.[3]

In our days there are still those who minimize evangelism. They look disparagingly on the office of evangelist. They claim that the results are not enduring. However, the results of professions of faith made under expository preaching do not prove to be 100% solid. Often those who make profession of faith under regular pastoral ministering fall from the ranks and do not mature. I have a hunger in my heart for more of the old-fashioned hell-fire and brimstone preaching that causes men to realize they are sinners in need of the world's only Savior! I would much prefer to see tears in our audiences than to observe yawns of indifference that are often apparent among congregations today. Let us pray that in our lifetime we might again see old time conviction that leads to life-changing conversions.

Ours is a heritage of revival type preaching. One of the gifts to the church is that of evangelist. Let us pray for a return to revival type preaching in our Bible-believing churches.

DLC

[1]John T. Christian, *A History of the Baptists* (Nashville, TN: Broadman Press, 1926), 2:324

[2]Ibid., 2:324-325

[3]Ibid.

October 2

The Bible: The Battle Ground

Scripture: 2 Timothy 3:16-17; 2 Peter 1:19-21

There is a danger that Bible-believing Baptists of the twenty-first century will become completely ignorant of the battle for the Bible that raged early in the twentieth century. Complete confidence in an infallible, inerrant, integral revelation from God to man was at the very heart of the strife. Modernists denied that the Bible is the Word of God indeed, while Fundamentalists defended the premise that the Bible is God's authoritative message to mankind.

The battle lines were not only drawn in the United States, but Canadian Baptists divided over the same issue. On October 2, 1919, the *Canadian Baptist* contained an editorial entitled, "The Inspiration and Authority of Scripture." It reads, "Some fifteen or twenty years ago the question of the inspiration and authority of the Scriptures agitated the evangelical churches of Great Britain a great deal more than it does today. This agitation has now largely ceased in the old land because the leading men in whom these churches had large confidence have brought themselves and their people into clearer light. Occasional echoes of the old acrimonious disputations are still heard there, but in the main they have ceased to interest or influence intelligent Christian people.

". . . on this continent a considerable number of Christian people, including a fair proportion of ministers, are still threshing away at many questions touching the Scriptures, which are regarded as settled questions in Great Britain. To some extent this is true among churches in Canada, and it is especially true in the United States, where some crude theological views still prevail in many quarters, in which some partially educated but very dogmatic preachers are still making loud proclamations of views and theories as to the Scriptures, which were laid aside years ago in England and Scotland.

"Any of our readers, who are still perplexed as to the disputations that occasionally prevail in our midst, touching the inspiration and authority of the Scriptures, will be greatly helped by the recital of the story of how light and relief came to Christian people in the old land."

Dr. T. T. Shields immediately challenged the editorial, declaring that the editorial was ". . . an attack on the Word of God." He determined that he would confront this heresy at the next meeting of the convention, which was scheduled for October 24, 1919. Supposed friends had betrayed Dr. Shield's trust and had warned the Convention leaders that Dr. Shields planned to present a resolution reaffirming faith in the Bible as the very Word of God. The night prior to the meeting, Dr. Shields agonized alone in prayer. He read Paul's closing words to Timothy: "At my first answer no man stood with me, but all men forsook me: I pray God that it may not be laid to their charge. Notwithstanding the Lord stood with me, and strengthened me, that by me the preaching might be fully known, and that all the Gentiles might hear: and I was delivered out of the mouth of the lion."

Upon attending the Convention meeting, Dr. Shields asked the Convention President whether the Convention approved of the principles of the editorial at issue so that he might determine his own future association. The President responded, "I hear you have a resolution you would like to present, and permission was granted." For the next hour and a half Dr. Shields spoke, and then he made his proposal. He asked the Convention to declare its disapproval of the editorial of October 2.

When the man of God concluded his oration, a hearty applause came from the audience and his resolution was seconded and approved. That battle was temporarily won for truth, but the modernists (liberals) continued the war, and in time they captured the Convention. However, the war has never concluded. For the most part today, fundamental Baptists have had to disassociate themselves from Baptist conventions. Once again, Baptists who avow complete faith in God's Word have had to separate themselves from ecclesiastical alignments and to stand in the realization that one with God is a majority! May we today determine faithfully to walk in the truth of God's Word.

DLC

October 3

The Tinkerman's Logic

Scripture: Acts 26:1-3

One of the most significant finds related to the legal history of England in the years immediately following the Commonwealth Period was the discovery among the papers of Thomas Breedlove, of nearly a thousand verbatim accounts of primarily minor trials conducted between 1660 and 1675. Among the sheaves found were these recording the proceedings of His Majesty, King Charles II, against John Bunyan, the author of *Pilgrim's Progress*, who spent over twelve years in an English prison for his religious convictions. The devotions of October 3 through October 6 shall deal with this matter, although the proceedings all took place on October 3, 1660.

> PROCEEDINGS, being a true account of the trial of John Bunyan, Tinker, of Bedfordshire, His Lordship, Judge Wingate presiding at the Courthouse in Bedfordshire on October 3, in the year of our Lord 1660. The Accused is charged with willful and deliberate violation of various and sundry Royal and Parliamentary Edicts. His Trial this Day, however respects a single Charge: namely, Violation of the Conventicle Acts, first proposed by Her Most High and Mighty Majesty, our Late and Beloved Queen

Elizabeth, and reinstated by His Beneficent Highness, King Charles II. All Parties being in Place, and the Witnesses having been sworn, the trial proceeds.

Judge Wingate: Mr. Bunyan, you stand before this Court accused of persistent and willful transgression of the Conventicle Act, which prohibits all British subjects from absenting themselves from worship in the Church of England, and from conducting worship services apart from our Church. You come, presumably, with no legal training, and yet without counsel. I must warn you, sir, of the gravity of the charge, the harshness of the penalty, in the event of your conviction, and the foolhardiness of acting as your own counsel in so serious a matter. Are you cognizant of these facts, and do you understand the charge?

Bunyan: I am, and I do, M'lord.

Judge Wingate: In truth, I hope you do. Now, I hold in my hand the depositions of the witnesses against you. In each case, they have testified that, to their knowledge, you have never, in your adult life, attended services in the church of this parish. Each further testifies that he has observed you, on numerous occasions, conducting religious exercises in and near Bedford. These depositions have been read to you, have they not?

Bunyan: They have, M'lord.

Judge Wingate: In that case, then, this Court would be profoundly interested in your response to them.

Bunyan: Thank you, M'lord. And may I say that I am grateful for the opportunity to respond. Firstly, the depositions speak the truth. I have never attended services in the Church of England, nor do I intend ever to do. Secondly, it is no secret that I preach the Word of God whenever, wherever, and to whomsoever He pleases to grant me opportunity to do so.

Having said that, M'lord, there is a weightier issue that I am constrained to address. I have no choice but to acknowledge my awareness of the law which I am accused of transgressing. Likewise, I have no choice but to confess my guilt in my transgression of it. As true as these things are, I must affirm that I neither regret breaking the law, nor repent of having broken it. Further, I must warn you that I have no intention in future of conforming to it. It is, on its face, an unjust law, a law against which honorable men cannot shrink from protesting. In truth, M'lord, it violates an infinitely higher law, the right of every man to seek God in his own way, unhindered by any temporal power. That, M'lord, is my response.

Judge Wingate: This Court would remind you, sir, that we are not here to debate the merits of the law. We are here to determine if you are, in fact, guilty of violating it.

Bunyan: Perhaps, M'lord, that is why you are here, but it is most certainly not why I am here. I am here because you compel me to be here. All I ask is to be left alone to preach and to teach as God directs me. As, however, I must be here, I cannot fail to use these circumstances to speak against what I know to be an unjust and odious edict.

DLC

October 4

The Court Verses John Bunyan

Scripture: John 4:22-26

We continue today with John Bunyan's brilliant defense in the English Court.

Judge Wingate: Let me understand you. You are arguing that every man has a right, given him by Almighty God, to seek the Deity in his own way, even if he chooses, without benefit of the English Church?

Bunyan: That is precisely what I am arguing, M'lord. Or without benefit of any church.

Judge Wingate: Do you know what you are saying? What of Papists and Quakers? What of pagan Mohammedans? Have these the right to seek God in their own misguided way?

Bunyan: Even these, M'lord.

Judge Wingate: May I ask if you are particularly sympathetic to the views of these or other such deviant religious societies?

Bunyan: I am not, M'lord.

Judge Wingate: Yet, you affirm a God-given right to hold any alien religious doctrine that appeals to the warped minds of men?

Bunyan: I do, M'lord.

Judge Wingate: I find your views impossible of belief. And what of those who, if left to their own devices, would have no interest in things heavenly? Have they the right to be allowed to continue unmolested in their error?

Bunyan: It is my fervent belief that they do, M'lord.

Judge Wingate: And on what basis, might I ask, can you make such a rash affirmation?

Bunyan: On the basis, M'lord, that a man's religious views or lack of them are matters between his conscience and his God, and are not the business of the Crown, the Parliament, or even, with all due respect, My lord, of this Court.

However much I may be in disagreement with another man's sincerely held religious beliefs, neither I nor any other may disallow his right to hold these beliefs. No man's right in these affairs are secure if every other man's rights are not equally secure.

Judge Wingate: It is obvious, sir, that you are a victim of deranged thinking. If my ears deceive me not, I must infer from your words that you believe the State to have no interest in the religious life of its subjects.

Bunyan: The State, M'lord, may have an interest in anything in which it wishes to have an interest. But the State has no right whatever to interfere in the religious life of its citizens.

Judge Wingate: You are a tinker by trade, are you not, Mr. Bunyan?

Bunyan: That is correct, M'lord.

Judge Wingate: Would you mind apprising this Court of the extent of your formal schooling?

Bunyan: Not at all, M'lord. Able I am to read and write, and that with difficulty.

Judge Wingate: I surmised as much. I think I perceive why you are unable to appreciate the disaster that would accompany your views should ever they hold sway in our society. I myself and I say this in all modesty am not inconsiderably trained in the historian's discipline. If you were half so well-versed yourself, you would instantly recognize the fatal flaw in your reasoning. Throughout history, virtually every significant human tragedy has come about as a result of divergent religious views. Nation against nation. Brother against brother. War, Destruction. Devastation. Time and time again. And why? I shall tell you why, sir. It is because men cannot agree on which God to worship, and how to worship Him.

Now, after a long and arduous struggle, we have succeeded in forging a conformity in the religious beliefs of all Englishmen. All our problems will be resolved when everyone agrees to accommodate himself, and adopt the same orthodoxy of religious opinion. No more religious wars. No more divisive doctrinal disputes! Think of it, Mr. Bunyan! Does this not portend a society of which any man would be proud and happy to be a part?

Cummins' Comment: How interesting that we live in a day when ecumenism makes the similar claim that one world-wide religion would solve the problems of mankind. The stage is surely be set for the coming of Antichrist— the man of sin —

who will, during the Tribulation period, demand a one-world church as men bow before him.

DLC

October 5

The Logic of a State Church

Scripture: Daniel 3:13-18

We concluded yesterday's section of the Thomas Breedlove papers and the trial of John Bunyan with the statement and question of the Judge Wingate to Mr. Bunyan. I shall pick up the Judge's last statement again as we see the legal arguments again from that point.

> **Judge Wingate:** I think I perceive why you are unable to appreciate the disaster that would accompany your views should ever they hold sway in our society. I myself, and I say this in all modesty, am not inconsiderably trained in the historian's discipline. If you were half so well-versed yourself, you would instantly recognize the fatal flaw in your reasoning. Throughout history, virtually every significant human tragedy has come about as a result of divergent religious views. Nation against nation. Brother against brother. War. Destruction. Devastation. Time and time again. And why? I shall tell you why, sir. It is because men cannot agree on which God to worship, and how to worship Him.
>
> Now, after a long and arduous struggle, we have succeeded in forging a conformity in the religious beliefs of all Englishmen. All our problems will be resolved when everyone agrees to accommodate himself, and adopt the same orthodoxy of religious opinion. No more religious wars. No more divisive doctrinal disputes! Think of it, Mr. Bunyan! Does this not portend a society of which any man would be proud and happy to be a part?
>
> **Bunyan:** To a degree, M'lord, it admittedly does. But only if everyone can be convicted by

virtue of reasoning alone to adopt identical views of God. The society that you describe is an appealing one, but I fear the cost is far too high. It would necessitate that honest men repudiate convictions honestly held.

Judge Wingate: You are, Mr. Bunyan, a strong-willed and opinionated man. Yet, this Court finds it fascinating to speak with you, and wishes time permitted further discussion of our respective philosophies. But, alas, time is passing swiftly, and other cases await our attention. Let us move, then, to the matter before us, shall we? The evidence I hold in my hand, even apart from your own admission of guilt, is sufficient to convict you, and the Court is within its rights to have you committed to prison for a considerably long time. I do not wish to send you to prison, Mr. Bunyan. I am aware of the poverty of your family, and I believe you have a little daughter who, unfortunately, was born blind. Is this not so?

Bunyan: It is, M'lord.

Judge Wingate: Very well. The decision of the Court is this: In as much as the accused has confessed his guilt, we shall follow a merciful and compassionate course of action. We shall release him on the condition that he swear solemnly to discontinue the convening of religious meetings, and that he affix his signature to such an oath prior to quitting the Courtroom. That will be all, Mr. Bunyan. I hope not to see you here again. May we hear the next case?

Bunyan: M'lord, if I may have another moment of the Court's time?

Judge Wingate: Yes, but you be quick about it. We have other matters to attend to. What is it?

Bunyan: I cannot do what you ask of me, M'lord. I cannot place my signature upon any document in which I promise henceforth not to preach. My calling to preach the Gospel is from God, and He alone can make me discontinue what He has appointed me to do. As I have had no word from Him to that effect, I must continue to preach, and I shall continue to preach.

> **Judge Wingate**: Mr. Bunyan, you are trying the patience of this Court!
>
> **Bunyan**: That is not my intention, M'lord.

As we have seen, Mr. Bunyan agreed completely with Peter and the others when, before the Sanhedrin, they said: ". . . we ought to obey God rather than men." May God give us the strength of conviction to stand on that principle as well.

DLC

October 6

Which Man Was Forgotten?

Scripture: Matthew 10:37-39

Today we conclude the material concerning the trial of John Bunyan, the man whom Judge Wingate claimed would soon be forgotten. If only the Judge had known that they that do the will of God abideth forever. Through the many years, John Bunyan's *Pilgrim's Progress* and other writings have continued among the best sellers of the English speaking world. Yea, *Pilgrim's Progress* has been translated into many languages around the world. We could well say that John Bunyan lives on in the lives of children of God because he determined as did Caleb, to fully follow the Lord.

May we, the followers of the Lord Jesus Christ in the twenty-first century, also determine to obey the Lord regardless of the cost.

But let me present the remainder herewith of the Thomas Breedlove papers.

> **Judge Wingate**: I warn you, sir, the Court has gone the second mile to be lenient with you, out of concern for your family's difficult straits. Truth to tell, it would appear that the Court's concern for family far exceeds your own. Do you wish to go to prison?
>
> **Bunyan**: No, M'lord. Few things there are that I would wish less.

Judge Wingate: Very well, then, Mr. Bunyan. This Court will make one further attempt in good faith to accommodate what appears to be strongly held convictions on your part. In his compassion and beneficence, our Sovereign, Charles II, has made provision for dissenting preachers to hold some limited meetings. All that is required is that such ministers procure licenses authorizing them to convene these gatherings. The Court will not require you to sign any documents, but will require only your verbal commitment to proceed through proper channels to obtain licenses. You will not find the procedure burdensome, and even you, Mr. Bunyan, must surely grant the legitimacy of the State's interest in ensuring that any fool with a Bible does not simply gather a group of people together and begin to preach to them. Imagine the implications were that to happen! Can you comply with this condition, Mr. Bunyan? Before you answer, mark you this: should you refuse, the Court will have no alternative but to sentence you to a prison term. Think, sir, of your poor wife. Think of your children, and particularly of your pitiful, sightless little girl. Think of your flock, who can hear you to their hearts' content when you have secured your licenses. Think of these things, and give us your answer, sir!

Bunyan: M'lord, I appreciate the Court's efforts to be as you have put it accommodating. But again, I must refuse your terms. I must repeat that it is God who constrains me to preach, and no man or company of men may grant or deny me leave to preach. These licenses of which you speak, M'lord, are symbols not of a right, but of a privilege. Implied therein is the principle that a mere man can extend or withhold them according to his whim. I speak not of privileges, but of rights. Privileges granted by men may be denied by men. Rights are granted by God, and can be legitimately denied by no man. I must therefore refuse to comply.

Judge Wingate: Very well, My Bunyan. Since you persist in your intractability, and since you reject this Court's honest effort at compromise, you leave us no choice but to commit you to Bedford jail for a period of six years. If you manage to survive, I should think that your experience will correct your thinking. If you fail to survive, that will be unfortunate. In any event, I strongly suspect that we have heard the last we shall ever hear from Mr. John Bunyan. Now, may we hear the next case.

Cummins' Comments: Well, there you have it. A complete word by word account of the trial of John Bunyan before Judge Wingate. Many times in the hearing Mr. Bunyan might well have compromised. He might have reasoned that his wife and family, and particularly blind Mary, needed him desperately. He might have concluded that he could accomplish more in freedom for the ongoing of the Gospel than ever he could fulfill in a jail cell. He might even have reasoned that his testimony would be impaired if he was imprisoned. But rather than that, John Bunyan was steadfast and immoveable, and thus he abounded to the praise of Christ's glory.

DLC

October 7

An Unknown Pioneer Hero

Scripture: Philippians 4:11-13

It is encouraging to realize how the Lord synchronizes His work around the world to bring glory to His name. A native of Ireland enlisted in the British army, and while serving abroad, his artillery corps was stationed at Madras. In 1830 he was sent on special assignment to Moulmein, Burma. Perhaps through loneliness, he found himself in the English-speaking Baptist church. There he came under the influence of the noted Baptist missionary, known as the "Champion Missionary," Reverend Eurgenio Kincaid. Though the young soldier had been raised in a Catholic home, he had always been tender toward the things of God. And now, hearing the clear-cut presentation of the gospel of Jesus Christ, the young man fell under heavy conviction, and ultimately he was gloriously saved.

Conversations ensued with Adoniram Judson, and the young man asked concerning the possibility of Christian service in America. Needless to say, Adoniram Judson encouraged him to get an education and prepare for that eventuality. The young Irishman secured his discharge from the British army and made his way to the States. He entered Hamilton in New York as a ministerial student, and upon the completion of his course, he was ordained in Broadalbin, New York, in 1838. He served several pastorates in the State of New York, and then determined to go to a pioneer country to preach Christ. Thus it was he made his way to Wisconsin.

He arrived in Racine, Wisconsin, in 1844, and set out for Janesville, Wisconsin. Winter was coming on, and no housing was available for rent. Thus the preacher purchased some land with a wooden shell upon it, and this was used as their home. The family determined that they needed bread, potatoes, and meat if they were to endure the coming winter. The preacher dug potatoes and took his salary in the product. He was given every seventh bushel, and his share was about forty bushels. Wheat was to be threshed, and he took his wages in the grain. The grain had to be hauled twenty-eight miles by an ox-team and ground at a mill. But, it provided bread and to spare. He was able to sell some wooden chairs to secure pork, and thus they endured that first winter. To resist the northern blasts, the preacher banked up soil making their dwelling appear like a dug-out. Without eggs, butter, cheese, sugar, milk, fish or foul, the family made it. Having no candles, they used lard from the pork as lamp oil.

But now, let me allow the unnamed pioneer to relate the story. "Notwithstanding all those difficulties, evangelical work had to be done, and attempts were made to do it. The first Sunday in October, 1844, I organized the Janesville Baptist Church. I had to take all the parts of the service. The number of members was thirteen, eleven women and two men. I tried to save the interest along that winter. There, at Janesville, was the county seat of Rock County. Religious meetings were held in the court room. Four denominations used it in turn; the Baptists were one of them. More than once I traveled on foot thirty or thirty-five miles to engage in a sermon. For years the church was in the condition of a weakly infant. At length appeared a young man, not the product of any college, but full of sacred zeal that came from a tender heart. He rallied, encouraged souls by personal talks and public addresses. Fresh life flowed through the whole interest. This young worker, O. J. Dearborn, was ordained and became to the church a successful pastor."[1]

I am sure that those who supported the missionary cause in Burma in the 1830s never realized that the work of God they were supporting abroad would return to our shores to assist here in the ongoing of the Gospel. But, it is important that we realize that the Irishman, who in the will of God, made such sacrifices in Wisconsin, will be rewarded on the same basis as Judson, Kincaid, and the other pioneer foreign missionaries. Again we are reminded that in the sight of God it is not foreign missions, or home missions, but simple submission to the Great Commission that the Lord desires.

DLC

---

[1] Justin A. Smith, *A History of the Baptists In the Western States East of the Mississippi* (Philadelphia: American Baptist Publication Society, 1896), 72.

October 8

Ridiculed for Christ

Scripture: Matthew 5:10-11; Romans 8:17-18

Though he wrote forty-three books, it was a small volume for children that resulted in a prison sentence and two days in the pillory for twenty-four-year-old Benjamin Keach, youthful Baptist preacher in England. The booklet entitled *The Child's Instructor; or, A New and Easy Primmer* was seized, and Keach was summoned to appear before Chief-Justice Hyde on October 8, 1664. The charge read by the clerk stated, "Thou art here indicted by the name of Benjamin Keach, of Winslow, in the county of Bucks, for that thou being a seditious, schismatic person, evilly and maliciously disposed and disaffected to his Majesty's government, and the government of the Church of England, didst maliciously and wickedly of the fifth of May, . . . write, print, and publish, or cause to be written, printed, and published, one seditious and venomous book . . . wherein are contained, by way of question and answer, . . . damnable positions, contrary to the Book of Common Prayer and the liturgy of the Church of England; that is to say, in one place you have thus written: Q. Who are the right subjects for baptism? A. Believers, or godly men and women, who, make profession of their faith and repentance."

Needless to say, the court found Benjamin Keach guilty of the horrendous crime of denying infant baptism as he taught believer's baptism. The Judge said: "Benjamin Keach, you are here convicted for writing, printing, and publishing a seditious and schismatical book, for which the court's judgment is this: . . . That you shall go to gaol for a fortnight without bail . . . and the next Saturday . . . stand upon the pillory at Aylesbury in the open market, from eleven o'clock till one, with a paper upon your head with this inscription: For writing, printing, and publishing a schismatical book . . . . And the next Thursday to stand, in the same manner and . . . time, in the market at Winslow; and then your book shall be openly burnt before your face by the common hangman, in disgrace of you and your doctrine. And you shall forfeit to the King's majesty the sum of twenty pounds, and shall remain in gaol until you find sureties for your good behavior, and for your appearance at the next assizes; then to renounce your doctrines, and make such public submission as shall be enjoined you. Take him away, keeper!"[1]

Keach replied, "I hope I shall never renounce the truths which I have written in that book."

At the pillory in Aylesbury, Keach addressed the spectators by saying, ". . . my Lord Jesus was not ashamed to suffer on the cross for me; and it is for His cause that I am made a gazing stock. A clergyman challenged Keach, but before the clergyman could say much, one of the crowd accused the priest of recently having been drunk. At that the people began laughing and turned their derision on the priest. In utmost shame the priest fled the scene."

As Mr. Keach continued witnessing, the sheriff became greatly angered and threatened to gag him if he persisted in such testifying. The prisoner was thus primarily silenced, but as his time in the pillory expired, he called out: "Blessed are they that are persecuted for righteousness' sake; for their's is the kingdom of heaven."

As one would expect, Mr. Keach' public trial and sufferings attracted growing multitudes to his message. In 1668 he became pastor of the Baptist Church in Horsleydown, London. For years his congregation was forced to meet in private houses, but in 1672 they were able to build their first house of worship. From that time onward the congregation expanded. The building was continually enlarged, and ultimately, their building held a thousand worshipers.

The Edict of Toleration in 1689 allowed a modicum of religious freedom, and the years of frequent imprisonment and violence gradually came to an end for heroes of the faith such as Benjamin Keach. These fearless, intrepid, valiant, champions of the faith must never be forgotten. In these days as our freedoms are being undermined, may we determine to stand boldly for God's eternal truth.

DLC

---

[1]C. H. Spurgeon, *The Metropolitan Tabernacle And Its Work*, 18-26.

October 9

Faithfulness: His Trademark

Scripture: 1 Corinthians 4:2

Those who sat at his feet would tell you that Dr. Roberson's favorite expression was, "Everything rises and falls on leadership." Thinking of his life, another adage fills my mind: "The greatest ability is dependability." That proverb succinctly sketches the life of Dr. Lee Roberson.

The Roberson family lived in a humble farmhouse on a fifty acre farm in English, Indiana, where Lee was born on November 24, 1909. When he was small, the family moved to Louisville, Kentucky. There Lee's father purchased a nine-acre farm a few miles from the city. Lee's father continued employment in Louisville as he could find it, and the family raised chickens to supplement their living. Lee completed a two-year commercial course at Louisville Male High, and then graduated from the Fern Creek High School.

Through the instruction of Mrs. Daisy Hawes, a faithful Sunday school teacher, Lee saw himself as a lost sinner in need of the Savior. One Sunday morning, Lee went home after church and called upon the Lord Jesus Christ for salvation. The following Sunday, he made public his confession of faith. During those days, the Roberson family attended the Cedar Creek Baptist Church. It was there, while a high-schooler, that Lee Roberson answered God's call to Christian service.

Lee was gifted with a fine voice and began voice instruction in Louisville under the direction of a noted German voice instructor. After completing one year of study at Old Bethel College, Lee returned to study at the University of Louisville. He resumed voice instruction and sang in the University Glee Club. Radio was the popular media of the day, and Lee was featured as soloist on many programs.

Following collegiate training, Lee Roberson was asked to serve as choir director and assistant pastor at the Virginia Avenue Baptist Church in Louisville. There he learned the importance of visitation, personal soul-winning, and the art of drawing the net with a Gospel invitation.

In 1932 Lee Roberson was called to his first pastoral charge. The Baptist Church in Germantown, Tennessee, (then a small suburb of Memphis) provided many leadership lessons. The Lord blessed with souls saved and good growth. However, in ten months, Lee Roberson was overwhelmed by an invitation to become the assistant pastor of the prestigious Temple Baptist Church of Memphis. His responsibilities would include music and visitation. Without seeking God's will, he accepted the call. In the matter of five months he become discontented and severed that arrangement. The Lord soon opened the door for Lee Roberson to pastor the Greenbrier Baptist Church in Greenbriar, Tennessee. For the next three years, the Lord taught our subject many important truths. While pastoring at Greenbriar, Lee was brought to the knowledge of premillennialism. The truth of the imminence of Christ's return became the impetus for his faithful service. Lee's ability in the pulpit produced many invitations for evangelistic meetings. During this ministry, an outstanding offer was given by the leading voice instructor of the Memphis Conservatory. Acceptance would have terminated Lee Roberson's work in the Gospel. Again the Lord gave victory.

On October 9, 1937, Lee Roberson married Miss Carolyn Allen in Homewood, Alabama. Following their honeymoon, the couple moved into the parsonage of the First Baptist Church of Fairfield, Alabama. During the next five years, the Lord used Lee Roberson as pastor-evangelist. The local church experienced the blessings of God with souls saved and great growth. Fifty-five revivals were conducted in adjoining areas as well.

When a call was extended to Reverend Roberson from the Highland Park Baptist Church in Chattanooga, there was great reluctance to accept the challenge. But the Lord made clear to the Robersons that this was His will. On November 17, 1942, Lee Roberson began his ministry at Highland Park Baptist Church, and the history from that time until his resignation in 1982 is amazing. Consider just three of the outreaches of Dr. Roberson's vision. Tennessee Temple University, where multitudes have been trained for Christian service, was established. Camp Joy, where 3,000 children per summer enjoyed free camping under the Gospel, was founded. A thriving chapel extension with seventy-three chapels in a three-state area was formed.

However, retirement did not mean idleness for Dr. Roberson. As I write, the 94 year-old Lee Roberson continues preaching the ageless message. He still challenges the present generation to continue faithfully in their service of the Lord. May faithfulness be our trademark as well.

DLC

October 10

Results of Revival

Scripture: Psalm 138:7; 85:6; Habakkuk 3:2

Surely every genuine born-again believer would agree that America's greatest need today is spiritual revival. I have passed the threescore and ten year mark, but I cannot truly say that I have ever seen a bona fide revival. I have been in evangelistic campaigns where many have been brought to know Christ, but that is not revival. It is thrilling to read accounts of the Great Awakening our Lord sent America in desperate days of spiritual need. It is inspiring also to read of the second great awakening that was experienced among believing settlers in Kentucky and Tennessee at the beginning of the eighteenth century. In reading of such movements, one experiences a hunger and cries out that God might do it again!

From periods of barrenness, how wonderful to witness the moving of the Holy Spirit in seasons of refreshing and blessedness! I grant that the word revival has been often used to describe times of mere emotional exhilaration, but when one can measure such a movement with lasting results, there can be no question that God's people experienced a genuine moving of the Holy Spirit in their midst.

In the moving of the Holy Spirit in the second great awakening, one thrills to witness tangible evidences of the work of God. The effects of the revival, aside from the numbers it added to the churches, were exceedingly salutary. Before the revival, the morals of the people, under the predominating influence of infidelity, were extremely bad. Rev. J. M. Peck, writing to the *Christian Review* in 1852, says, "Infidelity received its death blow during that period. Not a few continued infidels and scoffers, but they were shorn of their strength. So many of their number had been converted, some of whom became efficient preachers of the gospel, that infidelity could no longer boast."[1]

Secondly, there was an amazing growth numerically in the churches of Kentucky. One such report states, "At the beginning of the revival, in 1800, . . . there were seven associations, 106 churches, and 5,119 members. In 1803, there were ten associations, 219 churches, and 15,495 members. This was a clear gain of three associations, 111 churches, and 10,380 members, or a little more than trebling the number of Baptists in the State in three years."[2] So-called ecumenical evangelism has produced very little by way of results in church growth! But it is apparent that a genuine revival transforms sinners and generates numerical growth in local churches.

But the second great awakening also produced a harmony that was evident among the brethren. For years the Regular and Separate Baptists in Kentucky had been at odds with each other. Several efforts had been made at reconciliation, but they were all to no avail. However, under the influence of spiritual renewal, difficulties had disappeared, and a lasting union was consummated.

The Elkhorn Association appointed five of their men to meet with five leaders of the South Kentucky Association for discussion. In time, the joint committee agreed on such terms as they believed would be acceptable to both groups. A united conclave was held at Howards Creek (Old Providence Meetinghouse), in Clark County on October 10, 1801. The recommended terms were discussed and unanimously approved, and all the Baptists of the state experienced a new harmony.

In the spiritual drought that is commonly witnessed in America in the twenty-first century, let us pray that the Lord of Heaven will send revival anew. Our Scripture sequence today is most fitting. First we must pray, "Lord, revive me." Then our prayer should be, "Lord, revive us." Finally, we ought to cry out, "Lord, revive Thy work." Our greatest need is revival. Let us pray and trust to that end.

DLC

---

[1]J. H. Spencer, *A History of Kentucky Baptists* (Cincinnati: J. R. Baumes, 1885), 1:542.

[2]Ibid., 541.

October 11

In the Crucible of Testing

Scripture: Job 13:1-15

Along a busy four-lane highway between Columbia and Sumter, South Carolina, stands a white church with four colonial style columns on the front porch. Beside the church there is a small cemetery. The church is the Good Hope Baptist Church, organized in 1866, after having been the arm of Congaree Baptist Church for many years. The cemetery holds the remains of many of its distinguished members. There is one grave in particular that attracts our attention for today's devotional. It is the grave of Pastor Charles Augustus Stiles.

Sunday, October 11, 1908, was an unusual day. Ordinarily Pastor Stiles would be exalting the Lord Jesus Christ in a pulpit somewhere, but, on that date he was in heaven bowing before his Lord while family and friends were conducting his funeral. A large number of church members, friends, and acquaintances gathered to pay their final tribute of respect to that faithful pastor of many years. He was even then resting from his labors, burdens, and the many tragedies he had suffered in this vale of sorrow.

C. A. Stiles was born April 9, 1836, near Charleston, South Carolina. His parents were Copeland and Amelia Stiles. His father supported the family as a schoolteacher. When the 1850 Federal Census was taken for Sumter District, Charles was 14 years old and still living at home; ten years later the census found him still at home, but now he was 24 years.

C. A. was saved at the First Baptist Church in Sumter, pastored by W. D. Rice, during special meetings held by Dr. J. O. B. Dargan. He was baptized on December 9, 1855. Two years later his home congregation licensed him to preach. In the fall of 1860 he entered Furman University, but the country was on the verge of the dread Civil War which started in the spring of 1861. On November 15, 1861, C. A. joined the Confederate Army and served for twelve months. He became a Sergeant in Company K of the 23rd Regiment of the South

Carolina Volunteers, and was slightly wounded in Boonesborough, Maryland, on September 14, 1862. C. A. was discharged from the service on February 14, 1863.

In considering C. A's tragedies, we must consider the fact that his first two wives passed away early in their marriages. Mary K. Wheeler Stiles, died March 31, 1871, and left her husband with the care of four small children. His second wife, Sallie Catherine Wheeler Stiles, died October 4, 1874. His first two wives were sisters. C. A.'s third marriage was to a widow, Mrs. C. N. Sealy. Two daughters by his first wife and one daughter by his third wife survived him. Another great tragedy of the man of God's life was the accidental death of his oldest son, Arville Legare Stiles. His son was only fifteen-years-old when he was killed as the result of an explosion that took place on the steamer *Marion*, near Red Bluff, on the Wateree River.

His ordination had taken place on January 3, 1869, in the Bethany Baptist Church in Sumter County. His longest pastorates were at the Good Hope, Beulah, and Congaree Baptist churches. For a shorter period, he pastored churches in Mayesville and Timmonsville, and for a year he served the congregation of the First Baptist Church in Florence, South Carolina. He often had to walk from Timmonsville to Florence because he had no horse to ride. He was actively involved in the Charleston Baptist Association, having served as clerk and moderator.

Charles Augustus Stiles died at his home in Eastover, on Saturday, October 10, 1908. He was 72 years old. For over 50 years he was a consecrated and faithful preacher. He had the love and confidence of his people, and he left behind an irreproachable record. He possessed a quiet spirit, and was modest, unassuming, courteous, and kind. He was a loyal and patriotic citizen. Loyal friends in Lower Richland erected a monument over his grave in his memory. And as one drives by Good Hope Baptist Church cemetery today on that busy four-lane highway between Columbia and Sumter, the gravestone stands out as a testimony to that good and godly pastor, C. A. Stiles.

May God raise up faithful pastors in our day whose victory in trials encourage their flocks to similar faithfulness to God's calling even through pathways of sorrow.

DCB

October 12

A Pattern for Others

Scripture: 2 Timothy 3:10-16

Arno Q. Weniger was born in Lime Springs, Iowa, on October 12, 1907.[1] His father was a Presbyterian pastor at the time, who later came to Baptist convictions and left a record of faithful service to Christ (See the entry for November 22). His parents named him Arno after Dr. Arno C. Gaebelein, the noted Bible teacher and friend of the family. When Arno was just four years of age his father was ordained as a Baptist preacher.

Arno grew up in a series of parsonages across Iowa and Minnesota. His character was shaped by the services, godly leadership, and influence of his parents. He records that, "My heart was warm toward the Lord," and he came to know Christ as a young boy. He surrendered his life to the Lord for full-time service as he listened to his dad preach at his high school graduation. Just seventeen, he set off to enter Northwestern Schools in Minneapolis. W. B. Riley, pastor of First Baptist Church of Minneapolis, was the founder and president of Northwestern.

Arno Weniger's zeal for the Lord revealed itself during his college days. He spent weekends preaching in remote places in southern Minnesota. At one point during his college career, he preached in three different places north of Rochester every Sunday. His older brother graduated from Northwestern ahead of him, and served as an assistant pastor in Bisbee, Arizona. Arno spent a summer filling in for his brother while Dwight traveled with a Gospel quartet. That summer's work yielded a harvest of souls, and upon Dwight's return, the two brothers were ordained to the Gospel ministry on September 20, 1927. He returned to Minneapolis for his last year of school, a year which was marked by a serious illness and physical testing. Yet he graduated on time with his class in the spring of 1928.

Weniger enjoyed many years of fruitful ministry. In the 1930s he pastored in Medford, Oregon. His last pastorate at the Hamilton Square Baptist Church in San Francisco, California, extended over 35 years. This ministry began during World War II. The growing church needed to build during a time when steel was rationed due to the war effort. The War Production Board finally granted their request for some building materials, and on January 7, 1945 the church broke ground for their building, which stands today at Franklin and Geary Streets in that great city. The building was filled and people regularly came to Christ. In 1947 Northwestern Schools conferred the honorary Doctor of Divinity degree on Arno Q. Weniger. This is especially noteworthy because Weniger received his degree from the hand of William Bell Riley, his hero. Later that year Riley passed away, and Weniger had the distinction of receiving the last degree Riley conferred in his long ministry.

Arno Weniger pastored in San Francisco in momentous years. Hamilton Square Baptist Church left the Northern Baptist Convention in the battle over theological modernism. The church then affiliated with the Conservative Baptist Association of America. Dr. Weniger served as a leader in the movement. He served one year as president of the Conservative Baptist Association and traveled extensively across the country representing that ministry. When the Conservative Baptist Association began its decline into New Evangelicalism, Dr. Weniger stood with the separatist fundamentalists in the movement. He served as the first president of the San Francisco Baptist Theological Seminary, which Hamilton Square Baptist Church graciously housed. When Baptist World Mission was formed as a protest to the compromise in the Conservative Baptist mission agencies, Dr. Weniger served with distinction for many years on its board.

Arno Q. Weniger retired from the pastorate of the Hamilton Square church in 1976. He passed away in his sleep at the age of 87 on July 1, 1995.

His life is characterized by love for God, a zeal for souls, a commitment to biblical truth, the courage to stand for that truth, and a willingness to invest in training others for the Lord's work.

FJM

---

[1]All information in this entry is from Arno Q. Weniger, "My Start in Life," unpublished autobiography (Lucerne, CA: n.d.).

October 13

Better Than Brass or Marble

Scripture: Colossians 3:12-13

Pastor James Garnett, the grandson of James Garnett (who pastored the Crooked Run Baptist Church from a time predating the Revolutionary War until 1825 or 1826) and the son of Edmond and Sarah Garnett, was born in Culpeper County, Virginia, February 4, 1792.

While still a child, his parents moved to Kentucky, where he grew up and received his education. After entering the ministry, he had some additional training in Transylvania University. In his nineteenth year he received Christ as Saviour and surrendered completely to Him. He was later baptized into church membership. Very soon after church membership, he was impressed to preach the Gospel to warn people of their danger and point them to the "...the Lamb of God, which taketh away the sin of the world" (John 1:29). So acceptable and useful was his ministry that his church requested his ordination, which took place at Bullettsburg Baptist Church, Boone County, Kentucky, on October 13, 1816.

After his ordination, he returned to Virginia and was married to Elizabeth Garnett, who was his intelligent, affectionate, and faithful helpmeet. They settled in Culpeper County and lived there until the close of his earthly career. He pastored four churches: Cedar Run, Gourdvine, Bethel, and Crooked Run. One biographer says he pastored for more than fifty-five years.[1] Interestingly, he pastored all four churches at the same time.

Mr. Taylor says, "He has erected a monument more imposing and durable than brass or marble. He has impressed himself on the loving remembrance of his people, and put into operation moral influences which will be perpetuated through all coming time; while many hundreds, brought to the Saviour by his instrumentality, will rise up to call him blessed. The history of his labors, in this extensive and important field, presents nothing more novel than the unexciting and monotonous routine of pastoral work among rural churches, varied by seasons of depression and revival, with perhaps an occasional case of discipline."[2]

For the praise of divine grace magnified in Pastor Garnett's life and ministry, it is worthy to recall his character and influence. In the natural relations of life with people, he was upright and exemplary, diligent in business, as well as fervent in spirit. Pastor Garnett was a good provider for the family and a firm but kind ruler of his household. He was a good husband, father, and an honest man. Clearness of concepts and accuracy of statements characterized his preaching. Most of his illustrations were from the Bible, causing his people to become more familiar with the Scripture.

In regard to church administration, he was known for sound and judicious decisions. His advice in church matters was often sought after and highly prized, even from those of other churches.

It has been noted that his whole life illustrated a fidelity to truth and right, and his word was truly his bond. All pastoral duties he deemed binding and carried them out with cheerfulness and earnestness. He watched over his people with conscientious interest and unselfish devotion as one who would give account at the Judgment Seat. As a pastor, he was a friend to ministerial education and missions, promoting and raising money for them. In addition, he had a very great interest in the black people of his communities. The Crooked Run Church had two meeting houses, which had ample accommodations for the black folk who desired to come to services. When Pastor Garnett had special services for them, the whole church was given to them.

Dear Brother Garnett practiced the instruction of our text. He put on "bowels of mercies, kindness, humbleness of mind, meekness, longsuffering; forbearing one another and forgiving one another." Because of this, he won the respect and affectionate regard and love of a multitude of people of every walk of life. Few men were ever held in more tender esteem or have left behind them more loving memories.

He was gathered to his fathers at a good old age on July 12, 1875. He was sustained by an unshaken trust in God and a well-founded hope of eternal life.

How will people remember our faith, love, and life for God?

EGC

---

[1]George Braxton Taylor, *Virginia Baptist Ministers*, (Lynchburg, VA: J. P. Bell Company, 1912), 204.

[2]Ibid., 204.

October 14

A Model Gospel Minister

Scripture: 1 Timothy 3:1-7

The small obituary notice that appeared in the *Richmond Enquirer* on October 14, 1823, perhaps meant little to the average citizen, for Reuben Ford (1742-1823), was not well-known to the world in general. Elder Reuben Ford entered the presence of His Lord on October 6, 1823. His home-going occurred at his residence in Hanover County, in the eighty-second year of his earthly sojourn. The man of God had suffered a distressing affliction of nearly three years. Many of his peers had already passed from the scene.

Reuben Ford was about twenty years of age when he fell under conviction through the preaching of George Whitefield, and was gloriously regenerated. Seven years later he was immersed and professed himself of the Baptist persuasion. As he matured in the faith he expressed a desire to preach, and his gifts became evident to the saints. He was ordained, and his ministry led to the conversion of many in Goochland County, Virginia. His career in the pastoral ministry is set forth in the histories of that county. Goochland Baptist Church was organized December 23, 1771 with ninety-seven members, and Reuben Ford became its first minister. "Such was the success of his ministrations, that this church greatly increased in numbers, and efficiency. In the year 1799, a season of refreshing, from the presence of the Lord, was enjoyed, during which one hundred and twenty were added . . . from time to time, did the Lord attend the efforts of His servant . . . ."[1]

Through that ministry, other churches came into being, and a number of men were called from that congregation to serve in ministry. The historian of the Virginia Baptists authored his volume when Elder Ford was sixty-eight years of age. He provided this glowing report of the man of God: "No man ever sees him, who does not view him with reverence at his first appearance, and no one ever was disappointed in him. Grave, without the least moroseness; cheerful and affectionate in his manners, yet firm in his purposes; he has everything out of the pulpit which might serve as a model of a Gospel minister; his life is truly spotless; his talents are of the useful kind . . . ."[2]

When Committees of Safety were organized in Virginia in 1776 in preparation for the Revolutionary War, Reuben Ford was a member, and his service qualified him as a Minute Man. Reuben Ford was known as a man of sound judgment; and he was a natural leader. Though complete records of the early actions of the United States Senate are incomplete, family tradition has it that on one occasion Elder Ford addressed the new national congress. It is also passed down in family tradition, that as the Baptists led the way in securing an amendment to the Constitution assuring religious freedom, this man of God is said to have consulted with George Washington on the subject.

Prior to the Revolutionary War, only the clergy of the Church of England were permitted to perform marriage ceremonies. Baptist preachers chafed under such restrictions, and Reuben Ford and John Leland were appointed to present the Baptist protest of the ruling. Interestingly, "It appears that many of the Baptist preachers, among other dissenters, presuming on a future sanction of government, had ventured to marry those who applied to them. For a set of preachers to proceed to solemnize the rites of matrimony, without any law to authorize them, may, at first view, appear to be a heedless and censurable measure. But we are informed that they were advised to it by their friend Patrick Henry, as being the most certain method of obtaining the law which they had in view. Their attempts succeeded . . . ."

In 1784 the law finally allowed Baptist pastors the privilege of legally marrying their own members.[3]

In the last days of his life, though deathly ill, Elder Ford prevailed upon friends to transport him to the house of God that he might exhort the people to faithfulness in the work of God. Throughout his lifetime, with no spiritual relapse, he fulfilled his calling until his Lord took him home. May we so live that such a testimony might be given concerning our service for the Savior.

DLC

---

[1]J. B. Taylor, *Virginia Baptist Ministers* (Richmond: Yale & Wyatt, 1838), 53.

[2]Robert Baylor Semple, *History of the Baptists in Virginia* (Lafayette, TN: Church History Research and Archives, 1976), 140-141.

[3]David Benedict, *A General History of the Baptist Denomination* (Boston: Lincoln & Edmonds, 1813), 2:85-86.

October 15

Strong Local Churches are Vital

Scripture: 1 Timothy 3:15; Acts 20:28

It was to a local church that Paul wrote, admonishing them that they were the "pillar and ground of the truth." We appreciate godly leadership, and surely solid Christian colleges and seminaries are helpful, but autonomous local churches have epitomized Baptist progress throughout the years. Faithful missionaries and fruitful preachers are usually produced through godly families that make the local church the center of their lives. The churches that encourage families in producing such Christian workers are built upon and bounded by the Word of God, and they acknowledge the Lord Jesus Christ as their sovereign Head.

Such a congregation attracts our attention in this devotional, and we will consider the Hopewell Baptist Church in Hopewell, New Jersey. Baptists began arriving in the area of Hopewell early after the beginning of the

18th century, but the congregation did not build its first building until 1747. In time the congregation began to take root and grow, and "this church (became) remarkable for the number of ministers who have been raised up in it. Thomas Curtis, John Alderson, John Gano, Joseph Power, Hezekiah Smith, John Blackwell, Charles Thompson, and James Ewing, were all licensed or ordained at Hopewell."[1] Surely some of these names are known by every Baptist history reader.

For many years itinerant preachers filled the pulpit for the congregation, and the first settled pastor of the church was Isaac Eaton. His ministry began in April 1748 and lasted until July 4, 1772, when the Lord saw fit to take him home at the early age of forty seven. He was buried in the church building near the pulpit, and on a marble plate the following words are incised:

> In him, with grace and eminence did shine,
> The man, the Christian, scholar, and divine.[2]

Mr. Eaton established the first Baptist school to train preachers in America in 1756. In so doing he earned the distinction of honor of being the first Baptist leader in America to provide for the training of young men for the work of the ministry.

Approximately two years following Pastor Eaton's death, on October 15, 1774, Reverend Benjamin Coles was called to the pastorate. He pastored the church during the dreadful days of the Revolutionary War, and he served the congregation until the spring of 1779. In fact, it is pleasing to note that soon after he assumed the pastorate, the congregation experienced a spirit of revival that produced 105 converts in his first two years of ministry there.

At the very outset of the Revolutionary War, the congregation had gathered to worship. On that fateful day when word was received of Concord and Lexington, the members were gathered in the house of God. As the service continued, a messenger arrived informing Colonel Joab Houghton of the military situation. The Colonel sat through the service, and at the conclusion of the meeting, he retired to a great stone block in front of the meeting house. He beckoned to the people to stop.

"Men and women paused to hear, curious to know what so unusual a sequel to the service of the day could mean. At the first words a silence, stern as death, fell on all. The Sabbath quiet of the hour and of the place was deepened into a terrible solemnity. He told them all the story of the cowardly murder at Lexington by the royal troops; the heroic vengeance following hard upon it; the retreat of Percy; the gathering of the children of the Pilgrims round the beleaguered hills of Boston: then pausing, and looking over the silent throng, he said slowly: 'Men of New Jersey, the red coats are murdering our brethren of New England! Who follows me to Boston?' and every man of that audience stepped out into line, and answered: 'I!' There was not a coward nor a traitor in old Hopewell Baptist Meeting-house that day."[3]

The local church is still the "pillar and ground of truth" today. Loyalty to one's church is often indicative of one's loyalty to Christ. May we be found faithful to our local churches which, if they are true to the Word of God, have been purchased with the blood of our Savior.

DLC

---

[1] David Benedict, *A General History of the Baptist Denomination in America*, (Dayton, OH: Church History Research & Archives, 1985) 1:571.

[2] Ibid., 572.

[3] William Cathcart, *Baptist Patriots and the American Revolution* (Grand Rapids, MI: Guardian Press, 1976), 56-57.

October 16

A Biblical Separatist

Scripture: Timothy 2:15-26

Elsewhere in this volume we consider the life of Dr. Ernest D. Pickering. Merely recounting the high points of his life does not do justice to his memory.

Dr. Pickering was well known as a theologian. His ministry as seminary dean, professor, and college and seminary president has left generations of men who bless his memory. We who studied under him remember the rigorous demands he placed upon us, the love of God's Word he imparted to us, the evangelistic burden he demonstrated and urged upon us, and the meek example he set for us.

Perhaps Ernest Pickering's greatest legacy is his writing. While he served as dean at Central Seminary, he wrote numerous pamphlets, articles, and sermons for publication. Later, he wrote several volumes of Sunday school lessons for the Regular Baptist Press. He also authored numerous books, the most notable of which are *Biblical Separation: The Struggle for A Pure Church* and *The Tragedy of Compromise.* The first book continues as the classic exposition of biblical separation from both history and Scripture. The second documents the degeneration of Christianity in the New Evangelical movement from its inception until 1994. Both are must reading for every preacher. Laymen would also be well advised to read them. In the classroom, pulpit, and on paper Dr. Pickering had unusual ability to make profound truth simple and understandable.

Dr. Pickering articulated biblical separatism, *and he truly articulated it!* While serving as pastor of Woodcrest Baptist Church and dean of Central Conservative Baptist Theological Seminary in Minneapolis, he led in the struggle for biblical obedience in the Conservative Baptist movement. The Conservative Baptists, largely influenced by the leadership of Vernon Grounds, began its inexorable move toward New Evangelicalism in the late 1950s. Pickering was one of the men in the movement who opposed the ecumenical practices in the CB movement. Those who advocated cooperation in ecumenical evangelism (such as Billy Graham) practiced what was called the inclusive policy. Dr. Pickering wrote against this and opposed it in various Conservative Baptist ministries. When things came to a head, he led in the 1961 formation of the World Conservative Baptist Mission, which was a protest to the compromise and inclusivism within the Conservative Baptist Foreign and Home Mission societies. From 1961-1965, he served as vice-president of the board of the fledgling mission agency. He was the chief author of its constitution and doctrinal statement. From 1965 until 1988, he served churches and schools within the General Association of Regular Baptist Churches. He was known as a consistent separatist leader in the GARBC. For many years he served on the board of the Association of Baptists for World Evangelism (ABWE). In 1988 he returned to Minneapolis to serve as pastor of the Fourth Baptist Church. A year later he was elected to serve on the board of the mission agency he had helped to start, now known as Baptist World Mission. In 1993 the Lord led him to serve in the administration of BWM as deputation director. I was overwhelmed when my former professor, a man whom I loved and admired, came to work with his former student. He was a godly, positive influence in this ministry, a great promoter of BWM in the churches, a teacher and helper to the missionaries as they raised support, and an encouragement to the entire mission family. His wife, Yvonne, served as his secretary and did outstanding work as she also typed his voluminous writings. Baptist World Mission still publishes many of his booklets.

Ernest Pickering also modeled the life of a biblical separatist. As the text for today says, he did not strive. He was never contentious. In meekness, without regard for the personal cost, he always stood for biblical truth. He was the consummate Christian gentleman, but he never wavered in his obedience to Christ. He dedicated himself fervently and selflessly to the service of his Savior.

At the end of his life, Pickering fought a long battle with cancer. Never once did he complain. He trusted implicitly in the sovereign God Who saved him and Whom he served. He glorified God in his death (John 21:19). On October 16, 2000 the suffering ended and he met the Lord he loved and served.

May God help us to obey God's Word, to evidence a biblical spirit, and to faithfully serve our Lord.

FJM

October 17

Taxing or Coveting?

Scripture: Exodus 20:17

It is not my intention to belabor the point, but I am convinced that Baptists in the twenty-first century are very poorly informed concerning religious freedom in the early days of our Republic. Thus I would like to quote lengthy portions of a letter that was sent to the brethren of the Philadelphia Baptist Association to be read in their annual meeting of October 16, 17, and 18, 1770. As you will see, the letter was sent from Baptists in Massachusetts.

> The laws of this province were never intended to exempt the Baptists from paying towards building and repairing Presbyterian meeting houses, and making up Presbyterian ministers' salaries; for, besides other insufficiencies, they are all limited both as to extent and duration. The first law extended only five miles round each Baptist meeting house; those without this circle had no relief, neither had they within: for, though it exempted their polls, it left their estates to the mercy of harpies, and their estates went to wreck. The Baptists sought a better law, and with great difficulty and waste of time and money, obtained it; but this was not universal. It extended not to any parish until a Presbyterian meeting house should be built, and a Presbyterian minister settled there; in consequence of which the Baptists have never been freed from the first and great expenses of their parishes, expenses equal to the current expenses of ten or twelve years. This is the present case of the people of Ashfield, which is a Baptist settlement. There were but five families of other denominations in the place when the Baptist church was constituted; but those five, and a few more, have lately built a Presbyterian meeting house there, and settled

an orthodox minister, as they call him; which last cost them ,200 pounds. To pay for both, they laid a tax on the land; and, as the Baptists are the most numerous, the greatest part fell to their share. The Presbyterians, in April last, demanded the money. The Baptists pleaded poverty, alleging that they had been twice driven from their plantations by the Indians last war; that they were but new settlers, and had cleared but a few spots of land, and had not been able to build commodious dwelling houses. Their tyrants would not hear. Then the Baptists pleaded the ingratitude of such conduct; for they had built a fort there at their own expense, and had maintained it for two years, and so had protected the interior Presbyterians, as well as their neighbors who now rose up against them; that the Baptists to the westward had raised money to relieve Presbyterians who had like them suffered by the Indians; and that it was cruel to take from them what the Indians had left! But nothing touched the hearts of these cruel people. Then the Baptists urged the law of the province; but were soon told that that law extended to no new parish till the meeting house and minister were paid for. Then the Baptists petitioned the general court. Proceedings were stopped till further orders, and the poor people went home rejoicing, thinking their property safe; but had not all got home before said order came; and it was an order for the Presbyterians to proceed. Accordingly, in the month of April they fell foul on their plantations; and not on skirts and corners, but on the cleared and improved spots; and so have mangled their estates and left them hardly any but a wilderness. They sold the house and garden of one man, and the young orchards, meadows, and corn fields of others; nay, they sold their dead, for they sold their graveyard. The orthodox minister was one of the purchasers. These spots amounted to three hundred and ninety-five acres, and have since been valued at 363 pounds 8 shillings. But were sold for 35 pounds and 10 shillings. This was the first payment. Two more are coming, which will not leave

> them an inch of land at this rate. The Baptists waited on the assembly five times this year for relief, but were not heard, under the pretense they had no business; but their enemies were heard, and had their business done. At last the Baptists got together about a score of the members of Cambridge, and made their complaints known; but in general, they were treated very superciliously. One of them spoke to this effect, "The general assembly have a right to do what they did, and if you don't like it you may quit the place!" SS But, alas they must leave their all behind![1]

How we ought to thank God for our forefathers who secured our religious freedom at great cost!

DLC

---

[1]A. D. Gillette, Editor, *Minutes of the Philadelphia Baptist Association* (Springfield, MO: Particular Baptist Press, 2002), 115-116.

October 18

A Churchman Who Defended Immersion

Scripture: Colossians 2:12

An interesting bit of history may be gleaned concerning a Church of England pastor in England who became an immersionist by conviction in the seventeenth century. It will, however, be necessary to paraphrase the wordy account given by Isaac Backus.

A law was passed in Boston in 1644 to banish Baptists from the colony. An attempted revision was made on October 18, 1645. Hearing of this effort, John Tombes wrote a letter to ministers in New England in an effort to relieve some of the pressure the Baptists were enduring. Tombes never left the Church of England, but he stoutly defended the ordinance of adult-believers' baptism by immersion.

> John Tombes was born at Bewdly, Worcestershire, in 1603. At the age of fourteen he was admitted at Magdalen Hall, Oxford, and at the age of twenty-one was

made Catechetical Lecturer there. Six years later he entered the ministry, and was settled at Lemster and afterwards at Bristol. Driven from these places successively by the civil war, in 1643 he went to London. For several years he had questioned the scriptural authority of infant baptism and held that there was only one passage, 1 Corinthians 7:14, on which it could be defended. He had recently been led to yield this passage also, as affording it no support. . . .

Mr. Tombes became pastor of Fenchurch, London, agreeing with the church that he would not preach against infant baptism, and that they should admit no one to preach in their pulpit in its favor. Here he published two treatises against infant baptism, one of which was his *Examen of Mr. Marshall's Sermon,* and, as the result, he was dismissed from his church. He next assumed charge of a parish in Bewdly, his native town. While here, he was immersed upon his profession of faith, and gathered a church of those who were in agreement with him. He still continued to act as minister of the parish, and because of his acknowledged learning and ability, and of services which he had rendered to the government, he was held in repute, was entrusted with important offices in the national church and enjoyed the friendship of leading men in the country notwithstanding his religious views and practice. Several times he held public disputes upon baptism, once with Richard Baxter, (Presbyterian) when, says Anthony Wood, "all scholars there and present, who knew the way of disputing and managing arguments, did conclude that Tombes got the better of Baxter by far." . . . A catalogue of his writings gives the titles of twenty-six works, fourteen of which are against infant baptism.

The manuscript copy of his *Examen of Mr. Marshall's Sermon* which was sent to New England, is now in the library of the American Antiquarian Society, Worcester. With it is the following letter: "To all the elders of the churches of Christ in New England and to each in particular by name; to the pastor and teacher of the church of God at Boston, these present:

Reverend Brethren: Understanding that there is some disquiet in your churches about pedobaptism, and being moved by some that honor you much in the Lord, and desire your comfortable account at the day of Christ, that I would yield that a copy of my *Examen* of Master Marshall his sermon on infant baptism might be transcribed to be sent to you; I have consented thereto, and do commend it to your examination in like manner, as you may perceive by reading of it, I did to Master Marshall, not doubting but that you will, as in God's presence, and accountable to Christ Jesus, weigh the thing; remembering that your Lord Jesus Christ, John 7,24. 'Judge not according to appearance but judge righteous judgment.' To the blessings of him who is your God and our God, your judge and our Judge, I leave you and the flock of God over which the Holy Ghost hath made you overseers, and rest.

Your brother and fellow-servant,

John Tombes

From my study at the Temple in London, May 25th, 1645."[1]

In reality, the ordinance of believers' immersion has a continued history from the New Testament to the present. It pictures beautifully our Lord's death, burial and resurrection, and identifies true believers with the Lord from glory.

DLC

---

[1]Isaac Backus, *A History of New England* (Newton, MA: Backus Historical Society, 1871), 1:146-147.

October 19

Pioneering for Christ

Scripture: Romans 15:20

The expansion of the United States was greatly enhanced with the Louisiana Purchase in 1803. The purchase more than doubled the territory of our nation, and allowed for enlargement of the burgeoning population. The purchase was almost a gift from Napoleon who desired to avert the prospect of humiliation with the possible capture of the area by the British. The cost to America was about two cents per acre! But with the consummation of that purchase, the challenge of home missions in America greatly expanded.

Iowa was part of that purchase. On June 28, 1834, Congress made what is today Iowa a part of the Territory of Michigan. This was done to establish a more stable government. Twelve years later, December 28, 1846, the state of Iowa was formed with its present boundaries. In 1834, a young couple - William and Hepzibah Mathes-Manley were united in marriage in Kentucky. Wanting to establish a homestead, they traveled to Iowa. In what is now Burlington, Iowa, they found four or five log huts. There they set up housekeeping in the unbroken wilderness. Across the river in Illinois was a Baptist preacher, Elder John Logan, and the young couple invited him to the new settlement to preach. Thus on October 19, 1834, John Logan preached the first sermon in Iowa. A few Baptists from Illinois had moved into the area, and the following day the first Baptist church in Iowa was formed. The Articles of Faith had been carried by William and Hepzibah from the Brush Creek Baptist Church in Green County, Kentucky. They were adopted and ". . . eleven people organized the Long Creek Baptist church. This later became the Danville church."[1]

The first Baptist minister known to have settled in Iowa was Elder Hezekiah Johnson. Born in the home of a Baptist preacher in Maryland on March 6, 1799, young Hezekiah soon came to know the Savior. His parents moved to Ohio when he was a teenager, and Hezekiah was licensed to preach in 1825. He married the following year, and was ordained in April of 1827.

The next seven years found him preaching in the Buckeye State, but he traveled and preached as far as Iowa. Hezekiah Johnson was commissioned as a missionary under the American Baptist Home Mission Society in 1838, and he made his way to Iowa, where, as we have noted, he became the first settled Baptist pastor. In 1845, Hezekiah Johnson and Ezra Fisher were asked by the Home Society to go to Oregon to pioneer that ministry. Hezekiah settled there in Oregon City, and established a church. He was one of the early Baptist preachers in that state as well. In the course of years, Reverend Johnson's health degenerated, and the Lord called him home on August 28, 1866.[2]

How challenging to pioneer a work for Christ! That was the spirit of the early Baptists in America. Though they did not catch the burden of foreign missions until early in the nineteenth century, our Baptist forefathers in America saw the need of expanding to the West and they rose to accomplish that task. Make no mistake about it; they were in the religious vanguard of the day. For instance, consider the following quotation: "The first volume, now given to the public, deals with the Baptists because these groups *were the first to take an active interest in the frontier* situation as migrations moved westward when the territory between the Alleghenies and the Mississippi was settled[3] (Italics not in original)."

Unfortunately, numerical and financial expansion often produces apathy. Our Lord warned the Church at Laodicea against this very attitude in Revelation 3:17. With the receding spiritual impact of the Gospel today, it is time that fundamental Baptist churches in America re-seed the countryside with vibrant, victorious local congregations to reach others for Christ. Pray that your local church will gain such a vision today.

DLC

---

[1]G. P. Mitchell, *A Century of Iowa Baptist History* (Pella, IA: The Baptist Record, 1934), 18.

[2]C. H. Mattoon, *Baptist Annals of Oregon* (McMinnville, OR: Telephone Register Publishing Co., 1905), 1:47.

[3]William Warren Sweet, *Religion On The American Frontier* (New York: Cooper Square Publishers, 1964), VI.

October 20

A Sacrificial Leader

Scripture: John 1:47

Abram Burwell Brown was born on October 20, 1821, into a rich heritage. His father, Martin Brown, was the son of Jeremiah Brown, a Revolutionary soldier of English descent. His mother was of Huguenot extraction. Her great-grandfather, Abram Seay, fled from persecution in France, first to England and then to Virginia. Abram was the oldest child in the family. Though his mother died when he was only eleven, the memory of her intelligence, faith, and unusual beauty remained with him throughout life. Of his father, Abram said, "My father loved learning and loved me, and so he made many sacrifices to give me educational advantages." [1]

As was often the case in those days, Abram taught school before his own education was complete. During his first teaching experience, he lived with the William Waller family and attended an Episcopal church with them. He made a profession of faith, joined the church, and expected to become a preacher. Later, however, through studying the Bible and Dr. Carson's classic work on Baptism, Abram became a Baptist.

He attended Washington College in 1841-42, and spent the 1846-47 school year at the University of Virginia. John A. Broadus, a fellow student, later wrote, "In Moral Philosophy I was his classmate. Before the middle of the session it was apparent to me that he was the foremost man of the class."

Upon graduation Abram taught school and did some preaching. He then engaged in missionary work in both Virginia and West Virginia. During that time he met and married Miss Sallie Wimbish.

When the Civil War broke out, he gave up teaching to minister to the troops. He joined the Southern forces and became missionary chaplain to Carter's artillery battalion. The South was decimated following the war, and Abram, as did many other former pastors, returned to an impoverished, country church. Of course, it was necessary to supplement one's salary, and, once again, he reverted to farming and teaching.

An incident that reveals his compassion and missionary vision is noted during the difficult war years. His wife had sacrificially saved money for her Pastor/husband to buy a vest. She surprised him with the money as he left for a fellowship meeting with instructions that he was to purchase the vest following the sessions. However, at the meeting, Dr. A. M. Poindexter, missionary leader of the Southern Baptists, made an impassioned plea for foreign missions. Pastor Brown rose and said, "Here is money my wife gave me to buy a vest, but the vest may go and I will do without it, and foreign missions can have it."[2]

Soon after the war, Richmond College conferred upon Abram Brown the degree of Doctor of Divinity, and in 1884 he was given the degree of LL. D. from the University of Tennessee.

In 1871 the General Association confronted a serious crisis. They were faced with an indebtedness of $5,000. That was a mint of money in those post-war days of economic disaster. Many preachers had spoken in an effort to rally the association members, but doom enveloped the atmosphere. Dr. Brown arose and spoke. He emphasized the fact that Virginia needed the Gospel and the Virginia Baptists were able to meet that need. He pled for cooperation. He preached that the missionaries were at the front of the battle, and those at the rear should freely support them. He continued: "Mr. President, I suppose that the Battle of Gettysburg decided the fate of the Confederacy. At the time that Pickett's Division made its splendid charge, the angel of history hovered over the scene to write down, *a nation is born,* but the division which was to *support* Pickett's Northern Army rallied, and plucked from their hands their hard-earned victory; and the angel turned away with tears of iron, and with a pen of fate wrote *the lost cause.*"[3]

The day was saved. Dr. Brown's message persuaded a collection which took care of the debt and gave them a new lease on life.

Pastor Brown passed away November 27, 1885. The funeral was held on Sunday afternoon. It was a terrible day with torrents of water and flooded streets. However, a great congregation gathered to express appreciation and respect for him.

EGC

[1]George Braxton Taylor, *Virginia Baptist Minister,* Third Series, (Lynchburg,VA: J. P. Bell Company, 1912), 402

[2]Ibid., 412.

[3]Ibid., 413.

October 21

Independence Verses Interdependence

Scripture: Galatians 2:1-10

Oliver Hart's name is synonymous with growth among early Baptists of the South. He was an outstanding leader, and in 1749 he became pastor of the First Baptist Church of Charleston, South Carolina. Previously he had been active in the work of the Philadelphia Association of Baptists, and through that contact, he had become aware of the benefits of local churches pooling resources to accomplish together what a single church could not do alone. The Philadelphia Association had been established in 1707. On October 21, 1751, Reverend Hart was instrumental in inviting messengers from several area Baptist churches to join in considering action in establishing an association of Baptist churches in his vicinity. As a result, messengers from First Baptist Church of Charleston, Ashley River Baptist Church, and Welch Neck met in Charleston, and the Charleston Association came into being. Soon thereafter the Sandy Creek Association in North Carolina, the Ketocton Association in Virginia, the Salisbury Association in Maryland, the Georgia Association, the Elkhorn Association in Kentucky, and a number of other associations came into being.

What was the purpose of these associations?

"The object of [these] unions was declared to be the promotion of the Redeemer's kingdom, by the maintenance of love and fellowship, and by mutual consultations for the peace and welfare of the churches. The independency of the churches was asserted, and the powers of the Association restricted to those of a Council of Advice."[1]

In the early days of the growth of Baptist influence in our land, there was a realization among Baptist leaders that, though the Bible teaches the autonomy of each local assembly, it also pictures an interdependence of one congregation to another. This conclusion was surely evidenced at the conclusion of the first church council at Jerusalem. Vital doctrinal issues were discussed. Nothing could be more important than a thorough understanding and reiteration of the matter of salvation! Was it to be wholly of grace by faith, or was it to be by faith plus works such as keeping the Mosaic Law? Make no mistake about it. The matter of being saved was at the crux of the council (Acts 2:21, 47; 4:12; 15:11; 16:30-331). The issue was gloriously resolved, and Pastor James of Jerusalem summed up the verdict. The saints concurred with Paul's assessment, "For by grace are ye saved through faith; and that of yourselves, it is the gift of God." However, at the conclusion of the gathering, the apostles reminded Paul and Banabas of the need of interdependence. As they traveled among the churches that had a Gentile background, they were to remind those congregations of the need of those in Jerusalem. Those who embraced Jesus as their Messiah in Jerusalem, were being shunned for leaving Judaism to accept the pure Gospel message of grace. In other words, one congregation was to strengthen another congregation. They were each independent, but they were nonetheless interdependent.

In the twentieth century, fundamental Baptists saw the need of strengthening local church autonomy, but, I fear, that needed emphasis has led many congregations to become isolationists in nature. There is surely a need today for local churches to unite in assisting church planting in America. The need is great, and it is often impossible for a local church to birth another church alone. A changing society is no longer willing to gather in a store front. Acquisition of property and building restrictions can lead to astronomical costs. A young church-planting pastor in America is just as worthy of financial assistance as is a missionary in a foreign land. Rather than building colossal super- churches, there is the need to reach into unchurched communities. This is often best done in a cooperative effort. An Association is never to dictate to a local congregation, but local congregations need to consider re-seeding needy areas by cooperating with sister churches of like faith and practice.

Let us pray for a rebirth of a spirit of cooperation among Bible-believing, fundamental Baptist churches today that we might abandon isolation and practice interdependence to the glory of our Lord and Savior.

DLC

[1]Robert A. Baker, *A Baptist Source Book* (Nashville, TN: Broadman Press, 1966), 16.

October 22

The Secret of Revival

Scripture: 2 Chronicles 7:14

The greatest need among Bible believers today in America is revival. There is a spiritual dearth in our land, but it seems only to be recognized by mature saints. The fear of God is unknown among our citizenry, and many local churches have become mere entertainment centers. Rather than having prophets to call the twenty-first century believers to repentance, we are in danger of idolizing so-called Christian comedians. Philosophical casuistry has overtaken many pastors, and they have concluded, "Whatever it takes to get folks in, we will do!"

In days gone by in American history, saints of God knew what to do during times of spiritual decline. Rather than attempting to attract the unsaved by lowering biblical standards, they determined to pray and seek the face of God. In reading the history of the Sandy Creek Baptist Association in North Carolina, it is revealing to observe their close observance of the spiritual condition of their day. Time and again the saints gathered in association meetings called the local congregations to pray. When the Association met on October 23, 1824, the minutes stated, "This year the Lord blessed many of the churches with extensive revivals. *Prayer meetings* were frequent, and much blessed in the conversion of souls; they ought to be more generally in use in our churches."[1]

As early as 1816 the Association recommended to the churches that "they observe the monthly concern of prayer, on the evening of the first Monday in every month, for the spread of the gospel."[2]

This Day in Baptist History III

At their annual meeting in 1835, the minutes state, "*Resolved*, that Saturday before the second Sabbath in December next, be observed by all the members of the several churches composing this association, as a day of fasting and prayer, for a revival in this association, and generally throughout the world."[3]

As the Association met on October 22, 1836, the apparent need for revival called for action. A report was made as to the reasons that revival was needed. The committee listed the following conditions that demanded that serious prayer might be made: "...pride, arising from worldly prosperity; A conformity to the world, its fashions, and customs; The neglect of secret prayer, self-examination, and personal holiness; The neglect of Family prayer, and training up of our children in the nurture and admonition of the Lord; The omission of keeping the Sabbath Day holy, and suffering our children ...to violate the holy command; We think that the making, using, and vending of ardent spirits, is a bane to the life of religion, both in the soul of the individual and the community; and The neglect of the Bible and attending on the administration of the Word of Life."[4]

As I read of their concerns, I could not help but wonder what our forefathers would think of Baptists today. Brethren, if ever our local churches needed reviving, it is today! What an amazing day in which to live. It is undeniable that we have the greatest opportunity in the history of man for living and preaching the Gospel. But it is also true that no time in history have believers missed the mark more miserably than in this day. As I write this entry, our nation faces a great challenge from organized, demonically led terrorism, and yet there is a complacency that can only lead to devastation. Frankly the apathy of the average professed Baptist in America portends an omen of dark days ahead. America needs revival NOW. Thankfully our God is not the Great I Was. He is the Great I Am. And His promise from our text is still true. It is time that genuine believers in America unite to pray for personal, church-wide, and national revival. We are at a crossroads. It is revival or ruin.

DLC

[1]George W. Purefoy, *A History of the Sandy Creek Baptist Association* (New York: Sheldon & Co., 1859), 129.

[2]Ibid., 107.

[3]Ibid., 164.

[4]Ibid., 167.

October 23

Revival in the Land

Scripture: Psalm 85:6

In a letter to a friend, dated Logan County, Kentucky, October 23, 1801, M'Gready gives a "Narrative of the Commencement and Progress of the Revival of 1800." The description is amazing as month after month believers got right with God, and souls were saved. Apparently as Elder Lemuel Burkitt heard of the revival, he determined to visit Kentucky to see for himself. A most abbreviated account is all for which we have room. He reported,

> The first appearance that was discovered was, great numbers of people attended the ministry of the Word, and the congregations kept increasing. . . . The audience was more solemn and serious than usual. . . . The Word preached was attended with such a divine power that at some meetings two or three hundred would be in floods of tears, and many crying out loudly, What shall we do to be saved? . . . Old Christians were so revived they were all on fire to see their neighbors . . . so much engaged. . . . The work increasing, many were converted and they began to join the churches. Some churches, which had not received a member by baptism for a year or two, would now frequently receive at conference meeting, several members, sometimes twelve, fourteen, eighteen, twenty, and twenty-four at several times in one day. . . . Some of the churches in the revival received 200 members each.

The Lord was pleased to make use of weak and simple means to effect great purposes, that it might be manifest that the work was His and not man's. . . . Giving the people an invitation to come up and be prayed for was also blessed. . . . And when the ordinance of baptism was administered, nothing had a more solemn effect . . . . To see fifteen or twenty persons suitably attired, to go in the water, in a row, hand in hand and the minister at the head, march down into the water regularly, like soldiers of Jesus, singing as they went . . . would make a solemn effect on the numerous assembly. Numbers would be in floods of tears, and so greatly affected [they] could hardly stand while . . . . Sometimes they had the pleasure to see the father and the son, the mother and her daughter, the wife and the husband, go into the water together hand in hand.

Evening meetings were greatly blessed. Some years past it was customary to hold night meetings, but for some time they were disused. When the revival commenced they began to revive. In some neighborhoods they met once a week on an evening, and numbers would attend. Sometimes and in some places nearly 200 would meet, and some people would come ten miles to a night meeting . . . .

Union meetings have also been attended with a blessing. A Union meeting consists of several churches, being convenient to the other and of the same faith and practice, who meet at stated times to confer in love about matters relating to peace, brother union and general fellowship. The time the meeting holds is usually three days. . . .At times three or four thousand people would meet, and sometimes fifteen or sixteen ministers attend. Great numbers were solemnly affected and at times, we have reason to believe, many got converted.

At the Union Meeting at Parker's meeting house, August, 1803, it is supposed 4,000 people were present. The weather proved very rainy on Sunday. There was a stage erected in the meeting house yard; and at about half after 11 o'clock,

> Elder Burkitt ascended the stage to preach. It was expected from the appearance of the clouds it would rain every moment, and before he was done preaching it did so. Yet notwithstanding the numerous congregation still kept together; and although every effort was used to shut the rain, by umbrellas, blankets, etc., yet we believe 1,000 people were exposed to the rain without any shelter, some crying . . . some begging the ministers to pray for them.[1]

How thrilling to realize that the hearers of this report in North Carolina began crying out to God for such a revival in their state. The ministers carried the sacred flame to their congregations, and the fire began to kindle and North Carolinian Baptists too were honored in the Divine visit from Heaven with revival.

America's greatest need today is for revival! As we read of God's faithfulness in days gone by, let us cry out to Him to send revival in this twenty-first century. May we seek the Lord's face in humility that He might move in our hearts to the praise and glory of His name.

DLC

---

[1]George Washington Paschal, *History of North Carolina Baptists* (Raleigh: North Carolina State Convention, 1930), 1:540-541.

October 24

Pray for Those in Public Places

Scripture: Romans 13

Modern day Americans cannot conceive of the awful burden of paying Clergy Taxes to support pastors in churches they do not attend. It is even more incongruous for Bible-believing Baptists to accept that plan. Sincere Bible-believing Baptists all believe in tithing to their local church. On top of that, many, embracing the concept of Love Offerings and Faith Promise giving, give substantially more through their local churches. This means that these give a minimum of 10% to their churches, and many, with a desire to support missionaries, give well in excess of that. The Clergy Tax forced the Baptist believers to pay for services they did not want, and would even reject! Yet this was the procedure throughout the young colonies in New England.

Apparently such laws with regard to religion were not made in the Colony of Vermont until 1797. Then an act was passed for the support of the ministry. The substance of the law actually empowered the inhabitants of every town or parish that consisted of at least twenty-five voters, to collect taxes, to build meeting houses, and to hire and support religious teachers of such denomination as a majority of the population thought proper.

Every person of "adult age, was, by said act, considered as being of the religious opinion and sentiment of such society, and liable to be taxed, after residing in said town or parish one year, unless he should, previous to the vote for raising taxes, &c. obtain, and procure to be recorded in the Town Clerk's office in said town, a certificate of his different belief, signed by some minister of the gospel, deacon, elder, moderator, or clerk of the church, congregation, sect or denomination, to which he belonged."[1]

A slight modification of this law was granted on November 3, 1801, but still the individual seeking exemption had to present a written declaration of his objection and intent. Finally the legislature on October 24, 1807, repealed all the statutes on the subject of taxation aimed at supporting religious organizations.

It is interesting that this action of the legislature was championed by two Baptists who had entered into the political arena. Aaron Leland was Speaker of the Lower House while Ezra Butler was an active member of the State Senate. In the Lower House the bill was debated by a committee of the whole and Mr. Leland spoke to it. Both he and Senator Butler zealously advocated the adoption of the rescinding bill.

Often times the participation of Baptists in the political arena has been questioned and debated in our circles. Surely with tender consciences men ought to prayerfully seek to know the mind of God concerning His will for their lives. From time to time in our national Baptist history, Baptist men have been used of God in political positions to accomplish His Divine Will. Romans 13 sets forth clearly the relationship of the believer to the law.

I do not believe that any God-called man to the ministry ought under any consideration leave his God called position to serve in a political role. When Mr. Spurgeon's son wrote his father that he sensed God's call upon his life, Mr. Spurgeon is said to have responded, "Son, if God has called you to preach the Gospel, don't stoop to becoming the King of England."

On the other hand, as we have entered into the twenty-first century, we need godly men to become members of the House and Senate to stand solidly upon principles concerning homo-sexuality (same sex marriages), abortion, legalized prostitution, and the entire spectrum of issues of morality that will impact society. Surely Messrs, Aaron Leland, and Ezra Butler were in the right place at the right time. In the Old Testament the Lord positioned Joseph and Daniel in the very place where they could have the greatest impact. Let us pray for sincere, godly men who seek to serve our Republic in the political arena.

DLC

---

[1]David Benedict, *A General History of the Baptist Denomination* (Boston: Lincoln & Edmands, 1813), 1:351-352.

October 25

Godly Laymen

Scripture: Acts 6:1-4

The Baptist cause in America has been greatly forwarded by godly laymen. This has been true because Baptists practice the priesthood of the believer which encourages the participation of fellow helpers. Men such as Thomas Waford and Allen Wyley, who lived near Culpeper County, Virginia, in the latter half of the eighteenth century are examples. As Baptist preachers were being hauled off to jail for preaching without license, the laymen were also willing to share their fate.

Thomas Waford was a devout layman who delighted in traveling ahead of preachers to arrange for Gospel meetings. He was physically attacked near one of the meeting-places and severely beaten. Though he lived many years, he bore to his grave the scars of that brutal violence. Allen Wyley was baptized by David Thomas in 1765, and he desired a Baptist preacher to come to Culpeper to enlighten others. He heard of the Separate Baptist preacher, Samuel Harris, and he set out hardly knowing where he was going. In the will of God he came upon one of Samuel Harris' meetings. When he entered the meeting house, Mr. Harris sensed that Wyley had a message from God. He asked Wyley who he was and from where he had come. Mr. Wyley told him his errand. After deliberation, Mr. Harris believed he had been sent from God, and he returned with him to preach in Culpeper.[1] The Baptist preachers were treated roughly in Culpeper with both violence and imprisonment being their lot, but the Gospel was preached!

Later, in Orange County, Mr. Wyley was with a group of Baptist pastors who were tried and imprisoned. The court record reads, "This day Allan Wiley, John Corbley, Elijah Craig and Thomas Chambers [are] charged as Vagrant and Itinerant Persons . . . for Assembling themselves unlawfully at Sundry Times and Places Under the Denomination of Anabaptists and for Teaching & preaching Schismatick Doctrines. Whereupon the Court [is] of the opinion that the said Allen Wiley, John Corbley, Elijah Craig and Thomas Chambers are Guilty . . . and [are] Ordered [to] enter into Bond each in the sum of 50 pounds . . . Each . . . until the 25th of October next and in case they fail to Enter into Such Bond as aforesaid that Each of Them so failing Shall be Committed to Gaol Until the Same Shall be performed."[2]

Though never ordained, in time Mr. Wyley began preaching and moved to Stafford County, Virginia. On March 26, 1771, he became a constituent member of the Potomack Baptist Church, and served as assistant pastor with William Fristoe, a famous Regular Baptist pastor. Wyley's ministry was primarily that of exhortation, but he was a faithful brother.[3]

The jail could not stop those early-day Baptists. The historian, Robert Howell, wrote:

> A venerable gentleman, recently gone to his rest, some years ago said to his friend: "I have often heard, in my youth, the Baptist ministers preach from the windows of the Jail at Chesterfield Court House. The effects were sometimes most extraordinary. On one occasion Webber was preaching; the heavy iron gratings partially concealed him; his appeals were most touching. A man that I did not know, came up and stood by my side. In a few minutes this man began to tremble violently; presently he fell upon his knees, and then upon his face; and there he lay during the service, praying audibly and agonizingly to God for mercy and salvation through Jesus Christ. 'This,' he added, 'was no unusual occurrence. Scores and fifties were often at the same time similarly exercised.'"[4]

May God give us such leadership of both pastors and laymen in these days of tremendous vacillation.

DLC

---

[1]Robert Baylor Semple, *History of the Baptists in Virginia* (Lafayette, TN: Church History Research and Archives, 1976), 19-20.

[2]Lewis Peyton Little, Imprisoned Preachers and Religious Liberty in Virginia (Lynchburg, VA: J. P. Bell Co., 1938), 135-136.

[3]Ibid., 139

[4]Robert Boyle C. Howell, *The Early Baptists of Virginia* (Philadelphia: The Bible and Publication Society, 1857), 80.

October 26

A Vanishing Church

Scripture: Proverbs 29:18

Recently I was given a copy of the history of the First Baptist Church of St. Albans, West Virginia. As the author presented the heritage of that church, reference was made to the efforts of the Old Kanawha Baptist Church@ to establish two arms or branch works at the beginning of the nineteenth century. The churches to be planted were the Peter's Creek Church and the Mouth of Cole Church.

In tracing the growth of the Mouth of Cole church, an amazing phenomenon was observed. Suddenly the church vanished! Let me share some background. The original name might well have been Coalsmouth and is presently known as St. Albans. Jonathan Hilliard was assigned to promote the work of God and build the congregation on August 16, 1800. Immediate progress became evident, for in 1801, forty-five members were listed. The church was officially organized by Reverends John Alderson, Jr. and James Johnson in 1807, and again forty-five were listed as charter members of the work.

Minutes of the church are minimal, but the congregation opted to associate with the Teays Valley Association in 1812. Like most churches, numerical growth was not always forward and upward, and at the association meeting in 1814, the membership had fallen to twenty-nine. The membership was reported to the association as thirty-nine members in 1823, but the numbers had grown again, for the next year's report recorded one hundred and three members. However, at that time the congregation requested assistance from the association because the church was experiencing a church crisis.[1]

The crisis was not explained, but from this vantage point in history, one would have to conclude the trouble had to do with missions. A special business meeting was called for Sunday, October 26, 1834, and four churches were to form a council. Nothing more is ever heard of the crisis or of the church!

What happened? History is totally silent on the issue, but knowing something of Baptist history, it is possible for strong, logical conjectures to be made. The date 1834 provides a strong clue. During the period of 1834 to 1842, the Baptists of America were in crisis. The first Baptist missionary agency for foreign missions in America had been formed in 1814. During the next twenty years, men examined that movement and their own theologies very closely. Slowly but surely, opposition began to mount against sending missionaries to the heathen around the world. Those who held to that position became known by several names. They were called Primitive, Regular, or Old School Baptists. Primarily men of that persuasion also opposed Sunday schools, the use of hymnals, an educated ministry, and paying preachers. The battle raged during the period from 1834 to about 1842, and the end result was that approximately eighty percent of the Baptists approved of missions. These became known as Missionary Baptists. Foreign missions was a new concept in the thinking of many at that time, and thus the difference in the names of Old School and New School. Through the years some Primitive Baptists modified their position and were assimilated among the Missionary Baptists, but some never did. Many of those congregations shriveled and died!

With this background, we can surmise what happened to the Mouth of Cole Church. The answer is quite evident. An anti-missionary attitude removed all vision, and the local congregation ultimately expired. Without a Sunday school, children were poorly trained in the things of God. An uneducated ministry causes the Bible to be a closed book. Part-time pastors often lead to part-time members. The whole picture produces a scene of decline. Many Baptist churches during that period ceased to exist.

May we learn the lesson well! Missions begin at home and extends to the whole wide world. If a church fails to see Africa or Europe as a mission field, it will soon lose the vision for those in the immediate neighborhood. Let us realize that the purpose of the church is missions!

DLC

---

[1]Linda and Bill Troutman, *Heritage and History of the First Baptist Church of St. Albans, WV* (Valley Forge, PA: American Baptist Churches USA, 2003), 21.

October 27

Vavasor Powell, the Whitefield of Wales

Scripture: Matthew 10:1-34

Vavasor Powell was one of the strongest characters of 17th century England. He was born in Radnorshire, Wales, in 1617 into one the leading families in North Wales. His special status resulted in an excellent education, and he graduated from Jesus College, Oxford. He was ordained into the Anglican Church, although he was not yet a believer. One day a Puritan reproved him for breaking the Sabbath by taking part in the Sports, and this led to two years of mental agony over his sins. By reading Puritan books, by hearing sermons they preached, and by personal conversations with them, Powell came to the Savior. His heart and character were completely changed. After his conversion, he stated of his days as an Anglican minister that he "was a reader of common prayers, in the habit of a foolish shepherd, that he slighted the Scriptures, was a stranger to secret and spiritual prayer, and a great profaner of the Sabbath."[1] He left the Anglican Church, became an Independent, and began to preach the Gospel in earnest.

In 1642 Powell went to London and joined the parliamentary army, under Cromwell, as a chaplain. Four years later, after a short time as pastor in Dartford, Kent, he returned to Wales. The people there regarded him almost as an apostle. The country was more free from a persecuting spirit than it had ever been. The people of Wales were in great ignorance about the salvation provided by the Savior, with only a few ministers to point them to the light of Christ. When he returned to Wales, he carried a certificate from the Assembly of Divines as an accredited Presbyterian preacher. In Wales he preached as an itinerant, a common practice there, because the churches were small and scattered. He was constantly in the pulpit or the saddle, preaching two or three times a day, in two or three places, frequently riding more than a hundred miles a week. There was scarcely a church, chapel, market-place, or field where he did not preach during the fourteen years of liberty from 1646 to 1660.

In 1656 Powell changed his religious sentiment. He was immersed and became a Baptist at that time. In his "Confession of Faith" he taught that baptism was immersion and believers were the only subjects.[2] His change from Presbyterian to Baptist brought persecution. He, with fifty or sixty of his hearers, were once arrested about 10 p.m. in Brecknockshire, and confined during the night in a church. At midnight, he preached a sermon to his companions and captors from the words "Fear not them who kill the body." During the sermon, many of his persecutors wept bitterly. When he was brought to the house of the justice the next morning, the justice was temporarily absent. While waiting for his return, Powell preached again. The justice was indignant to find his house turned into a church, but two of his daughters were deeply moved by the truth preached by the fearless man of God. By 1660 Powell had formed more than twenty churches, with a total membership of over 20,000. He has appropriately been called "the Baptist Whitefield of Wales."

Powell was a strong republican. When Cromwell dismissed Parliament and declared himself the Protector of England, Powell openly denounced Cromwell. Cromwell was so concerned about the potential influence of Powell that he arrested him. Powell spent the next eight years in thirteen prisons before he finally was moved to the Fleet Jail in London. There he died in the eleventh year of his incarceration, October 27, 1671. His death was unusually blessed; the power and love of God filled his soul with enthusiasm in the miseries of a cell and in the agonies of his imprisonment.[3]

The footprints of Powell were seen all over Wales for years after his death. In addition, many of his Baptist descendants crossed the Atlantic to build up the Baptists of America, where true liberty of conscience was finally to be found.

LRO

---

[1]William Cathcart, *The Baptist Encyclopedia* (Philadelphia: Louis H. Everts, 1883), 932.

[2]Thomas Armitage, *A History of the Baptists* (New York: Bryan, Taylor, and Co., 1890), 600.

[3]Cathcart, 933.

October 28

A Stabilizing Pioneer

Scripture: Philippians 2:14-16

It is interesting to observe that as Baptist presence entered each of the states in America, the Lord provided some outstanding and unusual pioneers to lead the way. Such a man for Alabama was Alexander Travis. Alexander was born in South Carolina on August 23, 1790. He was converted and baptized into the membership of the Addiel Baptist Church when he was nineteen. He had made such growth in his spiritual life that he was licensed to preach when he was twenty. Three years later, Mr. Travis was ordained. As was the custom in that day, the young man of God served several churches simultaneously during the next few years.

In 1817 Reverend Travis moved to Alabama territory and invested the remainder of his ministry there. Tall, muscular of build, erect, handsome, and possessed of a good common school education, gentle and persuasive of manner, he would have been chosen a leader in any assembly. He was now in the flush of young manhood, being about twenty-seven. Though unassuming, he soon became popular, and was hailed as a preacher of remarkable force. Entering into the hard life of a pioneer, he soon gave evidence of his enterprising and administrative judgment as a citizen, while commanding a swaying influence as a preacher. He was founder of the town of Evergreen, to which he gave the name because of the magnificent foliage of the magnolia in the region.[1] He gathered a few believers about him, and established the Beulah Baptist Church in Conecuh County. That was to be the base of his ministry for the next thirty-five years.

On October 28, 1823, the Baptist State Convention of Alabama was formed. It had come about as an outgrowth of missionary interest that had been caused by the ministries of William Carey, Adoniram Judson, and the missionary challenge by the ubiquitous ministry of Luther Rice. Pastor Travis had already revealed missionary interest with outstanding leadership in missions, and thus at the first meeting of the Baptist State Convention, the man of God was appointed a domestic missionary. His labors in that realm were concurrent with those as pastor. "On . . . long and lonesome trips through the piney solitudes, Mr. Travis would now and then have to spend nights, with no food save the frugal luncheon which he might chance to have in his saddle-bags, and with no shelter but the tall pines. Tethering his horse that he might feed on the wiregrass and native peavines, the lonely missionary would sleep on a mattress of straw within the sound of howling wolves, and of yelping frogs in the distant lakes."[2]

He counted these privations as inconsequential if he could share the wonderful Gospel and solidify small congregations in the faith.

Difficulty developed in the matter of church planting in Montgomery, Alabama. The first effort in 1829 had failed because of factions in the congregation. In 1835 at the second effort to plant a church in Montgomery, the feud continued and created tension. The internal discord threatened to abort the new effort. A crisis was apparent, and Reverend Travis was asked to intervene. He consented, and upon arriving on the scene, he began a series of daily prayer meetings. He graciously declined to accept the hospitality and fellowship of any, for fear he might be considered biased. He continued the devotional meetings until they flamed into a spirit of deep love for the Savior. When the saints filled their vision with the Lord Jesus Christ, the problems began to dissolve. Folk began to weep, and confession of sin with the acknowledgment of mutual guilt, produced such a spirit of revival that the church was healed and began to grow.

At that time, Reverend Travis mounted his horse and returned to Beulah Baptist and his home near Evergreen. The man of God was called to his eternal home in 1852, but no one exceeded his godly influence in Alabama to that time.

I cannot help but think that many sickly local congregations could be healed today if only they prayed together and refocused upon the loveliness of our Lord and Savior.

DLC

---

[1]B. F. Riley, *A Memorial History of the Baptists of Alabama* (Philadelphis: Judson Press, 1923), 17.

[2]Ibid., 43.

October 29

A Church on the Move

Scripture: John 10:16

From time to time, modern day Americans express great interest in knowing how the West was won. Those who know Christ and rejoice in the impact that the Gospel has had historically in our republic ought to have interest in the subject of the expansion of the Gospel ministry into what was then the uncharted and wild West. To be sure there were Baptists among the first pre-revolutionary hunters and Indian fighters, those of the Daniel

Boone type. Squire Boone, brother of Daniel Boone, was a Baptist preacher, and others too were among that number. But it is rather the migration of settlers who moved westward and carved out farms from forests and planted towns and cities in the wilderness that come to mind. "Among the first Baptist preachers to permanently settle in the west was William Marshall. . . .Other preachers followed Marshall . . . including Joseph Barnett, John Whitaker, James Skaggs, Benjamin Lynn, all of whom were ordained, and John Gerrard, a licensed preacher. . . .[These] were responsible for forming the first Baptist church west of the mountains, the Severns Valley which was constituted June 18, 1781."[1]

Baptists had a decided edge in such expansion among the various religious denominations, for, "The Baptist preachers lived and worked exactly as did their flocks; their dwellings were little cabins with dirt floors and, instead of bedsteads, skin-covered pole-bunks; they cleared the ground, split rails, planted corn, and raised hogs on equal terms with their parishioners" (President Theodore Roosevelt, 111, 101).

Some of the migration came through what was known as "Traveling Churches." One such example is the church that had been known as the Upper Spottsylvania Church in Virginia.

It had as its pastor Lewis Craig, one of the most successful of the Virginia Baptist preachers. In 1781 Craig decided to remove to Kentucky, and so great was the attachment of his members to their minister, that a majority of them decided to migrate with him. Their organization was kept up on the march over the mountains, and their pastor preached again and again as they camped along the way, and there were several baptisms. On the route they came upon other Baptist emigrants from their own section and these Craig helped to form into a church. At Abington, Virginia, they heard the news of the surrender of Cornwallis at Yorktown, and they made the hills ring with the firing of their rifles in their glad rejoicing. In the midst of winter, after great hardship and danger, they arrived at their chosen destination, quickly made a clearing and established Craig's Station on Gilbert's Creek. Here on the second Sunday of December, 1781, they gathered for worship around the same old Bible they had used in Spottsylvania.[2]

Space does not permit a report, but the famed John Taylor's church too became a Traveling Church and relocated to the land of need.

These saints were not willing to become isolated enclaves of spiritual truth. They intended to become witnesses throughout the expanding West. As a result, as churches were established, they gather into associations to assist in evangelizing onward. The association, without impairing the autonomy of any local church, was meant to become an effort to accomplish collectively what a single church could not accomplish alone. Thus on September 30, 1785, six churches formed the Elkhorn Association, the first Baptist association formed west of the Allegheny Mountains. Four churches too far removed to become part of the Elkhorn Association, met on October 29, 1785, at Cox's Creek Church and formed the Salem Association,[3] and Kentucky soon became a hot-bed of Baptist enterprise.

Vision, fortitude, and sacrifice are words that describe our Baptist forebears who sought to win the West for Christ. What sacrifices are we willing to make for the ongoing of the Gospel into the heathen world where Christ has never been named? Thank God for our heritage, but what legacy will we leave the next generation? Surely if we cannot go to the heathen world without Christ, we ought to use our affluence to send others.

DLC

---

[1]William Warren Sweet, *Religion on The American Frontier* (New York: Cooper Square Publishers, 1964), 19.

[2]Ibid., 20-21.

[3]Ibid., 23.

October 30

Baptists Verses Slavery

Scripture: Acts 5:29; Romans 14:5b

Not only did many Baptists in the North oppose slavery, but a large number of Baptists in the South also held to the same position. John Leland, outstanding Baptist spokesman who led in obtaining the First Amendment to our national constitution, was very outspoken on the subject. He wrote, "The horrid work of bartering spirituous liquor for human souls, plundering the African coast, and kidnapping the people, brought the poor slaves into this state [Virginia]; and notwithstanding their usage is much better here than in the West Indies, yet human nature unbiased by education, shudders at the sight." He continued to decry the terrible iniquity of slavery![1] Nor can we forget the work of William H. Brisbane in purchasing land in Ohio and resettling his former slaves in freedom (Vol. 1:139-140).

Another outstanding example is David Barrow, eminent pioneer Baptist preacher of Virginia and Kentucky. He was born on October 30, 1753, and was baptized when he was seventeen. He began preaching the next year. "In 1754 he was ordained and became pastor of three Baptist churches in his native state. As he began an itinerant ministry in Virginia and North Carolina, he became the target of persecution. In 1778, he received an invitation to preach at the house of a gentleman who lived on Nansemond River, near the mouth of James River. A ministering brother accompanied him. They were informed, on their arrival, that they might expect rough usage; and so it happened. As soon as the hymn was given out, a gang of well dressed men came up to the stage, which had been erected under some trees, and sung one of their obscene songs. They then undertook to plunge both of the preachers. They plunged Mr. Barrow twice, pressing him into the mud, and holding him down, and nearly succeeded in drowning him. In the midst of their mocking, they asked him if he believed, and throughout, treated him with the most barbarous insolence and outrage. . . . The whole assembly was shocked, the women shrieked, but no one durst interfere, for about twenty stout fellows were engaged in this horrid measure."[2]

On yet another occasion, he was dragged from a house where he had been preaching and driven away brutally.

David Barrow had served in the army during the Revolutionary War, and it is believed that while contending for the liberty of the American colonies, he imbibed the notion of universal liberty. Upon this principle, he came to the conclusion that it was sinful to hold slaves. Accordingly, he freed all his Negroes, of which he owned a considerable number.[3]

In 1798 Barrows moved to Kentucky and accepted the call to pastor the Mount Sterling Baptist Church in Montgomery County. Here he became a very zealous advocate for the abolition of slavery. This led to a division of his church, the majority adhering to their pastor.[4] His opposition to slavery led to his church being expelled from the North District Association in Kentucky in 1806. Associations have prided themselves in never infringing upon the autonomy of a local church, but the members of the North District Association violated their own principle in the matter.

Following that action, Barrow became the catalyst in forming the Licking-Locust Association, and he became the motivator for many joining the Friends of Humanity movement. David Barrow passed into the presence of his Lord on November 14, 1819.

Generally Baptists have majored in preaching the Word of God, and thus social interests have never been their main thrust. Soul liberty insists that the individual believer must live with a tender conscience before his Lord. May we, led of the Holy Spirit through the principles of His Word, stand strong in these days upon moral issues to the glory of our Savior.

DLC

---

[1]John Leland, *The Writings of Elder John Leland* (New York: G. W. Wood, 1845), 94.

[2]James B. Taylor, *Virginia Baptist Ministers* (Richmond: Yale & Wyatt, 1838), 1:157.

[3]J. H. Spencer, *A History of Kentucky Baptists* (Cincinnati: J. R. Baumes, 1885), 1:105.

[4]William Cathcart, *The Baptist Encyclopaedia* (Philadelphis: Louis H. Everts, 1881), 1:83.

October 31

Fear None of These Things

Scripture: 2 Timothy 3:12; John 16:33

The era of John Bunyan's lifetime in England must have been most oppressive for our Baptist forebears. That was the period when the Baptist minister John James was martyred for the cause of Christ (Vol. 1:433-434). "The Baptists," says Sir James McIntosh, "suffered more than any others under Charles II, because they had publicly professed the principle of religious liberty."[1] A series of laws were passed to pressure all non-conformists to bow to the authority of the established state church. Some of the laws were aimed specifically at our Baptist forefathers.

"The first bill passed in 1662, to enforce uniformity in religion and to eject all the ministers from established churches who could not give unfeigned assent and consent to the articles of the Church of England, and of everything contained in the Book of Common Prayer, and also that would not declare upon oath that it was not lawful on any pretense whatever, to take up arms against the king. By this act many of the godliest men in England were driven from the established church, and among them were some Baptists who it seems had retained churches belonging to the establishment from the time of Cromwell."[2]

"The Conventicle Act of 1664 prohibited any person, over sixteen years of age, from being present at any meeting for religious worship, in any other manner than is allowed by the liturgy of the Church of England. The penalty for the first and second offenses was imprisonment or a fine. For the third offense, a heavy fine or banishment to the American Plantation; the name by which the American colonies were then known; and in case of their return from banishment before the expiration of their term they were to suffer death . . . ."[3]

The Five-Mile Act was established on October 31, 1665. This act required all nonconformist ministers to take an oath declaring it unlawful under any pretense to take up arms against the king, and that resistance to the king, or his officers was treasonable. Many ministers refused to take the oath, and as a penalty, they were forbidden to go within five miles of any city, or town, that sent members to Parliament, or within five miles of any place where they had formerly ministered. For every offense they were fined the equivalent of two hundred dollars.

To be sure, that era was all part of the dispensation of grace in which we are living. This era has been called by some, "the Day of man." In this, the Church age, God is allowing mankind to have his day, but it is apparent from time to time the Lord intervenes and brings mankind up short to get his attention. At any rate, during the time that Charles II ranted and raved against Bible-believing non-conformists, London was visited with the plague. It extended out into the surrounding country side. It is estimated that in London alone about one hundred thousand fell victims to its rages in less than a year. At that point an amazing event took place. For the most part, the clergymen of the Church of England fled for fear. At that time non-conformists, including many Baptist preachers, ministered to the suffering multitudes. In his *History of the English Baptists*, Joseph Ivimey, (pp. 357-358) quotes Daniel Neal, the historian of the Puritans, as saying, "that at a time both of war and of the plague, and when the nonconformist ministers were hazarding their lives in the service of the poor distressed congregations of London, the prime minister, Lord Clarendon and his creatures, instead of mourning for the sin of the nation and mediating a reformation of manners, should pour out all their vengeance upon nonconformists in order to make their condition insufferable."[4]

In some parts of the world today our brethren in the faith are suffering untold persecution. It is possible that such resistance could be experienced in our blessed land. Yea, the Scripture reminds us that "All who will live Godly in Christ Jesus shall suffer persecution," but, at such times, our Savior reassures us by telling us, "Be of good cheer; I have overcome the world."

May we dare to stand for truth regardless of the consequences.

DLC

---

[1]D. C. Haynes, *The Baptist Denomination* (New York: Sheldon, Blakeman & Co., 1856), 294.

[2]Richard B. Cook, *The Story of the Baptists* (Baltimore: H. M. Wharton & Co., 1886), 119-120.

[3]Ibid., 120-121.

[4]Ibid., 122.

November 1

Needed: Heaven-Sent Revival

Scripture: Psalm 85:6

The name of John Gano will long live in the annals of Baptist history in America. He was born in 1727 in Hopewell, New Jersey. Though his father was an ardent Presbyterian, through his study of the Word of God, John Gano was baptized and joined the Hopewell Baptist Church. When called of God to preach, Mr. Gano was ordained on March 29, 1754.[1] Seeing the great need in North Carolina, the Philadelphia Association paid the expenses of two young men of God to minister as itinerant preachers in that area. Rev. Gano was used of the Lord in assisting the Jersey Baptist Church in its establishment about 1755. The next few years found him in North Carolina. But facing great dangers from Indian attacks, he moved his family to New York City and became pastor of the First Baptist Church. You can read much of Rev. Gano in volumes one and two of this series.

Our attention is drawn however to the Jersey Baptist Church of Jersey Settlement in North Carolina. Most Bible-believing churches go through cycles of decline and of revival. The church at Jersey Settlement had reached a spiritual valley in its existence when, on November 1, 1874, the congregation called J. B. Richardson as its pastor. Hopes of instant growth were not to be realized. In fact, in two years the church had suffered a net loss of 97 members as discipline was brought to bear upon the congregation. When he felt the work was ready to respond to evangelism, Pastor Richardson invited Elder F. M. Jordan to come for meetings. All Heaven broke out! Let me share the evangelist's report of the meetings as related in his autobiography:

> Saturday night I took the car at Hillsboro and Sunday morning I was at old Jersey Church. The congregation had assembled when I arrived. I don't know that I ever felt or witnessed more of the presence and power of the Holy Spirit, both in the

> heart of saint and sinner. I preached a short sermon and many came forward for prayer. Strong men and women shouted and praised the Lord, and sinners cried for mercy. Some trembling mourners were rejoicing because of pardoned sin, and telling it around what a dear Savior they had found. The meeting continued nine days. We had a prayer meeting every morning at 10 . . . and by 9 o'clock the hill was lined with people, and inquiring souls were finding the Savior precious to their souls. . . . The whole community was moved by the power of the Holy Ghost. It was difficult to preach, indeed it did not seem to require much preaching; just pray and sing and rejoice. Sunday, the last day of the meeting, was a memorable day in the history of old Jersey Church.
>
> A large number had been received, and were to be baptized. There was a nice stream running near the church, through a body of large timber; a beautiful place for baptism. The brethren prepared two large tents near each other. The males prepared for baptism in one, and the females in the other. Brother Richardson and I were both to baptize. We marched out of our tent in double file, by the door of the sisters, when they fell in, in like manner. We marched down to the creek to the place appointed. Brother Richardson and I took our places in the middle of the creek. The deacons went in with us to convey the candidates to us, and then to the shore. And then alternately we began to baptize the candidates; and as we would baptize the columns would move up. The number baptized was sixty-seven. . . . It was a wonderful scene to behold. . . . There must have been between one and two thousand people present to witness the solemn scene. I would look up occasionally upon the vast assembly, and almost everybody seemed to be bathed in tears of love and gratitude to God for the wonderful displays of His grace and goodness.[2]

I cannot read such accounts without hungering to be in such a demonstration of spiritual power. How we need to pray that the Lord will again revive our churches and make of them soul-winning stations for His glory.

DLC

---

[1]William Cathcart, *The Baptist Encyclopedia* (Philadelphia: Louis H. Everts, 1881), 433.

[2]Garland A. Hendricks, *Saints and Sinners at Jersey Settlement* (Charlotte, NC: The Delmar Company, 1988), 80-81.

November 2

A Prophet From Texas

Scripture: Psalm 71:10-18

Texas has boasted of its size for years, but surely it never produced a man with a bigger heart than Lester Roloff who was born on June 28, 1914 in Dawson, Texas. Lester was saved when he was twelve years old at Shiloh Baptist Church. He completed his high schooling at Dawson, and then entered Baylor University in 1933. Before graduating in 1937, he pastored several Baptist churches. The next three years were invested at Southwestern Seminary in Fort Worth. During those years he was used of the Lord in the field of evangelism. On August 10, 1936, he married Miss Marie Brady. Lester pastored the Magnolia Baptist Church from 1941 to 1944 in Houston and experienced the blessings of Heaven. The Park Avenue Baptist Church in Corpus Christi extended him a call in 1944, and he invested the remainder of his life in service in that area.

A fire consumed the church building in October of 1944, and the congregation purchased new property and relocated. They also changed the name to Second Baptist Church, and Brother Roloff pastored from 1944 to 1951. Great growth was experienced, and a branch church was started. Lester Roloff began a radio ministry on May 8, 1944, and the *Family Altar Program*, was broadcast locally. This ministry flourished, and early in the 1980s it was aired nationally. Because he was considered controversial, some stations refused to broadcast his programs, but the Lord overruled, and the ministry expanded.

Pastor Roloff saw the need of Christian education, and in 1946 he founded the Park Avenue Christian Day School. The work was growing, and continual calls were coming for Brother Roloff to conduct evangelistic campaigns. Thus in April of 1951 he resigned as pastor of the Second Baptist Church to enter into full-time evangelism. At that juncture in his ministry, Roloff established the Roloff Evangelistic Enterprises, a non-profit organization.

In August of 1954 Lester Roloff broke all ties with the Southern Baptist Convention and declared himself an independent Baptist. The Alameda Baptist Church was founded in Corpus Christi with over a hundred members. Brother Roloff pastored there until 1961. His greatest work was yet in the future as he envisioned ministries to assist all who were in need. The Good Samaritan Rescue Mission was begun. The City of Refuge was established at Lexington, Texas, to assist alcoholics. In time that ministry was moved to Culloden, Georgia, on a 270 acre spread. The Lighthouse houseboat was taken down the Intercoastal Canal in 1958 to be located forty miles from Corpus Christi. It was used of God in serving those overcome with drugs, and could only be reached by plane or boat. The Peaceful Valley Home for retired elderly believers opened near Edinburg, Texas. The Anchor Home for Boys, located at Zapata, Texas, provided a capacity to serve three hundred wayward boys. The Bethesda Home for Girls in Hattiesburg, Mississippi, provided a home for girls in trouble. The Rebekah Home for Girls, located in Corpus Christi, Texas, was the largest of the homes. Fifteen hundred girls were helped in the first seven years of its existence. The Rebekah Christian Academy was established to provide an educational opportunity for these. How Satan has hated these ministries.

The major attack of Satan was launched upon the Rebekah Home for Girls. State Social Services could not help but realize their failure when they examined the records of this stellar Christian ministry. Roloff took the state's cast-offs, and many of these were transformed in salvation. The Welfare Department, in an effort to control, insisted upon licensing the home. Roloff recognized this for what it was and refused to comply. Room does not permit the rehearsal of events; Roloff was fined, imprisoned, and maligned, but he stood his ground on the First Amendment. In time the court system closed the ministry, but continual appeals were made to higher courts.

While this was going on, Brother Roloff continued to fly himself from meeting to meeting, rallying support for the ministry. On November 2, 1982, he boarded his plane to fly to a rally at Calvary Baptist Church in Kansas City, Missouri. At 10 A.M. the plane disappeared from radar screens, and apparently was lost in stormy weather about a hundred miles north of Houston. Sheriff's deputies found the wreckage. Though the battle was not over for the Roloff Enterprises, Lester entered into the rest of pure delight to be forever with His Lord.

May believers today be willing to stand on principle regardless of the cost.

DLC

November 3

Honoring the Untitled

Scripture: 1 Peter 5:1-4

The modern-day philosophy of "bigger is better" attached itself to the Baptist cause in the mid-twentieth century. Many Baptist parishioners developed the hero syndrome as they exalted gifted pastors whose vision seemed to be that of building a local church that embraced all of the population of their city. Bus ministries were established that reached far into the hinterland, and no consideration was ever given of planting sister churches that could better serve the extended areas. Soon competition began to emerge for the title, "Ten Largest Sunday schools" or "churches," and pastors became CEOs of burgeoning corporations. Surely we ought not to underestimate what the Lord would be pleased to do in and through a faithful Baptist church, but our goal must ever and only be the Will and Glory of the Lord.

Today I invite you to think with me of countless numbers of untitled, self-sacrificing pastors who have labored in small towns and rural areas to accomplish the Will of God and to bring honor to His name. Such a man was Richard M. Miller who was born in Sevier County, Tennessee, on November 3, 1815. When a teenager he came under conviction of sin and was converted. His family soon thereafter moved to Missouri, and he united with an area Baptist church. The young man was poorly educated, but he soon developed a desire to witness to those around him. In time, he began to attempt to preach, and he was overcome with a deep craving to minister the Gospel in the backwoods, as he said, knowing that his limited education disqualified him for the pastoral work of a town or city.[1]

The Union Baptist Church in Osage County, Missouri, called for his ordination on July 8, 1843. The ordination council, being fully satisfied concerning the doctrinal understanding of the candidate, recommended that the church ordain the brother. Elder Miller was married the following year to Miss Hornsby, a perfect co-laborer for what the Lord planned for the preacher. He entered into the work with full purpose of heart, and soon extended his labors into the counties of Johnson, Cass, Miller, Maries, and Pulaski.

None of these counties contained a single thriving metropolis, but the man of God saw the worth of each individual soul. He finally settled in the town of Pisgah in Pulaski County, Missouri in 1851, and through his faithful presentation of Divine truth, he was enabled to establish a strong Baptist church in 1852. Of course, it was necessary during his entire ministry to supplement with his own labor what little he was paid by the congregation. Elder Miller worked on his own farm to supply the necessities of life.

Three days before his death, while he was toiling in the fields, he was smitten with a paralysis. His wife found him on the ground helpless and almost speechless. In a short time, His Lord welcomed him into the presence of His Heavenly Father.

Across our nation today, tucked away in small towns and hamlets, are faithful men who are unknown by the world. These are preachers who have no agenda but the glory of the Lord. They are not lusting for a bigger pulpit, for they have discovered that the will of God is all that is important. These men must supplement their meager income by working on the side. You might find them driving a school bus or employed as a carpenter, but they gladly do it for the joy of preaching the Word of God to those who would otherwise not hear.

Hats off to these men of God! And hats off to their faithful wives who live sacrificially to assist their husbands in God's work. Perhaps you were raised in a rural area and remember that faithful couple who impacted your life so greatly for Christ. Why not drop them a note of thanks today, and it might be meaningful if you included a monetary expression of thanks. Praise God for a host of such godly men!

DLC

[1]R. S. Duncan, *A History of the Baptists in Missouri* (St. Louis: Scammell & Company, 1882), 537.

November 4

Infirmity in the Flesh

Scripture: 2 Corinthians 12:5-7b

Andrew Broaddus was born November 4, 1770, in Caroline County, Virginia. Through his mother's family, the Pryors, he was a descendent of Pocahontas. His educational opportunities were limited, but he had a great mind and was an eloquent speaker. At the age of eighteen, he was converted and baptized into the Baptist Church of Upper King and Queen.

He preached his first sermon on December 24, 1789, in a home where the noted Robert S. Semple also preached on that occasion. He was ordained October 16, 1791, in the same church where he was baptized. Among the first churches he served were Burruss and Bethel in Caroline County, and the Fredericksburg church. He succeeded John Waller, one of the imprisoned preachers, at the Burruss Church. Although Mr. Broaddus was known by few outside of Virginia, he received numerous invitations to become pastor of many large churches in major cities. Some of these churches were the First Baptist Church in Boston in 1811; the First Baptist Church in Philadelphia, in 1811; the First Baptist Church in Baltimore, in 1819; the New Market Street Baptist Church in Philadelphia in 1824; and the First Baptist Church in New York City in 1832. However, he turned them all down to devote his time and talents to the services of country churches, his Baptist Association, and literary pursuits. It was said that he possessed a delicate nervous structure, unfitting him for confronting difficulties. This involved large crowds.

In his course of life, he had the sad experience of burying three wives. He had both an embarrassing and interesting experience regarding his second marriage. There was a great deal of gossip and a question about the legality of this marriage. It was all put to rest by having a second ceremony. The *Fredericksburg Virginia Herald* of March 13, 1816, reported this: "Remarried in the City of Washington, on Tuesday the 8th by the Rev. Obadiah Brown, the Rev. Andrew Broaddus and Mrs. Jane Broaddus of Virginia. This connection which has made so much noise in Virginia is now completely legalized according to the law of Maryland and that part of the District of Columbia which formerly belonged to Maryland."[1]

The record shows that he had at least nine children by the four wives. His son, Andrew Broaddus, Jr., succeeded him in the pastorate of Salem and Upper King and Queen, in which he continued for 43 years. One of his daughters married a preacher from Essex County. Thus he was blessed with a good family.

His literary work was very productive and of high quality. He wrote a small volume entitled *The Age of Reason and Revolution,* published in 1795, which was a reply to Thomas Paine's attack on Christianity. In 1816 he published *A Bible History, with Occasional Notes, to Explain and Illustrate Difficult Passages.* He also wrote an excellent *Catechism for Children.* He wrote, collected, and published *Sacred Ballads, The Dover Selections,* and *Virginia Selections.* These were hymns in popular use at that time. He also wrote and published a series of *Controversial Arguments Against Alexander Campbell* and was a frequent contributor to the *Religious Herald.*[2]

Pastor Broaddus did not allow his delicate nervous system to be a stumbling block but used it as a stepping stone. He was head and shoulders above those of his generation. From the very beginning, he was a popular preacher. He excelled in exposition of the Scriptures. Some said his greatest sermons were not preached on special occasions or rallies but regular sermons in his pulpit. Dr. Broaddus succeeded Dr. Robert Semple as moderator of the Dover Association of Churches and continued in that office without a single interruption until 1840. He was a very brilliant man with unusual intellectual gifts. He was also a man so kind and so considerate that young preachers felt at home in his presence.[3] He was a man of genuine faith and a biblical scholar.

Dr. Andrew Broaddus died December 1, 1848, and is buried at Old Salem Church near Sparta in Caroline County.

What is our attitude and practice toward any infirmities we may have? Can we make them stepping stones and use them for God's glory as well?

EGC

[1]Oscar H. Darters, *The History of Fredericksburg Baptist Church*, (Richmond: Garrett and Massie, 1960), 52.

[2]William Cathcart, *The Baptist Encyclopedia*, (Philadelphia: Louis H. Everts, 1881), 138.

[3]W.O. Turpin, *Words spoken to the Dover Association*, Minutes 1883.

November 5

Faithful Unto Death

Scripture: Matthew 10:22-28

Believers in the United States of America enjoy complete religious freedom. We little understand the trials that our counterparts around the world have endured and still experience. Unspeakable suffering among Christian people is experienced in these early days of the twenty-first century in Africa. Yet today's liberal news media seems to be oblivious to any and all attacks against followers of Christ. Little was known by Americans of the religious persecution endured in Russia under the hands of the Communist regime. However, recent discoveries have unearthed the facts that those who professed faith in the Lord Jesus Christ in Russia suffered greatly under the hand of atheistic leaders. It is clear too that the non-registered Baptists of the Council of Evangelical (fundamental) Baptist Churches were a special target of the communists. As one becomes acquainted with the imprisonments, tribulations, and even martyrdom of Bible-believing Baptists in the Soviet Union during those godless regimes, one exclaims involuntarily the words of Hebrews 11:38: These are Bible believers ". . . Of whom the world was not worthy." Surely Revelation 2:10 was a reality to the multiplied thousands of persecuted Baptists in the Soviet Union in those days: "Fear none of those things which thou shalt suffer. . . be thou faithful unto death, and I will give thee a crown of life."

Nikolai Khmara was born in 1916. We know little concerning his life, but his wife's name was Maria, and the couple had four children. In July of 1963, when Nikolai was forty-seven years of age, he came personally to know Jesus

Christ and the divine forgiveness of sins. With a burning heart for the salvation of others, he soon opened his home for worship services of the local Baptist congregation. Within a matter of weeks, on November 5, 1963, Nikolai was arrested and incarcerated until his appearance before the tribunal. His actual trial extended from December 24 to December 27, 1963, and he was found guilty. His sentence decreed that Nikolai should serve a three-year term.

The condition of the prisons in Russia during that period defied description. Each of the prisons had isolation cells where physical and psychological pressures were brought to bear. One such prison had a cell for special punishment called the Afrikanka. The cell was exceedingly small, and the floor was covered with four-inch iron spikes laid out in checkerboard fashion. The spikes were twelve inches apart, making it difficult to walk and impossible to sit down. Being in the Northern reaches of the Soviet Union, the cold was almost unbearable. Little sleep could be managed, for the prisoner would have to lean or squat against the wall. Eventually prisoners would collapse and fall onto the spikes. The cell was called the Afrikanka, for when prisoners were released from the cell, they would come out black with bruises and dried blood.

One can only imagine the treatment that Nikolai endured, for his wife Maria received a telegram on January 11, 1964, requesting she make arrangements to pick up the dead body of her husband. When the broken-hearted widow went to secure the body, she found it covered with bruises and burn marks on the hands and feet. Nikolai's stomach had been punctured, and his tongue had been cut out.[1]

It was only six years later on November 14, 1969, that Aleksandr Solzhenitsyn described his land as a "sick society." In a letter to the writer's union of the Russian Federated Republic, he wrote, "In this time of crisis of our seriously sick society, you are not able to suggest anything good, only your hate-vigilance." Ten years later on April 27, 1979, Reverend Georgi Vins, imprisoned Russian Baptist preacher, and four other Russian dissidents were exchanged for two Russian spies that had been held in America. Persecution was a way of life for the Baptists in Russia! But most importantly, the cause of Christ continued to expand in the Soviet Union.

America has long experienced religious freedom, but would our type of Christianity endure the persecutions that befell the Russian saints? It is a question worth asking ourselves.

DLC

[1]Georgi Vins, Compiler, *Let the Waters Roar* (Grand Rapids, MI: Baker Book House, 1989), 262.

November 6

Contrasting Two Evangelists

Scripture: 1 Timothy 1:18-19

The story of Elijah Baker, his imprisonment, deportation, and relocation from Virginia to Delaware has been told in volume 1, pp. 495-497 of this set, but now let me tell you the rest of the story. It was in 1778 that Elijah Baker was dropped off on the shore of Delaware after having been banished to a privateer from his home state of Virginia. Immediately he set out preaching the Gospel in his new environment. The following year he was joined by Philip Hughes, also from Virginia. The two men were influential in founding twenty-one churches in Virginia, Maryland, and Delaware, and spent much time in visiting them, as fathers do their children.[1] The Salisbury Association was also organized by those two men.

Mr. Baker's life story is set forth in several volumes that depict the history of the early Baptists in Virginia. One of the volumes quotes a letter from Dr. Robert Lemon, for years Moderator of the Salisbury Association. Dr. Lemon reported the death of Elijah Baker in his home on November 6, 1798. He wrote, "In Mr. Baker I found the Israelite indeed, the humble Christian; the preacher of the gospel in the simplicity of it; and the triumphant saint, in his last moments. In his preaching he was very plain, and generally experimental: always very express on the doctrine of regeneration; never entering upon the doctrines by which he conceived he should give offence to one or the other. In his last illness, I attended his bed-side, day and night, for three weeks; and had many most agreeable conversations with him, on the glorious things of the kingdom of Christ. He retained his senses to the last minute; and seemed rather translated, than to suffer pain in his dissolution. Death was to him as familiar in his conversation, as if he talked of an absent friend from whom he expected a visit."[2]

Morgan Edwards provides an account of Reverend Philip Hughes, and I must share that as well. Edwards said, "Rev. Philip Hughes shares in the praise of Mr. Baker, as they were fellow-laborers in most of the good that was done in this and other states. He was born in Colver County, November 28, 1750, bred a Churchman, avowed his present sentiments, August 10, 1773, when he was baptized by Rev. David Thompson, called to the ministry in Rowanty Church, was ordained at an Association held in Virginia, August 13, 1776."

How thrilling to read of the blessings in those early days among the churches of Delaware. They believed that Christ had tasted death for every man. They were missionary-minded. They were evangelistic. But in 1856 a drastic change took place. For the first time, the minutes of the Association refer to the group as the "Delaware *Old School* Baptist Association." Some pastors had embraced hyper-Calvinism and had followed that road to its logical conclusion – antinomianism. They lost their zeal to see souls saved These changed the Baptist image from aggressive evangelistic to becoming what historically came to be called "Primitive Baptists." History verifies that evangelism ultimately dies when five-point Calvinism is embraced.

The historian, Richard Cook, wrote as follows: "Rev. Philip Hughes, who, after laboring so zealously in the cause of missions, embraced Antinomian views, and thus became widely separated from his former companion in labor, Mr. Baker."[3] Following his adopting the hyper-Calvinistic position, his name is hardly mentioned by the historian Semple, and not at all by Taylor. Semple has a brief footnote decrying his Antinomianism.

Dr. J. D. Fulton once said that "A Baptist Church is an illuminated edition of the New Testament."[4] That being the case, our churches ought to train our membership in witnessing and soul-winning for the Lord adds to the church when the saints are faithful. In these days of spiritual declension in America, may the Lord revive and burden us to go with Christ after the lost!

DLC

---

[1]Richard B. Cook, *The Early and Later Delaware Baptists* (Philadelphia: American Baptist Publication Society, 1880), 23.

[2]James B. Taylor, *Virginia Baptist Ministers* (Richmond: Yale & Wyatt, 1838), 1:113.

[3]Cook, 96.

[4]Ibid., 8.

November 7

A Diatribe That Produced A Deacon

Scripture: Acts 5:38-39

Some would call it an audacious spirit! Morgan Edwards, the historian, preferred to refer to it as the preternatural and invisible hand of God. But name it what you will, the Separate Baptists were wonderfully used in the great spiritual awakening in the South at the close of the eighteenth century. Without great theological training, the Separate Baptist preachers were used of God to move hearts, and this resulted in an elevated society that ultimately produced religious freedom.

The life of Dutton Lane is a case in point. Dutton was born on November 7, 1732, near Baltimore, Maryland. In the course of time, the family moved to Virginia. It was as a young adult in 1758 that Dutton was soundly converted under the preaching of Shubal Stearns, father of the Separatist Baptists. Shortly after being baptized, Dutton began to preach. As you would surmise, Dutton Lane was not educated for the ministry, but he possessed a robust constitution, a strong voice, and an undying enthusiasm. The Lord coupled those attributes together to produce a dynamic preacher. One would have to conclude that his ministry was extraordinary.

The year following his conversion, Dutton Lane began to preach just north of the Dan River. Other Separate Baptist preachers also entered the neighborhood, and soon a large number of believers were assembled. Up to that time, Mr. Lane had not been ordained, and as a result, Daniel Marshall came to the area to administer the Ordinance of Baptism. On the 4th Friday of August 1760, Philip Mulkey joined with Daniel Marshall in constituting these believers into the first Separate Baptist Church in Virginia. Traveling preachers continued to minister to the congregation until Dutton Lane was ordained on October 11, 1764. At that time, Reverend Lane assumed the pastorate. One must keep in mind that serving as pastor did not preclude a continuing evangelistic ministry by those early Separate Baptist pastors.

Though he was never imprisoned for preaching without a state-church license, Dutton Lane suffered continual threats made upon him. Some of these accounts have been mentioned in the first two volumes of this set. However, in this entry I would like to share the wonderful dealing of God through His servant in Lunenburg County. In 1758 as the young preacher held forth the Word of Truth, Joseph Williams, a magistrate, interrupted the service and charged him not to return there to preach again. The preacher assured the magistrate that there were other places where he could preach without such provocation. He brought his message to a close, and then wished peace to those who had gathered. But before leaving, he addressed the magistrate and said: "Little, Sir, as you now think it, my impressions tell me that you will become a Baptist, a warm espouser of the cause which you now persecute."[1]

Ten years later Samuel Harris and Jeremiah Walker preached again in that vicinity, and a number were saved and baptized, and united with the Nottoway Church, the nearest church to them. However in 1770, the Lunenburg County Court granted the petition of dissenters for a place of public worship on their land. The following year 108 members of Nottaway were dismissed to form the Meherrin Baptist Church. Interestingly, Joseph Williams, the magistrate, had been one of the petitioners to the county court, and he became a deacon in the newly formed church[2]. Jeremiah Walker served the church as pastor until a prominent citizen, John Williams, a former sheriff of the county, was ordained and became pastor. In time the Meherrin church became the mother of churches, and from its membership came outstanding preachers such as Elijah Baker, James Shelburne, and John King.

Expository gems heard in Baptist churches today are excellent for feeding the saints, but we could surely use some evangelistic fire in our midst once again. May the Lord raise up some young daring evangelists in this twenty-first century.

DLC

---

[1]Morgan Scott, *History of the Separate Baptist Church* (Indianapolis: Hollenbeck Press, 1901), 181.

[2]Garnett Ryland, *The Baptists of Virginia* (Richmond, VA: The Virginia Baptist Board of Missions and Education, 1955), 54-55.

November 8

The Man Who Married A Community

Scripture: Colossians 3:23

Some preachers do not like to be addressed as Reverend. This stems from the fact that the only reference to the word reverend in the Scriptures is to God. That was the case with Norman Grady Lemmons who began his ministry as an evangelist and considered himself an evangelist throughout his years as pastor.

Grady Lemmons went to Shelby, North Carolina, in September of 1941 to conduct a tent revival. He had previously been in the town for an eight-week revival at the Martin Street Methodist Church. During that time the Holy Spirit impressed upon his heart the need for an independent Baptist church in the area. At the close of the four-week tent meeting, the Davidson Memorial Baptist Church was organized with 34 charter members. Some of these were converts from the tent meetings.[1] Grady served as pastor for 33 years during which time the church grew to over 750 members.

His life span of 79 year began on November 8, 1909, when he was born in Westminster, South Carolina. He was fourth in a family of seven children born to Palmer and Lizzie Lemmons. His life with God began in 1938 at the age of 29. The Holy Spirit spoke to Grady's heart through a radio message by Evangelist J. Harold Smith one morning at his home in Spartanburg, South Carolina. He was saved while walking down Johnston Street toward work that very morning.[2]

The Lord called Grady to preach, and he began correspondence study from the Moody Bible Institute in Chicago, Illinois. Those courses, along with independent study and experience, helped to hone his preaching skills. He was not an ordinary man and did not fit any particular mold. He was a humble man, but others saw the gifts that God had given this magnanimous individual.

Grady's three sons were born in his hometown. His first wife, the mother of his children, died at an early age, and the three boys lived with different relatives. After eight years, the family was reunited in 1939 when Grady married Elmina Riddle. Elmina never had children of her own but became a wonderful mother to his boys. Her work at a textile mill provided financial support during the years of the Great Depression until the church could better support them.

During Grady's tenure at Davidson Memorial Baptist Church, he had a radio broadcast for over 25 years, helped organize seven churches, and preached several revivals during each year. However, he was seldom out of his own pulpit on the Lord's Day. In the course of time, the church built a beautiful complex on a main street in town. Over 100 men were in the men's Bible class every Sunday morning. The 100-voice choir captivated many with beautiful singing that filled the auditorium.

The highlight of Davidson Memorial Baptist Church was the annual preachers' fellowship. The church would be filled to capacity each year with preachers from all parts of the country. At least 100 preachers and their wives attended as well as many others who traveled great distances to enjoy the informal preaching and inspirational singing that uplifted Christ. The church underwrote the expenses of the week of fellowship. Grady did not schedule preachers in advance for the preachers' fellowship. He expected those preachers who attended to share in the ministry. As a result, preachers came prepared to preach. Grady would come by and whisper to a preacher, "Got your guns loaded?" That was his invitation to preach. Friendships that lasted a lifetime were made in those old-fashioned meetings.

During this day when everything is so scheduled, it is refreshing to remember those days with Brother Lemmons who relied on the Holy Spirit to direct him. He was a prince of a man who loved God. His children called him blessed and were proud to be part of his great ministry in the small city of

Shelby. Brother Lemmons was laid to rest on July 15, 1988, in the community he loved and into which he poured his life.

DCB

[1]June 28, 2004, telephone conversation with Paul Lemmons, son of Grady Lemmons.

[2]1970 article on Davidson Memorial Baptist Church's 29th Anniversary.

November 9

Campbellism Exposed

Scripture: Isaiah 59:19; 1 John 4:1

One of the saddest chapters of the history of Baptists in America is that which was written by the reintroduction of the heresy of baptismal regeneration by Alexander Campbell. With great charisma, Campbell claimed that people must be dipped or damned! The center of the conflict raged in Kentucky, Virginia, Ohio, and Pennsylvania, and it boiled over into other states as well. Withstanding this incursion of heresy stood three outstanding Baptist leaders: J. B. Jeter of Virginia, Silas M. Noel of Kentucky, and A. P. Williams of Missouri. We shall center our attention in this entry on the latter of the three.

Alvin Peter Williams was born in St. Louis County, Missouri on March 13, 1813. His father was a Baptist pastor, and he trained his son early in the Word of God. At the age of sixteen the lad was converted, and amazingly, he was ordained when he was only seventeen. He had no formal training, and primarily ministered in churches that required him to do manual labor to support his family. Early in his ministry he was challenged by John Mason Peck to enter into personal Bible study, and despite his work schedule, he found time to study the Greek and Hebrew languages while riding horseback to preaching assignments. A. P. Williams was blessed with great natural gifts. His retentive mind, allowed him to memorize much of the New Testament. It was said that if the New Testament was destroyed, he could reproduce it. His logic was masterful. His expositions of the Scripture were compelling. His cheerful disposition coupled with boldness, fitted him well to deal with controversy. All of these gifts earned for him the title, the Andrew Fuller of America. That in itself was a great honor when one considers the impact of Andrew Fuller upon the theology of Great Britain and modern-day Baptists.

A. P. Williams pastored a number of churches in Missouri, and established three churches. He was primarily known, however, for his itinerant ministry in central and western Missouri. He was a gifted evangelist, and in the course of his ministry he baptized in excess of 3,000 people. At one time he was indited for daring to preach without taking the controversial test oath. In 1867 the Supreme Court ruled the act unconstitutional, but Reverend Williams was never tried in the matter.

The baptismal regeneration heresy arose in Missouri due to the preaching of one, Moses Lard, who continually challenged the Baptist position of believer's baptism. He had been overwhelmed by the fallacious teaching of Alexander Campbell, and he seemed well on the way to carrying many away with him into spiritual oblivion. But the Lord had prepared the God-gifted scholar for this very situation. Williams wrote a significant book entitled *Campbellism Exposed.* The volume proved to be unanswerable, and the danger subsided. The General Baptist Association also requested their champion to write a volume on *The Lord's Supper*, and that work also was blessed of God among His children.

Reverend Williams' accomplishments were acknowledged as he was granted a doctorate by Bethel College. On November 9, 1868, the Lord called his servant home. The Baptists of Missouri greatly grieved over their loss.

As we think of men such as A. P. Williams, there is danger for young pastors to believe that they too can preach and win the world for Christ without formal training. They are introduced to the history of a man such as A. P. Williams. Then Charles Haddon Spurgeon also comes to mind. However men such as Williams and Spurgeon were specially gifted of God. The Lord prepared them and brought them to the kingdom for such a time as they were needed. But the usual plan of the Lord is for a man to study to show himself approved unto God, and this is best accomplished in a formal setting. We thank God for fundamental Bible colleges in our day where average young men can be trained theologically to become superior preachers.

In the life of A. P. Williams we are also mindful that when the enemy shall come in like a flood, the Spirit of the

Lord shall lift up a standard against him. We thank the Lord for such men, and ask of Him that we might too know His will as to how and where he would have us serve.

DLC

November 10

The Hinges of Opposition

Scripture: Revelation 3:7-8

Someone has said that the door to the room of success turns on the hinges of opposition. William Cate experienced both opposition and heaven-sent success. Born June 17, 1807 in Jefferson County, Tennessee, William was the sixth son of a family of eight sons and three daughters born to John and Mary Cate. (Two of William's brothers, Michael and Noah, also became Baptist preachers.) He grew up in east Tennessee with few opportunities for formal education. William and his wife, Mary, followed the Lord in believer's immersion on November 10, 1837. William was ordained to the gospel ministry January 24, 1840, and a year later began his labors as a missionary-at-large within the Holston Association. After one year of service, he reported, "[P]rotracted meetings held, 23; sermons preached, 200; addresses delivered, about the same; number of conversions witnessed, 500."

In 1842 he organized churches in Jonesboro, Elizabethton, and Blountsville. In later years he also organized churches in New Salem, Rogersville, and Bristol. From 1842 until his death on February 2, 1860, he served as pastor of the Jonesboro church. At the close of his life, the membership of the church numbered 170. In addition to his pastoral labors, he continued to work as an evangelist and as a fundraiser for various missionary and educational ministries. Having no children of his own, he devoted himself to helping in the education of other people's children, especially girls.

When Cate's ministry began, the Baptist cause in east Tennessee was floundering. The workers were few and discouraged. Cate's example of courage and success, combined with widespread revivals in 1841 and 1845, breathed new life into the work.

But Cate's tireless activity provoked opposition too. As William Keen said, "No man ever stirred up so much interest, or aroused such fierce opposition, or made so deep an impression upon the people as did William Cate. He was a full Baptist, and preached the gospel fearlessly, attacking the very stronghold of the enemy. From the very start his preaching was a sensation. He proclaimed the duty of Baptists to go up and possess the land, and led the way. But every step of the way was opposed and every foot of the territory was stoutly contested by Pedobaptist opponents. Every day was a battle, but every battle was a victory; for the hand of the Lord was with him."[1]

One cannot attribute these victories to a forceful appearance or a strong voice-he had neither. His preaching style was not what was considered popular, though he was popular as a preacher. He was not a professional evangelist, but he was nonetheless an effective soul winner. Although he lacked the advantages of education, he had a trained mind and a persevering spirit. "[I]f he failed today, he was sure that he would succeed tomorrow."[2]

Among Cate's opponents in Jonesboro was Wm. G. Brown Parson Brownlow, a preacher, politician, and newspaper editor. This Parson used the pages of his newspaper to mock Cate, and wrote a whole book attacking the Baptists. The mean spirit of these attacks helped to expose the weakness of Brownlow's arguments. Cate was also attacked for his fundraising efforts.

On the Dumplin Church records of December 7, 1851, is the copy of a "notice" posted on a tree close by the church-house and addressed to "Mr. William Cate." The notice reads as follows: "It is generally believed you had better not come to this camp-meeting at Dumplin, lest you cause sinners to be lost; for they have no confidence in you. They believe you are not seeking souls, but money. Now for the cause of God and your good, you had better stay away." It is gratifying to note that the Dumplin Church branded the notice as a "base falsehood and a foul slander," and endorsed Elder Cate as a "successful minister of the Gospel and an efficient agent in raising funds for benevolent purposes."[3]

In 1860 Cate traveled west to Fayetteville, Arkansas, to visit relatives, hold meetings and explore the possibility of further labors in the West. Upon arrival he contracted pneumonia and departed to be with the Lord on February 2.

DRP

---

[1] Burnett, J. J., *Sketches of Tennessee's Pioneer Baptist Preachers*, (Nashville, TN: Press of Marshall & Bruce Company, 1919), 101-106, http://www.knoxcotn.org/tnbaptists/cate william.htm

[2] Ibid.

[3] Ibid.

November 11

Christ's Kingdom is Not of This World

Scripture: John 18:36; Matthew 22:21

The Word of God makes it clear that God formed only three institutions. God first established the family unit, the home. Secondly, in Genesis 9:6 the Lord provided capital punishment as the foundation of human government. In the New Testament God ordained the church which our Lord Jesus purchased with His own blood. Israel in the Old Testament was to be a theocracy, but through rebellion and unbelief, Israel was temporarily set aside. We do well to understand that God's purpose today is not accomplished with the intertwining of church and state. God is not building a theocracy upon the earth today, but rather, He is calling out a people for His name. Confusion at this point has caused, and continues to produce great problems. The Lord God does not mean the state to be the right hand of the church, nor does He mean to use the state to recruit men and women and conscript them into the church. The two units are to exist side by side with each serving its own capacity. The state is to deal with the secular while the church deals with the spiritual.

The early pilgrims in America emulated the philosophy of the Reformation. They failed to understand God's purpose in government. As a result, religious freedom was not allowed. Massachusetts was extremely cruel to any other than those who were part of the state-church. The first two

Quakers to arrive in New England landed in Boston in July 1656. Both were women. Immediately arrested, they were imprisoned, interrogated, and inspected for signs of witchcraft. Their Quaker tracts were burned by the hangman. After five weeks in jail, with windows boarded lest anyone hear their heretical views, they were ordered back to Barbados.[1]

As those holding Baptist convictions multiplied in number, they fled or were banished and established the colony of Rhode Island. Total religious freedom was granted there to every citizen. In 1651 Obadiah Holmes had been severely beaten for daring to visit and encourage a Baptist friend in Massachusetts (Vol. 1:366-367). Yet in 1656, the contiguous Colonies urged Rhode Island to join them, and crush the Quakers; but she returned this answer: "We shall strictly adhere to the foundation principles on which the colony was first settled: i.e., liberty of conscience in religious concernments."[2]

Revealing the reality of this conviction, when the legislature of Georgia, in 1784, passed a law "giving three-pence per pound of moneys in the treasury to the support of any minister that might be called to his parish by thirty families,"[3] the Baptist Association of Georgia protested the law, and led in its repeal. Virginia offered patronage under the Assessment Bill of November 11, 1784, which stated "That the people of this Commonwealth, according to their respective abilities, ought to pay a moderate tax or contribution annually for the support of the Christian religion."[4] The bill allowed each citizen to designate which denomination should receive his taxes. However, the Baptists saw it for what it was. They recognized that the state has no right to meddle in ecclesiastical affairs, and thus the Baptists of Virginia led the way in opposing and ultimately defeating that measure.

The historic Baptist position, which our American Republic finally adopted, assures that no man's religious opinions shall affect his civil capacity. Man has total freedom to worship as he pleases with the proviso that if his religious acts disturb the peace or in any way violate the law of the land, he shall be punished by civil authorities. Thank God for the understanding of our Baptist forefathers! Let freedom ring!

DLC

---

[1]William G. McLoughlin, *Rhode Island a Bicentennial History* (New York: W. W. Norton & Company, 1978), 35.

[2]George C. Lorimer, *The Great Conflict* (Boston: Lee and Shepherd, 1877), 66.

[3]Ibid., 66.

[4]Rhys Isaac, *The Transformation of Virginia* (New York: W. W. Norton & Co., 1988), 284.

November 12

Bunyan's Heroic Wife

Scripture: Luke 18:1-8

Three years after the death of his first mate, John Bunyan took Elizabeth to be his wife in 1659. What an outstanding lady she proved to be. On November 12, 1660, at Lower Samsell in South Bedfordshire, Bunyan was brought before a local magistrate and charged with preaching without the authorization of the Church of England. Being unwilling to promise that he would cease his ministry, he was imprisoned. Unbelievable hardship began in earnest for Elizabeth. Throughout the next twelve long years of his imprisonment, Elizabeth cared for his four children from his first wife as though they were her very own. During his imprisonment, Elizabeth made three tedious trips to London to plead with the judges for Bunyan's release. Surely that action caused Bunyan to meditate upon the importunate widow whom the Savior mentioned in Luke chapter eighteen, and to write with his wife in mind. The report of Elizabeth's courage and daring inspired Bunyan with great admiration for her. Her faithfulness doubtless also caused the man of God to write his will leaving everything he possessed to her.

The trip from Bedford to London was difficult for Elizabeth, but she appeared before the judges and presented her husband's cause with great honor. John Bunyan recorded the events as follows:

> **Elizabeth**: My Lord, I make bold to come again to your lordship to know what may be done with my husband.

Judge: Woman, I told thee before I could do thee no good, because they have taken that for a conviction which thy husband spoke at the sessions; and unless there be something done to undo that, I can do thee no good.

Elizabeth: My Lord, he is kept unlawfully in prison. They clapped him up before there was any proclamation against the meetings. The indictment also is false. Besides they never asked him whether he was guilty or not of preaching without a license. Neither did he confess the indictment.

Another judge: Will your husband leave preaching? If he will do so, then send for him.

Elizabeth: My, Lord, he dares not leave preaching so long as he can speak . . . . He desires to live peaceably and to follow his calling that his family may be maintained. Moreover, my lord, I have four small children that cannot help themselves, one of which is blind, and we have nothing to live upon but the charity of good people. I am but a stepmother to them, having not been married to my husband yet two full years. Being young and unaccustomed to such things, I became dismayed at the news of his imprisonment and fell into labor, and so continued for eight days, and then was delivered, but my child died.

Judge: Alas! poor woman, you make poverty your cloak. I understand that your husband is maintained better by running up and down a-preaching than by following his calling. What is his calling?

Some of the company: A tinker, my lord.

Elizabeth: Yes, and because he is a tinker and a poor man, therefore he is despised and cannot have justice. . . . As for preaching, he preacheth nothing but the Word of God. . . . God hath owned him, and done much good by him.

Judge: God! Your husband's doctrine is the doctrine of the devil.

Elizabeth: My lord, when the righteous Judge shall appear, it will be known that his doctrine is not the doctrine of the devil.

Judge: I am sorry, woman, that I can do thee no good.

With this Elizabeth broke into tears, not too much because they were so hard-hearted against me and my husband, but to think what a sad account such poor creatures will have to give at the coming of the Lord, when they shall there answer for all things whatsoever they have done, whether it be good or bad.[1]

May God increase such godly ladies to stand beside their serving husbands. Surely we concur with Solomon that when such godly ladies are found, "...her husband...praiseth her."

DLC

[1]Edith Deen, Great Women of the Christian Faith (Westwood, NJ: Barbour and Company, 1959), 350-351.

November 13

The Land of the Free

Scripture: Psalm 33:8-18

Somehow the average American envisions our Land as always having been The Land of the Free. Surely those Pilgrims who came to our shores seeking religious freedom would establish a new land where freedom would reign supreme! At least, this is what most Americans think. They are often time shocked to realize that this was not true. The Pilgrims rather envisioned a theocracy, and to accomplish that goal, they planted a State church. To be sure the State church in England led to their trials and ultimate departure from Great Britain, but they perpetrated the same error in the new land from which they had fled in the old.

In 1620 the Pilgrims landed, but others soon began to come, and among them were some Baptists. Soon the Pilgrims learned that coercion would not convert Baptists to the Puritan theological persuasion. They would have to be dealt with in a different manner. Thus it was on November 13, 1644, the General Court framed and passed the following act:

> Forasmuch as experience hath plentifully and often proved, that since the first rising of the Anabaptists, about one hundred years since, they have been the incendiaries of the commonwealths, and the infectors of persons in main matters of religion, and the troublers of churches in all places where they have been, and that they who have held the baptizing of infants unlawful, have usually held other errors or heresies together therewith, though they have (as other heretics use to do) concealed the same till they spied out a fit advantage and opportunity to vent them, by way of question or scruple; and whereas divers of this kind have since our coming into New England appeared amongst ourselves, some whereof (as other before them) denied the ordinance of magistracy, and the lawfulness of making war, and others the lawfulness of magistrates, and their inspection into any branch of the first table; which opinions, if they should be connived at by us, are like to be increased among us, and so must necessarily bring guilt upon us, infection and trouble to the churches, and hazard to the whole commonwealth; it is ordered and agreed, that if any person or persons, within the jurisdiction, shall either openly condemn or oppose the baptizing of infants, or go about secretly to seduce others from the appropriation or use thereof, or shall purposefully depart the congregation at the ministration of the ordinance, or shall deny the ordinance of magistracy, or their lawful right and authority to make war, or to punish the outward breaches of the first table, and shall appear to the Court willfully and obstinately to continue therein after due time and means of conviction, every such person or persons shall be sentenced to banishment.[1]

Mr. Backus goes into the corrections necessary to explain that the effort of the Pilgrim officials to tie the Baptist cause historically into the few radical Anabaptists was totally fallacious. He deals as well with the illogical efforts of otherwise virtuous men with so distorting truth.

Be that as it may, even after the acceptance of the Edict of Toleration in Great Britain in 1689, American citizens in Massachusetts were still determined to run a closed shop. Elsewhere in this volume, along with the other two volumes of this set, we have dealt with the persecutions of early Baptists in Massachusetts and throughout New England.

Our religious freedom was not obtained easily. Our forefathers paid a severe price to obtain soul liberty and religious freedom. But tragically in our day, our freedoms are in danger. Benjamin Franklin, in a letter dated April 17, 1787, wrote, "Only a virtuous people are capable of freedom. As nations become corrupt and vicious, they have more need of masters."[2] It is one thing to sing, *God Bless America*, but we need to pray for revival and live righteously that our Lord shall indeed preserve our once-great Republic.

DLC

---

[1]Isaac Backus, *A History of New England* (Newton, MA: Backus Historical Society, 1871), 1:126.

[2]William J. Federer, *America's God and Country Encyclopedia of Quotations* (Coppell, TX: Fame Publishing, 1994), 247.

November 14

A Better Resurrection

Scripture: Hebrews 11:32-38

We recognize Hebrews chapter 11 as the Hall of Heroes of Faith. The chapter records one triumph after another beginning with Noah in verse 7, but a strange thing happens in the middle of verse 35 which says, "others were tortured . . ." Far from indicating a false or weak faith, persecution proved that the tortured were men "of whom the world was not worthy" (verse 38).

The records of the Baptist church in Bristol, England, for the date November 14, 1683, read in part as follows: "A day of prayer, having some hours together in the wood, between London and Sodbury Road, the enemy came upon us unawares, and seized about eight persons; but the brethren escaped to admiration. The bushes were of great service to us."

The history of the Bristol church is full of persecutions. When their pastor died in 1670, they invited Thomas Hardcastle to take his place. By the time he received the invitation, Hardcastle was in prison in London for preaching. After his release he became pastor in 1671. Three years free of disturbance followed before the persecution resumed. Hardcastle was arrested on February 4, 1675, and jailed for six months, but the church continued to meet undaunted, even though arrests took place every Sunday. The meetings took place in upper rooms of houses. A cord with a curtain attached hung across the room to protect the preacher. Women and children sat on the stairway, so that when the authorities arrived, they had difficulty climbing the stairs, allowing the congregation time to pull the curtain while the preacher sat down amidst the group, thus preventing his identification.

Hardcastle was arrested again just two weeks after his first imprisonment. From his cell he wrote letters of encouragement and instruction to his flock. "By the end of the year, the church meetings were grown very poor and lean, through fines, imprisonments, and constant worrying of us every day."

A four-year lull in the persecution followed, during which time Pastor Hardcastle died and was succeeded by George Fownes in 1679. The pastor and a large number of members having been arrested in December of 1681, secured their release by appealing to the Court of King's Bench at London. The court, nevertheless, maintained that Fownes could not preach in public based on the Five Mile Act. The next two years were very difficult, as the church met in private homes and open fields. According to the church records for March of 1683, "This week about 150 Dissenters were convicted by our recorder, on the statute of 23rd Eliz., for 20 a month, for not coming to [the state] church." On March 25, Fownes returned to jail. Several members had their property confiscated to pay their fines.

The entry for April 10, 1684, reads, "Brother Warren was fined £10 for a riot, being at a meeting near Roe Gate, and fees 47s., which he paid in the hall at Gloucester. But Lugg was forsworn in it, for he swore it was on the 27th, and it was on the 28th day that the meeting was. Old brother Cornish was bound to appear again next sessions, and several others. Some were fined 40s. and their fees, and released. Sister Fowles was put in prison at Gloucester. Some were fined five marks, as Mr. Jos. Wey; some £5, as the justices pleased, and to lie in prison till paid. About this time Pug Read died miserably, being an informer about twenty years old had his skull broke, as was said, by one of his companions; he was one that broke into Mr. Terrill's house."[1]

We read further that, "On the 29th of November, 1685, *our pastor, brother Fownes, died in Gloucester jail*, having been kept there for two years and about nine months a prisoner, unjustly and maliciously, for the testimony of Jesus and preaching the Gospel." The original sentence was six months, but the magistrates would not release him unless he promised not to resume preaching. Fownes was an example of those who would not accept deliverance, so that they might obtain a better resurrection.

DRP

---

[1]J. M. Cramp, (1871; 2003). *Baptist History: From the Foundation of the Christian Church to the Close of the Eighteenth Century* (310-311). Roger Williams Heritage Archives.

November 15

Is Autonomy Important?

Scripture: 1 Timothy 3:15; Matthew 18:17

Let me affirm that there are several reasons that Baptists have not apostatized as rapidly as those in other denominations. Surely the Bible is our foundation, and it is our only rule of faith and practice. Furthermore, we believe in a regenerate church membership. But another great reason is the fact that Bible-believing Baptists affirm local church autonomy. Other denominations have fallen quickly when their leadership has repudiated the faith. After all, in most denominations a hierarchy hold the title to the church property, and they appoint the ministers.

Let me illustrate this point from the history of my home state. Michigan was part of the Wild West in 1818 when the first Baptists arrived from New York in the Territory. Indians still roamed the countryside, and as the white population expanded into the Territory, a ministry to the Indians was established as well. In October 1822, Reverend Isaac McCoy, great Baptist missionary to the Indian population of America, was commissioned to enter the Territory of Michigan. By November 15, 1824, he had baptized a number of Indian converts in the St. Joseph River. The Baptist work in Michigan made great strides among both the aborigines and the pioneers.

As the Caucasian population grew, Baptist churches were quickly established in Pontiac (1822), Stoney Creek (1824); Troy (1825), Farmington, (1826) and Detroit (1827). Soon it was felt wise that an Association be formed to strengthen the fellowship and sustain numerically weaker churches. Associations have been, and can be, a blessing when it is realized that local churches participate voluntarily, and associations are not to infringe upon the autonomy of any local assembly. The first Baptist association in America was established in Philadelphia in 1707, and the purpose of the association then was just what has been stated.

However, as the years continue and churches multiply, associations can often become political organizations. Elected officers may contrive to gain power and control to assure their continuance in office. Such officials often curry the favor of larger churches, and, when pastoral changes take place, they can almost dictate whom each congregation might consider in calling a new pastor.

In reading the History of Baptists in Michigan, it was quite revealing to observe the very steps that lead an association for assistance into becoming a convention of control. I shall merely quote three sections of the historic account, and allow the reader to come to his or her own conclusion.

"In 1885 Rev. Z. Grenell of Detroit proposed to the Convention . . . (that) a Bureau of Ministerial Supply, which should consist of five brethren, elected at stated periods by the Convention to serve as a medium of communication between churches seeking pastors and pastors seeking churches; only so far, however, as churches and ministers made direct application."[1]

Six years later the accusation was made that some churches were ordaining men without discrimination, and thus a new proposition was offered. A proposal was made that "A . . . a standing committee be formed to examine all candidates for ordination privately, and that no council for ordination should be called except upon the recommendation of this committee."[2] This, of course, removed the authority of ordination from local church control.

Finally, two years later it was suggested that churches might do well to deed their property over to the convention.[3]

In the course of time the Michigan Baptist Convention, as part of the Northern Baptist Convention, went over the slippery slope of compromise and into modernism. Thankfully, a large number of the churches in Michigan, because they were totally independent and thus autonomous, were able to withstand the liberal onslaught, and Michigan became a leading state of the fundamental Baptist movement in America.

Participation in a fellowship or association, allowing local churches to do collectively what a single church could not do alone, has advantages, but we must make sure the autonomy of each local church is protected. After all, being composed of a regenerate church membership, God the Holy Spirit is able to move upon the congregation through every individual to accomplish His will collectively without outside interference.

DLC

---

[1]M. E. D. Trowbridge, *History of Baptists in Michigan* (Michigan Baptist State Convention, 1909), 168-169.

[2]Ibid., 170-171.

[3]Ibid., 179.

November 16

Answering the Call of God

Scripture: Isaiah 6:1-8

It would be well to read the entries of December 8 and February 9 with this material as it all pertains to Fred Donnelson, "Mr. Missions."

Following a rainstorm, as Mable Peck went out to look for any pigs that might have wandered off, she happened to notice that rain had washed away a railroad tie. Realizing the evening run was close at hand, she removed her cape, flagged down the train, and averted a disaster. Railroad officials rewarded her with a lifetime pass. Soon a crew was out to repair the damage. One of the crewmen, A. H. Donnelson happened to meet and, in time, married Mabel. On this date seven years later, Fred Sheldon Donnelson was born into that home.

The railroad company moved the Donnelson family to Marshalltown, Iowa, after the senior Donnelson lost a leg. Billy Sunday, the well known evangelist, decided to return to his hometown for an evangelistic campaign. At that time Fred was twelve years old and was wonderfully saved. Soon thereafter, all in his family were baptized and joined the First Baptist Church. Fred became very active in the church, and served in various capacities during the next few years.

When America entered the First World War, Fred entered the Army, but not until he had admitted to his lady friend that God had called him to preach. Fred and Effie wrote during the next two years, and when Fred returned from his military service, he asked Effie to marry him. She loved Fred, but thought it would be best to first get their education out of the way. However, after two years, on September 25, 1920, they were married. Fred had studied one year in the University of Chicago, but the liberal theology caused him to transfer to Wheaton College. After a year at Wheaton, Fred entered Northern Baptist Theological Seminary, graduating in 1925. He then returned to Wheaton and obtained another degree in 1928.

During his academic training, Fred served part-time in a small church north of Chicago. In time Fred was called to pastor Messiah Baptist Church and served there for eight years. It will be remembered that this was the time of the major battles between the fundamental and liberal forces in the Northern Baptist Convention. Fred was a solid fundamentalist, and found his fellowship in the Baptist Bible Union. He served for a time as editor of *The Trumpet*, the paper of the B. B. U. One of the missionaries supported by Messiah Baptist Church was Mrs. W. S. Sweet. She was known as Mother Sweet, and she served the Lord faithfully in China for forty years.

Following their service at Messiah Baptist Church, Fred accepted a call to the First Baptist Church of Plainfield, Illinois. In 1932 Mrs. Sweet visited the Donnelsons in Plainfield. She was nearly seventy years old. Mr. Sweet had passed away, and everyone thought Mrs. Sweet would remain in

America. But she was determined to return to the field of her love. At their breakfast table, Mrs. Sweet told the Donnelsons she sensed that the Lord was about to call an American pastor and his family to serve in China where there was a great need for a man to supervise the work.

The following Lord's Day Pastor Donnelson had a hard time composing his thoughts as he stood before his people. He finally said, "I believe that God is doing a work in our midst and desires some of us to make a new surrender to His will." He was met by Effie at the altar, and God did a significant work in calling that thirty-four-year-old pastor and his wife to China! How amazing is the story! In 1933 in the depths of the Great Depression, without a single church supporting them, the Donnelsons boarded the *Empress* of Canada, and departed from Vancouver, British Columbia, on February 25, 1933.[1] Their trip took them via Hawaii, Japan, and then to Shanghai, China.

Amazingly, in six months Fred Donnelson preached his first sermon in Chinese, and soon he was teaching preacher boys. During his first term in China, Fred was used of God in establishing twenty-five chapels. It is a thrilling story, but we will have to pick up the account in the entry of December 8. But, is it possible that God the Holy Spirit has been speaking to you as this account has been read? If so, I must remind you that the safest place for the child of God is in the center of His will.

DLC

---

[1]Fred Donnelson, *Finding Freedom In A Japanese Prison Camp* (Chicago: World Fundamental Baptist Missionary Fellowship, n.d.), 17.

November 17

Revive Thy Word, O Lord!

Scripture: Habbakuk 3:2; Psalm 85:6; 138:7

As we have entered the twenty-first century, it is apparent that there is great spiritual degeneration in America! Such was also the case at the beginning of the nineteenth century. Believers recognized that iniquity was abounding, and only a Divine intervention by the Lord would be sufficient to withstand the onslaught of the devilish enemy. Thus it was that men and women of God throughout Kentucky and Tennessee began crying out to Heaven for revival. For instance, on this date in 1798, the saints from the Sinking Creek Baptist Church in Tennessee met for their business meeting. The minutes reveal that no business was brought forward but a "...fast [was] proclaimed." These folk were desperate, and they began to agonize before God for revival!

And God answered! Oh, that we today might come to the realization that our hope is not in the modern-day attempts to conform the church to the world's standards that we might impact the world! How ridiculous is such an idea! We need God's empowerment of the church to confront the world! At the outset of the nineteenth century, saints prayed, and God did what they could not do! Burkitt and Read in *A Concise History of the Kehukee Baptist Association* reported, "Persons of the most dissolute lives, as drunkards, swearers, liars, thieves, &c., became sober, punctual, honest, virtuous persons. Surely that religion must be of *God* that makes people *godly* from *good principles*; that makes better husbands, better wives, better children, more obedient servants, better masters, better neighbors, and better citizens. This the work has evidently done."

Not only did Baptists experience revival, but Presbyterians and Methodists knew the blessings of Heaven as well. The noted Presbyterian preacher, Gideon Blackburn, wrote, "The ball room, tippling shops, and taverns have, in a number of instances, been . . . converted into places of prayer and praise . . . . The most profane settlements, where religion was not known, or the name of God mentioned only in blasphemy, are ... formed into societies, and meet weekly for social prayer."[1]

And the impact was not merely a temporary emotional experience bearing no continuing results. For instance, J. M. Peck, Baptist hero of home missions, wrote in an 1852 issue of *The Christian Review*, "Multitudes of strong men, proud of their habits of free-thinking, were converted in so sudden and impressive a mode as to perplex and confound their associates."[2]

The wonderful spiritual awakening of 1800-1803 resulted in great benefits both in society and in the work of the church. Prior to the season of revival, as we have seen, under the godless influence of infidelity, the morality of the citizenry was miserably bad. Had it continued long, America would have been consumed in its own vices. Spiritually, prior to the revival season, churches were floundering. Growth was very slow. Even those in the churches were half-hearted and indifferent. But, mercifully the Lord undertook. To be sure some agnostics remained following the revival season, but their power was broken. Society in general was saved from perpetuating the cesspool of iniquity. Spiritually the churches grew greatly. For instance, at the beginning of the nineteenth century there were 106 Baptist churches and 5,119 members. In the report of 1803, there were 219 Baptist churches and 15,495 members. In other words, the Baptist presence in Kentucky had more than trebled in the three year period. Other denominations too had grown in membership and influence.

As we have entered the twenty-first century, humanism has become America's religion. Christianity is all but outlawed in American society. Immorality seems to be the standard of the world. Sexual perversion and pornography are championed in the colleges and protected by the courts of our land. Wedded life without marriage, same sex marriage, and homosexuality seem to have become the norm. All this should drive believers to their knees! Oh, let us pray that He Who is the same yesterday, today, and forever might visit saints in America again with life-transforming revival! America's hope is not political. Our only hope is the Lord. Let us seek His face!

DLC

---

[1]O. W. Taylor, *Early Tennessee Baptists* (Nashville: Tennessee Baptist Convention, 1957), 172.

[2]Ibid., 152

November 18

The Inspired Word of God

Scripture: 2 Peter 1:20-21

One of the keenest minds among Bible believers in the nineteenth century was that of Dr. A. T. Pierson. His ability to express truth uniquely and succinctly has rarely been equaled. We have mentioned his immersion in the first volume of this set, but I should like to quote an extended portion of a message he delivered at a conference centered on the inspiration of God's Word in Philadelphia in 1887. Dr. Pierson's message climaxed the conference, and it was titled, "The Organic Unity of the Bible" and was delivered on the above denoted date.

> We find the Old Testament is patent in the New; the New latent in the Old. In such a book, then, it is not likely that there would be unity; for all the conditions were unfavorable, all the circumstances disadvantageous to a harmonious moral testimony and teaching. Here are some sixty or more separate documents, written by some forty different persons, scattered over wide intervals of space and time, strangers to each other; these documents are written in different languages, in different lands, among different and sometimes hostile peoples, with marked diversities of literary style, and by men of all grades of culture and mental capacity, from Moses to Malachi; and when we look into these productions, there is even in them great unlikeness, both in matter and manner of statement; and yet they all constitute one volume.
>
> Imagine another book, compiled by as many authors, scattered over as many centuries! Herodotus, in the fifth century before Christ, contributes an historic fragment on the origin of all things; a century later, Aristotle adds a book on moral philosophy; two centuries pass, and Cicero adds a work on law and government; still another hundred years,

and Virgil furnishes a grand poem on ethics. In the next century, Plutarch supplies some biographical sketches; and nearly two hundred years after, Origen adds essays on religious creeds and conduct; a century and a half later, Augustine writes a treatise on theology and Chrysostom a book of sermons; then seven centuries pass away, and Abelard completes the compilation by a magnificent series of essays on rhetoric and scholastic philosophy. And, between these extremes, which, like the Bible, span fifteen centuries, all along from Herodotus to Abelard, are thirty other contributors, whose works enter into the final results, men of different nations, periods, habits, languages, and education. Under the best conditions, how much real unity could be expected, even if each successive contributor had read all that preceded his own fragment? Yet here all are entirely at agreement. There is diversity in unity, and unity in diversity. It is *e pluribus unum*. If, at first sight, there be apparent divergence, a further search shows real harmony. As in a stereoscope, the two pictures sometimes appear as distinct, and will not come together, but, as we continue to look, and as the eye rests on some particular point, one view is seen; so in the Word of God. The more we study it, the more do its unity and harmony appear. Even the Law and the Gospels are not in conflict. They stand, like the cherubim, facing different ways, but their faces are toward each other. And the four gospels, like the cherubic creatures in Ezekiel's vision, facing in four different directions, move in one. All the criticism of more than three thousand years has failed to point out one important or irreconcilable contradiction in the testimony and teachings of those who are farthest separated. There is no collision, yet there could be no collusion!

How can this be accounted for? There is no answer which can be given unless you admit the supernatural element. If God actually superintended the production of this book, so that all who contributed to it were guided by Him, then its unity is the unity of a Divine plan and its harmony the harmony of a supreme intelligence and will.[1]

DLC

[1]Arthur T. Pierson, Editor, *The Inspired Word* (London: Hodder & Stoughton, 1888), 339-341.

November 19

On Calling A Pastor

Scripture: Acts 1:14; 2:46-47

I have often sat in a church auditorium and wished that the sacred walls could speak. The walls in the average Bible-believing Baptist church building have absorbed so much history, and they could testify of such vital truth if they possessed the ability to communicate. But let me briefly chronicle one congregation and bear down on one important truth.

Barnstaple, England was without a Baptist witness until 1814. Then a young, nineteen-year-old man, Charles Veysey, through reading the New Testament came under conviction, was gloriously saved, and requested believer's immersion. He had not previously known a Baptist, nor read any Baptist literature, but the Holy Spirit did a wonderful work in his life. In 1815 he was baptized in the river Taw with four other candidates. The Bible study group that emerged grew to the point that on November 19, 1817, a church of twelve members was formed. The history of the Barnstaple Baptist Church parallels the account of many other such congregations. There were months of revival and years of retrogression. There were times of prosperity and periods of penury. There were summers of growth and seasons of drought.

The church historian painstakingly lists the comings and going of twenty-two pastors during the first sixty-five year period of the church's existence. It is interesting to note that the church seemed to prosper most during the more lengthy terms of pastoral ministry. Indeed, it became necessary for the church to expand the chapel to accommodate the growing flock on two occasions. A certain Mr. S. Newman provided outstanding leadership for the flock. He and his ministry are described as follows: "Tall in person, serious in aspect, a glistening penetrating eye, peculiar in word-setting, deliberate in expression, pathetic in intonation, his whole soul full of the Divine Message, he could not fail to interest and impress. So that from the commencement of his ministry there was the gradual tide flow of prosperity."[1]

Unfortunately Pastor Newman's health declined, and he was given a 'years leave of absence in Switzerland that he might regain his strength. During his absence a new auditorium was dedicated. Soon after returning to his pastoral duties, Mr. Newman's health again failed, and he was forced to resign.

The continued ebb and flow of the congregation would almost become tedious if were not for the insertion of reminders of the Divine, sovereign intervention of our Lord Who loved the church and purchased it with His own blood. Surely the Great Head of the church realizes the importance of that which is the pillar and ground of the truth. And He oversees and protects His investment. Thus the Gospel was continually preached, souls saved and trained in truth, and God's work went forward.

However, one is caused to wonder in reading how the various pastors were called by the congregation. Then a tragic account reminds one of twenty-first century Baptist congregations. In 1880 Reverend J. N. Rootham accepted the call to pastor the Barnstaple Baptist Church. His ministry embraced five years, and during his tenure the chapel was renovated, a new organ was purchased, and the debt was removed. New members were also added, but, there was a continual undertone that ultimately caused the man of God to resign.

What had happened to cause dissension? Apparently the pulpit committee had made the fatal blunder of having more than one candidate at a time. To be sure, Reverend Rootham had received the majority of votes, but enough negative votes were cast to reveal that a sizeable minority were interested in securing the services of a different pastor. Reverend Rootham understood the situation but believed he would be able to win them over, but unanimity of spirit was broken and could not be restored.

What an important lesson for deacons and pulpit committees in this day! The harmony of a congregation can be destroyed if great care is not taken in securing God's man.

The best way to be assured of this leading is by considering one pastoral candidate at a time until unanimously the church family can get behind the leadership of the new pastor and move forward from victory unto victory. May we learn from history so as not to fail in the task set before us.

DLC

---

[1]D. Thompson, *A Book of Remembrance* (Watertown, WI: Roger Williams Heritage Archives, 1885-2003), 20.

November 20

A Dangerous Exception to the Rule

Scripture: Amos 3:3; 2 Corinthians 6:14

One of the most influential Baptist pastors in the early American history was surely Hezekiah Smith. He had a unique ministry of evangelism, church-planting, and pastoring. He served with honor as a chaplain during the Revolutionary War, and he led in the formation of the Baptists' first missionary society and was the deciding factor in the formation of the Warren Association of Baptist churches. We have featured him in both of the first two volumes of this set, and yet we acknowledge that God's men are unworthy servants.

We rejoice in acknowledging the hand of God upon outstanding servants of the past, but we must also learn from their failures. One of the evidences of the Bible's Divine inspiration is the fact that God honestly sets forth His followers declaring both good and bad in each life. We see Abraham lying concerning his relationship to Sarah. Dear David is painted truthfully in his moral failure with Bathsheba. And Moses, the meekest of men, spoke unadvisedly with his lips. Thus in honesty, that we might learn from failure, we submit this devotion of the day.

We are blessed indeed that the diary of Hezekiah Smith has been preserved. From it we can deduce several factors. The young preacher had been a bachelor well into his successful career of ministry. When he was thirty-five years old, apparently, he decided it was time to consider marriage. The entry in his diary of November 20 states, "I went to see Hephzibah Kimball, of Boxford, for the first time." From that date on through June of 1771 one reads often such entries as follow: "Tues., 11, went to Boston and stayed at Widow Harris'; assisted in getting Miss Hephzibah Kimball's household goods on board of Capt. Mullikin. Mon., 17. Went to Boxford to see Miss Hephzibah Kimball. Tues., 18. Preached at Stephen Wheeler's at North Salem, from 1 Pet. 2:11. That evening went to see Miss Hepzy Kimball and stay with her till Thursday. Thurs., 20, and Fri., 21. Went home and assisted in putting up the household stuff which came the Monday before. Thurs., June 27. Went to Boxford, and was married to Miss Hephzibah Kimball, by Mr. Holyoke."[1]

Hephzibah Kimball was apparently an attractive young lady who had many suitors. She possessed a good mind, strength of character, and some wealth. However, she made no profession of personal faith in Christ. It is apparent that her religious background was in the Congregational church, for the Mr. Holyoke who married the couple was the Reverend Elizur Holyoke, Pastor of the First Congregational Church in Boxford, from 1759 to 1793.

An interesting extract from a letter sent to Reverend Smith by Reverend Francis Pelot, of South Carolina, dated April 8, 1772, sheds some additional light on the matter. He wrote, "I again congratulate you on your nupitals and am glad you are so well suited. I pray the Lord to expose your lady to Himself, and then you will be happy indeed. Truly the want of a changed heart makes a chasm in the most happy marriages; but that is the gift of God, which no doubt you earnestly pray for. Her being so earnestly sought after by other ministers is a sign that she must be a sedate, serious person."[2]

Hezekiah and Hephzibah were blessed with many children, but only four lived to maturity. We can only surmise that Hephzibah came to personally trust Jesus Christ alone as her Savior, for she proved to be an excellent wife. A note affixed to the record states, "Mrs. Smith survived her husband many years. She died December 9, 1824, greatly beloved and lamented. Although not a member of the church, she was a generous contributor to its funds, and her life abounded in deeds of mercy."[3]

We will never know how much more fruitful Reverend Smith's ministry would have been had Hapzy declared her faith in baptism and united with the church. But we must be reminded that God calls us to obedience to His declared will. God demands, "Be not unequally yoked together."

DLC

---

[1]Reuben Aldridge Guild, *Chaplain Smith and the Baptists* (Philadelphia: American Baptist Publication Society, 1885), 149.

[2]Ibid., 150.

[3]Ibid., 374.

November 21

Well-Known to God

Scripture: 1 Corinthians 1:26-31

How I would love to know more about Reverend Thomas Dungan, the first Baptist preacher to minister in Pennsylvania. We know he was born in Ireland, and due to the bitter hostilities toward the Baptists under the regime of Charles II, he left his native land and sailed to America. He located in Rhode Island and united with the First Baptist Church of Newport, the church that Dr. John Clarke had founded. In 1684 Mr. Dungan moved to Pennsylvania and settled at Cold Spring in Bucks County, about three miles north of Bristol. This was only three years after William Penn had obtained his patent to form Pennsylvania. Mr. Dungan struck up a personal friendship with William Penn before Mr. Penn returned to England on August 12, 1684. David Benedict points out that William Penn, though a Quaker, had respect for Baptists. His father, Admiral Penn, was a Baptist in England. In quick order, Mr. Dungan established a Baptist church in Cold Springs.

The congregation never grew to any size, and in the course of time the membership of the church died off and the church ceased to exist. Morgan Edwards reported that Rev. Thomas Dungan died in 1688 and was buried in the graveyard at the side of the church building. Unfortunately that location has been lost from view.

However, the Lord placed His servant at the right place at the right time. We have reported in volume one of this set how Elias Keach had come as a teenager to America from England. He was the son of the famed Baptist preacher, Benjamin Keach. Dr. Benedict says of him: "On his landing he dressed in black, and wore a band in order to pass for a minister. The project succeeded to his wishes, and many people resorted to hear the young London divine. He performed well enough till he had advanced pretty far in the sermon. Then, stopping short, he looked like a man astonished. The audience concluded he had been seized with a sudden disorder, but on asking what the matter was, received from him a confession of his imposture, with tears in his eyes, and much trembling. Great was his distress, though it ended happily; for from this time he dated his conversion. He heard there was a Baptist minister at Cold Spring, in Bucks County, between Bristol and Trentown. To him did he repair to seek counsel and comfort, and by him was he baptized and ordained."[1]

This resulted in Elias Keach becoming an outstanding Baptist preacher and the leader among Baptists in Pennsylvania. Dr. Benedict says of Mr. Keach that he may be considered as "the chief apostle among the Baptists in these parts of America." This was possible because an unknown Irish Baptist preacher, Thomas Dungan, made himself available to the Will of God.

Immediately Elias Keach devoted himself to the work of the ministry at Pennypack, now a part of Philadelphia. The Lord blessed his ministry, and on November 21, 1687, he baptized Joseph and Jane Ashton along with William Fisher and John Watts. These were the first fruits of many to follow. In the course of time Philadelphia became the center of Baptist ministry in all of America. Mission agencies, publication facilities, and Baptist educational efforts centered in the City of Brotherly Love.

Mr. Keach resigned the church in 1689 and gave himself to an itinerant ministry throughout Pennsylvania and New Jersey. He and his family returned to his native land in the Spring of 1692. The Edict of Toleration had been granted in 1689, and Elias Keach had a very successful ministry in the land of his birth.

However, the elderly and hardly-known Thomas Dungan played a vital role in the ongoing of Baptist work in America, all because he obeyed the leading of the Lord. Your name may never be known broadly in the world, but it is encouraging to know that the Lord will bless and use you if you are willing to trust and obey.

DLC

[1]David Benedict, *A General History of the Baptist Denomination* (Boston: Lincoln & Edmans, 1813), 1:581-582.

November 22

A Faithful Pastor and a Godly Family

Scripture: Exodus 20:4-6

Our Scripture today gives us the promise that God shows mercy to thousands of those who love Him and obey His Word. Though God's judgment comes to three and four generations of those who hate Him, His mercy extends to thousands who obey Him in love.

That truth is certainly demonstrated in the life of Frederick William Weniger. His father, Henry Charles Weniger, was born in Germany in 1825. He came to America and was married in 1856. Frederick was born December 12, 1869, in Crawford County, Wisconsin.[1] He was saved in February of 1894 in the First Baptist Church of St. Paul, Minnesota. He immediately sensed that God was calling him to the ministry and took his training for the ministry in the Northwestern Bible School in St. Paul. (This school preceded the famous Northwestern Bible and Missionary Training School founded in 1902 by W. B. Riley. That school was in Minneapolis, Minnesota.

After completing his training, F. W. Weniger sailed for Venezuela in March 1899. Alice Mabel Bunch later joined him, and they were united in marriage on January 18, 1900. They labored in a difficult (then pioneer) mission field until failing health forced him to return to

America in the early 1900s. During the rest of his ministry, he gave himself to evangelism and to helping small churches. Over the next several years, he ministered to small churches in the Presbyterian, Methodist, and Congregational denominations. It is interesting that he never received ordination from these groups or identified with them. These churches were located in Minnesota and Iowa. Weniger would move on when a church had gained sufficient strength to support its own pastor. His son has recorded that the largest salary he ever received from the ministry at any time in his life was $1,800 per year.

His Baptist convictions apparently solidified through these ministries, and on November 22, 1911, while serving as the pastor of the First Baptist Church of Clinton Falls, Minnesota, he was ordained to the Gospel ministry as a Baptist. He invested the rest of his ministry in serving Baptist churches in the upper Midwest. He stood for the fundamentals of the faith, and when the battle over modernism was joined in the Northern Baptist Convention, he stood with W. B. Riley of Minneapolis and the fundamentalists.

This is only part of the story. The rest of the story is that this godly man and his wife achieved eminent success in raising their children. Their sons Dwight, Arno, Guy Archer, Ortiz, and Max all entered the ministry and left records of success in Baptist leadership. Their only daughter Helen, married the brother of Dr. B. Myron Cedarholm, and that couple invested their lives in missionary service. Succeeding generations of Wenigers have known Christ as their Savior, and a number have also followed on in the ministry.

All this record of godly generations springs from the godliness and conviction of one man and his wife. Here is the story of a man who was willing to serve the Lord faithfully in small places and in a sacrificial manner. This is a man who was loyal to the Word of God and stood for Baptist fundamentalism without apology. This is the account of a man who lived a consistent Christian life before his family and communicated his love for God, for the souls of men, and his firm convictions to children and children's children. God does show mercy to thousands of them that love Him and keep His commandments!

This Day in Baptist History III

Let this account be an encouragement to the pastor who serves in a place of seeming insignificance. It is not insignificant to God! Be faithful and "stay by the stuff"! May this account be an encouragement to Christian parents. God does honor consistent obedience to His Word! Let us live for God in the place where He puts us, and let us determine to follow Him.

FJM

[1]All information for this entry is taken from Arno Q. Weniger, "My Start in Life," unpublished autobiography (Lucerne, CA: n.d.).

November 23

The Young Man with the Old Message

Scripture: 2 Timothy 2

Radio preaching continues to be a real Gospel outreach. In years gone by, Maze Jackson had a 30-minute radio program that was carried on 53 stations called *The Truck Drivers' Special* from the young man with the old message. Old recorded tapes of the program are still aired on the East coast of North Carolina. Sometime while you are driving through the Southland and turn the radio on, you may hear the recorded voice of "one of God's cheerleaders," as some called him.

Most people called him "Brother Maze." He was a popular southern evangelist who preached like the old Separatist Baptists of the 18th century. Brother Maze was born on November 23, 1923, and grew up in Hendersonville, North Carolina, where he attended the Flat Rock Baptist Church. His dad was a fireman on the Southern Railway Company, and his mother worked in a sock mill. He enjoyed a typical childhood with his younger brother Frederick.

After high school, Maze left for North Carolina State University in Raleigh, North Carolina. In his freshman year he began reading the Bible his mother had stowed away in his luggage. In reading, he came under conviction, and was saved at the age of 19. When he called his mother to tell her the good news, he said, "You could hear her shout all over the neighborhood!" Thank the Lord for godly mothers.

Soon thereafter, Maze transferred to Columbia Bible College in Columbia, South Carolina. Under the tutelage of Dr. Frank Sells, he matured in the Lord. While in Columbia, he met Dorothy Whetstone who worked in a local bank. He immediately asked her for a date, but she responded that she usually did not go out with strangers; however she consented to attend a church service with him. During the service the pastor called upon Maze to lead in prayer. Maze stumbled through the prayer, but he was embarrassed for he had never prayed publicly before, and to top it off, Dot was present. Needless to report, their friendship sped along and eight months later, on June 4, 1945, they were married. Three sons were born to the lovely couple.

Maze did not finish his college course, but began pastoring. In all, Maze pastored three churches. Among them was the Jackson Street Baptist Church in Dentsville, South Carolina, where he and Dot were married. His gifts were apparent to one and all alike, and in time the Lord called His servant into full time evangelism. His habit was to open meetings on Tuesday night and conclude on Sunday. On Sunday night he traveled home. Mondays were spent in taping radio broadcasts, and then he would open another series of meetings on Tuesday. Fifty meetings a year kept him very busy. Most of his meetings were in the same churches year after year. Members of the various churches got to know Maze well as he was in their churches annually.

While Maze was in meetings in Danville, Virginia, my wife and I invited him to our home in Yanceyville, North Carolina, to have lunch. Knowing that he had an insatiable taste for steak, we grilled his specialty, and we never saw him thereafter without his commenting on them.

Mrs. Jackson traveled with Maze for five or six years before his home going on May 16, 1996. His funeral was held in the Belmont Baptist Church in Conyers, Georgia. His son, Nolan pastored the work there, and his widow lived with her son. The 1,500 seat auditorium was filled to capacity with folks standing outside. The choir loft was filled with preachers. Attendees saluted as his casket was being brought into the church. Four pastor friends preached his funeral message, and there were few dry eyes in the auditorium that day.[1]

Maze was an unusual man, but God often uses unusual men in the field of evangelism. Such men have schedules that are difficult to fulfill, and we would do well today to make these servants of our Savior the special target of our prayers. Pray for your pastor, but don't forget these who are called of God for a unique ministry.

DCB

[1]Telephone interview with Dorothy Jackson by Bettye Baughan, August 10, 2004.

November 24

Importunate Prayer

Scripture: Psalm 91:15

John Poindexter, Jr. was a man of considerable intelligence and well liked. However, he was opposed to spiritual and religious subjects. He resisted both the truth and the early Baptist preachers in Louisa County, Virginia, where he lived.

When his wife turned to the Lord and accepted Him as her Savior, John was both surprised and outraged. His opposition was now more definite and intense. His wife desired to be immersed and join the Baptists, but he strictly forbade it. We are told that she wept often and asked God to work in his heart for salvation and allow her to be obedient by immersion. Would God hear and answer her prayer?

The year was about 1788, and Poindexter's wife and Mrs. Henley, a friend, had both professed conversion but were not baptized because of their husbands' opposition. John not only opposed her baptism but also her attending services. The women met secretly, fellowshipped around the Word, and prayed that God would provide a meeting place. Although they considered permission unlikely, they asked Mr. Poindexter to allow preaching on his property. At first, he was indifferent but later thought that preaching might help his neighbors and their children, but he must be allowed to choose the preacher. He said he was against noisy preachers, but if an old gentleman by the name of Goodloe could be found, he could preach on his property. The ladies were thrilled and invited Preacher Goodloe, set the date, and had an arbor and seats built for the congregation. John did not plan to attend but came under conviction before the service took place. Pastor Goodloe came and preached, "Ye must be born again." A second service was planned for August 29. John Poindexter, Jr. thought he was too vile a sinner to be saved, but God opened his heart and mind and showed him he could be saved. Although he had despised Baptists, he esteemed them above all other groups after he was saved. He was also convinced that immersion was taught in the Scripture.

Nearly two years had passed since John's wife wanted to be baptized On August 29, 1790, he led her and Mrs. Henley into the water, and all three were baptized by Preacher Henry Goodloe. The service was well advertised, and a large crowd came from Louisa County and many others from adjacent counties. Many doubted that John's profession would last.

About a year after Poindexter's baptism, he began to speak publicly. In February of 1792, he was ordained to the ministry. A church near his home called him to be their pastor. During his first year of ministry, he baptized 100 and continued until more than 300 were added to his church. He was also instrumental in starting Bethel Baptist Church in Albermarle County. Through God's leading, he also had a revival of religion at Williams, where he labored for some time. He was elected moderator of the early Goshen Association of Churches for seventeen years. While moderator in 1795, he led the group to call for a day of solemn fasting and prayer to almighty God on November 24, 1795. This was prompted for deliverance from the dangers in consequence of the Treaty of Amity entered into with the Court of Great Britain.[1]

God truly answered the prayer of these people, but what kind of prayer warriors are we? We should thank God for our Baptist forefathers. In this country, or elsewhere, they were cradled amidst persecution and nurtured by the hatred of their foes. This has been their fortune in every age and in every land.

EGC

---

[1]Frederick Jarred Anderson, *A History of the Goshen Baptist Association of Virginia*, (Orange, VA: Goshen Baptist Association, 1992), 9.

November 25

Heavenly Melodies Midst Human Misery

Scripture: Job 35:10

Phillip Wachernagel, the celebrated musicologist of another day, has a section which he has entitled "Hymns of the Martyrs." These hymns, twelve in number, were published in 1583, and for the most part they are hymns of the so-called Anabaptists. When one considers the severe persecution that our forefathers were experiencing, the penetrating words of the hymns make one oblivious to any imperfections of the melodies.

After being well educated in Vienna, Leonhart Schiemer spent six years as a Franciscan friar. As he experienced only hypocrisy in the convent at Judenburg, Schiemer escaped in 1526, and soon met some of the leading Anabaptists of his day. Balthasar Hubmaier was used of God to challenge him,[1] and upon returning to his boyhood home of Vienna, he came under the influence of Hans Hut and came to the realization of personal salvation. Shortly thereafter he was baptized by Oswald Glaidt. Soon he was preaching the message of the grace of God, and he was greatly used of our Lord. At Steuer he baptized a number of converts. He traveled and preached in Austria and Bavaria, and everywhere he ministered he experienced the power of the Holy Spirit upon his ministry. In the Tyrol he was recognized by a Franciscan monk, who betrayed him. On November 25, 1527, his arrest took place. He was ultimately brought to trial, and was sentenced to death. His actual martyrdom took place in Rotenburg, in the valley of the Inn. "...by virtue of the mandate of the Emperor, and the edict of the King of Hungary and Bohemia, he was condemned delivered to the executioner, beheaded, and burnt to ashes, on the fourteenth day of January,"[2] 1528. In time, at the same place, some seventy of his followers also sealed their faith with their blood.

Leonhart Schiemer wrote the following hymn of substance:

Thine holy place they have destroyed,

Thine altars overthrown,
And reaching forth their bloody hands,
Have foully slain thine own.
And we alone, thy little flock,
The few who still remain,
Are exiles wandering through the land,
In sorrow and in pain.

We are, alas, like scattered sheep,
The shepherd not in sight,
Each far away from home and hearth,
And, like the birds of night
That hide away in rocky clefts,
We have our rocky hold,
Yet near at hand, as for the birds,
There waits the hunter bold.

We wander in the forests dark,
With dogs upon our track;
And like the captive, silent lamb
Men bring us, prisoners, back.
They point to us amid the throng,

And with their taunts offend;
And long to let the sharpened axe
On heretics descend.[3]

We in America have long enjoyed religious freedom. Surely our forefathers in this great land have procured it for us. However, the time may well come again that our faith will be tried by fire or by sword. May our faith sustain us to be witnesses unto death for our great Savior.

DLC

---

[1]George Huntston Williams, *The Radical Reformation* (Kirksville, MO: Truman State University Press, 1983), 273.

[2]Thieleman J. van Braght, *The Martrys Mirror* (Kitchener, ON: Herald Press, 1950), 424.

[3]Henry S. Burrage, *Baptist Hymn Writers and Their Hymns* (Portland: Brown Thurston & Co., 1888), 9.

November 26

Local Church Autonomy or Association Authority?

Scripture: Matthew 18:17

The middle Atlantic colonies provided a good nursery for producing Baptist ministers. Many Smigrated to that area from England and Wales, and of their progeny, many moved southward. Among the latter was the Newton family. John Newton was born September 6, 1732, in Kent County, Pennsylvania (now Delaware). He was reared in the Church of England, but when he was about 20-years-old he was saved. Soon he requested believer's immersion, and his baptism was administered by Pastor Joseph Potts at Southampton, Pennsylvania.

In 1753 John married Keziah Dorsett, and they parented six children, four boys and two girls. About this time the family moved to North Carolina. John was one of the first to identify with the Sandy Creek Baptist Church. On March 7, 1757, he became pastor of the Black River Baptist Church located in Duplin County. Black River was one of the churches present when the Sandy Creek Baptist Association organized in 1758. Through John's witness Philip Mulkey was saved. John continued to pastor the Black River church until the middle of the 1760s when he moved to the Congarees section of South Carolina.

Through the preaching of Daniel Marshall and Philip Mulkey in the Midlands of South Carolina, a number of people were saved, including Joseph Reese. John Newton, along with these new converts, organized the Congaree Baptist Church on November 30, 1765. Reese and Newton worked together for several years preaching throughout the area and organizing several other Baptist churches. God greatly blessed their ministry.

In February of 1768 Oliver Hart and Evan Pugh, both Regular Baptist preachers, ordained Joseph Reese and John Newton. Because Reese and Newton were connected with the Sandy Creek Baptist Association, but had accepted ordination at the hands of Regular Baptists, their home Association censored them. John Newton did not feel that he had done anything wrong, but Joseph Reese submitted to the censor.

The Sandy Creek Association then insisted that the Congaree church discipline Newton. They did so, allowing an association to infringe upon local church autonomy. As our Scripture text points out, the highest ecclesiastic authority is a local church.

Newton remained actively involved in Christian service until the end of his life. He remained in South Carolina until the early 1780s. His attendance is noted in the records of the Charleston Baptist Association (Regular Baptist) meetings of 1777 and 1779.

It is probable that in 1780 he moved his family to Wilkes County, Georgia. During the remainder of his life he kept a Journal that has been preserved at the University of Georgia. Though put on microfilm, some sections are difficult to read. However, a few entries throw light on his life of service for the Lord. The July 14, 1782, entry tells of a letter he sent his family in South Carolina mentioning that he preached at John Warrens. September 19, 1782, he preached at Tom Jones' Meeting House on "Of Him are ye in Christ Jesus." On June 17, 1783, he stayed with Mr. Richard Furman. He tells of attending the Charleston Baptist Association meeting in October of 1783, where Brother Cook preached and Richard Furman was chosen moderator. Another interesting tidbit recorded in his Journal is that he practiced medicine for a time and developed several remedies for certain diseases.

At the end of his life he was a member of the Providence Baptist Church in Wilkes County, Georgia. His Journal ends with the following entry: "Friday, Nov. the 26th day 1790 John Newton departed this life, after having arrived at a good old age, and living in the fear of God and obedience to the laws of his country and he had arrived at the age of 58 years, 2 months and 26 days. And on Sunday the 28th of Nov. he was buried on the Ogeechee River in the presence of a number of his Neighbors and Acquaintances. And on Thursday the 23rd day of Dec, 1790 a funeral sermon was preached on the occasion by the Rev. Thomas Mercer."

The only blot on the record of the Sandy Creek Association comes to light in this entry. An association has the right of censure, but it must not interfere with the autonomy of any local church. Let us ever defend and protect the New Testament principle of local church autonomy.

DCB

November 27

Following in a Path of Righteousness

Scripture: Proverbs 2:1-9

One of the greatest blessings that one could ever experience is that of being born and reared in a godly Christian home. Such was the case of E. L. Compere. His parents had left England in 1815 and had traveled to Jamaica to serve the Lord as missionaries. They served faithfully in Kingston, but in the course of time, health problems brought on by the weather caused Lee Compere and his wife to leave Jamaica. They sailed for Charleston, South Carolina, and became associated with Richard Furman. In the course of time, they applied to the Triennial Convention that they might serve the Lord among the Creek Indians in Alabama.

Ebenezer Lee Compere, the youngest of their nine children, was born into that blessed family on February 6, 1833, near Montgomery, Alabama.[1] As a teenager, E. L., as he was called, trusted Jesus Christ as his Savior, and on July 23, 1849, he was baptized by his father into the membership of the Montaches Creek Baptist Church in Mississippi. His mother had long prayed that E. L. would serve the Lord in the ministry, but he was reluctant to believe that the Lord could use him in that capacity. The saints in the local church, however, sensed God's call upon the young man, and they urged him to present himself to the Lord for ministry. After a long prayerful struggle, the young man surrendered to whatever the Lord had for him. He began his ministerial studies in Mercer University, and then completed his academic work in Mississippi College, graduating with honors in 1857. The following year he was ordained, and in 1859 he visited his brother, Elder T. H. Compere, in Arkansas.

Witnessing the spiritual destitution along the Arkansas border and the Indian Territory, E. L. resigned his churches, and without any financial support in view, he entered into the work at Fort Smith, Arkansas. He spent half of his time of ministry in Arkansas and the other half among the Cherokee Indians. The Lord burdened a Christian medical doctor to assist the man of God financially, and he pledged $500 annually toward the expenses of the preacher-missionary. To provide a base of operation, Reverend Compere established a church in Fort Smith, and he had a solid ministry there. However, his labor with the Cherokee Indians was interrupted for four years during the time of the Civil War. He spent those years ministering in Mississippi, and it was there that he met and married Miss Josephine Mullins of Copiah County, Mississippi.

When it became feasible for Reverend Compere to return to the field of his first love, he was again without funds. To avoid traveling on the Lord's Day, Reverend and Mrs. Compere remained in Memphis, Tennessee, during their journey. Attending church in Memphis, he was delighted to meet an old friend, Martin T. Sumner. As the Reverend Compere explained the Lord's dealing in his life, his friend promised him $500 a year to assist. Arriving back in Arkansas, the two-fold ministry was resumed, and the Lord continued to bless. Along with H. F. Buckner, missionary to the Creek Indians, Reverend Compere assisted in establishing the Buckner College and in the organization of the Baptist General Association of Western Arkansas and Indian Territory. He served that organization for nine years as Superintendent of Missions. On September 7, 1895, while participating in the annual meeting of the Association, Reverend Compere became ill. He was bed-ridden until his home-going on November 27, 1895.

General Douglas MacArthur once prayed, "Build me a son, O Lord, who will be strong enough to know when he is weak, and brave enough to face himself when he is afraid, one who will be proud and unbending in honest defeat, and humble and gentle in victory."[2] That could well have been the prayer of Reverend Lee Compere, and it was surely answered in the life of his youngest son.

DLC

---

[1]J. S. Rogers, *History of Arkansas Baptists* (Little Rock: Arkansas Baptist State Convention, 1948), 231.

[2]James B. Simpson, *Simpson's Contemporary Quotations* (Boston: Houghton Mifflin Company, 1988), 165.

November 28

Let Us Be Steadfast Unto the End

Scripture: 2 Timothy 1:13; 2 Timothy 2:19; Revelation 2:10

An interesting contrast is presented when one examines the lives of Elijah Baker and his partner, Reverend Philip Hughes. Elijah Baker was born in Virginia in 1748. At age 21, he was baptized by the renowned Separatist Baptist preacher, Samuel Harris. Philip Hughes was born on November 28, 1750. When he was 23, he was baptized by the prominent regular Baptist preacher, David Thompson.

The two men became fast friends, and both were greatly used of God. It will be remembered that Elijah Baker became one of the forty-four Baptist preachers who was incarcerated for preaching without the approval of Virginia's state church. Preaching through the prison grates, Baker became obnoxious to the jailer and was delivered into the hands of a ship captain with orders that he was not to be released on Colony territory. (Vol. 1:96) He was transferred from vessel to vessel when several ship captains became incensed with Baker's preaching. Finally he was delivered on to the Delaware shore. Baker began preaching with great power and wonderful results. Souls were saved and Baptist churches were planted. The following year, Philip Hughes joined his friend in Delaware, and the two formed a modern-day team of Paul and Barnabas. Everywhere they went souls were saved and churches were established. A faithful historian wrote, "They labored together as evangelists for about twelve months . . . . Many converts were baptized on profession of faith and repentance. They prepared materials and resolved to build churches. . . . They were not only well received and their labors approved, but, in their efforts to save souls, were aided on every hand by Baptist ministers and laymen, who helped them also in the constitution of churches and in the ordination of ministers. . . . Messrs. Baker and Hughes were instrumental in founding twenty-one churches in Virginia, Maryland, and Delaware, and spent much time in visiting them, as fathers do their children."[1]

In comparing these two men, it is apparent that Philip Hughes was the student, whereas Elijah Baker was the preacher. Twice during their ministry Hughes debated with Methodist clergymen over the subject of baptism. From both encounters, Hughes immersed former Methodists. He published a volume of hymns in 1782, many of which were his own expressions of praise to the Lord. Later, Hughes returned to Virginia, and on May 12, 1783, a letter to the Honorable Speaker and House of Delegates was sent by the Baptist State Association, and Mr. Hughes was the Moderator of the meeting.[2] Two years later Philip Hughes authored a volume on the subject of baptism.

However, in time Reverend Hughes changed theological courses. He apparently carried his Calvinism to its extreme and became Antinomian in his thinking. Cook refers to it as follows: ". . . Reverend Philip Hughes, who, after laboring so zealously in the cause of missions, embraced Antinomian views, and thus became widely separated from his former companion in labor, Mr. Baker. . . . He became intemperate in habit as well as Antinomian in view. His last days were a blot upon his first. He died at Dr. Lemon's, where Mr. Baker had ended his days so gloriously."[3]

In his Introduction to Cook's volume of the Delaware Baptists, Professor G. D. B. Pepper of Crozer Thological Seminary wrote the following: "Perhaps nowhere else in this country has Antinomianism, with its natural, if not inseparable, attendants of anti-Missionism, anti Sunday-schoolism, and all the other kindred anti-isms, so impressively by [their] fruits proved [their] origin, nature, and doom. In doing this it has also proved with like certainty its antagonism to the genuine Baptist faith and practice."[4]

May fundamental Baptists in this twenty-first century realize the necessity of balancing *head* and *heart* that we might preach the Gospel clearly to "whosoever will." May our hermeneutics be undergirded with a basic and literal faith in John 3:16.

DLC

[1]Richard B. Cook, *The Early and Later Delaware Baptists* (Philadelphia: American Baptist Publication Society, 1880), 22-23.

[2]Garnett Ryland, The Baptists of Virginia 1699-1926 (Richmond, VA: The Virginia Baptist Board of Missions and Education, 1955), 110.

[3]Cook, 96.

[4]Ibid., 7.

November 29

He Walked for God

Scripture: Philippians 4:13

William Cathcart, Baptist historian, relates that in 1798, John Clark, a Baptist in sentiment, though not a member, and Thomas R. Musick visited and preached in Missouri in "these times of proscription." i.e. "Proscription" refers to the Catholic law that demanded, "Liberty of conscience is not to be allowed beyond the first generation; the children of emigrants must be Catholics," and "No preacher of any religion but the Catholic must come into the province." Cathcart continued, "Clark's first trip was made in 1798; Musick's not long after. Clark was, we presume, the first Protestant minister that ever preached the Gospel west of the Mississippi River."[1]

In this entry we shall focus our attention upon the quasi Baptist, John Clark. John Clark was born on November 29, 1758, near the city of Inverness, Scotland.[2] He was raised as a strict Presbyterian, but moving to Georgia in 1786 or 1787, he united with the Methodist church. In 1791 he became a probationary Methodist preacher. Three years later, he was ordained. Though revering John Wesley as a reformer of the church of England, Clark determined that his only authority would be the Bible. From the New Testament he came to believe that the local church is the pillar and ground of the truth, and that each church should be autonomous.

This conviction grew, and in 1795 Clark severed his ties with the Methodists. The following year he set out on foot for a westward trip. He settled temporarily in Kentucky, and then went on to Illinois where he lived for some time. In reading the New Testament, he became dissatisfied with infant sprinkling and adopted immersion as the Biblical command. In Illinois he was often the guest of James Lemen (Cf. Vol. 1, pp. 10-11), and one can only surmise what influence Elder Lemen had on John Clark in relation to believer's immersion. At any rate, Clark was still only a Baptist in sentiment when first he traveled into Missouri.

John Clark never married, and thus he was free to do much itinerant work. There being no public conveyance, he traveled on foot throughout Missouri. Friends became so concerned that in time they presented him with a horse. However, whenever John Clark came to a creek, he would dismount, put his saddle-bags over his own shoulder, and lead his horse through the water. This slowed his travel, and on his return home he pled with his friends to take the horse back.

It was imperative to him that he rigidly keep to his schedule, and thus he would travel regardless of inclement weather. Clark's biographer recorded the following interesting event. John Clark was unaware that a certain ferry boat on the Missouri River had been destroyed in a flood. He had intended to use that boat, which would save him thirty miles. His next appointment was at a judge's home, and he was resolute on fulfilling his engagement and presenting Christ. Though 70 years old, he set out on foot traveling along a muddy pathway in thick darkness. He became fatigued, and repeatedly rested by leaning against a tree. He finally reached the house of a hospitable friend at break of day. He was excessively fatigued, and the family was astonished to learn that he had traveled the whole night and preceding day. Regarding such an effort as an undue sacrifice for a feeble old man, he was admonished to stop and rest. John Clark responded, "O, my dear brother, souls are precious, and God sometimes uses very feeble and insignificant means for their salvation. The people expect me to fill my appointments, and the only way was to reach here this morning. This is nothing to what our divine Master did for us." In actuality, John Clark had traveled sixty-six miles walking in a muddy path without sleep because he longed to serve His Lord.

Dare we do less than give Christ our best as we witness for Him in the 21st century?

DLC

---

[1]William Cathcart, *The Baptist Encyclopaedia* (Philadelphia: Louis H. Everts, 1881), 11: 805.

[2]R. S. Duncan, *A History of the Baptists in Missouri* (St.Louis: Scammell & Company, 1882), 46.

November 30

The Preacher's Partner

Scripture: Jeremiah 20:9; 1 Corinthians 9:16-17

We honor the revered memory of men such as B. E. Mullens, faithful, rural preacher of the South. We esteem such because they plowed their fields of red clay all week; then they mounted their steed and traveled to a distant church to minister spiritual sustenance. Such men are worthy of our praise. They were used of God to fashion stability throughout vast regions.

B. E. Mullens was born on November 30, 1831, in Georgia. In his infancy, his family moved to Alabama. During his youth, B. E.'s godly mother faithfully read God's Word aloud and prayed God's direction on each of her children. When he was eleven years of age, B. E. trusted Christ as his Savior. Though educational opportunities were limited, B. E. had an inquiring mind. By personal effort, he read extensively, and through this endeavor, he gained a great knowledge of the Scriptures. As a teen-ager, B. E. united with the Hopewell United Baptist Church in Walker County, Alabama. The membership soon observed that he was gifted of God, and long before he became convinced, they believed he should be ordained to preach the Gospel.

At the age of twenty, B. E. married Miss Mary L. Gravlee, a lady of sterling character. Their love was strong, and they little realized the poverty in which they lived. With great effort they eked out a living, but they continued as faithful church members. Through the congregation's continual urging, B. E. was ordained on September 24, 1854, and began a broader ministry. For the next thirteen years, Reverend Mullens remained at Hopewell church, but an extended ministry developed and carried him into many counties of the state. He labored on his farm during the week from necessity, and then on Saturday, he mounted his horse to make his way to a distant preaching appointment. Requests for his ministry were received from great distances.

My purpose, however, is primarily to present the sacrifice Mary Mullens made during this period. She was like many other faithful wives of country preachers, these ladies who are often forgotten. One of her sons wrote describing her anguish of soul, and it would be difficult to picture it any better.

". . . Let no one conclude that all the struggle is in the heart of the preacher, and that all the burdens fall on his shoulders. The young wife thus called upon to surrender husband and cherished hopes, and to take upon her shoulders cares that bend the stout heart and physical strength of the father under their weight, certainly undergoes an experience that is a sealed book to her sisters. As the first child of this sweet union of my parents, I . . . can testify truly on this point. In early childhood I stood many times at the side of my beautiful mother as she would watch the fading form of my father riding away to his appointments. When he had passed from her view, . . . I have seen her fall down in a flood of tears and prayer. Who knew beside herself and the Unseen Eye the wrestling and agony of her heart? Did the Comforter steal into her tempest-tossed soul in hours like these and breathe within His comforting peace? After the storm had passed the resolution and courage that spoke in actions and face were evidence that He often did.

"And at the end of three or four days, or a week perhaps, I watched with her, many times, far into the lonely hours of the night to catch the first signal of the dear one's return. At last from some distant hill-top, or high point on the road, that signal would come floating to us on the winds of the night in the words of some grand old hymn. Tears would again gush from the lovely eyes-tears this time born of the very joy of gladness. And what a happy greeting at the gate when the weary rider had dismounted!"[1]

May we be found faithful in the task given us by the Lord!

DLC

---

[1]W. W. Mullens, *The Old Paths* (Woodstock, VA: Power Print of W. N. Grabill, 1905), 274-275.

December 1

No Time for Retirement

Scripture: 1 Corinthians 15:58

William (Bill) Hopewell, Jr. was born on December 1, 1919, in Wilmington, Delaware, just prior to the beginning of the "Roaring Twenties". Bill was saved when he was sixteen years of age and was greatly impacted with the radio ministry of Dr. Harold S. Laird. Those were the days of the fierce battles between the fundamentalists and liberals. When Dr. Laird was defrocked and lost his church and sizable pension because he refused to support liberal missionaries, young Bill Hopewell threw his support to the fundamentalists, and this positioned him strongly as an ecclesiastical separatist.

Bill graduated from college, taking his undergraduate bachelor's degree when he was twenty-one. During his years in college, the Lord of the Harvest burdened his heart for missionary service, and in 1939 Bill volunteered to go on a survey trip to New Guinea. However, before those plans could be realized, World War II closed that door of opportunity. Knowing the call of God, Bill enrolled in seminary and received his bachelor of divinity degree in 1944. He entered the military service of our land and served for the last two years of the war as a naval chaplain. His wife, Ruth, completed her college training in 1943, and Bill and Ruth were married on July 23, 1943.

Following the war, Bill and Ruth sought the mind of the Lord for missionary service. Having served with the military in the Philippines, it was only natural that they should be burdened for that field. Thus in 1947 the Hopewells began their service. The Lord blessed them particularly in searching out scattered saints who had been dispersed due to the war and urging and assisting them to reestablish their churches. In a short time, as they ministered to these greatly despairing folk, they had encouraged about fifteen congregations to rebuild in and around the Manila area.

Their mission society needed helpers in Chile, South America, and because of their effective service in the Philippines, the Hopewells were asked to go. There in Chile they established a strong church (that continues to exist), and they constructed a Bible school building and started the needed school.

Because of Brother Hopewell's educational background, he was asked to return to the States and teach missions in a New York seminary. During his eleven-year tenure there, he completed his work for a Th.M. in missions. Many whom he trained went on to serve the Lord in mission fields of the world.

It was then that his mission agency requested Reverend and Mrs. Hopewell to return to their society and serve as a field director. During years to follow he served missionaries on three continents and opened eleven new fields for church planting. His was a rich service indeed.

After forty years of service, Reverend and Mrs. Hopewell stepped aside from the active role in their mission agency. Being unwilling to enter into a leisurely season of retirement, this fine couple offered their services as furlough replacement missionaries with Baptist World Mission in Decatur, Alabama. It was apparent that the missionary call of 1939 was still as vibrant in their hearts as it had been sixty-four years previously.

The Hopewell's first assignment took them to New Zealand, and their service was so blessed that another missionary in New Zealand requested their ministry. They served in each of those locations for nine months, and the missionaries returned to strengthened situations. The next assignment found them serving happily in Scotland for six months, and once again the blessings of heaven were attendant. But still they were not done. Though in their eighty-fourth year, they journeyed again to New Zealand to assist a young couple in church planting. Who were these missionaries? They were folk whom the Hopewells had led to the Lord during their first stint in New Zealand. The young couple had grown in grace, graduated from college, and now were themselves starting out in Christian service!

Bill and Ruth will tell you that there is no time for retirement in the eternal work of God! What an inspiration this couple is to all who know them. May God burden the hearts of other "senior citizens" to make their last years count for God.

DLC

December 2

Righteous Standards do not Vary

Scripture: Malachi 3:6a; Hebrews 13:8

One often wonders how 17th and 18th century Baptists would view 21st century Baptist standards of our day. It is surely true that one must observe the differences between cultural preferences and Biblical convictions, but it seems apparent to the author that there has been an extreme decadence in the standards of present day Bible believers. In fact, it would appear that a rapid acceleration of "worldliness" is presently being experienced in the religious world.

An interesting case in point confronts one while reading the volume by David Spencer, *Early Baptists of Philadelphia.* Mr. Spencer reported that on December 2, 1793, a committee of seven godly men was appointed by the Philadelphia Baptists to investigate and present recommendations as to what steps might be taken to suppress the worldliness caused by the theater. Please observe the date as being in the 18th century. The author well remembers that during his youth, rather early in the 20th century, attendance at the theater was still considered to be a sin. However, at the conclusion of the Second World War, television invaded American homes, and in the course of time the idols of Hollywood, along with their immoral life styles, became tolerated almost nationally by believers and unbelievers alike. Gradually the dress standards of Hollywood supplanted the modesty standards of God's Word even among believers. Tragically, four-letter words that would not have been allowed in Christian homes a few years before, now flow freely and without embarrassment over the media outlets in the average house. Christian youth apparently think of such conversation as a correct vehicle of communication.

It is apparent that the scientific second law of thermo dynamics in the physical world has a counterpart in the spiritual world. A gradual spiritual dissipation through seemingly harmless amusements was predicted by spiritual leaders in the early 20th century. This battle, of course, was not new. Surely in an earlier generation John Bunyan had portrayed it in his classic work *Pilgrim's Progress*.

During the author's youth, worldliness was often characterized as being theater attendance, dancing, and smoking. It was fully understood and preached that spirituality did not consist of what one did not do, but Spirit filled and Spirit led believers evidenced a life style that did not include those and other characteristics of the unsaved. At that point, Baptist believers were characterized, not only by the fact that they gave verbal testimony as to the redemptive work of Christ Jesus in their lives, but they also backed that testimony with a life style that seemed out of date with the world about.

Gradually spiritual erosion has developed, and believers are no longer discerned by their "unworldliness." In this 21st century it is difficult to distinguish many "believers" by their manner of living. They seemingly know Biblical doctrines, but there is little transformation of life. Tragically some professed "fundamental" Bible colleges (several which began as Bible Institutes during the days of the Fundamental vs. Modernism clashes), have done away with prohibitions of dancing, theater attendance and even smoking. Along with this anomaly, such institutions no longer produce missionaries who are willing to forego the luxuries of life to serve the Lord. This amazing development would have seemed impossible to the Godly founders of such institutions!

In light of all of the above, we do well to give serious thought to the fact that God's standards never change. What sin was in days gone by is still sin today.

The true church in the world is often pictured as a ship sailing in an ocean. As long as the water is kept outside the ship, all is well. But when leaks in the ship develop, danger persists. Our Lord told His disciples that they were in the world but not of the world. The greatest need of Bible-believing Baptists today is revival. How we need to pray that the Lord of Heaven shall bring conviction in our lives so that we shall not succumb to the methods and standards of the world, but that we might be a separate people to the praise and glory of our Savior's name.

DLC

December 3

Quit Ye Like Men!

Scripture: 2 Timothy 4:1-5

German rationalism invaded Great Britain even before being experienced on our shores in America. Of course this meant that Mr. Spurgeon confronted that dread evil of apostasy before it was experienced on this side of the Atlantic. He was doubtless looking for men who were built upon and bounded by the Word of God whom he could use in planting chapels all around London. He found such a man who was pastoring the Baptist church in Ilfracombe on the Bristol Channel.

The church at Ilfracombe had struggled since its formation in 1851. Several good pastors had assisted in the early days of the church, but one by one they had wearied or worn out in the battle, and had resigned. Discouragement had cut short the ministry of James J. Brown after he had labored in the vineyard for six years. He was followed by a young man of promise who had just graduated from college, Reverend J. E. Taylor, but after two years, the Lord called His servant home on December 3, 1867.

However, the congregation was greatly blessed when Reverend J. Douglas was called to assume the pastorate. I can do no better than to quote from the record of the church historian:

> A good and faithful pastor was found in the Reverend J. Douglas, M. A. He *proved* the minister for the place. A devoted people rallied around him. There were good congregations and many conversions. During the summer the place was too strait for the worshippers, so that increased sitting room was made by putting up an end gallery. They also greatly improved the internal look of the chapel. The expense incurred was £352,which has been paid.
>
> Mr. Douglas has scholarly parts, evinced by his M. A. degree, but these he subserves to sacred purposes. All he is and has he lays at the foot of the cross. Whatever his culture he is not one of

> those who unduly speculates in the pulpit, or gives forth uncertain sounds. Satisfied with the plain teaching of God's Word, his creed is that of Paul and the Puritans. The doctrines of sovereign grace he teaches without a falter. Some would call him too dogmatic, but in preaching cardinal truth there should be unflinching decidedness. Hesitancy in ministers robs them of power and weakens impression. "Thus saith the Lord," when declaring the essential verities cannot be too confidently spoken. A writer thus argues: "But what is dogmatism?" Dogmatism is the positive assertion that certain things are true. Are not first principles dogmatic? You never say two and two *ought* to make four, but you say dogmatically they *do* make four. You never say a straight line *ought* to be the shortest way between two points; you say it is so, and Euclid is as dogmatic as Paul. You never say, "*Perhaps* it is safer to build on a rock than on sand." There is no perhaps in the case. The King of nature never says, "You may if you like sow in August and reap in January; and no matter what you sow, you shall reap wheat." No; His teaching through nature is dogmatic, and you are shut up within the bars of sovereign limitations. The same King rules in Grace, and is *He* likely to be less decisive in the higher sphere than in the lower? Never. With a voice that puts down all other voices, and with the blow of a glory that turns all other glory into darkness, He declares positively that certain things are true, and we evangelists do but repeat the assertions. If you object to dogmatism, complain to the Master, not to the men.[1]

After a lengthy and blessed ministry, Mr. Douglas submitted his resignation mentioning that Mr. Spurgeon desired his services in establishing the Higgs' Memorial Chapel, Chapham. A heart-broken congregation gathered in a farewell appreciation service for their pastor on December 15, 1884.

Is your pastor dogmatic about truth? Thank God for him, and be sure and let him know that you appreciate the fact that he is presenting the truth as it is in Christ Jesus.

In these days of compromise, every solid, strong fundamental pastor needs the encouragement of God's children.

DLC

[1]D. Thompson, *A Book of Remembrance* (Watertown, WI; Roger Williams Heritage Archives, 1885-2003), 86.

December 4

An Ideal Pastor

Scripture: 1 Peter 5:6-7

Nathaniel Chambles was born on February 4, 1762, in Sussex, Virginia. He was the son of William and Elizabeth Chambles, who were faithful and godly Baptists. Though he was instructed in the Word of God throughout his youth, it was not until his twenty-sixth year that he was enabled to cast himself as a guilty, vile sinner upon the mercy of Christ Jesus. He was baptized in July of 1787, and received into the membership of the High Hills Baptist Church.

In 1803 he began exhorting, and in 1806 the congregation voted unanimously to recommend the calling of an ordination council to ordain Mr. Chambles. For years Elder Chambles served the High Hills church, but frankly, though he was a solid pastor, nothing of a remarkable nature was experienced until 1822. Elder Chambles was surely an excellent example of a godly pastor. He was not heartless and cold, but he loved his people and exhibited what we would call a "pastor's heart." He was known for his great humility. No man possessed a deeper sense of personal insufficiency than he did. Literally, he "esteemed others better than himself." He distinguished himself with acts of beneficence. He opened his home to those in financial difficulties, and at one time, entertained a minister in his own home, actually assisting the man financially from his own provisions. He never gained great fame, but the more popular and useful his brethren in the ministry became among the churches, the more he rejoiced. He was thrilled at the blessings pastors all around him received. Elder Chambles could never be accused of envy. He was always dignified and solemn in the pulpit.

In 1822, however, the man of God became deeply affected by the coldness that pervaded the churches. With unusual sincerity, he exhorted the members of his churches to be diligent in searching the Scriptures, faithful in self-examination, and fervent in prayer. A day of fasting, humiliation, and prayer was appointed by the church at High Hills. God was preparing them to receive a blessing. About this time, several itinerant evangelists were providentially sent into the area. A blessed revival began. In about a year, sixty or seventy people had been converted, baptized, and added to the church. During this season of "refreshing from the presence of the Lord," the heart of Elder Chambles was filled with gratitude, and he seemed once again to be young. With the warmth and tenderness of a young convert, he exhorted, prayed, and wept.[1]

Three years later, Elder Chambles' health began to fail. He was now sixty-three years of age, and he suffered from a disease in his lungs. He maintained his ministry, however, until within a few weeks of his home-going. His last sermon was taken from the text of 1 Peter 5:6-7. He spoke with freedom, and particularly he emphasized the latter part of the text. He urged his people to cast their cares upon the Lord in the realization that the Lord would care for their every need. Surely the Lord was preparing the congregation for the day when their under-shepherd would leave them and take his flight to glory.

For about two weeks, he was rendered speechless, as he suffered from a paralytic affliction. His countenance indicated the tranquility of his soul. On December 4, 1827, he fell asleep in Jesus. The funeral text chosen was Revelation 14:13: ". . . Blessed are the dead which die in the Lord from henceforth: Yea, saith the Spirit, that they may rest from their labors; and their works do follow them."

Perhaps these lines are being read by a "model pastor." Your name has never appeared in lights, and you are not well-known. But, you are faithful to the Lord, His Word, and to the sheep whom He has entrusted into your care. Let me urge you not to despair. Seek the Lord for His blessing, but it is merely required of pastors that we be found faithful. May the story of Elder Chalmers encourage your heart today.

DLC

---

[1]James B. Taylor, *Lives of Virginia Baptist Ministers* (Richmond: Yale & Wyatt, 1838), 331.

December 5

Freedom's Cost

Scripture: 1 Peter 3:14-17

The fact of the suffering of Baptists in the early days of our Republic comes as a shock to most modern-day Americans. After all, this is the "Land of the free and the home of the brave." But we do well to realize that the freedom we now enjoy has not always been a part of the fabric of this land. Consider the Colony of Connecticut. "As founded in 1635, Connecticut consisted of the three River Towns of Windsor, Hartford and Wethersfield, with Springfield temporarily included."[1] To be sure the governmental laws proliferated in the Colony, but Baptist oppression in the early days of its history has been permanently etched by faithful historians. As a case in point, Henry Stiles wrote, "The history of the Baptists in Windsor, [Connecticut] as in every part of the colony, is mainly a *record of persecution.*"[2] (Italics in original text)

In 1761 the State Church [Congregational] constructed a new church building in Windsor, Connecticut. Deacon Nathaniel Drake, Jr. refused to pay taxes which had been levied on him for that edifice. As a result, the good deacon was imprisoned. The case was mentioned in a book published in 1767 by Mr. Ebenezer Frothingham of Middletown, Massachusetts. Lengthy titles were used for books in those days, and this one is particularly long. The volume is quoted by Mr. Stiles and is entitled: *A Key to Unlock the Door that leads in to take a Fair View of the Religious Constitution established by Law, in the Colony of Connecticut.* Mr. Frothingham wrote, "Young Deacon Drake, of Windsor, now in Hartford prison, for the Minister's rates and building their meeting house, altho he is a Baptist, . . . is accounted a harmless, godly man, and he has pled the privilege of a Baptist through all the courts, and been at great expense, without relief, until at last the Assembly has given him *a mark in his hand* [a branding], and notwithstanding this, they have thrust him to prison to what the Constitution does to relieve the poor Deacon, he may there die, and the cry of blood, blood, go up into the ears of a just God. [Italics in original text]

"The Baptists . . . wanted . . . an end to taxes used exclusively for state-supported churches."[3]

In time, a slight variation was allowed. To escape the taxation imposed upon them by the established church, dissenters were obliged to file a certificate like the following: "Windsor, Dec. 5th, 1817. I now certify according as the law requireth that I belong to the Baptist Society in Windsor. Hezh. H. Palmer."[4]

Such a situation seems impossible to us in this day of religious freedom, but that was the plight of our Baptist forefathers in New England, as in most of the colonies. This condition persisted until the time following the Revolutionary War. With victory won, and with the support of the Baptists, Thomas Jefferson presented legislation in Virginia guaranteeing religious freedom in the Commonwealth. For seven years the Virginia Assembly debated the bill, and in 1786 the statute was finally passed. Disestablishment quickly followed in other states, particularly in the South, but in time the cause of religious freedom began to move forward in the New England states as well.

Freedom has come with a huge price tag. Our forefathers were willing to sacrifice their property and physical well-being for freedom. Surely one of the costs of maintaining our freedom is vigilance. Let us determine to use our soul liberty wisely as we faithfully worship the Lord without fear or favor. While the doors of God's house are open, let us be found faithful with our presence, praise, and purse for the ongoing of the Gospel.

DLC

---

[1]Wayne Andrews, *Concise Dictionary of American History* (New York: Charles Scribner's Sons, 1967), 233.

[2]Henry R. Stiles, *The History of Ancient Windsor* (Somersworth: New Hampshire Publishing Company, 1976), 1:392.

[3]James Kirby Martin, Randy Roberts, Steven Mintz, Linda O. McMurry, & James H. Jones, *America and Its People* (New York: HarperCollins College Publishers, 1993), 192.

[4]Daniel Howard, *The History of Old Windsor, Connecticut* (Salem, MA: Higginson Book Company, 1935), 214.

December 6

Religious Freedom or Judicial Bondage?

Scripture: Ephesians 6:10-19

Thank God for the "Land of the Free," but we surely need to understand that America has not always experienced the freedoms that we have today. And yet, I cannot help but wonder if the veneer of civility that seemingly allows for divergence of ideas and national tranquility will long endure. Baptists in time past knew what it was to be under physical surveillance and political pressure. But through the years America has cultivated an attitude that allows for a plurality of religions, and thus, though one might suffer verbal ridicule from society, there is a spirit of toleration that grants freedom of religious activity.

As we have said, this has not always been true. A case in point from New England will provide an illustration: "A Baptist church was formed at Salem, [Massachusetts], in 1780, and Mr. Samuel Fletcher was ordained their pastor, December 6, 1781. He was born in the county of Middlesex, in August 1747, born again in 1767, and began to preach in 1777. He was called to preach at Chelmsford in the spring of 1778, and preached there the main of the time for two years, and his labors were very successful in several other places, which appeared to be the cause of his meeting with uncommon abuse in one place."[1]

In our first volume of this set we describe the abuse of an angry mob vented against Reverend Fletcher when he attempted to baptize believers upon their profession of faith.

In the course of time, ". . . three officers of the town came into the house where the Baptist ministers were, and advised them immediately to depart out of that town for their own safety. Being asked whether their lives would be in danger if they did not depart, no answer was returned. But seeing their temper, the Baptists agreed to disperse, and to meet at a distant place of water; which was done, and . . . six persons were decently baptized, though further abuse was offered at the close of it."[2]

Similar violent occasions in the early Colonial days of our history could be cited. They were prevalent in New England and Virginia. However with victory in the Revolutionary War, and the provision of the Constitution and Bill of Rights, freedom has been assured to America. Yet it is apparent that these are radically changing days in America. Our liberal Supreme Court, with a convoluted logic that defies description, no longer applies "Original Intent" in the interpretation of our Constitution. Currently great emphasis is placed upon "precedent." The fact that the "precedent" is without constitutional foundation is meaningless. In other words, our Supreme Court is no longer a judicial branch of government. It looks upon itself now as a legislative branch. Laws are no longer merely interpreted by this legal body, but decisions are now superimposed upon American society. This has become evident as the Court has refused to rule on so-called cases of abortion, homosexuality, and so-called "same sex marriages." The judges' very indifference has allowed most liberal rulings of lower courts to stand. It is apparent to some that we are following the same procedure as our neighbor to the North. Soon it may well be considered illegal for pastors to quote the Bible concerning abortion, homosexuality, and "same sex marriages."

Let us firmly understand that these issues are not political! They are moral issues, and true believers must and will speak up. It is an infringement upon our religious freedom when we are told that we cannot present God's principles concerning society and life! In the near future, without the benefit of governmental protection, we may face indignant attacks from a hostile society. Again Bible-believing pastors may find themselves incarcerated for daring to proclaim a "Thus saith the Lord." May we in our day do all possible to defend our freedoms, but when and if the time shall come when our government, through the Supreme Court, shall attack our freedoms, may we be willing to pay the price and stand for truth!

DLC

[1]Isaac Backus, *A History of New England Baptists* (Newton, MA: Backus Historical Society, 1871), 535-536.

[2]Ibid., 220.

December 7

Let's Debate

Scripture: Acts 8:36-39

An interesting phenomenon of the expanding frontiers of nineteenth century America was the penchant for debating. Having little social entertainment, debating filled a desire that no longer exists. Our subject for consideration in today's entry was gifted with a quick mind, and he participated in debating skirmishes with great delight. In fact, the Lord used that inclination in his life to bring him to spiritual truth. Thomas Moor Rice was born in Jessamine County, Kentucky, on December 7, 1792. His education was limited to approximately ten months of formal training, but early in life, he developed an insatiable thirst for knowledge. His father, Samuel Rice, was a farmer, and to supplement his income, he ran a small distillery during the fall and winter. As a lad, Thomas was taught to manage the stills, and having ample free time in the brewery, the still-house became his academy. With an insistent appetite, he devoured the contents of every book available to him. He consumed whatever the subject was, and filed it in his mind until he had mastered the contents of each volume. He studied mathematics along with the Greek, Latin, and Hebrew languages. He studied with a zeal that assured success. When Thomas Rice was twenty years old, he was regarded as an accomplished mathematician, as well as a prodigy in the knowledge of those languages.

When the War of 1812 broke out, Mr. Rice enlisted as a volunteer. He served under General William Henry Harrison and fought in the famous battle of Tippecanoe. Following the war, Mr. Rice taught vocal music for a short time. In 1820 he married Miss Betsy Bane, and soon after the wedding he professed conversion. Though his father was a Presbyterian and his mother a Baptist, Thomas Rice united with the Methodists and became a circuit-riding preacher. However, after a few years he was forced to discontinue that activity due to a lung problem.

His next effort was at teaching school, and in the following several years, he served in that capacity in Perryville, Harrisburg, and Lagrange. His fame as an excellent teacher became well known. Thus in 1838, he was elected to the chair of mathematics in Georgetown College, but he declined the offer due to his wife's failing health. Mrs. Rice died the following year.

As opportunities presented themselves, Mr. Rice continued to preach occasionally. In his pulpit ministry he developed a taste for attacking controversial subjects, and in time, this led him to enter into debates. Possessing a quick mind, Mr. Rice experienced good success. He debated Thomas Fanning, a distinguished Campbellite preacher, and on another occasion he bested a Universalist in a well-publicized debate at Floydsburg, Kentucky. In 1839, he determined to prepare an unanswerable sermon on the "mode of baptism." He had frequently preached on the subject, but he had relied on the argumentation of those who favored sprinkling or pouring. He finally determined to undertake a thorough examination of the Bible texts and present an argument that immersionists could not refute.

As he studied, he was overwhelmed with material he had never considered. He reenacted the experiences of Adoniram Judson and Luther Rice in a similar examination. After carefully researching the subject, Mr. Rice came to the conclusion that water baptism as taught in the New Testament demands the immersion of believers. When he became fully convinced of this truth, Mr. Rice did not hesitate. He was baptized and united with the Pleasant Grove Baptist Church in Jefferson County, Kentucky, in 1840.

In that same year, he was ordained into the Baptist ministry. He was asked by a member of the ordination council how it was that he, being a classical scholar, had so long advocated sprinkling as baptism. Mr. Rice replied that he had simply taken the theory of his church leaders for granted. He had never examined the Scripture for himself. Reverend Rice lived only two more years, but he faithfully served Baptist churches in the role of pastor until, on October 3, 1842, he passed into the presence of His Savior.

Reader, have you obeyed the Lord in believer's immersion?

DLC

December 8

Confined in China

Scripture: 1 Peter 1:6-9

It would be well to read the entries of November 16 and February 9 with this material as it all pertains to Fred Donnelson, "Mr. Missions."

In our entry of November 16 we are told of the call of God upon Fred and Effie Donnelson to serve the Lord in China. The Great Depression made it impossible to gain needed support, but the Donnelsons dared to trust the Lord with only Divine financial assurance. Before leaving for the field, Mrs. Sweet, who was already there, had written them urging that they take an automobile. Fred's car was an old Model A Ford with over fifty thousand miles on it, and he knew that would not do. However, Donnelson got on his knees and prayed, "Lord show me Thy will in the matter." The Lord assured Fred through His Word that He would provide a car, and Fred thanked the Lord for His provision. A letter soon arrived from a believer in Minnesota offering Fred a new Ford V8 for China. Fred exchanged cars with the donor, and on February 11, 1933, the Donnelsons pulled out for Vancouver from where they would sail for China.

It is thrilling to read of the blessings of the Lord upon their ministry in China. As already mentioned, in one year Brother Donnelson was preaching in Chinese. However, of great interest is the fact that Brother Donnelson quickly learned an important principle of missions that many faithful men have never recognized. He wrote, "My biggest question, after arriving in China, was as to how best I could serve the Lord Jesus as a missionary there. I was thirty-five years of age and knew that learning the language would be difficult. Missionary children born and raised in China have an advantage over us adults who become missionaries. We can, by diligent study, learn the language and can talk and preach, but the missionaries who have been raised in the land not only can speak with the Chinese, but they can think with the Chinese . . . . Not having that advantage, I studied the question of how best I could invest my life. After seeing the fine young preachers and Bible women connected with our work—how zealous they were for the Lord and for souls and how able they were in reaching their own people with a little help from foreign friends—I decided that this is the method that God has honored in our mission in the past and is His will for the future. Dwight L. Moody used to say, 'It is better to put ten men to work than to try to do the work of ten men!' And so in the city and country churches around Hangchow I began to develop a special friendship with young men, for the purpose of enlisting them to become preachers."[1]

This method produced great results as twenty-five chapels were soon opened.

However in 1937 the Sino-Japanese War broke out, and the invading Japanese army soon began to penetrate inland. After three months the missionaries were forced to flee Hangchow, and they traveled by night in their car to Ningpo. There they boarded a steamer to Shanghai. After remaining in Shanghai for a period, the Lord burdened their hearts for the millions there, and they conceived an idea of reaching that City. First they would leave the war zone for furlough and return to the field as soon as it was feasible.

After eight months in America, the Donnelsons returned to Shanghai in 1938, and the blessings of the Lord were attendant upon the work. They again organized Chinese saints for service. The Shanghai Baptist Tabernacle became the center of spiritual activity. A Bible school with dormitories was built, and Fred followed the village chapel plan of attack.

When war between America and Japan began to seem possible, Paul Donnelson was sent back to the States to finish high school while living with his grandmother. Just a few months later, on December 7, 1941, the Japanese attacked Pearl Harbor. The Japanese had continued occupation of Hangchow and sections of Shanghai, and on December 8, Fred, Effie, and their fifteen year old daughter, Lois, were confined in their home by the Japanese. Soon they were interned, but we will tell that account in another entry.

Our God cares for His own, and the center of His will is the safest place for His children. Are you where the Lord wants you to be?

DLC

[1]Fred Donnelson, *Finding Freedom In A Japanese Prison Camp* (Chicago: World Fundamental Baptist Missionary Fellowship, n.d.), 57.

December 9

Another Scottish Evangelist

Scripture: Galations 6:1-6

John Linton was born in Edinburgh, Scotland, the oldest son of eleven children. Being reared in poverty, he responded with resentment, and often ran away. It appeared that his life would be one of a vagabond. Like others around him, he found that his life centered in cheating, lying, and stealing. God, however, intervened with grace when John was thirteen. While begging, a gracious lady - Mrs. McMichael, not only fed him but provided him with some better clothing. Then she invited John to attend Sunday school at the Bristo Baptist Church where her husband taught the teen-aged boys in Sunday school. It was in the Sunday school where John learned of the grace of the Lord Jesus Christ. Unfortunately, John had no encouragement at home, and in the course of time his love of the Savior cooled, and he found himself back with the old crowd of wayward boys.

Our Lord has promised, however, to complete the work of salvation when once a person is genuinely saved, and the Lord began working in John's life. He and a young friend decided to walk to a town about twenty miles from Edinburgh. In that town of Dunfermline a sweet lady treated John and his friend with such kindness that John was reminded of the loving Heavenly Father. He repented and made things right with the Lord.

John went from there onward to a mining town, and just before his fourteenth birthday he found employment in a coalpit. After a year of working and maturing there, John returned to Edinburgh and found employment with his father as an iron-molder. This allowed him again to attend the Bristo Place Church, and he began to grow in grace. When seventeen years of age, he was baptized and joined the church. It was then that John decided to emigrate to Canada. The trip took fourteen days, and John found himself in Hamilton, Ontario. He obtained employment and joined the James Street Baptist Church.

In the Fall of 1909 the Lord was moving upon John's heart for Christian service. Seeing an advertisement for the Gordon Bible College in Boston, he enrolled there. Under the consecrated teaching he received, Linton grew "like a plant in a hothouse."[1] His pastor persuaded him to go to a Baptist college in Woodstock, where he could finish high school work as well. All the while he was preparing to preach, he was busy "practicing preaching." In quick succession John Linton received a master's degree, married his childhood sweetheart, and became a pastor. His first pastoral experience was in Reston, Manitoba. Great blessings were experienced. From there the Lord led him to accept a call to the pastorate of High Park Baptist Church, in Toronto. After four blessed years there he was asked to accept a call to Montreal to the Point St. Charles Baptist Church. Souls were saved and the church was greatly revived, and it was there that Reverend Linton became vitally interested in revival and evangelism. An illustration of God's blessing is contained in the following letter:

> Morrisburg, Ontario
> December 9, 1923.
>
> My Dear Friend and Pastor,
>
> As I take my pen to write these lines in the little town of Morrisburg, you and the good people at Point St. Charles Baptist Church will be just about assembling in the house of God to render thanks to Him for the blessings of the week. . . . It is but a short while ago, that the writer, as you know, was a complete wreck, physical, mental and spiritual, miserable and helpless in the very depths

of sin, expecting the end at any moment, his wife brokenhearted, his little boy afraid of his daddy. This Sabbath day could you but see us in our comfortable home, I am sure you would utter a heartfelt prayer of thanksgiving to Him Who made such a transformation possible....[2]

With the call of God to evangelism, John Linton crisscrossed Canada and the United States with Heaven-blessed revivals and evangelistic campaigns. He left a trail of converts, and revived, restored, and rejoicing congregations. His compelling Scotch brogue, and his faithfulness to the Lord and His Word, were trademarks that followed John until his home-going in 1965. Just as he would have wanted, John Linton died in the pulpit while preaching the unsearchable riches of Christ. He was seventy-seven years old.

It would be well today to pray for local church evangelists who spend and are spent for Jesus Christ.

DLC

---

[1]John Linton, *From Coalpit to Pulpit* (Light and Life Press, 1947), 47.

[2]Linden, 96

December 10

A Great Influence and a Dilemma

Scripture: 1 Kings 18:17-21

Augustus Hopkins Strong was born on August 3, 1836, and died on November 29, 1921. His father, converted under the ministry of Charles Finney, was a newspaper executive in Rochester, New York. Strong was saved as a young man and prepared for the ministry. He graduated from Yale in 1857 and from the Rochester Theological Seminary in 1859. From 1861-1872, he pastored churches in Haverhill, Massachusetts, and Cleveland, Ohio. His illustrious career as president of Rochester Theological Seminary began in 1872 and lasted until 1912. He was memorialized in many publications shortly after his death. On December 10, 1921, Arthur W. Cleaves wrote an article in his honor entitled *A Great Leader Has Passed.*[1]

Strong's life was, and is, truly significant. He was one of the leading theological educators of his day. He led the Rochester Seminary for forty years. Six universities conferred honorary degrees on him in recognition of his leadership.

Strong was also a prolific writer. Of his lesser known works, I am privileged to own his *One Hundred Chapel Talks to Theological Students* (published in 1913) and *Popular Lectures on the Books of the New Testament* (published in 1914). The most significant of Strong's writings is *Systematic Theology*, published in 1886 and revised in 1907. The last edition of it remains in print. I have used Strong's work for all my ministry. Within the last two or three years, I found a used copy of the first edition and paid dearly to purchase it. Strong's *Systematic Theology* is still a valuable resource for a preacher. I personally own several systematic theology works. Every time I work with systematic theology I consult Strong, as well as newer works. Much of it is scriptural and rich with evidence of an intimate relationship with the Lord.

Strong possessed a droll wit. He often wrote of how he solved problems decisively, saying "I cut that dog's tail off behind his ears!" If one reads carefully, he will find Strong's humor embedded in his theology.

Strong's life is also a dilemma for one who studies him. He ministered in the years that evolution and higher criticism impacted the theological landscape. Strong was torn by these issues, and his life and work reveal that conflict. "The stress is not in his massive doctrinal system, but beneath the system, in the shadowy underworld of suppositions about the origin and nature of religious knowledge itself."[2] To put it simply, Strong held to orthodox doctrine, but simultaneously he was influenced by the liberal attack against the affirmation that the Bible is the revelation from God.

This struggle shows in Strong's theology. In 1886 he defended the biblical account of creation, but in 1907 he argued for theistic evolution. On his faculty he hired Walter Rauschenbusch, the father of the social gospel, and at the same time, he hired the conservative A. H. Newman. He was close friends with noted liberals of the day but also enjoyed fellowship with conservatives A. J. Gordon and Alva Hovey.[3] After hiring notorious liberals, he lamented the inroads that liberalism was making in the Northern Baptist Convention schools. At age 84, he wrote an article commending the

Fundamental Fellowship (now the FBF) after its first meeting. "To the end he clung to the conviction that the faith once delivered unto the fathers somehow stands above the vicissitudes of history, even as he became increasingly conscious that all things human are fragile creations of time and place."[4] Strong's life and ministry is a conundrum. We certainly remember with favor his good and positive work, and we can profit from his writings. We wonder how he could be so comfortable with liberals and their blasphemous teachings.

We look at Strong's life and learn a good lesson. *We must take God's Word for what it says it is!* Moses declared that God has revealed Himself to us (Deuteronomy. 29:29). Jesus affirmed that God's Word is truth (John. 17:17). Paul calls it ". . . the word of truth" (2 Timothy 2:15) and rebukes those who ". . . concerning the truth have erred" (2 Timothy 2:18). Let us take God at His word and believe His Word. We must determine not to limp between the opinions of modern thinkers and the affirmations of Scripture. Let us obey Scripture and proclaim it to a lost world.

FJM

---

[1]Arthur W. Cleaves, "A Great Leader Has Passed," *Baptist* (10 December 1921) cited in Grant Wacker, *Augustus H. Strong and the Dilemma of Historical Consciousness* (Macon, GA: Mercer University Press, 1985), 2.

[2]Ibid., 9.

[3]Ibid., 4-5.

[4]Ibid., 13.

December 11

Faithful to the End!

Scripture: 2 Timothy 3:12

Konshaubi Dzhangetov was a huge man; and as he approached Georgi Vins in the prison in the Russian Urals, the Baptist preacher did not know what to expect. Vins had just been delivered to the prison that would be his home for the next two years. Other prisoners confronted the Baptist preacher and were threatening; but when they discovered that Vins had no money, the angry crowd dispersed. Not so with Konshaubi Dzhangetov. The man's physical size caused Georgi Vins some concern until Konshaubi spoke. He had heard Vins tell the crowd: "I'm a Christian, sentenced to three years for my faith in God." When the others left, Konshaubi neared Vins and asked: "Are you a brother?" Vins could hardly believe that this man was indeed a believer; but he replied, "Yes, I'm a believer. What about you?" At that, Konshaubi grasped Vin's hand warmly and said, "I'm also a believer-"I'm your brother in Christ! . . . I used to be a Muslim, but at 19 I believed in Jesus Christ as my personal Savior. For over 20 years I've followed Him, and now I'm in prison for preaching the gospel."[1]

During Russia's communist regime, Baptists were continually arrested for daring to preach the gospel of God's Son. Konshaubi Dzhangetov was imprisoned three times, but he remained faithful. Just a bit of background might prove interesting. Konshaubi was a Circassian by birth and grew up in a Muslim village in the Caucasus Mountains in southern Russia. During his youth, communist leaders closed the mosque in his town. One day as young Konshaubi was pasturing sheep in a nearby field, an elderly Russian believer told him of the Lord Jesus Christ. The elderly gentleman invited young Konshaubi to attend the believers' meetings. There, Konshaubi was given a New Testament. In the course of time, the youth called upon the Lord Jesus Christ to save him. This led to great family pressure, and before long, Konshaubi had to choose between his family or his Lord. Making that difficult decision, Konshaubi determined to follow Christ, and he was forced to move from his family and town.

Soon the young man met his life partner, a godly lady named Tonya. They lived in a village about 60 miles from Konshaubi's former town. There was a Baptist church in their town, and at first they were very happy in it. However, the church leaders began to compromise so as to save their standing with the communist leaders. They decided to register, and thus they surrendered their autonomy. Furthermore, at the insistence of the communist leaders, they agreed that their youth suspend all Bible study and evangelism. Other compromises were made, and the power of God was lost. Realizing their spiritual destitution, Konshaubi challenged the congregation to be willing to suffer for the cause of Christ. A small minority of the church membership agreed, and private worship services were begun. Konshaubi became a leader. The new-found freedom of worship was enjoyable, but Konshaubi soon discovered the reality of the words of the Apostle. Paul had written to Timothy: "All that will live godly in Christ Jesus shall suffer persecution." In 1966, six months after establishing an independent Baptist church, Konshaubi was arrested and sentenced to three years imprisonment. In 1969 the three-year term was completed, and Konshaubi returned to faithful service for the Savior. In 1973 the man of God was again arrested and sentenced to three years' imprisonment in a camp in the far North near Archangelsk.

Konshaubi endured much there for the cause of our Savior. Upon the completion of his second incarceration, in 1976 Konshaubi again returned home. His prison terms had not dampened his spirit, and he continued to minister. Again the 56-year-old servant of God was arrested on October 30, 1985. His five-day trial took place on December 10, 11, 16, 17, 18, 1985. Once more he was found guilty. A three-year term of "strict regime" was imposed upon God's faithful witness for the third time.

As we read of such heroes as Konshaubi Dzhangetov we realize what little fundamental Christians in America know of suffering. May we ask the Lord to make us willing for any sacrifice, that we might be found faithful to the Savior.

DLC

---

[1]Georgi Vins, *Konshaubi - A True Story of Persecuted Christians in the Soviet Union* (Grand Rapids, MI: Baker Book House, 1988), 21.

December 12

Promotion From Captain to Preacher

Scripture: Hebrews 2:9-11

Robert Stockton was born in Albemarle County, Virginia, on December 12, 1743. His parents were Presbyterian, and early in life he became impressed with the matter of religion. Before he reached manhood, he united with the denomination of his parents. When he arrived at maturity, Robert Stockton joined the army as a captain in the service of the King of England.

While in the military, he became concerned about his salvation. He engaged in soul searching and private prayer until he experienced an adjustment in his feelings. He had never been taught anything concerning personal faith that leads to experiential Christianity, and thus he could not explain the peaceful state of mind that flooded him. Soon after that experience, he heard a Mr. Davis preach, and immediately he recognized the exercises of his own heart to be the work of divine grace. With a renewed interest in spiritual truth, he was caused to seriously investigate the Scriptures. Through that exercise, he became convinced of the duty of believer's baptism. When the opportunity became available, he presented himself as a candidate for baptism. He was immersed by Samuel Harris in 1771, and united with the Baptist church in Henry County, Virginia.

Immediately after his baptism, he called his troops together and directed them to stand at attention. He then addressed them as follows: "Gentlemen, I have found another King, and have enlisted in His service. I am now going to leave you. But, before we part, allow me to read from the order of my Commander."[1] He then read them a chapter from God's Word and called them to join with him in prayer. This done, he resigned his captaincy and entered into the service of the Lord Jesus Christ.

Few men in Virginia were ever more active and zealous in preaching the gospel than was Robert Stockton. He possessed an invincible boldness. He was a great soul-winner, and as a result, his efforts in church planting were greatly blessed of God.

During the Revolutionary War, and just before the Battle of Brandywine, the man of God, like David, visited the army to see how his brethren were doing and to encourage them. During the battle, he was captured by the British, and he spent two years as their prisoner. When he was given his freedom, he returned home to discover that his dear wife had not only supported the family, but she had paid off all their indebtedness. Robert Stockton took up his spiritual work immediately and continued his ministry in Virginia with great zeal until the close of the eighteenth century. In his history of Baptists in Virginia, Semple says, "Although his usefulness was so obvious in this country, and although he was among the richest men in those parts, his mind was not at rest. From some cause . . . he moved to Kentucky and settled within the limits of Green River Association."[2]

In the providence of God, Mr. Stockton arrived in Kentucky in 1799. This was just prior to a great revival, which swept through Kentucky during the first two years of the 19th century. In that great moving of God, Robert Stockton was very active. The Lord of the Harvest raised up many valuable young preachers during that time, and Mr. Stockton left his mark on many as he trained and encouraged them in the work. The man of God pastored the Dripping Spring church, which prospered tremendously under his leadership. He was elected to serve as Moderator of the Green River Association, and served in that capacity until he became too old and feeble to continue on. Mr. Stockton labored faithfully until he was summoned on high. The man of God died in great peace in his eighty-second year.

From captain, to preacher, to prisoner of war, Robert Stockton was found faithful. Let us determine to serve, whatever the circumstances and wherever His will leads, that we might be to the praise of His glory.

DLC

---

[1]J. H. Spencer, *A History of Kentucky Baptists* (Cincinnati: J. R. Baumes, 1885), 1: 380.

[2]Ibid., 381.

December 13

By Life or by Death

Scripture: Acts 12:1-17

The will of our omniscient God is at times past finding out. The Lord delivered Peter from prison, but James was allowed to suffer martyrdom for Christ's glory. Is God able to protect and deliver His own? Surely He is! We understand and recognize the *power* of God, but here on earth, we do not always know His *purpose*. Our responsibility is to walk in the center of His will and sincerely pray, "Thy will be done."

Our attention today is focused upon a rural Baptist preacher who ministered in North Carolina and Virginia. Ed ward Sylvester Pierce was born in Gates County, North Carolina, on December 13, 1870. He was privileged to have been born into a godly family, and his parents dedicated him to the Lord early in his life. After Edward Pierce had been saved at age sixteen, he sensed the hand of the Lord upon his life. As he grew it was evident that he was gifted in public speaking. He pursued his education to be better enabled to preach the Word of God. Thus, he took his undergraduate work at Wake Forest, and then graduated from Southern Baptist Seminary.

As a preacher, he was studious and well prepared, but he was also as bold as a lion and preached against sin. Because of his strong convictions and powerful preaching, Pastor Pierce cultivated many friendships, but he also made many enemies. You will remember that in 1920 with the passing of the eighteenth amendment to our national constitution, prohibition had become the law of the land. The Mafia immediately entered the arena, and bootlegging to provide illegal alcoholic beverages became the rage. Many Baptist preachers declared war on bootleggers, and Reverend Edward Pierce was such a preacher.

The preaching of the fifty-three-year-old pastor surely struck a nerve with some of the Mafia, and he was tragically cut down with gunfire in the presence of his wife and little six-week-old daughter. The article in the *Herald*, follows: "On the fifth day of June, 1923, two Garrett brothers armed approached and invaded the Baptist parsonage at the Cumberland Court House, Cumberland County, Virginia, about eight o'clock in the morning. Mrs. Pierce, with a cooing baby girl in her arms, met the armed Garretts at the door and informed the men that her husband was in bed. When the two men insisted on seeing the preacher he was called and came to the door, from which he was dragged into the yard, his nose broken, his face beat up, one eye beaten to a poultice. The second brother allowed no one to render any assistance to the struggling minister, not even his frail wife with the little six-week-old girl in her arms, for she was shoved aside and threatened. The minister finally broke away from his antagonist and went into the house marking his way on the grass and floor with a stream of blood. Seeming to be almost dazed he came back to order the intruders from his home when he was shot down, and repeatedly shot after he was prostrated, dead!"[1]

Needless to say, the death of this country preacher created great excitement far and wide as the daily newspapers heralded the account of the murder and court trial that followed.

But once again, anarchy is proliferating in America. The issue is no longer prohibition, but our major cities are experiencing gang warfare. Terror roams some districts. Drug abuse is "big business" in the underworld. Society and the Supreme Court have accepted abortion as the norm, and homosexuality with its so-called "same sex marriages" looms ever larger. Needless to say, the time will soon be upon us when euthanasia will be accepted as a program to "improve society." These issues are not merely political, they are moral, and though Baptist preachers are to "teach the Word," these issues impose themselves upon the texts of Scripture.

Will it become dangerous again to stand for truth and against error? Doubtless so, but we are called to preach the Word without fear or favor. Pray for your pastor today as the befuddled society of the twenty-first century challenges the very truth of God's Word.

DLC

---

[1]George Braxton Taylor, *Virginia Baptist Ministers* (Lynchburg, VA: J. P. Bell Company, 1935), 6:143.

December 14

Baptist by Conviction

Scripture: 2 Timothy 3:14-17

Often the life of a notable servant of Christ is the product of godly influence. That is certainly the case in the life of Ernest D. Pickering, who was born on December 14, 1928 in St. Petersburg, Florida. Ernest was the first of two boys born to Ernest J. and Evelyn Ida Pickering. The elder Pickerings were officers in the Salvation Army. When Evelyn was a teenage girl and already a Christian, she heard Evangeline Booth speak. The daughter of the Salvation Army's founder challenged the several hundred girls that day with the question: "Will you leave all for Christ?" Evelyn dedicated her life to the Lord's service, and she and Ernest J. Pickering invested their life together in God's service. After his retirement from the active service in the Salvation Army, the elder Pickering served several years as a nationwide motel chain's chaplains' administrator. He served the Lord until his death.

Ernest Pickering came to know Christ as his Savior as a lad. He enrolled in Bob Jones University after his high school years. After graduation in 1948, he entered Dallas Theological Seminary, where he earned the Th.M and Th.D. degrees. In 1952 he married Ariel Yvonne Thomas, a preacher's daughter.

Dr. Pickering's first pastorate was in New Kensington, Pennsylvania, from which he was called to be the national executive secretary of the Independent Fundamental Churches of America in 1957. Mrs. Pickering recounts that as he visited the churches in this fellowship, he saw several Baptist churches. He began studying the Scriptures and embraced Baptist principles by conviction.[1]

Ernest Pickering's fidelity to Scripture was nurtured in his home as a boy and in his theological training. When he saw and understood the principles of a New Testament church, he was quick to act upon them. After just two years in the position with the IFCA, he left this place of prominence to become pastor of the Woodcrest Baptist Church in Fridley, Minnesota, and dean of the fledgling Central Conservative Baptist Seminary in Minneapolis. God richly blessed his ministry. Woodcrest Baptist was a small church of one hundred or less. In just six years of ministry the church grew to about four hundred. At the same time, Central Seminary grew from just over thirty students to more than one hundred. (I count it an honor that he was my Systematic Theology professor during my seminary years.) Pickering challenged his students academically, instilled in them a fervor and enthusiasm for biblical preaching, and ignited a love for the souls of lost men. He was a preacher and a professor. His students did not learn theology from a dry academician, but from a man who loved God, built a growing, vibrant church, and lived his teaching and preaching.

At this point, we should comment on one other aspect of Dr. Pickering's ministry in Minnesota: It is readily apparent that as both pastor and seminary professor, he pursued two full-time ministries. Either ministry was in itself a full time occupation, but he did them both well and successfully.

Forced at that time to leave the upper Midwest by health concerns, the Pickerings moved to Kokomo, Indiana, where for four years Ernest served the Bible Baptist Church as its pastor. From there he was called to Clarks Summit, Pennsylvania he was first dean and then president of Baptist Bible College. Other ministries took him to Toledo, Ohio, Tacoma, Washington, back to Clarks Summit, and then back to Minneapolis, where he pastored the Fourth Baptist Church and served as president of Central Baptist Theological Seminary. In 1993 he became the deputation director at Baptist World Mission. When his final illness first took his sight in 1996, he continued as a field representative for BWM until his death on October 16, 2000.

This essay only begins to tell the story of Ernest Pickering's life, which we will consider again. It leaves us with some important lessons. Parents, it is vitally important that we who know the Lord serve Him faithfully and invest our lives in rearing our children for His glory. As Baptists we affirm that the Word of God is our only rule for what we believe and what we live. We must put that biblical conviction to work on our lives and obey the truth we believe and know.

FJM

---

[1]Interview with Yvonne Pickering, January 14, 2003.

December 15

The First Amendment and the "Remnant"

Scripture: John 4:24

From earliest time Baptists, both particular and general, have agreed unanimously that the government exists only for the collection of taxes, the restraint of lawbreakers, the punishment of crime, and the protection of all citizens of a nation. Historians have recognized that "the Novatians were persecuted by Constantine, the first to unite church and state. . . ."[1] From that time, true Bible-believers have been oppressed by Rome and later by the Reformers. It is a well-known fact that one of the results of the Reformation was the crushing of our Anabaptist forefathers in the pincer movement of persecution from both Rome and the Reformers. It is of interest that a member of the Westminster Assembly said: "Liberty of conscience and toleration of any and all religions is so prodigious an impiety that this religious parliament cannot but abhor the very meaning of it."[2]

On page ix of the preface of a most interesting volume, *That First Amendment and the Remnant*, Editor Richard Culp wrote, "The Anabaptists stood almost alone in Europe in championing this freedom [I.E. soul liberty]. Luther, Zwingli, and later Calvin likewise reacted against the ecclesiastical Rome's oppression of minorities. They all originally advocated freedom of choice in religion, believers' baptism, and nonresistance. But one by one these great leaders had what the author calls a 'second conversion.' They each compromised and established and maintained state churches, denying freedom of religious choice, and oppressing minorities within their countries."

Leonard Verduin, author of the volume referred to above, served for twenty years as chaplain at the University of Michigan for the Christian Reformed denomination. In an appendix he wrote: ". . . it is evident that the First Amendment was meant to put an end to an old debate as to *mode'd'integration* of church and state. We have seen that Christianity started with a new *mode'd'integration*, that this new mode was then, in the early fourth century, pushed aside as the other, the older, mode was adopted. And it has become evident (so we think) that from this moment on there was on the scene an element (to which the name 'Remnant' has been given) that was unable in-conscience to go-along with the new (but very old) view as to *mode'd'integration*. And we think it has become evident that, although there is a historiography that closes its eyes to the presence of this Remnant, the fact is that the First Amendment was in a very real way the product of the thought-system adhered-to by the Remnant."

Thank God, Bible believing Baptists are part of the "Remnant." The first amendment to our national constitution, which was adopted on December 15, 1792, was the gift to America of our Baptist forefathers. Reuben E. Alley in *A History of Baptists in Virginia* expounds on the historic meeting that was held between John Leland, Baptist preacher, and James Madison. The Baptists of Virginia opposed ratification of the constitution, and Virginia was a "swing" state. The vote was vital. Leland, at that meeting, carefully explained Baptist reluctance to accept the constitution without a Bill of Rights and assurance that the federal government would not establish a "State" church. It was there that Madison agreed to propose the Bill of Rights, and the Baptists of Virginia began to promote the ratification of the constitution. The result is evident. "If the researchers of the world were asked who was most responsible for the American guaranty for religious liberty, their prompt reply would be 'James Madison'; but if James Madison might answer, he would as quickly reply, 'John Leland and the Baptists.'"[3]

DLC

---

[1]David Burcham Ray, *The Baptist Succession* (Gallatin, TN: 1984), 179.

[2]Leonard Verduin, *That First Amendment and the Remnant* (Sarasota, FL: The Christian Hymnary Publishers, 1998), 322.

[3]Joseph Martin Dawson, *Baptists and the American Republic* (Nashville, TN: Broadman Press, 1956), 117.

December 16

Taxing for God?

Scripture: 1 Samuel 17:29b

Boston was a hot-bed of rebellion against the British in American Colonial days, and the British General, Thomas Gage, had sent in two regiments to maintain peace. Sentries were posted and armament was put in place, and citizens were often challenged. Frequent quarrels took place between the populace and the British troops. On March 5, 1770, a crowd of men and boys, maddened by the military presence, insulted the city guard. A fight ensued in which three citizens were killed and eight wounded. Bells were rung; the country people rushed in to help; and it was only with great difficulty that quiet was restored.

The British government had rescinded the taxes, with the exception of that on tea—which was left to maintain the principle. An arrangement was made whereby tea was furnished at a lower price in the colonies than that maintained in England. This subterfuge exasperated the patriots. They were fighting for a great principle, not against a paltry tax. The citizenry determined to boycott the product. At Charleston, the tea was stored in damp cellars, and it soon spoiled. The tea ships at New York and Philadelphia were sent home. The British authorities, however, refused to let the tea ships return from Boston. On December 16, 1773, a party of men, disguised as Indians, boarded the vessels and emptied three hundred and forty-two chests of tea into the water.

You are aware of the continuing history as General Gage fortified Boston Neck. Companies of Americans called "Minute Men" were formed, and the words of Patrick Henry, "Give me liberty or give me death," rang from every quarter of the area.

But, in the midst of all of this, Isaac Backus, as the representative of the Baptists in Massachusetts, was weighing in against the "church tax" that was so grievous to the Baptists. The British tax on tea, which had led to the "Boston Tea Party," was not as bad as the clergy tax that Massachusetts imposed upon Baptists. Isaac Backus wrote thus to the Massachusetts Assembly on December 2, 1774: "All America is alarmed by the tea tax, though, if they please, they can avoid by not buying the tea; but we have no such liberty. We must either pay the little tax, or else your people appear, even in this time of extremity, determined to lay the great one upon us." Of course, Isaac Backus was referring to the clergy tax whereby Baptists were forced to contribute to the support of ministers of the state church. "These lines are written," he continued, "to let you know that Baptists will not pay the clergy tax, not only under your principle of taxation without representation, but because we dare not render homage to an earthly power which we are convinced belongs only to God."[1]

How amazing that those who were part of the state church despised taxation without representation and fought against the British taxing system side by side with Baptist neighbors. Yet they sought to impose the clergy tax on Baptists without realizing the parallel that could so easily be seen. As representative of the Baptist churches in

Massachusetts, Mr. Backus brought to light many cases of Baptists who had been fined and imprisoned for refusing to pay the tax. As Mr. Backus made his strong appeals, John Adams responded: "They might as well expect the stars to change their course as to expect Massachusetts to give up the established church." Samuel Adams said that the Baptists making complaint were no more than "enthusiasts who make a show of suffering persecution."

Nine of the thirteen colonies had state churches. Baptists opposed the state-supported church system, and they stood firm in refusing to bow to such pressure. Thank God, America became the "Land of the Free." May we ever be alert to maintain the wonderful freedom that God has allowed our forefathers to secure.

DLC

---

[1]Alvah Hovey, *A Memoir of the Life and Times of the Rev. Isaac Backus* (Harrisonburg, VA: Gano Books, 1991), 220-221.

December 17

120,000 Miles on Horseback for Christ

Scripture: Romans 10:13-17

Barnet Grimsley was born in Culpeper County, Virginia, and he spent his entire life and ministry there. Just a few years before, the Separate Baptists had experienced great persecution in that very setting, but at his birth on December 17, 1807, the Gospel had free course in the countryside. The horizon on the West provided a long line of miles of the beautiful Blue Ridge Mountains. These accentuated the glory and dignity of the landscape. When he was nine years of age young Barnet revealed evidence of an unusual memory. At twelve years of age, though he was not saved, he preached his first sermon on *The Being and Perfections of God.*

Until he was eighteen the lad worked with his father on the farm, but during that time, in any spare moments, he read all he could. Although his books were few, those he had, he memorized. At twenty years of age he started a milling business for farmers, and he operated the mill for five years. During that time, two important events took place in his life. Chronologically, the first was his marriage to Ruth Updek, a farmer's daughter. Secondly, Barnet and Ruth trusted Christ personally and were baptized in November of 1831. Barnet gave himself to the Word of God, and in only a year's time he was licensed to preach. Soon thereafter he gave up the milling business that he might give himself to the ministry. On November 25, 1833, he was ordained to the gospel ministry and became pastor of Cedar Creek Baptist Church, which he had founded.

Pastor Grimsley began his ministry when the anti-missionary movement was widespread. In those days, those who were anti-missionary minded were referred to as the "Old School," while those who favored missions were designated as the "New School." There was no question as to Barnet's position in the controversy, for he served as a missionary throughout the area for a few years, receiving partial support from the Board of the Salem Union Association.

His was a fruitful and distinguished ministry for over half a century. As was often the pattern in those days, he sometimes pastored four churches at a time. The length of the pastorates varied, but it appears that he had unvarying success in all of them. After his first year of ministry, his reputation grew and he was known as an excellent preacher. He had the unique ability of making practical applications, and his marvelous memory was a great benefit to him.

While traveling from church to church in the saddle, he would commit to memory his sermon material. Often he was asked to repeat a sermon that had proved to be a special blessing when first he delivered it, and he could recall the sermon word for word.

Regarding his preaching Dr. John A. Broadus said, "Into his exhortations he poured all the tremendous earnestness of strong convictions, great-hearted love, and a deep sense of ministerial responsibility. All that he said was admitted as true and binding, and his own straightforward sincerity and consuming earnestness were fully recognized. Many a time the building seemed to shake with the passion of his appeals."

Yet another gives this illustration of the tenderness and effectiveness of his preaching: "On one occasion, at his own church, his sermon was so powerful that the whole congregation was melted to tears, many coming forward and asking the prayers of God's people. As soon as quiet was restored, one of the brethren rose and suggested that the meeting be continued through the week. He stated that they all intended sowing their wheat that week; it was the best time, but it was far more important that their children should be converted than that their wheat should be seeded. The meeting was continued with gracious results. It was noted that at the next harvest the wheat crop was unusually good.

Toward the end of his life, Pastor Grimsley estimated he had traveled 125,000 miles on horseback through that beautiful mountain area. His keynote was faithfulness. Is that true of your life? Someone has well said, "The greatest ability is dependability." May that characteristic be real in our lives of service today.

EGC

December 18

Ready to Preach, Pray, or Die

Scripture: Numbers 27:15-17

In Colonial America, Baptist preachers had to be fearless. Old John Courtney served the First Baptist Church of Richmond, Virginia, as pastor for thirty-six years. He surely must be considered a dauntless leader. He had battled for religious freedom against Virginia's state church system, and he had served in the Continental Army during the Revolutionary War. There is, however, an historical account of the white-haired, stooped-shouldered, old pastor that will ever be etched in my mind: "During the War of 1812, there was sounded a false alarm that enemy troops, proceeding up the James River from Norfolk, were nearing Richmond. Armed men appeared in the public square. Among them was the seventy-year-old Baptist minister and Revolutionary War veteran, John Courtney, his old musket in his hand, ready once more to defend his country."[1]

His manly character, godly sincerity, consistent and faithful life, commanded universal respect.

John Courtney was born in 1744 into an Episcopalian family. His father died when John was but a child, and the family inheritance was given to an older brother. John was apprenticed to a carpenter, and other than this, we know little of his youth. He was led to Christ under the preaching of a Separate Baptist preacher, and in time he became the first pastor of Rehoboth Baptist Church in King William County. The church flourished, but the young pastor left that charge to serve during that period in the Continental Army.

In his forty-fifth year, in 1788, Elder Courtney assumed the pastorate of Richmond's First Baptist Church, and he served exclusively as pastor or senior pastor until his death thirty-six years later. Under his pastoral care the congregation flourished. At the time of his death, there were 820 members. But his ministry was surely unique.

Elder Courtney wanted to reveal a decided difference between the polity of his congregation and that of the state church. As a result, he received no stipulated salary. "At the close of the morning service on the Lord's Day, a hat collection was taken by Deacons at each door of the Church. The money thus collected was emptied into the handkerchief of the senior Deacon, wrapped up, carried to the Pastor's house, and put into a bowl in the cupboard. This same, much or little, was his salary."[2]

Because the Church of England preachers were afforded a home paid for by the "clergy tax," Elder Courtney never wanted to own a home. From time to time in his preaching, he enjoyed quoting the couplet:

> No foot of land do I possess,
> Nor cottage in this wilderness.

As a result of this conviction, he rented a house for his family. But in time, a generous benefactor gave him a house and lot. On the next occasion that Elder Courtney began to quote the couplet, he stopped and corrected himself. The following week, he went to his friend and returned the property, saying, he would rather have his lines than the house.

Elder Courtney never "retired" from the call of God. "Even when too old and infirm to dismount from his horse he rode, cane in hand, from door to door, and calling the friends out to him would encourage, counsel, and exhort them, sometimes closing his interview with prayer on horseback in the street."[3]

As he grew older and the congregation grew larger, an assistant pastor was secured, and Elder Courtney graciously trained him in the work. The dear old man of God died on December 18, 1824, but he had stamped his godly influence upon those of his generation. May God give us twenty-first century pastors who preach without fear or favor, and who practice fidelity and faithfulness to the Lord and His work.

DLC

---

[1]Theodore F. Adams, *First Baptist Church Richmond 1780-1955* (Richmond, VA: Whittet & Shepperson, 1955), 26.

[2]J. L. Burrows, *The First Century of The First Baptist Church of Richmond, Virginia* (Richmond: Carlton McCarthy, 1880), 119-120.

[3]Ibid., 122.

December 19

An Eye Single for His Glory

Scripture: Isaiah 42:1-8

Elsewhere we have meditated on the conversion, call to the ministry, and first pastorates of Richard V. Clearwaters. His last ministry is so significant that it deserves its own consideration.

After a fruitful ministry at Calvary Baptist Church in Cedar Rapids, Iowa, Clearwaters was called to Fourth Baptist Church in Minneapolis, Minnesota. He began his ministry there January 1, 1940. Fourth Baptist was organized on December 19, 1881, and had become a strong, influential church.

This ministry is first significant because of its *longevity*. Dr. Clearwaters pastored this church for forty-two years. That in itself is noteworthy.

Dr. Clearwaters' ministry is notable because it was marked by *evangelism*. For years he made twenty-five calls per week, personally winning many to Christ. He told me that at one time, when people were saved at Fourth Baptist Church, three things were generally true. First, the family had somehow been influenced by the church's ministry for five years. Second, he knew them personally by first and last name. Third, in the soul-winning process he himself had been in their homes to witness to them. With such a pastoral example, it is no wonder the church was filled with folks who involved themselves in soul winning.

His ministry at Fourth Baptist Church is significant because it is a record of *unparalleled growth*. The congregation numbered about four hundred in 1940. Untold numbers of people came to Christ through the ministries of the church. At its zenith, attendance averaged more than 1,200. High attendances exceeded that number many times. The church grew numerically and in strength and influence. Over the years the church started a Christian day school, built educational facilities and a 2,400 seat auditorium, purchased land in Wisconsin to establish Camp Clearwaters, and led in the formation of Central Baptist Theological Seminary.

Clearwaters' ministry at Fourth Baptist Church is a study in *biblical separatism*. Clearwaters had completed his education in Kalamazoo College and the University of Chicago, both liberal institutions. He had seen the growing liberalism within the Northern (now American) Baptist Convention. He had "locked horns" with convention liberals in Iowa. He was a patient leader, but eleven years after arriving in Minneapolis, he led Fourth Baptist Church to separate from the Convention. The church sought fellowship within the Conservative Baptist movement. Clearwaters, along with others, fought the encroaching New Evangelicalism within that movement, and in the 1960s led the church out of that organization. The church remains an independent, fundamental Baptist church.

Clearwaters' ministry is notable because of his *educational influence*. In his early years in Minneapolis he served as Dean of Northwestern Seminary, founded by Dr. W. B. Riley. When that school closed, Fourth Baptist Church formed Central

Baptist Theological Seminary in 1956. In 1957 "Doc" led in the formation of Pillsbury Baptist Bible College in Owatonna, Minnesota. Thousands of young people have been trained for the ministry in the institutions he founded. That influence has reached around the world.

Clearwaters' ministry was notable because of his *personal character.* He influenced those who came into his life by his own personality. Keen insight, a lively sense of humor, solid preaching, and strong convictions characterized him. In seminary, I was privileged to have him for twelve hours of practical theology courses in one year. To sit in his classes was to "catch" a philosophy of the ministry, a firm commitment to the authority of Scripture, a zeal for preaching, a love for lost souls, and a passion to do one thing:glorify God. Clearwaters' life verse was a verse we have read today-Isaiah 42:8. He would often say that in all the ministry, preachers must "keep an eye single for His glory." The determination to glorify God dominated Clearwaters' thinking.

Dr. Clearwaters retired from his forty-two year ministry on April 4, 1982. Old age took its toll, and he entered the Lord's presence on September 26, 1996. His life stands as a challenge to us. May we live in the firm conviction that God has revealed Himself to us in His Word, for we will never fail when we obey that Word. May we determine to love the souls of men and seek their salvation, as we invest our lives in living for God's glory.

FJM

December 20

Christ in the Military Camps

Scripture: 2 Timothy 2:1-4

Reverend John William Jones, chaplain, minister, and author was mentioned in a previous volume. He was born in Virginia on September 25, 1836, and was born again while a teenager. In 1855 he entered the University of Virginia, where he took his undergraduate work. He matriculated as the first student at Southern Baptist Theological Seminary in Greenville, South Carolina, in 1859, and the following year he was appointed as a missionary for service in China. On December 20, 1860, John William Jones was married to Judith Page Helm. However, with the outbreak of the Civil War, his plans for foreign missionary service never came to fruition. Enlisting in the Confederate Army as a private, he was soon appointed as a chaplain, and in a short time he was serving as an army evangelist.

Chaplain Jones played a major role in the many revivals that swept through General Lee's troops, and following the tragic nation-dividing Civil War, he wrote a thrilling volume entitled *Christ in the Camp*. We have commented several times that well in excess of 100,000 men personally trusted Christ as Savior. In his volume, published in 1887, Jones observed, "Any history of this army which omits an account of the wonderful influence of religion upon it—which fails to tell how the courage, discipline, and morale was influenced by the humble piety and evangelical zeal of many of its officers and men—would be incomplete and unsatisfactory."[1]

In another important affirmation of this truth, Chaplain Jones stated, "It is believed that no army in the world's history ever had in it so much of genuine, devout piety, so much of active work for Christ, as the Army of Northern Virginia, under the command of our noble Christian leaders.

"None but the most severe revisionists in America would dare deny the fact that both General Robert E. Lee and General Stonewall Jackson were born-again believers. When Chaplains Jones and B. T. Lacey, visited General Robert E. Lee and mentioned to him the fact that all the chaplains were praying for him, the great General responded by saying: 'Please thank them for that, sir—I warmly appreciate it. And I can only say that I am nothing but a poor sinner, trusting in Christ alone for salvation, and need all the prayers they can offer for me.'"[2]

When calling for a "day of fasting, humiliation, and prayer," on April 8, 1864, General Lee gave the following proclamation: "Soldiers! Let us humble ourselves before the Lord, our God, asking through Christ, the forgiveness of our sins, beseeching the aid of God of our forefathers in the defense of our homes and our liberties, thanking

Him for His past blessings, and imploring their continuance upon our cause and our people."[3]

Doubtless the fact that the outstanding generals of the Confederate Army were Bible-believing Christians would have impacted the Southern troops. On yet another occasion, Chaplain Jones told of a captain in the Georgia Brigade who had accepted Christ and had publicly declared his testimony. He said: "Men, I have led you into many a battle . . . . Alas! I have (also) led you into all manner of wickedness and vice. . . . I have enlisted under the banner of the Cross, and mean, by God's help, to prove a faithful soldier of Jesus. . . . I call upon you, my brave boys, to follow me, as I shall try to follow 'the Captain of our salvation.'"[4]

As I write this entry, America is at war! This time it is the War against Terror. It was begun when America was attacked on what is popularly called "9/11." Using our own airplanes, the enemy struck from the sky and killed over a thousand on the second enemy attack on New York. The English did it the first time, Arab Terrorists did it the second time. Again young American soldiers have been called to battle. Pray for our soldiers! But pray too that God will give us Bible-believing chaplains to present the claims of Christ to our troops of the twenty-first century.

DLC

---

[1]J. William Jones, *Christ in the Camp,* (Harrisonburg, VA: Sprinkle Publications, 1986), 5-6

[I]Ibid., 50.

[3]Ibid., 58.

[4]Ibid.,398.

December 21

The Price of Freedom

Scripture: 1 Corinthians 15:58

Twenty-first century Baptists in America can hardly envision the sufferings that our forefathers experienced in early American colonial days. The pilgrims came to our shores in 1620, but soon thereafter, those of Baptist persuasion arrived. By 1644, the Massachusetts hierarchy grew so concerned lest Baptist principles spread that they passed a law directed specifically against Baptists. The law promised banishment for anyone who ". . . shall either openly condemn or oppose the baptizing of infants, or go about secretly to seduce others from the approbation or use thereof, or shall purposely depart the congregation at the ministration of the ordinance . . . ."[1]

The First Baptist Church in Boston was born midst such anguish. The first pastors were continually called before the magistrates and were fined and threatened with banishment. The first pastor was Thomas Goold. "For ten stormy years, in prison and out of prison, Thomas Goold had led his little flock, and himself had borne the brunt of sufferings. He passed away on October 27, 1675. He died a martyr. He had been despoiled of home, property, and health; but he never faltered."[2]

With the death of Pastor Goold, the flock needed a new undershepherd, and was desirous of obtaining the pastoral services of John Miles of Swansea, Massachusetts. He had occasionally preached for them, and they knew him to be a man of sterling character. However, when his services could not be secured, the flock looked within their own number and chose one of their beloved deacons as their new pastor. Mr. John Russell was selected. He was known to be a man of solid certitude and had already suffered for his convictions. On June 25, 1675, he had been fined "40 shillings & six shillings costs." Again in December 1677, "John Russell, John Wilson, Sen & Caleb Farlow were sentenced to pay twenty shillings a.p.s. & costs."[3] He had been with the congregation almost from its beginning, so he knew well the personal cost of assuming the spiritual leadership of the church.

The congregation had previously begun the clandestine building of a facility to house the growing congregation. They attempted to make the appearance of the building other than that of a "church building," and were successful in disguising the structure. On February 15, 1679, they met in their own building for the first time. However, in the month of May, a law was passed that disallowed continued use of the building for church gatherings. It was demanded that the congregation give assurance they would not use the building for worship purposes. Being unwilling to acquiesce to such demands, in March of 1680, the court ordered the building to be nailed shut! During those days of strain, John Russell was ordained to the gospel ministry. His ordination took place on July 28, 1679.

The Pilgrims had repudiated the Church of England, and upon coming to these shores, they had established a state church that was Congregational. However, they existed under Colonial rights granted by the king of England. As he desired freedom of worship for those of the Church of England, the king had directed that adherents to the Church of England in Massachusetts "be declared capable of all freedoms and privileges as any other person whosoever." Thus it became impossible for the Colonial government to enforce the laws against Baptists without countermanding the king's command regarding Episcopalians. They too were non-conformists in New England.

Thus, during the pastorate of John Russell, the Baptists in Massachusetts gained the unwilling acquiescence of the authorities and were able to permanently use their own meetinghouse. The ministry of Reverend Russell continued until his death on December 21, 1680. He only served for one year and five months, but he proved to be steadfast and devout as a servant of the Lord.

We have religious freedom because of such men. Let us so live as to assure that blessing to those who follow us.

DLC

---

[1]Isaac Backus, *Your Baptist Heritage* (Little Rock, AK: The Challenge Press, 1976), 42.

[2]Nathan E. Wood, *The History of The First Baptist Church of Boston* (Philadelphia: American Baptist Publication Society, 1899), 122.

[3]Ibid., 123.

December 22

Where Thomas Jefferson Learned

Scripture: 1 Timothy 4:16

Andrew Tribble was one of the first Baptist converts in Virginia. He often remarked that he was the fifty-third Baptist on the north side of the James River in the State.[1] No account of his youthful days has been preserved, but we know that he was born in March 1741. In the strength of his youth, he married Miss Sally Burns, and the Lord blessed that union with a large family of children. One of his sons, Peter, became a Baptist preacher.

During the days of his early manhood, Separate Baptists made great inroads into the area as Lewis and Elijah Craig, John Waller, and James Childs preached throughout the region. Andrew Tribble was saved during that era, and was probably baptized by James Reed. The Craigs, Waller, and Childs were not yet ordained, and thus Elijah Craig went to North Carolina and induced James Reed to go to Orange County, Virginia, and the surrounding neighborhood to baptize the first converts in the Baptist faith.

Following his baptism, Andrew Tribble united with the Goldmine Baptist Church in Louisa County. In 1771 he was sent as a messenger by that congregation to the first meeting of the General Association of Virginia. Doubtless he began preaching soon thereafter, for he was one of the forty-four imprisoned Baptist preachers in Virginia. Morgan Edwards wrote that Mr. Tribble ". . . was put in gaol [jail] at Fredericksburg for forty eight days."[2] Incarceration was, of course, given for preaching without a license from the state church.

In time he was extended a call to pastor the Baptist church in Albemarle County, Virginia. This church was near the home of Thomas Jefferson, and an interesting story has made the rounds of Virginia history since that time. The Albemarle church was constituted in 1773 and was the oldest Baptist church in the county. The July 16, 1925, issue of the *Religious Herald* contained the following item: "The story is told in the *Christian Watchman* by a minister who received the account of the incident from the Baptist pastor with whom Jefferson had the conversation. The minister was Rev. Dr. Fishback, of Lexington, Ky., and he wrote as follows. 'Mr. Editor: The following circumstances, which occurred in the State of Virginia relative to Mr. Jefferson, were detailed to me by elder Andrew Tribble about six years ago, who since died about 92 or 93 years old.... Andrew Tribble was the parson of a small Baptist church which held monthly meetings at a short distance from the Jefferson home nine or ten years before the American Revolution. Mr. Jefferson attended the meeting of the church several months in succession and after one of them asked Elder Tribble to go home and dine with him, with which he complied. Mr. Tribble asked Mr. Jefferson how he was pleased with their church government. Mr. Jefferson replied that it struck him with great force and had interested him much, that he considered it the only pure form of democracy that then existed in the world and had concluded that it would be the best plan of government for the American colonies. This was several years before the Declaration of Independence.'"[3]

In 1783 the Tribbles moved to Kentucky and became members of the Howard Creek Baptist Church where Robert Elkin served as pastor. During that time Mr. Tribble evangelized in the Tates Creek area, and in 1786, he established the converts into the Tates Creek Baptist Church. He served that congregation until his death on December 22, 1822.

His last illness was protracted and painful; however, he entered into glory triumphantly. A few hours before his home going, Peter, his son, and another young preacher were standing at his bedside. He addressed them and said, "Boys, you see me here now. In a few days I shall be gone. I give you this charge. Play the man for your God!"

DLC

---

[1]J. H. Spencer, *A History of Kentucky Baptists* (Cincinnati: J. R. Barmes, 1885), 128.

[2]Morgan Edwards, *Materials Towards a History of the Baptists* (Danielsville, GA: Heritage Papers, 1984), 1:65.

[3]Lewis Peyton Little, *Imprisoned Preachers and Religious Liberty in Virginia* (Lynchburg, VA: J. P. Bell Co., 1938), 142.

December 23

A Tenor Soloist in Heaven

Scripture: Acts 16:25

The reason for the choice of title for this entry will be evident as one reads the account of Joost Joosten of the Netherlands. The fourteen-year-old lad was singing in the choir of the local Catholic church in his hometown of Goes in the Netherlands, when King Philip II was in the audience. The lyric tenor voice of the youth so attracted the king that he purposed to take the soloist back to Spain with him. The King requested an interview with the lad. Upon hearing of the king's interest, young Joost was honored, but when told of the king's wishes, the lad's Dutch pride would not allow it. Asking the king's servant to wait a moment, the boy exited by another door and made his way home. He quickly gathered a few belongings, and slipped through the back streets of town to an abandoned boathouse. Joost remained secluded there until he knew that King Philip II had returned to Spain.

Upon hearing of the actions of the youth, the locals looked upon Joost as a hero. He was a good scholar and earnest in his studies. He had an interest in the matters of belief expressed in the Roman, Lutheran, Reformed, and Anabaptist systems of theology. The respect he gained among the citizenry allowed him some freedom to move in various circles, and in the course of time he crossed the pathway of the Anabaptists. As he listened to the preaching, it became clear to Joost that Christ's atonement was personal, and that he was included. In time he professed faith in Christ Jesus and was baptized. His life was transformed, and he began to witness publicly. Now, however, he discovered that he lost his hero's status and he was roundly criticized. Joost's clear thinking allowed him to declare and defend his faith. The authorities soon became aware of Joost's conversion, but they determined to reconvert him to Romanism by debate. After all, he was a youthful hero, and the authorities did not want to lose the respect of the citizens.

When Joost reached his eighteenth birthday and they had been unable to dissuade him, the officals arrested him in the neighboring city of Veere. King Philip II had renewed the mandate of his father, Charles V, which had been issued on September 25, 1550, against the Anabaptists. The edict called for the death penalty for those proposing Anabaptist doctrines.

Joost had been imprisoned, and at first inquisitors attempted to cause him to recant by confrontation. At times, such as inquisitorial session would feature four debaters, but their efforts failed. Soon Joost experienced the other methods used in the Inquisition, as he was placed on the rack and stretched until he would faint. He would be revived with cold water, and as he then suffered excruciating pain, he would again be bombarded with the demands to recant!

A uniquely new method was utilized to break young Joost's will. Van Braght's description is graphic.[1] As young Joost was tied to a chair, jailers would insert what was called a "iron teerlingen" in the top of his knee. They would drive the long thin rod of metal down through his leg until it came out at his ankle. The jailers who were forced to inflict such injury were themselves physically shaken, but yet the will of Joost could not be moved. Amazingly, all during his imprisonment, while in his cell Joost would sing to encourage himself and other prisoners. When it became clear that the young hero could not be broken, Joost was condemned to being burned to death. A straw hut was built in the marketplace at Veere where Joost would be sent to glory. Even as he was forced to walk on his bruised legs to the place of execution, Joost's clear voice rang out with a witness for Christ. As he approached the hut, he sang a favorite hymn: *"O Lord, you are forever in my Thoughts."* On the Monday before Christmas, 1560,[2] the hut was ignited and a new tenor voice joined the heavenly choir of our great God and Savior Jesus Christ.

May we realize in the small vicissitudes of life that we suffer, "It will be worth it all when we see Jesus."

DLC

---

[1]Thieleman J. Van Braught, *The Martyr's Mirror* (Scottsdale, PA: Herald Press, 1950), 651.

[2]Myron S. Augsburger, *Faithful Unto Death* (Waco, TX: Wood Books, 1978), 64.

December 24

A Gifted Servant

Scripture: Romans 10:14-15

James Barnett Taylor was born in Lincolnshire, England, on March 19, 1804. The year after the lad's birth, his parents, George and Chrisanna Taylor, determined to travel to America to seek financial security. Once upon the ocean, a British man-of-war attacked their vessel, and Mr. Taylor was seized for service in a war against France. However, for reasons known only to God, the Taylors were transferred to another ship on its way to America, and finally they arrived in New York.

The next twelve years found the little family in New York City. On one occasion as the family passed a church, young James persuaded his father to enter the building to hear the lovely music. In time, his parents were saved, and then in his thirteenth year James was converted. The family united with the First Baptist Church. In 1817 the Taylors moved to Virginia, and the next nine years were spent in Mecklenburg and Granville counties. James grew to maturity during those years, and proved himself faithful to the Lord and to God's Word. As a result, he was licensed to preach in 1824, and two years later he was ordained and called to pastor the Second Baptist Church, Richmond. During that ministry, on October 30, 1828, Mr. Taylor was married to Miss Mary Williams from Beverly, Massachusetts. The union proved most beneficial and lasted for almost forty-three years until his home going on December 22, 1871.

In the short span of space allotted, it would be impossible to briefly comment on the many accomplishments of James B. Taylor. I shall merely list a résumé of some of his attainments in catalogue form. Later I will comment on what I believe to have been his outstanding contribution.

On the basis of recommendations by a committee of which Taylor was a member, the Virginia Baptist Education Society was organized in 1830. The school that resulted ultimately became the Virginia Baptist Seminary, and Taylor served as a trustee. In 1839 he became chaplain of the University of Virginia. He later returned to Richmond as pastor of the Third Baptist Church. When the Foreign Mission Board of the Southern Baptist Convention was constituted, Taylor was urged to accept the position of secretary. He debated the decision in his mind whether to accept that offer or to continue in his pastorate. He finally decided to remain with Third Baptist Church. However he did agree to give two days a week to the service of the board, and to make a tour of the South in behalf of foreign missions. As the Lord would have it, just prior to leaving on tour, Taylor met Adoniram Judson. That great veteran missionary was in America for his only furlough, and the Lord arranged for that Divine appointment in Richmond. This was the turning point, and as Taylor traveled, he realized God would have him give himself to the foreign mission enterprise. This decision resulted in his serving as secretary of the Foreign Mission Board for twenty-six years. The work must have been arduous through both the Civil War, and reconstruction period. The Southern Baptist Convention did not convene every year during that period; Taylor had to be the catalyst that kept the mission afloat. It must be remembered that the last six years of Taylor's life was the period of reconstruction in the South. Though his personal strength was waning, still he exerted physical and spiritual reserve sufficient to allow him to continue raising the needed funds for the operation of the mission. Though he was a great administrator, Taylor kept his hand upon the pulse of local churches by preaching regularly. He corresponded by hand with missionaries, and it has been commented that his epistles were "frequent, full, and fatherly."[1]

In 1855 Columbian College conferred on Taylor the honorary D.D. degree, but out of humility, he declined the honor.[2] However, the school personnel persisted, claiming that if anyone deserved such an honor, it was James B. Taylor!

I rejoice in the accounts of his humility and desire for Christlikeness, but personally, in my estimation, his highest accomplishment is in the literary field. He authored the *Memoir of Luther Rice,* and *Life of Lott Carey.* But most meaningful to me are his two volumes entitled *Lives of Virginia Baptist Ministers.* May the Lord raise up men of his stature today to promote missions and to inform the Christian public of our glorious history.

DLC

---

[1]George Braxton Taylor, *Virginia Baptist Ministers* Third Series (Lynchburg, VA: J. P. Bell Company, 1912), 117.

[2]Ibid., 121.

December 25

Obeying the Great Commission

Scripture: Psalm 102:15

John Bates was born at Bugbrook, Northamptonshire, England, on January 26, 1805. On Christmas Day, 1829, he was baptized into the membership of the Eagle Street Baptist Church where Reverend Joseph Irving was the pastor.

Fortunately, Pastor Irving was an encourager of young men, and as John Bates matured, the pastor challenged him to consider service on a needy mission field. Just about that time, as young Mr. Bates began praying about the need, William Knibb, British Baptist missionary to Jamaica, was giving flamboyant speeches to arouse the general populace of England concerning the evils of slavery. The English Baptists in the 1830s began a correspondence with the Baptists in America concerning the subject of abolition of slavery. This was a hot topic of the day throughout Great Britain, and young Mr. Bates purposed in his heart to go to the West Indies to minister among the heathen. For additional information concerning William Knibb and his leading role in the anti-slavery movement in England, please see volume one of this set, pages 475-476. Doubtless, it was the debate concerning slavery that caused young Mr. Bates to give consideration to the West Indies.

Bates' plan to serve in the West Indies never came to fruition. Service for Christ, however, continued foremost in the mind of the young man. In 1833, when he was twenty-eight years old, he offered himself to the Baptist Irish Society for missionary service in Ireland. He was accepted, and his appointment followed. His initial ministry in the difficult field of Ireland proved to be fruitful as he served in Ballina and Sligo. There he had the joy of baptizing a number of converts, and establishing a healthy church. He then became somewhat itinerant in his service, and in all he served the Baptist Irish Society for seventeen fruitful years.

At the age of forty-five, in the spring of 1850, Reverend Bates relocated to the United States and settled in

Cascade, Iowa. Shortly he became pastor of the Baptist church. His ministry in the States was blessed of the Lord, and soon his counsel was sought among Baptist pastors throughout the area. However, Iowa seemed too settled an area for the man of God, and in 1864 he moved to Canada to become pastor of the Baptist church in Dundas. Three years later he was called to the church in Woodstock, and there he identified himself with the interests of the Canadian Literary Institute.

Reverend Bates never lost his interest in foreign missions, and while serving the Lord in Woodstock, he was privileged to commission two of his daughters, Mrs. A. Timpany and Mrs. John McLaurin to foreign missionary service in Africa.

Never a man to rest, Reverend Bates went forward at full tilt until his ministry had completely consumed him. Though only sixty-eight years of age, in 1873 he was forced to accept partial retirement. Canada has never been a stronghold for Baptist ministries, but his pastorate at Woodstock had been very fruitful. In his six year pastorate there, he had received over two hundred members into the church family. For nearly a year he remained without a regular pastoral charge, but his health continued to deteriorate. On May 8, 1875, in his seventieth year, the Lord graciously called His servant home.

Pastor John Bates was a man of great power and ardent piety, and he was sorely missed by his brethren. Two years following his death, Dr. J. A. Smith of Chicago compiled a book of nearly five hundred pages as a memoir to the labors of this servant of the Lord.

This whole matter brings to the author's mind the fact that the Great Commission is not satisfied only with foreign missions or home missions. It is a matter of submission to the will of God. How wonderful to realize that though Mr. Bates never got to the West Indies, he so lived and preached that this daughters were called and obeyed the voice of the Lord to serve in Africa. May our homes so magnify the Lord that our children might seriously consider the call of God to carry the Gospel to the heathen world.

DLC

December 26

How God Answered Whitefield's Prayer

Scripture: James 5:16a-18

Perhaps no preacher of the Gospel has ever had the impact upon America as did George Whitefield, the famed English Methodist preacher. One author wrote, "...George Whitefield . . . blazed across the New England landscape for six weeks during the fall of 1740. This evangelistic tour, which took him to all the towns of the seaboard and the Connecticut Valley, set the pattern for revivalism in New England for the remainder of the century." Another wrote, "The year 1740-1741 marks the high tide of the revival in the middle colonies. Whitefield's preaching had stirred all classes and all the churches. Even the deistic Franklin became his admirer and lifelong friend, and the revival became exceedingly popular with the common people."[1] Testimonies of his spiritual success are numberless, and they are thrilling to consider.

However, when George Whitefield visited New Bern, North Carolina, the man of God witnessed an indifference that overwhelmed him. On Christmas Day 1739, Whitefield made an entry in his journal describing the situation. He wrote, "Went to public worship . . . but mourned much in spirit, to see in what an indifferent manner everything was carried on . . . ." He continued, "Wrote this morning to the minister of New-born, [New Bern] who I heard countenanced a dancing-master, by suffering his son to be one of his learners. Several of the inhabitants, I was informed, had subscribed to his assemblies, and they were generally attended with ill consequences . . . . It grieves me to find that in every little town there is a settled dancing-master, but scarcely anywhere a settled minister to be met with . . . ."[2]

On December 26, Whitefield's entry in his journal contained the following petition: "Oh that the Lord would send forth some who, like John the Baptist, might preach and baptize in the wilderness! I believe they would flock to him from all the country round about."[3]

Just sixteen years later, the Lord of the Harvest abundantly answered Whitefield's prayer by sending Shubal Stearns and Daniel Marshall, two Separate Baptists who had a vision of victory, to North Carolina. These men had been saved under Whitefield's ministry, and both men were much like John the Baptist. Both men were burning and shining lights. They established the Sandy Creek Baptist Church in North Carolina, and soon the entire area was set aglow with the Gospel. In time, all of the southern colonies were impacted. Morgan Edwards is quoted as referring to the south-wide revival in the following terms: "Soon after [the establishment of the Sandy Creek Church] the neighborhood was alarmed and the Spirit of God listed to blow as a mighty rushing wind in so much that in three years' time they had increased . . . not only eastward towards the sea, but westward towards the great river Mississippi, . . . northward to Virginia and southward to South Carolina and Georgia. The word went forth from this Zion, and great was the company of them who published it, in so much that her converts were as drops of morning dew."[4]

George Whitefield prayed, God abundantly blessed, and the entire area became known through the years as "The Bible Belt!"

As we in this twenty-first century are confronted with a godless society that seems totally indifferent to the divine message of grace, we would do well to bombard heaven with our prayers for spiritual refreshing. "Is anything too hard for the Lord?" Praise God there is no prayer that He cannot answer. There is no problem that he cannot solve. There is no place too hard for Him to revive. And there is no person too hard for God to save. In the face of present-day indifference, let us not faint. Rather let us pray.

DLC

---

[1]William Warren Sweet, *The Story of Religion in America* (New York: Harper & Row Publishers, 1950), 142.

[2]George Whitefield, *George Whitefield's Journals* (Gainesville, FL: Scholars' Facsimiles & Reprints, 1969), 376.

[3]Ibid., 376.

[4]George Washington Paschall, *History of North Carolina Baptists* (Raleigh: The General Board North Carolina Baptist State Convention, 1930), 271.

December 27

Unsaved Church Members?

Scripture: John 6:67-69

Baptists maintain the principle of a regenerate church membership. This flies in the face of so-called "state-churches" where one becomes a member by natural generation. However, no one can definitely know the workings of the Holy Spirit in the life of another. There are doubtless multitudes of Baptist "church members" who know nothing of salvation. These are professors but not possessors of eternal life. How tragic to realize that many will stand before the Savior and hear Him say, "Depart from me, ye workers of iniquity, I never knew you"(Luke 13:27).

Such an illustration is found in the life of Dr. B. H. Carroll, one of the best known Baptist theologians of America. B. H. Carroll was born on December 27, 1843, into the family of a Baptist preacher-father and a devoted Christian mother in Carroll County, Mississippi. As a youth he united with the church, yet he gave testimony to the fact that he was not then saved. As is reported in our first volume on pages 462-463, early in his life, B. H. Carroll had become an infidel. He stated the case thus: "...my infidelity related to the Bible and its manifest doctrines. I doubted that it was God's book.... I doubted miracles. I doubted the divinity of Jesus of Nazareth. But more than all, I doubted the vicarious expiation for the sins of men.... I never doubted that the Scriptures claimed inspiration, nor that they taught unequivocally the divinity and vicarious expiation of Jesus. If the Bible does not teach these, it teaches nothing. The trifling expedient of accepting the Bible as 'inspired in spots,' never occurred to me."[1]

There is a great difference between believing that the Bible *claims* to teach truth, and believing that it really teaches truth which must be personally accepted.

During a "protracted" meeting, great pressure was brought upon the thirteen-year-old lad to join the church though he was still in his state of infidelity as described. Sincere adults asked questions which elicited stereotyped answers. With a nodding head affirming that he believed the Bible and that he believed in Jesus Christ, these adults approached the preacher stating, "Here is a lad who believes the Bible, believes in Jesus Christ, and believes that he is saved. Shouldn't he join the church?" With peer pressure, the transaction was completed, and the thirteen-year-old entered the waters of baptism as a dry sinner and came up a wet sinner. How often that scene is duplicated in Baptist churches today!

In time, young Mr. Carroll determined never to set foot in a church again. Fortunately, when he was twenty-two years of age, his mother convinced him to attend another evangelistic campaign. Still he was unmoved by the preaching. However, during that brush arbor type meeting, one of the preachers challenged the scorners to give consideration to a great proposition. He said, "You that stand aloof from Christianity and scorn us simple folks, what have you got? Answer honestly before God. Have you found anything worth having where you are? Is there anything else out there worth trying that has any promise in it?" As the questions penetrated the minds of the hearers, the preacher continued: "Well, then, admitting there's nothing there, if there is a God, mustn't there be something somewhere? If so, how do you know it is not here? Are you willing to test it? I don't ask you to read any book, nor study any evidences, nor make any difficult and tedious pilgrimages; that way is too long and time is too short. Are you willing to try it now: to make a practical experimental test?"

He then confronted his hearers with two Scripture passages: John 7:17: "If any man will do His will, he shall know of the doctrine, whether it be of God...." And Hosea 6:3: "Then shall we know if we follow on to know the LORD...."

The Holy Spirit used those Scriptures to move the heart of B. H. Carroll. In faith he responded and was gloriously transformed. Friend, perhaps you are a church member but there is no reality in your experience. I urge you to reach out in faith and see what God will do in your life.

DLC

---

[1]*Sermons and Life Sketch of B. H. Carroll* (Dallas, TX: Evangel Press, 1957), 11.

December 28

The Right Kind of Missionaries

Scripture: Matthew 10:32-42

We face a great task in fulfilling the Great Commission in our age. Jesus taught us to pray that God would send workers into the harvest (Matt. 9:37-38). Then, after spending an entire night in prayer, Jesus called the twelve Apostles (Lk. 6:12-16). Our selected Scripture passage for today is the conclusion of the sermon Jesus preached to these twelve men when he sent them on their first preaching ministry. We can rightly call Christ's words in Matthew 10 the first missionary commissioning sermon. We note that in the words of the text, Jesus emphasized that His servants must love Him above all others, follow Him at all cost, and be willing to suffer for His sake in the work.

It is imperative that we not only have missionaries who are willing to go to the field, but that we have missionaries who are of the right spirit for the work. Jesus emphasized both of these truths in Matthew 9 and 10.

That biblical truth, taught by our Lord, has been recognized throughout church history. William Carey, pioneer of the modern missionary movement, emphasized the need for the right kind of missionaries on several occasions.

On December 28, 1796, Carey wrote from India to the missionary society back in England. He pled for an increased number of missionaries of the right kind, saying, "Let the number of Missionaries be increased as much as the finances of the Society will admit of and let the Missionaries be either married or single as they may be procured. There are many advantages attending Families engaging in the work provide proper rules are adhered to, and the Missionaries' Wives are as much impressed with the missionary spirit as they themselves are, and are people of prudence, and not afraid of hardship, but if they are otherwise, they will prove a far greater Burden than you can well conceive of as many things will occur that will feed a discontented mind as full as it can well be."[1]

Concerning their talents and gifts, he went on to say, "Let the missionaries be men possessed of Gifts such as are not despicable; but perhaps the gift of utterance or rather eloquence may be accounted at present one of the best; a readiness to communicate knowledge to others; inward Godliness, meekness, and Zeal are the principal, but headlong rashness either in speaking, judging, or acting if it predominates should determine the Society to reject such."[2]

Three years earlier, on December 26, 1793, he wrote to John Ryland of the missionary society in a similar spirit, saying: "A Missionary must be one of the companions, and equals of the people to whom he is sent and many dangers and temptations will be in his way . . .. It will be very important to missionaries to be men of calmness and evenness of temper, and rather inclined to suffer hardships than to court the favour of Men and such who will be indefatigably employed in the Work set before them, an inconstancy of mind being quite injurious to that Work."[3]

We know that conflicts have occurred between missionaries from the time of Paul and Barnabas (Acts 15:36-41). That, however, is no excuse for self-will and pride which produces contention. The pressures of a foreign culture will only exacerbate the weaknesses of our flesh. May we be a people who love Christ supremely, follow Him submissively, and serve Him exclusively. May we be willing to suffer hardship in His work as He suffered to save us from sin (Matt. 10:25-26, 38-39; 1 Pet. 2:20-21).

Let us pray that God will raise up another generation of missionaries to go to this lost world. May they be the right kind of missionaries! May we be Christ-like Christians!

FJM

---

[1]Terry G. Carter, *The Journal and Selected Letters of William Carey* (Macon, GA: Smyth & Helwys, 2000), 133.

[2]Ibid., 133.

[3]Ibid., 132.

December 29

The Living Word of God

Scripture: Isaiah 40:3-8

The Waldenses surely had a godly influence not only in the Valley of Piedmont, but throughout all of Europe. We are not claiming a direct line of succession from the Waldenses when we consider their exploits in a Baptist devotional history, but it is apparent that they long preceded the Reformation, and surely they had distinctives that remind us of the Baptists.

One great historian wrote, "The persecutions of this remarkable people form one of the most heroic pages of the Church's history. These persecutions, protracted through many centuries, were endured with a patience, a constancy, a bravery, honourable to the gospel as well as to those simple people, whom the Gospel converted into heroes and martyrs."[1]

Fortunately, from time to time, several Dukes favored and protected the Waldenses such as the action of the Duke of Savoy in his concessions to the Evangelical professors of the Valley of Piedmont in the years 1603 and 1620. He confirmed that action on June 2 and 4 and December 29, 1653.[2]

Actually, the influence of the Waldenses was felt throughout Europe. For instance, one historian stated: ". . . Early as the year 1176, we find in Hungary many adhering to the doctrines of the Waldenses, who had sought here an asylum before the vengeance of Rome. . . ."[3]And again, "Thus lived the Waldenses in free Hungary, under the protection of the powerful, almost independent nobility, with little to annoy them till the reign of Emperor Sigismund, when they received the name *Hussites*, and at which time the days of trouble and visitation came."[4]

In the years following, those who stood for gospel truth received brutal treatment from the hand of Rome. "It was . . . Stephen Pilarick who had been turned out of Beczko by a military escort sent from Count Francis Nádasdy, and all his books had been brought to the castle of Cseithe; the count here ordered a fire to be made in the castle, and all the property and books of the pastor, with the exception of his official gown, to be thrown into the fire, the Bible was put on a spit and turned round before the fire, while he and some of his court stood by enjoying the spectacle. By some sudden blast several leaves of the Bible were blown about in the hall, and one was driven directly towards the count's breast; Baran Ladislaus Revay caught at it, but it was seized out of his hand by the count, who began to read. It happened to be a portion of the fortieth chapter of Isaiah, and the first words he read were these, "The grass withereth, the flower fadeth, but the word of our God shall stand for ever." The count Nádasdy, turning pale, rose immediately and retired, and, when he was leaving the hall, the court fool cried after him, 'How shall you feel, Sir Count, when the Devils are roasting you on a spit in hell?'"[5]

We rejoice when we consider the wonderful gloriously fruitful ministry of the great Baptist preacher, Kornya Mihály, in the late nineteenth and early twentieth century as he planted many Baptist congregations during his ministry. But again today, fundamental Baptist missionaries are re-seeding the area with Bible-believing Baptist congregations. Let us pray that the Word of God, which shall stand forever, will again penetrate hardened hearts in Hungary.

DLC

---

[1]J. A. Wylie, History of the Waldenses (New York: Cassell & Company, n.d.), 20.

[2]Samuel Morland, The History of the Evangelical Churches of the Valleys of Piemont (London: Henry Hills, 1658), 47.

[3] J. H. Merle D'Aubigné, History of the Protestant Church in Hungary (Boston: Phillips, Sampson, and Co., 1854), 12.

[4]Ibid., 20.

[5]D'Aubigné, 208-209.

December 30

Cleanliness is Next to Godliness

Scripture: Mark 2:17; Jeremiah 8:22

Miss Adele M. Fielde was surely a missionary heroine on the strength of her ministry in China. It was she who envisioned organizing groups of Chinese Christian women and training them carefully in the Word of God. These ladies were then sent throughout the community to teach the Word of God to other ladies. Ultimately, this impacted the lives of entire communities with the gospel. Miss Fielde was a heroine as well, for she had entered the work of missions in the anticipation of marrying Reverend Cyrus Chilcott, a Baptist missionary in Siam. However, upon arriving on the field of Siam early in 1866, Miss Fielde discovered that her beloved had died on December 30, 1865, with typhoid fever (Vol. 2:174-175). Being for months on an old sailing ship, there was no way of informing her of the tragedy. Rather than returning to the States in despair, Miss Fielde determined to give herself to the spiritual needs of ladies in China, and she became an outstanding missionary in that land.

In one of her interesting accounts of the locale in which she served, she related a visit to a pharmacy owned by one of the believers of the local church. In describing the shop, she mentioned that the store was enclosed on three sides, and the counter ran the entire length on the open side by the street. Customers would stand in the street and make their needs known over the counter. The boxes holding the various medications were against the rear wall, and the pharmacist could easily fill the requests or prescriptions for the many purchasers.

Miss Fielde became so enthralled with the various "cures" of that day, that she made a list of the most unique "drugs." Among the catalogue were the following: "A great variety of barks, tubers, bulbs, roots, seeds, and leaves with the stamens, petals, and seed-vessels of the lotus in separate compartments. Unhusked rice and wheat, sprouted and then dried.

"The flower of the honeysuckle, the leaves of the arbor-vitae, the pith of a large reed, and fungi from decayed wood. Various species of seaweed and bones of the cuttle-fish.

"Dried caterpillars, snails and worms, and the cast-off skin of locusts. Silk worms and the chrysalides of moths and butterflies.

"Shavings of goat, ibex and deer horn, the scales of the armadillo, and charred tiger bones.

"The shell of the box-turtle, and the horn of a rhinoceros, valued at three dollars for a piece three inches in diameter, centipedes six inches long stretched and dried on splints, and the gall-bladder of a bear, valued at ten dollars and used as a tonic. Medicated tea in small, hard cakes."[1]

Fortunately medical care in the third world is somewhat better than what was practiced back in the nineteenth century. However, most Americans would cringe at the realization of the primitive methods of sanitation and the medications used in many clinics in the third world. Often times, meals are not provided for the patients at all. Family members or friends are expected to care for this chore at mealtime. There is no such thing as twenty-four hour care. Family or friends must provide the oversight for the patients on a continuing daily basis. Cleanliness is totally unknown, not to mention sterilization. We are thankful for the improvements in the medical care offered our missionaries in some parts of the world, but third world countries leave much to be desired.

Why would I include such an entry in a serious devotional book? No, I am not making light of the "strange" herbal concoctions that are being advocated anew in America. The reason for the entry is that we might be reminded to pray for the health of our missionary heroes and heroines who serve the Lord in many places on this earth under conditions that it is difficult for an American to even imagine. Our missionaries need our prayer support that the God of Heaven shall not only heal them but that He shall protect them from disease itself.

DLC

---

[1]Adele M. Fielde, *Fifty Missionary Stories* (New York: Fleming H. Revell Company, 1903), 138.

December 31

Do Men See Christ in Me?

Scripture: John 3:30; 12:21

You doubtless have never heard of the man who is the subject of our consideration today, for his name never flashed on lights of a marquee, and he never conducted a citywide revival campaign. But then, most faithful men of God go through life without notoriety and fame. Most preachers' names are unknown except among the circle of friends with and to whom they minister.

Such a man was William J. Reynolds, whose ministry was pretty well circumscribed in the Shiloh Association in Virginia. The young couple, Joseph D. Reynolds and June Blair, in Pittsylvania County, were thrilled at the birth of their baby December 31, 1871. The baby grew into a boy and saw his sinful condition. Repenting of his sin, he trusted Jesus Christ as his Savior and at the age of eleven he was baptized and united with the Sharon Baptist Church. After completing the education offered locally, young William entered and graduated from both the University of Tennessee and the Southern Baptist Seminary. In the course of time he was licensed, and then proving the hand of God upon his life, he was ordained by the First Baptist Church of Danville, Virginia.

Reverend Reynolds was never robust physically, and he went West in search of complete health. Arriving in the town that had been recommended to him, he discovered there was no housing available. However, he found that an eastern millionaire owned a lovely mountainside home, and it was only occupied by his dissipated but gifted son, a bachelor. Reynolds in time was enabled to prevail upon the young man to allow him to rent a room for a short period. During the course of his stay, the two young men became friends. They hiked in the mountain air, and the young preacher determined to testify by his "life" rather than by his "lips." He lived his Christian life before his frivolous partner. Of course, the preacher gave his testimony, but he did not "ram it down the throat" of the young man. However, ". . . one day the young householder came rushing into his companion's room exclaiming: 'You have what I have not got and I want it.' Young Reynolds led him to Christ and [in time] both of them were preachers, one on the Pacific Coast and the other in Virginia."[1]

On November 12, 1912, William J. Reynolds took Miss Caroline Rust Miller as his wife. The two were married in the Mt. Lebanon Church, and two of the well-known preachers of that day Dr. George W. McDaniel and Dr. John Roach Straton performed the marriage. You will remember that Dr. John Roach Straton later became the outstanding leader of fundamental Baptists as he served the Calvary Baptist Church in New York City (Vol. 1:448-449).

Reverend Reynolds was never robust, but he fervently entered into ministering. He served the Woodville, Washington, Oakley, and Sperryville churches. Some of these ministries were singular while at other times he had the oversight of a combination of the works simultaneously. The amazing impact he had upon the communities in which he served did not come from a unique pulpit ministry. He was not known because he possessed the voice of an orator, or was unusual in any way in the pulpit. Rather his consistent and practical Christian life caused deep spiritual impressions on the minds of neighbors all about him.

Reverend Reynolds' life span was comparatively short. His physical problems had called for surgery in a Richmond hospital, and he never rallied to health again. He was only forty-nine years of age, in the prime of his ministerial life, when His Lord called His servant to rest. The funeral was conducted at the Woodville Church in the presence of many who had learned to love the man of God for what he was and not only for what he said.

As we close out another year, we would do well to ask ourselves the question: "Does my life point men to the Lord Jesus Christ?" Perhaps in our devotions today we ought to confess our failures and ask the Lord to live His life out through us that those around us might see Jesus only.

DLC

---

[1]George Braxton Taylor, *Virginia Baptist Ministers* (Lynchburg, VA: J. P. Bell Company, 1936), 6:104.

BIBLIOGRAPHY

Adams, Theodore F. *First Baptist Church Richmond 1780-1955.* Richmond, VA: Whittet & Shepperson, 1955).

Alexander, Walter R. *All Out For God.* Chicago: Moody Press, 1946.

Allen, I. M. *The Triennial Baptist Register.* Philadelphia: Baptist General Tract Society, 1839.

Allen, William Cox. *History of the Beulah Baptist Church.* Columbia: Vogue Press, 1962.

Anderson, Courtney. *To the Golden Shore.* Boston: Little, Brown and Company, 1956.

Anderson, Frederick Jarred. *A History of the Goshen Baptist Association of Virginia.* Orange, VA: Goshen Baptist Association, 1992.

Andrews, Wayne. *Concise Dictionary of American History.* New York: Charles Scribner's Sons, 1967.

Annual Report, American Missionary Union (ABMU), Detroit, 1900, 215; Year Book, ABC, 1982.

Annual, NBC, 1928, 27; Directory, ABC, 1983.

Armitage, Thomas. *A History of the Baptists.* New York: Bryan, Taylor, and Co., 1890.

Asplund, John. *The Annual Register of the Baptist Denomination in North America.* Lafayette, Tennessee: Church History and Research and Archives, 1979.

Augsburger, Myron S. *Faithful Unto Death.* Waco, Texas: Word Books, 1978.

Babb, Winston C. *Encyclopedia of Southern Baptists.* Nashville, Tennessee: Broadman Press, 1958.

Babcock, Rufus. Editor of Journals. *Memoir of John Mason Peck.* Carbondale, Illinois: Southern Illinois University Press, 1965.

Backlund, J. O. *Swedish Baptists in America.* Chicago, Conference Press, 1933.

Backus, Isaac. *A History of the Baptists in New England.* Newton, Massachusetts: Backus Historical Society, 1871.

Backus, Isaac. *Your Baptist Heritage.* Little Rock, Arkansas: The Challenge Press, 1976.

Backus, Issac. *The Diary of Isaac Backus.* Providence: Brown University Press, 1979.

Bacon, Leonard Woolsey. *A History of American Christianity.* New York: The Christian Literature Co., 1897.

Bainton, Roland H. *The Reformation of the Sixteenth Century.* Boston: Beacon Press, 1985.

Baker, Robert A. *A Baptist Source Book.* Nashville, Tennessee: Broadman Press, 1966.

Baptist Fundamentals: Being Addresses Delivered at the Pre-Convention Conference at Buffalo June 21 and 22, 1920. Philadelphia: Judson Press, 1920.

Barnes, Lemuel Call. *Two Thousand Years of Missions Before Carey.* Philadelphia: American Baptist Publication Society, 1900.

Barrows, C. Edwin, editor. *The Diary of John Comer.* Rhode Island Historical Society, 1893.

Bauder, Kevin Thomas. "*Biography of O. W. Van Osdel.*" Unpublished Th.M. Thesis, Denver Baptist Theological Seminary, 1983.

Belcher, James. *The Religious Denominations in the United States.* Philadelphia: John E. Potter, 1856.

Beller, James R. *America in Crimson Red.* Arnold, Missouri: Prairie Fire Press, 2004.

Benedict, David. *A General History of the Baptist Denomination in America, and other Parts of the World.* Boston: Lincoln & Edmands, 1813.

Benedict, David. *Fifty Years Among the Baptists.* New York: Sheldon & Company, 1860.

Billy Kelly, 1932-1997. Old Paths Radio Program article, n.d.

Bitting, C. C. *Bible Societies and the Baptists.* Philadelphia: American Baptist Publication Society, 1897.

Bogard, Ben M. *Pillars of Orthodoxy, or Defenders of the Faith.* Louisville, Kentucky: Baptist Book Concern, 1900.

Boykin, Samuel. *History of the Baptist Denomination in Georgia.* Atlanta, Georgia: Jas. P. Harrison & Co., 1881.

Broadbent, E. H. *The Pilgrim Church.* London, Pickering & Inglis, 1935.

Brooks, Charles Wesley. *A Century of Missions in The Empire State.* Philadelphia: American Baptist Publication Society, 1909.

Brown, J. Newton. *Memorials of Baptist Martyrs.* Philadelphia: American Baptist Publication Society, 1854.

Bunker, Alonzo. *Fifty Missionary Stories.* New York: Fleming H. Revell Company, 1903.

Burnett, J. J. *Sketches of Tennessee's Pioneer Baptist Preachers.* Nashville, Tennessee: Marshall & Bruce Coming, 1919.

Burrage, Henry S. *A History of the Anabaptists in Switzerland.* Philadelphia: American Baptist Publication Society, 1882.

Burrage, Henry. *Baptist Hymn Writers and Their Hymns.* Portland, Maine: Brown Thurston & Company, 1888.

Burrows, J. L. *The First Century of The First Baptist Church of Richmond, Virginia.* Richmond: Carlton McCarthy, 1880.

Carey, S. Pearce. *Samuel Pearce, The Baptist Brainerd.* London: The Carey Press, n.d.

Carlile, John C. *The Story of the English Baptists.* London: James Clarke & Co., 1905.

Carroll, J. M. *A History of Texas Baptists.* Dallas, Texas: Baptist Standard Publishing Co., 1923.

Carter, Terry G., Editor. *The Journal and Selected Letters of William Carey.* Macon, Georiga: Smyth and Helwys, 2000.

Cathcart, W. *The Baptist Encyclopedia.* Philadelphia: The Baptist Standard Bearer, 1881.

Cathcart, William. *Baptist Patriots and the American Revolution.* Grand Rapids, Michigan: Guardian Press, 1976

Champion, L. G. *Baptist Church Life in the Twentieth Century: Some Personal Reflections in Clements.*

Ray, Charles. *Mrs. C. H. Spurgeon*. Pasadena, Texas: Pilgrim Publications, 1979.

Christian, John T. *A History of the Baptists.* Nashville, Tennessee: Broadman Press, Vol. 1, 1926

Christian, John T. *A History of the Baptists.* Texarkana, Arkanas-Texas: American Baptist Association, Vol. 2, 1922.

Clearwaters, Richard V. *On The Upward Road.* Minneapolis: Nystrom Publishing, 1991.

Cleaves, Arthur W. "A Great Leader Has Passed," Baptist (10 December 1921) cited in Grant Wacker, *Augustus H. Strong and the Dilemma of Historical Consciousness.* Macon, GA: Mercer University Press, 1985.

Clement, J. *Fifth Thousand Memoir of Adoniram Judson: Being a Sketch of His Life and Missionary Labors.* Auburn: Derby and Miller, 1853.

Comer, John. *The Diary of John Comer.* Providence: The Rhode Island Historical Society, 1893.

Cook, Richard B. *The Early and Later Delaware Baptists.* Philadelphia: American Baptist Publication Society, 1880.

Bibliography

Cook, Richard R. *The Story of the Baptists in all Ages and Countries.* Baltimore: H. M. Wharton & Co, 1886.

Cramp, J. M. (1871; 2003). *Baptist History: From the Foundation of the Christian Church to the Close of the Eighteenth Century.* Roger Williams Heritage Archives.

Crismon, Leo T. and Harold Stephens. *Encyclopedia of Southern Baptists.* Nashville, Tennessee: Broadman Press, 1958.

Crismon, Leo Taylor, Editor. *Baptists in Kentucky, 1776-1976 - A Bicentennial Volume.* Middletown, Kentucky: Kentucky Baptist Convention, 1975.

Crosby, Thomas. *The History of the English Baptists.* London: John Robinson, 1740.

D'Aubigné, J. H. Merle, *History of the Protestant Church in Hungary.* Boston: Phillips, Sampson, and Co., 1854.

Daniel, Clifton, Editor-in-Chief. *20th Century Day by Day.* London: Dorling Kindersley, 2000.

Darters, Oscar H. *The History of Fredericksburg Baptist Church.* Richmond: Garrett and Massie, Inc. 1960.

David Brainerd's Personal Testimony. Grand Rapids, Michigan: Baker Book House, 1979.

Davis, J. *History of the Welch Baptists.* Pittsburgh: D. M. Hogan, 1835.

Dawson, Joseph Martin. *Baptists and the American Republic.* Nashville, Tennessee: Broadman Press, 1956.

De Chalandeau, Alexander. *The Christians in the U.S.S.R.* Chicago: Harper and Company, 1978.

Deen, Edith. *Great Women of the Christian Faith.* Westwood, NJ: Barbour and Company, Inc.,1959.

Denyes, Don. *For the Love of Preaching: The Life Story of Howard F. Sugden.* Lansing, Michigan: Wellington House Publishers, 2004.

Dillow, Myron D. *Harvesttime on the Prairie.* Franklin, Tennessee: Providence House Publishers, 1996.

Donnelson, Fred. *Finding Freedom in a Japanese Prison Camp.* Chicago: World Fundamental Baptist Missionary Fellowship, n.d.

Drumond, Lewis A. *Spurgeon: Prince of Preachers.* Grand Rapids, Michigan: Kregel Publications, 1992.

Duncan, R. S. *A History of the Baptists in Missouri.* Saint Louis: Scammell & Company, Publishers, 1882.

Durant, Will. *The Story of Civilization: Part VI, The Reformation.* New York: Simon and Schuster, 1957.

Dyck, Cornelius J. *An Introduction to Mennonite History.* Scottdale, Pennsylvania: Herald Press, 1976.

Eaton, W. H. *Historical Sketch of the Massachusetts Baptist Missionary Society and Convention 1802-1902.* Boston: Baptist Convention, 1903.

Edwards, Morgan. *Materials Towards A History of the Baptists.* Danielsville, Georgia: Heritage Papers, 1984.

Ella, George M. and Isaac McCoy. *Apostle of the Western Trail.* Springfield, Missouri: Particular Baptist Press, 2003.

Elliott, L. R. *Centennial Story of Texas Baptists.* Dallas, Texas: Baptist General Convention of Texas, 1936.

English, E. Schuyler. *Robert G. Lee, A Chosen Vessel.* Grand Rapids, Michigan: Zondervan Publishing House, 1949.

Estep, W. R. Jr. *Encyclopedia of Southern Baptists.* Nashville, Tennessee: Broadman Press, 1958.

Estep, William R. *The Anabaptist Story.* Nashville, Tennessee: Broadman Press, 1963.

Estep, William R. *Whole Gospel Whole World.* Nashville, Tennessee: Broadman & Holman Press, 1994.

Estep, William. *Renaissance and Reformation.* Grand Rapids, Michigan: Eerdmans Publishing Company, 1986.

Federer, William J. *America's God and Country Encyclopedia of Quotations.* Coppell, Texas: Fame Publishing, Inc., 1994.

Fielde, Adele M. *Fifty Missionary Stories.* New York: Fleming H. Revell Company, 1903.

Fitts, Leroy. *A History of Black Baptists.* Nashville, Tennessee: Broadman Press, 1985.

Ford, S. H. *Christian Repository.* August 1871.

Friesen, Abraham. *Erasmus, the Anabaptists, and the Great Commission.* Grand Rapids: Wm. B. Eerdmans Publishing Co., 1998.

From history notes of the Shiloh Baptist Church, Shiloh, NC.

Fuller, Thomas. *The Church History of Britain from the Birth of Jesus Christ until the year MDCXLVIII.* London, England: Thomas Tegg and Son, 1837.

Gardner, Robert G. *A History of the Georgia Baptist Association.* Atlanta, Georgia: Baptist Historical Society, 1988.

Gaskin, J. M. *Baptist Milestones in Oklahoma.* Oklahoma City: Good Printing Company, 1966.

Gillette, A. D., Editor. *Minutes of the Philadelphia Baptist Association 1707 to 1807.* Springfield, Missouri: Particular Baptist Press, 2002.

Goen, C. C. *Revivalism and Separatism in New England, 1740-1800.* Middletown, Connecticut: Wesleyan University Press, 1987.

Graham, B. J. W. *Baptist Biography.* Atlanta, Georgia: Index Printing Company, 1920.

Graham, B. J. W. *Baptist Biography.* Atlanta, Georgia: Index Printing Company, 1923.

Greene, David B. *From Disgrace to Grace.* Greenville: The Gospel Hour, Inc., 1996.

Griffiths, Thomas S. *A History of Baptists in New Jersey.* Hightown, New Jersey: Barr Press Publishing Company, 1904.

Griffits, Thomas S. *A History of Baptists in New Jersey.* Hightown, New Jersey: Barr Press Publishing Company, 1904.

Grime, J. H. *History of Middle Tennessee Baptists.* Nashville, Tennesse: Baptist and Reflector, 1902.

Guild,Reuben Aldridge. *Chaplain Smith and the Baptists.* Philadelphia: American Baptist Publication Society, 1885.

Halleck, Reuben Post. *History of our Country.* New York: American Book Company, 1923.

Haskell, Samuel. *Heroes and Hierarchs.* Published for the Michigan Baptist Convention, 1895.

Haykin, Michael A. G. *One Heart and One Soul, John Sutcliff of Olney, his Friends and his Times.* Durham, England: Evangelical Press, 1994.

Haynes, D. C. *The Baptist Denomination.* New York: Sheldon, Blakeman & Co., 1856.

Hendricks, Garland A. *Saints and Sinners at Jersey Settlement.* Charlotte: The Delmar Company, 1988.

Hill, James L. *The Immortal Seven.* Philadelphia: American Baptist Publication Society, 1913.

Hovey, Alvah. *A Memoir of the Life and Times of the Rev. Isaac Backus.* Harrisonburg, Vrigina: Gano Books, 1991.

Howard, Daniel. *The History of Old Windsor.* Connecticut Salem, Massachusetts: Higginson Book Company, 1935.

Howell, Robert Boyle C. *The Early Baptists of Virginia.* Philadelphia: The Bible and Publication Society, 1857.

Hubbard, Ethel Daniel. *Ann of Ava.* Philadelphia: Missionary Education Movement of the United States and Canada, 1913.

Hubbard, Ethel Daniels. *Ann of Ava.* New Hampshire: Ayer Company, 1941.

Huggins, M. A. *A History of North Carolina Baptists.* Raleigh: The General Board Baptist State Convention of North Carolina, 1967.

Interview with Yvonne Pickering, January 14, 2003.

Ironside, H. A. *The Lamp of Prophecy.* Grand Rapids, Michigan: Zondervan Publishing House, 1962.

Isaac, Rhys. *The Transformation of Virginia.* New York: W. W. Norton & Co., 1988.

Ivimey, Joseph. *A History of the English Baptists.* London, England: Printed for the Author, 1811.

Ivison, Stuart, and Fred Rosser, *The Baptists in Upper and Lower Canada Before 1820.* Toronro: University of Toronto Press, 1956.

James, Charles F. *Documentary History of the Struggle for Religious Liberty in Virginia.* New York: Da Capo Press, 1971.

Jewson, Charles Boardman. *The Baptists in Norfolk.* London: The Carey Kingsgate Press Limited, 1957.

Jones, J. William. *Christ in the Camp.* Harrisonburg, Virginia: Sprinkle Publications, 1986.

Jordan, Anne Devereaux and J. M. Stifle. *The Baptists.* New York: Hippocrene Books, 1990.

Keach's Catechism.

Keller, Ludwig, *The Reformation and the Older Reform Parties.* Quoted in J. W. Porter, *The World's Debt to the Baptists.* Louisville: Baptist Book Concern, 1914.

Knight, Richard. *History of the General or Six Principle Baptists.* Providence: Smith and Parmenter, 1827.

Landels, William. *Baptist Worthies.* London: Baptist Tract and Book Society, 1883.

Leland, John. *The Writings of Elder John Leland.* New York: G. W. Wood, 1845.

Linton, John. *From Coalpit to Pulpit.* Light and Life Press, 1947.

Littell, Franklin Hamlin. *The Origins of Sectarian Protestantism.* New York: The Macmillan Company, 1964.

Little, Lewis Peyton. *Imprisoned Preachers and Religious Liberty in Virginia.* Lynchburg, Virginia: J. P. Bell Co., Inc., 1938.

Lorimer, George C. *The Great Conflict.* Boston: Lee and Shepherd, Publishers, 1877.

Lumpkin, William L. *Baptist Confessions of Faith.* Philadelphia: The Judson Press, 1959.

Lumpkin, William Latane. *The Portsmouth Baptist Association, 1791-1991.* Clawrenceville, Virginia: Edmonds Printing Company, 1991.

Mallary, Charles D. *Memoirs of Elder Jesse Mercer.* New York: Printed by John Gray, 1844.

Martin, James Kirby, Randy Roberts, Steven Mintz, Linda O. McMurry, and James H. Jones. *America and Its People.* New York: HarperCollins College Publishers, 1993.

Martin, T. T. *God's Plan With Men.* Orlando, Florida: Daniels Publishing Co., 1978.

Materials gathered from personal conversations and written material supplied by Rev. Farrington's daughter, Clara (Farrington) Long of Colfax, North Carolina.

Mattoon, C. H. *Baptist Annals of Oregon.* McMinnville, Oregon: Telephone Register Publishing Co., 1905.

Maxon, Zane Allen. *Frontiersmen of the Faith.* San Antonio, Texas: The Naylor Company, 1970.

McBeth, H. Leon. *A Sourcebook For Baptist Heritage.* Nashville, Tennessee: Broadman Press, 1990.

McBeth, H. Leon. *The Baptist Heritage, Four Centuries of Baptist Witness.* Nashville: Broadman, 1987.

McComas, Wm. K. *50 Years of Plowing, Planting and Watering.* Newton, Kansas: United Printing, Inc., 1973.

McCoy, Isaac. *History of Baptist Indian Missions.* Springfield, Missouri: Particular Baptist Press, 2003.

McCoy, Isaac. *The Annual Register of Indian Affairs.* Springfield, Missouri: Particular Baptist Press, 1998.

McInturff, J. B., Editor. *The Old Paths.* New Market, Virginia: Henkel & Co., 1893.

McInturff, J. B., Editor. *The Old Paths.* New Market, Virginia: Henkel & Company, 1891.

McInturff, J. B., Editor. *The Old Paths.* Woodstock, Virgina: Power Print, 1905.

McLoughlin, William G. *Rhode Island a Bicentennial History.* New York: W. W. Norton & Company, Inc., 1978.

Mission Handbook. Billy Graham Center. 2000.

Mitchell, G. P. *A Century of Iowa Baptist History.* Pella, Iowa: The Baptist Record, 1934.

Morland, Samuel. *The History of the Evangelical Churches of the Valleys of Piemont.* London: Henry Hills, 1658.

Mosteller, James Donovan. *A History of the Kiokee Baptist Church in Georgia.* Ann Arbor, Michigan: Edwards Brothers, Inc., 1952.

Mullens, W. W. *The Old Paths.* Woodstock, VA: Power Print of W. N.Grabill, 1905.

Neander, Augustin. *History of the Christian Religion and Church.* Boston: Crocker & Brewster, 1872.

New Testament Association of Independent Baptist Churches. Spring 1974.

Newman, A. H. *A Century of Baptist Achievement.* Philadelphia: American Baptist Publication Society, 1901.

Newman, A. H. *A History of the Baptist Churches in the United States.* New York: Charles Scribner's Sons, 1915.

Oyer, John S. and Robert S. Kreider. *Mirror of the Martyrs.* Intercourse, Pennslyvania: Good Books, 1990.

Parker, Monroe. *Through Sunshine and Shadows, My First 77 Years.* Murfreesboro, Tennessee: Sword of the Lord Publishers, 1987.

Paschal, George Washington. *History of North Carolina Baptists.* Raleigh: The General Board North Carolina State Convention, 1930.

Pegues, A. W. *Our Baptist Ministers and Schools.* Cincinnati, Ohio: Lyons Brothers Publishing Co., 1891.

Personal correspondents with Mrs. Jean Myers Smith of Greer, South Carolina, who has written a history of the Myers family.

Personal letter from Wanda Kallam Stewart, daughter of B.W. Kallam, to Bettye Baughan, dated May 17, 2004.

Phone conversation with Faye Gaulden, Church Clerk at McLeansville Baptist Church, on June 5, 2004.

Pierson, Arthur T., Editor. *The Inspired Word.* London: Hodder & Stoughton, 1888.

Pius, N. H. *An Outline of Baptist History.* Nahsville, Tennessee: National Baptist Publishing Board, 1911.

Purefoy, George W. *A History of the Sandy Creek Baptist Association.* New York: Sheldon & Co., Publishers, 1859.

Ray, David Burcham. *The Baptist Succession.* Gallatin, Tennessee: 1984.

Recorded sermon by Rev. B.H. Farrington titled From The Blockade Still to the Pulpit, 1954.

Renfree, Henry A. *Heritage & Horizon.* Mississauga, Ontario: Canadian Baptist Federation, 1988.

Renstrom, Billy. *Darkness is Light.* Murfreesboro, Tennessee: Bill Rice Ranch, Inc, 1976.

Riley, B. F. *A Memorial History of the Baptists of Alabama.* Philadelphia: Judson Press, 1923.

Riley, B. F. *History of the Baptists of Texas.* Dallas, Texas: Published for the Author,1907.

Riley, B. F. *The Baptists in the Building of the Nation.* Watertown, Wisconsin: Roger Williams Heritage Archives, Maranatha Baptist Bible College, n.d.

Rogers, J. S. *History of Arkansas Baptists.* Little Rock: Arkansas Baptist State Convention, 1948.

Rosser, John Leonidas. *A History of Florida Baptists.* Nashville, Tennessee: Broadman Press, 1949.

Routh, E. C. *Encyclopedia of Southern Baptists.* Nashville, Tennessee: Broadman Press, 1958.

Rush, L. and Tom J. Nettles. *Baptists and the Bible.* Nashville: Broadman, 1999.

Ryland, Garnett. *The Baptists of Virginia 1699-1926.* Richmond, Virginia: The Virginia Baptist Board of Missions and Education, 1955.

Scott, Morgan. *History of the Separate Baptist Church.* Indianapolis: Hollenbeck Press, 1901.

Segler, Franklin M. *Encyclopedia of Southern Baptists.* Nashville, Tennessee: Broadman Press, 1958.

Semple, Robert B. *History of the Rise and Progress of the Baptists in Virginia.* Richmond, Virginia: 1910.

Sermons and Life Sketch of B. H. Carroll. Dallas, Texas: Evangel Press, 1957.

Shwe Wa, Maung. *Burma Baptist Chronicle.* Rangoon: Board of Publications Burma Baptist Convention, 1963.

Sightler, Harold B. *The Story of My Life.*

Sightler, James H. *50 Years of the Greer Baptist Campmeeting.* July 4, 1997.

Sightler, James. *Personal Recollections of Dr. Harold B. Sightler's Early Ministry and the Heritage of Tabernacle Baptist Church.*

Simons, Menno. *The Complete Writings.* Trans. Leonard Verduin, ed. John C. Wenger. Scottdale, Pennsylvania: Herald Press, 1956.

Simpson, James B. *Simpson's Contemporary Quotations.* Boston: Houghton Mifflin Company, 1988.

Skinner, Craig. *Spurgeon and Son, The Forgotten Story of Thomas Spurgeon and His Famous Father, Charles Haddon Spurgeon.* Grand Rapids, Michigan: Kregel, 1999.

Smith, Al. *Treasury of Hymn Histories.* Greenville: Better Music Publications, Inc., 1985.

Smith, Justin A. *A History of the Baptists In the Western States East of the Mississippi.* Philadelphia: American Baptist Publication Society, 1896.

Spencer, David. *Early Baptists of Philadelphia.* Philadelphia: William Syckelmoore, 1877.

Spencer, J. H. *A History of Kentucky Baptists.* Cincinnati: J. R. Barnes, 1885.

Sprague, William B. *Annals of the American Pulpit.* New York: Robert Carter & Brothers, 1865.

Spurgeon, C. H. *The Metropolitan Tabernacle And Its Work.*

Spurgeon, Charles H. *Metropolitan Tabernacle Publications.* Pasadena, Texas: Pilgrim Publications, 1973 reprint.

Spurgeon, Charles Haddon. Metropolitan Tabernacle Pulpit. Pasadena, Texas: Pilgrim Publications 1969.

Stanley, Brian. *The History of the Baptist Missionary Society 1792-1992.* Edinburgh: T & T Clark, 1992.

Stewart, I. D. *The History of the Freewill Baptists.* Dover: Freewill Baptist Printing Establishment, 1862.

Stiles, Henry R. *The History of Ancient Windsor.* Somersworth, NH: New Hampshire Publishing Company, 1976.

Sweet, William Warren. *Religion on the American Frontier.* New York: Cooper Square Publishers, Inc., 1964.

Sweet, William Warren. *The Story of Religion in America.* New York: Harper & Row Publishers, 1950.

Taylor, Adam. *Memoirs of the Rev. Dan Taylor.* London: T. Bore, 1818.

Taylor, George Braxton. *Virginia Baptist Minister, Third Series.* Lynchburg, Virginia: J.P.Bell Company, Inc., 1912.

Taylor, George Braxton. *Virginia Baptist Ministers, Fourth Series.* Lynchburg, Virginia: J.P. Bell Company, Inc., 1913.

Taylor, George Braxton. *Virginia Baptist Ministers.* Lynchburg, Virginia: J. P. Bell Company, Inc, 1936.

Taylor, George Braxton. *Virginia Baptist Ministers.* Lynchburg, Virginia: J.P. Bell Company, Inc. 1912.

Taylor, George Braxton. *Virginia Baptist Ministers.* Lynchburg, Virginia: J. P. Bell Company, Inc., 1935.

Taylor, James B. *Lives of Virginia Baptist Ministers.* Richmond: Yale & Wyatt, 1838.

Taylor, James B. *Memoir of Rev. Luther Rice.* Nashville, Tennessee: Broadman Press, n.d.

Taylor, O. W. *Early Tennessee Baptists.* Nashville, Tennessee: Tennessee Baptist Convention, 1957.

The First Annual Report of The Baptist Board of Foreign Missions for the United States. Philadelphia: William Fry, 1815.

The Franklin Times. February 29, 1992.

The Greenville News, August 10, 2001.

The Missionary Jubilee. New York: Sheldon and Company, 1865.

The News and Herald, September 3, 1964, Volume 120, No. 31.

The State, Columbia, SC, February 25, 1917.

The Sword and the Trowel, May 1878.

The Unforgettable Glen Schunk. FRONTLINE MAGAZINE, January-February, 1991.

Thieleman, J. Van Braught. *The Martyr's Mirror* Scottsdale, PA: Herald Press, 1950.

Thompson, D. *A Book of Remembrance.* Watertown, Wisconsin: Roger Williams Heritage Archives, 1885-2003.

Thompson, Evelyn Wingo. *LUTHER RICE - Believer in Tomorrow.* Nashville, Tennessee: Broadman Press, 1967.

Torbet, Robert G. *A History of the Baptists.* Philadelphia: The Judson Press, 1950.

Townsend, Leah. *South Carolina Baptists 1670-1805.* Baltimore: Genealogical Publishing Co., Inc., 1978.

Troutman, Linda and Bill. *Heritage and History of the First Baptist Church of St. Albans, WV.* Valley Forge, Pennsylvania: American Baptist Churches USA, 2003.

Trowbridge, M. E. D. *History of Baptists in Michigan.* Michigan Baptist State Convention, 1909.

Tulga, Chester E. *The Foreign Missions Controversy in the Northern Baptist Convention.* Chicago: Conservative Baptist Fellowship, 1950.

Turpin, W. O. Words spoken to the Dover Association, Minutes 1883.

Underwood, A. C. *A History of the English Baptists.* London: The Baptist Union of Great Britain and Ireland, 1970.

Verduin, Leonard. *That First Amendment and the Remnant.* Sarasota, FL: The Christian Hymnary Publishers, 1998.

Bibliography

Verduin, Leonard. *The Anatomy of a Hybrid.* Grand Rapids, Michigan: William B. Eerdmans Publishing Company, 1976.

Verduin, Leonard. *The Reformers and Their Stepchildren.* Grand Rapids, Michigan: William B. Eerdmans Publishing Company, 1964.

Vins, George. Compiler. *Let the Waters Roar.* Grand Rapids, Michigan: Baker Book House, 1989.

Vins, Georgi. *Konshaubi - A True Story of Persecuted Christians in the Soviet Union.* Grand Rapids, MI: Baker Book House, 1988.

Vins, Natasha. *Children of the Storm.* Greenville, South Carolina: Bob Jones University Press, 2002.

Wallace, Isaiah. *Autobiographical Skeetch - Reminiscences of Revival Work.* Halifax, Nova Scotia: Press of John Burgoyne, n.d.

Warns, Johannes. *Baptism - Studies in the Original Christian Baptism.* London, The Paternoster Press, 1957

Wayland, Francis. *A Memoir of the Life and Labors of the Rev. Adoniram Judson.* New York: Sheldon & Company, 1860.

Wegner, John Christian. *Even Unto Death.* Richmond, Virginia: John Knox Press, 1961.

Weiss, Benjamin. *God in American History.* Grand Rapids, Michigan: Zondervan Publishing House, 1966.

Weniger, Arno Q. "My Start in Life," unpublished autobiography. Lucerne, California: n.d.

Weston Henry Griggs. *Appleton's Cyclopedia of American Biography.* Editor, James Grant Wilson and John Fiske. New York: D. Appleton and Company, 1887-1889.

Weston, Henry Griggs. *In Remembrance.* American Baptist Publication Society, n.d.

Whitefield, George. *George Whitefield's Journals.* Gainesville, Florida: Scholars' Facsimiles & Reprints, 1969.

Whitley, W. T. *Calvinism and Evangelism in England.* London: Kingsgate, n.d.

Whitley, W. T., Editor. *Fourth Baptist World Congress.* Toronto: Stewart Printing Service, n.d.

Whitted, J. A. *A History of the Negro Baptists of North Carolina.* Raleigh: Edwards & Broughton Printing Co., 1908.

Whyte, William, *Revival in Rose Street.* Edinburgh, Scotland: Lindsay & Co. Ltd., n.d.

Williams, George Huntston. *The Radical Reformation.* Kirksville, Missouri: Truman State University Press, 2000.

Wilson, James Grant and John Fiske, editors. *"Ebenezer Kinnersley," Appleton's Cyclopedia of American Biography.* New York: D. Appleton and Company, 1887-1889.

Winebarger, W. L. *A History of the Muhlenberg County Baptist Association in Kentucky.* Greenville, Kentucky: The Western Recorder, 1966.

Wood, Nathan E. *The History of The First Baptist Church of Boston.* Philadelphia: American Baptist Publication Society, 1899.

Woolley, Davis. *Encyclopedia of Southern Baptists.* Nashville, Tennessee: Broadman Press, 1958.

Wylie, J. A. *History of the Waldenses.* New York: Cassell & Company, n.d.

INDEX